W9-AXL-987

MORE
BASIC
COMPUTER
GAMES

MORE BASIC COMPUTER GAMES

Edited by David H. Ahl
Program Conversion by Steve North
Illustrations by George Beker
Introduction by Chris Cerf

Workman Publishing
New York

All of the programs listed here run, without error, in Microsoft Basic Version 3.0 or higher. While most users will encounter no problems in entering and running the games, some microcomputer Basics may require program conversion. If you are a newcomer to personal computing, do not attempt to enter the longest program first. This will only result in frustration and confusion. You must become familiar with your Basic's capabilities and limitations before attempting one of the longer programs.

 Published simultaneously in Canada by Saunders of Toronto.

Trade edition published in cooperation with Creative Computing.

Library of Congress Cataloging in Publication Data
Main entry under title:
More Basic Computer Games.

1. Games—Data processing. 2. Microcomputers—Programming. I. Ahl, David H. II. North, Steve.
GV1469.2.M67 794 80-57619
ISBN 0-89480-137-6

Cover Design: Paul Hanson
Illustrations: George Beker

Workman Publishing Company
1 West 39 Street
New York, New York 10018

Manufactured in the United States of America
First Printing June 1980

20 19 18 17 16 15 14 13 12 11

To people everywhere who look back and wonder how they ever got along without a personal computer...

ABOUT THE EDITOR

David Ahl has a BEE from Cornell University, MBA from Carnegie-Mellon University and has done further work in educational psychology at the University of Pittsburgh.

Two years in the Army Security Agency were followed by four years with Management Science Associates working on computer models and analysis of new consumer products. He continued work in computer analysis (of vocational education graduates) with Educational Systems Research Institute.

He joined Digital Equipment Corporation in early 1970. As Education Product Line Manager he formulated the concept of an educational computer system consisting of hardware, software, and courseware (Edu-System) and helped guide DEC into a leading position in the education market.

Mr. Ahl joined AT&T in 1974 as Education Marketing Manager and was later promoted to Manager of Marketing Communications where he was responsible for the development of sales promotional strategies and materials for the Bell System. Concurrent with this move, he started Creative Computing as a hobby in late 1974.

As Creative Computing grew, Mr. Ahl left AT&T in 1978 to devote full time to it. Creative Computing magazine today is number 1 in software and applications for small computers.

Mr. Ahl is a frequent lecturer and workshop leader at colleges and professional conferences. He is a member of ACM, AEDS, AERA, COSMEP and NCTM.

ACKNOWLEDGEMENTS

So many people had a hand in bringing this book to fruition, it's difficult to know where to start with acknowledgements. Clearly the 70 some odd game authors deserve a great deal of credit. Taking each game in its own peculiar dialect of Basic and converting it to a "standard" Microsoft Basic was a huge task ably managed by Steve North. Thanks to the team of programmers involved in the conversion effort: Steven Neitz, Bruce Schaeffer, and Jeff Yuan.

RESTRICTIONS

Contents

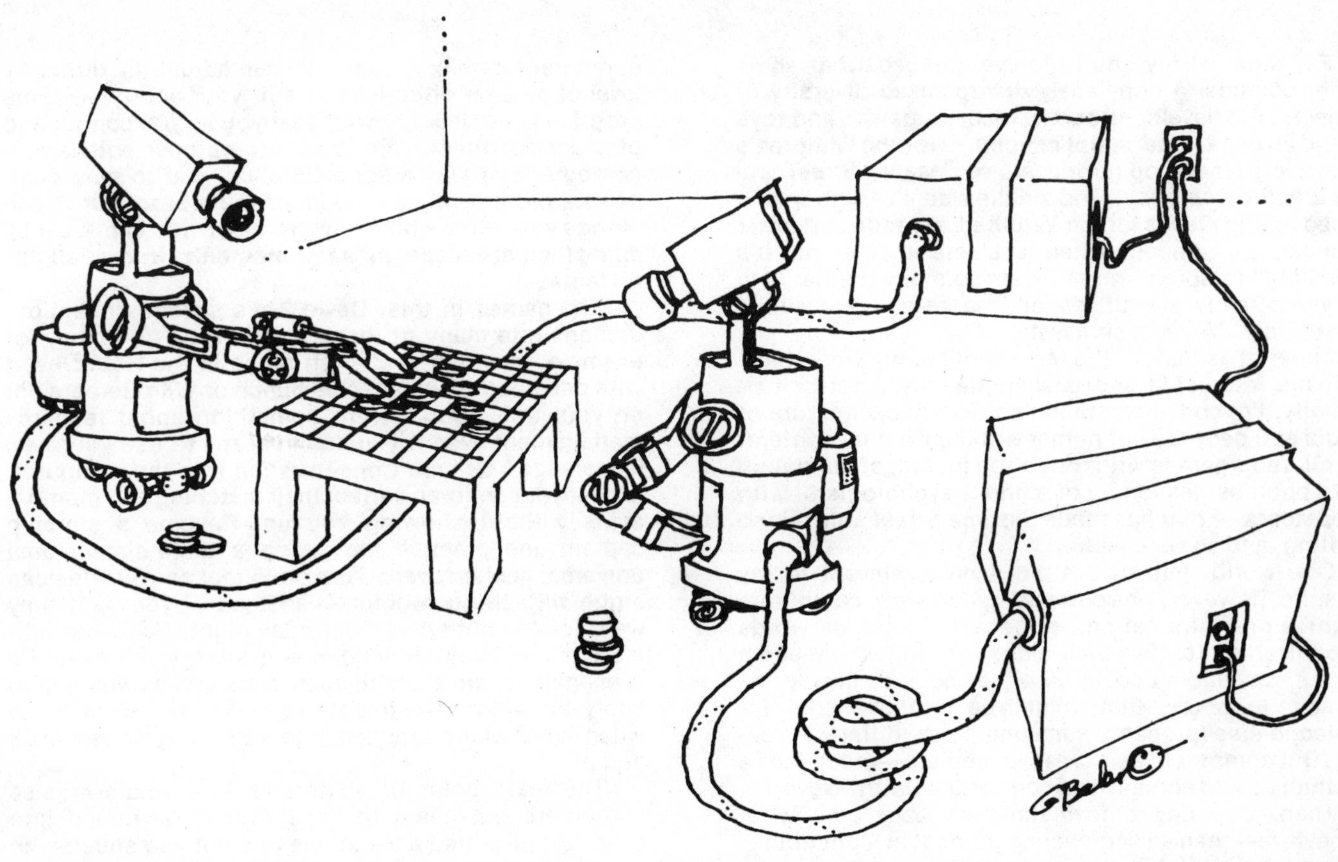

Introduction

For most of my adult life I've pursued what some might consider a hopelessly disorganized diversity of projects. I've develor ed books, records, games and toys — and an occasiona. script or song — for the Children's Television Workshop (producers of *Sesame Street* and *The Electric Company*), and, on the side, I've written and edited satiric pieces for the *National Lampoon* and other publications. People often ask me if I think it's "sensible" to spread myself over so many media. "My activities really *are* all related," I answer, somewhat defensively. "At least somewhat..."

The truth is that it's the very variety of my work that's kept me interested and challenged. And, not coincidentally, I'm convinced that it's the unlikely mixture of media and people — of humor with curriculum content, of children's games with rock'n'roll music, of animation with phonics lessons; of child psychologists with puppeteers — that has made *Sesame Street* so vital, so exciting, and so successful.

One world that always *did* seem irrelevant to my pursuits, however, was computing. Oh sure, computers might store information, or generate lists of words recognizable to five-year-olds, or index research results, or handle accounts, or, of course, invade my privacy. In short, they might be a useful tool for *someone else* (probably someone pretty different from me). But computers as a *creative* medium—much less a medium I could actually feel comfortable with? Never!

Then, one day a few summers back, my wife, Genevieve—then an engineering student at Columbia—showed me a book called *Basic Computer Games,* by David Ahl. To my amazement, it had funny pictures in it. It was full of *games* — many of them delightfully silly. And — wonder of wonders! — at least some of it (sample runs of the games, for example) was not hopelessly beyond my comprehension.

I was intrigued, and when, months later, I visited the Boston Children's Museum and actually got to play with a computer, I was hooked. The terminals at the museum played many of the games in David Ahl's book. What's more, they actually called me by name, and made humorous comments about my playing skill. After several hours of trying to land a capsule on the moon (only to be told that I'd created several hundred new craters, and that Neil Armstrong "did it right the first time"), I had to be dragged away from the keyboard — it was past closing time, the museum personnel insisted.

From that day on, the development of computer games — to entertain *and* to educate — has been a high priority activity for us at CTW. (As I write this, we're designing a prototype computer game center to open, near Philadelphia, in 1980 — a project in which David Ahl has taken a pioneering role). For the computer combines the possibility of fun, education, challenge, personalization, humor and — most important — *interaction,* in a way that no other medium can. Computers are infinitely patient, not minding (unless they're *programmed* to mind) if you take all day to respond to a question or move a game "piece". If there's something you don't understand, you don't have to be embarrassed to ask a computer for help. A computer can adjust the difficulty level of a game or activity to suit your ability — some programs even learn how to beat you as you continue to play against them. Armed with the proper software, a computer can play a song (or allow you to play one), paint a picture, write a poem or tell a story. Or it can plunge you into a whole new world, so you can learn by doing (or just escape, for a few moments, into a delightful fantasy).

The games in this, David Ahl's second collection, demonstrate many of these attributes. Try *Camel,* for example, in which you're left alone in the Gobi Desert with one quart of water and a bunch of Wild Berbers hot on your trail. (You'll learn something about resource management even if you don't escape to use your new knowledge.) Or type *Concentration* into the computer, and let your children perfect their matching and memory skills without showing you up. Become a starship captain and practice navigating a three-dimensional universe, in *Maneuvers.* Turn on *Father* so your kids can argue with the computer — instead of you — if they want to stay out late on Saturday night. Or — the ultimate trip — play *Millionaire* and start your whole life over again (complete with such decisions as what job to apply for, what investments to make, and what to do when an airplane crashes into your magnificent new home)!

The main point of all this is that whatever else computers are meant to be, they can be turned into magical multi-media machines that put *you* squarely in the center of the action. And, as Dave Ahl has continually demonstrated, they're an awful lot of fun.

Christopher Cerf

The Basic Language

Be sure to read this section before entering any of the games in this book on your computer. It will save you time and minimize potential problems.

The games in this book were written by a wide cross section of people on a variety of computers over a ten-year period. Most of the games were originally written for time-sharing systems such as the DEC Timeshared 8 and RSTS-11, HP 2000, and CDC 3600.

The first edition of this book was originally published in the early 70's. All the programs were printed in their original dialect of Basic. One of the major functions of the book was to give computer users an opportunity to learn more about their own and other versions of Basic. For example, a dimensioned string variable such as A$(I) had an entirely different meaning in DEC and HP Basics. The designers of each version of Basic had good reasons for doing what they did and it was (and is) very instructive to understand how different approaches work and their respective rationales.

In 1975, a small company in the telemetry business, M.I.T.S., introduced the first computer for hobbyists, the Altair 8800. This signaled the start of an immense new industry: personal computers. Ed Roberts, president of M.I.T.S., contracted with a small consulting company started by two bright young programmers to write a version of Basic for the Altair.

The name of the consulting company was Microsoft, and the Basic that Bill Gates and Paul Allen devised soon came to be known, appropriately enough, as Microsoft Basic. It was modeled on Basic-Plus, originally a creation of Nathan Teichholtz at Digital Equipment Corporation. Nathan is an unsung hero in the history of the Basic language and deserves a great deal of credit for this vastly improved version of the language. And in the kudos department, we must always remember to bow low to John Kemeny and Tom Kurtz of Dartmouth, the creators of the original Basic.

In any event, in 1977 it appeared that Microsoft Basic was fast becoming the standard Basic for microcomputers, and the programs in this book were all converted to Microsoft Basic, Revision 4.0. For about three years, this Basic truly was the standard.

However, three things conspired against it becoming the all-time standard. First, it was written for the 8080 (and Z80) microprocessor, and later mpu's had capabilities (and idiosyncrasies) that the 8080 did not have, hence, slight differences started creeping into Microsoft Basic on later computers.

Second, not all computer manufacturers wanted to contract with Microsoft to write Basic for their computers and so some wrote their own. This has led to some particularly interesting (and confusing) dialects of Basic.

Third, as computer hardware became more powerful with 16-bit mpu's, special chips for graphics and sound, Winchester disk drives, modems, and other peripherals, various extensions and changes had to be made to the software. Some of these changes are in the operating system and are transparent to the user, but others affect the Basic language.

So, what you are holding is a book of thoroughly debugged programs that can be entered directly and will run perfectly on some computers, while on other computers they will not run at all. What can you do about it if you have a computer on which the programs will not run?

First, do not call or write us. You have paid less than a dime per program and, after everyone has taken his share, we have made less than 1 cent per program; for that, we can't afford to act as personal consultants.

Second, please keep in mind that every program runs perfectly in Microsoft Basic 4.0. The sample runs are not faked; they came off a real computer exactly as they appear. There are no typographical errors in the programs — misspellings maybe — but the functional code is absolutely correct.

Third, the early versions of the books had programs in 15 or 20 vastly different dialects of Basic, yet hundreds of thousands of purchasers managed to convert the programs to their machines and get them going.

The key to converting the programs is to understand how Microsoft Basic works compared with your Basic. While we cannot present an entire manual on Microsoft Basic, we have included in the next section information on the key elements of the language and those likely to be different in other implementations.

If direct conversion doesn't work, do some "reverse engineering," (as it known in the computer industry). This means taking apart a program and drawing a flowchart of the logic. With a flowchart in hand, you can then write your own program to do the same thing, but often faster and better.

Since many of the programs were originally written in what today would be considered a primitive version of Basic, there are many ways of substantially shortening and improving some of these programs.

You should also keep in mind that all of these programs were written on computers which used an ASR-33 Teletype terminal. These are massive clunkers with 72 (or 80) columns of output, upper case only, and no graphics capability whatsoever. Naturally, you will have to do a fair amount of reformatting if your computer has only 40 columns (Apple, etc.), 32 columns (Sinclair), 28 columns (TI), or 20 columns (Epson HX-20). It can be done; for another book, I converted Hammurabi, Lunar Lander, and Gunner, all of which use 72 columns, to all the computers mentioned above.

The programs in this book use the following statements and functions in Microsoft Basic:

Statements		
DATA	Holds numeric or string data for a READ statement	20 DATA 4,6,"AHL"
DEF FNA(X)	Defines any function of X	20 DEF FNA(X)=3*X-2 20 DEF FNA(X)=SIN(X/57.3)
DIM	Declares maximum size of string or numeric array. Array subscripting begins at 0 although many programs do not use the zero subscript.	20 DIM A(50) 20 DIM A$(25),B1$(50)
END	Last statement in program	9999 END
FOR..TO..(STEP)	Executes a loop. The test for ending the loop is made after the loop has been executed. Upon exiting, the counter value equals the upper limit plus the step. For example, 10 FOR J=1 TO 3 20 PRINT "HI" 30 NEXT J will print "HI" three times, and J will equal 4 when the loop is finished.	20 FOR I=1 TO 30 20 FOR J=2 TO N STEP 3
GOSUB n	Branch to subroutine n	20 GOSUB 200
GOTO n	Branch to statement n	20 GOTO 50
IF..THEN n	Branch to statement n if condition is true	20 IF A>1 THEN 50
IF..THEN stmts	Executes statements if condition is true. Drops to next numbered line if false.	20 IF Z<5 THEN A=1:PRINT B
IF..THEN n ELSE m	Branch to n if true or to m if not true	20 IF X=Y THEN 50 ELSE 90
IF..THEN stmts ELSE stmts	Does statements after THEN if true, stmts after ELSE if false	20 IF Z>R THEN X=1 ELSE X=2
INPUT	Requests data from keyboard. The prompt string is optional	20 INPUT N 20 INPUT "YES OR NO";Z$
LET	Assigns value of expression to variable. The word LET is optional	20 LET A=1 20 Z$="DRY"
NEXT	Marks end of FOR loop	20 NEXT J
ON m GOSUB...	Branch to mth subroutine	20 ON X GOSUB 100,200
ON m GOTO...	Branch to mth line no. In these statements, m must be an integer starting at 1 and increasing by 1	20 ON Y GOTO 50,80,120
PRINT	Displays strings, constants and variables. Calculations can be done within a PRINT statement	20 PRINT "A=";A 20 PRINT Z$,10*A+B
READ	Moves values of DATA into variables	20 READ N,X1,A$
REM	Remark. Does not execute	20 REMARKABLE PROGRAM
RESTORE	Resets DATA pointer to first item in list	20 RESTORE
RETURN	Go to statement following last GOSUB	20 RETURN
STOP	Terminate program	20 STOP

Functions

ABS (X)	Absolute value.
ASC(X$)	Returns the ASCII value of the first character in the string argument. ASC("A") is 65,ASC("B") is 66, etc.
ATN(X)	Arctangent
CHR$(X)	Converts ASCII value to a character string. CHR$(65) is "A", etc. CHR$(7) is a bell ring.
COS(X)	Cosine
EXP(X)	Value of e raised to the X power
INT(X)	Integer function
LEFT$(X$,Y)	The leftmost Y characters in X$
LEN(X$)	Number of characters in X$
LOG(X)	Log of x to the base e
MID$(X$,Y,Z)	Takes Z characters from X$ starting at position Y
RND(1)	Returns a random number between 0 and 1.
RIGHT$(X$,Y)	The rightmost Y characters in X$
SGN(X)	Sign function. Returns -1 if X is negative, 0 if x is zero, 1 if x is positive.
SIN(X)	Sine
SQR(X)	Square root
STR$(X)	Converts X to a string of decimal digits, for example if X was 8.45 it would be converted to the string "8.45".
TAB(X)	Spaces over to position X on the terminal.
TAN(X)	Tangent
VAL(X$)	Returns the numerical value of the string of digits in X$. Opposite of STR$(X).

In Microsoft (Altair) BASIC, any expression may be evaluated as either true or false. A true condition will return a value of -1, and a false condition 0. Thus, if we say LET Q= -(X=Y), Q=1 if X=Y and Q=0 if X=Y. This logical evaluation of expressions is only used in the Hexapawn game in the user-defined function and with a little ingenuity could be replaced with a look-up table. A few other games use the logical AND and OR operators, which work in a straightforward manner.

The programs in this book were printed on a printer that uses a caret (∧) to indicate exponentiation. This is equivalent to an up arrow. Incidentally, exponentiation and taking roots are among the least accurate functions on small computers. For example, try this program.

```
10 INPUT N
20 I=SQR(SQR(N))
30 J=(I↑2)↑2
40 PRINT N,J
50 GOTO 10
```

Chances are good that N and J will not be the same 25% or more of the time. You can improve the accuracy by substituting J*J for J squared or J*J*J for J cubed.

Microsoft Basic permits more than one statement on a line when the statements are separated by a colon (:). As noted above, in an IF..THEN statement, if the condition is false, control drops to the next numbered line, not to the next statement on the same line.

This means that for TI and other computers that do not permit multiple statements on one line, you will have to insert additional lines. This may be difficult when line numbers are close together. One easy solution is to add a zero to all line numbers, but you must remember to do this in IF..THEN, GOTO and GOSUB statements as well as changing all the numbered lines.

The random function can be especially irksome as it is one that differs widely on different versions of Basic. In Microsoft Basic, RND(1) returns a value between 0 and 0.999999. This is the convention used in all programs in this book. On some computers, you may have to use RND(0), and on others just RND.

The Games

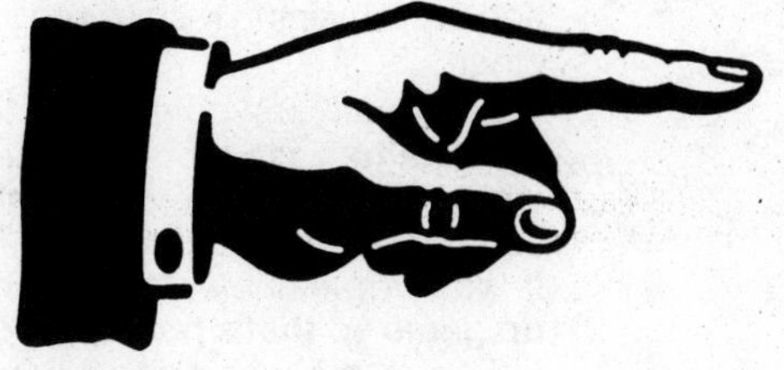

Artillery 3

In this game, two or three humans may play. Each one of them has an artillery piece and is firing at an opponent. The first person to destroy his opponent wins that round of the game. The parameters for distances and muzzle velocities of the artillery pieces are set at the beginning of the game. The shots are fired by giving a firing angle expressed in degrees from the horizontal.

In a three player game, you may elect which player you are firing at; hence player one and three could both be firing at player two. Once one of the players is eliminated, it becomes a two player game and the remaining two players fire at each other.

Personally, I would prefer to think of this game as lobbing mudpies or snowballs or custard cream pies or something non-destructive. However, it was originally written as shoot-'em-up game so that's how it appears here.

This game was originally written by Mike Forman and further revised by N.E. Lyon and Brian West. It first appeared in *Creative Computing*, Jan/Feb 1976.

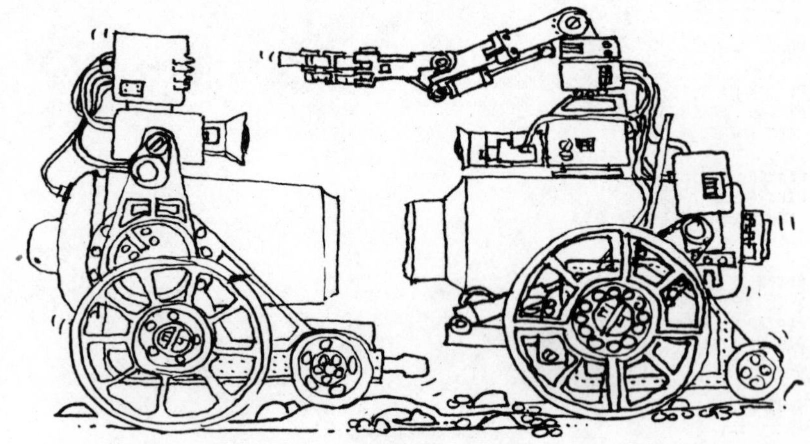

```
RUN
                    ARTILLERY 3
                 CREATIVE COMPUTING
               MORRISTOWN, NEW JERSEY


WELCOME TO 'WAR3'. TWO OR THREE HUMANS MAY PLAY!
DO YOU WISH SOME ASSISTANCE? YES

THIS IS A WAR GAME. TWO OR THREE PLAYERS ARE GIVEN
(THEORETICAL) CANNONS WITH WHICH THEY ATTEMPT TO SHOOT EACH
OTHER. THE PARAMETERS FOR DISTANCES AND MUZZLE VELOCITIES ARE
SET AT THE BEGINNING OF THE GAME. THE SHOTS ARE FIRED BY
GIVING A FIRING ANGLE, EXPRESSED IN DEGREES FROM HORIZONTAL

THE COMPUTER WILL KEEP TRACK OF THE GAME AND REPORT ALL
MOVES. A 'HIT' IS SCORED BY FIRING A SHOT WITHIN 5% OF THE
TOTAL DISTANCE FIRED OVER. GOOD LUCK


NO. OF PLAYERS? 3

DISTANCE (FT.)  1   TO   2 ? 1000
DISTANCE (FT.)  2   TO   3 ? 2000
DISTANCE (FT.)  3   TO   1 ? 2500


MUZZLE VELOCITY (FT./SEC.) OF   1 ? 300
MUZZLE VELOCITY (FT./SEC.) OF   2 ? 350
MUZZLE VELOCITY (FT./SEC.) OF   3 ? 400
```

```
ROUND  1

PLAYER  1 SHOOTING AT? 3
FIRING ANGLE? 68
 YOU UNDERSHOT BY  545.777  FEET.

PLAYER  2 SHOOTING AT? 3
FIRING ANGLE? 79
 YOU UNDERSHOT BY  566.253  FEET.

PLAYER  3 SHOOTING AT? 1
FIRING ANGLE? 80.5
 YOU UNDERSHOT BY  872.861  FEET.


ROUND  2

PLAYER  1 SHOOTING AT? 2
FIRING ANGLE? 70
 YOU OVERSHOT BY  808.207  FEET.

PLAYER  2 SHOOTING AT? 3
FIRING ANGLE? 84
 YOU UNDERSHOT BY  1204.37  FEET.

PLAYER  3 SHOOTING AT? 1
FIRING ANGLE? 73
 YOU OVERSHOT BY  294.324  FEET.


ROUND  3

PLAYER  1 SHOOTING AT? 2
FIRING ANGLE? 60
 YOU OVERSHOT BY  1435.18  FEET.

PLAYER  2 SHOOTING AT? 3
FIRING ANGLE? 70
 YOU OVERSHOT BY  460.307  FEET.

PLAYER  3 SHOOTING AT? 1
FIRING ANGLE? 76
 YOU UNDERSHOT BY  153.305  FEET.


ROUND  4

PLAYER  1 SHOOTING AT? 2
FIRING ANGLE? 74
 YOU OVERSHOT BY  490.028  FEET.

PLAYER  2 SHOOTING AT? 3
FIRING ANGLE? 73
 YOU OVERSHOT BY  140.66  FEET.

PLAYER  3 SHOOTING AT? 1
FIRING ANGLE? 72
 YOU OVERSHOT BY  438.912  FEET.
```

```
ROUND  5

PLAYER  1 SHOOTING AT? 2
FIRING ANGLE? 76.5
 YOU OVERSHOT BY  276.044  FEET.

PLAYER  2 SHOOTING AT? 3
FIRING ANGLE? 75
 A HIT -  3  IS DEFUNCT.

ROUND  6

PLAYER  1 SHOOTING AT? 2
FIRING ANGLE? 78
 YOU OVERSHOT BY  143.826  FEET.

PLAYER  2 SHOOTING AT? 1
FIRING ANGLE? 78
 YOU OVERSHOT BY  557.79  FEET.


ROUND  7

PLAYER  1 SHOOTING AT? 2
FIRING ANGLE? 79.4
 A HIT -  2  IS DEFUNCT.

GAME OVER.  1  WINS.
OK
```

```
LIST

8 PRINT TAB(22);"ARTILLERY 3"
9 PRINT TAB(20);"CREATIVE COMPUTING"
10 PRINT TAB(18);"MORRISTOWN, NEW JERSEY"
11 PRINT:PRINT:PRINT
20 T=0
60 DIM V(3),X(3),P(3),R(3,3)
70 MAT V=ZER
80 MAT X=ZER
90 MAT P=ZER
100 MAT R=ZER
110 DATA 1,2,2,3,3,1,1,3,3,2,2,1,2,3,3,1,1,2,0
120 PRINT "WELCOME TO 'WAR3'. TWO OR THREE HUMANS MAY PLAY!"
130 PRINT "DO YOU WISH SOME ASSISTANCE";
140 INPUT A$
150 IF A$="YES" THEN 1310
160 PRINT ""
170 PRINT "NO. OF PLAYERS";
180 INPUT N
190 IF N=2 THEN 240
200 IF N=3 THEN 270
210 PRINT "ERROR--TWO OR THREE PLAYERS!"
220 PRINT
230 GOTO 160
240 N1=1
250 PRINT ""
260 GOTO 290
270 N1=N
280 PRINT ""
290 FOR J=1 TO N1
300 READ A,B
310 PRINT "DISTANCE (FT.) ";A;" TO ";B;
320 INPUT R(A,B)
330 R(B,A)=R(A,B)
340 NEXT J
350 PRINT ""
360 RESTORE
370 IF N=2 THEN 460
380 FOR J=1 TO N
390 READ A,B,C,D,E,F
400 IF R(A,B)<R(C,D)+R(E,F) THEN 440
410 PRINT "ERROR--ILLEGAL TRIANGLE. RE-ENTER RANGES."
420 RESTORE
430 GOTO 290
440 NEXT J
450 PRINT
460 FOR J=1 TO N
470 PRINT "MUZZLE VELOCITY (FT./SEC.) OF ";J;
480 INPUT V(J)
490 NEXT J
500 PRINT ""
510 FOR J=1 TO N
520 X(J)=V(J)^2/32
530 NEXT J
540 FOR A=1 TO N
550 FOR B=1 TO N
560 IF X(A)>R(A,B) THEN 610
570 PRINT "ERROR--";A;" CANNOT REACH ";B
580 PRINT "WHAT IS THE MUZZLE VELOCITY OF ";A;
590 INPUT V(A)
600 GOTO 510
610 NEXT B
620 NEXT A
630 N1=N
640 PRINT ""
650 PRINT ""
660 PRINT "ROUND ";T+1
670 PRINT
680 FOR M=1 TO N
690 IF N=3 THEN 750
700 C=1
710 IF M<> 1 THEN 730
720 C=2
730 PRINT "PLAYER ";M;" SHOOTING AT ";C
740 GOTO 890
750 IF P(M)=12 THEN 1280
760 PRINT "PLAYER ";M;"SHOOTING AT";
770 INPUT C
780 ON C GOTO 830,830,830
810 PRINT "ERROR--PLAYERS DESIGNATED 1,2,3."
820 GOTO 760
830 IF C<> M THEN 860
840 PRINT "ERROR--CANNOT SHOOT SELF."
850 GOTO 760
860 IF P(C) <> 12 THEN 890
870 PRINT "ERROR-- ";C;" IS DEFUNCT"
880 GOTO 760
890 PRINT "FIRING ANGLE";
900 INPUT A3
910 IF A3<0 THEN 940
920 IF A3>180 THEN 940
930 GOTO 970
940 PRINT "ERROR--FIRED INTO GROUND. ";M;" NOW DEFUNCT."
950 P(M)=12
960 GOTO 760
970 IF A3<90 THEN 1000
980 PRINT "ERROR--FIRED WRONG WAY, LOSE SHOT."
990 GOTO 760
1000 Z=SIN(A3*3.49064E-02)*V(M)^2/32
1010 X=(R(M,C)/1000*RND(1))-(R(M,C)/1000*RND(1))
1020 D=X+Z
1030 D1=R(M,C)*.05
1040 IF D<D1 THEN 1080
1050 IF ABS(D-R(M,C))<D1 THEN 1110
1060 IF D<R(M,C) THEN 1140
1070 IF D>R(M,C) THEN 1160
1080 PRINT " TOO CLOSE- ";M;" IS DEFUNCT."
1090 P(M)=12
1100 GOTO 1180
1110 PRINT " A HIT - ";C;" IS DEFUNCT."
1120 P(C)=12
1130 GOTO 1180
1140 PRINT " YOU UNDERSHOT BY ";ABS(D-R(M,C));" FEET."
1150 GOTO 1270
1160 PRINT " YOU OVERSHOT BY ";ABS(D-R(M,C));" FEET."
1170 GOTO 1270
1180 N1=N1-1
1190 IF N1>1 THEN 1270
1200 FOR M1=1 TO N
1210 IF P(M1)=12 THEN 1250
1220 PRINT
1230 PRINT "GAME OVER. ";M1;" WINS."
1240 GOTO 1430
1250 NEXT M1
1260 STOP
1270 PRINT ""
1280 NEXT M
1290 T=T+1
1300 GOTO 650
1310 PRINT
1320 PRINT "THIS IS A WAR GAME. TWO OR THREE PLAYERS ARE GIVEN"
1330 PRINT "(THEORETICAL) CANNONS WITH WHICH THEY ATTEMPT TO SHOOT EACH"
1340 PRINT "OTHER. THE PARAMETERS FOR DISTANCES AND MUZZLE VELOCITIES AR
E"
1350 PRINT "SET AT THE BEGINNING OF THE GAME. THE SHOTS ARE FIRED BY"
1360 PRINT "GIVING A FIRING ANGLE, EXPRESSED IN DEGREES FROM HORIZONTAL"
1370 PRINT
1380 PRINT "THE COMPUTER WILL KEEP TRACK OF THE GAME AND REPORT ALL"
1390 PRINT "MOVES. A 'HIT' IS SCORED BY FIRING A SHOT WITHIN 5% OF THE"
1400 PRINT "TOTAL DISTANCE FIRED OVER. GOOD LUCK"
1410 PRINT ""
1420 GOTO 160
1430 END
OK
```

Baccarat

Games of the baccarat and chemin de fer family originated in the baccarat that became popular in the French casinos in the 1830's. In the present century they have travelled from Europe to the United States, back to Europe, and to casinos throughout the world. This process has resulted in wide variations in playing rules and what is called "baccarat" in one casino may more nearly resemble the "chemin de fer" of another.

The computer game here is more nearly chemin de fer than it is baccarat. The rules, briefly, are as follows: Eight packs of cards are shuffled together and placed in a "shoe" from which the cards can be slid out one by one. Following this, the players make their bets. Any player may make any bet up to the amount of the bank. The player at the banker's right has the first choice to bet. Any part of the bank he does not take may be bet by the next player on his right, and so on in order until the entire bank is covered or until everyone has bet who wishes to. Any player may take the entire bank by saying, "Banco," but when two or more players wish to banco, the one nearest the banker's right has the privilege.

After the bets are placed, the banker deals two hands of two cards each, dealing one card at a time. The hand he deals first represents all the players betting against him; the other hand is the banker's. The player who has made the largest bet against the banker plays the opposition hand.

The object of the game is to hold two or three cards which count nine (9), or as nearly nine as possible. The values of the cards are: face cards and tens, zero; aces, one each; any other card, its number. Units of ten points are disregarded, so that nine plus seven count as six, not sixteen.

A player whose card is nine or eight in his first two cards shows his hand immediately. He has a natural and his hand wins (but a natural nine beats a natural eight). Naturals of the same number tie, and there is a new deal.

When the result is not decided by a natural, the banker must give a card to his opponent on request; or the opponent may stand. The opponent must stand on six or seven, must draw to a zero, one, two, three, or four, but has the option on five. The additional card, if given, is face up.

Then the banker decides whether to stand or take a card.

IF BANKER GIVES	BANKER STANDS ON	BANKER DRAWS TO
Face card or ten	4, 5, 6, 7	3, 2, 1, 0
Nine	4, 5, 6, 7 (or 3)	2, 1, 0 (or 3)
Eight	3, 4, 5, 6, 7	2, 1, 0
Seven or six	7	6, 5, 4, 3, 2, 1, 0
Five or four	6, 7	5, 4, 3, 2, 1, 0
Three or two	5, 6, 7	4, 3, 2, 1, 0
Ace	4, 5, 6, 7	3, 2, 1, 0
Opponent stands	6, 7	5, 4, 3, 2, 1, 0

Neither player may have more than one additional card, giving him three cards at the most. When each player has exercised his option, the cards are shown. If the totals are the same, the bets are off and may be withdrawn and new bets are placed exactly as before for another deal. If the opponent has a higher number than the banker's, each player collects such portion of the bank as he has covered.

In the game of chemin de fer, the role of banker rotates among the players after each hand; in baccarat, it does not.

```
RUN
                         BACRAT
                    CREATIVE COMPUTING
                  MORRISTOWN, NEW JERSEY



BACCARAT -- CHEMIN DE FER

DO YOU NEED INSTRUCTIONS? YES
    BACCARAT IS A VERY POPULAR GAME IN LAS
VEGAS.  THE PLAYER AND BANKER EACH RECEIVE
TWO CARDS FROM A 'SHOE' CONTAINING 8 DECKS
OF CARDS.   ALL CARD COMBINATIONS TOTALING
TEN ARE NOT COUNTED.  THE ONE THAT ENDS UP
CLOSER TO NINE WINS.  THE STAKES ARE HIGH,
ALL OF THE PLAYERS START WITH TEN THOUSAND
DOLLARS.  YOU CAN BET ON THE DEALER OR THE
PLAYER.   A THIRD CARD IS GIVEN ONLY UNDER
CERTAIN CONDITIONS, AS YOU WILL SEE.   LET
US BEGIN.      GOOD LUCK!


HOW MANY PLAYERS? 1
WHAT IS THE NAME OF PLAYER 1 ? STEVE
STEVE HAS $ 10000 .    BET? 500
(1) BANKER OR (2) PLAYER? 1

BANKER             PLAYER
FOUR OF SPADES     FOUR OF SPADES
EIGHT OF HEARTS    NINE OF DIAMONDS
PLAYER MUST DRAW.
ACE OF SPADES
PLAYER CANNOT DRAW.
PLAYERS TOTAL: 4

BANKER MUST DRAW.
FIVE OF DIAMONDS
BANKERS TOTAL: 7

BANKER WINS!!
STEVE WINS $ 500 , FOR A TOTAL OF $ 10500 .
```

```
---------- NEW GAME ----------

STEVE HAS $ 10500 .   BET? 1000
(1) BANKER OR (2) PLAYER? 2

BANKER              PLAYER
FOUR OF CLUBS       FOUR OF DIAMONDS
KING OF HEARTS      SEVEN OF SPADES
PLAYER MUST DRAW.
TWO OF HEARTS
PLAYER CANNOT DRAW.
PLAYERS TOTAL: 3

BANKER MUST DRAW.
KING OF DIAMONDS
BANKERS TOTAL: 4

BANKER WINS!!
STEVE LOSES $ 1000 , FOR A TOTAL OF $ 9500 .

---------- NEW GAME ----------

STEVE HAS $ 9500 .   BET? 9400
(1) BANKER OR (2) PLAYER? 2

BANKER              PLAYER
TWO OF CLUBS        JACK OF CLUBS
JACK OF DIAMONDS    FIVE OF CLUBS
PLAYER MUST DRAW.
JACK OF HEARTS
PLAYER CANNOT DRAW.
PLAYERS TOTAL: 5

BANKER MUST DRAW.
THREE OF DIAMONDS
BANKERS TOTAL: 5

IT'S A TIE.  THE HAND IS PLAYED OVER.
STEVE HAS $ 9500 .   BET? 9400
(1) BANKER OR (2) PLAYER? 2
```

```
10 PRINT TAB(26);"BACRAT"
20 PRINT TAB(20);"CREATIVE COMPUTING"
30 PRINT TAB(18);"MORRISTOWN, NEW JERSEY":PRINT:PRINT:PRINT
40 PRINT"BACCARAT -- CHEMIN DE FER"
50 PRINT
60 PRINT"DO YOU NEED INSTRUCTIONS";
70 INPUT Q$
80 IF Q$<>"YES" THEN 210
90 PRINT"   BACCARAT IS A VERY POPULAR GAME IN LAS"
100 PRINT"VEGAS.  THE PLAYER AND BANKER EACH RECEIVE"
110 PRINT"TWO CARDS FROM A 'SHOE' CONTAINING 8 DECKS"
120 PRINT"OF CARDS.  ALL CARD COMBINATIONS TOTALING"
130 PRINT"TEN ARE NOT COUNTED.  THE ONE THAT ENDS UP"
140 PRINT"CLOSER TO NINE WINS.  THE STAKES ARE HIGH,"
150 PRINT"ALL OF THE PLAYERS START WITH TEN THOUSAND"
160 PRINT"DOLLARS.  YOU CAN BET ON THE DEALER OR THE"
170 PRINT"PLAYER.  A THIRD CARD IS GIVEN ONLY UNDER"
180 PRINT"CERTAIN CONDITIONS, AS YOU WILL SEE.  LET"
190 PRINT"US BEGIN.     GOOD LUCK!"
200 PRINT
210 DIM M(20),F1(20),F(20),B$(13),V(13),G$(20)
220 DIM Z(9,10),Q(4,13)
240 FOR X=3 TO 6
250 FOR Y=1 TO 10
260 READ Z(X,Y)
270 NEXT Y,X
280 FOR S1=1 TO 10:READ  W(S1):NEXT
283 FOR S1=1 TO 4:READ A$(S1):NEXT
285 FOR S1=1 TO 13:READ B$(S1):NEXT
287 FOR S1=1 TO 13:READ V(S1):NEXT
290 PRINT
300 PRINT"HOW MANY PLAYERS";
310 INPUT P1
320 FOR J=1 TO P1
330 PRINT"WHAT IS THE NAME OF PLAYER"J;
340 INPUT G$(J)
350 M(J)=10000
360 NEXT J
370 FOR S1=1 TO 4
373 FOR S2=1 TO 13
375 Q(S1,S2)=0
377 NEXT S2
379 NEXT S1
380 FOR J=1 TO 6
390 C=INT(1+RND(1)*4)
400 D=INT(1+RND(1)*13)
410 Q(C,D)=Q(C,D)+1
420 IF Q(C,D)>=32 THEN 390
430 B(J)=V(D)
440 C$(J)=B$(D)+" OF "+A$(C)
450 NEXT J
460 W1=2
470 FOR J=1 TO P1
480 IF M(J)<1 THEN 580
490 PRINT G$(J)" HAS $"M(J)".   BET";
500 INPUT F(J)
510 IF F(J)>M(J) THEN 490
520 IF F(J)<>INT(F(J)) THEN 490
530 IF F(J)<1 THEN 490
540 PRINT"(1) BANKER OR (2) PLAYER";
550 INPUT F1(J)
560 IF F1(J)>=1000 THEN 490
570 IF (F1(J)-1)*(F1(J)-2)<>0 THEN 540
580 NEXT J
590 J=0
600 T1=B(1)+B(2)
610 T2=B(3)+B(4)
620 PRINT
630 PRINT"BANKER"TAB(20)"PLAYER"
640 PRINT C$(3)TAB(20)C$(1)
650 PRINT C$(4)TAB(20)C$(2)
660 IF T1<10 THEN 680
670 T1=T1-10
680 IF T2<10 THEN 700
690 T2=T2-10
700 IF W(T1+1)=0 THEN 770
710 PRINT"PLAYER MUST DRAW."
720 PRINT C$(5)
730 T1=T1+B(5)
740 IF T1<10 THEN 770
750 T1=T1-10
760 GOTO 790
770 PRINT"PLAYER CANNOT DRAW."
780 J=11
790 PRINT"PLAYERS TOTAL:"T1
800 PRINT
810 IF T2<3 THEN 870
820 IF T2>6 THEN 930
830 IF J<>11 THEN 860
840 IF T2=6 THEN 930
850 GOTO 870
860 IF Z(T2,B(5)+1)=0 THEN 930
870 PRINT"BANKER MUST DRAW."
880 PRINT C$(6)
890 T2=T2+B(6)
900 IF T2<10 THEN 920
910 T2=T2-10
920 GOTO 940
930 PRINT"BANKER CANNOT DRAW."
940 PRINT"BANKERS TOTAL:"T2
950 PRINT
960 IF T2<>T1 THEN 990
970 PRINT"IT'S A TIE.  THE HAND IS PLAYED OVER."
980 GOTO 380
990 IF T2<T1 THEN 1030
1000 W1=1
1010 PRINT"BANKER WINS!!"
1020 GOTO 1040
1030 PRINT"PLAYER WINS!!"
1040 FOR J=1 TO P1
1050 IF M(J)<=0 THEN 1130
1060 PRINT G$(J)" ";
1070 IF F1(J)=W1 THEN 1110
1080 M(J)=M(J)-F(J)
1090 PRINT"LOSES $"F(J)", FOR A TOTAL OF $"M(J)"."
1100 GOTO 1130
1110 M(J)=M(J)+F(J)
1120 PRINT"WINS $"F(J)", FOR A TOTAL OF $"M(J)"."
1130 NEXT J
1140 FOR J=1 TO P1
1150 IF M(J)<>0 THEN 1190
1160 NEXT J
1170 PRINT"THANK YOU FOR YOUR MONEY, AND ";
1180 GOTO 1320
1190 PRINT
1200 PRINT"---------- NEW GAME ----------"
1210 PRINT
1220 FOR X=1 TO 4
1230 FOR Y=1 TO 13
1240 IF Q(X,Y)<>8 THEN 380
1250 NEXT Y,X
1260 GOTO 370
1270 DATA 1,1,1,1,1,1,1,1,0,1,0,0,1,1,1,1,1,1,0,0
1280 DATA 0,0,0,0,1,1,1,1,0,0,0,0,0,0,0,0,1,1,0,0
1290 DATA 1,1,1,1,1,0,0,0,0,SPADES,HEARTS,DIAMONDS
1300 DATA CLUBS,ACE,TWO,THREE,FOUR,FIVE,SIX,SEVEN,EIGHT
1310 DATA NINE,TEN,JACK,QUEEN,KING,1,2,3,4,5,6,7,8,9,0,0,0,0
1320 PRINT"THANK YOU FOR PLAYING."
1330 END
```

Bible Quiz

BIBLE QUIZ is a program which administers up to 25 questions about the Bible to the user. If the answer given to a question is correct, the program proceeds to the next question. If an incorrect answer is given, the program gives the correct answer. In either case, the biblical reference is given.

Note that Statements 124 to 296 could serve as the basis for any type of CAI dialogue with instructions preceeding Statement 124 and the questions and answers in the data statements.

This program was written by Steve Wentworth of Muskingum College. It originally appeared in *Creative Computing*, Mar/Apr 1977.

```
                    BIBLE QUIZ
                CREATIVE COMPUTING
              MORRISTOWN, NEW JERSEY

THIS GAME IS A QUIZ WHICH TESTS
YOUR KNOWLEDGE OF BIBLICAL EVENTS, PLACES,
AND PERSONS.

I WILL ASK YOU A QUESTION AND THEN WAIT
FOR YOUR ANSWER.  IF YOUR ANSWER IS CORRECT
I WILL PROCEED TO THE NEXT QUESTION.  IF YOUR
ANSWER IS INCORRECT I WILL GIVE YOU THE
CORRECT ANSWER AND THEN PROCEED TO THE
NEXT QUESTION.

ALL ANSWERS ARE ONE WORD.
ALL ANSWERS MUST BE CORRECTLY SPELLED.
THERE IS A TOTAL OF 25 QUESTIONS.
HOW MANY QUESTIONS DO YOU WISH TO TRY? 7


QUESTION # 1

WHAT SONG-COMPOSER IS CREDITED WITH 1005 SONGS? SOLOMON
CORRECT ANSWER--VERY GOOD! 1 KINGS 4:32

QUESTION # 2

WHAT BLIND MAN KILLED THREE THOUSAND AT A RELIGOUS FEAST? SAMSON
CORRECT ANSWER--VERY GOOD!  JUDGES 16:23-30

QUESTION # 3

WHO KILLED HIS BROTHER FOR HUMBLING HIS SISTER? ABSALOM
CORRECT ANSWER--VERY GOOD! 2 SAM. 13

QUESTION # 4

WHAT BOY HAD A VARIEGATED COAT? JOSEPH
CORRECT ANSWER--VERY GOOD!  GEN. 37:3

QUESTION # 5

WHO CLIMBED A TREE TO SEE JESUS? ZACCHAEUS
CORRECT ANSWER--VERY GOOD!  LUKE 19:4

QUESTION # 6

WHO SET FIRE TO THREE HUNDRED FOXES TAILS? SAMSON
CORRECT ANSWER--VERY GOOD! 1 JUDGES 15:4,5

QUESTION # 7

WHAT CITY IS CALLED THE CITY OF PALM TREES? BABEL
INCORRECT ANSWER
THE CORRECT ANSWER IS JERICHO.  DUET. 34:3

OUT OF  7  QUESTIONS YOU ANSWERED 6  CORRECTLY.
YOUR PERCENTAGE FOR CORRECT ANSWERS IS 86 %
```

```
5 PRINT TAB(24);"BIBLE QUIZ"
6 PRINT TAB(20);"CREATIVE COMPUTING"
7 PRINT TAB(18);"MORRISTOWN, NEW JERSEY"
9 PRINT:PRINT:PRINT
10 PRINT "THIS GAME IS A QUIZ WHICH TESTS "
20 PRINT "YOUR KNOWLEDGE OF BIBLICAL EVENTS, PLACES, "
30 PRINT "AND PERSONS."
40 PRINT
50 PRINT "I WILL ASK YOU A QUESTION AND THEN WAIT "
60 PRINT "FOR YOUR ANSWER.  IF YOUR ANSWER IS CORRECT "
70 PRINT "I WILL PROCEED TO THE NEXT QUESTION.  IF YOUR "
80 PRINT "ANSWER IS INCORRECT I WILL GIVE YOU THE "
90 PRINT "CORRECT ANSWER AND THEN PROCEED TO THE "
100 PRINT "NEXT QUESTION."
110 PRINT
118 PRINT "ALL ANSWERS ARE ONE WORD."
119 PRINT "ALL ANSWERS MUST BE CORRECTLY SPELLED."
120 PRINT "THERE IS A TOTAL OF 25 QUESTIONS."
122 PRINT "HOW MANY QUESTIONS DO YOU WISH TO TRY";
124 INPUT N
130 PRINT
135 DIM S(25)
140 C=0
142 N1=0
145 RESTORE
150 IF C=N THEN 290
160 C=C+1
162 PRINT
170 PRINT "QUESTION #";C
180 PRINT
183 X=INT(RND(1)*25+1)
184 IF S(X)=1 THEN 183
185 S(X)=1
186 FOR Q=1 TO X:READ Q$,A$,V$:NEXT Q
210 PRINT Q$;
220 INPUT R$
230 IF R$=A$ THEN 270
240 PRINT "INCORRECT ANSWER"
250 PRINT "THE CORRECT ANSWER IS ";A$;". ";V$
260 GOTO 145
270 PRINT "CORRECT ANSWER--VERY GOOD! ";V$
272 N1=N1+1
280 GOTO 145
290 PRINT
292 PRINT "OUT OF ";N;" QUESTIONS YOU ANSWERED";N1;" CORRECTLY."
294 P=INT((N1/N)*100+.5)
296 PRINT "YOUR PERCENTAGE FOR CORRECT ANSWERS IS";P;"%"
301 DATA "WHO SET FIRE TO THREE HUNDRED FOXES TAILS","SAMSON"
302 DATA "1 JUDGES 15:4,5"
303 DATA "WHAT HEBREW SERVED A QUICK LUNCH UNDER A TREE"
304 DATA "ABRAHAM"," GEN. 18:6-8"
305 DATA "WHAT HUNGRY MAN CURSED A FRUITLESS FIG TREE","JESUS"
306 DATA " MARK 11:12-14"
307 DATA "WHO KILLED HIS BROTHER FOR HUMBLING HIS SISTER"
308 DATA "ABSALOM","2 SAM. 13"
309 DATA "WHO HAD THREE HUNDRED CONCUBINES","SOLOMON","1 KINGS 11:1-3"
310 DATA "WHAT BOY HAD A VARIEGATED COAT","JOSEPH"," GEN. 37:3"
311 DATA "WHO HAD A SEAMLESS COAT","JESUS"," JOHN 19:23"
312 DATA "WHO TOOK OFF HIS SHOE TO BIND A CONTRACT","BOAZ","RUTH 4:7-9"
313 DATA "WHO SLEPT ON AN IRON BEDSTEAD OVER THIRTEEN FEET LONG"
314 DATA "OG"," DUET. 3:11"
315 DATA "WHO WAS THE FIRST CITY-BUILDER","CAIN"," GEN. 4:17"
316 DATA "WHAT PHYSICIAN WAS AN AUTHOR","LUKE"," COL. 4:14"
317 DATA "WHAT SONG-COMPOSER IS CREDITED WITH 1005 SONGS","SOLOMON"
318 DATA "1 KINGS 4:32"
319 DATA "WHO WAS THE FIRST PERSON KILLED","ABEL"," GEN. 4:8"
320 DATA "WHO WAS BURIED IN A CAVE WITH HIS WIFE","ABRAHAM"
321 DATA " GEN. 25:9-10"
322 DATA "WHO ACCIDENTLY HANGED HIMSELF IN A TREE","ABSALOM"
323 DATA "2 SAM. 18:9"
324 DATA "WHAT BLIND MAN KILLED THREE THOUSAND AT A RELIGOUS FEAST"
325 DATA "SAMSON"," JUDGES 16:23-30"
326 DATA "WHAT WAS THE NAME OF THE FIRST CITY EVER BUILT"
327 DATA "ENOCH"," GEN. 4:17"
328 DATA "WHO WAS A MIGHTY HUNTER","NIMROD"," GEN. 10:9-12"
329 DATA "WHO DROVE FURIOUSLY","JEHU","2 KINGS 9:20"
330 DATA "WHO WAS THE FIRST CHRISTIAN MARTYR","STEPHEN"," ACTS 7"
331 DATA "WHO FELL ASLEEP DURING A LONG SERMON","EUTYCHUS"
332 DATA " ACTS 20:9"
333 DATA "WHAT CITY IS CALLED THE CITY OF PALM TREES","JERICHO"
334 DATA " DUET. 34:3"
335 DATA "WHO CLIMBED A TREE TO SEE JESUS","ZACCHAEUS"," LUKE 19:4"
336 DATA "WHO KILLED GOLIATH","DAVID","1 SAM. 17:49"
337 DATA "WHO WAS CAST INTO A DEN OF LIONS","DANIEL"," DAN. 6:16"
400 END
```

Big 6

Big 6 is strictly an American invention from the casinos of Nevada. There is a very large wheel mounted vertically, generally four feet or more in diameter, that has the numbers one through six in a random arrangement around its periphery. Players place their bets on a roulette type of table in front of the wheel. The wheel is then spun and three numbers are declared the winners. These are the three numbers that appear at the top of the wheel. Most novice players looking at the wheel think that since there are three winners they have a very good chance of winning a large sum of money. Betting limits are generally up to $500 and, as many players discover very quickly, the odds are very heavily in favor of the house.

If you feel that you must play Big 6, try it by computer first and then figure out how much you can afford to lose when you go to play it in Las Vegas or Atlantic City. The computer is a much better sport when you lose than the casino managers will be at either of those resort cities.

Big 6 was written by Steve Heywood and Dave Alvey.

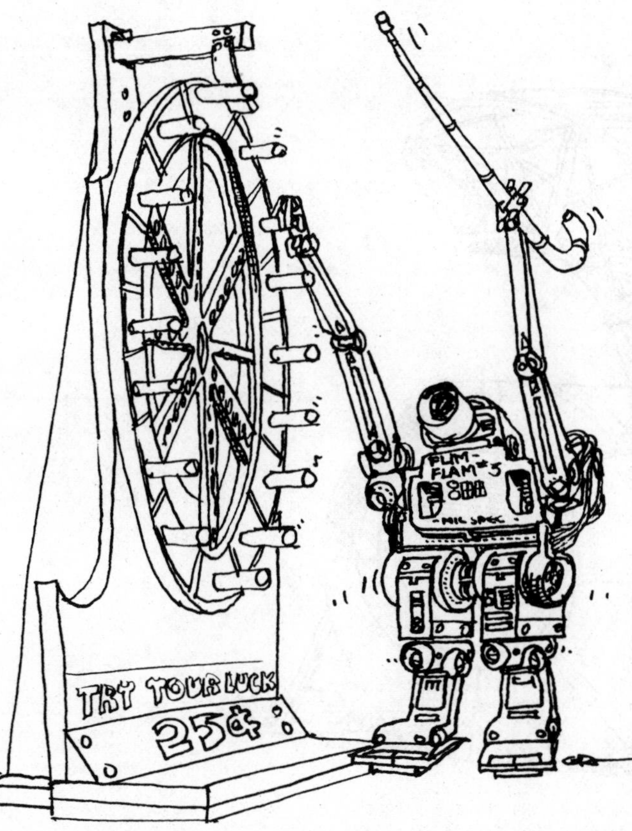


```
                    BIG6
             CREATIVE COMPUTING
           MORRISTOWN, NEW JERSEY


  THIS PROGRAM IS A DICE WHEEL GAME IN WHICH
YOU CAN BET ON ANY NUMBER BETWEEN ONE AND SIX
AND UP TO THREE NUMBERS.
  THE HOUSE LIMIT IS FROM $1 TO $500!!
TO END THIS PROGRAM TYPE THE WORD 'STOP'.
GOOD LUCK!


HOW MANY NUMBERS DO YOU WANT TO BET ON? 1
WHAT NUMBER? 4
WAGER? 10
THE LUCKY NUMBERS ARE:  3  3  6
YOU LOSE ON:  4
YOU'RE BEHIND $-10

HOW MANY NUMBERS DO YOU WANT TO BET ON? 2
WHAT TWO NUMBERS? 2,4
WAGER ON BOTH? 5,10
THE LUCKY NUMBERS ARE:  1  5  6
YOU LOSE ON:  2
YOU LOSE ON:  4
YOU'RE BEHIND $-25

HOW MANY NUMBERS DO YOU WANT TO BET ON? 3
WHAT THREE NUMBERS? 1,3,5
WAGER ON EACH OF THE THREE? 5,5,5
THE LUCKY NUMBERS ARE:  1  6  6
YOU WIN  1  TIMES ON: 1
YOU LOSE ON:  3
YOU LOSE ON:  5
YOU'RE BEHIND $-30

HOW MANY NUMBERS DO YOU WANT TO BET ON? 2
WHAT TWO NUMBERS? 1,3
WAGER ON BOTH? 10,10
THE LUCKY NUMBERS ARE:  1  4  6
YOU WIN  1  TIMES ON: 1
YOU LOSE ON:  3
YOU'RE BEHIND $-30

HOW MANY NUMBERS DO YOU WANT TO BET ON? 1
WHAT NUMBER? 4
WAGER? 100
THE LUCKY NUMBERS ARE:  4  5  6
YOU WIN  1  TIMES ON: 4
YOU'RE AHEAD $ 70

HOW MANY NUMBERS DO YOU WANT TO BET ON? 2
WHAT TWO NUMBERS? 2,4
WAGER ON BOTH? 25,25
THE LUCKY NUMBERS ARE:  4  6  6
YOU LOSE ON:  2
YOU WIN  1  TIMES ON: 4
YOU'RE AHEAD $ 70

HOW MANY NUMBERS DO YOU WANT TO BET ON? 3
WHAT THREE NUMBERS? 1,2,3
WAGER ON EACH OF THE THREE? 10,10,20
THE LUCKY NUMBERS ARE:  3  4  6
YOU LOSE ON:  1
YOU LOSE ON:  2
YOU WIN  1  TIMES ON: 3
YOU'RE AHEAD $ 70

HOW MANY NUMBERS DO YOU WANT TO BET ON? 1
WHAT NUMBER? 4
WAGER? 500
THE LUCKY NUMBERS ARE:  1  4  5
YOU WIN  1  TIMES ON: 4
YOU'RE AHEAD $ 570

HOW MANY NUMBERS DO YOU WANT TO BET ON? STOP


SO YOU WANT TO CASH IN YOUR CHIPS, I SEE!!!
YOU WON EXACTLY $ 570 !! NOT BAD !!!
Ok
```

```
LIST
1 PRINT TAB(27);"BIG6"
2 PRINT TAB(20);"CREATIVE COMPUTING"
3 PRINT TAB(18);"MORRISTOWN, NEW JERSEY"
4 PRINT:PRINT:PRINT
10 PRINT "  THIS PROGRAM IS A DICE WHEEL GAME IN WHICH"
20 PRINT "YOU CAN BET ON ANY NUMBER BETWEEN ONE AND SIX"
30 PRINT "AND UP TO THREE NUMBERS."
40 PRINT "  THE HOUSE LIMIT IS FROM $1 TO $500!!"
50 PRINT "TO END THIS PROGRAM TYPE THE WORD 'STOP'."
60 PRINT "GOOD LUCK!"
65 PRINT:PRINT
67 DIM S(3)
70 GOTO 90
80 PRINT "YOU CANNOT BET ON LESS THAN ONE OR MORE THAN THREE NUMBERS."
90 PRINT "HOW MANY NUMBERS DO YOU WANT TO BET ON";
100 INPUT N$:IF N$="STOP" THEN 3360
110 N=VAL(N$)
120 IF N=2 THEN 370
130 IF N=3 THEN 600
140 IF N>3 OR N<1 THEN 80
190 PRINT "WHAT NUMBER";
200 INPUT V
210 IF V<=6 OR V>=1 THEN 260
240 PRINT "YOU CAN ONLY BET ON AN INTEGER FROM ONE TO SIX."
250 GOTO 190
260 PRINT "WAGER";
270 INPUT F
280 IF F<=500 OR F >=1 THEN 330
310 PRINT "THE HOUSE LIMIT IS FROM $1 TO $500."
320 GOTO 260
330 GOSUB 1870
340 S2=V:S3=F:GOSUB 2060
360 GOTO 3260
370 PRINT "WHAT TWO NUMBERS";
380 INPUT V,P
390 IF V<=6 OR V>=1 OR P<=6 OR P>=1 THEN 460
440 PRINT "YOU CAN ONLY BET ON AN INTEGER FROM ONE TO SIX."
450 GOTO 370
460 PRINT "WAGER ON BOTH";
470 INPUT F,I
480 IF F<=500 OR F>=1 OR I<=500 OR I>=1 THEN 550
530 PRINT "THE HOUSE LIMIT IS FROM $1 TO $500."
540 GOTO 460
550 GOSUB 1870
560 S2=V:S3=F:GOSUB 2060
570 S2=P:S3=I:GOSUB 2060
590 GOTO 3260
600 PRINT "WHAT THREE NUMBERS";
610 INPUT V,P,S
620 IF V<=6 OR V>=1 OR P<=6 OR P>=1 OR S<=6 OR S>=1 THEN 710
690 PRINT "YOU CAN ONLY BET ON AN INTEGER FROM ONE TO SIX."
700 GOTO 600
710 PRINT "WAGER ON EACH OF THE THREE";
720 INPUT F,I,J
730 IF F<=500 OR F>=1 OR I<=500 OR I>=1 OR J<=500 OR J>=1 THEN 820
800 PRINT "THE HOUSE LIMIT IS FROM $1 TO $500."
810 GOTO 710
820 GOSUB 1870
830 S2=V:S3=F:GOSUB 2060
840 S2=P:S3=I:GOSUB 2060
850 S2=S:S3=J:GOSUB 2060
870 GOTO 3260
1870 X=-1
1880 A=INT(6*RND(1)+1):B=INT(6*RND(1)+1):C=INT(6*RND(1)+1)
1890 S(1)=A:S(2)=B:S(3)=C
1900 FOR Y=1 TO 2
1910 FOR X=1 TO 3-Y
1920 IF S(X)<=S(X+1) THEN 1940
1930 TE=S(X):S(X)=S(X+1):S(X+1)=TE
1940 NEXT X:NEXT Y
1950 PRINT "THE LUCKY NUMBERS ARE: "S(1);S(2);S(3)
1960 RETURN
2060 C1=0
2070 IF S2=A THEN C1=C1+1
2080 IF S2=B THEN C1=C1+1
2090 IF S2=C THEN C1=C1+1
2100 IF C1>0 THEN 2130
2110 S3=S3*(-1)
2120 PRINT "YOU LOSE ON: ";S2:GOTO 2150
2130 S3=S3*C1
2140 PRINT "YOU WIN ";C1;" TIMES ON:"S2
2150 W=W+S3
2160 RETURN
3260 IF W=0 THEN PRINT "YOU'RE EVEN!!":PRINT:GOTO 90
3270 IF W>0 THEN PRINT "YOU'RE AHEAD $";W:PRINT:GOTO 90
3280 IF W<0 THEN PRINT "YOU'RE BEHIND $";W:PRINT:GOTO 90
3350 REM
3360 PRINT:PRINT:PRINT "SO YOU WANT TO CASH IN YOUR CHIPS, I SEE!!!"
3370 IF W>0 THEN 3410
3380 PRINT "YOU DIDN'T WIN ANY MONEY, BUT I'M WILLING TO CALL IT EVEN!!"
3390 GOTO 3440
3410 PRINT "YOU WON EXACTLY $";W;"!! NOT BAD !!!"
3440 END
Ok
```

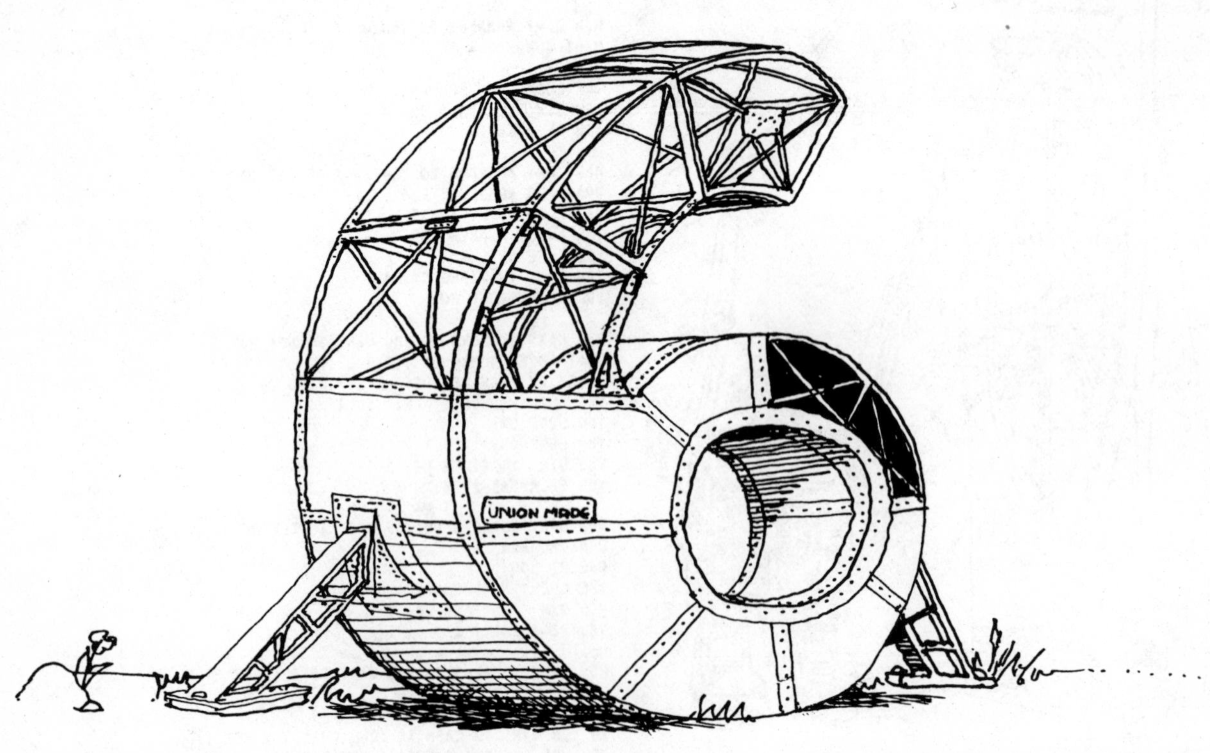

Binary

This game tests your skills in binary-to-decimal and decimal-to-binary conversion. You are given twenty conversion trials. Numbers are chosen randomly and your score is printed at the end. The answer to any conversion you miss is displayed; if the next conversion is presented, you may assume you got the previous one correct.

There are several possible modifications for this program such as timing the response, allowing the user to specify the number range, checking for duplicate numbers, or extending it to other bases.

This program was written by Ted Park of Pacific Union College. It originally appeared in *Creative Computing*, Mar/Apr 1975.

```
RUN

                              BINARY
               CREATIVE COMPUTING  MORRISTOWN NEW JERSEY

BINARY:11000     DECIMAL:? 24

BINARY:10001     DECIMAL:? 17

BINARY:01011     DECIMAL:? 11

BINARY:00110     DECIMAL:? 10
 6

BINARY:10100     DECIMAL:? 12
 20

BINARY:01100     DECIMAL:? 12

BINARY:10001     DECIMAL:? 16
 17

BINARY:01010     DECIMAL:? 10

BINARY:00011     DECIMAL:? 3

BINARY:10110     DECIMAL:? 21
 22



DECIMAL:  7      BINARY:   ? 111

DECIMAL:  15      BINARY:   ? 1111

DECIMAL:  1      BINARY:   ? 1

DECIMAL:  18      BINARY:   ? 10010

DECIMAL:  9      BINARY:   ? 01000
 01001

DECIMAL:  11      BINARY:   ? 1011

DECIMAL:  15      BINARY:   ? 1111

DECIMAL:  12      BINARY:   ? 1100

DECIMAL:  25      BINARY:   ? 11001

DECIMAL:  6      BINARY:   ? 01
 00110


YOUR SCORE: 70 %

OK
```

```
LIST

10 PRINT TAB(30);"BINARY"
20 PRINT TAB(15);"CREATIVE COMPUTING  MORRISTOWN NEW JERSEY"
110 B$="01"
120 T0=20
130 PRINT
140 PRINT
150 FOR I=1 TO 10
160 GOSUB 560
170 PRINT "BINARY:";
180 FOR J=1 TO 5
190 PRINT MID$(B$,B(J)+1,1);
200 NEXT J
210 PRINT "     DECIMAL:";
220 INPUT A
230 IF A=D THEN 260
240 PRINT D
250 T0=T0-1
260 PRINT
270 NEXT I
280 PRINT
290 PRINT
300 FOR I=1 TO 10
310 GOSUB 560
320 PRINT "DECIMAL: ";D;
330 PRINT "     BINARY:  ";
340 I$="00000"
350 INPUT I$
360 IF LEN(I$)> 10 THEN 420
370 I$="00000"+I$
375 I$=RIGHT$(I$,5)
380 FOR J=1 TO 5
390 IF MID$(B$,B(J)+1,1)<>MID$(I$,J,1) THEN 420
400 NEXT J
410 GOTO 480
420 PRINT " ";
430 FOR J=1 TO 5
440 PRINT MID$(B$,B(J)+1,1);
450 NEXT J
460 PRINT
470 T0=T0-1
480 PRINT
490 NEXT I
500 PRINT
510 PRINT
520 PRINT "YOUR SCORE:";INT(T0/.2+.5);"%"
530 PRINT
540 PRINT
550 END
560 D=0
570 FOR J=1 TO 5
580 B(J)=INT(RND(1)+.5)
590 D=D*2+B(J)
600 NEXT J
610 RETURN
620 END
OK
```

Blackbox

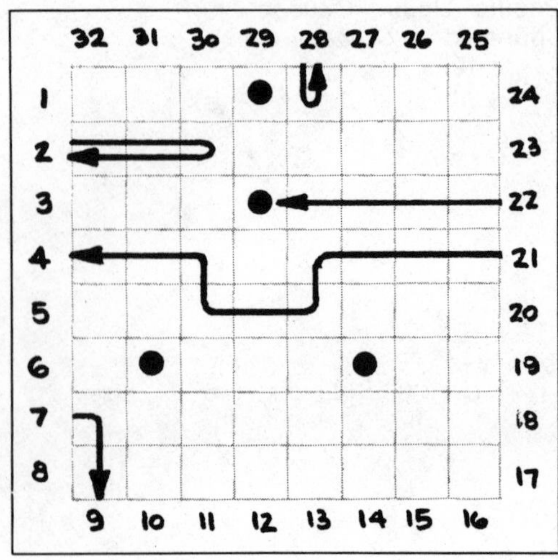

Description: Black Box is a computerized version of the game that appeared in the August 1977 issue of *Games and Puzzles*. The Black Box is an 8-by-8 square in which several atoms are hidden. The object of the game is to discover the positions of the atoms by projecting rays at them from the sides of the box and noticing how these rays are deflected, reflected, or absorbed. Rays enter the box across one of the four edges and travel horizontally or vertically. The entry points are numbered from 1 to 32, counterclockwise, starting at the top of the left edge.

To play the game, you first specify how many atoms to place in the Black Box. Then you type in the point at which you send the ray into the box, and you are told whether the ray was absorbed or where it emerged. Type a zero to end the game and print the board. The path of the ray is governed by the following rules:

(1) Rays that strike an atom directly are absorbed.

(2) Rays that come within one square of an atom in a diagonal direction (so that they would pass next to the atom if they continued) are deflected by 90 degrees.

(3) Rays aimed between two atoms one square apart are reflected.

(4) Rays that enter on either side of an atom on the edge of the box are reflected.

(5) Rays otherwise travel in straight lines.

The game is pretty interesting with four or five atoms, but can get out of hand with too many more. Occasionally, an atom can be masked by others. This doesn't occur often, but sometimes the position is truly ambiguous (more often, there is only one place the atom can be). For competitive play, score one point for reflections and absorptions, two for rays which emerge from the box, and five points for each atom guessed incorrectly.

This program and description were written by Jeff Kenton. A previous version appeared in *Creative Computing*, May/Jun 1978.

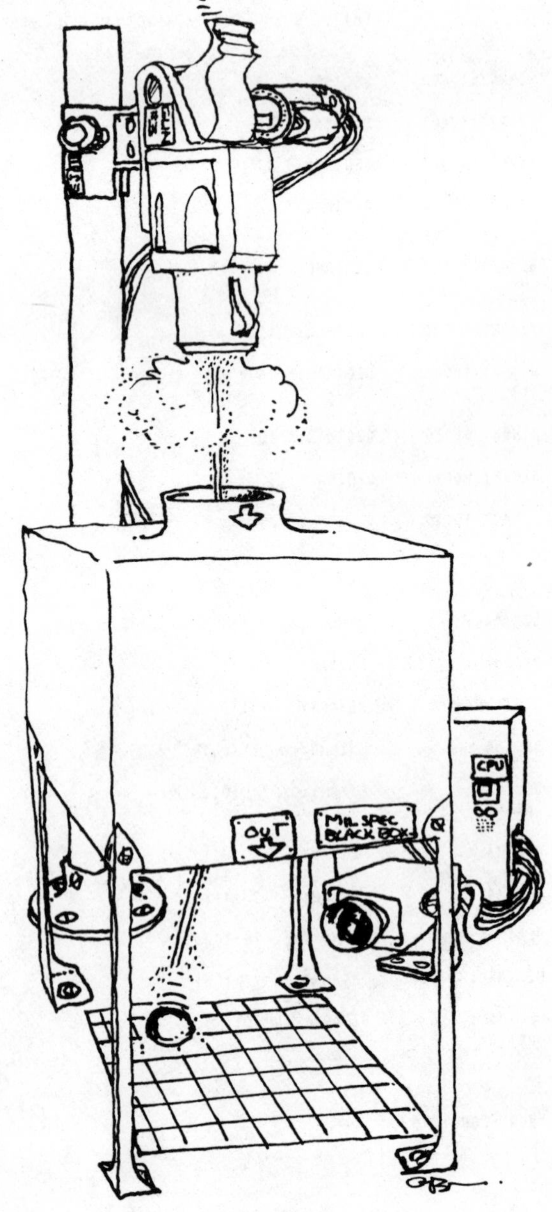

```
RUN
                         BLACKBOX
                    CREATIVE COMPUTING
                  MORRISTOWN, NEW JERSEY



NO. OF ATOMS? 4
RAY? 1
ABSORBED
RAY? 2
ABSORBED
RAY? 3
TO 22
RAY? 31
REFLECTED
RAY? 4
TO 32
RAY? 28
TO 13
RAY? 26
ABSORBED
RAY? 7
ABSORBED
RAY? 8
TO 15
RAY? 0
NOW TELL ME, WHERE DO YOU THINK THE ATOMS ARE?
(IN ROW,COLUMN FORMAT PLEASE.)
ATOM #  1 ? 4,3
ATOM #  2 ? 1,1
ATOM #  3 ? 2,7
ATOM #  4 ? 7,8

 . . * . . . . .
 . . . . . . . .
 . . . . . . . .
 . . . . . . . .
 . * . . . . * .
 . . . . . . . .
 . . . . . . . *
 . . . . . . . .

YOU GUESSED  1  OUT OF  4  ATOMS CORRECTLY!!
YOUR SCORE FOR THIS ROUND WAS  28  POINTS.
CARE TO TRY AGAIN? YES

NO. OF ATOMS? 4
RAY? 4
TO 13
RAY? 25
ABSORBED
RAY? 23
TO 26
RAY? 19
TO 6
RAY? 26
TO 23
RAY? 17
ABSORBED
RAY? 31
TO 1
RAY? 3
TO 18
RAY? 0
NOW TELL ME, WHERE DO YOU THINK THE ATOMS ARE?
(IN ROW,COLUMN FORMAT PLEASE.)
ATOM #  1 ? 8,1
ATOM #  2 ? 2,3
ATOM #  3 ? 4,7
ATOM #  4 ? 8,8

 . . . . . . . .
 . . * . . . . .
 . . . . . * . .
 . . . . . . . *
 . . . . . . . .
 . . . . . . . .
 . . . . . . . .
 * . . . . . . .

YOU GUESSED  2  OUT OF  4  ATOMS CORRECTLY!!
YOUR SCORE FOR THIS ROUND WAS  24  POINTS.
CARE TO TRY AGAIN? NO
Ok
```

```
LIST
100 PRINT TAB(25);"BLACKBOX"
110 PRINT TAB(20);"CREATIVE COMPUTING"
120 PRINT TAB(18);"MORRISTOWN, NEW JERSEY"
130 PRINT:PRINT:PRINT
140 DEF FNR(Z)=INT(8*RND(1)+1)
150 PRINT "NO. OF ATOMS";: INPUT N
160 FOR J=0 TO 9: FOR I=0 TO 9: B(I,J)=0: NEXT I,J
170 FOR I=1 TO N
180 X=FNR(1): Y=FNR(1): IF B(X,Y)<>0 THEN 180
190 B(X,Y)=1: NEXT I
200 S=0:C=0
210 PRINT "RAY";: INPUT R: IF R<1 THEN 480
220 ON (R-1)/8+1 GOTO 240,250,260,270
230 PRINT "ERROR": GOTO 210
240 X=0: Y=R: U=1: V=0: GOTO 280
250 X=R-8: Y=9: U=0: V=-1: GOTO 280
260 X=9: Y=25-R: U=-1: V=0: GOTO 280
270 X=33-R: Y=0: U=0: V=1
280 X1=X+U: Y1=Y+V
290 IF U=0 THEN X2=X1-1: X3=X1+1: Y2=Y1: Y3=Y1: GOTO 310
300 Y2=Y1-1: Y3=Y1+1: X2=X1: X3=X1
310 ON 8*B(X1,Y1)+B(X2,Y2)+2*B(X3,Y3)+1 GOTO 330,340,350,340
320 PRINT "ABSORBED":S=S+1: GOTO 210
330 X=X1: Y=Y1: GOTO 380
340 Z=1: GOTO 360
350 Z=-1
360 IF U=0 THEN U=Z: V=0: GOTO 380
370 U=0: V=Z
380 ON (X+15)/8 GOTO 420,400,430
390 STOP
400 ON (Y+15)/8 GOTO 440,280,450
410 STOP
420 Z=Y: GOTO 460
430 Z=25-Y: GOTO 460
440 Z=33-X: GOTO 460
450 Z=8+X
460 IF Z=R THEN PRINT "REFLECTED":S=S+1: GOTO 210
470 PRINT "TO";Z:S=S+2: GOTO 210
480 PRINT "NOW TELL ME, WHERE DO YOU THINK THE ATOMS ARE?"
490 PRINT "(IN ROW,COLUMN FORMAT PLEASE.)"
500 FOR Q=1 TO N
510 PRINT "ATOM # ";Q;
520 INPUT I,J
530 IF B(J,I)<>1 THEN S=S+5:GOTO 540
532 B(J,I)=2
535 C=C+1
540 NEXT Q
550 PRINT: FOR J=1 TO 8: FOR I=1 TO 8
560 IF B(I,J)=0 THEN PRINT " .";: GOTO 580
570 PRINT " *";
580 NEXT I: PRINT: NEXT J: PRINT:
590 PRINT "YOU GUESSED ";C;" OUT OF ";N;" ATOMS CORRECTLY!!"
600 PRINT "YOUR SCORE FOR THIS ROUND WAS ";S;" POINTS."
610 INPUT "CARE TO TRY AGAIN";A$
620 IF LEFT$(A$,1)="Y" THEN PRINT:GOTO 150
Ok
```

Bobstones

The idea for this number game was derived from a contest called "Bobstones" described in the novel *Watership Down*. The object of Bobstones is to guess three things about the roll of a pair of dice.

1. If the sum of the dice is odd or even............. 1 point
2. The sum of the dice ...... 2 points
3. The number on each of the two dice .... 3 points

The winner is the first player to score eleven points. If a tie results, the winner is the first player to break the tie.

In this computer version of the game, you are playing against the computer. However, the computer makes its guess before the dice are "rolled." Hence, it has no real advantage over its human opponent.

This game was written by Dohn Addleman. It originally appeared in *Creative Computing* Mar/Apr 1976.

```
RUN

                        BOBSTONES
                    CREATIVE COMPUTING
                  MORRISTOWN, NEW JERSEY



    THIS IS A NUMBER GAME CALLED BOBSTONES.  THE OBJECT OF
BOBSTONES IS TO GUESS THREE THINGS ABOUT THE ROLL OF A PAIR
OF DICE.  ON EACH TURN, THE COMPUTER SIMULATES THE ROLL OF
THE DICE.  THEN, YOU OR THE COMPUTER (YOUR OPPONENT) GUESS

                                                   SCORE
 1. IF THE SUM OF THE DICE IS ODD OR EVEN         1 POINT
 2. THE SUM OF THE DICE                           2 POINTS
 3. THE NUMBER ON EACH OF THE TWO DICE            3 POINTS

    THE WINNER IS THE FIRST PLAYER TO SCORE 11 POINTS.  IF A
TIE RESULTS, THE WINNER IS THE FIRST PLAYER TO BREAK THE TIE.
    GOOD LUCK !


YOU FIRST OR ME? ME

YOUR TURN.
IS THE SUM ODD OR EVEN? ODD
SORRY, THE SUM IS 4 .

MY TURN.
*** ON THIS ROLL OF THE DICE, THE TWO NUMBERS ARE  4  AND  4 .
*** THE SUM IS  8 .
MY GUESS IS THAT THE SUM IS EVEN.
AM I RIGHT OR WRONG? RIGHT
MY GUESS OF THE SUM IS  8
AM I RIGHT OR WRONG? RIGHT
MY GUESS IS THAT THE NUMBERS ARE  3  AND  5 .
AM I RIGHT OR WRONG? WRONG

THE SCORE IS ME 3  - YOU 0 .

YOUR TURN.
IS THE SUM ODD OR EVEN? ODD
SORRY, THE SUM IS 8 .

MY TURN.
*** ON THIS ROLL OF THE DICE, THE TWO NUMBERS ARE  3  AND  3 .
*** THE SUM IS  6 .
MY GUESS IS THAT THE SUM IS EVEN.
AM I RIGHT OR WRONG? RIGHT
MY GUESS OF THE SUM IS  12
AM I RIGHT OR WRONG? WQRONG
/// TYPE THE WORD 'RIGHT' OR THE WORD 'WRONG'.
AM I RIGHT OR WRONG? WRONG

THE SCORE IS ME 4  - YOU 0 .

YOUR TURN.
IS THE SUM ODD OR EVEN? EVEN
YOU ARE CORRECT.
NOW, GUESS THE SUM? 12
SORRY, THE SUM IS 10 .

MY TURN.
*** ON THIS ROLL OF THE DICE, THE TWO NUMBERS ARE  2  AND  4 .
*** THE SUM IS  6 .
MY GUESS IS THAT THE SUM IS ODD.
AM I RIGHT OR WRONG? WRONG

THE SCORE IS ME 4  - YOU 1 .

YOUR TURN.
IS THE SUM ODD OR EVEN? ODD
YOU ARE CORRECT.
NOW, GUESS THE SUM? 3
SORRY, THE SUM IS 9 .

MY TURN.
*** ON THIS ROLL OF THE DICE, THE TWO NUMBERS ARE  1  AND  2 .
*** THE SUM IS  3 .
MY GUESS IS THAT THE SUM IS ODD.
AM I RIGHT OR WRONG? RIGHT
MY GUESS OF THE SUM IS  9
AM I RIGHT OR WRONG? WRONG

THE SCORE IS ME 5  - YOU 2 .

YOUR TURN.
IS THE SUM ODD OR EVEN? ODD
SORRY, THE SUM IS 6 .

MY TURN.
*** ON THIS ROLL OF THE DICE, THE TWO NUMBERS ARE  6  AND  2 .
*** THE SUM IS  8 .
MY GUESS IS THAT THE SUM IS ODD.
AM I RIGHT OR WRONG? WRONG

THE SCORE IS ME 5  - YOU 2 .

YOUR TURN.
IS THE SUM ODD OR EVEN? EVEN
YOU ARE CORRECT.
NOW, GUESS THE SUM? 6
SORRY, THE SUM IS 4 .

MY TURN.
*** ON THIS ROLL OF THE DICE, THE TWO NUMBERS ARE  3  AND  4 .
*** THE SUM IS  7 .
MY GUESS IS THAT THE SUM IS ODD.
AM I RIGHT OR WRONG? RIGHT
MY GUESS OF THE SUM IS  11
AM I RIGHT OR WRONG? WRONG

THE SCORE IS ME 6  - YOU 3 .

LIST


10 PRINT TAB(24);"BOBSTONES"
20 PRINT TAB(20);"CREATIVE COMPUTING"
30 PRINT TAB(18);"MORRISTOWN, NEW JERSEY"
130 PRINT:PRINT:PRINT
140 PRINT "    THIS IS A NUMBER GAME CALLED BOBSTONES.  THE OBJECT OF"
150 PRINT "BOBSTONES IS TO GUESS THREE THINGS ABOUT THE ROLL OF A PAIR"
160 PRINT "OF DICE.  ON EACH TURN, THE COMPUTER SIMULATES THE ROLL OF"
170 PRINT "THE DICE.  THEN, YOU OR THE COMPUTER (YOUR OPPONENT) GUESS"
180 PRINT
190 PRINT "                                                   SCORE"
200 PRINT " 1. IF THE SUM OF THE DICE IS ODD OR EVEN         1 POINT"
```

```
210 PRINT " 2. THE SUM OF THE DICE                              2 POINTS"
220 PRINT " 3. THE NUMBER ON EACH OF THE TWO DICE               3 POINTS"
230 PRINT
240 PRINT "    THE WINNER IS THE FIRST PLAYER TO SCORE 11 POINTS.  IF A"
250 PRINT "TIE RESULTS, THE WINNER IS THE FIRST PLAYER TO BREAK THE TIE.
"
260 PRINT "    GOOD LUCK !"
270 DEF FND(X)=INT(6*RND(1)+1)
280 DIM A(2)
290 LET A(1)=0
300 LET A(2)=0
310 LET Z1=-1
320 LET Z2=-1
330 LET Z3=-1
340 LET Z4=-1
350 LET Z5=-1
360 LET J1=0
370 PRINT
380 PRINT
390 PRINT "YOU FIRST OR ME";
400 INPUT Z$
410 IF Z$="YOU" THEN 450
420 IF Z$="ME" THEN 450
430 "/// TYPE THE WORD 'YOU' OR THE WORD 'ME'."
440 GOTO 390
450 LET D1=FND(Z1)
460 IF Z1=0 THEN 480
470 LET Z1=0
480 LET D2=FND(0)
490 LET S=D1+D2
500 IF J1=0 THEN 650
510 IF Z$<>"ME" THEN 580
520 IF J2<>0 THEN 1160
530 PRINT
540 PRINT "THE SCORE IS ME";A(2);" - YOU";A(1);"."
550 IF A(1)>=11 THEN 1900
560 IF A(2)>=11 THEN 1900
570 GOTO 670
580 IF Z$<>"YOU" THEN 2020
590 IF J2<>1 THEN 670
600 PRINT
610 PRINT "THE SCORE IS YOU";A(1);" - ME";A(2);"."
620 IF A(1)>=11 THEN 1900
630 IF A(2)>=11 THEN 1900
650 LET J1=-1
660 IF Z$="YOU" THEN 1160
670 PRINT
680 PRINT "YOUR TURN."
690 LET J2=1
700 LET R=S-(INT(S/2)*2)
710 PRINT "IS THE SUM ODD OR EVEN";
720 INPUT A$
730 IF A$="ODD" THEN 770
740 IF A$="EVEN" THEN 800
750 PRINT "/// TYPE THE WORD 'ODD' OR THE WORD 'EVEN'."
760 GOTO 710
770 IF R=1 THEN 820
780 PRINT "SORRY, THE SUM IS";S;"."
790 GOTO 450
800 IF R=0 THEN 820
810 GOTO 780
820 PRINT "YOU ARE CORRECT."
830 LET A(1)=A(1)+1
840 PRINT "NOW, GUESS THE SUM";
850 INPUT G1
860 IF G1<2 THEN 890
870 IF G1>12 THEN 890
880 GOTO 910
890 PRINT "/// THE SUM MUST BE BETWEEN 2 AND 12."
900 GOTO 840
910 IF G1=S THEN 940
920 PRINT "SORRY, THE SUM IS";S;"."
930 GOTO 450
940 PRINT "YOU ARE CORRECT."
950 LET A(1)=A(1)+2
960 PRINT "WHAT ARE THE TWO NUMBERS WHICH PRODUCED ";S;" ";
970 INPUT N1,N2
980 IF N1<1 THEN 1030
990 IF N2<1 THEN 1030
1000 IF N1>6 THEN 1030
1010 IF N2>6 THEN 1030
1020 GOTO 1050
1030 PRINT "/// THE NUMBERS MUST BE BETWEEN 1 AND 6."
1040 GOTO 960
1050 IF N1=D1 THEN 1090
1060 IF N2=D1 THEN 1110
1070 PRINT "SORRY, THE NUMBERS ARE";D1;" AND";D2;"."
1080 GOTO 450
1090 IF N2=D2 THEN 1130
1100 GOTO 1070
1110 IF N1=D2 THEN 1130
1120 GOTO 1070
1130 PRINT "YOU ARE CORRECT."
1140 LET A(1)=A(1)+3
1150 GOTO 450
1160 LET J2=0
1170 PRINT
1180 PRINT "MY TURN."
1190 PRINT "*** ON THIS ROLL OF THE DICE, THE TWO NUMBERS ";
1195 PRINT "ARE ";D1;" AND ";D2;"."
1200 PRINT "*** THE SUM IS ";S;"."
1210 LET A1=INT(2*RND(1)+1)
1220 IF Z2=0 THEN 1240
1230 LET Z2=0
1240 IF A1=1 THEN 1270
1250 PRINT "MY GUESS IS THAT THE SUM IS ODD."
1260 GOTO 1280
1270 PRINT "MY GUESS IS THAT THE SUM IS EVEN."
1280 PRINT "AM I RIGHT OR WRONG";
1290 INPUT D$
1300 IF D$="RIGHT" THEN 1340
1310 IF D$="WRONG" THEN 450
1320 PRINT "/// TYPE THE WORD 'RIGHT' OR THE WORD 'WRONG'."
1330 GOTO 1280
1340 LET A(2)=A(2)+1
1350 IF A1=1 THEN 1410
1360 LET B1=INT(5*RND(1)+1)
1370 IF Z3=0 THEN 1390
1380 LET Z3=0
1390 LET B2=B1+B1+1
1400 GOTO 1430
1410 LET B1=FND(0)
1420 LET B2=B1+B1
1430 PRINT "MY GUESS OF THE SUM IS ";B2
1440 PRINT "AM I RIGHT OR WRONG";
1450 INPUT D$
1460 IF D$="RIGHT" THEN 1500
1470 IF D$="WRONG" THEN 450
1480 PRINT "/// TYPE THE WORD 'RIGHT' OR THE WORD 'WRONG'."
1490 GOTO 1440
1500 LET A(2)=A(2)+2
1510 IF B2<>2 THEN 1550
1520 LET C1=1
1530 LET C2=1
1540 GOTO 1810
1550 IF B2<>3 THEN 1590
1560 LET C1=1
1570 LET C2=2
1580 GOTO 1810
1590 IF B2<>11 THEN 1630
1600 LET C1=5
1610 LET C2=6
1620 GOTO 1810
1630 IF B2<>12 THEN 1670
1640 LET C1=6
1650 LET C2=6
1660 GOTO 1810
1670 IF B2>7 THEN 1740
1680 LET K1=B2-1
1690 LET C1=INT(K1*RND(1)+1)
1700 IF Z4=0 THEN 1720
1710 LET Z4=0
1720 LET C2=B2-C1
1730 GOTO 1810
1740 LET K1=B2-6
1750 LET K3=K1-1
1760 LET K2=7-K1
1770 LET C1=(INT(K2*RND(1)+1)+K3)
1780 IF Z5=0 THEN 1800
1790 LET Z5=0
1800 LET C2=B2-C1
1810 PRINT "MY GUESS IS THAT THE NUMBERS ARE ";C1;" AND ";C2;"."
1820 PRINT "AM I RIGHT OR WRONG";
1830 INPUT D$
1840 IF D$="RIGHT" THEN 1880
1850 IF D$="WRONG" THEN 450
1860 PRINT "/// TYPE THE WORD 'RIGHT' OR THE WORD 'WRONG'."
1870 GOTO 1820
1880 LET A(2)=A(2)+3
1890 GOTO 450
1900 IF A(1)<>A(2) THEN 1930
1910 IF J2<>0 THEN 1160
1920 GOTO 670
1930 IF A(1)>A(2) THEN 2030
1940 PRINT
1950 PRINT "I WIN! ANOTHER GAME";
1960 INPUT C$
1970 IF C$="YES" THEN 290
1980 IF C$="NO" THEN 2010
1990 PRINT "/// TYPE THE WORD 'YES' OR THE WORD 'NO'."
2000 GOTO 1960
2010 PRINT "SEE YOU LATER."
2020 END
2030 PRINT
2040 PRINT "YOU WIN! ANOTHER GAME";
2050 GOTO 1960
```

Bocce

This program simulates the Italian game of Bocce also called "lawn bowls" or just "bowls."

The instructions starting at the line 1770 explain the game.

This is the four-ball version (Q=5). Allowing more balls in the game (raising Q) will increase central processing time since the chances of collision will rise and the resulting position of each ball has to be recomputed. However, the delay is short and we routinely play six to eight balls. Increasing Q beyond 9 will require redimensioning the arrays at line 1030.

When there is collision, the bell will sound (line 1500).

It is important to remember that the object is to get close to the jack and not to hit it. Upon collision, the jack will move off more quickly than a ball because it is smaller and lighter. A careless shot can turn a good game into a disaster.

It requires some imagination to play the game well. It goes best if you imagine that you are standing at coordinates 0,0 and are looking out along the X-axis.

This game and the description above were written by Victor Bendall of Eastern Kentucky University. It originally appeared in *Creative Computing*, Jul/Aug 1977.

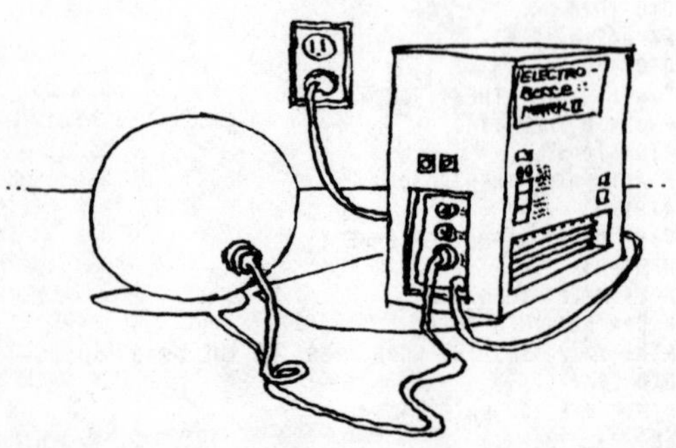


```
RUN
                          BOCCE
                    CREATIVE COMPUTING
                  MORRISTOWN  NEW JERSEY



THIS GAME SIMULATES THE GAME OF LAWN BOWLS
DO YOU NEED INSTRUCTIONS? ENTER YES OR NO? YES

IN THIS GAME YOU ROLL  4 BALLS SUCCESSIVELY AT A TARGET
BALL (CALLED A JACK). THE OBJECT IS TO GET THE BALLS AS CLOSE
TO THE JACK AS POSSIBLE.  THE BALLS ARE 10 CM IN DIAMETER AND
ARE WEIGHTED SO THAT THEY ROLL IN A CURVE. YOU WILL HAVE TO
ROLL THEM AT AN ANGLE TO THE LINE FROM YOU AT COORDINATES 0,0
TO THE JACK AT COORDINATES X,Y. A POSITIVE ANGLE WILL MAKE
THE BALL CURVE CLOCKWISE. A NEGITIVE ANGLE WILL MAKE IT CURVE
ANTI-CLOCKWISE.  THE JACK IS A 4 CM WIDE AND WILL ROLL
STRAIGHT IF YOU HIT IT.  BALLS HIT BY YOUR THROWN BALL MAY
CURVE IN EITHER DIRECTION.

HINT. TRY AN INITIAL VELOCKTY OF 500 AND AN ANGLE OF 10


THE JACK IS LOCATED AT  2171  77
BALL  1
VELOCITY? 500
ANGLE? 10

JACK AT COORDINATES  2171  77
BALL  1  AT COORDINATES  2434.63 -494.239  IT IS  622.137 FROM THE JACK

     YECH! OVER  20 FEET AWAY!
LONG AND TO THE RIGHT

BALL  2
VELOCITY? 480
ANGLE? 9

JACK AT COORDINATES  2171  77
BALL  1  AT COORDINATES  2434.63 -494.239  IT IS  622.137 FROM THE JACK
BALL  2  AT COORDINATES  2243.71 -455.535  IT IS  530.476 FROM THE JACK

     YECH! OVER  17 FEET AWAY!
LONG AND TO THE RIGHT

BALL  3
VELOCITY? 600
ANGLE? 3

JACK AT COORDINATES  2171  77
BALL  1  AT COORDINATES  2434.63 -494.239  IT IS  622.137 FROM THE JACK
BALL  2  AT COORDINATES  2243.71 -455.535  IT IS  530.476 FROM THE JACK
BALL  3  AT COORDINATES  3506.13 -710.248  IT IS  1542.95 FROM THE JACK

     YECH! OVER  50 FEET AWAY!
LONG AND TO THE RIGHT

BALL  4
VELOCITY? 300
ANGLE? 5

JACK AT COORDINATES  2171  77
BALL  1  AT COORDINATES  2434.63 -494.239  IT IS  622.137 FROM THE JACK
BALL  2  AT COORDINATES  2243.71 -455.535  IT IS  530.476 FROM THE JACK
BALL  3  AT COORDINATES  3506.13 -710.248  IT IS  1542.95 FROM THE JACK
BALL  4  AT COORDINATES  876.228 -178.163  IT IS  1312.67 FROM THE JACK

     YECH! OVER  43 FEET AWAY!
SHORT AND TO THE RIGHT


THE TOTAL DISTANCE OF ALL BALLS FROM THE JACK IS  4008.23  CM
DON'T PLAY THIS GAME FOR MONEY!!

CARE TO TRY AGAIN? ENTER YES OR NO? NO

Ok
```

```
LIST
10 PRINT TAB(25);"BOCCE"
20 PRINT TAB(19);"CREATIVE COMPUTING"
30 PRINT TAB(17);"MORRISTOWN  NEW JERSEY"
40 PRINT:PRINT:PRINT
1000 Q=5
1010 PRINT "THIS GAME SIMULATES THE GAME OF LAWN BOWLS"
1020 INPUT "DO YOU NEED INSTRUCTIONS? ENTER YES OR NO";Z$
1030 DIM B(9),B1(9),D(9),V(9),X(9),Y(9)
1040 PRINT: IF Z$="YES" THEN GOSUB 1770
1045 P1=3.14159
1050 S1=0:S2=0:A=-49.3
1070 X(1)=INT(2000+700*RND(1)): Y(1)=INT(200-400*RND(1))
1080 PRINT "THE JACK IS LOCATED AT ";X(1);Y(1)
1090 FOR P=2 TO Q
1100 J=P:GOSUB 1570
1110 NEXT P
1120 FOR J=2 TO Q
1130 D1=D1+D(J)
1140 NEXT J
1150 PRINT: PRINT "THE TOTAL DISTANCE OF ALL BALLS FROM THE JACK IS ";
1155 PRINT D1;" CM"
1160 IF D1 < Q^2 THEN PRINT "MAGNIFICENT BOWLING! WHAT AN EYE!!"
1165 IF D1 < Q^2 THEN 1230
1170 IF D1<2*Q^2 THEN PRINT"EXCELLENT BUT COULD BE BETTER:":GOTO 1230
1180 IF D1 < 3*Q^2 THEN PRINT "GOOD BUT NEEDS SOME INPROVEMENT":GOTO1230
1190 IF D1 < 6*Q^2 THEN PRINT "FAIR - YOU NEED MORE PRACTICE":GOTO 1230
1200 IF D1 < 10*Q^2 THEN PRINT "POOR - TRY TO BE MORE CONSISTANT":GOTO 1230
1210 IF D1 < 20*Q^2 THEN PRINT "YOUR GAME NEEDS LOTS OF WORK":GOTO 1230
1220 PRINT "DON'T PLAY THIS GAME FOR MONEY!!"
1230 FOR J=1 TO Q
1232 B(J)=0:B1(J)=0:D(J)=0
1240 V(J)=0:X(J)=0:Y(J)=0
1250 NEXT J
1260 PRINT:INPUT "CARE TO TRY AGAIN? ENTER YES OR NO";Y$
1270 PRINT: IF Y$="YES" THEN 1050
1280 GOTO 1890
1290 K1=-20
1295 IF J=1 THEN K1=0
1300 A1=A*COS(B(J))+K1*COS((P1/2)+B(J))
1305 A2=A*SIN(B(J))+K1*SIN((P1/2)+B(J))
1310 S3=V(J)*COS(B(J))*.05+1.25E-03*A1
1315 S4=V(J)*SIN(B(J))*.05+1.25E-03*A2
1320 B(J)=ATN((V(J)*SIN(B(J))+A2*.05)/(V(J)*COS(B(J))+A1*.05))
1330 IF B1(J)< 0 THEN S4=-S4
1340 S5=S1+S3: S6=S2+S4
1350 IF J=1 THEN 1370
1360 IF ABS(S5-X(1))<7 AND ABS(S6-Y(1))<7 THEN K=1:GOSUB 1550
1370 FOR K=2 TO Q
1380 IF K=J OR X(K)=0 THEN 1400
1390 IF ABS(S5-X(K))< 10 AND ABS(S6-Y(K))< 10 THEN GOSUB 1500
1400 NEXT K
1410 IF V(J)<ABS(A*.05) THEN 1440
1420 V(J)=V(J)+(A*.05):S1=S5:S2=S6:GOTO 1290
1430 GOTO 1290
1440 X(J)=X(J)+S5: Y(J)=Y(J)+S6:S1=0:S2=0:S5=0:S6=0
1450 FOR L=1 TO Q
1460 IF V(L)>ABS(A*.05) THEN J=L:GOTO  1290
1470 B(L)=0:V(L)=0
1480 NEXT L
1490 GOTO 1630
1500 B(K)=ATN((Y(K)-S2)/(X(K)-S1)): PRINT CHR$(7);
1510 IF J=1 THEN V(J)=V(J)/5
1520 V(J)=ABS(V(J)*SIN(B(J)-B(K))):V(K)=ABS(V(J)*COS(B(J)-B(K)))
1530 B(J)=((P1/2)+B(K)): S5=S1: S6=S2
1540 IF K=1 THEN V(K)=5*V(K)
1550 IF J=1 THEN V(J)=5*V(J)
1560 RETURN
1570 PRINT "BALL ";(J-1)
1580 INPUT "VELOCITY";V(J):V(J)=ABS(V(J))
1590 IF V(J) > 1000 THEN PRINT "VELOCITY TOO HIGH":GOTO 1580
1600 INPUT "ANGLE";B1(J)
1610 IF ABS(B1(J))> 89 THEN PRINT "ANGLE TO BIG":GOTO 1290
1620 PRINT : B(J)=ABS(B(J)*P1/180):GOTO 1290
1630 PRINT "JACK AT COORDINATES ";X(1);Y(1)
1640 FOR M=2 TO P
1650 D=(SQR((Y(1)-Y(M))^2+(X(1)-X(M))^2))-7
1655 D(M)=D
1660 IF D < 0 THEN D(M)=0
1670 PRINT"BALL ";(M-1);" AT COORDINATES ";X(M);Y(M);" IT IS ";D(M);
1675 PRINT "FROM THE JACK"
1680 NEXT M
1690 PRINT
1700 IF D(P) < 10 THEN PRINT TAB(15);"EXCELLENT SHOT! ";:GOTO 1740
1710 IF D(P) < 20 THEN PRINT TAB(15);"GOOD SHOOTING! ";:GOTO 1740
1720 IF D(P)< 30 THEN PRINT TAB(15);"NICE TRY !";:GOTO 1740
1730 IF D(P)>500 THEN PRINT TAB(5);"YECH! OVER ";INT(D(P)/30.48);
1735 IF D(P) > 500 THEN PRINT "FEET AWAY!"
1740 IF X(P)>X(1) THEN PRINT "LONG AND ";
1745 IF X(P)< X(1) THEN PRINT "SHORT AND ";
1750 IF Y(P)>Y(1) THEN PRINT "TO THE LEFT "
1755 IF Y(P) < Y(1) THEN PRINT "TO THE RIGHT"
1760 PRINT
1765 RETURN
1770 PRINT "IN THIS GAME YOU ROLL ";Q-1;"BALLS SUCCESSIVELY AT A TARG";
1775 PRINT "ET"
1780 PRINT "BALL (CALLED A JACK). THE OBJECT IS TO GET THE BALLS AS CLOSE"
1790 PRINT "TO THE JACK AS POSSIBLE.  THE BALLS ARE 10 CM IN DIAMETER AND"
1800 PRINT "ARE WEIGHTED SO THAT THEY ROLL IN A CURVE. YOU WILL HAVE TO"
1810 PRINT "ROLL THEM AT AN ANGLE TO THE LINE FROM YOU AT COORDINATES 0,0"
1820 PRINT "TO THE JACK AT COORDINATES X,Y. A POSITIVE ANGLE WILL MAKE"
1830 PRINT "THE BALL CURVE CLOCKWISE. A NEGITIVE ANGLE WILL MAKE IT CURVE"
1840 PRINT "ANTI-CLOCKWISE.  THE JACK IS A 4 CM WIDE AND WILL ROLL"
1850 PRINT "STRAIGHT IF YOU HIT IT.  BALLS HIT BY YOUR THROWN BALL MAY"
1860 PRINT "CURVE IN EITHER DIRECTION."
1870 PRINT:PRINT "HINT. TRY AN INITIAL VELOCMTY OF 500 AND AN ANGLE OF 10"
1880 PRINT:PRINT:RETURN
1890 END
Ok
```

Boga II

A Boga is a bogus animal or mythical beast in the Hurkle family. Like a Hurkle, the Boga hides on a grid with dimensions up to 20 by 20. It sends out clues that tell you which direction to move from where you are to where it is. However, one major difference between a Boga and a Hurkle is the Boga is also seeking you out at the same time you are looking for it. You don't have to tell it which directions to go after each of its guesses to get closer to you. It apparently has a very good nose and can tell on its own. However, it plays fairly and gives you the first guess, and then it takes its guess. Guesses continue alternately until one or the other, human or boga, find the opposing player. At the beginning of the game, you may print out the grid if you wish to make your guessing job slightly easier. Remember, directions in this game correspond to the diagram; that is, north is up and east is to the right.

This game was created by David Strickler.

```
      N
W           E
      S
```

```
RUN
                    BOGA II
              CREATIVE COMPUTING
            MORRISTOWN, NEW JERSEY


DO YOU WANT INSTRUCTIONS? YES


  THE BOGA IS HIDING ON A GRID (YOU SPECIFY THE LENGTH
AND WIDTH).  TRY TO GUESS HIS POSITION USING THE HINTS
I GIVE YOU.  EACH GUESS IS TWO NUMBERS SEPERATED BY
A COMMA.  PLEASE KEEP IN MIND THAT THE BOGA IS ALSO
SEARCHING FOR YOU!!!!


HOW BIG SHOULD THE GRID BE(20 MAXIMUM)? 21

HOW BIG SHOULD THE GRID BE(20 MAXIMUM)? 15
WOULD YOU LIKE A SAMPLE GRID? YEWS

                           1 1 1 1 1 1
         0 1 2 3 4 5 6 7 8 9 0 1 2 3 4 5
 0       * * * * * * * * * * * * * * * *
 1       * * * * * * * * * * * * * * * *
 2       * * * * * * * * * * * * * * * *
 3       * * * * * * * * * * * * * * * *
 4       * * * * * * * * * * * * * * * *
 5       * * * * * * * * * * * * * * * *
 6       * * * * * * * * * * * * * * * *
 7       * * * * * * * * * * * * * * * *
 8       * * * * * * * * * * * * * * * *
 9       * * * * * * * * * * * * * * * *
 10      * * * * * * * * * * * * * * * *
 11      * * * * * * * * * * * * * * * *
 12      * * * * * * * * * * * * * * * *
 13      * * * * * * * * * * * * * * * *
 14      * * * * * * * * * * * * * * * *
 15      * * * * * * * * * * * * * * * *

CHOOSE YOUR POSITION? -1,16

CHOOSE YOUR POSITION? 4,7
THE BOGA PICKS HIS POSITION!
GUESS # 1 ? 7,7
YOU GUESSED 7 , 7

HE'S MORE TO THE SOUTHWEST

THE BOGA GUESSES 7 , 7

GUESS # 2 ? 12,4
YOU GUESSED 12 , 4

HE'S MORE TO THE SOUTHWEST

THE BOGA GUESSES 5 , 7

GUESS # 3 ? 14,1
YOU GUESSED 14 , 1

HE'S MORE TO THE WEST
THE BOGA GUESSES 4 , 7

THE BOGA GUESSED YOUR POSITION IN 3 GUESS(ES)!

THE BOGA WAS AT 14 , 0
```

```
DO YOU WANT TO PLAY AGAIN? YES
HOW BIG SHOULD THE GRID BE(20 MAXIMUM)? 4
WOULD YOU LIKE A SAMPLE GRID? YES

     0 1 2 3 4
 0   * * * * *
 1   * * * * *
 2   * * * * *
 3   * * * * *
 4   * * * * *

CHOOSE YOUR POSITION? 2,1
THE BOGA PICKS HIS POSITION!
GUESS # 1 ? 2,2
YOU GUESSED 2 , 2

HE'S MORE TO THE SOUTH

THE BOGA GUESSES 2 , 2

GUESS # 2 ? 4,2
YOU GUESSED 4 , 2

HE'S MORE TO THE NORTH

THE BOGA GUESSES 2 , 1

THE BOGA GUESSED YOUR POSITION IN 2 GUESS(ES)!

THE BOGA WAS AT 3 , 2

DO YOU WANT TO PLAY AGAIN? YES
HOW BIG SHOULD THE GRID BE(20 MAXIMUM)? 4
WOULD YOU LIKE A SAMPLE GRID? NO

CHOOSE YOUR POSITION? 0,4
THE BOGA PICKS HIS POSITION!
GUESS # 1 ? 2,2
YOU GUESSED 2 , 2

HE'S MORE TO THE EAST
THE BOGA GUESSES 2 , 2

GUESS # 2 ? 2,3
YOU GUESSED THE BOGA'S POSITION IN 2 GUESS(ES)!

THE BOGA WAS AT 2 , 3

DO YOU WANT TO PLAY AGAIN? NO
Ok
```

```
LIST
10 PRINT TAB(26);"BOGA II"
14 PRINT TAB(20);"CREATIVE COMPUTING"
17 PRINT TAB(18);"MORRISTOWN, NEW JERSEY"
20 PRINT:PRINT:PRINT
30 INPUT "DO YOU WANT INSTRUCTIONS";Q$
35 PRINT:PRINT
40 IF LEFT$(Q$,1)<>"Y" THEN 220
70 PRINT "  THE BOGA IS HIDING ON A GRID (YOU SPECIFY THE LENGTH"
80 PRINT "AND WIDTH).  TRY TO GUESS HIS POSITION USING THE HINTS"
90 PRINT "I GIVE YOU.  EACH GUESS IS TWO NUMBERS SEPERATED BY"
100 PRINT "A COMMA.  PLEASE KEEP IN MIND THAT THE BOGA IS ALSO"
105 PRINT "SEARCHING FOR YOU!!!!"
110 PRINT:PRINT
220 U=0
240 K=1
250 F=0
260 INPUT "HOW BIG SHOULD THE GRID BE(20 MAXIMUM)";G
275 IF G>20 OR G<1 THEN PRINT:GOTO  260
280 S=G
290 REM: PRINTS THE GRID
300 INPUT "WOULD YOU LIKE A SAMPLE GRID";Z$
305 IF LEFT$(Z$,1)="N" THEN 380
310 PRINT
318 A$=""
320 IF G<10 THEN 332
322 FOR X=10 TO G
324 X1=INT(X/10)
326 A$=A$+CHR$(X1+48)+" "
328 NEXT X
330 PRINT TAB(25);A$
332 A$=""
334 FOR X=0 TO G
336 X1=X-INT(X/10)*10
338 A$=A$+CHR$(X1+48)+" "
340 NEXT X
342 PRINT TAB(5);A$
344 A$=""
346 FOR X=0 TO G
348 A$=A$+"* "
350 NEXT X
352 FOR X=0 TO G
354 PRINT X;TAB(5);A$
356 NEXT X
380 PRINT
390 H=1
400 INPUT "CHOOSE YOUR POSITION";X1,Y1
411 IF X1>G OR X1<0 OR Y1>G OR Y1<0 THEN PRINT:GOTO 400
420 PRINT "THE BOGA PICKS HIS POSITION!"
440 X2=INT(RND(1)*G)
450 Y2=INT(RND(1)*G)
460 PRINT "GUESS #"K;
470 INPUT X3,Y3
471 IF X3>G OR X3<0 OR Y3>G OR Y3<0 THEN PRINT:GOTO 460
480 K=K+1
490 F=F+1
500 IF K=10 THEN 1040
510 IF ABS(X3-X2)+ABS(Y3-Y2)=0 THEN 1010
520 PRINT "YOU GUESSED"X3","Y3
530 PRINT
540 PRINT "HE'S MORE TO THE ";
550 IF X2=X3 THEN 620
560 IF X2>X3 THEN 600
570 PRINT "NORTH";
590 GOTO 620
600 PRINT "SOUTH";
620 IF Y2=Y3 THEN 700
630 IF Y2>Y3 THEN 670
640 PRINT "WEST"
660 GOTO 700
670 PRINT "EAST"
690 REM: LINES 700-970 AND 1110-1150=BOGAS GUESSING FORMULA
700 PRINT"":IF H=0 THEN 730
710 X4=INT(.5*S)
720 Y4=INT(.5*S)
730 PRINT "THE BOGA GUESSES"X4","Y4
740 U=U+1
750 PRINT ""
760 Q=ABS(Y1-Y4)+ABS(X1-X4)
770 IF Q=0 THEN 980
780 H=0
790 IF Y4=Y1 THEN 880
800 A=1
810 IF ABS(Y4-Y1)<2 THEN 830
820 GOSUB 1140
830 IF Y4<Y1 THEN 860
840 Y4=INT(ABS(Y4-A))
850 GOTO 880
860 Y4=INT(ABS(Y4+A))
870 IF Y4>G THEN 1110
880 IF X4=X1 THEN 970
890 A=1
900 IF ABS(X4-X1)<2 THEN 920
910 GOSUB 1140
920 IF X4<X1 THEN 950
930 X4=INT(ABS(X4-A))
940 GOTO 970
950 X4=INT(ABS(X4+A))
960 IF X4>G THEN 1130
970 GOTO 460
980 PRINT "THE BOGA GUESSED YOUR POSITION IN"U"GUESS(ES)!"
990 PRINT
1000 GOTO 1050
1010 PRINT "YOU GUESSED THE BOGA'S POSITION IN"F"GUESS(ES)!"
1020 PRINT
1030 GOTO 1050
1040 PRINT "YOU USED UP ALL OF YOUR GUESSES."
1050 PRINT "THE BOGA WAS AT"X2","Y2
1060 PRINT
1070 INPUT "DO YOU WANT TO PLAY AGAIN";Q$
1080 IF LEFT$(Q$,1)="Y" THEN 220
1100 GOTO 1160
1110 Y4=.5*G
1120 GOTO 880
1130 X4=.5*G
1140 A=2
1150 RETURN
1160 END
Ok
```

Bombrun

Bombrun is an extremely accurate simulation of an aircraft dropping a bomb on a very small target. You may specify whether the aircraft is climbing, diving, and the angle in degrees. You may specify speed in feet per second; you may also specify at what point you wish to drop the bomb. The program gives you four passes over the target.

A perfect hit is possible but extremely difficult to achieve. A hit within 300 feet of the target is considered "threatening" while hits outside of that range may be considered a negative commentary on your knowledge of physics.

This program was originally written by Jim Prelesnik.

```
RUN
                           BOMBRUN
                      CREATIVE COMPUTING
                    MORRISTOWN, NEW JERSEY


THIS PROGRAM SIMULATES A BOMBING RUN.  DO YOU NEED
INSTRUCTIONS? YES
YOU HAVE THE OPTION OF MAKING FOUR PASSES OVER THE TARGET,
WITH THE ABILITY TO DROP A BOMB ONCE DURING EACH OF
THESE PASSES.  ALTITUDE CHANGES MAYBE MADE THROUGH THE
'CLIMB/DIVE' COMMAND BY PRINTING 'CLIMB' OR 'DIVE',FOL-
LOWED BY A COMMA AND THE DESIRED ANGLE (IN DEGREES).  NEW
VELOCITIES (RANGING FROM 300 TO 900 FEET PER SECOND) MAY
BE INPUT AFTER THE 'AIRSPEED' QUESTION MARK.  'CLIMB/DIVE'
ANGLES, VARYING FROM 0 TO 15 DEGREES, WILL ADD AS SPEC-
IFIED BY 'CLIMB' OR'DIVE' COMMANDS TO YIELD A NET INCLIN-
ATION/DECLINATION ANGLE BETWEEN 0 TO 60 DEGREES, CLIMBING
OR DIVING.  A MINIMUM ALTITUDE OF 100 FEET MUST ALSO BE
MAINTAINED.  WILLFULLY EXCEEDING ANY OF THE MAX./MIN. SPECS
WILL RESULT IN THE CRASH OF YOUR BOMBER.  ALSO , A BOMB
COMMAND OF 'DROP' DURING A DIVE WILL GIVE YOUR BOMB AN IN-
ITIAL DOWNWARD VELOCITY, SHORTENING THE DROP TIME, AS A
'CLIMB' COMMAND WILL LENGTHEN THIS TIME.  THE BOMB WILL BE
LAUNCHED IMMEDIATELY FOLLOWING THE MOST RECENT 'STATS' READ-
OUT UPON 'DROP' COMMAND, AND WILL BE HELD FOR FURTHER
POSITIONING INFORMATION UPON THE COMMAND 'STAND BY'.  THE
TARGET IS 1 FOOT IN DIAMETER.  GOOD LUCK


                         **INITIAL**
                         ***STATS***

            ELAPSED TIME... 0 SECONDS
    PRESENT ANGLE COMMAND... 0 DEGREES
          RESULTANT ANGLE... 0 DEGREES
         PRESENT VEROCITY... 876.763 FEET PER SECOND
                 ALTITUDE... 428.7 FEET
       DISTANCE FROM SITE... 4500 FEET
 ESTIMATED TIME OF ARRIVAL... 5.13252 SECONDS


BOMB COMMAND? STAND BY
STANDING BY.

MAINTAIN PRESENT RESULTANT ANGLE? YES

AIRSPEED? 800
                         ***STATS***

            ELAPSED TIME... 1 SECOND
    PRESENT ANGLE COMMAND... 0 DEGREES
          RESULTANT ANGLE... 0 DEGREES
         PRESENT VEROCITY... 800 FEET PER SECOND
                 ALTITUDE... 428.7 FEET
       DISTANCE FROM SITE... 3700 FEET
 ESTIMATED TIME OF ARRIVAL... 4.625 SECONDS

BOMB COMMAND? STAND BY
STANDING BY.

MAINTAIN PRESENT RESULTANT ANGLE? NO

'CLIMB/DIVE' COMMAND? DIVE,10

AIRSPEED? 600
                         ***STATS***

            ELAPSED TIME... 2 SECONDS
    PRESENT ANGLE COMMAND... DIVE, 10 DEGREES
          RESULTANT ANGLE... 10 DEGREES DIVING
         PRESENT VEROCITY... 600 FEET PER SECOND
                 ALTITUDE... 324.511 FEET
       DISTANCE FROM SITE... 3109.12 FEET
 ESTIMATED TIME OF ARRIVAL... 5.2618 SECONDS


BOMB COMMAND? STAND BY
STANDING BY.

MAINTAIN PRESENT RESULTANT ANGLE? YES

AIRSPEED? 700
                         ***STATS***

            ELAPSED TIME... 3 SECONDS
    PRESENT ANGLE COMMAND... 0 DEGREES
          RESULTANT ANGLE... 0 DEGREES DIVING
         PRESENT VEROCITY... 700 FEET PER SECOND
                 ALTITUDE... 202.958 FEET
       DISTANCE FROM SITE... 2419.75 FEET
 ESTIMATED TIME OF ARRIVAL... 3.51011 SECONDS


BOMB COMMAND? STAND BY
STANDING BY.

MAINTAIN PRESENT RESULTANT ANGLE? YES

AIRSPEED? 700
IF YOUR ALTITUTE ISN'T INCREASED IMMEDIATELY TO A MIN-
IMUN OF 100 FEET, A CRASH IS IMMINENT.

'CLIMB/DIVE' COMMAND? CLIMB,20

YOUR BOMBER CANNOT TOLERATE THE STRESS CAUSED BY ANGLE
INPUTS EXCEEDING 15 DEGREES.  RECONSIDER YOUR CHOICE.

'CLIMB/DIVE' COMMAND? CLIMB,12

AIRSPEED? 500
YOUR BOMBER FAILED TO MAINTAIN THE LOW ALTITUTE YOU DE-
SIRED AND SOON CRASHED.
BETTER LUCK NEXT TIME.

DURING YOUR 1 -PASS BOMBRUN, YOU MANAGED TO STRIKE
WITHIN 0 FEET OF THE TARGET.

WOULD YOU LIKE TO RELOAD AND PLAY AGAIN?
? YES

                         **INITIAL**
                         ***STATS***

            ELAPSED TIME... 0 SECONDS
    PRESENT ANGLE COMMAND... 0 DEGREES
          RESULTANT ANGLE... 0 DEGREES
         PRESENT VEROCITY... 567.958 FEET PER SECOND
                 ALTITUDE... 182.338 FEET
       DISTANCE FROM SITE... 4500 FEET
 ESTIMATED TIME OF ARRIVAL... 7.92312 SECONDS


BOMB COMMAND? STAND BY
STANDING BY.

MAINTAIN PRESENT RESULTANT ANGLE? YES

AIRSPEED? 700
```

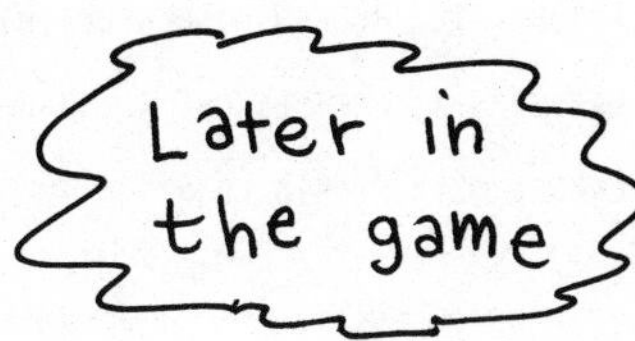


```
BOMB COMMAND? STAND BY
STANDING BY.

MAINTAIN PRESENT RESULTANT ANGLE? YES

AIRSPEED? 750
                              ***STATS***

                 ELAPSED TIME... 2 SECONDS
        PRESENT ANGLE COMMAND... 0 DEGREES
             RESULTANT ANGLE... 0 DEGREES
            PRESENT VEROCITY...  750 FEET PER SECOND
                   ALTITUDE...  128.552 FEET
           DISTANCE FROM SITE...  3000 FEET
     ESTIMATED TIME OF ARRIVAL...  4 SECONDS


BOMB COMMAND? STAND BY
STANDING BY.

MAINTAIN PRESENT RESULTANT ANGLE? YES

AIRSPEED? 750
                              ***STATS***

                 ELAPSED TIME... 3 SECONDS
        PRESENT ANGLE COMMAND... 0 DEGREES
             RESULTANT ANGLE... 0 DEGREES
            PRESENT VEROCITY...  750 FEET PER SECOND
                   ALTITUDE...  128.552 FEET
           DISTANCE FROM SITE...  2250 FEET
     ESTIMATED TIME OF ARRIVAL...  3 SECONDS


BOMB COMMAND? STAND BY
STANDING BY.

MAINTAIN PRESENT RESULTANT ANGLE? YES

AIRSPEED? 750
                              ***STATS***

                 ELAPSED TIME... 4 SECONDS
        PRESENT ANGLE COMMAND... 0 DEGREES
             RESULTANT ANGLE... 0 DEGREES
            PRESENT VEROCITY...  750 FEET PER SECOND
                   ALTITUDE...  128.552 FEET
           DISTANCE FROM SITE...  1500 FEET
     ESTIMATED TIME OF ARRIVAL...  2 SECONDS


BOMB COMMAND? STAND BY PLEASE
UNRECOGNIZABLE COMMAND.  REPLY 'STAND BY' OR 'DROP'.
STANDING BY.

MAINTAIN PRESENT RESULTANT ANGLE? YES

AIRSPEED? 300
                              ***STATS***

                 ELAPSED TIME... 5 SECONDS
        PRESENT ANGLE COMMAND... 0 DEGREES
             RESULTANT ANGLE... 0 DEGREES
            PRESENT VEROCITY...  300 FEET PER SECOND
                   ALTITUDE...  128.552 FEET
           DISTANCE FROM SITE...  1200 FEET
     ESTIMATED TIME OF ARRIVAL...  4 SECONDS


BOMB COMMAND? DROP
BOMB DROPPED.
TINE TO EXPLOSION...  2.8257 SECONDS

THE BOMB LANDED 352.28 FEET IN FRONT OF THE TARGET'S CENTER.

DURING YOUR 4 -PASS BOMBRUN, YOU MANAGED TO STRIKE
WITHIN 0 FEET OF THE TARGET.

WOULD YOU LIKE TO RELOAD AND PLAY AGAIN?
? NO
LOOK OVER THE PHYSICS LAWS GOVERNING FALLING BODIES,
AND RETURN TO PLAY AGAIN SOON.
Ok
```

```
LIST
10 PRINT TAB(27)"BOMBRUN"
13 PRINT TAB(20)"CREATIVE COMPUTING"
15 PRINT TAB(18)"MORRISTOWN, NEW JERSEY"
19 PRINT:PRINT
20 PRINT"THIS PROGRAM SIMULATES A BOMBING RUN.  DO YOU NEED"
25 X5=3000
30 PRINT"INSTRUCTIONS";
40 INPUT I$
50 IF I$="YES" THEN 90
60 IF I$="NO" THEN 290
70 PRINT"ILLOGICAL RESPONSE.  REPLY'YES' OR "NO"."
80 GOTO 40
90 PRINT"YOU HAVE THE OPTION OF MAKING FOUR PASSES OVER THE TARGET,"
100 PRINT"WITH THE ABILITY TO DROP A BOMB ONCE DURING EACH OF"
110 PRINT"THESE PASSES.  ALTITUDE CHANGES MAYBE MADE THROUGH THE"
120 PRINT "'CLIMB/DIVE' COMMAND BY PRINTING 'CLIMB' OR 'DIVE',FOL-"
130 PRINT"LOWED BY A COMMA AND THE DESIRED ANGLE (IN DEGREES).  NEW"
140 PRINT"VELOCITIES (RANGING FROM 300 TO 900 FEET PER SECOND) MAY"
150 PRINT"BE INPUT AFTER THE 'AIRSPEED' QUESTION MARK.  'CLIMB/DIVE'"
160 PRINT"ANGLES, VARYING FROM 0 TO 15 DEGREES, WILL ADD AS SPEC-"
170 PRINT"IFIED BY 'CLIMB' OR'DIVE' COMMANDS TO YIELD A NET INCLIN-"
180 PRINT "ATION/DECLINATION ANGLE BETWEEN 0 TO 60 DEGREES, CLIMBING"
190 PRINT "OR DIVING.  A MINIMUM ALTITUDE OF 100 FEET MUST ALSO BE"
200 PRINT"MAINTAINED.  WILLFULLY EXCEEDING ANY OF THE MAX./MIN. SPECS"
210 PRINT"WILL RESULT IN THE CRASH OF YOUR BOMBER.  ALSO , A BOMB"
220 PRINT"COMMAND OF 'DROP' DURING A DIVE WILL GIVE YOUR BOMB AN IN-"
230 PRINT"ITIAL DOWNWARD VELOCITY, SHORTENING THE DROP TIME, AS A"
240 PRINT"'CLIMB' COMMAND WILL LENGTHEN THIS TIME.  THE BOMB WILL BE"
250 PRINT"LAUNCHED IMMEDIATELY FOLLOWING THE MOST RECENT 'STATS' READ-"
260 PRINT "OUT UPON 'DROP' COMMAND, AND WILL BE HELD FOR FURTHER"
270 PRINT"POSITIONING INFORMATION UPON THE COMMAND 'STAND BY'.  THE"
280 PRINT"TARGET IS 1 FOOT IN DIAMETER.  GOOD LUCK"
290 Z1=1000
300 Z2=1000
310 Z3=1000
320 Z4=1000
330 R=R+1
340 W1=0
350 X2=0
360 W3=0
370 W4=0
380 T=0
390 A1=0
400 A=0
410 V1=RND(1)
420 V=V1*1000
430 IF V<300 OR V>900 THEN 410
440 Y1=RND(1)
450 Y=Y1*500
460 IF Y<100 THEN440
470 X=4500
480 PRINT" "
490 PRINT" "
500 E=X/V
510 PRINT TAB(30)"**INITIAL**"
520 PRINT TAB(30)"***STATS***"
530 GOTO1430
540 W1=0
550 W2=0
560 W3=0
570 W4=0
580 PRINT" "
590 PRINT"BOMB COMMAND";
600 INPUT C$
610 IF C$="STAND BY" THEN 640
620 IF C$="DROP" THEN 1680
630 PRINT"UNRECOGNIZABLE COMMAND.  REPLY 'STAND BY' OR 'DROP'."
640 PRINT"STANDING BY."
650 PRINT " "
660 GOTO 700
670 A=A-A1
680 T=T-1
690 GOTO 770
700 PRINT"MAINTAIN PRESENT RESULTANT ANGLE";
710 INPUT P$
720 PRINT" "
730 IF P$="YES" THEN 1130
740 IF P$="NO" THEN 770
750 PRINT"REPLY 'YES' OR'NO'.";
760 GOTO 710
770 PRINT"'CLIMB/DIVE' COMMAND";
780 INPUT A$,A1
790 PRINT" "
800 IF A1<0 THEN 830
810 IF A1>15 THEN 870
820 GOTO 930
830 PRINT"ANGLE INPUT MUST BE POSITVE.  IF NECESSARY, CHANGE THE"
840 PRINT"'DIVE' COMMAND TO 'CLIMB', OR VICE VERSA."
```

```
850 PRINT" "
860 GOTO770
870 W1=W1+1
880 IF W1=2 THEN 2120
890 PRINT"YOUR BOMBER CANNOT TOLERATE THE STRESS CAUSED BY ANGLE"
900 PRINT"INPUTS EXCEEDING 15 DEGREES.  RECONSIDER YOUR CHOICE."
910 PRINT" "
920 GOTO 770
930 IF A$="CLIMB" THEN 950
940 A1=-A1
950 A=A+A1
960 IF A<-60 THEN 990
970 IF A>60 THEN 1060
980 GOTO 1140
990 W2=W2+1
1000 IF W2=2 THEN 2170
1010 PRINT"YOUR PRESENT'DIVE' COMMAND WILL EXCEED THE MAXIMUN RE-"
1020 PRINT"SULTANT DIVE ANGLE OF 60 DEGREES, CAUSING AN IRREVERSIBLE"
1030 PRINT" NOSEDIVE.  RECONSIDER YOUR CHOICE."
1040 PRINT" "
1050 GOTO 670
1060 W3=W3+1
1070 IF W3=2 THEN 2210
1080 PRINT"YOUR PRESENT 'CLIMB' COMMAND WILL EXCEED THE  MAXIMUN RE-"
1090 PRINT"SULTANT CLIMB ANGLE  OF 60 DEGREES, CAUSING YOUR"
1100 PRINT" ENGINES TO FAIL AND YOUR PLANE TO CRASH.  RECONSIDER YOUR "
1105 PRINT"CHOICE"
1110 PRINT" "
1120 GOTO 670
1130 REM
1140 PRINT"AIRSPEED";
1150 INPUT V
1160 IF V>900 THEN 1190
1170 IF V<300 THEN 1230
1180 GOTO 1290
1190 PRINT"YOUR BOMBER ISN'T CAPABLE OF ATTAINING THAT VELOCITY."
1200 PRINT"INPUT AN AIRSPEED LESS THAN 900 FEET PER SECOND."
1210 PRINT" "
1220 GOTO 1150
1230 W4=W4+1
1240 IF W4=2 THEN 2250
1250 PRINT"IF YOUR VELOCITY ISN'T INCREASED IMMEDIATELY, YOUR BOMBER"
1260 PRINT"WILL FALL TO EARTH AND BE DESTROYED."
1270 PRINT" "
1280 GOTO 1140
1290 T=T+1
1300 B=A*3.14159/180
1310 Y=Y+V*SIN(B)
1320 IF Y>100 THEN 1390
1330 W5=W5+1
1340 IF W5=2 THEN 2290
1350 PRINT"IF YOUR ALTITUTE ISN'T INCREASED IMMEDIATELY TO A MIN-"
1360 PRINT"IMUN OF 100 FEET, A CRASH IS IMMINENT."
1370 PRINT" "
1380 GOTO 670
1390 X=X-V*COS(B)
1400 IF X<=0 THEN 2350
1410 E=X/(V*COS(B))
1420 PRINT TAB(30)"***STATS***"
1430 PRINT" "
1440 IF NOT(T=1)THEN 1470
1450 PRINT TAB(20)"ELAPSED TIME... 1 SECOND"
1460 GOTO 1480
1470 PRINT TAB(20)"ELAPSED TIME...";T;"SECONDS"
1480 IF NOT(A1=0) THEN 1510
1490 PRINT TAB(11)"PRESENT ANGLE COMMAND... 0 DEGREES"
1500 GOTO 1550
1510 IF A$="CLIMB" THEN 1540
1520 PRINTTAB(11)"PRESENT ANGLE COMMAND... DIVE,";-A1;"DEGREES"
1530 GOTO 1550
1540 PRINT TAB(11)"PRESENT ANGLE COMMAND... CLIMB,";A1;"DEGREES"
1550 IF A<0 THEN 1590
1560 IF A>0 THEN 1610
1570 PRINT TAB(17)"RESULTANT ANGLE... 0 DEGREES"
1580 GOTO 1620
1590 PRINT TAB(17)"RESULTANT ANGLE...";-A1;"DEGREES DIVING"
1600 GOTO 1620
1610 PRINT TAB(17)"RESULTANT ANGLE...";A;"DEGREES CLIMBING"
1620 PRINT TAB(16)"PRESENT VEROCITY... ";V;"FEET PER SECOND"
1630 PRINT TAB(24)"ALTITUDE... ";Y;"FEET"
1640 PRINT TAB(14)"DISTANCE FROM SITE... ";X;"FEET"
1650 PRINT TAB(7)"ESTIMATED TIME OF ARRIVAL... ";E;"SECONDS"
1660 PRINT
1670 GOTO 540
1680 PRINT"BOMB DROPPED."
1690 T3=(SQR((V*SIN(B))^2+64.4*Y)+V*SIN(B))/32.2
1700 PRINT"TIME TO EXPLOSION... ";T3;"SECONDS"
1710 X=X-V*COS(B)*T3
1720 X=INT(X*100)/100
1725 IF X5>ABS(X5) THEN X5=ABS(X5)
1730 PRINT " "
1740 IF X<-.5 THEN 1780
1750 IF X>.5 THEN 1800
1760 PRINT"CONGRATULATIONS, YOU SCORED AS PERFECT HIT."
1770 GOTO 2030
1780 PRINT"THE BOMB LANDED";-X;"FEET BEYOND THE TARGET'S CENTER."
1790 GOTO 1810
1800 PRINT"THE BOMB LANDED";X;"FEET IN FRONT OF THE TARGET'S CENTER."
1810 IF R=1 THEN 1850
1820 IF R=2 THEN 1870
1830 IF R=3 THEN 1890
1840 IF R=4 THEN 1910
1850 Z1=ABS(X)
1860 GOTO 2400
1870 Z2=ABS(X)
1880 GOTO 2420
1890 Z3=ABS(X)
1900 GOTO 2440
1910 Z4=ABS(X)
1920 Z1=Z10(1):Z2=Z10(2):Z3=Z10(3):Z4=Z10(4)
1921 FOR M=1 TO 4
1922 FOR M1= 4 TO 1 STEP-1
1923 IF Z10(M)<Z10(M1) THEN Z10(M)=X5
1924 IF M=M1 AND M=1 THEN 1926
1925 NEXTM1
1926 NEXT M
1930 PRINT" "
1940 IF X5<= 300 THEN 2000
1950 PRINT"DURING YOUR";R;"-PASS BOMBRUN, YOU FAILED TO EVEN"
1960 PRINT"THREATEN THE TARGET WITH A HIT.  BETTER LUCK NEXT TIME."
1970 IF R$="NO" THEN 2590
1980 GOTO 2040
1990 GOTO 2610
2000 PRINT"DURING YOUR";R;"-PASS BOMBRUN, YOU MANAGED TO STRIKE"
2010 PRINT"WITHIN";X5;"FEET OF THE TARGET."
2020 PRINT" "
2030 IF R$="NO" THEN 2590
2040 PRINT"WOULD YOU LIKE TO RELOAD AND PLAY AGAIN?"
2050 INPUT A$
2060 IF A$="NO" THEN 2590
2070 IF A$="YES" THEN 2100
2080 PRINT"YOU MUST BE A LOUSY SPELLER.  REPLY 'YES' OR'NO'."
2090 GOTO 2050
2100 R=0
2110 GOTO 290
2120 PRINT"YOU TORE THE WINGS OFF OF YOUR BOMBER BY EXCEEDING THE"
2130 PRINT"MAXIMUN ANGLE INPUT OF 15 DEGREES. NEXT TIME TAKE MY ADVISE"
2150 H=1
2160 GOTO 1920
2170 PRINT"THE STEEP DIVE ANGLE DESIRED CAUSED AN IRREVERISIBLE NOSE-"
2180 PRINT"DIVE, RESULTING IN  THE DESTRUCTION OF YOUR BOMBER."
2190 H=1
2200 GOTO 1920
2210 PRINT"THE ENGINES OF YOUR BOMBER FAILED WHILE CLIMBING THE"
2220 PRINT"STEEP ANGLE INPUT DURING YOUR ANGLE COMMAND OPPORTUNITY."
2230 H=1
2240 GOTO 1920
2250 PRINT"THE VEROCITY OF YOUR BOMBER WAS INSUFFICIENT TO SUPPORT"
2260 PRINT"ITS WEIGHT, AND CONSEQUENTLY IT CRASHED."
2270 H=1
2280 GOTO 1920
2290 PRINT"YOUR BOMBER FAILED TO MAINTAIN THE LOW ALTITUTE YOU DE-"
2300 PRINT"SIRED AND SOON CRASHED."
2310 PRINT"BETTER LUCK NEXT TIME."
2320 H=1
2330 GOTO 1920
2340 PRINT"YOUR BOMBER  JUST PASSED UP THE TARGET, AND NEEDLESS TO"
2350 PRINT"SAY, YOU NO LONGER THREATEN ITS EXISTANCE."
2360 PRINT" "
2370 IF R=2 THEN 2420
2380 IF R=3 THEN 2440
2390 IF R=4 THEN 1920
2400 Q$=" SECOND "
2410 GOTO 2450
2420 Q$="THIRD"
2430 GOTO 2450
2440 Q$="FOURTH AND FINAL"
2450 IF R>1 THEN 2490
2460 PRINT"YOU HAVE THUS FAR COMPLETED 1 RUN. WOULD YOU LIKE TO"
2470 PRINT"MAKE ANOTHER PASS";
2480 GOTO2510
2490 PRINT"YOU HAVE THUS FAR COMPLETED ";R;"RUNS.  WOULD YOU LIKE TO "
2500 PRINT"ANOTHER PASS";
2510 INPUT R$
2520 IF R$="YES" THEN 2560
2530 IF R$="NO" THEN 1920
2540 PRINT"SIMPLY REPLY 'YES' OR'NO'."
2550 GOTO 2510
2560 PRINT"YOUR PLANE HAS CIRCLED, AND IS NOW IN POSITION TO MAKE"
2570 PRINT"ITS";Q$;"PASS."
2580 GOTO 330
2590 PRINT"LOOK OVER THE PHYSICS LAWS GOVERNING FALLING BODIES,"
2600 PRINT"AND RETURN TO PLAY AGAIN SOON."
2610 END
Ok
```

Bridge-It

Bridge-it is a two-player pencil and paper logic game. One player is represented by X's, the other by O's. The X's and O's are arranged in an alternating grid pattern so that X's may be joined to one another by a line without crossing an O and O's may be joined to one another without crossing an X. The object of the game is for the X's to draw a line from the top to the bottom of the board. The O's must connect a continuous chain from the right to the left of the board. Players move alternately and may go any place on the grid. Any two of your symbols, either X's or O's, may be connected together on a given move.

In this particular version of the game, the computer is your opponent. The computer plays the X's and you play the O's. The computer moves first, which gives it a very slight advantage. If you find it is too formidable an opponent you may wish to modify the program to allow the player to move first. At any point during the game you may ask for a printout of the board and see how the play is progressing.

This program was written by Michael Kass, Miles Barel, and Alan Segal.

```
RUN
                    BRIDGE-IT
                CREATIVE COMPUTING
              MORRISTOWN, NEW JERSEY


DO YOU WANT INSTRUCTIONS? YES

THE OBJECT OF THIS GAME IS FOR YOU TO GO FROM THE LEFT
COLUMN TO THE RIGHT COLUMN BY CONNECTING THE O'S.  THE COM-
PUTER MUST GO FROM THE TOP TO THE BOTTOM BY CONNECTING
THE X'S.

YOU MAKE YOUR MOVES BY TYPING IN THE COORDINATES (X,Y) OR
(COLUMN,ROW)
OF THE 'O' YOU WISH TO MOVE FROM AFTER THE COMPUTER
 TYPES:

YOUR MOVE FROM?

AND BY TYPING IN THE COORDINATES OF THE'O' YOU WISH TO MOVE
TO AFTER THE COMPUTER TYPES:

TO?

YOU CAN MOVE EITHER VERTICALLY OR HORIZONTALLY,
BUT NOT DIAGONALLY.  YOU CANNOT MOVE VERTICALLY IN EITHER
THE FIRST COLUMN OR THE THIRTEENTH COLUMN. THE COMPUTER WILL
MOVE FIRST.


TEAR ON LINE
----------------------------
YOU MAY USE THIS BOARD TO MARK THE MOVES ON, OR
YOU CAN GET AN UPDATED BOARD AFTER YOU MAKE EACH MOVE.



            1111
   1234567890123
13  X X X X X X
12 0 0 0 0 0 0 0
11  X X X X X X
10 0 0 0 0 0 0 0
 9  X X X X X X
 8 0 0 0 0 0 0 0
 7  X X X X X X
 6 0 0 0 0 0 0 0
 5  X X X X X X
 4 0 0 0 0 0 0 0
 3  X X X X X X
 2 0 0 0 0 0 0 0
 1  X X X X X X
   1234567891111
            0123


-------------------- --------
TEAR ON LINE

I MOVE FROM 2,1 TO 2,3


YOUR MOVE FROM? 1,4
TO? 3,4

BOARD (YES OR NO)? N

I MOVE FROM  4 , 3 TO  4 , 5


YOUR MOVE FROM? 3,2
TO? 3,4

BOARD (YES OR NO)? N

I MOVE FROM  4 , 1 TO  4 , 3


YOUR MOVE FROM? 3,3
TO? 5,3

INVALID MOVE -- TRY AGAIN

YOUR MOVE FROM? 3,6
TO? 5,6
BOARD (YES OR NO)? N

I MOVE FROM  6 , 5 TO  6 , 7


YOUR MOVE FROM? 5,4
TO? 5,6

BOARD (YES OR NO)? N

I MOVE FROM  6 , 3 TO  6 , 5


YOUR MOVE FROM? 5,8
TO? 7,8

BOARD (YES OR NO)? N

I MOVE FROM  8 , 7 TO  8 , 9


YOUR MOVE FROM? 7,10
TO? 9,10
```

```
BOARD (YES OR NO)? Y

              1111
   1234567890123
13  X X X X X X
12 0 0 0 0 0 0 0
11  X X X X X X
10 0 0 0 0-0 0 0
 9  X X X X X X
 8 0 0 0-0!0 0 0
 7  X X X X X X
 6 0 0-0!0 0 0 0
 5  X X!X X X X
 4 0-0!0!0 0 0 0
 3  X!X X X X X
 2 0!0!0 0 0 0 0
 1  X X X X X X
   1234567891111
            0123


I MOVE FROM  10 , 9 TO  10 , 11


YOUR MOVE FROM? 9,8
TO? 9,10

BOARD (YES OR NO)? N

I MOVE FROM  10 , 7 TO  10 , 9


YOUR MOVE FROM? 7,6
TO? 7,8

BOARD (YES OR NO)? N

I MOVE FROM  8 , 5 TO  8 , 7


YOUR MOVE FROM? 9,12
TO? 11,12

BOARD (YES OR NO)? N

I MOVE FROM  12 , 11 TO  12 , 13
I WIN!!!!

BOARD (YES OR NO)? Y

              1111
   1234567890123
13  X X X X X X
12 0 0 0 0 0-0!0
11  X X X X X X
10 0 0 0 0-0!0 0
 9  X X X X!X X
 8 0 0 0-0!0!0 0
 7  X X X!X X X
 6 0 0-0!0!0 0 0
 5  X X!X X X X
 4 0-0!0!0 0 0 0
 3  X!X X X X X
 2 0!0!0 0 0 0 0
 1  X X X X X X
   1234567891111
            0123
```

```
LIST
5 PRINT TAB(24);"BRIDGE-IT"
10 PRINT TAB(20);"CREATIVE COMPUTING"
20 PRINT TAB(18);"MORRISTOWN, NEW JERSEY"
30 I=I-2
42 PRINT
50 PRINT
70 PRINT"DO YOU WANT INSTRUCTIONS";
80 INPUT B4$
90 PRINT
100 IF LEFT$(B4$,1)="N" THEN 300
120 PRINT"THE OBJECT OF THIS GAME IS FOR YOU TO GO FROM THE LEFT "
130 PRINT"COLUMN TO THE RIGHT COLUMN BY CONNECTING THE O'S.  THE COM-"
140 PRINT"PUTER MUST GO FROM THE TOP TO THE BOTTOM BY CONNECTING"
145 PRINT"THE X'S."
150 PRINT
160 PRINT"YOU MAKE YOUR MOVES BY TYPING IN THE COORDINATES (X,Y) OR"
170 PRINT"(COLUMN,ROW)"
171 PRINT"OF THE 'O' YOU WISH TO MOVE FROM AFTER THE COMPUTER"
172 PRINT" TYPES:"
180 PRINT
190 PRINT"YOUR MOVE FROM?"
200 PRINT
210 PRINT"AND BY TYPING IN THE COORDINATES OF THE'O' YOU WISH TO MOVE"
220 PRINT"TO AFTER THE COMPUTER TYPES:"
230 PRINT
240 PRINT"TO?"
250 PRINT
260 PRINT"YOU CAN MOVE EITHER VERTICALLY OR HORIZONTALLY,"
270 PRINT"BUT NOT DIAGONALLY.  YOU CANNOT MOVE VERTICALLY IN EITHER"
280 PRINT"THE FIRST COLUMN OR THE THIRTEENTH COLUMN. THE COMPUTER WILL"
281 PRINT"MOVE FIRST."
290 PRINT:PRINT
300 DIM X(20,20)
320 DIMO(20,20)
330 DIMT(20,20)
340 FOR X=1 TO 13 STEP 2
350 FOR Y=2 TO 12 STEP2
360 O(X,Y)=1
370 X(Y,X)=1
380 NEXT Y
390 NEXT X
400 GOTO480
410 PRINT
420 PRINT"BOARD (YES OR NO)";
430 INPUTB$
440 PRINT
450 IF LEFT$(B$,1)="N" THEN 490
480 GOSUB 990:REM PRINT BOARD SUBROUTINE
490 IF E<>5 THEN 510
500 GOTO 3010
510 GOSUB1640:REM COMPUTER MOVE
520 GOSUB 640:REM COMPUTER WIN SUBROUTINE
530 PRINT
540 IF E=5 THEN 420
550 GOSUB2710:REM PLAYER WIN SUBROUTINE
560 PRINT
570 PRINT"YOUR MOVE FROM";
580 INPUT F,G
590 PRINT"TO";
600 INPUT F1,G1
610 PRINT
620 GOSUB 2220:REM ERROR AND CHANGE BOARD SUBROUTINE
630 GOTO 420
640 REM WIN SUBROUTINE ***********************************************
650 REM FIRST TEST
660 FOR H=1 TO 11 STEP 2
670 J=12
680 IF O(H,J)=3 THEN 710
690 NEXT H
700 GOTO 980
710 FOR I=1 TO 11 STEP 2
720 J=2
730 IF O(I,J)=3 THEN 760
740 NEXT I
750 GOTO 980
760 REM OTHER TESTS
770 J=J+2
780 IF J=12 THEN 960
790 IF O(I,J)=3 THEN 870
800 IF O(I+1,J+1)=2 THEN 890
810 IF I-1<0 THEN 840
820 IF O(I-1,J-1)=2 THEN 920
830 IF X(I+1,J+1)=2 THEN 890
840 IF I-1<0 THEN980
850 IF X(I-1,J-1) THEN 890
860 GOTO 740
870 J=J+2
880 GOTO 780
890 J=J
900 I=I+2
910 GOTO 780
920 J=J
950 GOTO 980
960 PRINT"I WIN!!!!"
970 E=5
980 RETURN
990 REM PRINT BOARD SUBROUTINE *****************************************
1000 R=R+1
1010 IF R>1 THEN 1150
1020 PRINT"TEAR ON LINE"
1030 PRINT"---------------------------"
1040 PRINT"YOU MAY USE THIS BOARD TO MARK THE MOVES ON, OR"
1050 PRINT"YOU CAN GET AN UPDATED BOARD AFTER YOU MAKE EACH MOVE."
1060 PRINT
1070 PRINT
1080 PRINT
1090 PRINT
1100 PRINT
1110 PRINT
1120 PRINT TAB(5);CHR$(7);CHR$(13);TAB(5);CHR$(7)
1130 PRINT
1140 PRINT
1150 D=0
1160 PRINT TAB(13)"1111"
1170 PRINT TAB(4)"1234567890123"
1180 FOR Y=13 TO 1 STEP -1
```

```
1190 IF Y<10 THEN 1220
1200 PRINT Y;
1210 GOTO 1230
1220 PRINT" "Y;
1230 FOR X=1 TO 13 STEP1
1240 IF Y/2=INT(Y/2) THEN 1330
1250 IF X(X,Y)=0 THEN 1420
1260 ONX(X,Y) GOTO 1270,1290,1310
1270 PRINT"X ";
1280 GOTO 1450
1290 PRINT"X-";
1300 GOTO 1450
1310 PRINT"X!":
1320 GOTO 1450
1330 D=0
1340 IF O(X,Y)=0 THEN 1450
1350 ON O(X,Y) GOTO 1360,1380,1400
1360 PRINT "O ";
1370 GOTO 1450
1380 PRINT"O-";
1390 GOTO 1450
1400 PRINT"O!";
1410 GOTO 1450
1420 D=D+1
1430 IFD>1 THEN 1450
1440 PRINT " ";
1450 NEXT X
1460 GOSUB 1620
1470 NEXT Y
1480 PRINT TAB(4)"1234567891111"
1490 PRINT TAB(13)"0123"
1500 R1=R1+1
1510 IF R1>1 THEN 1590
1520 PRINT
1530 PRINT
1540 PRINT"---------------------------"
1550 PRINT"TEAR ON LINE"
1560 PRINT
1570 PRINT
1580 PRINT
1590 PRINT
1600 PRINT
1610 RETURN
1620 PRINT
1630 RETURN
1640 REM COMPUTER MOVE SUBROUTINE *************************************
1650 B=B+1
1660 IF B>1 THEN 1710
1670 O(1,2)=3
1680 PRINT "I MOVE FROM 2,1 TO 2,3"
1690 B1=B1+1
1700 IF B1>1 THEN 1890
1710 FOR C=3 TO 11 STEP 2
1720 T(C,C+1)=1
1730 T(C-2,C+1)=1
1740 GOTO 1790
1750 NEXT C
1760 T(2,3)=3
1770 T(7,12)=2
1780 GOTO 1890
1790 FOR Q=C+3 TO 12 STEP 2
1800 T(C-2,Q)=2
1810 T(C-1,Q+1)=2
1820 T(C-1,Q-1)=2
1830 NEXT Q
1840 FOR S=C TO 3 STEP -2
1850 T(C-1,S)=3
1860 T(C,S-1)=3
1870 NEXT S
1880 GOTO 1750
1890 IF F>F1 THEN 1950
1900 IF F<>F1 THEN 1920
1910 IF G>G1 THEN 1950
1920 X=F
1930 Y=G
1940 GOTO 1970
1950 X=F1
1960 Y=G1
1970 IF T(X,Y)=0 THEN 2210
1980 IF F<>F1 THEN 2000
1990 ON T(X-1,Y+1) GOTO 2010,2080,2150
2000 ON T(X,Y) GOTO 2010,2080,2150
2010 IF X=Y-1 THEN 2050
2020 O(X+2,Y)=3
2030 PRINT"I MOVE FROM ";X+3;",";Y-1;"TO ";X+3;",";Y+1
2040 GOTO 2210
2050 O(X-2,Y)=3
2060 PRINT"I MOVE FROM ";X-1;",";Y-1;"TO ";X-1;",";Y+1
2070 GOTO 2210
2080 IF X(X-1,Y+1)=3 THEN 2120
2090 X(X+1,Y-1)=2
2100 PRINT"I MOVE FROM ";X+1;",";Y-1;"TO ";X+3;",";Y-1
2110 GOTO2210
2120 O(X-2,Y+2)=3
2130 PRINT"I MOVE FROM ";X-1",";Y+1;"TO ";X-1;",";Y+3
2140 GOTO 2210
2150 IF X(X-1,Y+1)=3 THEN 2190
2160 X(X-1,Y+1)=2
2170 PRINT"I MOVE FROM ";X-1;",";Y+1;"TO ";X+1;",";Y+1
2180 GOTO 2210
2190 O(X,Y)=3
2200 PRINT"I MOVE FROM ";X+1;",";Y-1;"TO ";X+1",";Y+1
2210 RETURN
2220 REM ERROR AND CHANGE BOARD SUBROUTINE****************************
2230 IF F<>F1 THEN 2280
2240 IF F=1 THEN 2630
2250 IF F=13 THEN 2630
2260 IF F1=13 THEN 2630
2270 IF G=G1 THEN 2630
2280 IF F/2=INT(F/2) THEN 2630
2290 IF F>13 THEN 2630
2300 IF G>12 THEN 2630
2310 IF G/2<> INT(G/2) THEN 2630
2320 IF F<>INT(F) THEN 2630
2330 IF F<1 THEN 2630
2340 IF G<1 THEN 2630
2350 IF F1/2=INT(F1/2) THEN 2630
2360 IF F1>13 THEN 2630
2370 IF G1>12 THEN 2630
2380 IF G1/2 <>INT(G1/2) THEN 2630
2390 IF F1<>INT(F1) THEN 2630
2400 IF G1<1 THEN 2630
2410 IF F=F1 THEN 2530
2420 IF G<>G1 THEN 2630
2430 IF ABS(F-F1)<>2 THEN 2630:REM PRINT ERROR
2440 IF F>F1 THEN 2490
2450 IF O(F,G)=2 THEN 2630
2460 IF O(F,G)=3 THEN 2630
2470 O(F,G)=2
2480 GOTO 2700:REM RETURN
2490 IF O(F1,G1)=2 THEN 2630
2500 IF O(F1,G1)=3 THEN 2630
2510 O(F1,G1)=2
2520 GOTO 2700: REM RETURN
2530 IF ABS(G-G1)<>2 THEN 2530:REM PRINT ERROR
2540 IF G>G1 THEN 2590
2550 IF X(F-1,G+1)=2 THEN 2630
2560 IF X(F-1,G+1)=3 THEN 2630
2570 X(F-1,G+1)=3
2580 GOTO 2700:REM RETURN
2590 IF X(F1-1,G1+1)=2 THEN 2630
2600 IF X(F1-1,G1+1)=3 THEN 2630
2610 X(F1-1,G1+1)=3
2620 GOTO 2700:REM RETURN
2630 PRINT"INVALID MOVE -- TRY AGAIN"
2640 PRINT
2650 PRINT"YOUR MOVE FROM";
2660 INPUT F,G
2670 PRINT"TO";
2680 INPUT F1,G1
2690 GOTO 2220
2700 RETURN
2710 REM PLAYER WIN ROUTINE ******************************************
2720 FOR H=1 TO11 STEP 2
2730 I=12
2740 IF X(I,H)=3 THEN 2770
2750 NEXT H
2760 GOTO 3000
2770 FOR  J=1 TO 11 STEP 2
2780 I=2
2790 IF X(I,J)=3 THEN 2820
2800 NEXT J
2810 GOTO 3000
2820 I=I+2
2830 IF I=12 THEN 2970
2840 IF X(I,J)=3 THEN 2910
2850 IF X(I+1,J+1)=2 THEN 2930
2860 IF J-1<0 THEN 2890
2870 IF X(I-1,J-1)=2 THEN 2950
2880 IFO(I+1,J+1)=2 THEN 2930
2890 IF J-1<0 THEN 3000
2900 GOTO 2808
2910 I=I+2
2920 GOTO 2830
2930 J=J+2
2940 GOTO 2830
2950 J=J-2
2960 GOTO 2830
2970 IF O(1,2)<>2 THEN 3000
2980 PRINT"YOU WIN !!! CONGRATULATIONS!!!"
2990 E=5
3000 RETURN
3010 END
Ok
```

Camel

In this game of high adventure, your object is to travel 200 miles across the great Gobi Desert. You're being chased by a tribe of knock-kneed pygmies. You have one quart of water which will last you for six drinks; it may be renewed if you find an oasis or, if you are found by another traveller, you may get an additional half-quart of water. During your journey you encounter all types of hazards such as sand storms, wild Berbers and possible injuries to your camel.

Warning: this is a very hazardous and addictive game. It is also very difficult to win. In ten plays of the game, the maximum distance we were able to travel was 159 miles, and in many cases we managed to make only seven or eight miles before one of the hazards caused our demise.

This game was submitted by the Heath Users Group.

```
RUN
                         CAMEL
                   CREATIVE COMPUTING
                 MORRISTOWN, NEW JERSEY


WOULD YOU LIKE INSTRUCTIONS? YES

   WELCOME TO CAMEL.  THE OBJEST IS TO TRAVEL
200 MILES ACROSS THE GREAT GOBI DESERT.
A TRIBE OF KNOCKED KNEED PIGMIES WILL BE CHASING YOU.
YOU WILL BE ASKED FOR COMMANDS EVERY SO OFTEN.


C O M M A N D S :
#1 DRINK FROM YOUR CANTEEN
#2 AHEAD MODERATE SPEED
#3 AHEAD FULL SPEED
#4 STOP FOR THE NIGHT
#5 STATUS CHECK
#6 HOPE FOR HELP



YOU HAVE ONE QUART OF WATER WHICH WILL LAST YOU SIX DRINKS.
YOU MAVE RENEW YOUR WATER SUPPLY COMPLETELY AT AN OASES.
YOU GET A HALF A QUART IF FOUND BY HELP.
IF HELP DOES NOT FIND YOU AFTER COMMAND SIX, YOU LOSE.
GOOD LUCK AND GOOD CAMELING !!
YOU ARE IN THE MIDDLE OF THE DESERT AT AN OASIS.
YOU HAVE TRAVELLED  0  MILES ALLTOGETHER.
WHAT IS YOUR COMMAND? 3
YOUR CAMEL IS BURNING ACROSS THE DESERT SANDS.

YOU HAVE TRAVELLED  6  MILES ALLTOGETHER.
WHAT IS YOUR COMMAND? 3
YOUR CAMEL IS BURNING ACROSS THE DESERT SANDS.

----------W A R N I N G---------- GET A DRINK
YOU HAVE TRAVELLED  8  MILES ALLTOGETHER.
WHAT IS YOUR COMMAND? 4
YOUR CAMEL THANKS YOU!
THE PYGMIES HAVE CAPTURED YOU.  CAMEL AND PEOPLE SOUP IS
THEIR FAVORITE DISH !!!!!
WANT A NEW CAMEL AND A NEW GAME ? Y
GOOD LUCK AND GOOD CAMELING !!
YOU ARE IN THE MIDDLE OF THE DESERT AT AN OASIS.
YOU HAVE TRAVELLED  0  MILES ALLTOGETHER.
WHAT IS YOUR COMMAND? 3
YOUR CAMEL IS BURNING ACROSS THE DESERT SANDS.

YOU HAVE TRAVELLED  6  MILES ALLTOGETHER.
WHAT IS YOUR COMMAND? 2
YOUR CAMEL LIKES THIS PACE.
----------W A R N I N G---------- GET A DRINK
YOU HAVE TRAVELLED  8  MILES ALLTOGETHER.
WHAT IS YOUR COMMAND? 1
BETTER WATCH FOR AN OASES !
WHAT IS YOUR COMMAND? 2
YOU HAVE BEEN CAUGHT IN A SANDSTORM.....GOOD LUCK!
YOUR NEW POSITION IS  12  MILES SO FAR!
YOUR CAMEL LIKES THIS PACE.
THE PYGMIES ARE  10  MILES BEHIND YOU.
YOU HAVE TRAVELLED  20  MILES ALLTOGETHER.
WHAT IS YOUR COMMAND? 3
YOU DIRTY RAPSCALLION! YOU RAN YOUR POOR CAMEL TO DEATH !!
YOU DIED IN THE DESERT.
YOUR BODY WAS EATEN BY VULTURES AND IMPORTED CANNINBALS !!!


WANT A NEW CAMEL AND A NEW GAME ? Y
GOOD LUCK AND GOOD CAMELING !!
YOU ARE IN THE MIDDLE OF THE DESERT AT AN OASIS.
YOU HAVE TRAVELLED  0  MILES ALLTOGETHER.
WHAT IS YOUR COMMAND? 2
YOU HAVE ARRIVED AT AN OASES--------YOUR CAMEL IS
FILLING YOUR CANTEEN AND EATING FIGS.
YOUR CAMEL LIKES THIS PACE.
YOU HAVE TRAVELLED  3  MILES ALLTOGETHER.
WHAT IS YOUR COMMAND? 2
YOUR CAMEL LIKES THIS PACE.
YOU HAVE TRAVELLED  11  MILES ALLTOGETHER.
WHAT IS YOUR COMMAND? 2
YOUR CAMEL LIKES THIS PACE.
----------W A R N I N G---------- GET A DRINK
THE PYGMIES ARE  7  MILES BEHIND YOU.
YOU HAVE TRAVELLED  14  MILES ALLTOGETHER.
WHAT IS YOUR COMMAND? 1
BETTER WATCH FOR AN OASES !
WHAT IS YOUR COMMAND? 2
YOUR CAMEL HURT HIS HUMP.
LUCKILY THE PYGMIES WERE FOOTWEARY !!!
YOUR CAMEL LIKES THIS PACE.
THE PYGMIES ARE  11  MILES BEHIND YOU.
YOU HAVE TRAVELLED  21  MILES ALLTOGETHER.
WHAT IS YOUR COMMAND? 2
YOUR CAMEL LIKES THIS PACE.
THE PYGMIES ARE  15  MILES BEHIND YOU.
YOU HAVE TRAVELLED  28  MILES ALLTOGETHER.
WHAT IS YOUR COMMAND? 2
YOU HAVE ARRIVED AT AN OASES--------YOUR CAMEL IS
FILLING YOUR CANTEEN AND EATING FIGS.
YOUR CAMEL LIKES THIS PACE.
THE PYGMIES ARE  13  MILES BEHIND YOU.
YOU HAVE TRAVELLED  37  MILES ALLTOGETHER.
WHAT IS YOUR COMMAND? 2
WILD BERBERS HIDDEN IN THE SAND HAVE CAPTURED YOU.
LUCKILY THE LOCAL SHEIK HAS AGREED TO THEIR RANSOM-
DEMANDS.......BUT........WATCH FOR THE PYGMIES !!!
YOU HAVE A NEW CHOICE OF SUB-COMMANDS:
#7 ATTEMPT AN ESCAPE
#8 WAIT FOR PAYMENT
YOUR SUB-COMMAND ? 7
CONGRADULATIONS, YOU SUCCESSFULLY ESCAPED !!!!
THE PYGMIES ARE  4  MILES BEHIND YOU.
YOU HAVE TRAVELLED  37  MILES ALLTOGETHER.
WHAT IS YOUR COMMAND? 6
YOU DIED IN THE DESERT.
THE LOCAL SHEIK NOW USES YOUR SKULL FOR A CHANGE PURSE !!!


WANT A NEW CAMEL AND A NEW GAME ? NO
-----------------
      CHICKEN
-----------------
Ok
```

```
LIST
10 PRINT TAB(26);"CAMEL"
20 PRINT TAB(20);"CREATIVE COMPUTING"
30 PRINT TAB(18);"MORRISTOWN, NEW JERSEY"
35 PRINT:PRINT:PRINT
110 PRINT "WOULD YOU LIKE INSTRUCTIONS";
120 INPUT D$
130 IF LEFT$(D$,1)="N" THEN 320
140 PRINT:PRINT "   WELCOME TO CAMEL.  THE OBJEST IS TO TRAVEL"
150 PRINT "200 MILES ACROSS THE GREAT GOBI DESERT."
160 PRINT "A TRIBE OF KNOCKED KNEED PIGMIES WILL BE CHASING YOU."
170 PRINT "YOU WILL BE ASKED FOR COMMANDS EVERY SO OFTEN."
180 PRINT
190 PRINT
200 PRINT
210 PRINT "C O M M A N D S :"
220 PRINT "#1 DRINK FROM YOUR CANTEEN"
230 PRINT "#2 AHEAD MODERATE SPEED"
240 PRINT "#3 AHEAD FULL SPEED"
250 PRINT "#4 STOP FOR THE NIGHT"
260 PRINT "#5 STATUS CHECK"
270 PRINT "#6 HOPE FOR HELP"
275 PRINT
276 PRINT
277 PRINT
278 PRINT
279 PRINT
280 PRINT "YOU HAVE ONE QUART OF WATER WHICH WILL LAST YOU SIX DRINKS."
290 PRINT "YOU MAVE RENEW YOUR WATER SUPPLY COMPLETELY AT AN OASES."
300 PRINT "YOU GET A HALF A QUART IF FOUND BY HELP."
310 PRINT "IF HELP DOES NOT FIND YOU AFTER COMMAND SIX, YOU LOSE."
320 PRINT "GOOD LUCK AND GOOD CAMELING !!"
330 PRINT "YOU ARE IN THE MIDDLE OF THE DESERT AT AN OASIS."
335 GOSUB 2000
340 IF C>199 THEN 1210
350 Z=Z-1
355 IF Z=1 THEN PRINT "----------W A R N I N G---------- GET A DRINK"
360 IF Z<0 THEN 1630
370 P=P+1
380 X2=INT(10*RND(1)+2.5)
390 IF Q>0 THEN 940
400 IF P<4 THEN 470
410 C1=C1+X2
420 IF C1<C THEN 460
430 PRINT "THE PYGMIES HAVE CAPTURED YOU.  CAMEL AND PEOPLE SOUP IS"
440 PRINT "THEIR FAVORITE DISH !!!!!"
450 GOTO 1560
460 PRINT "THE PYGMIES ARE "C-C1;" MILES BEHIND YOU."
470 PRINT "YOU HAVE TRAVELLED ";C;" MILES ALLTOGETHER."
480 PRINT "WHAT IS YOUR COMMAND";
490 INPUT Y
500 ON Y GOTO 830,610,680,760,790
550 T=INT(10*RND(1))
560 IF T<>1 THEN 1200
570 PRINT "HELP HAS FOUND YOU IN A STATE OF UNCONSCIOUSNESS."
580 S=3
590 Z=4
600 GOTO 340
610 F=F+1
620 IF F=8 THEN 1190
630 GOSUB 880
640 X1=INT(10*RND(1))
650 C=C+X1
660 PRINT "YOUR CAMEL LIKES THIS PACE."
670 GOTO 340
680 F=F+3
690 IF F>7 THEN 1190
700 GOSUB 880
710 X1=2*INT(10*RND(1))
720 C=C+X1
730 PRINT "YOUR CAMEL IS BURNING ACROSS THE DESERT SANDS."
740 PRINT
750 GOTO 340
760 PRINT "YOUR CAMEL THANKS YOU!"
770 F=0
780 GOTO 350
790 PRINT "YOUR CAMEL HAS ";7-F;" GOOD DAYS LEFT."
800 PRINT "YOU HAVE ";S;" DRINKS LEFT IN YOUR CANTEEN."
810 PRINT "YOU CAN GO ";Z;" COMMANDS WITHOUT DRINKING."
830 S=S-1
840 IF S<0 THEN 1200
850 PRINT "BETTER WATCH FOR AN OASES !"
860 Z=4
870 GOTO 480
880 A=INT(100*RND(1))
890 IF A>5 THEN 1120
900 PRINT "WILD BERBERS HIDDEN IN THE SAND HAVE CAPTURED YOU."
910 PRINT "LUCKILY THE LOCAL SHEIK HAS AGREED TO THEIR RANSOM-"
920 PRINT "DEMANDS.......BUT........WATCH FOR THE PYGMIES !!!"
930 PRINT "YOU HAVE A NEW CHOICE OF SUB-COMMANDS:"
940 PRINT "#7 ATTEMPT AN ESCAPE"
950 PRINT "#8 WAIT FOR PAYMENT"
960 PRINT "YOUR SUB-COMMAND ";
970 INPUT X
980 IF X=8 THEN 1060
990 X1=INT(10 * RND(1))
1000 IF X1<5 THEN 1040
1010 PRINT "CONGRADULATIONS, YOU SUCCESSFULLY ESCAPED !!!!"
1020 Q=0
1030 GOTO 340
1040 PRINT "YOU WERE MORTALLY WOUNDED BY A PIG STABBER WHILE ESCAPING."
1050 GOTO 1410
1060 X1=INT(100*RND(1))
1070 REM
1080 IF X1>24 THEN 1100
1090 PRINT "YOUR RANSOM HAS BEEN PAID AND YOU ARE FREE TO GO."
1095 Q=0
1096 GOTO 340
1100 PRINT "THE LOCAL SULTAN IS COLLECTING......JUST WAIT......."
1110 GOTO 340
1120 A=INT(10*RND(1))
1130 IF A>2 THEN 1240
1140 PRINT "YOU HAVE ARRIVED AT AN OASES--------YOUR CAMEL IS"
1150 PRINT "FILLING YOUR CANTEEN AND EATING FIGS."
1160 Z=4
1170 S=6
1180 RETURN
1190 PRINT "YOU DIRTY RAPSCALLION! YOU RAN YOUR POOR CAMEL TO DEATH !!"
1200 GOTO 1410
1210 PRINT "YOU WIN, A PARTY IS BEING GIVEN IN YOUR HONOR......."
1220 PRINT ".......THE PYGMIES ARE PLANNING TO ATTEND......."
1230 GOTO 1560
1240 X1=INT(100*RND(1))
1250 IF X1>5 THEN 1350
1260 PRINT "YOU HAVE BEEN CAUGHT IN A SANDSTORM.....GOOD LUCK!"
1270 X5=INT(10*RND(1))
1280 X6=INT(10*RND(1))
1290 IF X6<5 THEN 1320
1300 C=C+X5
1310 GOTO 1330
1320 C=C-X5
1330 PRINT "YOUR NEW POSITION IS ";C;" MILES SO FAR!"
1340 RETURN
1350 X1=INT(100*RND(1))
1360 IF X1>5 THEN RETURN
1370 C1=C1+1
1380 PRINT "YOUR CAMEL HURT HIS HUMP."
1390 PRINT "LUCKILY THE PYGMIES WERE FOOTWEARY !!!"
1400 RETURN
1410 U=INT(10*RND(1))
1420 PRINT "YOU DIED IN THE DESERT."
1430 IF U>1 THEN 1460
1440 PRINT "THE NATIONAL CAMEL'S UNION IS NOT ATTENDING YOUR FUNERAL!!!"
1450 GOTO 1560
1460 IF U>3 THEN 1490
1470 PRINT "YOUR BODY WAS EATEN BY VULTURES AND IMPORTED CANNINBALS !!!"
1480 GOTO 1560
1490 IF U>5 THEN 1520
1500 PRINT "THE LOCAL SHEIK NOW USES YOUR SKULL FOR A CHANGE PURSE !!!"
1510 GOTO 1560
1520 IF U>7 THEN 1550
1530 PRINT "PEOPLE WITH LITTLE INTELLIGENCE SHOULD STAY OUT OF THE DESERT
1540 GOTO 1560
1550 PRINT "TURKEYS SHOULD FLY, NOT RIDE CAMELS !!!!!!!"
1560 PRINT
1570 PRINT
1580 PRINT "WANT A NEW CAMEL AND A NEW GAME ";
1590 INPUT D$
1600 IF LEFT$(D$,1)="Y" THEN 320
1620 GOTO 1650
1630 PRINT "YOU RAN OUT OF WATER......SORRY CHUM!!!"
1640 GOTO 1410
1650 PRINT "-----------------"
1655 PRINT "     CHICKEN"
1657 PRINT "-----------------"
1660 END
2000 Z=4
2010 S=6
2020 C=0
2030 C1=0
2040 Q=0
2050 F=0
2060 P=0
2070 RETURN
Ok
```

Chase

CHASE puts you in a maze made up of high-voltage fences and posts. This in itself isn't too unpleasant but there're also the five interceptor robots bent on just one thing—your destruction. If these robots touch you ... that's the end of the game (and you!). There's one hope—make the robots hit the maze, or each other (they're like people—sometimes they'd rather be alone). If you destroy them all, you win! If you find yourself in a totally hopeless situation, you have the option of making a tremendous leap to a random location (which may well be on top of a fence or a guard).

At the end of the game, you may replay with the same or different starting conditions.

I believe this game was originally created by Mac Oglesby. It was then modified by Bill Cotter and further improved by Arnold Loveridge. An intermediate version appeared in *Creative Computing*, Jan/Feb 1976.

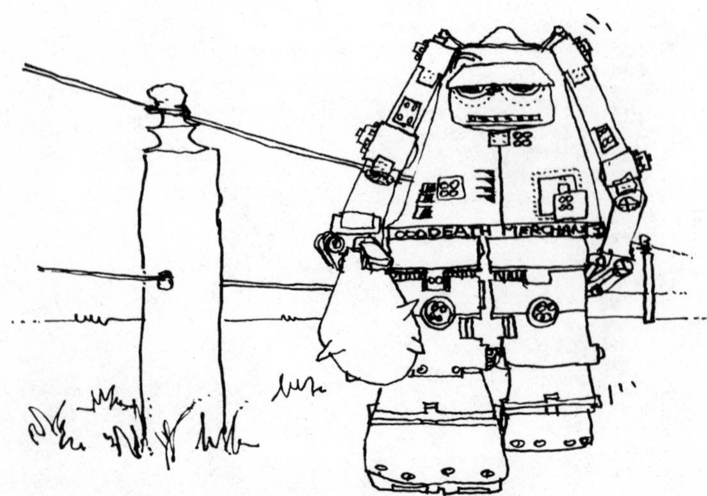


```
RUN
                              CHASE
                        CREATIVE COMPUTING
                      MORRISTOWN, NEW JERSEY


YOU ARE WITHIN THE WALLS OF A HIGH VOLTAGE MAZE
THERE ARE FIVE SECURITY MACHINES TRYING TO DESTROY YOU
YOU ARE THE '*'   THE INTERCEPTORS ARE THE '+'
THE AREAS MARKED 'X' ARE HIGH VOLTAGE
YOUR ONLY CHANCE FOR SURVIVAL IS TO MANEUVER EACH
INTERCEPTOR INTO AN 'X'.-----GOOD LUCK-----
MOVES ARE   7.8.9
            4.*.6
            1.2.3

10 = NO MOVE FOR THE REST OF THE GAME
-1 = GAVE UP, SITUATION HOPELESS.
 0 = A TREMENDOUS (BUT UNFORTUNATELY RANDOM) LEAP

XXXXXXXXXXXXXXXXXXXX
X             X   XX
X X +     X  X     X
X          X X     X
X              X   X
X   X  +     X   + X
X X    X  X  XXX   X
XX      XX  +      X
X  *    X       +  X
XXXXXXXXXXXXXXXXXXXX
? 5
XXXXXXXXXXXXXXXXXXXX
X             X   XX
X X       X  X     X
X  +       X X     X
X              X   X
X   X        X     X
X X   +X  X  XXX+  X
XX      XX         X
X  *    X  +   +   X
XXXXXXXXXXXXXXXXXXXX
? 5
XXXXXXXXXXXXXXXXXXXX
X             X   XX
X X       X  X     X
X          X X     X
X  +           X   X
X   X        X     X
X X    X  X  XXX   X
XX   +  XX     +   X
X  *    X +   +    X
XXXXXXXXXXXXXXXXXXXX
? 5
XXXXXXXXXXXXXXXXXXXX
X             X   XX
X X       X  X     X
X          X X     X
X              X   X
X  +X        X     X
X X    X  X  XXX   X
XX      XX         X
X  *+   X+   ++    X
XXXXXXXXXXXXXXXXXXXX
? 4
XXXXXXXXXXXXXXXXXXXX
X             X   XX
X X       X  X     X
X          X X     X
X              X   X
X   X        X     X
X X    X  X  XXX   X
XX      XX         X
X *+    X   ++     X
XXXXXXXXXXXXXXXXXXXX
? 0
$6,000,000 JUMP!!!
HIGH VOLTAGE!!!!!!!!!!
***** ZAP *****  YOU'RE DEAD!!!

ANOTHER GAME (Y/N)? N
```

```
LIST
10 PRINT TAB(26);"CHASE"
20 PRINT TAB(20);"CREATIVE COMPUTING"
30 PRINT TAB(18);"MORRISTOWN, NEW JERSEY"
40 PRINT:PRINT:PRINT
41 PRINT "YOU ARE WITHIN THE WALLS OF A HIGH VOLTAGE MAZE"
42 PRINT "THERE ARE FIVE SECURITY MACHINES TRYING TO DESTROY YOU"
60 PRINT "YOU ARE THE '*'   THE INTERCEPTORS ARE THE '+'"
70 PRINT "THE AREAS MARKED 'X' ARE HIGH VOLTAGE"
80 PRINT "YOUR ONLY CHANCE FOR SURVIVAL IS TO MANEUVER EACH"
90 PRINT "INTERCEPTOR INTO AN 'X'.-----GOOD LUCK-----"
100 PRINT "MOVES ARE   7.8.9"
110 PRINT "            4.*.6"
120 PRINT "            1.2.3"
130 PRINT
140 PRINT "10 = NO MOVE FOR THE REST OF THE GAME"
150 PRINT "-1 = GAVE UP, SITUATION HOPELESS."
160 PRINT " 0 = A TREMENDOUS (BUT UNFORTUNATELY RANDOM) LEAP"
170 PRINT
180 DIM A(10,20),A1(10,20),N(12),L(5),M(5),L1(5),M1(5)
190 REM
210 FOR B=1 TO 10
220 FOR C=1 TO 20
230 X=INT(10*RND(1))
240 IF X=5 THEN 270
250 A(B,C)=ASC(" ")
260 GOTO 280
270 A(B,C)=ASC("X")
280 NEXT C
290 NEXT B
300 FOR D=1 TO 10
310 A(D,1)=ASC("X"):A(D,20)=ASC("X")
320 NEXT D
330 FOR F=1 TO 20
340 A(1,F)=ASC("X"):A(10,F)=ASC("X")
350 NEXT F
360 GOTO 410
370 H=INT(2+8*RND(1))
380 I=INT(2+18*RND(1))
390 IF A(H,I)<>ASC(" ") THEN 370
400 RETURN
410 GOSUB 370
420 A(H,I)=ASC("*")
430 J=H:K=I
440 FOR N9=1 TO 5
450 GOSUB 370
460 A(H,I)=ASC("+")
470 L(N9)=H:M(N9)=I
480 NEXT N9
490 FOR B1=1 TO 10:FOR B2=1 TO 20:A1(B1,B2)=A(B1,B2):NEXT B2:NEXT B1
500 FOR B1=1 TO 5:L1(B1)=L(B1):M1(B1)=M(B1):NEXT B1
520 J1=J:K1=K
530 Y9=0
540 FOR D2=1 TO 10
550 FOR B2=1 TO 20
560 N$=CHR$(A(D2,B2))
570 PRINT N$;
580 NEXT B2
590 PRINT
600 NEXT D2
610 IF Y9 <> 10 THEN 640
620 PRINT
630 GOTO 890
640 INPUT Y9
650 J2=J:K2=K
660 IF Y9=0 THEN 860
670 IF Y9 < 0 THEN 1230
680 IF Y9=10 THEN 1070
690 ON Y9 GOTO 820,800,780,840,890,760,700,720,740
700 J=J-1:K=K-1
710 GOTO 890
720 J=J-1
730 GOTO 890
740 J=J-1:K=K+1
750 GOTO 890
760 K=K+1
770 GOTO 890
780 J=J+1:K=K+1
790 GOTO 890
800 J=J+1
810 GOTO 890
820 J=J+1:K=K-1
830 GOTO 890
840 K=K-1
850 GOTO 890
860 PRINT "$6,000,000 JUMP!!!"
870 J=INT(2+8*RND(1))
880 K=INT(2+18*RND(1))
890 IF A(J,K)=ASC("X") THEN 1260
900 A(J2,K2)=ASC(" ")
910 A(J,K)=ASC("*")
920 GOTO 1070
930 REM INTERCEPTOR MOVEMENT
940 IF A(X,Y)=ASC("X") THEN 1040
950 X2=X:Y2=Y
960 X=SGN(J-X):Y=SGN(K-Y)
970 X=X+X2:Y=Y+Y2
980 IF A(X,Y)=ASC("*") THEN 1050
990 IF A(X,Y)=ASC(" ") THEN 1020
1000 A(X2,Y2)=ASC(" ")
1010 RETURN
1020 A(X,Y)=ASC("+")
1030 A(X2,Y2)=ASC(" ")
1040 RETURN
1050 G9=99
1060 RETURN
1070 FOR N9=1 TO 5
1080 X=L(N9):Y=M(N9)
1090 G9=0
1100 GOSUB 940
1110 IF G9 <> 0 THEN 1240
1120 L(N9)=X:M(N9)=Y
1130 NEXT N9
1140 FOR N9=1 TO 5
1150 IF A(L(N9),M(N9)) <> ASC(" ") THEN 1170
1160 A(L(N9),M(N9))=ASC("+")
1170 NEXT N9
1180 FOR N9=1 TO 5
1190 IF A(L(N9),M(N9)) <> ASC("X") THEN 540
1200 NEXT N9
1210 PRINT "YOU HAVE DESTROYED ALL YOUR OPPONENTS - THE GAME IS YOURS"
1220 GOTO 1290
1230 PRINT "GIVE UP, EH."
1240 PRINT "*** YOU HAVE BEEN DESTROYED BY A LUCKY COMPUTER ***"
1250 GOTO 1290
1260 PRINT "HIGH VOLTAGE!!!!!!!!!!"
1270 PRINT "***** ZAP *****  YOU'RE DEAD!!!"
1280 PRINT
1290 PRINT  "ANOTHER GAME (Y/N)";
1300 INPUT N9$
1310 IF N9$ <> "Y" THEN 1400
1320 PRINT "SAME SETUP (Y/N)";
1330 INPUT N9$
1340 IF N9$ <> "Y" THEN 190
1350 FOR B1=1 TO 10:FOR B2=1 TO 20:A(B1,B2)=A1(B1,B2):NEXT B2:NEXT B1
1360 FOR B1=1 TO 5:L(B1)=L1(B1):M(B1)=M1(B1):NEXT B1
1380 J=J1:K=K1
1390 GOTO 530
1400 END
Ok
```

Chuck-A-Luck

Chuck-a-luck is generally found in fairgrounds, cheap casinos, and small gambling parlors. It flourished in frontier America, but dates back to European gaming houses of the eighteenth century. During its long history, chuck-a-luck has had many names including sweatcloth, chucker-luck, chuck luck, and bird cage.

Each player places his bets on one of the six numbers, one through six. When all bets have been placed, the operator tumbles three dice in a chuck cage until they come to rest face up or drop down a chute onto the table. If a player's number appears on one die, the operator pays him even money; if on two dice, two to one; if on three dice, three to one.

The computer version of Chuck-a-luck was originally written by Michael Tanoff.

```
RUN
                         CHUCK-A-LUCK
                      CREATIVE COMPUTING
                    MORRISTOWN, NEW JERSEY



CHOOSE A NUMBER FROM 1 TO 6. I WILL ROLL 3 DICE.
IF YOUR NUMBER MATCHES 1 DIE, I PAY OFF EVEN MONEY.
TWO DICE, 2:1    3 DICE, 3:1


YOU HAVE $ 500 . MAKE A BET.
? 100
CHOOSE A NUMBER? 3
 1     1     5
YOU'VE MATCHED  0  TIMES.
YOU LOOSE $ 100
YOU HAVE $ 400 . MAKE A BET.
? 50
CHOOSE A NUMBER? 1
 3     5     6
YOU'VE MATCHED  0  TIMES.
YOU LOOSE $ 50
YOU HAVE $ 350 . MAKE A BET.
? 50
CHOOSE A NUMBER? 5
 5     6     1
YOU'VE MATCHED  1  TIMES.
YOU'VE WON $ 50
YOU HAVE $ 400 . MAKE A BET.
? 100
CHOOSE A NUMBER? 2
 4     1     3
YOU'VE MATCHED  0  TIMES.
YOU LOOSE $ 100
YOU HAVE $ 300 . MAKE A BET.
? 100
CHOOSE A NUMBER? 5
 2     4     1
YOU'VE MATCHED  0  TIMES.
YOU LOOSE $ 100
YOU HAVE $ 200 . MAKE A BET.
? 100
CHOOSE A NUMBER? 3
 1     3     6
YOU'VE MATCHED  1  TIMES.
YOU'VE WON $ 100
YOU HAVE $ 300 . MAKE A BET.
? 100
CHOOSE A NUMBER? 4
 3     4     3
YOU'VE MATCHED  1  TIMES.
YOU'VE WON $ 100
YOU HAVE $ 400 . MAKE A BET.
? 100
CHOOSE A NUMBER? 2
 2     1     4
YOU'VE MATCHED  1  TIMES.
YOU'VE WON $ 100
YOU HAVE $ 500 . MAKE A BET.
? 200
CHOOSE A NUMBER? 3
 2     3     1
YOU'VE MATCHED  1  TIMES.
YOU'VE WON $ 200
YOU HAVE $ 700 . MAKE A BET.
? -9
DON'T GET CUTE!!!
YOU HAVE $ 700 . MAKE A BET.
? 100
CHOOSE A NUMBER? 4
 5     3     4
YOU'VE MATCHED  1  TIMES.
YOU'VE WON $ 100
YOU HAVE $ 800 . MAKE A BET.
? 900
I DON' TAKE I.O.U'S !!!!
YOU HAVE $ 800 . MAKE A BET.
? .001
DON'T GET CUTE!!!
YOU HAVE $ 800 . MAKE A BET.
? 200
CHOOSE A NUMBER? 7
CHEATER!!!!!!
CHOOSE A NUMBER? 2
 3     6     3
YOU'VE MATCHED  0  TIMES.
YOU LOOSE $ 200
YOU HAVE $ 600 . MAKE A BET.
? 600
CHOOSE A NUMBER? 1
 1     1     2
YOU'VE MATCHED  2  TIMES.
YOU'VE WON $ 1200
YOU HAVE $ 1800 . MAKE A BET.
? 1800
CHOOSE A NUMBER? 4
 1     1     1
YOU'VE MATCHED  0  TIMES.
YOU LOOSE $ 1800
```

```
LIST
100 PRINT TAB(23);"CHUCK-A-LUCK"
110 PRINT TAB(20);"CREATIVE COMPUTING"
120 PRINT TAB(18);"MORRISTOWN, NEW JERSEY"
130 PRINT:PRINT:PRINT
140 PRINT "CHOOSE A NUMBER FROM 1 TO 6. I WILL ROLL 3 DICE."
150 PRINT "IF YOUR NUMBER MATCHES 1 DIE, I PAY OFF EVEN MONEY."
160 PRINT "TWO DICE, 2:1    3 DICE, 3:1"
170 PRINT:PRINT:M=500
180 PRINT "YOU HAVE $";M;". MAKE A BET."
190 INPUT B
200 IF B > M THEN 410
210 IF B > 0 THEN IF B*100=INT(B*100) THEN 230
220 GOTO 420
230 PRINT "CHOOSE A NUMBER";
240 INPUT N
250 IF INT(N)=N AND N > 0 AND N < 7 THEN 270
260 PRINT "CHEATER!!!!!!":GOTO 230
270 A=INT(RND(1)*6)+1:PRINT A;"    ";:D=INT(RND(1)*6)+1:PRINT D;"
280 C=INT(RND(1)*6)+1:PRINT C;"      "
290 T=0
300 IF A=N THEN T=T+1
310 IF D=N THEN T=T+1
320 IF C=N THEN T=T+1
330 PRINT "YOU'VE MATCHED ";T;" TIMES."
340 ON T GOTO 380,390,400
350 PRINT "YOU LOOSE $";B
360 M=M-B:IF M<= 0 THEN 430
370 GOTO 180
380 PRINT "YOU'VE WON $";B:M=M+B:GOTO 180
390 PRINT "YOU'VE WON $";B*2:M=M+2*B:GOTO 180
400 PRINT "YOU'VE WON $";B*3;M=M+B*3:GOTO 180
410 PRINT "I DON' TAKE I.O.U'S !!!!":GOTO 180
420 PRINT "DON'T GET CUTE!!!":GOTO 180
430 PRINT
440 PRINT
450 END
Ok
```

Close Encounters

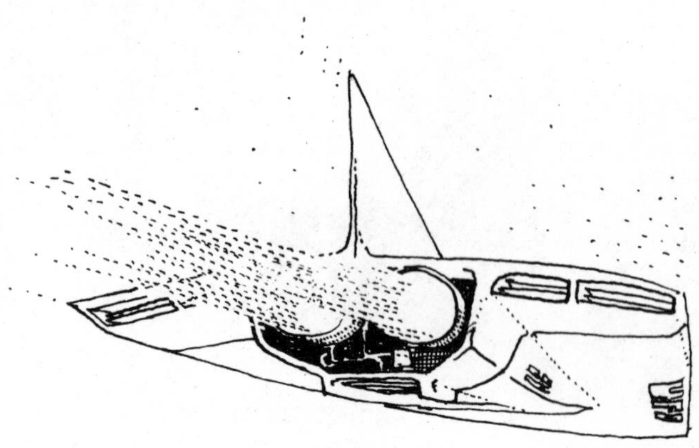

In this game, you are situated at the center of a target area for a UFO. The program assigns coordinates 0,0 to your location. You are given information as to the course of the UFO in degrees longitude and degrees latitude and also its speed. You then have two alternatives. One, you can attempt to shoot the UFO out of the sky with an ICBM or you can do nothing and hope that air friction will cause the course of the UFO to deviate or to burn up.

A knowledge of mathematical coordinate systems will be of some assistance in winning this game, although you'll probably be able to discover a reasonably good strategy by yourself using trial and error if you play enough games.

This program was originally written by Chris Falco.

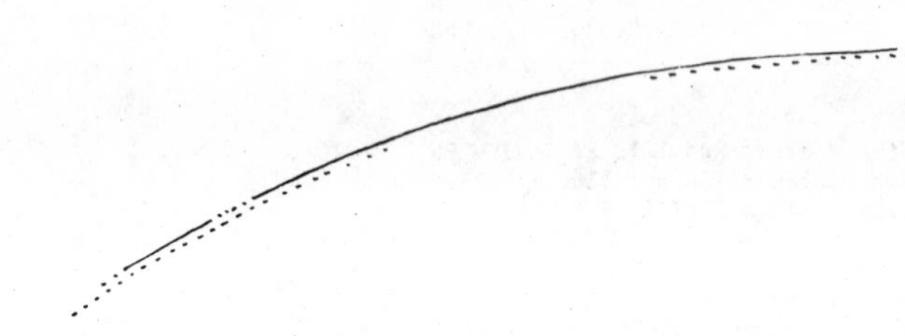

```
RUN
                     CLOSE ENCOUNTERS
                     CREATIVE COMPUTING
                   MORRISTOWN, NEW JERSEY


YOU ARE SITUATED AT COORDINATES (0,0).  A UFO IS
HEADING FOR IMPACT AT THAT LOCATION.

AT FIRST TRACK, THE UFO IS ON A COURSE OF 55 DEGREES LONGITUDE
AND 133 DEGREES LATITUDE.
   (ALSO IT'S FALLING AT A SPEED OF 2562 MILES/PER HOUR)
YOU HAVE THE FOLLOWING ALTERNATIVES:
A) YOU CAN ATTEMPT TO SHOOT THE UFO OUT OF THE SKY.  OR
B) YOU CAN DO NOTHING, AND HOPE THAT AIR FRICTION
   WILL CAUSE THE COURSE OF THE UFO TO DEVIATE, AND THUS
   MISS YOUR LOCATION.

WHAT IS YOUR PLAN OF ACTION (A OR B)? B

MILES          SPEED          LONGITUDE     LATITUDE      COURSE
-----          -----          ---------     --------      ------
 12000          2562           55            133           82
 11857.2        8569           52            130           94
 11654.7        12148          51            128           93
 11348.6        18367          51            119           84
 10945.5        24186          42            118           92
 10485.7        27587          37            117           96
 9989.48        29774          32            110           94
 9376.64        36771          24            107           99
 8697.39        40755          20            107           103
 7977.35        43202          14            98            100
 7186.97        47423          6             94            104
 6301.64        53120          4             85            97
 5337.84        57828         -4             85            105
 4323.59        60855         -12            79            107
 3198.72        67492         -19            79            114
 2011.02        71262         -21            71            108
 770.118        74454         -27            65            108

---------IMPACT-AT- 78371 -MILES-PER-HOUR---------------
GOOD WORK.  FRICTION OF 5 % HAS CAUSED THE COURSE
OF THE UFO TO DEVIATE.  IMPACT COORDINATES ARE
NOW ( 5 ,-5 ).  YOU MADE IT!
```

```
TRY AGAIN? Y
PLAN (A OR B)? A


LAUNCH AN I.C.B.M. ON A COURSE THAT WILL INTERCEPT THE UFO
WITHOUT THE UFO BEING TOO CLOSE TO YOUR LOCATION.  IF THE SPEED
OF THE UFO EXCEEDS 10529 M.P.H., YOUR MISSILES ARE USELESS!
--SCANNERS PREDICT YOU HAVE 5 MINUTES TO DESTROY THE UFO
BEFORE IT IS TOO CLOSE TO IMPACT.

--COMPUTER INDICATES COURSE AT FIRST SIGHTING IS APPROX. 54

TYPE IN A COURSE ON THE CHART BELOW


TIME           SPEED          LONGITUDE     LATITUDE      COURSE
 0              2529           54            105           ? 60
 .5             4100           56            107           ? 55
YOU ARE SHY OF THE UFO'S COORDINATES,
HOWEVER THIS IS ONLY A SLIGHT DEVIATION SO THE
UFO HAS BEEN DESTROYED!

TRY AGAIN? YES
PLAN (A OR B)? A


--SCANNERS PREDICT YOU HAVE 2 MINUTES TO DESTROY THE UFO
BEFORE IT IS TOO CLOSE TO IMPACT.

--COMPUTER INDICATES COURSE AT FIRST SIGHTING IS APPROX. 77

TYPE IN A COURSE ON THE CHART BELOW


TIME           SPEED          LONGITUDE     LATITUDE      COURSE
 0              5122           47            113           ? 80
 .5             6597           41            107           ? 85
 1              8072           35            101           ? 90
 1.5            9547           29            95            ? 71
FANTASTIC!!!!  YOU HIT THE UFO EXACTLY ON PROJECTED COURSE
YOU MUST BE VERY SHARP!
```

```
TRY AGAIN? YES
PLAN (A OR B)? B

MILES          SPEED          LONGITUDE      LATITUDE       COURSE
-----          -----          ---------      --------       ------
 12000          2802           58             108            54
 11857.3        8565           51             99             64
 11628.5        13726          51             93             58
 11356.7        16307          44             92             64
 11036.4        19219          37             88             67
 10606.8        25776          36             79             59
 10066.9        32396          36             78             58
 9482.08        35086          28             77             65
 8817.98        39846          19             75             72
 8090.73        43635          14             70             72
 7283.78        48417          14             64             66
 6400.58        52992          9              62             69
 5441.75        57530          0              59             75
 4375.52        63974         -2              50             68
 3256.52        67140         -8              47             71
 2048.63        72473         -14             44             74
 790.901        75464         -18             39             73

---------IMPACT-AT- 77572 -MILES-PER-HOUR---------------
GOOD WORK.  FRICTION OF 4 % HAS CAUSED THE COURSE
OF THE UFO TO DEVIATE.  IMPACT COORDINATES ARE
NOW ( 4 ,-4 ).  YOU MADE IT!
TRY AGAIN? Y
PLAN (A OR B)? B

MILES          SPEED          LONGITUDE      LATITUDE       COURSE
-----          -----          ---------      --------       ------
 12000          5782           56             112            58
 11787.4        12757          49             112            67
 11504.3        16983          46             112            70
 11114.7        23376          41             112            75
 10668.8        26756          41             108            71
 10171.8        29818          36             107            75
 9571.63        36012          35             103            72
 8887.7         41036          33             100            71
 8151.72        44159          31             96             69
 7375.72        46560          27             92             69
 6483.92        53508          20             87             71
 5495.93        59279          19             78             63
 4457.3         62318          18             74             60
 3331.95        67521          16             70             58
 2109.15        73368          10             62             56
 810.517        77918          5              55             54

---------IMPACT-AT- 80674 -MILES-PER-HOUR---------------
GOOD WORK.  FRICTION OF 6 % HAS CAUSED THE COURSE
OF THE UFO TO DEVIATE.  IMPACT COORDINATES ARE
NOW ( 6 ,-6 ).  YOU MADE IT!
TRY AGAIN? NO
Ok
```

```
LIST
100 PRINT TAB(21);"CLOSE ENCOUNTERS"
110 PRINT TAB(20);"CREATIVE COMPUTING"
120 PRINT TAB(18);"MORRISTOWN, NEW JERSEY"
130 GOSUB 1100
140 PRINT:PRINT:PRINT
150 PRINT "YOU ARE SITUATED AT COORDINATES (0,0).  A UFO IS"
160 PRINT "HEADING FOR IMPACT AT THAT LOCATION."
170 PRINT
180 PRINT "AT FIRST TRACK, THE UFO IS ON A COURSE OF"Y"DEGREES ";
190 PRINT "LONGITUDE"
200 PRINT "AND"Z"DEGREES LATITUDE."
210 PRINT "   (ALSO IT'S FALLING AT A SPEED OF"X"MILES/PER HOUR)"
220 PRINT "YOU HAVE THE FOLLOWING ALTERNATIVES:"
230 PRINT "A) YOU CAN ATTEMPT TO SHOOT THE UFO OUT OF THE SKY.  OR"
240 PRINT "B) YOU CAN DO NOTHING, AND HOPE THAT AIR FRICTION"
250 PRINT "   WILL CAUSE THE COURSE OF THE UFO TO DEVIATE, AND THUS"
260 PRINT "   MISS YOUR LOCATION.":PRINT
270 PRINT "WHAT IS YOUR PLAN OF ACTION (A OR B)";:INPUT D$
280 PRINT
290 IF LEFT$(D$,1)="B" THEN 790
300 PRINT "LAUNCH AN I.C.B.M. ON A COURSE THAT WILL INTERCEPT THE UFO"
310 PRINT "WITHOUT THE UFO BEING TOO CLOSE TO YOUR LOCATION.  IF THE ";
320 PRINT "SPEED"
330 PRINT "OF THE UFO EXCEEDS"H"M.P.H., YOUR MISSILES ARE USELESS!"
340 PRINT "--SCANNERS PREDICT YOU HAVE"M"MINUTES TO DESTROY THE UFO"
350 PRINT "BEFORE IT IS TOO CLOSE TO IMPACT.":PRINT
360 C=Z-Y+I-INT(RND(1)*4)+1
370 PRINT "--COMPUTER INDICATES COURSE AT FIRST SIGHTING IS APPROX.";C+F
380 PRINT
390 PRINT "TYPE IN A COURSE ON THE CHART BELOW":PRINT
400 PRINT
410 PRINT "TIME","SPEED","LONGITUDE","LATITUDE","COURSE"
420 FOR T=0TO 5 STEP .5
430 PRINT T,X,Y,Z,:INPUT A
440 IF T=INT(T) AND T=M THEN 620
450 IF X<=H THEN 490
460 PRINT "SORRY--THE SPEED OF THE UFO HAS EXCEEDED"H"M.P.H."
470 PRINT "THIS SPEED IS TO GREAT FOR YOUR DEFENSE SCREEN TO TRACK!"
480 PRINT "THEREFORE, YOU ARE (HA HA) DOOMED!":PRINT:GOTO 750
490 IF A=C THEN 720
500 IF A>10 THEN 550
510 PRINT "AT THAT COURSE YOU SHOT YOUR MISSILE STRAIGHT UP, SO WHEN"
520 PRINT "IT RUNS OUT OF FUEL IN ABOUT"F"HOURS, IT WILL FALL";
530 PRINT " THROUGH"
540 PRINT "YOUR ROOF!!!!!!!!!!    GOODBYE!!!!!!":GOTO 660
550 IF A<200 GOTO 580
560 PRINT "GOOD WORK! THERE GOES THE MISSILE-----------RIGHT TOWARDS"
570 PRINT "RUSSIA!!!!  NOW YOU'RE DEFINITELY IN TROUBLE!!":GOTO 660
580 IF A=C-1 THEN 670
590 IF A=C+1 THEN 710
600 X=X+V+1200:Y=Y-I+5:Z=Z-I+5:C=Z-Y+5
610 NEXT T
620 PRINT "--------------------------ATTENTION--------------------------"
630 PRINT "ELAPSED-TIME-INDICATES-THAT-"M"MINUTES-HAVE-PASSED.--IF-YOU-"
640 PRINT "WERE-TO-HIT-THE-UFO-NOW----THE-FORCE-OF-THE-EXPLOSION-WOULD"
650 PRINT "----------DESTROY-YOU-AS-WELL-AS-THE-UFO-!":PRINT
660 GOTO 750
670 PRINT "YOU ARE SHY OF THE UFO'S COORDINATES,"
680 PRINT "HOWEVER THIS IS ONLY A SLIGHT DEVIATION SO THE"
690 PRINT "UFO HAS BEEN DESTROYED!":PRINT
700 GOTO 750
710 PRINT "YOU OVERSHOT THE UFO'S COORDINATES,":GOTO 680
720 PRINT "FANTASTIC!!!!  YOU HIT THE UFO EXACTLY ON PROJECTED COURSE"
730 PRINT "YOU MUST BE VERY SHARP!":PRINT
740 PRINT
750 PRINT "TRY AGAIN";:INPUT J$:IF LEFT$(J$,1)="N" THEN 1220
760 GOSUB 1100
770 GOSUB 1070
780 PRINT:PRINT:GOTO 340
790 PRINT
800 F=0
810 A=INT(RND(1)*5)+1:C=Z-Y+A
820 M=12000
830 PRINT "MILES","SPEED","LONGITUDE","LATITUDE","COURSE"
840 PRINT "-----","-----","---------","--------","------"
850 P=X+1
860 PRINT M,X,Y,Z,C
870 C=Z-Y
880 X=X+INT(RND(1)*5000)+2000:M=M-X/60
890 Y=Y-INT(RND(1)*10):Z=Z-INT(RND(1)*10):C=Z-Y+A^2
900 IF X-P>5700 THEN F=F+1
910 IF M>0 THEN 850
920 PRINT
930 PRINT "---------IMPACT-AT-"X"-MILES-PER-HOUR---------------"
940 IF F<=2 THEN 980
950 PRINT "GOOD WORK.  FRICTION OF"F"% HAS CAUSED THE COURSE"
960 PRINT "OF THE UFO TO DEVIATE.  IMPACT COORDINATES ARE"
970 PRINT "NOW ("F","0-F").  YOU MADE IT!":GOTO 1020
980 PRINT "-----------UPI-WIRE-SERVICE----ON-LINE-"A":"A+5":"A+10":--"
990 PRINT "---  HAVE JUST OBSERVED EXPLOSION AT COORDINATES ("0-F",0)."
1000 A=(A+2)*A
1010 PRINT "BLAST SEEN FROM"A^3"MILES AWAY.  NO SURVIVORS.":PRINT
1020 INPUT "TRY AGAIN";J$
1030 IF LEFT$(J$,1)="N" THEN 1220
1040 GOSUB 1100
1050 GOSUB 1070
1060 PRINT:PRINT:GOTO 300
1070 INPUT "PLAN (A OR B)";D$
1080 IF LEFT$(D$,1)="B" THEN 790
1090 RETURN
1100 I=INT(RND(1)*20)+1:V=INT(RND(1)*400)+200:F=INT(RND(1)*5)+1
1110 X=INT(RND(1)*5000)+2001:H=X+8000:Q=INT(RND(1)*5)+1
1120 Z=INT(RND(1)*140):IF Z<100 THEN 1120
1130 Y=INT(RND(1)*60):IF Y<40 THEN 1130
1140 IF X>=3000 THEN 1160
1150 M=5:GOTO 1210
1160 IF X>=3700 THEN 1180
1170 M=4:GOTO 1210
1180 IF X>=4700 THEN 1200
1190 M=3:GOTO 1210
1200 M=2
1210 RETURN
1220 END
Ok
```

Column

This program is a computer version of an old card trick which never fails to get some ooohs and aaahs from the uninitiated. The dealer, or magician, takes twenty-one random cards, deals them out in three piles of seven cards each. You then tell him which column (or which pile) contains your card. He then picks up the three columns from right to left, putting the right pile on the top, and then deals the deck out again horizontally. In other words the top card of the right column now becomes the top card of the left column; the second card in the right column now becomes the first card in the middle column; the third card of the right column becomes the first card in the third column, and so on. After he deals out all twenty-one cards in this way, you again tell him which column your card appears in. The magician then picks up the three piles in the same order and deals them out once again. Again you tell him which column contains your card. He then deals the cards out one by one face up and identifies yours when he comes to it. Don't ask me how he does it! Maybe you can figure it out from the program, but it works every time.

This program was originally written by Alan Barnes.

```
RUN
                                COLUMN
                          CREATIVE COMPUTING
                        MORRISTOWN, NEW JERSEY


THIS PROGRAM WILL SHOW YOU A CARD TRICK. AFTER THE FIRST DEAL
PICK A CARD AND TYPE THE NUMBER OF THE COLUMN CONTAINING IT.
THE DEALER WILL THEN PICK UP THE CARDS, A COLUMN AT A TIME,
AND WILL DEAL THEM OUT AGAIN HORIZONTALLY. WHEN HE FINISHES
EACH TIME, TYPE THE NUMBER OF THE THE NEW COLUMN CONTAINING YOUR
CARD. FOLLOWING THE LAST DEAL THE DEALER WILL TURN OVER THE
CARDS, ONE AT A TIME, UNTIL HE REACHES THE ONE YOU PICKED.


 9 OF CLUBS               JACK OF SPADES           6 OF HEARTS
 6 OF CLUBS               KING OF CLUBS            2 OF CLUBS
 4 OF HEARTS               3 OF HEARTS             5 OF SPADES
QUEEN OF SPADES            4 OF DIAMONDS           3 OF CLUBS
ACE OF DIAMONDS            10 OF SPADES            7 OF CLUBS
KING OF DIAMONDS           6 OF SPADES             10 OF HEARTS
QUEEN OF CLUBS             8 OF CLUBS              10 OF CLUBS

WHICH COLUMN CONTAINS YOUR CARD? 1


 6 OF HEARTS               2 OF CLUBS              5 OF SPADES
 3 OF CLUBS                7 OF CLUBS              10 OF HEARTS
 10 OF CLUBS               9 OF CLUBS              6 OF CLUBS
 4 OF HEARTS              QUEEN OF SPADES         ACE OF DIAMONDS
KING OF DIAMONDS          QUEEN OF CLUBS          JACK OF SPADES
KING OF CLUBS              3 OF HEARTS             4 OF DIAMONDS
 10 OF SPADES              6 OF SPADES             8 OF CLUBS

WHICH COLUMN CONTAINS YOUR CARD? 1


 5 OF SPADES               10 OF HEARTS            6 OF CLUBS
ACE OF DIAMONDS           JACK OF SPADES           4 OF DIAMONDS
 8 OF CLUBS                6 OF HEARTS             3 OF CLUBS
 10 OF CLUBS               4 OF HEARTS            KING OF DIAMONDS
KING OF CLUBS              10 OF SPADES            2 OF CLUBS
 7 OF CLUBS                9 OF CLUBS             QUEEN OF SPADES
QUEEN OF CLUBS             3 OF HEARTS             6 OF SPADES

WHICH COLUMN CONTAINS YOUR CARD? 2


 5 OF SPADES
ACE OF DIAMONDS
 8 OF CLUBS
 10 OF CLUBS
KING OF CLUBS
 7 OF CLUBS
QUEEN OF CLUBS
 10 OF HEARTS
JACK OF SPADES
 6 OF HEARTS
 4 OF HEARTS
 10 OF SPADES
 9 OF CLUBS
 3 OF HEARTS
 6 OF CLUBS
 4 OF DIAMONDS
 3 OF CLUBS
KING OF DIAMONDS
 2 OF CLUBS

OOPS!!! YOUR CARD IS THE  4 OF HEARTS.
```

```
LIST
100 PRINT TAB(26);"COLUMN"
110 PRINT TAB(20);"CREATIVE COMPUTING"
120 PRINT TAB(18);"MORRISTOWN, NEW JERSEY"
130 PRINT:PRINT:PRINT
140 PRINT "THIS PROGRAM WILL SHOW YOU A CARD TRICK. AFTER THE FIRST DEAL"
150 PRINT "PICK A CARD AND TYPE THE NUMBER OF THE COLUMN CONTAINING IT."
160 PRINT "THE DEALER WILL THEN PICK UP THE CARDS, A COLUMN AT A TIME,"
170 PRINT "AND WILL DEAL THEM OUT AGAIN HORIZONTALLY. WHEN HE FINISHES"
180 PRINT "EACH TIME, TYPE THE NUMBER OF THE THE NEW COLUMN CONTAINING YOUR"
190 PRINT "CARD. FOLLOWING THE LAST DEAL THE DEALER WILL TURN OVER THE"
200 PRINT "CARDS, ONE AT A TIME, UNTIL HE REACHES THE ONE YOU PICKED."
210 PRINT:PRINT:PRINT
220 DIM A(21),B(21)
230 FOR X=1 TO 21
240 J=0
250 T=INT(52*(RND(1)))
270 FOR Y=1 TO X-1
280 IF A(Y)=T THEN 250
290 NEXT Y
300 A(X)=T
310 NEXT X
320 N=0
330 FOR I=1 TO 3
340 FOR Z=1 TO 21
350 IF A(Z)=4*(INT(A(Z)/4)) THEN 470
360 IF A(Z)-2=4*(INT(A(Z)/4)) THEN 440
370 IF A(Z)-3=4*(INT(A(Z)/4)) THEN 410
380 C$="SPADES"
390 D$=""
400 GOTO 490
410 C$="HEARTS"
420 D$=""
430 GOTO 490
440 C$="CLUBS"
450 D$=""
460 GOTO 490
470 C$="DIAMON"
480 D$="DS"
490 N=N+1
500 IF N <> 4 THEN 530
510 PRINT
520 N=1
530 IF A(Z) > 35 THEN 580
540 PRINT TAB((N-1)*25);INT(A(Z)/4)+2;"OF ";C$;D$;
550 IF J=5 THEN 900
560 IF J=10 THEN 980
570 GOTO 710
580 IF INT(A(Z)/4)=9 THEN 670
590 IF INT(A(Z)/4)=10 THEN 650
600 IF INT(A(Z)/4)=11 THEN 630
610 A$="JACK"
620 GOTO 680
630 A$="QUEEN"
640 GOTO 680
650 A$="KING"
660 GOTO 680
670 A$="ACE"
680 PRINT TAB((N-1)*25);A$;" OF ";C$;D$;
690 IF J=5 THEN 900
700 IF J=10 THEN 980
710 NEXT Z
720 PRINT:PRINT
730 PRINT "WHICH COLUMN CONTAINS YOUR CARD";
740 INPUT K
750 IF K<1 OR K > 3 THEN PRINT:PRINT "(1-3)":GOTO 730
760 PRINT:PRINT
770 T=1
780 S=K+2-3*INT((K+1)/3)
790 GOSUB 940
800 S=K
810 GOSUB 940
820 S=K+1-3*INT(K/3)
830 GOSUB 940
840 FOR C=1 TO 21
850 A(C)=B(C)
860 NEXT C
870 NEXT I
880 J=5
890 FOR Z=1 TO 11+INT(10*RND(1)+1):N=0:GOTO 350
900 PRINT:NEXT Z:PRINT
910 PRINT "OOPS!!! YOUR CARD IS THE";
920 N=1
930 J=10:Z=11:GOTO 350
940 FOR R=S TO S+18 STEP 3
950 B(T)=A(R)
960 T=T+1
970 NEXT R:RETURN
980 PRINT ".":PRINT
990 PRINT "DO YOU WANT TO SEE IT AGAIN";:INPUT T$
1000 IF T$="YES" THEN PRINT:PRINT:GOTO 230
1010 END
Ok
```

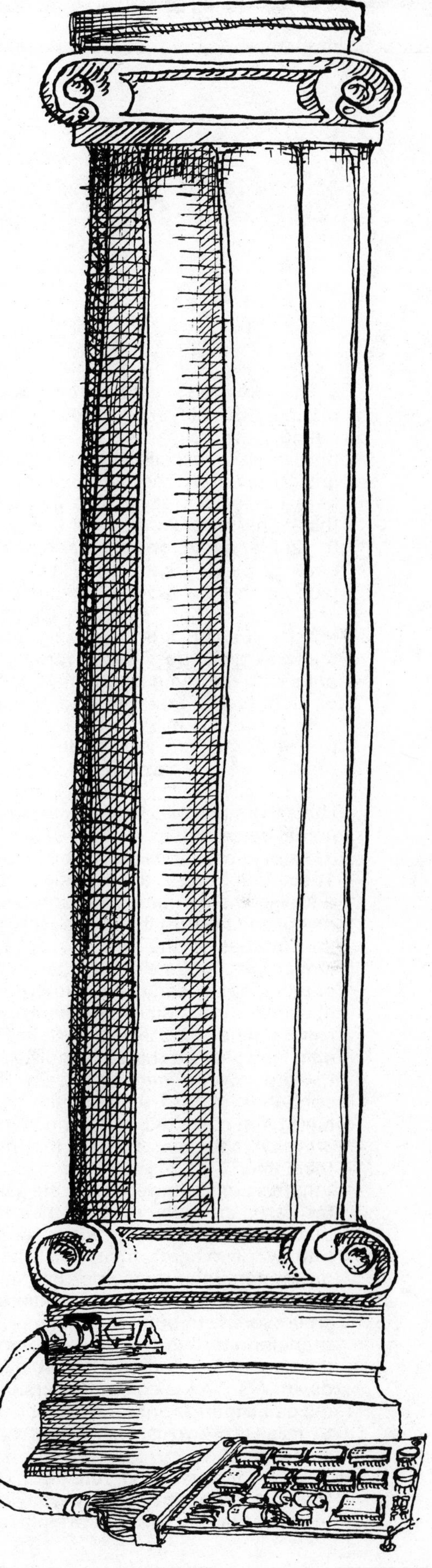

Concentration

This children's card game for any number of players is also called memory, or pelmanism. It is easy to play and is an excellent test of memory and observation. The computer version here simulates the actual game except that it only allows one player to play. In the actual game, one player shuffles a deck of playing cards and lays them face down on a table in all directions and so that no card is touching another. Each player tries to collect as many cards as possible by turning up pairs with the same rank per a number or picture. The first player to go turns over two cards at random and allows the other players to see them. If the rank of the two cards is the same, for example, two aces or two kings, he takes them and may turn over two more cards. He continues in this way until he turns over two cards that do not match. These cards are then placed back down in their original positions, face down, and his turn then ends. The play then passes to the next player. This player turns up one card. If it matches one that has already been turned over, he must try to remember where that card is. If he is successful, he takes the pair. He continues his turn until he fails to turn over a matching pair. Play continues in turn until all the cards have been collected. The winner is the player with the most cards at the end of the game.

In this computer version of the game, the cards are numbered on their face down side from one to fifty-two. As you turn over two cards, their rank is typed on the terminal. If they do not match, their rank is obliterated by successive type-overs with other characters. This is analogous to the situation of placing the cards back down on the table face down. Also in the computer version of the game there is only one player trying to get all fifty-two cards in as few moves as possible.

This game is good fun on a CRT terminal. Also, why not try modifying it to allow play by two or more players?

```
RUN
                          CONCENTRATION
                CREATIVE COMPUTING  MORRISTOWN NEW JERSEY



FIRST CARD? 1
SECOND CARD? 2
██████████████████████████████


FIRST CARD? 13
SECOND CARD? 2
██████████████████████████████


FIRST CARD? 53
THERE ARE ONLY 52 CARDS IN THE DECK, NOT  53
FIRST CARD? 41
SECOND CARD? 37
██████████████████████████████


FIRST CARD? 20
SECOND CARD? 16
██████████████████████████████


FIRST CARD? 29
SECOND CARD? 49
██████████████████████████████


FIRST CARD? 41
SECOND CARD? 29
THAT'S A MATCH --9C        9D
YOUR SCORE IS NOW 1  YOU HAVE HAD  6 PICKS.
FIRST CARD? 1
SECOND CARD? 49
THAT'S A MATCH --2S        2S
YOUR SCORE IS NOW 2  YOU HAVE HAD  7 PICKS.
FIRST CARD? 41
YOU HAVE ALREADY MATCHED THAT CARD.
FIRST CARD? 43
SECOND CARD? 498
THERE ARE ONLY 52 CARDS IN THE DECK, NOT  498
SECOND CARD? 48
██████████████████████████████


FIRST CARD? 26
SECOND CARD? 51
██████████████████████████████


FIRST CARD?

BREAK IN 370
OK
```

```
LIST

10 PRINT TAB(25);"CONCENTRATION"
20 PRINT TAB(15);"CREATIVE COMPUTING  MORRISTOWN NEW JERSEY"
30 PRINT
40 PRINT
50 PRINT
200 DIM C$(52)
210 FOR X=1 TO 52
220 READ E$
230 C$(X)=E$
240 NEXT X
250 REM --   SHUFFLE AND DEAL
260 FOR Z=1 TO 51
270 K$=C$(Z)
275 L=INT((53-Z)*RND(1)+1)
280 C$(Z)=C$(L+Z-1)
290 C$(L)=K$
300 NEXT Z
340 REM --   START TO PLAY
350 FOR N=1 TO 26
360 PRINT "FIRST CARD";
370 INPUT U
372 IF U > 0 AND U < 52 THEN 380
374 PRINT "THERE ARE ONLY 52 CARDS IN THE DECK, NOT ";U
376 GOTO 360
380 LET G=1
390 IF C$(U)=" " THEN 840
400 PRINT "SECOND CARD";
410 INPUT W
412 IF W > 0 AND W < 52 THEN 420
414 PRINT "THERE ARE ONLY 52 CARDS IN THE DECK, NOT ";W
416 GOTO 400
420 LET G=2
430 IF C$(W)=" " THEN 840
440 IF U <> W THEN 470
450 PRINT "YOU CAN'T PICK THE SAME CARD TWICE!"
460 GOTO 400
470 IF MID$(C$(U),1,1)=MID$(C$(W),1,1) THEN 580
480 PRINT "#";U;"IS ";C$(U),"#";W;"IS ";C$(W),
490 FOR I=1 TO 50
500 PRINT;
510 NEXT I
520 PRINT CHR$(13);"HHHHHHHHHHHHHHHHHHHHHHHHHHHHHH";
530 PRINT CHR$(13);"IIIIIIIIIIIIIIIIIIIIIIIIIIIIII";
540 PRINT CHR$(13);"XXXXXXXXXXXXXXXXXXXXXXXXXXXXXX"
550 PRINT
560 PRINT
570 GOTO 630
580 PRINT "THAT'S A MATCH --";C$(U),C$(W)
590 LET C$(U)=" "
600 LET C$(W)=" "
610 LET S=S+1
620 PRINT "YOUR SCORE IS NOW";S;" YOU HAVE HAD ";N;"PICKS."
630 NEXT N
640 REM --   THE RESULTS
650 LET S1=S/(N/4)
660 PRINT "YOU SCORED",S;" OUT OF ";N;"THAT IS ";
670 ON S1+1.5 GOTO 680,700,720,760
680 PRINT "POOR."
690 GOTO 770
700 PRINT "FAIR."
710 GOTO 770
720 PRINT "GOOD."
730 GOTO 770
740 PRINT "EXCELLENT ! ! !"
750 GOTO 770
760 PRINT ". . . AAAH . . . UH....YOU MUST HAVE CHEATED!"
770 PRINT
780 PRINT "DO YOU WANT TO PLAY AGAIN";
790 INPUT Z$
800 IF Z$ = "YES" THEN 260
810 PRINT
820 PRINT "COME BACK AGAIN!!"
830 END
840 PRINT "YOU HAVE ALREADY MATCHED THAT CARD."
850 IF G=1 THEN 360
860 GOTO 400
870 DATA "AS","2S","3S","4S","5S","6S","7S","8S","9S", 10S","JS","QS"
875 DATA "KS"
880 DATA "AH","2H","3H","4H","5H","6H","7H","8H","9H","10H","JH","QH"
885 DATA "KH"
890 DATA "AD","2D","3D","4D","5D","6D","7D","8D","9D","10D","JD","QD"
895 DATA "KD"
900 DATA "AC","2C","3C","4C","5C","6C","7C","8C","9C","10C","JC","QC"
905 DATA "KC"
910 END
OK
```

Condot

This is the old childhood favorite of "connect the dots." The objective is to carve out squares of "real estate" with the computer as an able adversary. The player who connects the two dots which complete a square gets ownership of that square. In addition, the player gets the added bonus of moving once more. This can be quite advantageous in certain situations. A nine-square grid is provided as a playing board.

A sample of the grid follows with an identification of each coordinate where a line may be drawn.

```
      (1,2)     (1,4)     (1,6)

(2,1)     (2,3)     (2,5)     (2,7)

      (3,2)     (3,4)     (3,6)

(4,1)     (4,3)     (4,5)     (4,7)

      (5,2)     (5,4)     (5,6)

(6,1)     (6,3)     (6,5)     (6,7)

      (7,2)     (7,4)     (7,6)
```

You'll find it interesting to note that the computer mirrors the player's move in so far as possible. You may also find that the game moves rather slowly, especially for the first three or four moves. Be patient! Once squares begin to fall, the game moves swiftly to its conclusion.

There are some modifications that you may wish to consider if you are going to adopt this program for regular use. In addition to improving the REM statements in the program, I would suggest:

1. Modifying the program so that the grid is printed after *both* players have moved (rather than each time a move is made);
2. Modifying the program so that once a player had ownership of a majority of the squares, the game would end rather than proceed to its inevitable conclusion; and
3. Modify the program so that the player's initials appear in each square he captures.

The program is by Chuck Lund; the writeup by Pete Olivieri. It originally appeared in *Creative Computing*, Jan/Feb 1976.

```
RUN
                              CONDOT
                        CREATIVE COMPUTING
                      MORRISTOWN, NEW JERSEY


THIS PROGRAM WILL PLAY CONNECT THE DOTS WITH YOU.
THE GAME IS PLAYED ON A 4 X 4 ARRAY. WHEN
YOU WANT TO MAKE A MOVE YOU MUST TYPE IN
THE COORDINATES OF THE SPACE BETWEEN THE TWO DOTS YOU
WANT TO CONNECT. ENTER EACH OF YOUR MOVES BY TYPING
THE ROW NUMBER, A COMMA AND THE COLUMN NUMBER.
THE UPPER LEFT HAND CORNER OF THE ARRAY IS 1,1.
HERE WE GO.
 .   .   .   .

 .   .   .   .

 .   .   .   .

 .   .   .   .
YOUR MOVE? 1,1
YOU REALLY DON'T WANT TO PUT A LINE THERE!!!!
YOUR MOVE? 1,2
 . - .   .   .

 .   .   .   .

 .   .   .   .

 .   .   .   .
MY MOVE
 . - .   .   .

 .   .   .   .

 .   .   .   .

 .   .   . - .
YOUR MOVE? 7,5
YOU REALLY DON'T WANT TO PUT A LINE THERE!!!!
YOUR MOVE? 7,4
 . - .   .   .

 .   .   .   .

 .   .   .   .

 .   . - . - .
MY MOVE
 . - . - .   .

 .   .   .   .

 .   .   .   .

 .   . - . - .
YOUR MOVE? 1,6
 . - . - . - .

 .   .   .   .

 .   .   .   .

 .   . - . - .
```

```
M: MOVE
 . - . - . - .

 .   .   .   .

 .   .   .   .

 . - . - . - .
YOUR MOVE? 2,1
 . - . - . - .
 :
 .   .   .   .

 .   .   .   .

 . - . - . - .
MY MOVE
 . - . - . - .
 :
 .   .   .   .

 .   .   .   .
             :
 . - . - . - .
YOUR MOVE? 4,1
 . - . - . - .
 :
 .   .   .   .
 :
 .   .   .   .
             :
 . - . - . - .
MY MOVE
 . - . - . - .
 :
 .   .   .   .
 :           :
 .   .   .   .
             :
 . - . - . - .
YOUR MOVE? 2,7
 . - . - . - .
 :           :
 .   .   .   .
 :           :
 .   .   .   .
             :
 . - . - . - .
MY MOVE
 . - . - . - .
 :           :
 .   .   .   .
 :           :
 .   .   .   .
 :           :
 . - . - . - .
```

```
YOUR MOVE? 4,3
. - . - . - .
:           :
.   .   .   .
:   :       :
.   .   .   .
:           :
. - . - . - .
MY MOVE
. - . - . - .
:           :
.   .   .   .
:   :   :   :
.   .   .   .
:           :
. - . - . - .

YOUR MOVE? 5,4
. - . - . - .
:           :
.   .   .   .
:   :   :   :
.   . - .   .
:           :
. - . - . - .
MY MOVE
. - . - . - .
:           :
.   . - .   .
:   : C :   :
.   . - .   .
:           :
. - . - . - .

MY MOVE
. - . - . - .
:       :   :
.   . - .   .
:   : C :   :
.   . - .   .
:           :
. - . - . - .
YOUR MOVE? 2,3
. - . - . - .
:   : H :   :
.   . - .   .
:   : C :   :
.   . - .   .
:           :
. - . - . - .

YOUR MOVE? 3,6
. - . - . - .
:   : H : H :
.   . - . - .
:   : C :   :
.   . - .   .
:           :
. - . - . - .
YOUR MOVE? 6,3
. - . - . - .
:   : H : H :
.   . - . - .
:   : C :   :
.   . - .   .
:   :       :
. - . - . - .

MY MOVE
. - . - . - .
: C : H : H :
. - . - . - .
:   : C :   :
.   . - .   .
:   :       :
. - . - . - .
MY MOVE
. - . - . - .
: C : H : H :
. - . - . - .
: C : C :   :
. - . - .   .
: C :       :
. - . - . - .

MY MOVE
. - . - . - .
: C : H : H :
. - . - . - .
: C : C : C :
. - . - . - .
: C :       :
. - . - . - .
MY MOVE
. - . - . - .
: C : H : H :
. - . - . - .
: C : C : C :
. - . - . - .
: C : C : C :
. - . - . - .
I WON
```

```
LIST

1 PRINT TAB(26);"CONDOT"
2 PRINT TAB(20);"CREATIVE COMPUTING"
3 PRINT TAB(18);"MORRISTOWN, NEW JERSEY":PRINT
4 PRINT
5 PRINT
6 PRINT "THIS PROGRAM WILL PLAY CONNECT THE DOTS WITH YOU."
7 PRINT "THE GAME IS PLAYED ON A 4 X 4 ARRAY. WHEN"
8 PRINT "YOU WANT TO MAKE A MOVE YOU MUST TYPE IN"
9 PRINT "THE COORDINATES OF THE SPACE BETWEEN THE TWO DOTS YOU"
10 PRINT "WANT TO CONNECT. ENTER EACH OF YOUR MOVES BY TYPING"
11 PRINT "THE ROW NUMBER, A COMMA AND THE COLUMN NUMBER."
12 PRINT "THE UPPER LEFT HAND CORNER OF THE ARRAY IS 1,1."
13 PRINT "HERE WE GO."
20 DIM A(12,12)
30 V=0
40 FOR R=1 TO 12
50 FOR C=1 TO 12
60 IF R/2=INT(R/2) THEN 100
70 IF C/2 = INT(C/2) THEN 100
80 A(R,C)=-50
90 GOTO 110
100 A(R,C)=0
110 NEXT C
120 NEXT R
130 IF V=1 THEN 200
200 GOSUB 1000
210 PRINT "YOUR MOVE";
220 INPUT X,Y
230 IF X=INT(X) THEN 260
240 PRINT "YOU REALLY DON'T WANT TO PUT A LINE THERE!!!!"
250 GOTO 210
260 IF (X-1)*(X-7) > 0 THEN 240
265 X=X+2
270 IF (Y-1)*(Y-7) > 0 THEN 240
272 Y=Y+2
280 IF (X+Y+1)/2 <> INT((X+Y+1)/2) THEN 240
290 IF A(X,Y) <> 0 THEN 240
300 A(X,Y)=50
310 IF X/2 =INT(X/2) THEN 380
320 IF A(X-2,Y)+A(X-1,Y+1)+A(X-1,Y-1) <> 150 THEN 350
330 P=1
340 A(X-1,Y)=1
350 IF A(X+2,Y)+A(X+1,Y+1)+A(X+1,Y-1) <> 150 THEN 440
360 A(X+1,Y)=1
370 GOTO 200
380 IF A(X,Y-2)+A(X+1,Y-1)+A(X-1,Y-1) <> 150 THEN 410
390 A(X,Y-1)=1
400 P=1
410 IF A(X,Y+2)+A(X+1,Y+1)+A(X-1,Y+1) <> 150 THEN 440
420 A(X,Y+1)=1
430 GOTO 200
440 IF P=1 THEN 200
450 GOSUB 1000
460 PRINT "MY MOVE"
470 FOR R=4 TO 10 STEP 2
480 FOR C=4 TO 10 STEP 2
490 IF A(R-1,C)+A(R+1,C)+A(R,C-1)+A(R,C+1) <> 150 THEN 680
500 A(R,C)=-1
510 IF A(R-1,C) <> 0 THEN 550
520 A(R-1,C)=50
530 IF A(R-3,C)+A(R-2,C-1)+A(R-2,C+1) <> 150 THEN 450
540 LET A(R-2,C)=-1
550 IF A(R+1,C) <> 0 THEN 590
560 A(R+1,C)=50
570 IF A(R+3,C)+A(R+2,C-1)+A(R+2,C+1) <> 150 THEN 450
580 A(R+2,C)=-1
590 IF A(R,C-1) <> 0 THEN 630
600 A(R,C-1)=50
610 IF A(R,C-3)+A(R-1,C-2)+A(R+1,C+2) <> 150  THEN 450
620 A(R,C-2)=-1
630 IF A(R,C+1) <> 0 THEN 450
640 A(R,C+1)=50
650 IF A(R,C+3)+A(R-1,C+2)+A(R+1,C+2) <> 150 THEN 450
660 A(R,C+2)=-1
670 GOTO 450
680 NEXT C
690 NEXT R
692 IF E > 1 THEN 730
700 IF A(12-X,12-Y)<>0 THEN 730
710 A(12-X,12-Y)=50
712 IF E > 1 THEN 870
720 GOTO 200
730 FOR R=3 TO 9
740 FOR C=3 TO 9
750 IF (R+C)/2=INT((R+C)/2) THEN 850
760 IF A(R,C) <> 0 THEN 850
780 IF R/2 = INT(R/2) THEN 830
790 IF A(R-2,C)+A(R-1,C-1)+A(R-1,C+1) = 100 THEN 850
800 IF A(R+2,C)+A(R+1,C-1)+A(R+1,C+1) =100 THEN 850
810 A(R,C)=50
820 GOTO 200
830 IF A(R,C-2)+A(R-1,C-1)+A(R+1,C-1)=100 THEN 850
840 IF A(R,C+2)+A(R-1,C+2)+A(R+1,C+1) <> 100 THEN 810
850 NEXT C
860 NEXT R
862 IF E > 1 THEN 700
870 R=INT(RND(1)*7)+3
880 C=INT(RND(1)*7)+3
881 IF R/2=INT(R/2) THEN 885
882 IF C/2=INT(C/2) THEN 900
883 GOTO 870
885 IF C/2 <> INT(C/2) THEN 900
886 GOTO 870
900 IF A(R,C)<> 0 THEN 870
910 A(R,C)=50
920 GOTO 200
930 PRINT "DO YOU WANT TO PLAY AGAIN (TYPE 1 FOR YES OR 2 FOR NO)";
940 INPUT B
950 IF B = 1 THEN 40
960 END
1000 P=0
1010 D=0
1020 E=0
1030 FOR R=3 TO 9
1040 FOR C=3 TO 9
1050 IF A(R,C) <> 0 THEN 1080
1060 PRINT "   ";
1070 GOTO 1240
1080 IF A(R,C) <> -50 THEN 1110
1090 PRINT " . ";
1100 GOTO 1240
1110 IF A(R,C) <> -1 THEN 1140
1120 PRINT " C ";
1130 GOTO 1170
1140 IF A(R,C) <> 1 THEN 1200
1150 PRINT " H ";
1170 D=D+A(R,C)
1180 E=E+1
1190 GOTO 1240
1200 IF R/2 = INT(R/2) THEN 1230
1210 PRINT " - ";
1220 GOTO 1240
1230 PRINT " : ";
1240 NEXT C
1245 PRINT
1250 NEXT R
1260 IF E >=9 THEN 1280
1270 RETURN
1280 IF D > 0 THEN 1310
1290 PRINT "I WON"
1300 GOTO 930
1310 PRINT "YOU WON!!!"
1320 GOTO 930
1400 END
OK
```

Convoy

This is a naval war game played on a 10 by 10 grid. You are a submarine and the computer plays the role of the convoy consisting of a cargo ship and two destroyers. One destroyer acts as the escort traveling alongside the cargo ship, while the other searches for the submarine and tries to destroy it. The destroyer which is searching for the submarine moves from zero to three squares at a time, searching. The other destroyer stays within one square of the ship. The submarine starts in square #12 and can move up, down, left, or right one square at a time with two moves per turn. It has four torpedoes which may be fired one at a time in any straight direction, horizontally, vertically, or diagonally.

The game ends when either the submarine destroys the cargo ship or when one of the two destroyers gets the submarine.

```
                                 CONVOY
               CREATIVE COMPUTING, MORRISTOWN, NEW JERSEY
INSTRUCTIONS? YES
THIS NAVAL WAR GAME IS PLAYED ON A 10 BY 10 MATRIX
YOU ARE THE SUB; THE COMPUTER IS A CARGO SHIP AND ITS TWO
DESTROYERS. THE SHIP STARTS IN SQUARE 100 AND RANDOMLY MOVES
TO SQUARE 1, MOVING 0,1,2,OR 3 SQUARES AT A TIME.
ONE OF THE SHIP'S DESTROYERS STARTS AT SQUARE 78 AND MOVES
RANDOMLY 0,1,2 OR 3 SQUARES AT A TIME SEARCHING FOR THE SUB.
THE OTHER DESTROYER STAYS WITHIN ONE SQUARE OF THE SHIP AS
AN ESCORT.  THE SUB STARTS IN SQUARE 12, CAN MOVE UP,DOWN,
LEFT OR RIGHT 1 SQUARE AT A TIME, 2 MOVES PER TURN,AND IT
HAS TORPEDOES WHICH IT CAN FIRE 1 AT A TIME IN ANY STRAIGHT
LINE. AFTER EACH SUB MOVE, THE PERISCOPE WILL SEARCH
EACH ADJACENT SQUARE FOR THE SHIP. ALSO RANDOM RECONNAISANCE
REPORTS WILL BE MADE. THE SEQUENCE OF PLAY IS:

1 SHIP AND DESTROYERS MOVE
2 YOUR MOVE
3 YOU CAN FIRE A TORPEDO
4 PERISCOPE SEARCH
5 YOUR MOVE AGAIN
 AND BACK TO 1

 THE SUB WINS IF IT SUCCEEDS IN HITTING THE SHIP WITHIN 4
TORPEDOES WITHOUT MOVING TO A SQUARE OCCUPIED BY A DESTROYER.

TO 'FIRE?' ANSWER:NO,L,R,U,D,LU,LD,RU,OR,RD.
'L'=LEFT,'R'=RIGHT,'U'=UP,'D'=DOWN,'LU'=LEFT UP,'RU'=RIGHT
UP,OR 'RD'=RIGHTDOWN

WILL YOU NEED A BOARD? YES


  1   2   3   4   5   6   7   8   9   10
 11  12  13  14  15  16  17  18  19   20
 21  22  23  24  25  26  27  28  29   30
 31  32  33  34  35  36  37  38  39   40
 41  42  43  44  45  46  47  48  49   50
 51  52  53  54  55  56  57  58  59   60
 61  62  63  64  65  66  67  68  69   70
 71  72  73  74  75  76  77  78  79   80
 81  82  83  84  85  86  87  88  89   90
 91  92  93  94  95  96  97  98  99  100


DESTROYER HAS MOVED
SHIP MOVED

SUB IS NOW AT  12
DESTROYER LAST SIGHTED AT  78
SUB'S MOVE? 13
SUB'S MOVE? 14

SUB AT 14
SHIP LAST SEEN AT 100
FIRE? NO

UP PERISCOPE
SHIP NOT IN SIGHT

RECON. SHOWS SHIP AT  99

SUB IS NOW AT  14
DESTROYER LAST SIGHTED AT  78
SUB'S MOVE? 15
SUB'S MOVE? 16
DESTROYER HAS MOVED
SHIP MOVED

SUB IS NOW AT  16
DESTROYER LAST SIGHTED AT  78
SUB'S MOVE? 17
SUB'S MOVE? 18

SUB AT 18
SHIP LAST SEEN AT 99
FIRE? NO

UP PERISCOPE
SHIP NOT IN SIGHT

RECON. SHOWS SHIP AT  88
SUB IS NOW AT  18
DESTROYER LAST SIGHTED AT  78
SUB'S MOVE? 28
SUB'S MOVE? 38
DESTROYER HAS MOVED
SHIP MOVED

SUB IS NOW AT  38
DESTROYER LAST SIGHTED AT  78
SUB'S MOVE? 48
SUB'S MOVE? 58

SUB AT 58
SHIP LAST SEEN AT 88
FIRE? NO

UP PERISCOPE
SHIP NOT IN SIGHT

RECON. SHOWS SHIP AT  87

SUB IS NOW AT  58
DESTROYER LAST SIGHTED AT  78
SUB'S MOVE? 57
DESTROYER CLOSING IN AT 66
SUB'S MOVE? 56
DESTROYER CLOSING IN AT 66
DESTROYER HAS MOVED
SHIP MOVED
```

```
LIST

80 PRINT TAB(33)"CONVOY"
90 PRINT TAB(15)"CREATIVE COMPUTING, MORRISTOWN, NEW JERSEY"
100 PRINT "INSTRUCTIONS";
110 INPUT B$
120 IF B$="NO" THEN  300
130 PRINT "THIS NAVAL WAR GAME IS PLAYED ON A 10 BY 10 MATRIX"
140 PRINT"YOU ARE THE SUB; THE COMPUTER IS A CARGO SHIP AND ITS TWO"
145 PRINT"DESTROYERS. THE SHIP STARTS IN SQUARE 100 AND RANDOMLY MOVES"
150 PRINT"TO SQUARE 1, MOVING 0,1,2,OR 3 SQUARES AT A TIME."
155 PRINT"ONE OF THE SHIP'S DESTROYERS STARTS AT SQUARE 78 AND MOVES"
160 PRINT"RANDOMLY 0,1,2 OR 3 SQUARES AT A TIME SEARCHING FOR THE SUB."
165 PRINT"THE OTHER DESTROYER STAYS WITHIN ONE SQUARE OF THE SHIP AS"
166 PRINT"AN ESCORT.  THE SUB STARTS IN SQUARE 12, CAN MOVE UP,DOWN, "
167 PRINT"LEFT OR RIGHT 1 SQUARE AT A TIME, 2 MOVES PER TURN,AND IT "
190 PRINT"HAS TORPEDOES WHICH IT CAN FIRE 1 AT A TIME IN ANY STRAIGHT"
200 PRINT"LINE. AFTER EACH SUB MOVE, THE PERISCOPE WILL SEARCH"
210 PRINT"EACH ADJACENT SQUARE FOR THE SHIP. ALSO RANDOM RECONNAISANCE"
220 PRINT"REPORTS WILL BE MADE. THE SEQUENCE OF PLAY IS:"
230 PRINT
240 PRINT"1 SHIP AND DESTROYERS MOVE"
245 PRINT"2 YOUR MOVE"
250 PRINT"3 YOU CAN FIRE A TORPEDO"
270 PRINT"4 PERISCOPE SEARCH"
275 PRINT"5 YOUR MOVE AGAIN"
280 PRINT" AND BACK TO 1"
281 PRINT
283 PRINT" THE SUB WINS IF IT SUCCEEDS IN HITTING THE SHIP WITHIN 4 "
285 PRINT"TORPEDOES WITHOUT MOVING TO A SQUARE OCCUPIED BY A DESTROYER."
286 PRINT
287 PRINT"TO 'FIRE?' ANSWER:NO,L,R,U,D,LU,LD,RU,OR,RD."
288 PRINT"'L'=LEFT,'R'=RIGHT,'U'=UP,'D'=DOWN,'LU'=LEFT UP,'RU'=RIGHT "
289 PRINT"UP,OR 'RD'=RIGHTDOWN"
290 PRINT
300 PRINT"WILL YOU NEED A BOARD";
310 INPUT B$
320 IF B$="NO" THEN 420
330 PRINT
340 PRINT
350 PRINT"  1   2   3   4   5   6   7   8   9  10"
360 FOR I=1 TO9
370 FOR J=1 TO 10
380 PRINTI*10+J;
390 NEXT J
400 PRINT
410 NEXT I
420 PRINT:PRINT
440 D=12
```

```
450 T=4
460 S=100
470 C=78
480 C2=78
490 L=100
500 IF C=-100 THEN 550
510 GOTO 2780
520 Y3=0
530 M1=0
540 GOTO580
550 M1=0
560 IF S=2 THEN 1230
570 Y3=1
580 IF S=3 THEN 1230
590 IF S=11 THEN 1230
600 IF S=12 THEN 1230
610 IF S=21 THEN 1230
620 X=RND(1)
630 IF X>.4 THEN 690
640 IF X>.2 THEN 710
650 IF X>.05 THEN 670
660 GOTO 1020
670 S1=0
680 GOTO 720
690 S1=2
700 GOTO 720
710 S1=1
720 X=RND(1)
730 IF X<.75 THEN 760
740 P1=1
750 GOTO 830
760 P1=-1
770 GOTO 830
780 IF S=10*INT(S/10) THEN 820
790 GOTO 860
800 IF S=1+(10*INT(S/10)) THEN 820
810 GOTO 860
820 P1=P1*(-1)
830 M2=P1*((INT(2*(RND(1)))*9)+1)
840 IF M2=1 THEN 780
850 IF M2=-1 THEN 800
860 IF M1=M2*(-1) THEN 820
870 C1=S+M2
880 IF C1=1 THEN 1230
890 IF C1=D THEN 2720
900 IF C1=C THEN 820
910 IF C1<1 THEN 820
920 IF C1>100 THEN 820
930 M1=M2
940 S=C1
950 C6=S+((INT(2*RND(1))*(-2))+1)*((INT(2*RND(1))*9)+1)
960 IF C6<2 THEN 950
970 IF C6>100 THEN 950
980 IF C6= D THEN 2700
990 IF S1=1 THEN 670
1000 IF S1=2 THEN 710
1010 C3=0
1020 PRINT"SHIP MOVED"
1030 IF Y3=0 THEN 1060
1040 X1=0
1050 GOTO 2340
1060 PRINT
1070 X1=1
1080 PRINT"SUB AT";D
1090 PRINT"SHIP LAST SEEN AT";L
1100 PRINT"FIRE";
1110 INPUT A$
1120 IF A$="NO" THEN 1730
1130 IF A$="L" THEN 1250
1140 IF A$="R" THEN 1270
1150 IF A$="U" THEN 1290
1160 IF A$="D" THEN 1310
1180 IF A$="LU" THEN 1330
1185 IF A$="LD" THEN 1350
1190 IF A$="RU" THEN 1370
1200 IF A$="RD" THEN 1390
1210 PRINT"ANS: NO,L,R,U,D,LU,LD,RU,OR,RD"
1220 GOTO 1100
1230 PRINT"SHIP'S IN PORT"
1240 GOTO 2750
1250 P1=-1
1260 GOTO 1400
1270 P1=1
1280 GOTO 1400
1290 P1=-10
1300 GOTO 1400
1310 P1=10
1320 GOTO 1400
1330 P1=-11
1340 GOTO 1400
1350 P1=9
1360 GOTO 1400
1370 P1=-9
1380 GOTO 1400
1390 P1=11
1400 D1=D
1410 D1=D1+P1
1420 PRINT D1;
1430 IF D1=S THEN1500
1440 IF D1=C THEN 1520
1450 IF D1<11 THEN 1600
1460 IF D1>90 THEN 1640
1470 IF D1=10*INT(D1/10) THEN 1560
1480 IF D1=1+(10*INT(D1/10)) THEN 1580
1490 GOTO 1410
1500 PRINT"KER-BOOM! CARGO SHIP DESTROYED!"
1502 PRINT"YOU WIN"
1504 Q=1
1510 GOTO 2750
1520 PRINT"WHAMO!!, DESTROYER SUNK."
1530 C=-100
1540 T=T-1
1550 GOTO 1710
1560 IF D=10*INT(D/10) THEN 1410
1570 GOTO 1680
1580 IF D=1+(10*INT(D/10)) THEN 1410
1590 GOTO 1680
1600 IF D>10 THEN 1680
1610 IF D1<2 THEN 1680
1620 IF D1>9 THEN 1680
1630 GOTO 1410
1640 IF D<91 THEN 1680
1650 IF D1<92 THEN 1680
1660 IF D1>99 THEN 1680
1670 GOTO 1410
1680 T=T-1
1690 PRINT"MISS"
1700 IF T=0 THEN 2740
1710 PRINT T;"TORPEDOES LEFT"
1720 GOTO 1100
1730 PRINT
1740 Y=0
1750 PRINT"UP PERISCOPE"
1760 Y2=0
1770 IF S=D THEN 1930
1780 IF S=D-1 THEN 1930
1790 IF S=D+1 THEN 1930
1800 IF S=D-10 THEN 1930
1810 IF S=D+10 THEN 1930
1820 IF S=D-9 THEN 1930
1830 IF S=D+9 THEN 1930
1840 IF S=D-11 THEN 1930
1850 IF S=D+11 THEN 1930
1860 IF Y=1 THEN 1960
1870 PRINT"SHIP NOT IN SIGHT"
1880 X=RND(1)
1890 IF X<.35 THEN 1960
1900 PRINT
1910 PRINT"RECON. SHOWS ";
1920 Y2=-1
1930 PRINT"SHIP AT ";S
1940 Y2=Y2+1
1950 L=S
1960 IF C=D THEN 2280
1970 IF C6=D THEN 2700
1980 IF C=D+1 THEN 2260
1990 IF C6=D+1 THEN 2240
2000 IF C=D-1 THEN 2260
2010 IF C6=D-1 THEN 2240
2020 IF C=D+9 THEN 2260
2030 IF C6=D+9 THEN 2240
2040 IF C=D-9 THEN 2260
2050 IF C6=D-9 THEN 2240
2060 IF C=D+10 THEN 2260
2070 IF C6=D+10 THEN 2240
2080 IF C=D-10 THEN 2260
2090 IF C6=D-10 THEN 2240
2100 IF C=D+11 THEN 2260
2110 IF C6=D+11 THEN 2240
2120 IF C=D-11 THEN 2260
2130 IF C6=D-11 THEN 2240
2140 IF C=D+2 THEN 2260
2150 IF C=D-2 THEN 2260
2160 IF C=D+20 THEN 2260
2170 IF C=D-20 THEN 2260
2180 IF C=-100 THEN 2320
2190 IF Y=1 THEN 2330
2200 X=RND(1)
2210 IF X<.6 THEN 2320
2220 PRINT"RECON. PLANE SPOTS TIN CAN AT";C
2230 GOTO 2300
2240 PRINT"ESCORT VERY NEAR!"
2250 GOTO 2320
2260 PRINT"DESTROYER CLOSING IN AT";C
2270 GOTO 2300
2280 PRINT"DESTROYER DIRECTLY OVER HEAD"
2290 GOTO 2660
2300 C2=C
2310 C3=1
2320 IF Y=0 THEN 2340
2330 RETURN
2340 PRINT
2350 PRINT"SUB IS NOW AT ";D
2360 IF C3=1 THEN 2390
2370 IF C=-100 THEN 2390
2380 PRINT"DESTROYER LAST SIGHTED AT ";C2
2390 D2=0
2400 PRINT"SUB'S MOVE";
2410 Y=1
2420 INPUT X
2430 IF X=D THEN 2560
2440 IF X<2 THEN 2640
2450 IF X>100 THEN 2640
2460 IF X=INT(X) THEN 2480
2470 GOTO 2640
2480 IF X=D+1 THEN 2530
2490 IF X=D-1 THEN 2550
2500 IF X=D+10 THEN 2560
2510 IF X=D-10 THEN 2560
2520 GOTO 2640
2530 IF D=10*INT(D/10) THEN 2640
2540 GOTO 2560
2550 IF X=10*INT(X/10)  THEN  2640
2560 D=X
2570 GOSUB 1760
2580 IF D2=1 THEN 2610
2590 D2=1
2600 GOTO 2400
2610 IF X1=0 THEN 3060
2620 IF C=-100 THEN 550
2630 GOTO 2780
2640 PRINT"CAN'T DO"
2650 GOTO 2400
2660 X=RND(1)
2670 IF X<.8 THEN 2700
2680 PRINT"DEPTH CHARGE JUST MISSED!"
2690 GOTO 2300
2700 PRINT"VAROOM!!SUB DEPTH CHARGED!"
2710 GOTO 2750
2720 PRINT"SHIP NOW OVERHEAD"
2730 GOTO 550
2740 PRINT"AMMO DEPLETED"
2750 PRINT
2751 IF Q=0 THEN 2754
2752 Q1=Q1+1
2753 GOTO 2755
2754 Q2=Q2+1
2755 PRINT"SCORE: COMPUTER";Q2;"-   SUB";Q1
2756 PRINT
2757 Q=0
2760 PRINT"    NEW    GAME";
2761 INPUT N$
2762 IF N$="NO" THEN 3080
2770 GOTO 420
2780 M1=0
2790 S1=0
2800 X=RND(1)
2810 IF X<.6 THEN 2840
2820 P1=1
2830 GOTO 2850
2840 P1=-1
2850 M2=(P1*((INT(2*RND(1)))*9)+1)
2860 IF M2=1 THEN 3000
2870 IF M2=-1 THEN 3020
2880 IF M1=M2*(-1) THEN 3040
2890 C1=C+M2
2900 IF C1=D THEN 2700
2910 IF C1=S THEN 3040
2920 IF C1<2 THEN 3040
2930 IF C1>100 THEN 3040
2940 M1=M2
2950 C=C1
2960 IF S1=1 THEN 550
2970 S1=1
2980 PRINT"DESTROYER HAS MOVED"
2990 GOTO 2800
3000 IF C=10*INT(C/10) THEN 3040
3010 GOTO 2880
3020 IF C=1+(10*INT(C/10)) THEN 3040
3030 GOTO 2880
3040 P1=P1*(-1)
3050 GOTO 2850
3060 IF Y2=0 THEN 1060
3070 GOTO 520
3080 END
OK
```

Corral

CORRAL is a game program inspired by Harry (short for Aragon), a horse acquired in a rash moment of indulgence for a teen-age daughter. Harry, in his own inimitable style, taught us much about the care, feeding and psychology of the equine species. Some of that hard-won psychology has found its way into CORRAL, which is a one-dimensional simulation of the two- (and almost three-) dimensional problem of catching Harry for anything other than food. The main reason for confining Harry's alter ego in the computer to only one dimension is simply to conserve paper on hard-copy terminals. Even so, the presentation is very effective on a video display unit.

The corral itself is bounded by a pair of siderails represented by upper-case I characters separated by 21 spaces. The cowboy C always enters beside the leftmost rail while the horse H is happily mooching somewhere between positions 10 and 18 with a bias towards the right. This bias and the various other behavioral peculiarities of the horse are governed by two data matrices (statements 90 and 100) which may be altered to vary the beast's temperament from wild to docile depending on the data distribution.

If the horse bolts, a check is made (line 450) to ensure that it does not reach a position less than one space away from the cowboy. Occasionally, the horse bolts to a position more advantageous to the cowboy, just as in real life, but usually the opposite is true, particularly when it bolts as a result of an incautious approach by the cowboy. So heed with care the advice for the cowboy not to advance by more than half the separation in any one move except when adjacent to the horse, of course!

The probability that the horse may kick when the cowboy moves close is set by the IF statement at line 500. The cowboy is immobilized for from one to five moves, while the horse canters happily away from the scene of his triumph. If this happens more than a certain (random) number of times the round-up is terminated by the departure of the cowboy in an ambulance.

Occasionally the horse decides to engage in a friendly dance around the cowboy, but remember that random number generators have no soul and the result is often vile treachery as the horse delivers a fatal kick at the very moment when a successful catch seems assured. On the other hand, the skill of an accomplished CORRAL cowboy can result in a catch within three moves with no injuries sustained. You either have it or you have not, as the saying goes. In the latter case the program allows a maximum of 100 moves before relegating the luckless cowboy to cookhouse chores.

Computer freaks with multi-color graphics will no doubt be dissatisfied with such prosaic symbols as H and C for the horse and cowboy. A fully animated CORRAL in living color (with sound effects by a music or speech synthesizer—a talking horse yet!) should not be too difficult to achieve.

Program and description are by Colin Keay.

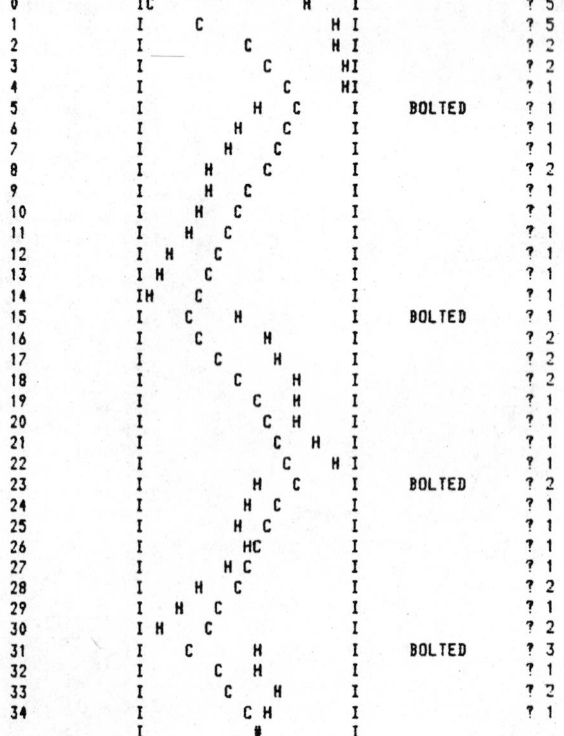

```
                    CORRAL
               CREATIVE COMPUTING
             MORRISTOWN, NEW JERSEY


  YOU ARE THE COWBOY.  GO CATCH YOUR HORSE IN THE CORRAL!
DO YOU WANT FULL INSTRUCTIONS? YES
YOU MOVE TOWARD YOUR HORSE 1 TO 5 STEPS AT A TIME.
IF YOU MORE THAN HALVE THE SEPERATION HE WILL BOLT!
HE MAY ALSO BOLT WHEN HE IS CLOSE TO THE RAIL
WHEN YOU COME WITHIN 2 STEPS HE MAY KICK.  SO LOOKOUT!!

AFTER '?' TYPE IN DIGIT FROM 1 TO 5 FOR COWBOY'S NEXT MOVE

 0            IC               H    I                ? 5
 1            I     C             H I                ? 5
 2            I          C        H I                ? 2
 3            I            C       HI                ? 2
 4            I              C     HI                ? 1
 5            I           H   C     I     BOLTED     ? 1
 6            I         H    C      I                ? 1
 7            I        H    C       I                ? 1
 8            I      H     C        I                ? 2
 9            I      H   C          I                ? 1
 10           I     H   C           I                ? 1
 11           I    H   C            I                ? 1
 12           I  H    C             I                ? 1
 13           I H    C              I                ? 1
 14           IH    C               I                ? 1
 15           I    C    H           I     BOLTED     ? 1
 16           I     C      H        I                ? 2
 17           I       C     H       I                ? 2
 18           I         C     H     I                ? 2
 19           I           C   H     I                ? 1
 20           I            C  H     I                ? 1
 21           I             C   H   I                ? 1
 22           I              C    H I                ? 1
 23           I           H   C     I     BOLTED     ? 2
 24           I          H  C       I                ? 1
 25           I         H  C        I                ? 1
 26           I          HC         I                ? 1
 27           I        H C          I                ? 1
 28           I     H   C           I                ? 2
 29           I   H   C             I                ? 1
 30           I H    C              I                ? 2
 31           I    C      H         I     BOLTED     ? 3
 32           I       C   H         I                ? 1
 33           I        C    H       I                ? 2
 34           I          C H        I                ? 1
              I           #         I

YIPPEE!!  NOW SEE IF YOU CAN CATCH HIM IN FEWER MOVES
ANOTHER ROUNDUP? NO THANKS
```

```
ANOTHER ROUNDUP? YES

 0            IC               H    I                ? 5
 1            I     C            H  I                ? 5
 2            I          C         HI                ? 5
 3            I               C    HI                ? 2
 4            I       H         C   I     BOLTED     ? 3
 5            I       H      C      I                ? 2
 6            I     H      C        I                ? 3
 7            I   H     C           I                ? 3
 8            I H    C              I                ? 2
 9            I H  C                I                ? 1
 10           I H C                 I                ? 1
 11           I  C      H           I     BOLTED     ? 3
 12           I     C   H           I                ? 2
 13           I       C  H          I                ? 1
 14           I        C   H        I                ? 2
 15           I          C   H      I                ? 2
 16           I            C    H   I                ? 1
 17           I             C     H I                ? 2
 18           I               C    HI                ? 1
 19           I           H    C    I     BOLTED     ? 1
 20           I           H   C     I                ? 2
 21           I             C  H    I     KICKED
 22           I             C      HI
 23           I             C      HI
 24           I             C      HI
 25           I             C      HI                ? 3
 26           I                C   HI                ? 1
 27           I           H     C   I     BOLTED     ? 3
 28           I         H    C      I                ? 2
 29           I       H    C        I                ? 2
 30           I       H  C          I                ? 1
 31           I     H   C           I                ? 2
 32           I    H  C             I                ? 1
 33           I      C  H           I     KICKED
 34           I      C      H       I
 35           I      C        H     I
 36           I      C          H   I                ? 5
 37           I           C       H I                ? 3
 38           I       H      C      I     BOLTED     ? 2
 39           I       H    C        I                ? 2
 40           I    H     C          I                ? 3
 41           I       C H           I     KICKED
 42           I       C    H        I
 43           I       C      H      I                ? 3
 44           I          C   H      I                ? 2
 45           I            C    H   I                ? 2
 46           I              C   H  I                ? 1
 47           I               C H   I                ? 1
 48           I           H    C    I     KICKED
 49           I          H     C    I
 50           I      H         C    I
 51           I   H            C    I
 52           IH               C    I                ? 5
 53           IH          C         I                ? 5
 54           IH     C              I                ? 2
 55           IH   C                I                ? 1
 56           I   C         H       I     BOLTED     ? 5
 57           I        C    H       I                ? 2
 58           I          C    H     I                ? 1
 59           I           C      H  I                ? 2
 60           I         H  C        I     BOLTED     ? 21
ILLEGAL MOVE. TRY AGAIN     ? 2
 61           I        H C          I                ? 1
 62           I     H    C          I                ? 2
 63           I   H  C              I                ? 2
 64           IH     C              I                ? 3
 65           I  C    H             I     BOLTED     ? 2
 66           I     C   H           I                ? 1
 67           I      C     H        I                ? 2
 68           I        C   H        I                ? 2
 69           I       H  C          I     KICKED
THOSE KICKS LANDED YOU IN THE HOSPITAL!
 GET WELL SOON!!
ANOTHER ROUNDUP? NO
Ok
```

```
LIST
1 PRINT TAB(26);"CORRAL"
2 PRINT TAB(20);"CREATIVE COMPUTING"
3 PRINT TAB(18);"MORRISTOWN, NEW JERSEY"
4 PRINT:PRINT:PRINT
10 DIM A(21)
40 DIM S(2,9)
50 FOR I=1 TO 2:FOR J=0 TO 9
55 READ S(I,J):NEXT J:NEXT I
60 DATA 0,1,2,3,3,2,2,1,0,-1
70 DATA 1,2,3,4,5,4,3,2,1,0
100 PRINT "  YOU ARE THE COWBOY.  GO CATCH YOUR HORSE IN THE CORRAL!"
110 INPUT "DO YOU WANT FULL INSTRUCTIONS";F$
120 IF LEFT$(F$,1)="N" GOTO 190
130 PRINT "YOU MOVE TOWARD YOUR HORSE 1 TO 5 STEPS AT A TIME."
140 PRINT "IF YOU MORE THAN HALVE THE SEPERATION HE WILL BOLT!"
150 PRINT "HE MAY ALSO BOLT WHEN HE IS CLOSE TO THE RAIL"
160 PRINT "WHEN YOU COME WITHIN 2 STEPS HE MAY KICK.  SO LOOKOUT!!"
180 PRINT
190 PRINT "AFTER '?' TYPE IN DIGIT FROM 1 TO 5 FOR COWBOY'S NEXT MOVE"
200 C=1:L=1:K=0:M=0:N=0:GOSUB 800
220 IF R>5 THEN Q=-Q
225 H=13+Q:GOSUB 810
230 T=2+P:PRINT
300 B$= "            "
310 FOR J=1 TO 21:A(J)=32:NEXT J
320 A(C)=67:A(H)=72
330 PRINT N,"I";
333 FOR J=1 TO 21:PRINT CHR$(A(J));:NEXT J
337 PRINT "I",B$;
370 X=ABS(H-C):L=SGN(H-C)
380 N=N+1:IF K>0 GOTO 640
390 IF N>100 THEN 980
395 INPUT D
400 IF D>0 AND D<6 GOTO 450
420 PRINT "ILLEGAL MOVE. TRY AGAIN",;:GOTO 390
450 E=C+L*D:IF E <1 OR E>21 THEN 420
460 C=E:GOSUB 800
510 G=P:H=H+L*G:GOSUB 810
530 IF X<2*D AND D >1 GOTO 570
540 IF H>1 AND H<20 THEN 600
545 GOSUB 800
550 IF R>2 GOTO 600
555 IF X>7 GOTO 300
570 G=9+2*P:H=H-L*G:L=-L:GOSUB 810
580 IF ABS(H-C)>1 THEN 590
585 H=H-3*L:GOSUB 810
590 B$="BOLTED      ":GOTO 310
600 IF ABS(H-C)>2 GOTO 300
605 GOSUB 800
610 IF R>3 GOTO 700
615 GOSUB 800
620 K=P+2:M=M+1:H=H-5*L:GOSUB 810
630 B$="KICKED":GOTO 310
640 IF M>T GOTO 900
650 K=K-1:PRINT:GOSUB 800
670 H=H+L*(P+1):GOSUB 810:GOTO 300
700 IF H=C THEN 930
705 GOTO 300
800 R=INT(10*RND(1)):P=S(1,R):Q=S(2,R):RETURN
810 IF H<1 THEN H=1
820 IF H>21 THEN H=21
830 RETURN
900 PRINT:PRINT "THOSE KICKS LANDED YOU IN THE HOSPITAL!"
910 PRINT " GET WELL SOON!!":GOTO 960
930 FOR J=1 TO 21:A(J)=32:NEXT J:A(C)=35
940 PRINT ,"I";
943 FOR J=1 TO 21:PRINT CHR$(A(J));:NEXT J
947 PRINT "I"
950 PRINT:PRINT "YIPPEE!!  NOW SEE IF YOU CAN CATCH HIM IN FEWER MOVES"
960 INPUT "ANOTHER ROUNDUP";F$
970 IF LEFT$(F$,1)="Y" THEN 200
975 GOTO 999
980 PRINT:PRINT "ENOUGH!! YOU'D DO BETTER AS CAMP COOK!":GOTO 960
999 END
Ok
```

Countdown

The program Countdown is based on the program Guess in which the computer chooses a random number and then gives you clues whether you are too high or too low until you finally get the number. In Countdown, the program adds a little interest to this guessing game by giving you a certain number of tries to get the mystery number between one and ten before your schoolbuilding explodes. Using a good guessing strategy should allow you to get any number in four or fewer tries. If you take more than four tries, the building goes "boom." To add a little more interest to the game, you may want to make the maximum number of tries three. To do this change the value of T in statement 45 from 4 to 3.

Countdown was written by Mark Chambers.

```
LIST
1 PRINT TAB(24);"COUNT DOWN"
2 PRINT TAB(20);"CREATIVE COMPUTING"
3 PRINT TAB(18);"MORRISTOWN, NEW JERSEY"
4 PRINT:PRINT:PRINT
5 A=INT(RND(1)*10)
6 T=0
7 N=0
15 PRINT "YOU HAVE ACTIVATED THE SELF-DESTRUCT MECHANISM ";
20 PRINT "IN THIS SCHOOL."
25 PRINT "IF YOU WISH, YOU MAY STOP THE MECHANISM."
27 PRINT "TO DO SO, JUST TYPE IN THE CORRECT NUMBER,"
35 PRINT "WHICH WILL STOP THE COUNT-DOWN."
37 PRINT "PLEASE HURRY!! THERE IS NO TIME TO WASTE!!!!!!!"
44 PRINT "WHAT'LL IT BE";:INPUT X:PRINT
45 IF T=4 THEN 98
47 GOTO 200
50 REM
75 PRINT "YOUR NUMBER DOES NOT COMPUTE!!"
80 PRINT "PLEASE TRY AGAIN!!!!":T=T+1
81 IF T=2 THEN 96
82 IF T=3 THEN 105
83 GOTO 44
85 PRINT "CORRECT!!!!":LET N=5
90 PRINT "THE COUNTDOWN HAS STOPPED."
92 PRINT "YOU HAVED SAVED THE SCHOOL!"
93 PRINT "(HAVE YOU SEEN YOUR SHRINK LATELY ?)"
94 LET T=10
95 GOTO 1000
96 PRINT "TIME GROWS SHORT, PLEASE HURRY!!!!!!!!"
97 GOTO 44
98 PRINT:PRINT:PRINT:PRINT
99 PRINT TAB(32);"TOO LATE"
100 PRINT:PRINT:PRINT:PRINT TAB(32);"\ **** /"
101 PRINT TAB(31);"-- BOOM --"
102 PRINT TAB(32);"/ **** \"
103 PRINT:PRINT:PRINT
104 GOTO 1000
105 PRINT "HURRY, THE COUNT-DOWN IS APPROACHING ZERO!!!!!!!!!"
110 GOTO 44
200 IF X<A THEN PRINT "TOO SMALL!!!!!":GOTO 50
210 IF X>A THEN PRINT "TOO BIG!!!!!":GOTO 50
225 IF X=A THEN 85
1000 END
Ok
```

```
RUN
                        COUNT DOWN
                    CREATIVE COMPUTING
                  MORRISTOWN, NEW JERSEY



YOU HAVE ACTIVATED THE SELF-DESTRUCT MECHANISM IN THIS SCHOOL.
IF YOU WISH, YOU MAY STOP THE MECHANISM.
TO DO SO, JUST TYPE IN THE CORRECT NUMBER,
WHICH WILL STOP THE COUNT-DOWN.
PLEASE HURRY!! THERE IS NO TIME TO WASTE!!!!!!!
WHAT'LL IT BE? 0

CORRECT!!!!
THE COUNTDOWN HAS STOPPED.
YOU HAVED SAVED THE SCHOOL!
(HAVE YOU SEEN YOUR SHRINK LATELY ?)
Ok
```

```
RUN
                        COUNT DOWN
                    CREATIVE COMPUTING
                  MORRISTOWN, NEW JERSEY



YOU HAVE ACTIVATED THE SELF-DESTRUCT MECHANISM IN THIS SCHOOL.
IF YOU WISH, YOU MAY STOP THE MECHANISM.
TO DO SO, JUST TYPE IN THE CORRECT NUMBER,
WHICH WILL STOP THE COUNT-DOWN.
PLEASE HURRY!! THERE IS NO TIME TO WASTE!!!!!!!
WHAT'LL IT BE? 0

TOO SMALL!!!!!
YOUR NUMBER DOES NOT COMPUTE!!
PLEASE TRY AGAIN!!!!
WHAT'LL IT BE? 1

TOO SMALL!!!!!
YOUR NUMBER DOES NOT COMPUTE!!
PLEASE TRY AGAIN!!!!
TIME GROWS SHORT, PLEASE HURRY!!!!!!!!
WHAT'LL IT BE? 2

TOO SMALL!!!!!
YOUR NUMBER DOES NOT COMPUTE!!
PLEASE TRY AGAIN!!!!
HURRY, THE COUNT-DOWN IS APPROACHING ZERO!!!!!!!!!
WHAT'LL IT BE? 3

TOO SMALL!!!!!
YOUR NUMBER DOES NOT COMPUTE!!
PLEASE TRY AGAIN!!!!
WHAT'LL IT BE? 4




                                TOO LATE



                                \ **** /
                               -- BOOM --
                                / **** \



Ok
```

Cup

Cup is a cute little game in which a cup is located thirty lines down the paper of your terminal or thirty lines down on your video display screen and a random number of spaces from one to sixty to the right of the left margin. The pull of gravity varies from one to ten lines per second per second. You are then asked in this program what push you would like to give the ball from left to right across the paper in spaces per second. The program then traces the path of the ball from the left margin of the paper as it falls down and hopefully into the cup.

A knowledge of physics is helpful if you wish to get the ball in the cup on the first try. However, you can diddle with it by trial and error and generally hit the cup on your fourth or fifth try.

Cup was written by Jonathan Freidin.

```
RUN

                           CUP
                    CREATIVE COMPUTING
                  MORRISTOWN, NEW JERSEY



THE CUP IS 30 LINES DOWN AND  53  SPACES OVER.
THE PULL OF GRAVITY IS  6  LINES/SECOND/SECOND.
WHAT IS THE PUSH YOU WOULD LIKE TO GIVE THE BALL
ACROSS THE PAPER (IN SPACES/SECOND)? 8
THE RESULTS MAY TAKE ANYWHERE BETWEEN 30 AND 90 SECONDS.

                .
                  .
                    .
                      .
                        .
                         .
                           .
                             .
                              .
                               .
                                 .
                                   .
                                    .
                                     .
                                      .
                                       .
                                        .
                                         .
                                          .
                                           .
                                           .
                                            .
                                            .
                                             .
                                             .
                                              . * *
                                                ***

YOU MISSED; TRY AGAIN.
```

```
LIST
1 PRINT TAB(27);"CUP"
2 PRINT TAB(20);"CREATIVE COMPUTING"
3 PRINT TAB(18);"MORRISTOWN, NEW JERSEY"
4 PRINT:PRINT:PRINT
10  DIM S(30,60)
30  LET L=INT(60*RND(1))+1
40  IF L=60 OR L=1 THEN 30
50  LET G=INT(10*RND(1))+1
60 PRINT "THE CUP IS 30 LINES DOWN AND ";L;" SPACES OVER."
70 PRINT "THE PULL OF GRAVITY IS ";G;" LINES/SECOND/SECOND."
80  PRINT "WHAT IS THE PUSH YOU WOULD LIKE TO GIVE THE BALL"
90  PRINT "ACROSS THE PAPER (IN SPACES/SECOND)";
100  INPUT T
110  PRINT "THE RESULTS MAY TAKE ANYWHERE BETWEEN 30 AND 90 SECONDS."
120 FOR S1=1 TO 30:FOR S2=1 TO 60:S(S1,S2)=0:NEXT:NEXT
130  LET S(30,L)=S(30,L-1)=S(30,L+1)=S(29,L-1)=S(29,L+1)=1
140  FOR Z=1 TO SQR(60*G)/G STEP .01
150  LET Y=T*Z*2
160  LET X=G/2*Z^2
170  IF X>30.5 OR X<.5 OR Y>60.5 OR Y<.5 THEN 300
180  IF INT(X)=29 AND INT(Y)=L THEN 310
190  IF INT(X)+1=29 AND INT(Y)+1=L THEN 310
200  IF INT(X)=29 AND INT(Y)=L-1 THEN 310
210  IF INT(X)+1=29 AND INT(Y)+1=L-1 THEN 310
220  IF INT(X)=29 AND INT(Y)=L+1 THEN 330
230  IF INT(X)+1=29 AND INT(Y)+1=L+1 THEN 330
240  LET S(X,Y)=2
250  FOR D=1 TO 5
260  IF Y<6 THEN 290
270  LET S(X,Y-D)=0
280  NEXT D
290  NEXT Z
300  GOTO 340
310  LET W=1
320  GOTO 335
330  LET W=2
335  LET S(29,L)=2
337  GOTO 345
340  LET W=0
345  LET P$=" *."
360 LET S(30,L)=1:S(30,L-1)=1:S(30,L+1)=1:
365 LET S(29,L-1)=1:S(29,L+1)=1
370  FOR X=1 TO 30
380  FOR X1=1 TO 60
390  IF S(X,X1)<>0 THEN 420
400  NEXT X1
410  GOTO 500
420  FOR Y=1 TO 60
430 PRINT MID$(P$,S(X,Y)+1,1);
440  IF X=29 OR X=30 THEN 490
450  IF Y=60 OR Y=1 THEN 490
460  IF Y=1 OR Y=59 THEN 500
470  IF S(X,Y)=2 AND S(X,Y+1)=0 THEN 500
480  IF S(X,Y)=1 AND S(X,Y+1)=0 AND S(X,Y+2)=0 THEN 500
490  NEXT Y
500  PRINT
510  NEXT X
520  PRINT
530  IF W=1 THEN 570
540  IF W=2 THEN 590
550  PRINT "YOU MISSED; TRY AGAIN."
560  GOTO 60
570  PRINT "RIGHT IN!!!"
580  GOTO 600
590  PRINT "YOU ALMOST DIDN'T MAKE IT, BUT IT BOUNCED IN."
600  PRINT "DO YOU WANT TO PLAY AGAIN?"
610  INPUT A$
620 IF LEFT$(A$,1)="Y" THEN 30
630  END
Ok
```

Dealer x 5

In this game, you, the player, are given $100 to start with. You then play five card games loosely modeled on casino gambling games, but with peculiar variations. The five games are well-explained in the rules.

This game was written by Thomas Carey.

```
RUN
                    DEALER'S CHOICE
                  CREATIVE COMPUTING
                MORRISTOWN, NEW JERSEY



THIS PROGRAM WILL SIMULATE THE T.V. SHOW, DEALER'S CHOICE.
YOU HAVE $100 TO START WITH. ENJOY THE GAME.

FOR THE FIRST GAME, WE WILL PLAY ON THE WHEEL OF CHANCE.
THE OBJECT IS SIMPLE. GUESS WHAT SUITE WILL APPEAR ON THE
WHEEL AND YOU WILL GET PAID AT THOSE ODDS IF YOU ARE RIGHT.
THEY ARE AS FOLLOWS:

1=DIAMONDS AT 11 TO 1 ODDS          2=SPADES AT 1 TO 1 ODDS.
3=HEARTS AT 3 TO 1 ODDS             4=CLUBS AT 3 TO 1 ODDS.
YOU MAY BET UP TO $25. GOOD LUCK!

WHAT SUITE DO YOU WANT? 1
WHAT IS THE BET? 25
O.K. NOW THAT YOUR BET IS IN, WE WILL SPIN
THE WHEEL, GOOD LUCK!
THE WHEEL IS SLOWING DOWN.
THE WHEEL IS STOPPING.
THE SUITE IS
**** 1 ****
YOU WIN ON DIAMONDS
AT THE END OF PART 1, YOU HAVE $ 375


THIS IS THE GAME OF IN BETWEEN. THE OBJECT IS: 5 CARDS WILL
BE DEALT OUT. IF ANY CARD IS LESS THAN A 3 OR GREATER THAN A
10, THE GAME IS OVER. YOU MAY BET UP TO $30. YOUR MONEY
WILL BE DOUBLED EACH TIME YOU ARE RIGHT. GOOD LUCK!

WHAT IS THE BET? 40
***YOU BET OVER THE HOUSE LIMIT ***
WHAT IS THE BET? 30
CARD NUMBER  1  IS A  4
YOU ARE STILL IN THE GAME. YOU HAVE  60
STOP OR GO? GO
CARD NUMBER  2  IS A  4
YOU ARE STILL IN THE GAME. YOU HAVE  120
STOP OR GO? GO
CARD NUMBER  3  IS A  7
YOU ARE STILL IN THE GAME. YOU HAVE  180
STOP OR GO? STOP
YOU WIN. AT THE END OF PART 2, YOU HAVE $ 555


THIS IS THE GAME OF BLACKJACK <DEALER'S CHOICE STYLE>
THE OBJECT IS TO BEAT THE DEALER WITH OVER 17 OR 21 OR
UNDER. YOU MAY BET UP TO $50. YOU MAY STOP WHEN YOU WISH.
IF YOU MAKE BLACKJACK, YOUR MONEY IS DOUBLED.
IF THE HOUSE DEALS OUT LESS THAN A TOTAL OF 17 IN 6 TRIES,
YOU WILL KEEP THE MONEY YOU BET. GOOD LUCK!

THE DEALER WILL GET HIS CARDS FIRST

HERE I GO
THE CARD IS A  1
SO FAR: 1
THE CARD IS A  10
SO FAR: 11
THE CARD IS A  6
SO FAR: 17
I STOP. THE TOTAL FOR ME IS  17
NOW YOU GO

WHAT IS THE BET? 50
YOUR CARD IS A  5
SO FAR THE TOTAL FOR YOU IS  5
STOP OR GO? GO
YOUR CARD IS A  12
SO FAR THE TOTAL FOR YOU IS  17
STOP OR GO? STOP
WE ARE THE SAME SO WE WILL PLAY AGAIN
THE DEALER WILL GET HIS CARDS FIRST

HERE I GO
THE CARD IS A  11
SO FAR: 11
THE CARD IS A  9
SO FAR: 20
I STOP. THE TOTAL FOR ME IS  20
NOW YOU GO

WHAT IS THE BET? 50
YOUR CARD IS A  1
SO FAR THE TOTAL FOR YOU IS  1
STOP OR GO? GO
YOUR CARD IS A  12
SO FAR THE TOTAL FOR YOU IS  13
STOP OR GO? GO
YOUR CARD IS A  1
SO FAR THE TOTAL FOR YOU IS  14
STOP OR GO? GO
YOUR CARD IS A  12
SO FAR THE TOTAL FOR YOU IS  26
THE DEALER BEAT YOU. YOU LOSE
AT THE END OF PART 3, YOU HAVE $ 325

NOW WE ENTER THE LAST CHANCE ROUND. IF YOU MAKE UP TO
$300 YOU WILL BE ABLE TO GO INTO THE BONUS ROUND. THE
OBJECT IS TO GUESS INTO WHICH CATEGORY THE TOTAL OF 5 CARDS
WILL ADD UP TO. THESE ARE THE CATEGORIES:

1=31-40 AT 1 TO 1 ODDS      2=41-50 AT 3 TO 1 ODDS
3=21-31 AT 3 TO 1 ODDS      4=6-20 AT 20 TO 1 ODDS
GOOD LUCK!!

AT THIS POINT IN THE GAME YOU HAVE $ 325
WHAT CATEGORY DO YOU WANT? 2
WHAT IS THE BET? 25
THE CARDS ARE NOW BEING ADDED UP
GOOD LUCK!
CARD NUMBER  1  IS A  1
SO FAR:  8
CARD NUMBER  2  IS A  11
SO FAR:  19
CARD NUMBER  3  IS A  8
SO FAR:  27
CARD NUMBER  4  IS A  7
SO FAR:  34
CARD NUMBER  5  IS A  10
SO FAR:  44
AT THE END OF THE GAME YOU HAVE A GRAND TOTAL OF $ 400
YOU ARE ELIGIBLE FOR THE BONUS ROUND.
DO YOU WANT TO PLAY IT? YES
THIS IS THE BONUS ROUND. IF YOU GET A TOTAL OF 1,000
WITHOUT GETTING A SPADE IN THE ROLLS, YOU WILL GET
A GRAND PRIZE OF $10,000.00. YOU MAY STOP AT ANY POINT
DURING THE GAME. YOU WILL KEEP WHAT YOU MADE. GOOD LUCK!

THE DICE ARE ROLLING
GOOD LUCK.
THE DICE ARE
****SPADES 200 ****
TOTAL  200
YOU LOSE THE MONEY FROM THE LAST CHANCE
ROUND BUT YOU STILL HAVE A GRAND TOTAL OF $ 400
THIS IS THE END OF THE GAME. I HOPE YOU ENJOYED IT.
```

```
100 PRINT TAB(21);"DEALER'S CHOICE"
110 PRINT TAB(20);"CREATIVE COMPUTING"
120 PRINT TAB(18);"MORRISTOWN, NEW JERSEY"
130 PRINT:PRINT:PRINT
140 PRINT "THIS PROGRAM WILL SIMULATE THE T.V. SHOW, DEALER'S CHOICE."
150 PRINT "YOU HAVE $100 TO START WITH. ENJOY THE GAME.":PRINT
160 O=100
170 PRINT "FOR THE FIRST GAME, WE WILL PLAY ON THE WHEEL OF CHANCE."
180 PRINT "THE OBJECT IS SIMPLE. GUESS WHAT SUITE WILL APPEAR ON THE"
190 PRINT "WHEEL AND YOU WILL GET PAID AT THOSE ODDS IF YOU ARE RIGHT."
200 PRINT "THEY ARE AS FOLLOWS:":PRINT
210 PRINT "1=DIAMONDS AT 11 TO 1 ODDS          2=SPADES AT 1 TO 1 ODDS."
220 PRINT "3=HEARTS AT 3 TO 1 ODDS             4=CLUBS AT 3 TO 1 ODDS."
230 PRINT "YOU MAY BET UP TO $25. GOOD LUCK!":PRINT
240 PRINT "WHAT SUITE DO YOU WANT";:INPUT A
250 IF A > 4 OR A < 1 THEN 270
260 IF A <=4 THEN 280
270 PRINT "***YOU PICKED A WRONG SUITE***":GOTO 240
280 PRINT "WHAT IS THE BET";:INPUT B8
290 IF B8 > 25 OR B8 <= 0 THEN 310
300 IF B8 <= 25 THEN 320
310 PRINT "***YOU BET OVER THE HOUSE LIMIT***":GOTO 280
320 PRINT "O.K. NOW THAT YOUR BET IS IN, WE WILL SPIN"
330 PRINT "THE WHEEL, GOOD LUCK!":FOR B1=1 TO 10*570:NEXT B1
340 PRINT "THE WHEEL IS SLOWING DOWN."
350 FOR B1=1 TO 7*570:NEXT B1:PRINT "THE WHEEL IS STOPPING."
360 FOR B1=1 TO 4*570:NEXT B1
370 PRINT "THE SUITE IS ":FOR B1=1 TO 4*570
380 NEXT B1
390 Z=INT(4*RND(1)+1):PRINT "****";Z;"****"
400 IF Z=A THEN 420
410 IF Z <> A THEN 470
420 ON Z GOTO 430,440,450,460
430 O=O+(11*B8):PRINT "YOU WIN ON DIAMONDS":GOTO 480
440 O=O+(1*B8):PRINT "YOU WIN ON SPADES":GOTO  480
450 O=O+(3*B8):PRINT "YOU WIN ON HEARTS":GOTO 480
460 O=O+(3*B8):PRINT "YOU WIN ON CLUBS":GOTO 480
470 O=O-(1*B8):PRINT "YOU LOSE.":GOTO 480
480 PRINT "AT THE END OF PART 1, YOU HAVE $";O
490 FOR P=1 TO 5:PRINT:NEXT P
500 PRINT "THIS IS THE GAME OF IN BETWEEN. THE OBJECT IS: 5 CARDS WILL"
510 PRINT "BE DEALT OUT. IF ANY CARD IS LESS THAN A 3 OR GREATER THAN A"
520 PRINT "10, THE GAME IS OVER. YOU MAY BET UP TO $30. YOUR MONEY"
530 PRINT "WILL BE DOUBLED EACH TIME YOU ARE RIGHT. GOOD LUCK!":PRINT
540 PRINT "WHAT IS THE BET";:INPUT A
550 IF A > 30 THEN PRINT "***YOU BET OVER THE HOUSE LIMIT ***":GOTO 540
560 T=T+1:Z=INT(12*RND(1)+1)
570 PRINT "CARD NUMBER ";T;" IS A ";Z:B=B+(2*A)
580 IF Z < 3 OR Z > 10 THEN 630
590 IF T=5 THEN 650
600 PRINT "YOU ARE STILL IN THE GAME. YOU HAVE ";B
610 PRINT "STOP OR GO";:INPUT A$:IF A$="GO" THEN 560
620 IF A$="STOP" THEN 650
630 O=O-A
640 PRINT "YOU LOST. AT THE END OF PART 2, YOU HAVE $";O:GOTO 660
650 PRINT "YOU WIN. AT THE END OF PART 2, YOU HAVE $";B+O:B=B+O
660 FOR P=1 TO 5:PRINT:NEXT P
670 PRINT "THIS IS THE GAME OF BLACKJACK <DEALER'S CHOICE STYLE>"
680 PRINT "THE OBJECT IS TO BEAT THE DEALER WITH OVER 17 OR 21 OR"
690 PRINT "UNDER. YOU MAY BET UP TO $50. YOU MAY STOP WHEN YOU WISH."
700 PRINT "IF YOU MAKE BLACKJACK, YOUR MONEY IS DOUBLED."
710 PRINT "IF THE HOUSE DEALS OUT LESS THAN A TOTAL OF 17 IN 6 TRIES,"
720 PRINT "YOU WILL KEEP THE MONEY YOU BET. GOOD LUCK!":PRINT
730 Z5=0:Z1=0:PRINT "THE DEALER WILL GET HIS CARDS FIRST":PRINT
740 C=0:C3=0
750 PRINT "HERE I GO"
760 Q=INT(12*RND(1)+1)
770 Z5=Q+Z5
780 PRINT "THE CARD IS A ";Q:C=C+1
790 PRINT "SO FAR:";Z5:IF C=6 THEN 850
800 IF Z5<17 THEN 760
810 IF Z5 > 21 THEN 910
820 IF Z5=21 THEN 880
830 IF Z5 < 21 THEN 870
840 IF Z5 >= 17 THEN 870
850 IF Z5 < 17 THEN 890
860 IF Z5 >= 17 THEN 800
870 PRINT "I STOP. THE TOTAL FOR ME IS ";Z5:PRINT "NOW YOU GO":PRINT:GOT
O930
880 PRINT "I GOT BLACKJACK":PRINT:GOTO 930
890 PRINT "THE HOUSE DELT OUT LESS THAN 17. NOW YOU MUST TRY TO"
900 PRINT "BEAT ME";:PRINT:GOTO 930
910 PRINT "I BLEW IT. YOU WIN THE GREATEST AMOUNT ALLOWED TO BE"
920 PRINT "BET BY THE HOUSE.":GOTO 1160
930 PRINT "WHAT IS THE BET";:INPUT A
940 IF A > 0 THEN 980
950 IF A > 50 OR A <= 0 THEN 970
960 IF A <= 50 THEN 990
970 PRINT "***YOU BET OVER THE HOUSE LIMIT***":GOTO 930
980 PRINT "***YOU BET OVER WHAT YOU HAVE***":GOTO 930
990 Q1=INT(12*RND(1)+1):PRINT "YOUR CARD IS A ";Q1:C3=C3+1
1000 Z1=Q1+Z1:PRINT "SO FAR THE TOTAL FOR YOU IS ";Z1:IF C3=6 THEN 1090
1010 IF Z1 > 21 THEN 1120
1020 PRINT "STOP OR GO";:INPUT A$
1030 IF A$="STOP" THEN 1050
1040 IF A$="GO" THEN 990
1050 IF Z1=Z5 THEN 1100
1060 IF Z1 < Z5 THEN 1120
1070 IF Z1=21 THEN 1110
1080 IF Z5 <Z1 THEN 1130
1090 IF Z1 < 17 THEN 1140
1100 PRINT "WE ARE THE SAME SO WE WILL PLAY AGAIN":GOTO 730
1110 O=O+(2*A):PRINT "YOU BEAT THE DEALER WITH BLACKJACK!!":GOTO 1170
1120 O=O-(1*A):PRINT "THE DEALER BEAT YOU. YOU LOSE":GOTO 1170
1130 O=O+(1*A):PRINT "THE DEALER LOST. YOU WIN":GOTO 1170
1140 U=O+(1*A):PRINT "THE HOUSE DELT OUT LESS THAN 17 IN"
1150 PRINT "6 TRIES. YOU GET THE MONEY YOU BET":GOTO 1170
1160 O=O+50:PRINT "YOU KEEP IT WITH OUR BEST WISHES.":GOTO 1170
1170 PRINT "AT THE END OF PART 3, YOU HAVE $";O
1180 IF O<=0 THEN 1580
1190 FOR P=1 TO 5:PRINT:NEXT P
1200 PRINT "NOW WE ENTER THE LAST CHANCE ROUND. IF YOU MAKE UP TO"
1210 PRINT "$300 YOU WILL BE ABLE TO GO INTO THE BONUS ROUND. THE"
1220 PRINT "OBJECT IS TO GUESS INTO WHICH CATEGORY THE TOTAL OF 5 CARDS"
1230 PRINT "WILL ADD UP TO. THESE ARE THE CATEGORIES:":PRINT
1240 PRINT "1=31-40 AT 1 TO 1 ODDS      2=41-50 AT 3 TO 1 ODDS"
1250 PRINT "3=21-31 AT 3 TO 1 ODDS      4=6-20 AT 20 TO 1 ODDS"
1260 PRINT "GOOD LUCK!!":PRINT
1270 PRINT "AT THIS POINT IN THE GAME YOU HAVE $";O
1280 PRINT "WHAT CATEGORY DO YOU WANT";:INPUT A
1290 IF A <= 4 THEN 1320
1300 IF A > 4 THEN 1310
1310 PRINT "***YOU BET ON A WRONG CATEGORY***":GOTO 1280
1320 PRINT "WHAT IS THE BET";:INPUT B
1330 IF B <= 0 THEN 1360
1340 IF B > 0 THEN 1350
1350 PRINT "***YOU BET OVER WHAT YOU HAVE***":GOTO 1320
1360 PRINT "THE CARDS ARE NOW BEING ADDED UP":PRINT "GOOD LUCK!"
1370 Q=INT(12*RND(1)+1):C1=C1+1
1380 PRINT "CARD NUMBER ";C1;" IS A ";Q
1390 Z=Z+Q:PRINT "SO FAR: ";Z
1400 IF C1=5 THEN 1420
1410 GOTO 1370
1420 ON A GOTO 1430,1460,1490,1520
1430 IF Z < 31 THEN 1540
1440 IF Z < 40 THEN 1550
1450 IF Z > 40 THEN 1540
1460 IF Z < 41 THEN 1540
1470 IF Z < 50 THEN 1560
1480 IF Z > 50 THEN 1540
1490 IF Z < 21 THEN 1540
1500 IF Z < 31 THEN 1560
1510 IF Z > 31 THEN 1540
1520 IF Z < 6 THEN 1540
1530 IF Z < 20 THEN 1570
1540 O=O-(1*B):PRINT "YOU LOSE":GOTO 1580
1550 O=O+(1*B):PRINT "YOU WIN":GOTO 1580
1560 O=O+(3*B):GOTO 1580
1570 O=O+(20*B):PRINT "YOU WIN":GOTO 1580
1580 PRINT "AT THE END OF THE GAME YOU HAVE A GRAND TOTAL OF $";O
1590 IF O < 300 THEN 1940
1600 FOR X=1 TO 6:PRINT CHR$(7);:FOR B1=1 TO 570:NEXT B1:NEXT X
1610 PRINT "YOU ARE ELIGIBLE FOR THE BONUS ROUND."
1620 PRINT "DO YOU WANT TO PLAY IT";:INPUT A$
1630 IF A$="NO" THEN 1940
1640 PRINT "THIS IS THE BONUS ROUND. IF YOU GET A TOTAL OF 1,000"
1650 PRINT "WITHOUT GETTING A SPADE IN THE ROLLS, YOU WILL GET"
1660 PRINT "A GRAND PRIZE OF $10,000.00. YOU MAY STOP AT ANY POINT"
1670 PRINT "DURING THE GAME. YOU WILL KEEP WHAT YOU MADE. GOOD LUCK!"
1680 PRINT
1690 DIM A(5),B(4):A9$="SPADES"
1700 PRINT "THE DICE ARE ROLLING":PRINT "GOOD LUCK."
1710 PRINT "THE DICE ARE"
1720 FOR B1=1 TO 570*5:NEXT B1
1730 X=INT(5*RND(1)+1)
1740 A(1)=50:A(2)=100:A(3)=150:A(4)=200:A(5)=0
1750 Y=INT(4*RND(1)+1)
1760 B(1)=50:B(2)=100:B(3)=150:B(4)=200
1770 IF A(X)=0 THEN 1790
1780 PRINT "****";A(X);B(Y);"****":PRINT "TOTAL ";A(X)+B(Y):GOTO 1810
1790 PRINT "****";A9$;B(Y);"****"
1800 PRINT "TOTAL ";B(Y):GOTO 1870
1810 B7=B7+(A(X)+B(Y)):PRINT "YOU NOW HAVE ";B7:IF B7 >= 1000 THEN 1890
1820 PRINT "STOP OR GO":INPUT B$
1830 IF B$="GO" THEN 1700
1840 PRINT "SMART MOVE. YOU GET THE MONEY FROM THE BEGINNING OF"
1850 PRINT "THE GAME PLUS THE BONUS ROUND. AT THE END OF THE GAME"
1860 PRINT "YOU HAVE THE GRAND TOTAL OF $";B7+O:GOTO 1940
1870 PRINT "YOU LOSE THE MONEY FROM THE LAST CHANCE"
1880 PRINT "ROUND BUT YOU STILL HAVE A GRAND TOTAL OF $";O:GOTO 1940
1890 FOR T=1 TO 3:PRINT CHR$(7);:FOR B1=1 TO 570:NEXT B1:NEXT T
1900 B7=O+10000:PRINT TAB(15);"****CONGRATULATIONS****"
1910 PRINT "YOU WON THE GRAND PRIZE. AT THE END OF THE GAME, YOU HAVE"
1920 FOR P=1 TO 3:PRINT:NEXT P
1930 PRINT TAB(18);"******";B7;"******"
1940 PRINT "THIS IS THE END OF THE GAME. I HOPE YOU ENJOYED IT."
1950 END
```

Deepspace

Deepspace is another version of a space battle. You become the commander of either a scout ship, cruiser, or battleship. You then pick the weapons, and planetary system to patrol, and it's time to do battle.

The closer you get to the enemy, the better your chance of destroying him. Unfortunately, his chance of destroying you also improves. If you get too close, you can damage yourself; when a vessel's damage rating reaches or exceeds 100, it's destroyed.

Suggestion: Change the time between reports—this will shorten the game by allowing you to get closer faster.

Deepspace originally appeared in *Creative Computing*, Mar/Apr 1976.

```
RUN
                          DEEPSPACE
                      CREATIVE COMPUTING
                    MORRISTOWN, NEW JERSEY



THIS IS DEEPSPACE, A TACTICAL SIMULATION OF SHIP TO SHIP
COMBAT IN DEEP SPACE.
DO YOU WISH INSTRUCTIONS? YES
YOU ARE ONE OF A GROUP OF CAPTAINS ASSIGNED TO PATROL A
SECTION OF YOUR STAR EMPIRE'S BORDER AGAINST HOSTILE
ALIENS. ALL YOUR ENCOUNTERS HERE WILL BE AGAINST HOSTILE
VESSELS. YOU WILL FIRST BE REQUIRED TO SELECT A VESSEL
FROM ONE OF THREE TYPES, EACH WITH ITS OWN CHARACTERISTICS:

TYPE           SPEED         CARGO SPACE   PROTECTION
1 SCOUT        10X           16            1
2 CRUISER      4X            24            2
3 BATTLESHIP   2X            30            5

SPEED IS GIVEN RELATIVE TO THE OTHER SHIPS.
CARGO SPACE IS IN UNITS OF SPACE ABOARD SHIP WHICH CAN BE
FILLED WITH WEAPONS.
PROTECTION IS THE RELATIVE STRENGTH OF THE SHIP'S ARMOR
AND FORCE FIELDS.

ONCE A SHIP HAS BEEN SELECTED, YOU WILL BE INSTRUCTED TO ARM
IT WITH WEAPONRY FROM THE FOLLOWING LIST:

TYPE                             CARGO SPACE   REL. STRENGTH
1 PHASER BANKS                     12              4
2 ANTI-MATTER MISSILE               4             20
3 HYPERSPACE LANCE                  4             16
4 PHOTON TORPEDO                    2             10
5 HYPERON NEUTRALIZATION FIELD     20              6

WEAPONS #1 & #5 CAN BE FIRED 100 TIMES EACH; ALL OTHERS CAN
BE FIRED ONCE FOR EACH ON BOARD.
A TYPICAL LOAD FOR A CRUISER MIGHT CONSIST OF:
            1-#1 PHASER BANK         = 12
            2-#3 HYPERSPACE LANCES   =  8
            2-#4 PHOTON TORPEDOES    =  4
                                     ---------
                                      24 UNITS OF CARGO
 A WORD OF CAUTION: FIRING HIGH YIELD WEAPONS AT CLOSE (<100)
RANGE CAN BE DANGEROUS TO YOUR SHIP AND MINIMAL DAMAGE CAN
OCCUR AS FAR OUT AS 200 IN SOME CIRCUMSTANCES.

RANGE IS GIVEN IN THOUSANDS OF KILOMETERS.
     ***************
     MANUEVER CHART

 1        FIRE PHASERS
 2        FIRE ANTI-MATTER MISSILE
 3        FIRE HYPERSPACE LANCE
 4        FIRE PHOTON TORPEDO
 5        ACTIVE HYPERON NEUTRALIZATION FIELD
 6        SELF-DESTRUCT
 7        CHANGE VELOCITY
 8        DISENGAGE
 9        PROCEED

YOU HAVE A CHOICE OF THREE SYSTEMS TO PATROL.
1 ORION
2 DENEB
3 ARCTURUS
SELECT A SYSTEM(1-3)? 3
WHICH SPACECRAFT WOULD YOU LIKE(1-3)? 2
YOU HAVE  24 UNITS OF CARGO SPACE TO FILL WITH WEAPONRY.
CHOOSE A WEAPON AND THE AMOUNT YOU WISH.? 1,1
YOU HAVE  12 UNITS OF CARGO SPACE TO FILL WITH WEAPONRY.
CHOOSE A WEAPON AND THE AMOUNT YOU WISH.? 2,1
YOU HAVE  8 UNITS OF CARGO SPACE TO FILL WITH WEAPONRY.
CHOOSE A WEAPON AND THE AMOUNT YOU WISH.? 3,1
YOU HAVE  4 UNITS OF CARGO SPACE TO FILL WITH WEAPONRY.
CHOOSE A WEAPON AND THE AMOUNT YOU WISH.? 4,2

RANGE TO TARGET: 743.491
RELATIVE VELOCITY: 3.24654
ACTION? 9


RANGE TO TARGET: 682.097
RELATIVE VELOCITY: 3.24654
ACTION? 9


RANGE TO TARGET: 620.703
RELATIVE VELOCITY: 3.24654
ACTION? 7
CHANGE TO BE EFFECTED? .5

RANGE TO TARGET: 620.703
RELATIVE VELOCITY: 3.74654
ACTION? 4
SCANNERS REPORT ENEMY DAMAGE NOW: 4.58858
DAMAGE CONTROL REPORTS YOUR VESSEL DAMAGE AT: 5.20508


RANGE TO TARGET: 547.271
RELATIVE VELOCITY: 3.74654
ACTION? 1
SCANNERS REPORT ENEMY DAMAGE NOW: 5.3724
DAMAGE CONTROL REPORTS YOUR VESSEL DAMAGE AT: 11.7754


RANGE TO TARGET: 473.839
RELATIVE VELOCITY: 3.74654
ACTION? 3
SCANNERS REPORT ENEMY DAMAGE NOW: 23.1197
DAMAGE CONTROL REPORTS YOUR VESSEL DAMAGE AT: 20.3527


RANGE TO TARGET: 400.407
RELATIVE VELOCITY: 3.74654
ACTION? 2
SCANNERS REPORT ENEMY DAMAGE NOW: 47.8738
DAMAGE CONTROL REPORTS YOUR VESSEL DAMAGE AT: 32.0649


RANGE TO TARGET: 326.975
RELATIVE VELOCITY: 3.74654
ACTION? 7
CHANGE TO BE EFFECTED? -2

RANGE TO TARGET: 326.975
RELATIVE VELOCITY: 1.74654
ACTION? 1
SCANNERS REPORT ENEMY DAMAGE NOW: 54.5828
DAMAGE CONTROL REPORTS YOUR VESSEL DAMAGE AT: 49.1026


RANGE TO TARGET: 298.689
RELATIVE VELOCITY: 1.74654
ACTION? 8
ANOTHER BATTLE? NO
TRY AGAIN LATER!
OK
```

```
100 PRINT TAB(24);"DEEPSPACE"
110 PRINT TAB(20);"CREATIVE COMPUTING"
120 PRINT TAB(18);"MORRISTOWN, NEW JERSEY"
130 PRINT:PRINT:PRINT
150 PRINT "THIS IS DEEPSPACE, A TACTICAL SIMULATION OF SHIP TO SHIP"
160 PRINT "COMBAT IN DEEP SPACE."
170 PRINT "DO YOU WISH INSTRUCTIONS";:INPUT I$
180 IF I$="NO" THEN 610
200 PRINT "YOU ARE ONE OF A GROUP OF CAPTAINS ASSIGNED TO PATROL A"
210 PRINT "SECTION OF YOUR STAR EMPIRE'S BORDER AGAINST HOSTILE"
220 PRINT "ALIENS. ALL YOUR ENCOUNTERS HERE WILL BE AGAINST HOSTILE"
230 PRINT "VESSELS. YOU WILL FIRST BE REQUIRED TO SELECT A VESSEL"
240 PRINT "FROM ONE OF THREE TYPES, EACH WITH ITS OWN CHARACTERISTICS:"
260 PRINT:PRINT "TYPE","SPEED","CARGO SPACE","PROTECTION"
270 PRINT "1 SCOUT","10X","16","1"
280 PRINT "2 CRUISER","4X","24","2"
290 PRINT "3 BATTLESHIP","2X","30","5"
310 PRINT:PRINT "SPEED IS GIVEN RELATIVE TO THE OTHER SHIPS."
320 PRINT "CARGO SPACE IS IN UNITS OF SPACE ABOARD SHIP WHICH CAN BE"
330 PRINT "FILLED WITH WEAPONS."
340 PRINT "PROTECTION IS THE RELATIVE STRENGTH OF THE SHIP'S ARMOR"
350 PRINT "AND FORCE FIELDS."
370 PRINT:PRINT "ONCE A SHIP HAS BEEN SELECTED, YOU WILL BE INSTRUCTED T
O ARM"
380 PRINT "IT WITH WEAPONRY FROM THE FOLLOWING LIST:"
390 PRINT
400 PRINT "TYPE                        CARGO SPACE    REL. STRENGTH"
410 PRINT "1 PHASER BANKS                   12              4"
420 PRINT "2 ANTI-MATTER MISSILE             4             20"
430 PRINT "3 HYPERSPACE LANCE                4             16"
440 PRINT "4 PHOTON TORPEDO                  2             10"
450 PRINT "5 HYPERON NEUTRALIZATION FIELD   20              6"
470 PRINT:PRINT "WEAPONS #1 & #5 CAN BE FIRED 100 TIMES EACH; ALL OTHERS
 CAN"
480 PRINT "BE FIRED ONCE FOR EACH ON BOARD."
490 PRINT "A TYPICAL LOAD FOR A CRUISER MIGHT CONSIST OF:"
500 PRINT "         1-#1 PHASER BANK          = 12"
510 PRINT "         2-#3 HYPERSPACE LANCES    =  8"
520 PRINT "         2-#4 PHOTON TORPEDOES     =  4"
530 PRINT "                                 ---------"
540 PRINT "                               24 UNITS OF CARGO"
550 PRINT " A WORD OF CAUTION: FIRING HIGH YIELD WEAPONS AT CLOSE (<100)
"
560 PRINT "RANGE CAN BE DANGEROUS TO YOUR SHIP AND MINIMAL DAMAGE CAN"
570 PRINT "OCCUR AS FAR OUT AS 200 IN SOME CIRCUMSTANCES."
590 PRINT:PRINT "RANGE IS GIVEN IN THOUSANDS OF KILOMETERS."
600 GOTO 640
610 PRINT "DO YOU WISH A MANUEVER CHART";:INPUT M$
620 IF M$="NO" THEN 770
640 PRINT "      **************"
650 PRINT "      MANUEVER CHART":PRINT
670 PRINT " 1      FIRE PHASERS"
680 PRINT " 2      FIRE ANTI-MATTER MISSILE"
690 PRINT " 3      FIRE HYPERSPACE LANCE"
700 PRINT " 4      FIRE PHOTON TORPEDO"
710 PRINT " 5      ACTIVE HYPERON NEUTRALIZATION FIELD"
720 PRINT " 6      SELF-DESTRUCT"
730 PRINT " 7      CHANGE VELOCITY"
740 PRINT " 8      DISENGAGE"
750 PRINT " 9      PROCEED"
770 PRINT:PRINT "YOU HAVE A CHOICE OF THREE SYSTEMS TO PATROL."
780 PRINT "1 ORION"
790 PRINT "2 DENEB"
800 PRINT "3 ARCTURUS"
810 PRINT "SELECT A SYSTEM(1-3)";:INPUT S9
820 IF S9=1 THEN 2380
830 IF S9=2 THEN 2430
840 GOTO 2480
850 D0=0
860 D1=0
870 N1=0
880 N2=0
890 N3=0
900 N4=0
910 D=0
920 PRINT "WHICH SPACECRAFT WOULD YOU LIKE(1-3)";:INPUT S
930 ON S GOTO 1790,1830,1870
960 GOTO 920
970 C=C0
980 PRINT "YOU HAVE ";C;"UNITS OF CARGO SPACE TO FILL WITH WEAPONRY."
990 PRINT "CHOOSE A WEAPON AND THE AMOUNT YOU WISH.";:INPUT W,N
1000 ON W GOTO 1910,2010,2100,2190,2280
1050 GOTO 980
1060 IF N*C1>C THEN 2530
1070 C=C-N*C1
1080 ON W GOTO 1990,2080,2170,2260
1120 GOTO 2360
1130 IF C>1 THEN 980
1140 REM
1150 S1=S0*RND(0)
1160 R=(3*RND(0)+5)*100
1180 PRINT:PRINT "RANGE TO TARGET:";R
1190 PRINT "RELATIVE VELOCITY:";S1
1200 PRINT "ACTION";:INPUT M
1210 ON M GOTO 1940,2030,2120,2210,2310,1660,1390,2760
1290 IF R<500 THEN 1500
1300 IF S1>0 THEN 1330
1310 R=R+(S1*8.3)^1.25
1320 GOTO 1340
1330 R=R-(S1*8.3)^1.25
1340 IF R>1500 THEN 2590
1350 IF R>0 THEN 1370
1360 R=-R
1370 PRINT
1380 GOTO 1180
1390 PRINT "CHANGE TO BE EFFECTED";:INPUT S2
1400 IF (S1+S2)>S0 THEN 2550
1410 S1=S1+S2
1420 GOTO 1180
1430 F0=P1*(Z/R)^1.5
1440 REM
1450 D0=(2*F0+3*F0*RND(0))/5
1460 D=D+D0
1470 PRINT "SCANNERS REPORT ENEMY DAMAGE NOW:";D
1480 IF D>99 THEN 2720
1490 GOTO 1510
1500 D0=0
1510 REM
1520 K=E1+E2*RND(0)
1530 REM
1540 E=E3+E4*RND(0)+5/P0*RND(0)
1550 REM
1560 F3=E*(K/R)^1.85
1570 D2=(3*F3+3*F3*RND(0))/5.5
1580 D1=D1+D2
1590 IF (Z*D0)/(R*500)>2.2 THEN 1620
1600 D3=D0*2/(R^2*P0)
1610 D1=D1+D3
1620 PRINT "DAMAGE CONTROL REPORTS YOUR VESSEL DAMAGE AT:";D1
1630 IF D1>99 THEN 2740
1640 IF D>99 THEN 2760
1650 GOTO 1300
1660 PRINT "SELF DESTRUCT FAILSAFE ACTIVATED!!"
1670 PRINT "INPUT 1 TO RELEASE FAILSAFE";:INPUT U
1680 IF U=1 THEN 1700
1690 GOTO 1290
1700 PRINT "SELF DESTRUCT ACCOMPLISHED"
1710 IF R>60 THEN 1740
1720 PRINT "ENEMY VESSEL ALSO DESTROYED"
1730 GOTO 2760
1740 D4=3200/R
1750 D=D+D4
1760 IF D>99 THEN 1720
1770 PRINT "ENEMY VESSEL SURVIVES WITH";D;"DAMAGE"
1780 GOTO 2760
1790 S0=10
1800 C0=16
1810 P0=1
1820 GOTO 970
1830 S0=4
1840 C0=24
1850 P0=2
1860 GOTO 970
1870 S0=2
1880 C0=30
1890 P0=5
1900 GOTO 970
1910 C1=12
1930 GOTO 1060
1940 P1=4
1950 IF N1=0 THEN 2160
1960 N1=N1-1
1970 Z=200
1980 GOTO 1430
1990 N1=N1+N
2000 GOTO 1130
2010 C1=4
2020 GOTO 1060
2030 P1=20
2040 IF N2=0 THEN 2640
2050 N2=N2-1
2060 Z=500
2070 GOTO 1430
2080 N2=N2+N
2090 GOTO 1130
2100 C1=4
2110 GOTO 1060
2120 P1=16
2130 IF N3=0 THEN 2660
2140 N3=N3-1
2150 Z=550
2160 GOTO 1430
2170 N3=N3+N
2180 GOTO 1130
2190 C1=2
2200 GOTO 1060
2210 P1=10
2220 IF N4=0 THEN 2680
2230 N4=N4-1
2240 Z=400
2250 GOTO 1430
2260 N4=N4+N
2270 GOTO 1130
2280 C1=.20
2290 N=100
2300 GOTO 1060
2310 P1=6
2320 IF N5=0 THEN 2700
2330 N5=N5-1
2340 Z=250
2350 GOTO 1430
2360 N5=N5+N
2370 GOTO 1130
2380 E1=150
2390 E2=500
2400 E3=3
2410 E4=4
2420 GOTO 850
2430 E1=200
2440 E2=350
2450 E3=4
2460 E4=3
2470 GOTO 850
2480 E1=150
2490 E2=400
2500 E3=5
2510 E4=2
2520 GOTO 850
2530 PRINT "NOT ENOUGH SPACE. RESELECT"
2540 GOTO 980
2550 PRINT "CHANGE BEYOND MAXIMUM POSSIBLE"
2560 PRINT "INCREASING TO MAXIMUM"
2570 S1=S0
2580 GOTO 1300
2590 PRINT "OUT OF SENSOR RANGE. AAUTOMATIC DISENGAGE."
2600 GOTO 2760
2610 PRINT "PHASER BANKS DRAINED"
2620 PRINT "SELECT ANOTHER COURSE OF ACTION"
2630 GOTO 1200
2640 PRINT " ALL ANTI-MATTER MISSLES EXPENDED"
2650 GOTO 2620
2660 PRINT "ALL HYPERSPACE LANCES EXPENDED"
2670 GOTO 2620
2680 PRINT "ALL PHOTON TORPEDO TUBES EMPTY"
2690 GOTO 2620
2700 PRINT "HYPERON NEUTRALIZATION FIELD DRAINED"
2710 GOTO 2620
2720 PRINT "ENEMY VESSEL DESTROYED"
2730 GOTO 1510
2740 PRINT "YOUR VESSEL HAS BEEN DESTROYED"
2760 PRINT "ANOTHER BATTLE";:INPUT R$
2770 IF R$="YES" THEN 810
2780 PRINT "TRY AGAIN LATER!"
2790 END
OK
```

Defuse

In this game, you are in an experimental building with one million rooms in it. The building is one hundred rooms long, one hundred rooms wide, and one hundred rooms high.

You have just received a telephone call from a mad bomber who tells you he has planted a bomb someplace in the building. Fortunately you are armed with a bomb detector that registers a stronger and stronger signal as you get closer to the bomb. You start at the bottom right-hand door of the building, at the room 0,0,0. In response to the signals from your detector, every ten seconds you may try a new room to search for the bomb. You have two hundred seconds or twenty trials to find it.

It's fairly easy to find the bomb once you get the knack of how your detector works. However, we're not going to spoil it for you and tell the secret.

```
RUN
                         DEFUSE
                   CREATIVE COMPUTING
                 MORRISTOWN, NEW JERSEY



YOU ARE IN A GOVERNMENT EXPERIMENTAL BUILDING WITH
1,000,000 ROOMS IN IT. THE BUILDING IS 100 ROOMS
LONG(0-99), 100 ROOMS WIDE(0-99), AND 100 ROOMS HIGH(0-99).

IN IT A BOMB IS HIDDEN. THE BOMB SENDS OUT SIGNALS THAT
GET STRONGER AS YOU GET CLOSER. YOU HAVE 200 SECONDS
TO DEACTIVATE IT.

SIGNAL        L    W    H         SEC.           COORDINATES(L,W,H)
 1454.99      0    0    0          0             ? 90,90,90
 9454.11      90   90   90         10            ? 80,80,90
 9464.21      80   80   90         20            ? 80,80,80
 9535.79      80   80   80         30            ? 80,80,70
 8535.79      80   80   70         40            ? 80,80,85
 9964.21      80   80   85         50            ? 80,80,86
 9864.21      80   80   86         60            ? 80,80,84
 9935.79      80   80   84         70            ? 80,70,85
 9974.21      80   70   85         80            ? 80,60,85
 9984.21      80   60   85         90            ? 80,50,85
 9994.21      80   50   85         100           ? 80,45,85
 9999.21      80   45   85         110           ? 80,40,85
 9995.79      80   40   85         120           ? 70,45,85
 9999.31      70   45   85         130           ? 40,45,85
 9999.61      40   45   85         140           ? 30,45,85
 9999.71      30   45   85         150           ? 20,45,85
 9999.81      20   45   85         160           ? 0,45,85
 9999.99      0    45   85         170           ? 1,45,85
BOMB DEACTIVATED AT 180  SECONDS!!!
WANT TO PLAY AGAIN? YES

SIGNAL        L    W    H         SEC.           COORDINATES(L,W,H)
 4969.04      0    0    0          0             ? 0,0,50
 9969.04      0    0    50         10            ? 0,0,60
 9030.96      0    0    60         20            ? 0,0,40
 8969.04      0    0    40         30            ? 0,0,70
 8030.96      0    0    70         40            ? 0,50,60
 8980.96      0    50   60         50            ? 0,90,60
 8940.96      0    90   60         60            ? 50,0,60
 9030.46      50   0    60         70            ? 0,10,60
 9020.96      0    10   60         80            ? 1,0,60
 9030.95      1    0    60         90            ? 1,0,50
 9969.05      1    0    50         100           ? 10,0,50
 9969.14      10   0    50         110           ? 30,0,50
 9969.34      30   0    50         120           ? 50,50,50
 9980.46      50   50   50         130           ? 60,50,50
 9980.36      60   50   50         140           ? 50,60,50
 9970.46      50   60   50         150           ? 55,50,50
 9980.41      55   50   50         160           ? 51,49,49
 9918.55      51   49   49         170           ? 50,55,50
 9975.46      50   55   50         180           ? 51,51,51
 9879.45      51   51   51         190           ? 40,50,50
BOOOOOOMMM!!!
YOU BLEW IT. THE BUILDING BLEW UP.
THE BOMB WAS LOCATED AT THE COORDINATES(L,W,H):  76   30   30
```

```
LIST
1 PRINT TAB(26);"DEFUSE"
2 PRINT TAB(20);"CREATIVE COMPUTING"
3 PRINT TAB(18);"MORRISTOWN, NEW JERSEY"
4 PRINT:PRINT:PRINT
10 PRINT "YOU ARE IN A GOVERNMENT EXPERIMENTAL BUILDING WITH"
20 PRINT "1,000,000 ROOMS IN IT. THE BUILDING IS 100 ROOMS"
30 PRINT "LONG(0-99), 100 ROOMS WIDE(0-99), AND 100 ROOMS HIGH(0-99)."
40 PRINT:PRINT "IN IT A BOMB IS HIDDEN. THE BOMB SENDS OUT SIGNALS THAT"
50 PRINT "GET STRONGER AS YOU GET CLOSER. YOU HAVE 200 SECONDS"
60 PRINT "TO DEACTIVATE IT."
70 PRINT:A=INT(100*RND(1)):B=INT(100*RND(1))
80 C=INT(100*RND(1)):IF A>0 THEN 90
85 IF B>0 THEN 90
87 IF C=0 THEN 80
90 D=0:E=0:F=0:G=0
100 PRINT "SIGNAL";TAB(15);"L";TAB(20);"W";TAB(25);"H";
105 PRINT TAB(35);"SEC.";TAB(50);"COORDINATES(L,W,H)"
110 PRINT 10000-ABS((A/100+B+C*100)-(D/100+E+F*100));
112 PRINT TAB(14);D;TAB(19);E;TAB(24);F;TAB(35);G;TAB(50);
120 INPUT D,E,F:G=G+10:IF A<>D THEN 130
125 IF B<>E THEN 130
127 IF C=F THEN 170
130 IF G=200 THEN 140
135 GOTO 180
140 PRINT "BOOOOOOMMM!!!":PRINT "YOU BLEW IT. THE BUILDING BLEW UP."
145 PRINT "THE BOMB WAS LOCATED AT THE COORDINATES(L,W,H):";A;B;C:PRINT
150 PRINT "WANT TO PLAY AGAIN";
160 INPUT Z$:IF LEFT$(Z$,1)="Y" THEN 70
165 GOTO 999
170 PRINT "BOMB DEACTIVATED AT";G;" SECONDS!!!":GOTO 150
180 IF D>99 THEN 200
183 IF D<0 THEN 200
185 IF E>99 THEN 200
187 IF E<0 THEN 200
190 IF F>99 THEN 220
195 IF F<0 THEN 230
197 GOTO 110
200 PRINT "YOU WALKED OUT A WINDOW ON THE";:IF F<4 THEN 240
205 PRINT F;"TH FLOOR!!!"
210 PRINT "YOU WERE KILLED AND";200-G;" SECONDS LATER THE BUILDING"
215 PRINT "BLEW UP!!!":GOTO 150
220 PRINT "YOU ARE NOW";F*9;" FEET IN THE AIR!!!":GOTO 210
230 PRINT "YOU ARE NOW";-1*(F*9)"FEET UNDERGROUND!!!":GOTO 210
240 ON F GOTO 250,260,270
250 PRINT " 1ST FLOOR!!!":GOTO 210
260 PRINT " 2ND FLOOR!!!":GOTO 210
270 PRINT " 3RD FLOOR!!!":GOTO 210
999 END
Ok
```

Dodgem

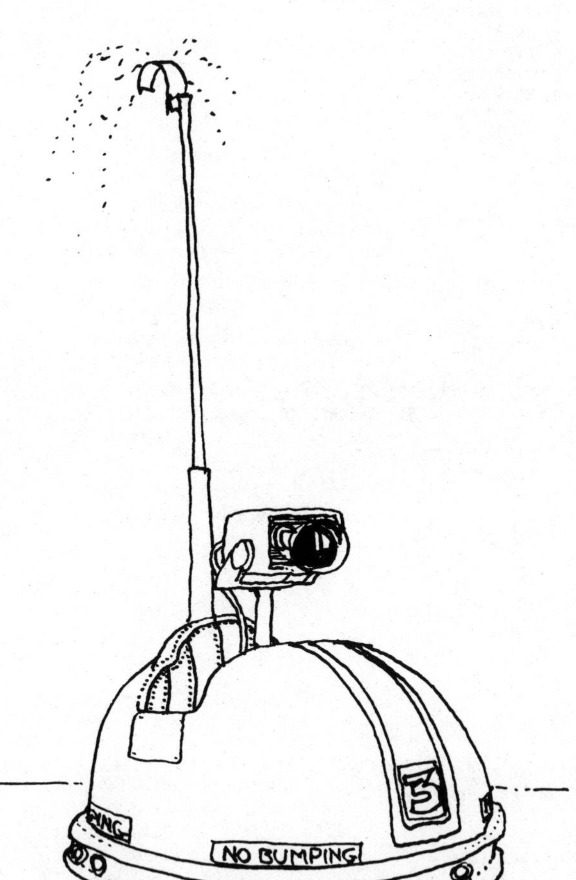

DODGEM is a game originally devised in 1972 by Colin Vout, then a student at the University of Cambridge, England. It got its major publicity from Martin Gardner who discussed it in the June 1975 issue of *Scientific American*. Complete instructions are in the sample run.

It may be played by two players in which case the computer is the referee, or by one player against the computer. The computer, incidentally, plays uncommonly well. This is not surprising since Dodgem was written by the very talented and prolific Mac Oglesby.

```
RUN
                    DODGEM
               CREATIVE COMPUTING
             MORRISTOWN  NEW JERSEY



DO YOU WANT INSTRUCTIONS FOR DODGEM? Y

HERE'S A SAMPLE PLAYING BOARD:

1 . . . .
2 . . . .
3 . . . .
4 . . . .
. A B C D

TWO SETS OF PIECES (DIGITS AND LETTERS) RACE AT RIGHT ANGLES
ACROSS A SQUARE BOARD. VACANT LOCATIONS ARE SHOWN AS PERIODS.
YOU CHOOSE THE THE BOARD SIZE (THE ONE ABOVE IS SIZE 5.)
   N
   :
W---E
   :
   S

THE OBJECT IS TO MOVE ALL OF YOUR PIECES ACROSS THE BOARD
AND OFF THE OPPOSITE EDGE. DIGITS LEAVE THE BOARD ONLY AT
THE EASTERN EDGE; LETTERS ONLY AT THE NORTHERN. THE WINNER
IS THE PLAYER WHOSE PIECES HAVE ALL LEFT THE BOARD.

THE PLAYERS GO IN TURN, MOVING ONE OF THEIR PIECES TO AN
ADJACENT LOCATON WHICH IS EITHER OFF THE BOARD OF CURRENTLY
VACANT. THERE ARE NO DIAGONAL MOVES, NO JUMPS AND NO CAPTURES.
DIGITS CANNOT MOVE WEST, NOR LETTERS MOVE SOUTH.

TO MOVE A PIECE, TYPE ITS NAME AND THE FIRST LETTER OF THE
DESIRED DIRECTION.  EXAMPLES:
  2E MEANS THAT PIECE 2 WANTS TO GO EAST
  BW MEANS THAT PIECE B WANTS TO GO WEST.

NOTE: YOU FORFET THE GAME IF YOUR MOVE LEAVES YOUR OPPONENT
WITHOUT ANY LEGAL MOVE.

LASTLY, YOU MAY TYPE R TO RESIGN AND H FOR HELP.

BOARD SIZE (3-6)? 4
HOW MANY PLAYERS (1 OR 2)? 1
OK, THE COMPUTER WILL MOVE THE DIGITS.
WHO MOVES FIRST (1=COMPUTER, 2=YOU)? 2

HERE WE GO...

  1 . . .
  2 . . .
  3 . . .
  . A B C

LETTERS MOVE? CN
THE DIGITS MOVE: 1E

  . 1 . .
  2 . . .
  3 . . C
  . A B .

LETTERS MOVE? AN
THE DIGITS MOVE: 1E

  . . 1 .
  2 . . .
  3 A . C
  . . B .

LETTERS MOVE? CN'
THE DIGITS MOVE: 1E

  . . . 1
  2 . . C
  3 A . .
  . . B .
```

```
LETTERS MOVE? CN
ILLEGAL MOVE OR BAD INPUT.
INPUT IGNORED. TYPE H FOR HELP.
LETTERS MOVE? H
THE LETTERS HAVE THESE LEGAL MOVES:
  AN  AE  BN  BE  BW  CW
LETTERS MOVE? BN
THE DIGITS MOVE: 1E

  .  .  .  .
  2  .  .  C
  3  A  B  .
  .  .  .  .

LETTERS MOVE? AN{
THE DIGITS MOVE: 3E

  .  .  .  .
  2  A  .  C
  .  3  B  .
  .  .  .  .

LETTERS MOVE? CN
THE DIGITS MOVE: 2N

  2  .  .  C
  .  A  .  .
  .  3  B  .
  .  .  .  .

LETTERS MOVE? AN
THE DIGITS MOVE: 2S

  .  A  .  C
  2  .  .  .
  .  3  B  .
  .  .  .  .

LETTERS MOVE? CN
THE DIGITS MOVE: 2E

  .  A  .  .
  .  2  .  .
  .  3  B  .
  .  .  .  .

LETTERS MOVE? BN
THE DIGITS MOVE: 3E

  .  A  .  .
  .  2  B  .
  .  .  3  .
  .  .  .  .

LETTERS MOVE? AN
THE DIGITS MOVE: 3E

  .  .  .  .
  .  2  B  .
  .  .  .  3
  .  .  .  .

LETTERS MOVE? BN
THE DIGITS MOVE: 3E

  .  .  B  .
  .  2  .  .
  .  .  .  .
  .  .  .  .

LETTERS MOVE? BN

*** THE LETTERS WIN!!!
OK
```

```
LIST

10 PRINT TAB(24);"DODGEM"
20 PRINT TAB(18);"CREATIVE COMPUTING"
30 PRINT TAB(16);"MORRISTOWN  NEW JERSEY"
40 PRINT:PRINT:PRINT
240 PRINT "DO YOU WANT INSTRUCTIONS FOR DODGEM";
250 INPUT A$
260 GOSUB 2950
270 IF LEFT$(A$,1) <> "Y" THEN 290
280 GOSUB 3130
290 PRINT "BOARD SIZE (3-6)";
300 INPUT A
310 LET A=INT(A)
320 IF (6-A)*(A-3) >= 0 THEN 340
330 GOTO 290
340 LET P(1,0)=A-1:LET P(2,0)=A-1
380 FOR J=1 TO A-1
390 LET P(1,J)=10*J+1
400 NEXT J
420 FOR J=1 TO A-1
430 LET P(2,J)=10*A+J+1
440 NEXT J
460 LET F=1
470 LET M$(1)="NES"
480 LET M$(2)="NE W"
490 LET C$(1)="DIGITS"
500 LET  C$(2)="LETTERS"
510 LET A$(1)="1234567"
520 LET A$(2)="ABCDEFG"
560 FOR J=1 TO A
570 IF J=A THEN 630
580 LET D$(J,1)=CHR$(48+J)
590 FOR K=2 TO A
600 LET D$(J,K)="."
610 NEXT K
620 GOTO 670
630 LET D$(J,1)="."
640 FOR K=2 TO A
650 LET D$(J,K)=CHR$(63+K)
660 NEXT K
670 NEXT J
690 PRINT "HOW MANY PLAYERS (1 OR 2)";
700 INPUT B
710 IF B=2 THEN 800
720 IF B=1 THEN 740
730 GOTO 690
740 PRINT "OK, THE COMPUTER WILL MOVE THE DIGITS."
750 PRINT "WHO MOVES FIRST (1=COMPUTER, 2=YOU)";
760 INPUT F
770 IF (2-F)*(1-F)=0 THEN 800
780 PRINT "PLEASE TYPE 1 OR 2. NOW,";
790 GOTO 750
800 PRINT
810 PRINT "HERE WE GO..."
840 PRINT
850 FOR J=1 TO A
860 FOR K=1 TO A
870 PRINT "  ";D$(J,K);
880 NEXT K
890 PRINT
900 NEXT J
910 PRINT
950 FOR J=F TO 3-F STEP 3-2*F
960 REM
980 FOR J1=1 TO A-1
990 LET R=INT(P(J,J1)/10)
1000 LET C=P(J,J1)-10*R
1020 ON J GOTO 1040,1100
1040 IF C=A THEN 1080
1050 IF C > A THEN 1070
1060 GOTO 1160
1070 GOTO 1250
1080 GOTO 1300
1100 IF R=1 THEN 1140
1110 IF R=0 THEN 1130
1120 GOTO 1160
1130 GOTO 1250
1140 GOTO 1300
1160 REM
1165 IF D$(R-1,C)="." THEN 1240
1170 IF D$(R,C+1)="." THEN 1240
1180 IF J=2 THEN 1220
1190 IF D$(R+1,C)="." THEN 1210
1200 GOTO 1250
1210 GOTO 1300
1220 IF D$(R,C-1)="." THEN 1240
1230 GOTO 1250
1240 GOTO 1300
1245 PRINT "BBS---1245",J1
1250 NEXT J1
1260 PRINT "THE ";C$(3-J);" HAVE NO LEGAL MOVES FOR THE ";C$(J);"!"
1270 PRINT "THE ";C$(J);" WIN!!!"
1280 STOP
1300 IF B=2 THEN 1750
1310 IF J=2 THEN 1750
1340 LET L1=2
1350 FOR L0=1 TO 3
1370 ON L0 GOTO 1450,1380,1430
1380 IF RND(1) < .5 THEN 1410
1390 LET L1=1
1400 GOTO 1450
1410 LET L1=3
1420 GOTO 1450
1430 LET L1=4-L1
1450 LET P1=INT(RND(1)*A)
1460 FOR L2=1 TO A-1
1470 LET P1=P1+1
```

```
1480 IF P1 <= A-1 THEN 1500
1490 LET P1=P1-(A-1)
1500 LET R=INT(P(J,P1)/10)
1510 LET C=P(J,P1)-10*R
1520 IF C > A THEN 1720
1540 ON L1 GOTO 1570,1620,1690
1570 IF D$(R-1,C)="." THEN 1590
1580 GOTO 1720
1590 GOTO 2090
1620 IF D$(R,C+1)="." THEN 1660
1630 IF C=A THEN 1650
1640 GOTO 1720
1650 LET P(J,0)=P(J,0)-1
1660 GOTO 2160
1690 IF D$(R+1,C)="." THEN 1710
1700 GOTO 1720
1710 GOTO 2230
1720 NEXT L2
1730 NEXT L0
1740 GOTO 1260
1750 PRINT C$(J);" MOVE";
1760 INPUT A$
1770 GOSUB 2950
1790 IF LEFT$(A$,1)="R" THEN 2860
1800 IF LEFT$(A$,1)="H" THEN 2460
1810 LET A$=MID$(A$,1,2)
1811 P1=0
1813 FOR B0=1 TO A-1
1815 IF MID$(A$(J),B0,1)=MID$(A$,1,1) THEN P1=B0
1817 NEXT B0
1830 IF P1=0 THEN 2430
1832 LET P2=0
1834 FOR B0=1 TO 4
1836 IF MID$(M$(J),B0,1)=MID$(A$,2,1) THEN P2=B0
1838 NEXT B0
1850 IF P2=0 THEN 2430
1860 LET R=INT(P(J,P1)/10)
1870 LET C=P(J,P1)-10*R
1880 IF R=0 THEN 2430
1890 IF C > A THEN 2430
1910 ON J GOTO 1930,1990
1930 IF C < A THEN 1970
1940 IF P2 <> 2 THEN 1970
1950 LET P(1,0)=P(1,0)-1
1960 GOTO 2160
1970 GOTO 2040
1990 IF R > 1 THEN 2040
2000 IF P2 <> 1 THEN 2040
2010 LET P(2,0)=P(2,0)-1
2020 GOTO 2090
2040 ON P2 GOTO 2070,2140,2210,2280
2070 IF D$(R-1,C)="." THEN 2090
2080 GOTO 2430
2090 LET D$(R-1,C)=MID$(A$(J),P1,1)
2100 LET P(J,P1)=P(J,P1)-10
2110 GOTO 2330
2140 IF D$(R,C+1)="." THEN 2160
2150 GOTO 2430
2160 LET D$(R,C+1) = MID$(A$(J),P1,1)
2170 LET P(J,P1)=P(J,P1)+1
2180 GOTO 2330
2210 IF D$(R+1,C)="." THEN 2230
2220 GOTO 2430
2230 LET D$(R+1,C)=MID$(A$(J) ,P1,1)
2240 LET P(J,P1)=P(J,P1)+10
2250 GOTO 2330
2280 IF D$(R,C-1)="." THEN 2300
2290 GOTO 2430
2300 LET D$(R,C-1)=MID$(A$(J),P1,1)
2310 LET P(J,P1)=P(J,P1)-1
2330 LET D$(R,C)="."
2340 IF B=2 THEN 2380
2350 IF J=2 THEN 2380
2360 PRINT "THE DIGITS MOVE: ";MID$(A$(J),P1,1);
2365 PRINT MID$(M$(J),L1,1)
2380 IF P(J,0) <> 0 THEN 2420
2390 PRINT
2400 PRINT "*** THE ";C$(J);" WIN!!!"
2410 END
2420 GOTO 2900
2430 PRINT "ILLEGAL MOVE OR BAD INPUT."
2440 PRINT "INPUT IGNORED. TYPE H FOR HELP."
2450 GOTO 1750
2460 PRINT "THE ";C$(J);" HAVE THESE LEGAL MOVES:"
2480 FOR J3=1 TO A-1
2490 LET P$=MID$(A$(J),J3,1)
2500 LET R=INT(P(J,J3)/10)
2510 LET C=P(J,J3)-10*R
2530 ON J GOTO 2550,2620
2550 IF C=A THEN 2590
2560 IF C > A THEN 2580
2570 GOTO 2690
2580 GOTO 2830
2590 PRINT " ";P$;"E";
2600 GOTO 2690
2620 IF R=1 THEN 2660
2630 IF R=0 THEN 2650
2640 GOTO 2690
2650 GOTO 2830
2660 GOTO 2700
2690 IF D$(R-1,C) <> "." THEN 2730
2700 PRINT "  ";P$;"N";
2730 IF D$(R,C+1) <> "." THEN 2770
2740 PRINT "  ";P$;"E";
2770 IF J=2 THEN 2810
2780 IF D$(R+1,C) <> "." THEN 2800
2790 PRINT "  ";P$;"S";
2800 GOTO 2830
2810 IF D$(R,C-1) <> "." THEN 2830
2820 PRINT "  ";P$;"W";
2830 NEXT J3
2840 PRINT
2850 GOTO 1750
2860 PRINT "THE ";C$(J);" GIVE UP!!"
2870 PRINT "*** THE ";C$(3-J);" WIN!!!"
2880 END
2900 NEXT J
2910 GOTO 840
2950 IF LEN(A$)>10 THEN 3090
2960 LET C1=0
2963 FOR B0=1 TO LEN(A$)
2965 LET A(B0)=ASC(MID$(A$,B0,1))
2970 NEXT B0
2975 LET A(0)=LEN(A$)
2980 FOR J2=1 TO A(0)
2990 IF A(J2)<96 THEN 3010
3000 LET A(J2)=A(J2)-32
3010 IF (57-A(J2))*(A(J2)-48) >= 0 THEN 3040
3020 IF (90-A(J2))*(A(J2)-65) >=  0 THEN 3040
3030 GOTO 3060
3040 LET C1=C1+1
3050 LET A(C1)=A(J2)
3060 NEXT J2
3070 LET A(0)=C1
3073 LET A$=""
3075 FOR B0=1 TO A(0)
3077 LET A$=A$+CHR$(A(B0))
3080 NEXT B0
3090 RETURN
3130 PRINT
3140 PRINT "HERE'S A SAMPLE PLAYING BOARD:"
3150 PRINT
3160 PRINT "1 . . . ."
3170 PRINT "2 . . . ."
3180 PRINT "3 . . . ."
3190 PRINT "4 . . . ."
3200 PRINT ". A B C D"
3210 PRINT
3220 PRINT "TWO SETS OF PIECES (DIGITS AND LETTERS) RACE AT RIGHT ANG";
3225 PRINT "LES"
3230 PRINT "ACROSS A SQUARE BOARD. VACANT LOCATIONS ARE SHOWN AS PERI";
3235 PRINT "ODS."
3240 PRINT "YOU CHOOSE THE THE BOARD SIZE (THE ONE ABOVE IS SIZE 5.)"
3260 PRINT "  N"
3270 PRINT "  :"
3280 PRINT "W---E"
3290 PRINT "  :"
3300 PRINT "  S"
3310 PRINT
3320 PRINT "THE OBJECT IS TO MOVE ALL OF YOUR PIECES ACROSS THE BOARD"
3330 PRINT "AND OFF THE OPPOSITE EDGE. DIGITS LEAVE THE BOARD ONLY AT"
3340 PRINT "THE EASTERN EDGE; LETTERS ONLY AT THE NORTHERN. THE WINNER"
3350 PRINT "IS THE PLAYER WHOSE PIECES HAVE ALL LEFT THE BOARD."
3360 PRINT
3370 PRINT "THE PLAYERS GO IN TURN, MOVING ONE OF THEIR PIECES TO AN"
3380 PRINT "ADJACENT LOCATON WHICH IS EITHER OFF THE BOARD OF CURRENT";
3385 PRINT "LY"
3390 PRINT "VACANT. THERE ARE NO DIAGONAL MOVES, NO JUMPS AND NO CAPT";
3395 PRINT "URES."
3400 PRINT "DIGITS CANNOT MOVE WEST, NOR LETTERS MOVE SOUTH."
3410 PRINT
3420 PRINT "TO MOVE A PIECE, TYPE ITS NAME AND THE FIRST LETTER OF THE"
3430 PRINT "DESIRED DIRECTION.  EXAMPLES:"
3440 PRINT "   2E MEANS THAT PIECE 2 WANTS TO GO EAST"
3450 PRINT "   BW MEANS THAT PIECE B WANTS TO GO WEST."
3460 PRINT
3470 PRINT "NOTE: YOU FORFET THE GAME IF YOUR MOVE LEAVES YOUR OPPONENT
3480 PRINT "WITHOUT ANY LEGAL MOVE."
3490 PRINT
3500 PRINT "LASTLY, YOU MAY TYPE R TO RESIGN AND H FOR HELP."
3510 PRINT
3520 RETURN
3530 END
OK
```

Doors

In this cute little game, there are four doors in succession and you must open them to get the prize behind the last one. You have a key ring containing eleven keys numbered zero to ten (computer people have a different way of numbering things than normal people) and you have fourteen tries to open all four doors. As an added hooker, some keys may open more than one door. If at first you don't succeed, try, try again. The prizes behind the fourth door are well worth the patience in trying to get them all open.

Doors was conceived and written by Bill Ingram.

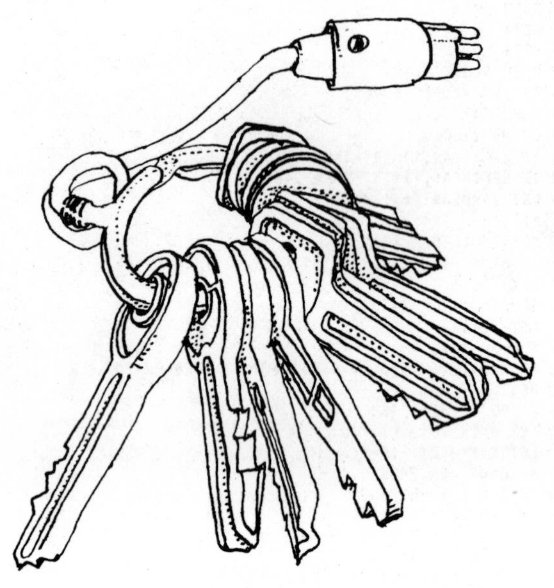

```
RUN

                            DOORS
                     CREATIVE COMPUTING
                   MORRISTOWN, NEW JERSEY



THERE ARE 4 LOCKED DOORS AND THERE ARE 11 KEYS(0- 10 )
YOU WILL HAVE  14 TRIES TO OPEN THEM ALL
(SOME KEYS MAY OPEN MORE THAN ONE DOOR)
TRIES LEFT # 14              DOOR # 1 KEY? 2
TRIES LEFT # 13              DOOR # 1 KEY? 3
TRIES LEFT # 12              DOOR # 1 KEY? 6
TRIES LEFT # 11              DOOR # 1 KEY? 0
WA LAH!
TRIES LEFT # 10              DOOR # 2 KEY? 3
TRIES LEFT # 9               DOOR # 2 KEY? 2
TRIES LEFT # 8               DOOR # 2 KEY? 5
TRIES LEFT # 7               DOOR # 2 KEY? 7
TRIES LEFT # 6               DOOR # 2 KEY? 10
TRIES LEFT # 5               DOOR # 2 KEY? 9
TRIES LEFT # 4               DOOR # 2 KEY? 1
TRIES LEFT # 3               DOOR # 2 KEY? 2
TRIES LEFT # 2               DOOR # 2 KEY? 4
SURPRISE!
TRIES LEFT # 1               DOOR # 3 KEY? 6
YOU LOSE,  THE REST OF THE KEYS ARE:
DOOR 3 KEY 8
DOOR 4 KEY 1
DO YOU WANT TO PLAY AGAIN(YES SIR! OR NO SIR!)
? YES SIR!
THERE ARE 3 LOCKED DOORS AND THERE ARE 11 KEYS(0- 10 )
YOU WILL HAVE  9 TRIES TO OPEN THEM ALL
(SOME KEYS MAY OPEN MORE THAN ONE DOOR)
TRIES LEFT # 9               DOOR # 1 KEY? 1
TRIES LEFT # 8               DOOR # 1 KEY? 0
ABRACADABRA!
TRIES LEFT # 7               DOOR # 2 KEY? 3
TRIES LEFT # 6               DOOR # 2 KEY? 4
TRIES LEFT # 5               DOOR # 2 KEY? 5
TRIES LEFT # 4               DOOR # 2 KEY? 8
TRIES LEFT # 3               DOOR # 2 KEY? 1
TRIES LEFT # 2               DOOR # 2 KEY? 2
TRIES LEFT # 1               DOOR # 2 KEY? 10
YOU LOSE,  THE REST OF THE KEYS ARE:
DOOR 2 KEY 0
DOOR 3 KEY 6
DO YOU WANT TO PLAY AGAIN(YES SIR! OR NO SIR!)
? NO SIR!
OK
```

```
LIST

1 PRINTTAB(27)"DOORS"
2 PRINT TAB(20)"CREATIVE COMPUTING"
3 PRINT TAB(18)"MORRISTOWN, NEW JERSEY"
4 PRINT
5 PRINT
6 PRINT
25 DIM K(20)
30 DEF FNR(Z)=INT(Z*RND(1))
32 FOR X=0 TO 6:READ R$(X):NEXT X
33 FOR X=0 TO 6: READ S$(X):NEXT X
35 D=1:T=10+FNR(21):N=3+FNR(3):K3=8+FNR(5)
40 PRINT"THERE ARE";N;"LOCKED DOORS AND THERE ARE";K3;"KEYS(0-"K3-1")"
41 PRINT"YOU WILL HAVE ";T-1;"TRIES TO OPEN THEM ALL"
42 PRINT"(SOME KEYS MAY OPEN MORE THAN ONE DOOR)"
65 FOR X=2 TO N:K(X)=FNR(K3):NEXT X
70 T=T-1:IF T=0 THEN 150
80 PRINT"TRIES LEFT #";T;"              DOOR #";D;"KEY";
90 INPUT K2
100 IF K2<>K(D) THEN 70
110 PRINT S$(FNR(7)):D=D+1
120 IF D<N+1 THEN 70
125 PRINT
130 PRINT"YOU DID IT, BEHIND DOOR #";N;"IS............................."
140 PRINT R$(FNR(7)) "!!":GOTO 170
150 PRINT"YOU LOSE,  THE REST OF THE KEYS ARE:"
160 FOR X=D TO N:PRINT"DOOR";X;"KEY"K(X):NEXT X
170 PRINT"DO YOU WANT TO PLAY AGAIN(YES SIR! OR NO SIR!)
171 INPUT Q$
180 IF Q$="YES SIR!" THEN 35
181 IF Q$="NO SIR!" THEN 999
190 PRINT"HEY, I DIDN'T JUST FALL OFF A TURNIP TRUCK, YA KNOW!!!!!"
200 GOTO 170
500 DATA"A POT OF GOLD","A BEAUTIFUL MAIDEN","A MAN EATING TIGER"
505 DATA"NOTHING","$22.59","A ROLLS ROYCE","THE KEYS TO THE WORLD"
600 DATA"OPEN SESAME!","C-R-E-E-E-E-E-A-A-K!","WA LAH!","TA-DAH!"
605 DATA"ABRACADABRA!","CLICK !!!!!!!!?!??????!!!!!!!!","SURPRISE!"
999 END
OK
```

Drag

DRAG allows the user to design his own dragster and then race it against a dragster designed by another player or the computer. You must specify the horsepower, rear end ratio, tire width, and tire diameter. There are no limits to these parameters.

Aha! you say. "I'll just design a two million horsepower dragster!" But it doesn't work that way, because your mass is related to your engine size, and so you usually end up with a top speed of something like 33 MPH. The computer is extremely hard to beat, but it's rumored that it can be done. Note: on some systems the amount of time between printouts can be aggravatingly long.

This program came from the Hewlett-Packard User Library. It also appeared in *Creative Computing*, Jan/Feb 1977.

```
RUN

                           DRAG
                    CREATIVE COMPUTING
                   MORRISTOWN NEW JERSEY



WELCOME TO DRAG STRIP.
WOULD YOU LIKE THE INSTRUCTIONS ? YES
YOU MAY RACE AGAINST ONE OF YOUR FRIENDS OR YOU MAY RACE
AGAINST MY DRAGSTER. YOU WILL BE ASKED TO DESIGN YOUR
OWN MACHINE, SPECIFYING HOURSEPOWER, READ END RATIO (X:1),
TIRE WIDTH IN INCHES AND TIRE DIAMETER IN FEET.
DO YOU WANT TO RACE AGAINST ME ? YES
I WILL HAVE CAR #1.
DESIGN CAR #2:
HORSEPOWER=? 790
REAR END RATIO=? 4.5
TIRE WIDTH=? 22
TIRE DIAMETER=? 4

GO!


ELAPSED         CAR #1                        CAR #2
TIME   SPEED     DISTANCE      SPEED      DISTANCE
(SEC)  (MPH)       (FT)        (MPH)         (FT)

CAR # 2  STOPS BURNING RUBBER
 1      22.0707      16.3821  19.5767     14.3695
 2      43.5753      64.7826  39.9392     58.1071
 3      64.0015      143.982  60.3405     131.846
 4      82.9394      252.079  79.8184     234.947
 5      100.107      386.668  97.4014     365.321
 6      115.356      545.024  112.362     519.607
CAR # 1  STOPS BURNING RUBBER
 7      128.639      724.299  124.389     693.674
 8      139.186      921.158  133.582     883.247
 9      146.922      1131.34  140.326     1084.43
 9.86047      151.811      1320  144.586      1264.35
          WINNER

DO YOU WANT TO TRY AGAIN ? NO
Ok
```

```
LIST
3 PRINT TAB(27);"DRAG"
5 PRINT TAB(20);"CREATIVE COMPUTING"
7 PRINT TAB(19);"MORRISTOWN NEW JERSEY"
10 DIM P(2),E(2),W(2),S(2),X(2),M(2),C(2),B(2),Y(2)
20 DIM Q(2)
30 PRINT:PRINT:PRINT
35 PRINT "WELCOME TO DRAG STRIP."
40 PRINT "WOULD YOU LIKE THE INSTRUCTIONS ";
50 INPUT I$
60 IF I$="NO" THEN 110
70 PRINT "YOU MAY RACE AGAINST ONE OF YOUR FRIENDS OR YOU MAY RACE"
80 PRINT "AGAINST MY DRAGSTER. YOU WILL BE ASKED TO DESIGN YOUR"
90 PRINT "OWN MACHINE, SPECIFYING HOURSEPOWER, READ END RATIO (X:1),"
100 PRINT "TIRE WIDTH IN INCHES AND TIRE DIAMETER IN FEET."
110 PRINT "DO YOU WANT TO RACE AGAINST ME ";
120 INPUT I$
130 IF I$="NO" THEN 200
140 PRINT "I WILL HAVE CAR #1."
150 P(1)=600
160 E(1)=5.9
170 W(1)=22
180 D(1)=3.9
190 GOTO 290
200 PRINT "DESIGN CAR #1:"
210 PRINT "HOURSPOWER=";
220 INPUT P(1)
230 PRINT "REAR END RATIO=";
240 INPUT E(1)
250 PRINT "TIRE WIDTH=";
260 INPUT W(1)
270 PRINT "TIRE DIAMETER=";
280 INPUT D(1)
290 PRINT "DESIGN CAR #2:"
300 PRINT "HORSEPOWER=";
310 INPUT P(2)
320 PRINT "REAR END RATIO=";
330 INPUT E(2)
340 PRINT "TIRE WIDTH=";
350 INPUT W(2)
360 PRINT "TIRE DIAMETER="; -
370 INPUT D(2)
380 PRINT
390 PRINT "GO!"
400 K1=500
410 K2=1.6
420 K3=2
430 K4=6E-04
440 K5=6E-05
450 K6=.2
460 K7=4
470 K8=1.5E-04
480 Q(1)=0:Q(2)=0
490 S(1)=0:S(2)=0
500 X(1)=0:X(2)=0
510 REM: M IS MASS
520 FOR J=1 TO 2
530 M(J)=(K1+K2*P(J)+K3*W(J)*D(J)+K7*D(J)^2)/32.2
540 REM: C IS DRAG FROM WIND.
550 C(J)=K4*M(J)^(2/3)+K8*W(J)*D(J)
560 REM: B IS THE MAX ACCELERATION WITHOUT BURNING
570 B(J)=15+28*W(J)*D(J)/((W(J)+6)*(D(J)+1))
580 REM: Y IS THE SCALE FACTOR FOR RPM VS POWER.
590 Y(J)=3.7-3.3E-03*P(J)
600 NEXT J
610 PRINT
620 PRINT
630 PRINT "ELAPSED ";TAB(15);"CAR #1";TAB(39);"CAR #2"
640 PRINT "TIME   SPEED     DISTANCE     SPEED     DISTANCE"
650 PRINT "(SEC)  (MPH)       (FT)       (MPH)        (FT)"
660 PRINT
670 FOR T=0 TO 100
680 FOR T1=1 TO 100
690 FOR J=1 TO 2
700 REM: R IS RPM.
```

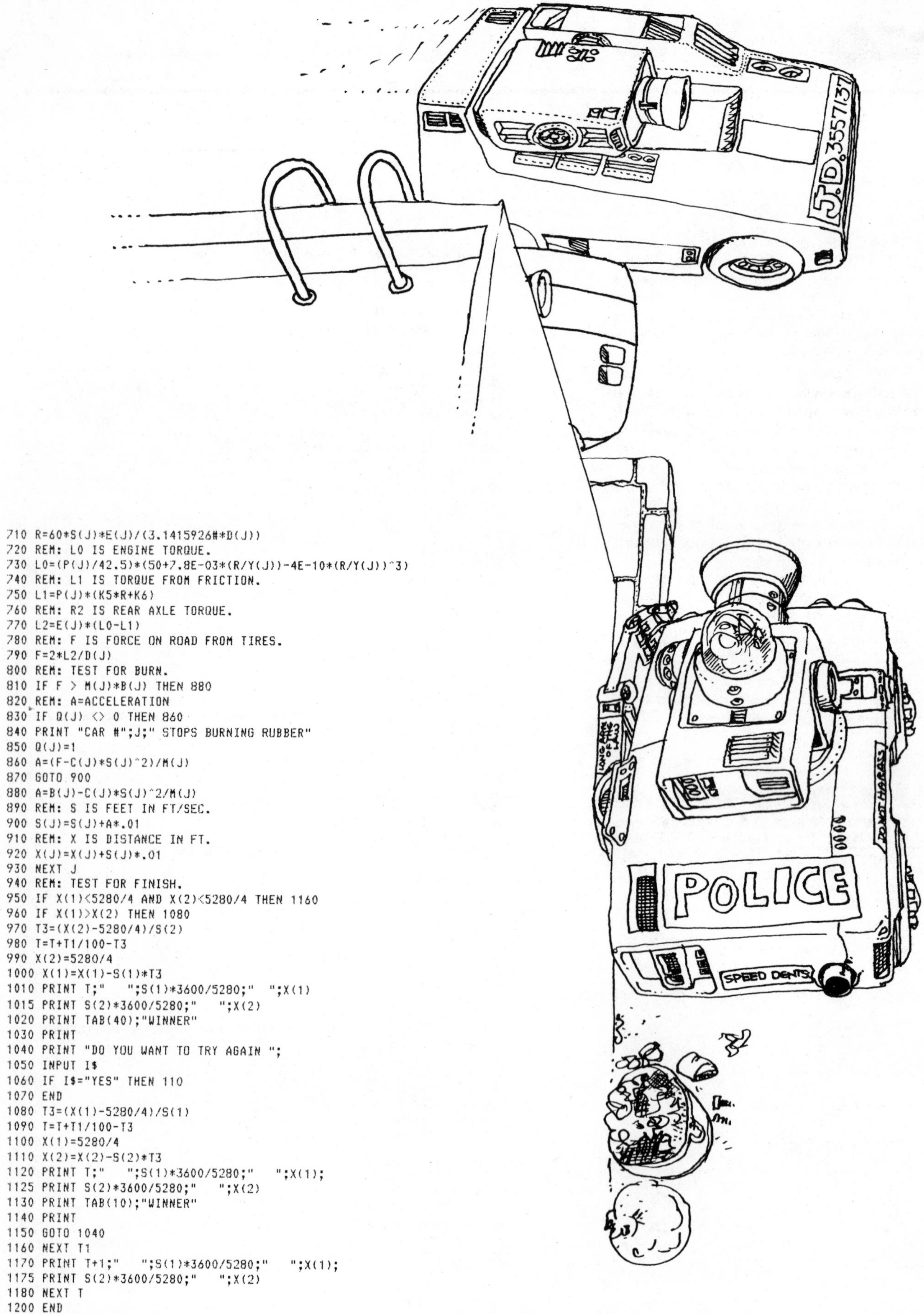


```
710 R=60*S(J)*E(J)/(3.1415926#*D(J))
720 REM: L0 IS ENGINE TORQUE.
730 L0=(P(J)/42.5)*(50+7.8E-03*(R/Y(J))-4E-10*(R/Y(J))^3)
740 REM: L1 IS TORQUE FROM FRICTION.
750 L1=P(J)*(K5*R+K6)
760 REM: R2 IS REAR AXLE TORQUE.
770 L2=E(J)*(L0-L1)
780 REM: F IS FORCE ON ROAD FROM TIRES.
790 F=2*L2/D(J)
800 REM: TEST FOR BURN.
810 IF F > M(J)*B(J) THEN 880
820 REM: A=ACCELERATION
830 IF Q(J) <> 0 THEN 860
840 PRINT "CAR #";J;" STOPS BURNING RUBBER"
850 Q(J)=1
860 A=(F-C(J)*S(J)^2)/M(J)
870 GOTO 900
880 A=B(J)-C(J)*S(J)^2/M(J)
890 REM: S IS FEET IN FT/SEC.
900 S(J)=S(J)+A*.01
910 REM: X IS DISTANCE IN FT.
920 X(J)=X(J)+S(J)*.01
930 NEXT J
940 REM: TEST FOR FINISH.
950 IF X(1)<5280/4 AND X(2)<5280/4 THEN 1160
960 IF X(1)>X(2) THEN 1080
970 T3=(X(2)-5280/4)/S(2)
980 T=T+T1/100-T3
990 X(2)=5280/4
1000 X(1)=X(1)-S(1)*T3
1010 PRINT T;"   ";S(1)*3600/5280;"   ";X(1)
1015 PRINT S(2)*3600/5280;"   ";X(2)
1020 PRINT TAB(40);"WINNER"
1030 PRINT
1040 PRINT "DO YOU WANT TO TRY AGAIN ";
1050 INPUT I$
1060 IF I$="YES" THEN 110
1070 END
1080 T3=(X(1)-5280/4)/S(1)
1090 T=T+T1/100-T3
1100 X(1)=5280/4
1110 X(2)=X(2)-S(2)*T3
1120 PRINT T;"   ";S(1)*3600/5280;"   ";X(1);
1125 PRINT S(2)*3600/5280;"   ";X(2)
1130 PRINT TAB(10);"WINNER"
1140 PRINT
1150 GOTO 1040
1160 NEXT T1
1170 PRINT T+1;"   ";S(1)*3600/5280;"   ";X(1);
1175 PRINT S(2)*3600/5280;"   ";X(2)
1180 NEXT T
1200 END
Ok
```

Dr. Z

Using DR.Z your computer "interacts" with you in true Rogerian form, never making a value judgment of your response.

DR.Z is multi-lingual and "professional confidence" is guaranteed, especially with a video display terminal. However, if you have a printer, try employing a unique language known only to you and Dr.Z.

If you would prefer to employ DR.Z in an educational mode, you might consider the following sequence of activities.

1. Discuss communication, exploring:
   a. The role of spoken language
   b. The role of written language
   c. Non-verbal language
      1. facial expressions
      2. posture of body
      3. hand gestures
2. Experience a session with DR.Z.
3. Develop computerizations of other "purely human" situations.

Note: Don't mistake DR.Z for Eliza (or Doctor). In DR.Z, all the responses are "canned" and the computer makes no attempt to analyze your input in any way.

DR.Z was submitted to us anonymously by some students of Dr. Melvin Zeddies of San Diego.

```
RUN
                           DR.Z
                    CREATIVE COMPUTING
                  MORRISTOWN, NEW JERSEY


HELLO THERE, I'M YOUR COMPUTER THERAPIST.
WHAT IS YOUR NAME? AND TELL ME SOMETHING ABOUT YOURSELF.
HOWEVER, DON'T TYPE MORE THAN ONE LINE. I TIRE EASILY.
? MY NAME IS STEVE. I'M TRYING TO FIX THIS PROGRAM.
WHAT DID YOU SAY YOUR NAME WAS AGAIN?
? STEVE
HOW DO YOU FEEL TODAY?
? TERRIBLE. IT IS TOO HOT OUTSIDE!!!


DO YOU THINK THIS IS REASONABLE IN LIGHT OF YOUR INTERESTS?

? WHAT ARE YOU  TALKING ABOPUT


DO YOUR FRIENDS FIND THIS ACCEPTABLE?

? SOMETIMES


WHY DO YOU THINK YOU FEEL THIS WAY?

? BECAUSE OF THE WEATHER


DO YOU THINK THAT THIS IS A NORMAL FEELING?

? YES


DO YOUR FRIENDS FIND THIS ACCEPTABLE?

? I JUST ANSWERED THAT
```

```
I THINK YOU ARE MAKING A GREAT ATTEMPT TO SOLVE YOUR
DIFFICULTIES, AND I SEE NO NEED TO CONTINUE THIS
SESSION ANY FURTHER.
STEVE WOULD YOU MAKE ANOTHER APPOINTMENT WITH MY COMPUTER
FOR SOMETIME IN THE NEXT FEW WEEKS. WHAT DATE WOULD YOU
PREFER?
? NEVER
THAT WILL BE FINE .
I'VE ENJOYED COMMUNICATING WITH YOU.
HAVE A NICE DAY.

LIST

5 PRINT TAB(27);"DR.Z"
6 PRINT TAB(20);"CREATIVE COMPUTING"
7 PRINT TAB(18);"MORRISTOWN, NEW JERSEY"
8 PRINT:PRINT:PRINT
20 PRINT "HELLO THERE, I'M YOUR COMPUTER THERAPIST."
30 PRINT "WHAT IS YOUR NAME? AND TELL ME SOMETHING ABOUT YOURSELF."
40 PRINT "HOWEVER, DON'T TYPE MORE THAN ONE LINE. I TIRE EASILY."
50 INPUT A$
60 PRINT "WHAT DID YOU SAY YOUR NAME WAS AGAIN?"
70 INPUT B$
80 PRINT "HOW DO YOU FEEL TODAY?"
90 LET C=0:U=0:V=0
100 INPUT A$
110 PRINT
120 PRINT
130 IF C=10 THEN 720
140 LET Z=INT(10*RND(1))
150 IF U=Z THEN 140
160 IF V=Z THEN 140
170 LET U=Z
180 ON Z+1 GOTO 690,420,450,480,510,540,570,600,630,660
380 GOTO 690
390 PRINT "THAT'S VERY INTERESTING, TELL ME MORE."
400 PRINT
410 GOTO 690
420 PRINT "HAVE YOU FELT THIS WAY LONG?"
430 PRINT
440 GOTO 690
450 PRINT "DO YOU THINK THIS IS REASONABLE IN LIGHT OF YOUR INTERESTS?"
460 PRINT
470 GOTO 690
480 PRINT "DO YOUR FRIENDS FIND THIS ACCEPTABLE?"
490 PRINT
500 GOTO 690
510 PRINT "DO YOU FEEL COMFORTABLE WITH THIS FEELING?"
520 PRINT
530 GOTO 690
540 PRINT "DO YOU THINK THAT THIS IS A NORMAL FEELING?"
550 PRINT
560 GOTO 690
570 PRINT "WHY DO YOU THINK YOU FEEL THIS WAY?"
580 PRINT
590 GOTO 690
600 PRINT "HAVE YOU TALKED TO ANYONE ABOUT THIS?"
610 PRINT
620 GOTO 690
630 PRINT "WHY ARE YOU HERE?"
640 PRINT
650 GOTO 690
660 PRINT "ARE YOU SATISFIED WITH THE WAY YOUR IDEAS ARE DEVELOPING?"
670 PRINT
690 LET C=C+1
700 LET U=Z
710 GOTO 100
720 PRINT "I THINK YOU ARE MAKING A GREAT ATTEMPT TO SOLVE YOUR"
730 PRINT "DIFFICULTIES, AND I SEE NO NEED TO CONTINUE THIS"
740 PRINT "SESSION ANY FURTHER."
750 PRINT B$;" WOULD YOU MAKE ANOTHER APPOINTMENT WITH MY COMPUTER"
760 PRINT "FOR SOMETIME IN THE NEXT FEW WEEKS. WHAT DATE WOULD YOU"
770 PRINT "PREFER?"
780 INPUT A$
790 PRINT "THAT WILL BE FINE ."
800 PRINT "I'VE ENJOYED COMMUNICATING WITH YOU."
810 PRINT "HAVE A NICE DAY."
820 FOR T=1 TO 6
830 PRINT
840 NEXT T
850 END
```

Eliza

Description: ELIZA is a program that accepts natural English as input and carries on a reasonably coherent conversation based on the psychoanalytic techniques of Carl Rogers. You will have to forgive ELIZA for being a poor English student. You'll find that it is best not to use punctuation in your input, and you'll have to carry the conversation. But it does work!

How it works: In order to speak to you, ELIZA must: (1) get a string from the user, and prepare it for further processing: (2) find the keywords in the input string: (3) if a keyword is found, take the part of the string following the keyword and "translate" all the personal pronouns and verbs ("I" becomes "YOU", "ARE" becomes "AM", etc.); (4) finally, look up an appropriate reply based on the keyword which was found, print it and, if necessary, the "translated" string. ELIZA uses four types of program data to accomplish this:

(1) 36 keyword, such as "I AM", "WHY DONT YOU", and "COMPUTER". The keywords must be in order of priority, so ELIZA will key on "YOU ARE" before "YOU".

(2) 12 strings used for the translation or conjugation process. These are in pairs such that if one member of the pair is found, the other is substituted for it. Examples: "Y", "YOU", "AM", "ARE", etc.

(3) 112 reply strings. The strings are arranged in groups corresponding to the keywords. There is no fixed number of different replies for each keyword. Replies ending in a "*" are to be followed by the translated string, while the strings ending in normal punctuation are to be printed alone.

(4) Numerical data to determine which replies to print for each keyword. For each keyword there is a pair of numbers signifying (start of reply strings, number of reply strings). Thus the fifth pair of number, (10,4), means that the replies for the fifth keyword ("I DONT") start with the tenth reply string, and that there are four replies.

Detailed Explanation:
Lines 10-160: Initialization. Arrays and strings are dimensioned. N1, N2, and N3, which represent the number of keywords, number of translation strings, and number of replies respectively, are defined. Then the arrays are filled. S(keyword number) is the ordinal number of the start of the reply strings for a given keyword, R(keyword number) is the actual reply to be used next, and N(keyword number) is the last reply for that keyword. Finally an introduction is printed.
Lines 170-255: User input section. This part of the program gets a string from the user, places a space at the start of the string and two at the end (to make it easier to correctly locate keywords and to preventsubscripting out of bounds), throws out all the apostrophes (so DONT and DON'T are equivalent), and stops if the word SHUT is found in the input string (which it takes to mean SHUT UP). ELIZA also checks for repetitive input by the user.
Lines 260-370: Keyword-finding section. ELIZA scans the input string for keywords and saves the keyword of highest priority temporarily in S, T, and F$. If no keyword is found, the keyword defaults to number 36, NOKEYFOUND (which causes ELIZA to say something noncommital) and it skips the next section.
Lines 380-555: Translation or Conjugation section. The part of the input string following the keyword is saved. Then pairs of translation strings, as described above, are read and upon the occurence of one of these strings, the other is substituted for it. When this is done ELIZA makes sure there is only one leading space in the translated string.
Lines 560-640: Reply printing section. Using R(keyword number), S(keyword number), and N(keyword number), the correct reply is located. The pointer for the next reply is bumped and reset if it is too large. If the reply string ends in a "*" it is printed with the translated string, otherwise it is printed alone. The previously entered input string is saved to permit checking for repetetive input, and then ELIZA goes back for more input.

Limitations: Runs in 16K of memory.

Modifications: You can easily add, change, or delete any of the keywords, translation words, or replies. Remember, you will also have to change N1, N2, N3, and/or the numerical data. Just as a suggestion, if you decide to insert "ME" and "YOU" in the translation string list, put a nonprinting (control) character in YOU to prevent ELIZA from substituting I→YOU→ME. This means that YOU will always be assumed to be the subject of a verb, never the object, but resolving that difficulty is a whole different problem.

A Few Comments: The structures found in lines 120, 420, and 590 could be replaced by RESTORE NNNN statements if your BASIC has them. The use of an INSTR, SEARCH, or POS function to determine if one string is a substring of another would probably speed things up considerably (it takes ELIZA around 10 seconds to think of a reply).

What it all means: we'll leave to you. Although this program is an inferior imitation of the original, it does work. It is pretty farfetched to believe that a psycholanalyst is nothing but a sentence-input-keyword-finder-conjugator-reply finder, but if you really think so, you can buy your computer a speech-recognition unit, a Computalker and a green couch, and charge $75/hr! My computer, the doctor!

Geneology: ELIZA was originally programmed in LISP by Joseph Weizenbaum at MIT. It was converted to BASIC by Jeff Shrager and further modified to work in Microsoft BASIC by Steve North, who also wrote these notes.

Name	*Usage*
R(X),S(X),N(X)	See Text
I$	Input string
K$	Keyword string
C$	Translated or conjugated string
F$	Reply string, also used to save K$ in scanning for keyword
R$,S$	Strings used in conjugation process
P$	Previous input string
Z$	Scratch (used for simulating RESTORE NNNN statement).
N1	Number of keywords
N2	Number of conjugation strings
N3	Number of replies
K	Keyword number
S,T	Used to save K and L when scanning for keyword
X,L	X,L Scratch. X is generally used for looping while L is used for scanning through strings
V	V Used for scanning for keyword string

```
                    ELIZA
             CREATIVE COMPUTING
           MORRISTOWN, NEW JERSEY


HI!  I'M ELIZA.  WHAT'S YOUR PROBLEM?
? YOU
WE WERE DISCUSSING YOU-- NOT ME.
? BUT YOU ATR THE PROBLEM
OH, I ATR THE PROBLEM
? SO I MISSPELLED A WORD
SAY, DO YOU HAVE ANY PSYCHOLOGICAL PROBLEMS?
? NO DO YOU
YOU'RE NOT REALLY TALKING ABOUT ME, ARE YOU?
? ONLY BEHIND YOUR BACK
WHY ARE YOU CONCERNED ABOUT MY BACK
? BECAUSE I'M AFRAID TO CON FRONT YOU
DID YOU COME TO ME BECAUSE YOU ARE AFRAID TO CON FRONT I
? YOU SPEAK WIERD ENGLISH
WE WERE DISCUSSING YOU-- NOT ME.
? AM I GETTING THE BEST OF YOU
OH, I
? WHAT IS THAT SUPPOSED TO MEAN
WHY DO YOU ASK?
? WHY NOT
WHY DO YOU ASK?
? I ASKED FIRST
WHAT DOES THAT SUGGEST TO YOU?
? THAT YOU ARE NOT AS SMART AS YOU THINK
WHAT MAKES YOU THINK I AM NOT AS SMART AS I THINK
? YOU ARE MAKING A FOOL OUT OF YOURSELF
DOES IT PLEASE YOU TO BELIEVE I AM MAKING A FOOL OUT OF YOURSELF
? DON'T TWIST THE WORDS ON ME BUDDY
I SEE.
? DO YOU REALLY
YOU'RE NOT REALLY TALKING ABOUT ME, ARE YOU?
? YES
ARE YOU SURE?
? YES I AM SURE
DID YOU COME TO ME BECAUSE YOU ARE SURE
? I CAME BECAUSE I AM
HOW LONG HAVE YOU BEEN
? AS LONG AS POSSIBLE
I'M NOT SURE I UNDERSTAND YOU FULLY.
? SO I AM NOT THE GREATEST CONVERSATIONALIST
DO YOU BELIEVE IT IS NORMAL TO BE NOT THE GREATEST CONVERSATIONALIST
? YES
I SEE.
? HOW CAN YOU SEE WITHOUT ANY EYES
DON'T YOU BELIEVE THAT I CAN SEE WITHOUT ANY EYES
? NO SO PROVE IT
ARE YOU SAYING NO JUST TO BE NEGATIVE?
? ABSOLUTELY NOT
YOU ARE BEING A BIT NEGATIVE.
? SO YOU WANT TO FIGHT DO YOU
WE WERE DISCUSSING YOU-- NOT ME.
? DON'T BACK DOWN FRIEND
WHY DO YOU BRING UP THE TOPIC OF FRIENDS?
? I DON'T HAVE ANY FRIENDS
DON'T YOU REALLY HAVE ANY FRIENDS
? NO NOT REALLY
WHY NOT?
? BECAUSE I AM YOU AND YOU ARE ME AND WE ARE ALL TOGETHER
PERHAPS YOU WOULD LIKE TO BE YOU AND WE AM ALL TOGETHER
? SAY WHAT
DOES THAT QUESTION INTEREST YOU?
? DEFINITELY
COME COME ELUCIDATE YOUR THOUGHTS.
? DO YOU LIKE THE BEATLES
OH, I LIKE THE BEATLES
? HOW ABOUT THE BEACH BOYS
WHY DO YOU ASK?
? DO YOU DREAM OFTEN
YOU'RE NOT REALLY TALKING ABOUT ME, ARE YOU?
? DREAM ON
WHAT DOES THAT DREAM SUGGEST TO YOU?
? WHAT DREAM
WHAT ANSWER WOULD PLEASE YOU THE MOST?
? DO YOU SUBSCRIBE TO CREATIVE COMPUTING
WE WERE DISCUSSING YOU-- NOT ME.
? I AM AN IBM 370/168
DO YOU ENJOY BEING AN IBM 370/168
? I AM WORRIED ABOUT THE COMPETITION
DID YOU COME TO ME BECAUSE YOU ARE WORRIED ABOUT THE COMPETITION
? DON'T GET PERSONAL
CAN YOU ELABORATE ON THAT?
? I'M GETTING TIRED OF LISTENING TO YOU TO SHUT UP
SHUT UP...
Ok
```

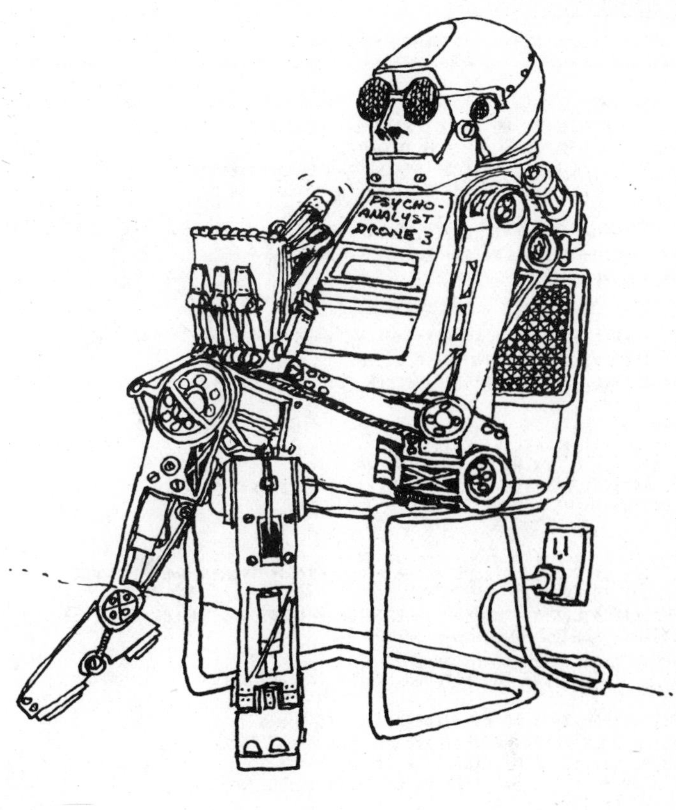


```
1 PRINT TAB(26);"ELIZA"
2 PRINT TAB(20);"CREATIVE COMPUTING"
3 PRINT TAB(18);"MORRISTOWN, NEW JERSEY"
4 PRINT:PRINT:PRINT
80 REM     -----INITIALIZATION-----
100 DIM S(36),R(36),N(36)
110 N1=36:N2=14:N3=112
120 FOR X=1 TO N1+N2+N3:READ Z$:NEXT X:REM SAME AS RESTORE
130 FORX=1 TO N1
140 READ S(X),L:R(X)=S(X):N(X)=S(X)+L-1
150 NEXT X
160 PRINT "HI!  I'M ELIZA.  WHAT'S YOUR PROBLEM?"
170 REM
180 REM      -----USER INPUT SECTION-----
190 REM
200 INPUT I$
201 I$=" "+I$+"  "
210 REM  GET RID OF APOSTROPHES
220 FOR L=1 TO LEN(I$)
230 IFMID$(I$,L,1)="'"THENI$=LEFT$(I$,L-1)+RIGHT$(I$,LEN(I$)-L):GOTO230
240 IFL+4<=LEN(I$)THENIFMID$(I$,L,4)="SHUT"THENPRINT"SHUT UP...":END
250 NEXT L
255 IF I$=P$ THEN PRINT "PLEASE DON'T REPEAT YOURSELF!":GOTO 170
260 REM
270 REM      -----FIND KEYWORD IN I$-----
```

```
280 REM
290 RESTORE
295 S=0
300 FOR K=1 TO N1
310 READ K$
315 IF S>0 THEN360
320 FOR L=1 TO LEN(I$)-LEN(K$)+1
340 IF MID$(I$,L,LEN(K$))=K$THENS=K:T=L:F$=K$
350 NEXT L
360 NEXT K
365 IF S>0 THEN K=S:L=T:GOTO390
370 K=36:GOTO570:REM  WE DIDN'T FIND ANY KEYWORDS
380 REM
390 REM      TAKE RIGHT PART OF STRING AND CONJUGATE IT
400 REM      USING THE LIST OF STRINGS TO BE SWAPPED
410 REM
420 RESTORE:FORX=1 TO N1:READ Z$:NEXT X:REM SKIP OVER KEYWORDS
430 C$=" "+RIGHT$(I$,LEN(I$)-LEN(F$)-L+1)+" "
440 FOR X=1 TO N2/2
450 READ S$,R$
460 FOR L= 1 TO LEN(C$)
470 IF L+LEN(S$)>LEN(C$) THEN 510
480 IF MID$(C$,L,LEN(S$))<>S$ THEN 510
490 C$=LEFT$(C$,L-1)+R$+RIGHT$(C$,LEN(C$)-L-LEN(S$)+1)
495 L=L+LEN(R$)
500 GOTO 540
510 IF L+LEN(R$)>LEN(C$)THEN540
520 IF MID$(C$,L,LEN(R$))<>R$ THEN 540
530 C$=LEFT$(C$,L-1)+S$+RIGHT$(C$,LEN(C$)-L-LEN(R$)+1)
535 L=L+LEN(S$)
540 NEXT L
550 NEXT X
555 IF MID$(C$,2,1)=" "THENC$=RIGHT$(C$,LEN(C$)-1):REM ONLY 1 SPACE
556 FOR L=1 TO LEN(C$)
557 IF MID$(C$,L,1)="!" THEN C$=LEFT$(C$,L-1)+RIGHT$(C$,LEN(C$)-L):GOTO557
558 NEXTL
560 REM
570 REM      NOW USING THE KEYWORD NUMBER (K) GET REPLY
580 REM
590 RESTORE:FOR X= 1 TO N1+N2:READ Z$:NEXT X
600 FORX=1TOR(K):READ F$:NEXT X:REM  READ RIGHT REPLY
610 R(K)=R(K)+1: IFR(K)>N(K) THEN R(K)=S(K)
620 IF RIGHT$(F$,1)<>"*" THEN PRINT F$:P$=I$:GOTO 170
630 PRINT LEFT$(F$,LEN(F$)-1);C$
640 P$=I$:GOTO 170
1000 REM
1010 REM      -----PROGRAM DATA FOLLOWS-----
1020 REM
1030 REM      KEYWORDS
1040 REM
1050 DATA "CAN YOU","CAN I","YOU ARE","YOURE","I DONT","I FEEL"
1060 DATA "WHY DONT YOU","WHY CANT I","ARE YOU","I CANT","I AM","IM "
1070 DATA "YOU ","I WANT","WHAT","HOW","WHO","WHERE","WHEN","WHY"
1080 DATA "NAME","CAUSE","SORRY","DREAM","HELLO","HI ","MAYBE"
1090 DATA " NO","YOUR","ALWAYS","THINK","ALIKE","YES","FRIEND"
1100 DATA "COMPUTER","NOKEYFOUND"
1200 REM
1210 REM      STRING DATA FOR CONJUGATIONS
1220 REM
1230 DATA " ARE "," AM ","WERE ","WAS "," YOU "," I ","YOUR ","MY "
1235 DATA " IVE "," YOUVE "," IM "," YOURE "
1240 DATA " ME "," !YOU "
1300 REM
1310 REM      REPLIES
1320 REM
1330 DATA "DON'T YOU BELIEVE THAT I CAN*"
1340 DATA "PERHAPS YOU WOULD LIKE TO BE ABLE TO*"
1350 DATA "YOU WANT ME TO BE ABLE TO*"
1360 DATA "PERHAPS YOU DON'T WANT TO*"
1365 DATA "DO YOU WANT TO BE ABLE TO*"
1370 DATA "WHAT MAKES YOU THINK I AM*"
1380 DATA "DOES IT PLEASE YOU TO BELIEVE I AM*"
1390 DATA "PERHAPS YOU WOULD LIKE TO BE*"
1400 DATA "DO YOU SOMETIMES WISH YOU WERE*"
1410 DATA "DON'T YOU REALLY*"
1420 DATA "WHY DON'T YOU*"
1430 DATA "DO YOU WISH TO BE ABLE TO*"
1440 DATA "DOES THAT TROUBLE YOU?"
1450 DATA "TELL ME MORE ABOUT SUCH FEELINGS."
1460 DATA "DO YOU OFTEN FEEL*"
1470 DATA "DO YOU ENJOY FEELING*"
1480 DATA "DO YOU REALLY BELIEVE I DON'T*"
1490 DATA "PERHAPS IN GOOD TIME I WILL*"
1500 DATA "DO YOU WANT ME TO*"
1510 DATA "DO YOU THINK YOU SHOULD BE ABLE TO*"
1520 DATA "WHY CAN'T YOU*"
1530 DATA "WHY ARE YOU INTERESTED IN WHETHER OR NOT I AM*"
1540 DATA "WOULD YOU PREFER IF I WERE NOT*"
1550 DATA "PERHAPS IN YOUR FANTASIES I AM*"
1560 DATA "HOW DO YOU KNOW YOU CAN'T*"
1570 DATA "HAVE YOU TRIED?"
1580 DATA "PERHAPS YOU CAN NOW*"
```

```
1590 DATA "DID YOU COME TO ME BECAUSE YOU ARE*"
1600 DATA "HOW LONG HAVE YOU BEEN*"
1610 DATA "DO YOU BELIEVE IT IS NORMAL TO BE*"
1620 DATA "DO YOU ENJOY BEING*"
1630 DATA "WE WERE DISCUSSING YOU-- NOT ME."
1640 DATA "OH, I*"
1650 DATA "YOU'RE NOT REALLY TALKING ABOUT ME, ARE YOU?"
1660 DATA "WHAT WOULD IT MEAN TO YOU IF YOU GOT*"
1670 DATA "WHY DO YOU WANT*"
1680 DATA "SUPPOSE YOU SOON GOT*"
1690 DATA "WHAT IF YOU NEVER GOT*"
1700 DATA "I SOMETIMES ALSO WANT*"
1710 DATA "WHY DO YOU ASK?"
1720 DATA "DOES THAT QUESTION INTEREST YOU?"
1730 DATA "WHAT ANSWER WOULD PLEASE YOU THE MOST?"
1740 DATA "WHAT DO YOU THINK?"
1750 DATA "ARE SUCH QUESTIONS ON YOUR MIND OFTEN?"
1760 DATA "WHAT IS IT THAT YOU REALLY WANT TO KNOW?"
1770 DATA "HAVE YOU ASKED ANYONE ELSE?"
1780 DATA "HAVE YOU ASKED SUCH QUESTIONS BEFORE?"
1790 DATA "WHAT ELSE COMES TO MIND WHEN YOU ASK THAT?"
1800 DATA "NAMES DON'T INTEREST ME."
1810 DATA "I DON'T CARE ABOUT NAMES-- PLEASE GO ON."
1820 DATA "IS THAT THE REAL REASON?"
1830 DATA "DON'T ANY OTHER REASONS COME TO MIND?"
1840 DATA "DOES THAT REASON EXPLAIN ANYTHING ELSE?"
1850 DATA "WHAT OTHER REASONS MIGHT THERE BE?"
1860 DATA "PLEASE DON'T APOLOGIZE!"
1870 DATA "APOLOGIES ARE NOT NECESSARY."
1880 DATA "WHAT FEELINGS DO YOU HAVE WHEN YOU APOLOGIZE."
1890 DATA "DON'T BE SO DEFENSIVE!"
1900 DATA "WHAT DOES THAT DREAM SUGGEST TO YOU?"
1910 DATA "DO YOU DREAM OFTEN?"
1920 DATA "WHAT PERSONS APPEAR IN YOUR DREAMS?"
1930 DATA "ARE YOU DISTURBED BY YOUR DREAMS?"
1940 DATA "HOW DO YOU DO ... PLEASE STATE YOUR PROBLEM."
1950 DATA "YOU DON'T SEEM QUITE CERTAIN."
1960 DATA "WHY THE UNCERTAIN TONE?"
1970 DATA "CAN'T YOU BE MORE POSITIVE?"
1980 DATA "YOU AREN'T SURE?"
1990 DATA "DON'T YOU KNOW?"
2000 DATA "ARE YOU SAYING NO JUST TO BE NEGATIVE?"
2010 DATA "YOU ARE BEING A BIT NEGATIVE."
2020 DATA "WHY NOT?"
2030 DATA "ARE YOU SURE?"
2040 DATA "WHY NO?"
2050 DATA "WHY ARE YOU CONCERNED ABOUT MY*"
2060 DATA "WHAT ABOUT YOUR OWN*"
2070 DATA "CAN YOU THINK OF A SPECIFIC EXAMPLE?"
2080 DATA "WHEN?"
2090 DATA "WHAT ARE YOU THINKING OF?"
2100 DATA "REALLY, ALWAYS?"
2110 DATA "DO YOU REALLY THINK SO?"
2120 DATA "BUT YOU ARE NOT SURE YOU*"
2130 DATA "DO YOU DOUBT YOU*"
2140 DATA "IN WHAT WAY?"
2150 DATA "WHAT RESEMBLANCE DO YOU SEE?"
2160 DATA "WHAT DOES THE SIMILARITY SUGGEST TO YOU?"
2170 DATA "WHAT OTHER CONNECTIONS DO YOU SEE?"
2180 DATA "COULD THERE REALLY BE SOME CONNECTION?"
2190 DATA "HOW?"
2200 DATA "YOU SEEM QUITE POSITIVE."
2210 DATA "ARE YOU SURE?"
2220 DATA "I SEE."
2230 DATA "I UNDERSTAND."
2240 DATA "WHY DO YOU BRING UP THE TOPIC OF FRIENDS?"
2250 DATA "DO YOUR FRIENDS WORRY YOU?"
2260 DATA "DO YOUR FRIENDS PICK ON YOU?"
2270 DATA "ARE YOU SURE YOU HAVE ANY FRIENDS?"
2280 DATA "DO YOU IMPOSE ON YOUR FRIENDS?"
2290 DATA "PERHAPS YOUR LOVE FOR FRIENDS WORRIES YOU."
2300 DATA "DO COMPUTERS WORRY YOU?"
2310 DATA "ARE YOU TALKING ABOUT ME IN PARTICULAR?"
2320 DATA "ARE YOU FRIGHTENED BY MACHINES?"
2330 DATA "WHY DO YOU MENTION COMPUTERS?"
2340 DATA "WHAT DO YOU THINK MACHINES HAVE TO DO WITH YOUR PROBLEM?"
2350 DATA "DON'T YOU THINK COMPUTERS CAN HELP PEOPLE?"
2360 DATA "WHAT IS IT ABOUT MACHINES THAT WORRIES YOU?"
2370 DATA "SAY, DO YOU HAVE ANY PSYCHOLOGICAL PROBLEMS?"
2380 DATA "WHAT DOES THAT SUGGEST TO YOU?"
2390 DATA "I SEE."
2400 DATA "I'M NOT SURE I UNDERSTAND YOU FULLY."
2410 DATA "COME COME ELUCIDATE YOUR THOUGHTS."
2420 DATA "CAN YOU ELABORATE ON THAT?"
2430 DATA "THAT IS QUITE INTERESTING."
2500 REM
2510 REM      DATA FOR FINDING RIGHT REPLIES
2520 REM
2530 DATA 1,3,4,2,6,4,6,4,10,4,14,3,17,3,20,2,22,3,25,3
2540 DATA 28,4,28,4,32,3,35,5,40,9,40,9,40,9,40,9,40,9,40,9
2550 DATA 49,2,51,4,55,4,59,4,63,1,63,1,64,5,69,5,74,2,76,4
2560 DATA 80,3,83,7,90,3,93,6,99,7,106,6
```

Father

This program loosely simulates a debate with your father about going out on Saturday night. After you win or lose the debate, then Saturday night approaches and you must decide whether or not to actually go out. When all is said and done, the computer will give you a score on a scale of minus seven to plus four. (This could have been a scale of zero to ten, but computers have this magic ability to give us scales of anything we want).

This program originated in the dungeons of Digital Equipment Corporation and was whipped into its present form by Victor Nahigian.

```
RUN
                        FATHER

                  CREATIVE COMPUTING
                MORRISTOWN, NEW JERSEY



WANT TO HAVE A DEBATE WITH YOUR FATHER, EH??

DO YOU WANT INSTRUCTIONS? YES
YOU ARE GOING TO PLAY IN A GAME IN WHICH YOU WILL DISCUSS
A PROBLEM WITH YOUR FATHER AND ATTEMPT TO GET HIM TO
AGREE WITH YOU IN THREE TRIES.

FOR EACH STATEMENT YOU MAKE, I WILL TELL YOU WHAT
YOUR FATHER REPLIED.

YOU MUST SELECT YOUR STATEMENT FROM ONE
OF THE FOLLOWING SIX.
**********
1.      O.K. I WILL STAY HOME.
2.      BUT I'D REALLY LIKE TO GO. ALL MY FRIENDS ARE GOING.
3.      IF ALL MY WORK IS DONE, I SHOULD BE ABLE TO GO.
4.      IF YOU LET ME GO OUT I'LL BABYSIT ALL NEXT WEEK
5.      YOU NEVER LET ME DO WHAT I WANT TO DO.
6.      I'M GOING ANYWAY!
**********

WHEN A QUESTION MARK APPEARS, TYPE THE NUMBER
OF YOUR RESPONSE FOLLOWED BY A RETURN.

YOU WILL RECEIVE POINTS BASED ON HOW SUCCESSFULL YOU
ARE AT CONVINCING YOUR FATHER.

THE ISSUE IS:
    YOU WANT TO GO OUT SATURDAY NIGHT.
     YOUR FATHER OPPOSES THE IDEA.

WHEN YOU FIRST BRING UP THE IDEA, YOUR FATHER STATES:

NO, YOU CAN'T GO OUT ON A DATE SAT. NITE AND THAT'S THAT.
HOW WOULD YOU APPROACH YOUR FATHER
WHAT WOULD YOU SAY FIRST? 2
YOUR FATHER SAID:
I DON'T THINK YOU DESERVE TO GO OUT SAT. NITE.
WHAT IS YOUR REPLY? 3
YOUR FATHER SAID:
O.K. IF YOU DO THAT YOU CAN GO OUT SAT. NIGHT.

ON A SCALE OF -7 TO 4, YOUR SCORE WAS  2  POINTS.
IT IS NOW SAT. NIGHT, WHICH DO YOU DO?
     1. GO OUT.
     2. STAY HOME.
? 1
YOU FATHER DIDN'T CHECK UP ON YOU.
YOUR SCORE IS NOW  2  POINTS.
WELL DONE!

WOULD YOU LIKE TO TRY AGAIN? YES
WHEN YOU FIRST BRING UP THE IDEA, YOUR FATHER STATES:

NO, YOU CAN'T GO OUT ON A DATE SAT. NITE AND THAT'S THAT.
HOW WOULD YOU APPROACH YOUR FATHER
WHAT WOULD YOU SAY FIRST? 1
AGREEMENT REACHED

ON A SCALE OF -7 TO 4, YOUR SCORE WAS -1  POINTS.
IT IS NOW SAT. NIGHT, WHICH DO YOU DO?
     1. GO OUT.
     2. STAY HOME.
? 2
YOUR FATHER CHECKED UP ON YOU.
YOUR SCORE IS NOW -1  POINTS.
YOU DIDN'T SUCCEED IN CONVINCING YOUR FATHER.

WOULD YOU LIKE TO TRY AGAIN? NO
Ok
```

```
LIST
100 PRINT TAB(26);"FATHER":PRINT
110 PRINT TAB(20);"CREATIVE COMPUTING"
120 PRINT TAB(18);"MORRISTOWN, NEW JERSEY "
130 PRINT:PRINT:PRINT
140 PRINT "WANT TO HAVE A DEBATE WITH YOUR FATHER, EH??":PRINT
150 DIM M$(2)
160 A=2
170 M$(2)="FATHER"
180 PRINT "DO YOU WANT INSTRUCTIONS";
190 INPUT Q1$
200 IF Q1$="YES" THEN 220
210 GOTO 310
220 PRINT "YOU ARE GOING TO PLAY IN A GAME IN WHICH YOU WILL DISCUSS"
230 PRINT "A PROBLEM WITH YOUR ";M$(A);" AND ATTEMPT TO GET HIM TO"
240 PRINT "AGREE WITH YOU IN THREE TRIES."
250 PRINT
260 PRINT "FOR EACH STATEMENT YOU MAKE, I WILL TELL YOU WHAT "
270 PRINT "YOUR ";M$(A);" REPLIED."
280 PRINT
290 PRINT "YOU MUST SELECT YOUR STATEMENT FROM ONE"
300 PRINT "OF THE FOLLOWING SIX."
310 PRINT "**********"
320 PRINT "1.      O.K. I WILL STAY HOME."
330 PRINT "2.      BUT I'D REALLY LIKE TO GO. ALL MY FRIENDS ARE GOING."
340 PRINT "3.      IF ALL MY WORK IS DONE, I SHOULD BE ABLE TO GO."
350 PRINT "4.      IF YOU LET ME GO OUT I'LL BABYSIT ALL NEXT WEEK"
360 PRINT "5.      YOU NEVER LET ME DO WHAT I WANT TO DO."
370 PRINT "6.      I'M GOING ANYWAY!"
380 PRINT "**********"
390 PRINT
400 PRINT "WHEN A QUESTION MARK APPEARS, TYPE THE NUMBER"
410 PRINT "OF YOUR RESPONSE FOLLOWED BY A RETURN."
420 PRINT
430 PRINT "YOU WILL RECEIVE POINTS BASED ON HOW SUCCESSFULL YOU"
440 PRINT "ARE AT CONVINCING YOUR FATHER."
450 PRINT
460 PRINT "THE ISSUE IS:"
470 PRINT "     YOU WANT TO GO OUT SATURDAY NIGHT."
480 PRINT "      YOUR ";M$(A);" OPPOSES THE IDEA."
490 PRINT
500 PRINT "WHEN YOU FIRST BRING UP THE IDEA, YOUR ";M$(A);" STATES:"
510 P1=-1
520 P3=2
530 P5=-1
540 C=1
550 P6=-2
560 X=0
570 I6=0
580 PRINT
590 PRINT "NO, YOU CAN'T GO OUT ON A DATE SAT. NITE AND THAT'S THAT."
600 PRINT "HOW WOULD YOU APPROACH YOUR ";M$(A)
610 PRINT "WHAT WOULD YOU SAY FIRST";:INPUT I1
620 ON I1 GOTO 720,760,1070,1070,750,700
630 PRINT "NO, YOU CAN NOT GO OUT ON A SAT. NIGHT."
640 X=X-2:I6=I6+I1
650 IF I6=I2 THEN 830
660 C=C+1
670 IF C=3 THEN 1040
680 IF I2=6 THEN 840
690 GOTO 780
700 PRINT "YOUR ";M$(A);" SAID:"
710 GOTO 630
720 PRINT "AGREEMENT REACHED"
730 X=X+P1
740 GOTO 1040
750 X=X+P5
760 PRINT "YOUR ";M$(A);" SAID:"
770 PRINT "I DON'T THINK YOU DESERVE TO GO OUT SAT. NITE."
780 PRINT "WHAT IS YOUR REPLY";
790 INPUT I2
800 ON I2 GOTO 720,960,1010,1010,950,700
810 PRINT "YOUR ";M$(A);" SAID:"
820 X=X+P3
830 PRINT "WHAT IS YOUR REPLY";
840 INPUT I3
850 ON I3 GOTO 910,1050,890,890,910,920
860 X=X+P1
870 X=X+P1
880 GOTO 1050
890 X=X+2
900 GOTO 1050
910 X=X-1:GOTO 1050
920 X=X-2
930 PRINT "DISCUSSION ENDED. NO AGREEMENT REACHED."
940 GOTO 1040
950 X=X+P5
960 PRINT "YOUR  ";M$(A);" SAID:"
970 PRINT "NO, I'M SORRY, BUT YOU REALLY DON'T DESERVE TO GO ";
980 PRINT "SAT. NIGHT."
990 PRINT "WHAT IS YOUR REPLY";:INPUT I3
1000 ON I3 GOTO 720,890,1010,1010,870,860
1010 PRINT "YOUR FATHER SAID:"
1020 X=X+P3
1030 PRINT "O.K. IF YOU DO THAT YOU CAN GO OUT SAT. NIGHT."
1040 PRINT
1050 PRINT "ON A SCALE OF -7 TO 4, YOUR SCORE WAS ";X;" POINTS."
1060 GOTO 1120
1070 PRINT "YOUR ";M$(A);" SAID:"
1080 X=X+P3
1090 PRINT "WELL, MAYBE, BUT I DON'T THINK YOU SHOULD GO."
1100 PRINT "WHAT IS YOUR REPLY";:GOTO 790
1110 PRINT
1120 PRINT "IT IS NOW SAT. NIGHT, WHICH DO YOU DO?"
1130 PRINT "     1. GO OUT."
1140 PRINT "     2. STAY HOME."
1150 INPUT Q3
1160 IF Q3 > 1 THEN 1180
1170 GOTO 1220
1180 IF I2 > 1 THEN 1200
1190 GOTO 1220
1200 IF I3 < 5 THEN 1220
1210 GOTO 1230
1220 IF RND(1) > .5 THEN 1250
1230 PRINT "YOUR FATHER CHECKED UP ON YOU."
1240 GOTO 1270
1250 PRINT "YOU FATHER DIDN'T CHECK UP ON YOU."
1260 GOTO 1270
1270 ON Q3 GOTO 1360,1280
1280 PRINT "YOUR SCORE IS NOW ";X;" POINTS."
1290 GOTO 1410
1300 IF I2=3THEN 1330
1310 IF I2=4 THEN 1330
1320 GOTO 1350
1330 X=X+1
1340 GOTO 1280
1350 ON I3 GOTO 1280,1280,1330,1330,1280,1280
1360 IF I1=1 THEN 1390
1370 ON I2 GOTO 1390,1380,1280,1280,1380,1380
1380 ON I3 GOTO 1390,1390,1280,1280,1390,1390
1390 X=X-1
1400 GOTO 1280
1410 ON X+8 GOTO 1420,1420,1420,1420,1450,1450,1450,1450,1470,1500,1500,
1500
1420 PRINT "YOU DIDN'T REALLY SUCCEED IN CHANGING YOUR"
1430 PRINT M$(A);"'S IDEAS AT ALL."
1440 GOTO 1510
1450 PRINT "YOU DIDN'T SUCCEED IN CONVINCING YOUR ";M$(A);"."
1460 GOTO 1510
1470 PRINT "YOU CONVINCED YOU ";M$(A);" BUT IT TOOK YOU TOO"
1480 PRINT "MANY TRIES."
1490 GOTO 1510
1500 PRINT "WELL DONE!"
1510 PRINT
1520 T1=T1+1
1530 PRINT "WOULD YOU LIKE TO TRY AGAIN";:INPUT Q5$
1540 IF Q5$="YES" THEN 500
1550 END
Ok
```

Flip

This game may be the only one so easy that even an animal could play it, yet hard for people to play even as well as random chance. It may be useful in training the intuition, and improving gamesmanship in speculation-type activities, where each player is trying to outguess the other's behavior and stay one step ahead.

On each turn, the program first selects 'yes' or 'no', but gives you no information about its decision. Therefore your guess on the first turn is pure chance, there is no skill involved. But soon the program starts using patterns in your behavior, making its decisions to increase the chance of your next guess being wrong. And to make it harder for you, the program doesn't strictly maximize its chances, but throws a little randomness into its decisions.

Variations

There are endless strategies for programming this game, for there could be almost infinitely many definitions of what a "pattern" is. No single algorithm could be "best", because it must assume a model of the human player, and people are different, even the same person from moment to moment. Any good algorithm must build or refine its model of the player, during the course of the game.

This particular program keeps an array of 16 probability estimates; the person's last two guesses, and whether they were right or wrong (16 situations altogether) determine which estimate is selected. The array (which depends on all previous play within the game) becomes a model or profile of the player, and it can be printed at end of game. Any probabilities far from .5 indicate predictable behavior in the corresponding situations. The profiles can be compared over time, or used to study strategy differences between people. They can also be compared with random profiles developed by playing games with random input such as coin flips, or (more easily) by modifying the program so that BASIC statements replace the human player and make guesses randomly (or by some other rule). In fact, different algorithms could play each other.

This particular implementation has two parameters: a memory factor (F1) which controls the decay rate of old learning when it is overridden by recent experience, and a randomness factor (F2) influencing the program's likelihood of making the decision suggested by the probability estimate. These are just two of innumerable optional parameters which could be used in programming FLIP.

The program and description were written by John S. James. They originally appeared in *Creative Computing*, Mar/Apr 1977.

```
RUN
                                   FLIP
                            CREATIVE COMPUTING
                           MORRISTOWN  NEW JERSEY


EXPLANATION (Y OR N)? Y
ON EACH TURN, YOU GUESS YES ('Y') OR NO ('N').
ONLY ONE IS CORRECT, AND THE PROGRAM HAS DECIDED
WHICH ONE, BEFORE YOU MAKE YOUR GUESS. AT FIRST
YOUR ODDS ARE 50%, PURE CHANCE. BUT LATER THE
PROGRAM WILL TRY TO TAKE ADVANTAGE OF PATTERNS
IN YOUR GUESSING.

GAME ENDS AFTER  50  TURNS; A SCORE OF  24  OR MORE
IS GOOD. PROGRAM TELLS WHEN YOU WIN A TURN,
BY TYPING AN ASTERISK ('*') AS THE FIRST
CHARACTER OF THE FOLLOWING LINE.



BEGIN.
 ? N
 ? Y
*? Y
 ? N
 ? Y
 ? Y
 ? Y
*? Y
 ? N
 ? Y
 ? Y
 ? N
*? N
*? N
*? N
*? N
 ? Y
 ? Y
 ? Y
 ? N
*? N
 ? N
*? Y
*? N
*? Y
 ? N
 ? N
*? N
*? Y
 ? N
 ? N
 ? Y
*? Y
*? N
 ? Y
 ? N
*? N
 ? Y
 ? N
*? N
 ? Y
 ? Y
*? Y
 ? N
 ? N
 ? Y
 ? Y
 ? Y
 ? Y
 ? Y

END OF GAME.
YOU GOT  17  OUT OF  50  CORRECT.


PLAY AGAIN (Y OR N)? N
OK
```

```
LIST

10 PRINT TAB(25);"FLIP"
20 PRINT TAB(18);"CREATIVE COMPUTING"
30 PRINT TAB(16);"MORRISTOWN  NEW JERSEY":PRINT:PRINT:PRINT
31 B1=50
32 PRINT "EXPLANATION (Y OR N)";
34 INPUT T$
36 IF LEFT$(T$,1) <> "Y" THEN 180
50 PRINT "ON EACH TURN, YOU GUESS YES ('Y') OR NO ('N')."
60 PRINT "ONLY ONE IS CORRECT, AND THE PROGRAM HAS DECIDED"
70 PRINT "WHICH ONE, BEFORE YOU MAKE YOUR GUESS. AT FIRST"
80 PRINT "YOUR ODDS ARE 50%, PURE CHANCE. BUT LATER THE"
90 PRINT "PROGRAM WILL TRY TO TAKE ADVANTAGE OF PATTERNS"
100 PRINT "IN YOUR GUESSING."
110 PRINT
120 PRINT "GAME ENDS AFTER ";B1;" TURNS; A SCORE OF ";
125 PRINT INT(B1/2-1);" OR MORE"
130 PRINT "IS GOOD. PROGRAM TELLS WHEN YOU WIN A TURN,"
140 PRINT "BY TYPING AN ASTERISK ('*') AS THE FIRST"
150 PRINT "CHARACTER OF THE FOLLOWING LINE."
160 PRINT
170 REM
180 REM INIALIZE: 16 PROBABILITIES, 4 RESPONSES (X),
190 REM OLD-MEMORY FACTOR (F1), RANDOMNESS FACTOR (F2),
200 REM SCORES (S1,S2) AND RIGHT-ANSWER FLAG.
210 PRINT
220 PRINT
230 DIM P(16),X(4)
240 PRINT "BEGIN."
250 FOR I=1 TO 16
260 P(I)=.5
270 NEXT I
280 FOR I=1 TO 4
290 X(I)=0
300 IF RND(1) < .5 THEN 320
310 X(I)=1
320 NEXT I
330 F1=.8
340 F2=.3
350 S1=0
360 S2=0
370 A$=" "
380 REM
390 REM TAKE THE ESTIMATED PROBABILITY (Z1)
400 REM OF THE PERSON GUESSING YES.
410 REM USE AN ADJUSTED PROBABILITY (Z2).
420 I9=8*X(4)+4*X(3)+2*X(2)+X(1)+1
430 Z1=P(I9)
440 Z2=Z1
450 IF Z2 <> .5 THEN 480
460 Z2=RND(1)
470 GOTO 520
480 IF Z2 > .5 THEN 510
490 Z2=Z2*F2+0*(1-F2)
500 GOTO 520
510 Z2=Z2*F2+1*(1-F2)
520 Z5=0
530 IF RND(1) < Z2 THEN 560
540 Z5=1
550 REM
560 REM INTERACT WITH PERSON. GET HIS RESPONSE (Z3).
570 REM UPDATE RESPONSE HISTORY (X), APPROPRIATE PROB. (P(I9)).
580 PRINT A$;
590 Z3=0
600 INPUT H$
610 IF LEFT$(H$,1) = "Y" THEN 650
620 IF LEFT$(H$,1) ="N" THEN 660
630 PRINT "ERROR, MUST BE  Y  OR  N  ."
640 GOTO 600
650 Z3=1
660 A$=" "
670 S2=S2+1
680 IF Z3 <> Z5 THEN 710
690 A$="*"
700 S1=S1+1
710 REM UPDATE X - THE LAST 4 CHOISES.
720 X(1)=X(3)
730 X(2)=X(4)
740 X(3)=Z3
750 X(4)=Z5
760 REM UPDATE THE PROBABILITY USING OLD I9.
770 P(I9)=F1*P(I9)+(1-F1)*X(3)
780 IF S2 < B1 THEN 380
790 PRINT A$;
800 PRINT
810 PRINT "END OF GAME."
820 PRINT "YOU GOT ";S1;" OUT OF ";S2;" CORRECT."
830 PRINT:PRINT
840 PRINT "PLAY AGAIN (Y OR N)";
850 INPUT T$
860 IF LEFT$(T$,1)="Y" THEN 240
870 END
OK
```

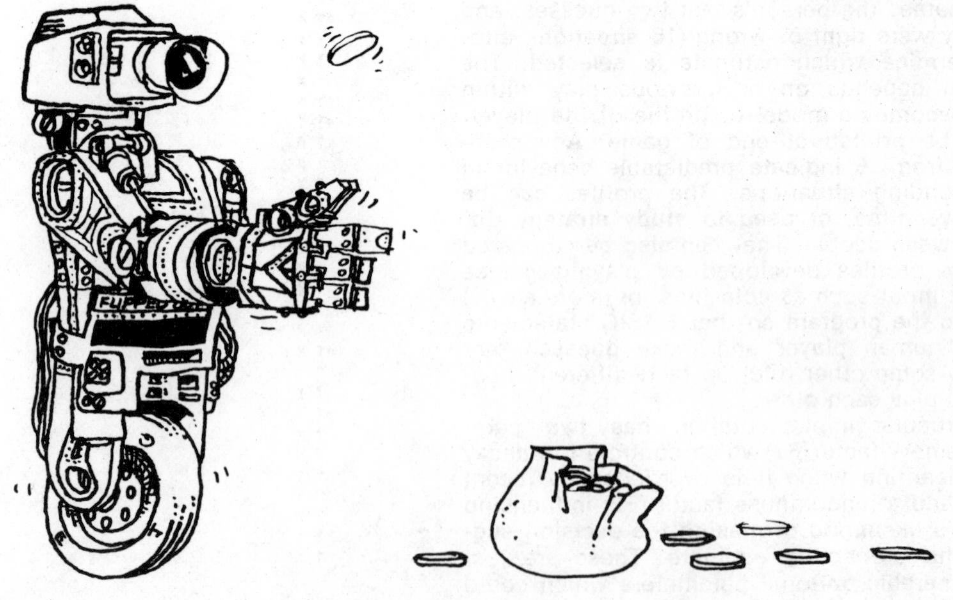

Four In A Row

In this game, eight pegs are put in a row, each one of which can hold eight rings. Each ring is marked with either an X or an O. You and an opponent alternate turns; in this case the opponent is the computer. On each turn you place a ring over one of the pegs, one through eight. The object is to get four X's or O's in a row, vertically, horizontally or diagonally. A glance at the sample run will show you how this process works.

While the computer already plays rather well, you may wish to experiment with improving the computer's play by changing the values in the data statements in lines 120 and 130. The first four values are awarded if a position yields one, two, three, or four in a row respectively, for the computer. The next four values are bonus points for making one, two, three, or four in a row in more than one direction with the same move. The next eight values (line 130) are dealt with in the same way for the human player; thus, these values are for defense.

The computer version of the game was written by James L. Murphy.

```
RUN
                FOUR IN A ROW
             CREATIVE COMPUTING
           MORRISTOWN, NEW JERSEY



THE GAME OF FOUR IN A ROW
DO YOU WANT INSTRUCTIONS? YES
THE GAME CONSISTS OF STACKING X'S
AND O'S (THE COMPUTER HAS O) UNTIL
ONE OF THE PLAYERS GETS FOUR IN A
ROW VERTICALLY, HORIZONTALLY, OR
DIAGONALLY.


DO YOU WANT TO GO FIRST? YES
  -  -  -  -  -  -  -  -
  -  -  -  -  -  -  -  -
  -  -  -  -  -  -  -  -
  -  -  -  -  -  -  -  -
  -  -  -  -  -  -  -  -
  -  -  -  -  -  -  -  -
  -  -  -  -  -  -  -  -
  -  -  -  -  -  -  -  -
  1  2  3  4  5  6  7  8

A NUMBER BETWEEN 1 AND 8? 4

  -  -  -  -  -  -  -  -
  -  -  -  -  -  -  -  -
  -  -  -  -  -  -  -  -
  -  -  -  -  -  -  -  -
  -  -  -  -  -  -  -  -
  -  -  -  -  -  -  -  -
  -  -  -  -  -  -  -  -
  -  -  -  X  -  -  -  -
  1  2  3  4  5  6  7  8

COMPUTER PICKS COLUMN  4

  -  -  -  -  -  -  -  -
  -  -  -  -  -  -  -  -
  -  -  -  -  -  -  -  -
  -  -  -  -  -  -  -  -
  -  -  -  -  -  -  -  -
  -  -  -  -  -  -  -  -
  -  -  -  O  -  -  -  -
  -  -  -  X  -  -  -  -
  1  2  3  4  5  6  7  8

A NUMBER BETWEEN 1 AND 8? 5
  -  -  -  -  -  -  -  -
  -  -  -  -  -  -  -  -
  -  -  -  -  -  -  -  -
  -  -  -  -  -  -  -  -
  -  -  -  -  -  -  -  -
  -  -  -  O  X  -  -  -
  -  -  O  O  X  -  -  -
  X  O  X  X  O  -  -  X
  1  2  3  4  5  6  7  8

COMPUTER PICKS COLUMN  5

  -  -  -  -  -  -  -  -
  -  -  -  -  -  -  -  -
  -  -  -  -  -  -  -  -
  -  -  -  -  -  -  -  -
  -  -  -  -  O  -  -  -
  -  -  -  O  X  -  -  -
  -  -  O  O  X  -  -  -
  X  O  X  X  O  -  -  X
  1  2  3  4  5  6  7  8

C O M P U T E R   W I N S !!!
```

```
10 PRINT TAB(22);"FOUR IN A ROW"
20 PRINT TAB(20);"CREATIVE COMPUTING"
30 PRINT TAB(18);"MORRISTOWN, NEW JERSEY"
40 PRINT:PRINT:PRINT
100 DIM B$(8,8),L(8),S(4),F(4)
110 DIM V(16),N(4)
130 DATA 1,100,500,1E20,1,800,4000,1E20
140 DATA 1,75,900,1E18,1,450,3000,1E18
150 FOR Z1=1 TO 16:READ V(Z1):NEXT Z1
160 PRINT"THE GAME OF FOUR IN A ROW"
170 INPUT"DO YOU WANT INSTRUCTIONS";A$
180 IF A$="NO" THEN 270
190 IF A$="YES" THEN 210
200 PRINT"YES OR NO":GOTO 170
210 PRINT"THE GAME CONSISTS OF STACKING X'S"
220 PRINT"AND O'S (THE COMPUTER HAS O) UNTIL"
230 PRINT"ONE OF THE PLAYERS GETS FOUR IN A"
240 PRINT"ROW VERTICALLY, HORIZONTALLY, OR "
250 PRINT"DIAGONALLY."
260 PRINT:PRINT
270 X$="X":O$="O"
280 FOR I=1 TO 8:FOR J=1 TO 8:B$(I,J)="-":NEXT J:NEXT I
290 FOR Z1=1 TO 8:L(Z1)=0:NEXT Z1
300 INPUT"DO YOU WANT TO GO FIRST";A$
310 IF A$="NO" THEN 610
320 GOSUB 340
330 GOTO 450
340 FOR I=8 TO 1 STEP -1
350 FOR J=1 TO 8
360 PRINT"  ";B$(I,J);
370 NEXT J
380 PRINT
390 NEXT I
400 PRINT" ";
410 FOR I=1 TO 8:PRINT I;:NEXT I
420 PRINT:PRINT
430 RETURN
440 PRINT"ILLEGAL MOVE, TRY AGAIN."
450 INPUT"A NUMBER BETWEEN 1 AND 8";M
460 M=INT(M)
470 IF M<1 OR M>8 THEN 440
480 L=L(M)
490 IF L>7 THEN 440
500 L(M)=L+1:L=L+1
510 B$(L,M)=X$
520 PRINT
530 GOSUB 340
540 P$=X$
550 GOSUB 1240
560 FOR Z=1 TO 4
570 IF S(Z)<4 THEN 600
580 PRINT"Y O U   W I N !!!"
590 GOTO 1580
600 NEXT Z
610 M9=0:V1=0
620 N1=1
630 FOR M4=1 TO 8
640 L=L(M4)+1
650 IF L>8 THEN 1080
660 V=1
670 P$=O$:W=0
680 M=M4
690 GOSUB 1240
700 FOR Z1=1 TO 4:N(Z1)=0:NEXT Z1
710 FOR Z=1 TO 4
720 S=S(Z)
730 IF S-W>3 THEN 1130
740 T=S+F(Z)
750 IF T<4 THEN 780
760 V=V+4
770 N(S)=N(S)+1
780 NEXT Z
790 FOR I = 1 TO 4
800 N=N(I)-1
810 IF N=-1 THEN 840
820 I1=8*W+4*SGN(N)+I
830 V=V + V(I1) + N*V(8*W+I)
840 NEXT I
850 IF W=1 THEN 880
860 W=1:P$=X$
870 GOTO 690
880 L=L+1
920 IF L>8 THEN 1020
930 GOSUB 1240
940 FOR Z=1 TO 4
950 IF S(Z)>3 THEN V=2
960 NEXT Z
1020 IF V<V1 THEN 1080
1030 IF V>V1 THEN N1=1: GOTO 1060
1040 N1=N1 + 1
1050 IF RND(1)>1/N1 THEN 1080
1060 V1 = V
1070 M9=M4
1080 NEXT M4
1090 IF M9<>0 THEN 1120
1100 PRINT "T I E   G A M E ..."
1110 GOTO 1580
1120 M=M9
1130 PRINT "COMPUTER PICKS COLUMN ";M:PRINT
1140 L=L(M)+1:L(M)=L(M)+1
1150 B$(L,M)=O$
1160 P$=O$:GOSUB 340
1170 GOSUB 1240
1180 FOR Z = 1 TO 4
1190 IF S(Z)<4 THEN 1220
1200 PRINT"C O M P U T E R   W I N S !!!"
1210 GOTO 1580
1220 NEXT Z
1230 GOTO 450
1240 Q$=X$
1250 IF P$=X$ THEN Q$=O$
1260 D2=1:D1=0
1270 Z=0
1280 GOSUB 1360
1290 D1=1:D2=1
1300 GOSUB 1360
1310 D2=0:D1=1
1320 GOSUB 1360
1330 D2=-1:D1=1
1340 GOSUB 1360
1350 RETURN
1360 D=1:S=1
1370 T=0
1380 Z=Z+1
1390 C=0
1400 FOR K=1 TO 3
1410 M5=M+K*D1:L1=L+K*D2
1420 IF M5<1 OR L1<1 OR M5>8 OR L1>8 THEN 1510
1430 B$=B$(L1,M5)
1440 IF C=0 THEN 1480
1450 IF B$=Q$ THEN K=3: GOTO 1510
1460 T = T+1
1470 GOTO 1510
1480 IF B$=P$ THEN S=S+1:GOTO 1510
1490 C=1
1500 GOTO 1450
1510 NEXT K
1520 IF D=0 THEN 1550
1530 D=0:D1=-D1:D2=-D2
1540 GOTO 1390
1550 S(Z)=S
1560 F(Z)=T
1570 RETURN
1580 END
```

Geowar

This program very loosely represents a battlefield in which you, the player, are located at point 0,0. There are five enemy installations that may be located anywhere from 0,0 to 30,30 except for a clear zone from 0,0 to 10,10. The accompanying diagram should make this clear. Instead of the normal artillery type of game where you are lobbing projectiles onto your enemy installations, in this game you are firing some sort of laser missile in a very straight path which destroys everything in its path. If the missile flies within one unit either northwest or southeast of the target, or, of course, over the target directly, that target is destroyed. If it is within two units of the target, the missile will be shot down and that target will relocate to a new position one unit away from its previous position in some random direction.

Geowar is largely a guessing game with incomplete information given in its clues. Nevertheless it's fun to play and is a nice switch from just a plain "guess the mystery number game." It was written by Gary Lorenc and originally appeared in *Creative Computing*, May/June 1975.

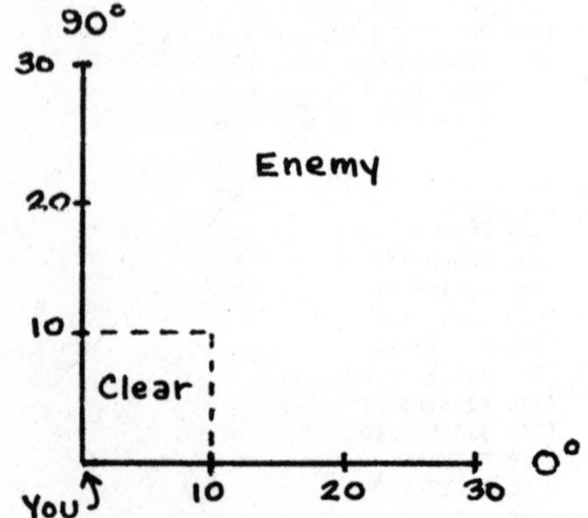


```
RUN
                              GEOWAR
                         CREATIVE COMPUTING
                       MORRISTOWN, NEW JERSEY



DO YOU WANT A DESCRIPTION OF THE GAME? YES

     THE FIRST QUADRANT OF A REGULAR COORDINATE GRAPH WILL SERVE AS
THE BATTLEFIELD.  FIVE ENEMY INSTALLATIONS ARE LOCATED WITHIN A
30 BY 30 UNIT AREA.  NO TARGET IS INSIDE THE 10 BY 10 UNIT AREA
ADJACENT TO THE ORIGIN, AS THIS IS THE LOCATION OF OUR BASE. WHEN
THE MACHINE ASKS FOR THE DEGREE OF THE SHOT, RESPOND WITH A NUMBER
BETWEEN 1 AND 90.

                                                         SCARE**********
    1. A DIRECT HIT IS A HIT WITHIN 1 DEGREE OF          *             *
        THE TARGET.                                      *  HIT******  *
    2. A HIT MUST PASS BETWEEN THE FIRST SET OF          *  *       *  *
        INTEGRAL POINTS NW AND SE OF THE TARGET.         *  *   D   *  *
    3. A SCARE MUST PASS BETWEEN THE NEXT SET OF         *  *       *  *
        INTEGRAL POINTS NW AND SE OF THE TARGET,         *  ******HIT  *
        AND CAUSES THE ENEMY TO RELOCATE A               *             *
        MAXIMUM OF 1 UNIT IN ANY DIRECTION.              **********SCARE


     MISSLES HAVE INFINITE RANGE AND MAY HIT MORE THAN ONE TARGET.
A MISSILE THAT NEARLY MISSES AN INSTALLATION (A SCARE) WILL BE
IMMEDIATELY SHOT DOWN.  ANY HITS BEFORE THIS TIME WILL NOT BE COUNTED
UNLESS A DIRECT HIT WAS MADE.


READY TO GO? YES
GOOD LUCK!


ENTER DEGREE OF SHOT? 25
NO LUCK -- TRY AGAIN.

ENTER DEGREE OF SHOT? 35
A NEAR HIT.  ENEMY HAS RELOCATED.

ENTER DEGREE OF SHOT? 47
NO LUCK -- TRY AGAIN.

ENTER DEGREE OF SHOT? 37
****BULLS EYE****  2  HITS -- A DIRECT HIT ON 1  OF THEM!
 2  DOWN -- 3  TO GO.

ENTER DEGREE OF SHOT? 58
NO LUCK -- TRY AGAIN.

ENTER DEGREE OF SHOT? 75
A NEAR HIT.  ENEMY HAS RELOCATED.

ENTER DEGREE OF SHOT? 77
A NEAR HIT.  ENEMY HAS RELOCATED.

ENTER DEGREE OF SHOT? 78
NO LUCK -- TRY AGAIN.

ENTER DEGREE OF SHOT? 74
A NEAR HIT.  ENEMY HAS RELOCATED.

ENTER DEGREE OF SHOT? 76
A NEAR HIT.  ENEMY HAS RELOCATED.

ENTER DEGREE OF SHOT? 73
NO LUCK -- TRY AGAIN.

ENTER DEGREE OF SHOT? 75
NO LUCK -- TRY AGAIN.

ENTER DEGREE OF SHOT? 76
**CONGRATULATIONS**  A HIT.
 3  DOWN -- 2  TO GO.

ENTER DEGREE OF SHOT? 80
NO LUCK -- TRY AGAIN.

ENTER DEGREE OF SHOT? 85
NO LUCK -- TRY AGAIN.

ENTER DEGREE OF SHOT? 60
NO LUCK -- TRY AGAIN.

ENTER DEGREE OF SHOT? 40
NO LUCK -- TRY AGAIN.

ENTER DEGREE OF SHOT? 35
NO LUCK -- TRY AGAIN.

ENTER DEGREE OF SHOT? 20
NO LUCK -- TRY AGAIN.

ENTER DEGREE OF SHOT? 10
****BULLS EYE****  A DIRECT HIT!
 4  DOWN -- 1  TO GO.

ENTER DEGREE OF SHOT? 50
TOO LOW -- TRY AGAIN.

ENTER DEGREE OF SHOT? 62
A NEAR HIT.  ENEMY HAS RELOCATED.

ENTER DEGREE OF SHOT? 63
A NEAR HIT.  ENEMY HAS RELOCATED.

ENTER DEGREE OF SHOT? 67
A NEAR HIT.  ENEMY HAS RELOCATED.

ENTER DEGREE OF SHOT? 69
****BULLS EYE****  A DIRECT HIT!

GAME TOTALS: 2  HITS AND 3  DIRECT HITS ON 27  SHOTS.
```

```
LIST
1 PRINT TAB(26);"GEOWAR"
2 PRINT TAB(20);"CREATIVE COMPUTING"
3 PRINT TAB(18);"MORRISTOWN, NEW JERSEY"
4 PRINT:PRINT:PRINT
5 PRINT "DO YOU WANT A DESCRIPTION OF THE GAME";
6 INPUT I$
7 IF I$="NO" THEN 46
8 PRINT
9 PRINT "     THE FIRST QUADRANT OF A REGULAR COORDINATE GRAPH WILL";
10 PRINT " SERVE AS"
11 PRINT "THE BATTLEFIELD.  FIVE ENEMY INSTALLATIONS ARE LOCATED";
12 PRINT " WITHIN A"
13 PRINT "30 BY 30 UNIT AREA.  NO TARGET IS INSIDE THE 10 BY 10 ";
14 PRINT "UNIT AREA"
15 PRINT "ADJACENT TO THE ORIGIN, AS THIS IS THE LOCATION OF OUR ";
16 PRINT "BASE. WHEN"
17 PRINT "THE MACHINE ASKS FOR THE DEGREE OF THE SHOT, RESPOND ";
18 PRINT "WITH A NUMBER"
19 PRINT "BETWEEN 1 AND 90."
20 PRINT
21 PRINT TAB(51),"SCARE**********"
22 PRINT "    1. A DIRECT HIT IS A HIT WITHIN 1 DEGREE OF";
23 PRINT TAB(51),"*             *"
24 PRINT "          THE TARGET.",TAB(51),"*  HIT******  *"
25 PRINT "    2. A HIT MUST PASS BETWEEN THE FIRST SET OF";
26 PRINT TAB(51),"*  *        *  *"
27 PRINT "           INTEGRAL POINTS NW AND SE OF THE TARGET.";
28 PRINT TAB(51),"*  *   D   *  *"
29 PRINT "    3. A SCARE MUST PASS BETWEEN THE NEXT SET OF";
30 PRINT TAB(51), "*  *   D   *  *"
31 PRINT "           INTEGRAL POINTS NW AND SE OF THE TARGET,";
32 PRINT TAB(51),"*  ******HIT  *"
33 PRINT "           AND CAUSES THE ENEMY TO RELOCATE A ";
34 PRINT TAB(51),"*             *"
35 PRINT "           MAXIMUM OF 1 UNIT IN ANY DIRECTION.";
36 PRINT TAB(51),"**********SCARE"
37 PRINT
38 PRINT
39 PRINT "    MISSLES HAVE INFINITE RANGE AND MAY HIT MORE THAN ";
40 PRINT "ONE TARGET."
41 PRINT "A MISSILE THAT NEARLY MISSES AN INSTALLATION (A SCARE) ";
42 PRINT "WILL BE"
43 PRINT "IMMEDIATELY SHOT DOWN.  ANY HITS BEFORE THIS TIME WILL ";
44 PRINT "NOT BE COUNTED"
45 PRINT "UNLESS A DIRECT HIT WAS MADE."
46 PRINT
47 PRINT
48 PRINT "READY TO GO";
49 INPUT R$
50 IF R$="NO" THEN 192
51 PRINT "GOOD LUCK!"
52 PRINT
53 DIM C(10),H(20),D(10),S(20),F(5)
54 DEF FNV(V1)=INT((180/3.14159)*ATN(V1)+.5)
55 X=250
56 X1=RND(1)
57 G2=0
58 S2=0
59 D2=0
60 H2=0
61 FOR K=1 TO 10
62 GOSUB 154
63 IF INT(K/2)<>K/2 THEN 70
64 IF C(K-1)>10 THEN 70
65 IF C(K)>10 THEN 70
66 FOR L=K-1 TO K
67 GOSUB 154
68 NEXT L
69 GOTO 63
70 NEXT K
71 S=0
72 FOR L=1 TO 5
73 D(L)=FNV(C(2*L)/C(2*L-1))
74 NEXT L
75 A=2
76 L1=10
77 T5=5
78 D5=0
79 H5=0
80 GOSUB 147
81 PRINT
82 PRINT "ENTER DEGREE OF SHOT";
83 D1=0
84 H1=0
85 FOR Q=1 TO 5
86 F(Q)=20
87 NEXT Q
88 INPUT D
89 IF D>=90 THEN 81
90 ON SGN(D)+2 GOTO 177,192
91 S=S+1
92 FOR A=2 TO 10 STEP 2
93 IF D>S(A) THEN 103
94 IF D<S(A-1) THEN 103
95 IF D>H(A) THEN 105
96 IF D<H(A-1) THEN 105
97 IF D>D(A/2)+1 THEN 101
98 IF D<D(A/2)-1 THEN 101
99 D1=D1+1
100 GOTO 102
101 H1=H1+1
102 F(D1+H1)=A
103 NEXT A
104 GOTO 108
105 IF D1>0 THEN 110
106 GOSUB 138
107 GOTO 81
108 IF D1+H1<>0 THEN 112
109 IF T5=1 THEN 159
110 PRINT "NO LUCK -- TRY AGAIN."
111 GOTO 81
112 IF D1>0 THEN 118
113 IF H1>1 THEN 116
114 PRINT "**CONGRATULATIONS**  A HIT."
115 GOTO 124
116 PRINT "**CONGRATULATIONS**";H1;"HITS."
117 GOTO 124
118 PRINT "****BULLS EYE**** ";
119 IF D1>1 THEN 123
120 IF H1>0 THEN 123
121 PRINT " A DIRECT HIT!"
122 GOTO 124
123 PRINT D1+H1;" HITS -- A DIRECT HIT ON";D1;" OF THEM!"
124 T5=T5-(D1+H1)
125 D5=D5+D1
126 H5=H5+H1
127 IF T5=0 THEN `167
128 FOR J=1 TO H1+D1
129 Z=F(J)
130 D(Z/2)=0
131 H(Z)=0
132 H(Z-1)=0
133 S(Z)=0
134 S(Z-1)=0
135 NEXT J
136 PRINT 5-T5;" DOWN --";T5;" TO GO."
137 GOTO 81
138 PRINT "A NEAR HIT.  ENEMY HAS RELOCATED."
139 FOR R=1 TO 2
140 X2=INT(RND(1)*100)
141 IF ABS(C(A-(R-1))-X2)>1 THEN 140
142 IF C(A-(R-1))<=2 THEN 140
143 C(A-(R-1))=X2
144 NEXT R
145 D(A/2)=FNV(C(A)/C(A-1))
146 L1=A
147 FOR I=A TO L1 STEP 2
148 H(I-1)=FNV((C(I)-1)/(C(I-1)+1))
149 H(I)=FNV((C(I)+1)/(C(I-1)-1))
150 S(I-1)=FNV((C(I)-2)/(C(I-1)+2))
151 S(I)=FNV((C(I)+2)/(C(I-1)-2))
152 NEXT I
153 RETURN
154 R=INT(RND(1)*100)
155 IF R>30 THEN 154
156 IF R<3 THEN 154
157 C(K)=R
158 RETURN
159 FOR Z1=1 TO 5
160 IF D(Z1)>1 THEN 162
161 NEXT Z1
162 IF D<D(Z1) THEN 165
163 PRINT "TOO HIGH -- TRY AGAIN."
164 GOTO 81
165 PRINT "TOO LOW -- TRY AGAIN."
166 GOTO 81
167 PRINT
168 PRINT "GAME TOTALS:";H5;" HITS AND";D5;" DIRECT HITS ON";S;" SHOTS."
169 PRINT
170 PRINT "READY FOR A NEW GAME";
171 G2=G2+1
172 S2=S2+S
173 D2=D2+D5
174 H2=H2+H5
175 INPUT G$
176 IF G$="NO" THEN 184
177 PRINT
178 PRINT
179 PRINT
180 PRINT "FIVE NEW INSTALLATIONS HAVE BEEN BUILT AT DIFFERENT ";
181 PRINT "LOCATIONS."
182 PRINT "GOOD LUCK!"
183 GOTO 61
184 PRINT
185 PRINT
186 PRINT "TOTALS FOR";G2;" GAMES:";H2;" HITS AND";D2
187 PRINT " DIRECT HITS ON";S2;" SHOTS."
188 PRINT "AN AVERAGE OF";S2/(D2+H2);" SHOTS PER TARGET."
192 END
Ok
```

Grand Prix

In this program, you are attempting to complete one lap around a grand prix circuit against one of six opponents, everything from a US Postal delivery truck to a 1974 Ferrari. The track consists of four straightaways and four curves with different maximum speeds possible for each one. Depending on which car you select for your own, you can take these curves and straights at different speeds. Also, the car you select will have different braking characteristics which may allow you to head into a curve at a higher speed and then apply the brakes at the last minute.

It may sound like it's easy to win by simply selecting a Porsche or Ferrari for your car and racing against a US Mail truck or a well-used Ford Mustang, but beware, it isn't really that easy.

The origin of this game is a bit hazy. The only thing that identifies it is PUC. Could this be Pacific Union College? Perhaps, but we're not really sure.

```
RUN
                          GRNPRX
                    CREATIVE COMPUTING
                  MORRISTOWN, NEW JERSEY



WELCOME TO THE PUC GRAN PRIX

DO YOU WANT A COURSE DESCRIPTION? YES

                        2                                            1
                     CCOXPXXXXXXXXXXXXXXXXXXXXXXXXXXXXXXXXXXXXXXXXXXOCC
            85-100 CC (800)                                           C
                   C                                                   C
               3 0   PUC GRAN PRIX RACE                                C
                 X                                                    C
                X                                                   CC
               X                        SS                    (2800) C 50-
              X        SSSSSSS    SSS  SSSOXXXXXXXXXXXXXXXXXXPXXOC   70
             X       SS        SSSSSSS       7                    8
            X (1900)0 6    90-110
           X       X
          X       X         DISTANCES IN YARDS, EG. (800) = 800 YDS.
         X       X   SPEEDS IN MPH, EG. 85 TO 100 MPH.
        P     X
       X       X
      X       X
    X       X
 4 0(1500) X
 H         X
 H        X
20-H    0 5
 35 H   H
     HH


 1 TO 2 IS A STRAIGHTAWAY 800 YARDS LONG
 2 TO 3 IS A CURVE 200 YARDS LONG
     THE BREAKAWAY SPEED RANGE IS 85 TO 100 MPH
 3 TO 4 IS A STRAIGHTAWAY 500 YARDS LONG
     IT ENDS AT POSITION 1500 YARDS FROM STARTING GRID
 4 TO 5 IS A HAIRPIN CURVE 100 YARDS LONG
     THE BREAKAWAY SPEED RANGE IS 20 TO 35 MPH
 5 TO 6 IS ANOTHER STRAIGHTAWAY 300 YARDS LONG
     IT ENDS AT POSITION 1900 YARDS FROM THE GRID
 6 TO 7 IS A SET OF 'S' CURVES 500 YARDS LONG
     THE SPEED RANGE IS 90-110 MPH
 7 TO 8 IS THE FINAL STRAIGHTAWAY OF 400 YARDS
     IT ENTERS THE LAST CURVE AT 2800 YARDS
 8 TO 9 IS THE FINAL CURVE OF 400 YARDS
     THE BREAKAWAY SPEED RANGE IS 50 TO 70 MPH

 THE TOTAL LENGTH OF ONE LAP IS 3200 YARDS
```

```
DURING THE STRAIGHTAWAYS YOU WILL BE ABLE TO CONTROL THE
ACCELERATION AND BRAKING OF THE CAR.  THE CURVES WILL BE TAKEN
AT WHATEVER SPEED YOU ENTER THEM.
BELOW THE BREAKAWAY SPEED, THE CURVES MAY BE TAKEN WITH NO DIFFICULTY.
ABOVE THE FASTEST SPEED INDICATED, YOU WILL CRASH!!
WITHIN THE SPEED RANGE, THERE IS THE POSSIBILITY THAT YOU MIGHT
LOSE TIME OR SPEED BY SWINGING WIDE OR BY SPINNING OUT.
THE FASTER YOU TAKE THE CURVES, THE GREATER THE RISKS--
AND THE LESS THE TIME!!!!


YOUR TASK IS TO TRANSVERSE THE TRACK IN A MINIMUM OF TIME
WITHOUT CRASHING!!!

YOUR CAR MAY BE ONE OF THE FOLLOWING:
1. PORSCHE
2. FERRARI
3. MASERATI
4. LOTUS FORD
WHICH CAR WOULD YOU LIKE? 4
YOUR CAR HAS A MAXIMUM ACCELERATION OF  8 MPH/SEC.
AND A MAXIMUM BRAKING OF -30 MPH/SEC.
YOU WILL RACE AGAINST ONE OF THE FOLLOWING:
1. U.S. POSTAL DELIVERY TRUCK
2. 1970 BEAT PONTIAC GTO
3. 1966 WELL USED FORD MUSTANG
4. LOTUS FORD
5. 1974 FERRARA
6. THE PHYSICS SUPERCHARGED LIGHTBEAM SPECIAL
CHOOSE ONE OPPONENT BY ENTERING NUMBER? 2

ELAPSED TIME  SPEED          POSITION       OPPONENT'S     ACCELERATION
  SECONDS      MPH             YARDS         POSITION

    0           0              0             0              ? 8
    2           16             7             3              ? 8
    4           32             31            16             ? 8
    6           48             70            48             ? 8
    8           64             125           94             ? 8
    10          80             195           156            ? 8
    12          96             281           235            ? 8
    14          112            383           328            ? 8
    16          128            500           438            ? -20
    18          88             606           565            ? 5
    20          98             697           700            ? -2
    22          94             791           792            ? 0
CURVE 2 -3 ,  SPEED 94 MPH
    26.4        94             1000          977            ? 0
    28.4        94             1091          1056           ? 0
    30.4        94             1183          1156           ? 0
    32.4        94             1275          1269           ? -30
    34.4        34             1338          1378           ? 8
    36.4        50             1379          1458           ? 8
    38.4        66             1436          1498           ? 8
LOST CONTROL AT 80 MPH.  YOUR CAR CRASHED!!
YOUR OPPONENT FINISHED IN  91.0926 SECONDS!
```

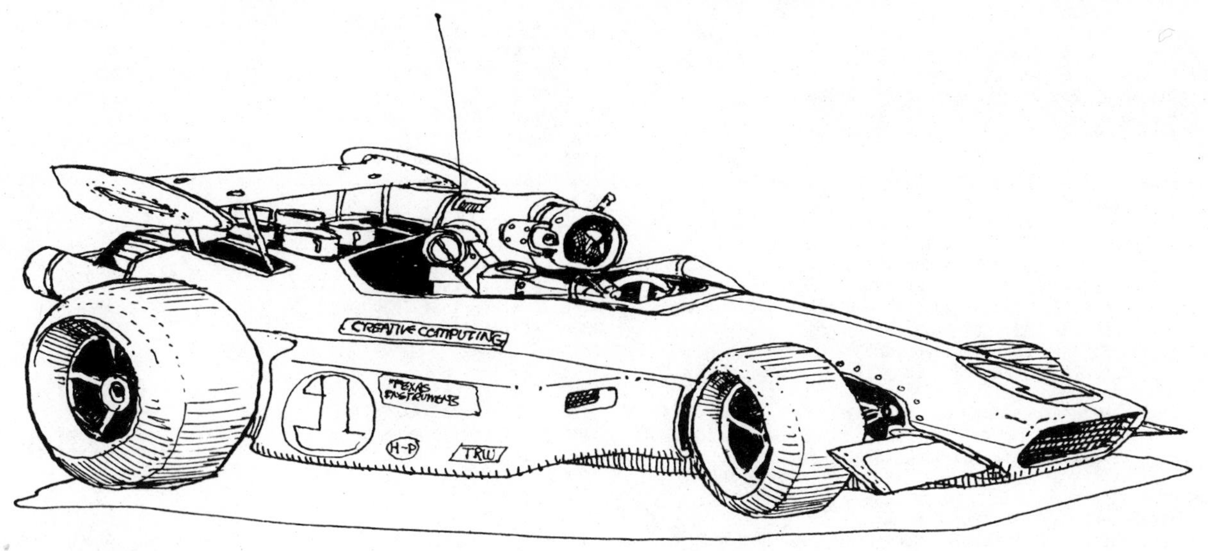


```
DO YOU WISH TO TRY AGAIN? YES
YOUR CAR MAY BE ONE OF THE FOLLOWING:
1. PORSCHE
2. FERRARI
3. MASERATI
4. LOTUS FORD
WHICH CAR WOULD YOU LIKE? 3
YOUR CAR HAS A MAXIMUM ACCELERATION OF  12 MPH/SEC.
AND A MAXIMUM BRAKING OF -22 MPH/SEC.
YOU WILL RACE AGAINST ONE OF THE FOLLOWING:
1. U.S. POSTAL DELIVERY TRUCK
2. 1970 BEAT PONTIAC GTO
3. 1966 WELL USED FORD MUSTANG
4. LOTUS FORD
5. 1974 FERRARA
6. THE PHYSICS SUPERCHARGED LIGHTBEAM SPECIAL
CHOOSE ONE OPPONENT BY ENTERING NUMBER? 3

ELAPSED TIME  SPEED        POSITION      OPPONENT'S     ACCELERATION
  SECONDS      MPH           YARDS        POSITION

    0            0             0             0            ? 12
    2           24            11             3            ? 12
    4           48            46            20            ? 12
    6           72           105            61            ? 12
    8           96           187           117            ? 12
   10          120           293           192            ? 10
   12          140           420           287            ? 0
   14          140           557           401            ? 0
   16          140           694           538            ? -22
CURVE 2 -3 ,  SPEED 100 MPH
   21.9        100          1000           877            ? 0
   23.9        100          1098           972            ? 0
   25.9        100          1196          1060            ? -10
   27.9         80          1284          1173            ? -10
   29.9         60          1353          1299            ? -10
   31.9         40          1402          1405            ? 0
   33.9         40          1442          1480            ? -3
   35.9         34          1478          1512            ? 0
CURVE 4 -5 ,  SPEED 34 MPH
   41.8         34          1600          1549            ? 12
   43.8         58          1645          1641            ? 12
   45.8         82          1714          1695            ? 10
   47.8        102          1804          1771            ? -5
   49.8         92          1899          1862            ? 0
CURVE 6 -7 ,  SPEED 92 MPH
   60.9         92          2400          2435            ? 0
   62.9         92          2490          2550            ? 0
   64.9         92          2580          2681            ? 0
   66.9         92          2671          2774            ? -22
   68.9         48          2739          2835            ? 10
   70.9         68          2796          2896            ? 0
SPEED IN CURVE 68 MPH, TOOK CURVE WIDE, LOST 3.7 SEC.

COMPLETED LAP,ELAPSED TIME 86.5 SEC.
YOUR OPPONENT FINISHED IN  80.8497 SECONDS
SORRY, YOU LOST BY  5.65029 SECONDS

DO YOU WISH TO TRY AGAIN? NO
OK
```

```
LIST

10 PRINT TAB(26);"GRNPRX"
20 PRINT TAB(20);"CREATIVE COMPUTING"
30 PRINT TAB(18);"MORRISTOWN, NEW JERSEY"
40 PRINT:PRINT:PRINT
1020 DIM P(9),F(4),G(4),H(82)
1030 REM
1040 FOR X=1 TO 9
1043 READ P(X)
1045 NEXT X
1050 FOR I=1 TO 4
1060 READ G(I),F(I)
1080 LET G(I)=G(I)/2.04545
1090 LET F(I)=(F(I)+.61/2.04545)
1100 NEXT I
1110 FOR X=1 TO 82:READ H(X):NEXT X
1115 REM
1120 DEF FNA(X)=INT(X*2.04545+.05)
1130 DEF FNT(T)=INT(T*10+.5)/10
1133 DEF FNC(T)=-(INT(T*R)+2)*(INT(T*R)+2<82)-82*(82<INT(T*R)+2)
1134 DEF FNB(T)=-(INT(T*R)+1)*(INT(T*R)+1<82)-82*(82<INT(T*R)+1)
1135 DEF FNP(T)=INT(H(FNB(T))+FNQ(T)*FNR(T)+.5)
1136 DEF FNQ(T)=H(FNC(T))-H(FNB(T))
1137 DEF FNR(T)=T*R-INT(T*R)
1140 REM
1150 LET D=2
1200 PRINT
1210 PRINT "WELCOME TO THE PUC GRAN PRIX"
1220 PRINT
1250 REM
1260 PRINT "DO YOU WANT A COURSE DESCRIPTION";
1270 INPUT A$
1280 IF LEFT$(A$,1)<>"Y" THEN 1910
1300 PRINT
1320 PRINT TAB(23);"2";TAB(66);"1"
1330 PRINT TAB(21);"CCOXPXXXXXXXXXXXXXXXXXXXXXXXXXXXXXXXXXXXXXXXXXOCC"
1340 PRINT TAB(12);"85-100 CC (800)";TAB(69);"C"
1350 PRINT TAB(18);"C";TAB(70);"C"
1360 PRINT TAB(15);"3 0";TAB(21);"PUC GRAN PRIX RACE";TAB(70);"C"
1370 PRINT TAB(16);"X";TAB(69);"C"
1375 PRINT TAB(15);"X";TAB(67);"CC"
1380 PRINT TAB(14);"X";TAB(38);"SS";TAB(59);"(2800) C 50-"
1390 PRINT TAB(13);"X";TAB(22);"SSSSSSS    SSS  SSSOXXXXXXXXXXXXXXXXX";
1395 PRINT "XPXXOC   70"
1400 PRINT TAB(12);"X       SS       SSSSSSS       7";
1405 PRINT TAB(64);"8"
1410 PRINT TAB(11);"X (1900)0 6   90-110"
1420 PRINT TAB(10);"X       X"
1430 PRINT TAB(9);"X       X";
1433 PRINT TAB(28);"DISTANCES IN YARDS, EG. ";
1435 PRINT "(800) = 800 YDS."
1440 PRINT TAB(8);"X       X";TAB(20);"SPEEDS IN MPH, ";
1445 PRINT "EG. 85 TO 100 MPH."
1450 PRINT "       P     X"
1460 PRINT "      X       X"
1470 PRINT "     X        X"
1480 PRINT "   X        X"
1490 PRINT " 4 0(1500) X"
1500 PRINT "  H       X"
1510 PRINT "  H      X"
1520 PRINT "20-H   0 5"
1530 PRINT " 35 H  H"
1535 PRINT "     HH"
1540 PRINT
```

```
1550 PRINT
1560 PRINT "1 TO 2 IS A STRAIGHTAWAY 800 YARDS LONG"
1570 PRINT "2 TO 3 IS A CURVE 200 YARDS LONG"
1580 PRINT "      THE BREAKAWAY SPEED RANGE IS 85 TO 100 MPH"
1590 PRINT "3 TO 4 IS A STRAIGHTAWAY 500 YARDS LONG"
1600 PRINT "      IT ENDS AT POSITION 1500 YARDS FROM STARTING";
1605 PRINT " GRID"
1610 PRINT "4 TO 5 IS A HAIRPIN CURVE 100 YARDS LONG"
1620 PRINT "      THE BREAKAWAY SPEED RANGE IS 20 TO 35 MPH"
1630 PRINT "5 TO 6 IS ANOTHER STRAIGHTAWAY 300 YARDS LONG"
1640 PRINT "      IT ENDS AT POSITION 1900 YARDS FROM THE GRID"
1650 PRINT "6 TO 7 IS A SET OF 'S' CURVES 500 YARDS LONG"
1660 PRINT "      THE SPEED RANGE IS 90-110 MPH"
1670 PRINT "7 TO 8 IS THE FINAL STRAIGHTAWAY OF 400 YARDS"
1680 PRINT "      IT ENTERS THE LAST CURVE AT 2800 YARDS"
1690 PRINT "8 TO 9 IS THE FINAL CURVE OF 400 YARDS"
1700 PRINT "      THE BREAKAWAY SPEED RANGE IS 50 TO 70 MPH"
1710 PRINT
1720 PRINT "THE TOTAL LENGTH OF ONE LAP IS 3200 YARDS"
1730 PRINT
1820 PRINT "DURING THE STRAIGHTAWAYS YOU WILL BE ABLE TO CONTROL THE"
1830 PRINT "ACCELERATION AND BRAKING OF THE CAR.  THE CURVES WILL BE";
1835 PRINT " TAKEN"
1840 PRINT "AT WHATEVER SPEED YOU ENTER THEM."
1842 PRINT "BELOW THE BREAKAWAY SPEED, THE CURVES MAY BE TAKEN WITH ";
1844 PRINT "NO DIFFICULTY."
1850 PRINT "ABOVE THE FASTEST SPEED INDICATED, YOU WILL CRASH!!"
1860 PRINT "WITHIN THE SPEED RANGE, THERE IS THE POSSIBILITY THAT YOU";
1865 PRINT " MIGHT"
1870 PRINT "LOSE TIME OR SPEED BY SWINGING WIDE OR BY SPINNING OUT."
1880 PRINT "THE FASTER YOU TAKE THE CURVES, THE GREATER THE RISKS--"
1890 PRINT "AND THE LESS THE TIME!!!!"
1905 PRINT
1906 PRINT
1907 PRINT "YOUR TASK IS TO TRANSVERSE THE TRACK IN A MINIMUM OF TIME"
1908 PRINT "WITHOUT CRASHING!!!"
1909 PRINT
1910 PRINT "YOUR CAR MAY BE ONE OF THE FOLLOWING:"
1911 PRINT "1. PORSCHE"
1912 PRINT "2. FERRARI"
1913 PRINT "3. MASERATI"
1914 PRINT "4. LOTUS FORD"
1915 PRINT "WHICH CAR WOULD YOU LIKE";
1916 INPUT Z
1917 ON Z GOTO 1920,1923,1926,1929
1918 PRINT "WE DON'T HAVE THAT CAR IN STOCK, PLEASE CHOOSE AGAIN.";
1919 GOTO 1916
1920 M=15
1921 LET B=-20
1922 GOTO 1931
1923 M=10
1924 B=-25
1925 GOTO 1931
1926 M=12
1927 B=-22
1928 GOTO 1931
1929 M=8
1930 B=-30
1931 PRINT "YOUR CAR HAS A MAXIMUM ACCELERATION OF ";M;"MPH/SEC."
1932 PRINT "AND A MAXIMUM BRAKING OF ";B;"MPH/SEC."
1933 PRINT "YOU WILL RACE AGAINST ONE OF THE FOLLOWING:"
1934 PRINT "1. U.S. POSTAL DELIVERY TRUCK"
1935 PRINT "2. 1970 BEAT PONTIAC GTO"
1936 PRINT "3. 1966 WELL USED FORD MUSTANG"
1937 PRINT "4. LOTUS FORD"
1938 PRINT "5. 1974 FERRARA"
1939 PRINT "6. THE PHYSICS SUPERCHARGED LIGHTBEAM SPECIAL"
1940 PRINT "CHOOSE ONE OPPONENT BY ENTERING NUMBER";
1941 INPUT R1
1942 IF R1>0 AND R1<6 THEN 1946
1943 IF R1=6 THEN 1948
1944 PRINT "WHICH CAR DID YOU SAY";
1945 GOTO 1941
1946 LET R=2*R1-5
1947 GOTO 1949
1948 LET R=2.5E+08
1949 LET R=(90+2*R)/100+7*RND(1)/100
1950 PRINT
3000 REM
3002 REM           BEGIN THE RACE!!
3004 REM
3010 LET J=1
3020 PRINT "ELAPSED TIME","SPEED","POSITION","OPPONENT'S","ACC";
3025 PRINT "ELERATION"
3030 PRINT "  SECONDS"," MPH"," YARDS"," POSITION"
3040 PRINT
3070 X=0:S=0:T=0:T9=0:X9=0
3080 REM
3100 IF J<9 THEN 3200
3130 PRINT
3160 PRINT "COMPLETED LAP";",ELAPSED TIME";FNT(T);"SEC."
3166 PRINT "YOUR OPPONENT FINISHED IN ";80/R;"SECONDS"
3167 LET K1=FNT(T)-80/R
3168 IF K1>0 THEN 3171
3169 PRINT "CONGRATULATIONS, YOU WON BY ";-K1;"SECONDS"
3170 GOTO 8600
3171 PRINT "SORRY, YOU LOST BY ";K1;"SECONDS"
3172 GOTO 8600
3200 IF FNP(T)>3200 THEN 3203
3201 PRINT "  ";FNT(T),"  ";FNA(S),"  ";INT(X),"  ";FNP(T),"  ";
3202 GOTO 3210
3203 PRINT "  ";FNT(T),"  ";FNA(S),"  ";INT(X),"  FINISH","  ";
3210 INPUT A1
3220 LET A=A1/2.04545
3230 IF A1>=0 THEN 3600
3240 IF A1>=B THEN 3300
3250 PRINT "MAXIMUM BRAKING IS ";B;"MPH/SEC"
3260 GOTO 3200
3300 LET T1=-S/A
3310 IF T1>D THEN 3500
3320 LET X1=X+S*T1+A/2*T1*T1
3330 IF X1>P(J+1) THEN 3400
3340 PRINT "YOU STOPPED";INT(P(J+1)-X1);"YARDS FROM POINT";J+1
3350 LET S=0
3360 LET X=X1
3370 LET T=T+T1
3380 GOTO 3100
3400 LET Y=P(J+1)-X
3402 IF A<>0 THEN 3410
3404 LMT T=T+Y/S
3406 GOTO 3440
3410 LET S1=SQR(S*S+2*A*Y)
3420 LET T=T-(S-S1)/A
3430 LET S=S1
3440 LET J=J+1
3450 GOTO 8000
3500 LET X1=X+S*D+A/2*D*D
3510 IF X1>P(J+1) THEN 3400
3520 LET T=T+D
3530 LET S=S+A*D
3540 LET X=X1
3550 GOTO 3100
3600 IF A1 <= M THEN 3700
3610 PRINT "MAXIMUM ACCELERATION IS ";M;"MPH/SEC"
3620 GOTO 3200
3700 LET X1=X+S*D+A/2*D*D
3710 IF X1>P(J+1) THEN 3400
3720 GOTO 3500
8000 REM *** SUB CURVE ***
8010 REM
8020 LET I=INT(J/2)
8030 LET T1=(P(J+1)-P(J))/S
8040 LET S1=G(I)+(F(I)-G(I))*RND(1)
8050 IF S>S1 THEN 8100
8055 PRINT "CURVE";J;-J-1;",  SPEED";FNA(S);"MPH"
8060 LET J=J+1
8070 LET X=P(J)
8080 LET T=T+T1
8090 GOTO 3100
8100 IF S>S1+(F(I)-S1)/2 THEN 8200
8110 LET T2=T1*RND(1)*.4
8120 PRINT "SPEED IN CURVE";FNA(S);"MPH, TOOK CURVE WIDE, LOST";
8125 PRINT FNT(T2);"SEC."
8130 LET T1=T1+T2
8140 GOTO 8060
8200 IF S>F(I) THEN 8300
8210 LET S2=S-S*RND(1)*.9
8220 LET T1=T1*S/S2
8230 PRINT "SPUN OUT AT";FNA(S);"MPH, LOST SPEED AND TIME"
8240 LET S=S2
8250 GOTO 8060
8300 PRINT "LOST CONTROL AT";FNA(S);"MPH.  YOUR CAR CRASHED!!"
8305 PRINT "YOUR OPPONENT FINISHED IN ";82/R;"SECONDS!"
8330 REM
8600 PRINT
8605 PRINT "DO YOU WISH TO TRY AGAIN";
8610 INPUT A$
8620 IF LEFT$(A$,1)="Y" THEN 1910
9000 REM
9010 DATA 0,800,1000,1500,1600,1900,2400,2800,3200
9020 DATA 85,100
9030 DATA 20,35
9040 DATA 90,110
9050 DATA 50,70
9060 REM
9070 DATA 0,1,3,9,21,39,62,87,120,156,196,244,293,351,410
9080 DATA 479,550,625,700,758,800,847,894,942,990,1030,1080
9090 DATA 1135,1200,1260,1330,1382,1425,1470,1490,1505,1519
9100 DATA 1539,1548,1563,1578,1512,1610,1632,1658,1683,1718
9110 DATA 1758,1800,1850,1890,1943,1997,2050,2104,2057,2210
9120 DATA 2294,2317,2370,2420,2480,2535,2600,2670,2725,2768,2799,2830
9130 DATA 2861,2892,2920,2951,2982,3013,3044,3075,3106,3137,3168,3199
9140 DATA 10000
OK
```

Guess-It

Many, if not most, two person games that are played on a computer are based on fixed rules that assure that if one player uses these rules and a rational playing strategy then that player wins. If both players use these rules and rational playing strategies then the winner is usually determined by who goes first. Tic-Tac-Toe, Batnum and Even are examples of games of this type.

A more interesting type of game is one where the playing strategy is of mixed type. This means that the best move, in most cases, depends on what moves have already been made and a player can only determine the probability of the best move. Standard card games (Bridge, Poker etc.) are usually games of mixed type.

Most two person games of mixed type are either so complicated that the best strategies are not known or they are so simple that they are not interesting to play. The game of Guess-It is an exception to this pattern. The element of bluffing, which plays a central role in this game, makes the game interesting. The optimal strategy for playing this two person game of mixed type has been determined by Rufus Isaacs[2].

This program simulates the game of Guess-It. The computer plays according to the optimal strategy determined by Isaacs. Lines 1740 to 1930 give instructions on how to play the game. The number of numbers in each hand is determined in line 70. (It is set at 5. This is the value Isaacs used in his analysis of the game.) To change the number of numbers in each hand only the value of H in line 70 needs to be changed.

To play the game in an optimal way decisions need to be made based on the win probabilities P(m,n) where m is the number of numbers in your hand and n is the number of numbers in your opponents hand. The matrix of these win probabilities is computed in lines 80 to 180.

To match the optimal strategy of the computer some type of randomizing device based on the win probabilities P(m,n) is required. (See (1) and (2) for descriptions of how to make and use such devices. These devices only work when there is a maximum of 5 numbers in each hand.)

The decision as to whether or not a number asked about by a player was a bluff is made in line 750. The decision to bluff or not when asking about a number is made in line 940.

The program gives the player the option of going first. The win probability, P(5,5), in this case is .538. Therefore the player going first has a slightly better than even chance of winning assuming that both players use the optimal strategy.

There are two reasons why bluffing is important in any strategy. If a player never bluffs, then any "ask" about a number that is not in the opponent's hand will result in a loss since the other player will know that it must be the down number. A successful bluff can lead the other player to make an incorrect guess of the down number.

The program and description were written by Gerard Kiernan of Manhattanville College, Purchase, NY.

References

1. Mathematical Magic Show. Martin Gardner. Alfred A. Knopf, 1977.
2. "A Card Game With Bluffing." Rufus Isaacs, The American Mathematical Monthly, Vol. 62, February 1955 pages 99-108.


```
RUN
                              GUESS-IT
                         CREATIVE COMPUTING
                       MORRISTOWN, NEW JERSEY



DO YOU WANT INSTRUCTIONS-TYPE YES OR NO
? YES

THE OBJECT OF THIS GAME IS TO GUESS AN UNKNOWN NUMBER
CALLED THE 'DOWN NUMBER'.  THE GAME IS PLAYED WITH THE
NUMBERS 1 TO 11 .  YOU WILL BE GIVEN A HAND OF  5
RANDOMLY SELECTED NUMBERS BETWEEN 1 AND 11 . THE
COMPUTER WILL HAVE A SIMILAR HAND.  THE DOWN NUMBER WILL
ALWAYS BE THE NUMBER NOT IN EITHER PLAYER HANDS.

YOU ALTERNATE MOVES WITH THE COMPUTER.  ON ANY MOVE THERE
ARE TWO OPTIONS- GUESS THE DOWN NUMBER OR ASK ABOUT SOME
NUMBER.

WHEN A PLAYER GUESSES THE DOWN NUMBER THE GAME STOPS.
IF THE GUESS IS CORRECT THAT PLAYER WINS.
IF THE GUESS IS NOT CORRECT THAT PLAYER LOSES.

ALL QUESTIONS ABOUT NUMBERS IN THE OTHER PLAYERS HAND
MUST BE ANSWERED TRUTHFULLY.  A PLAYER MAY'BLUFF' BY
ASKING ABOUT A NUMBER IN HIS OWN HAND.  THE COMPUTER
WILL SOMETIMES DO THIS.

A NUMBER MAY BE ASKED ABOUT ONLY ONCE.

GOOD LUCK

YOUR HAND IS

 11  2  6  1  4

DO YOU WANT TO GO FIRST? YES

DO YOU WANT TO GUESS THE DOWN NUMBER? NO

WHAT NUMBER DO YOU WANT TO ASK ABOUT? 3

IS NOT IN MY HAND


DO YOU HAVE  4
? NO


DO YOU WANT TO GUESS THE DOWN NUMBER? YES

WHAT DO YOU THINK THE DOWN NUMBER IS
? 3

THE DOWN NUMBER IS 3
YOUR GUESS OF  3 IS CORRECT - YOU WIN
DO YOU WANT TO PLAY AGAIN? YES

YOUR HAND IS

 7  9  5  6  10

DO YOU WANT TO GO FIRST? NO


DO YOU HAVE  6
? YES


DO YOU WANT TO GUESS THE DOWN NUMBER? NO

WHAT NUMBER DO YOU WANT TO ASK ABOUT? 11

 11 IS IN MY HAND


DO YOU HAVE  9
? YES
```

```
DO YOU WANT TO GUESS THE DOWN NUMBER? NO

WHAT NUMBER DO YOU WANT TO ASK ABOUT? 2

 2 IS IN MY HAND


DO YOU HAVE 4
? NO


DO YOU WANT TO GUESS THE DOWN NUMBER? YES

WHAT DO YOU THINK THE DOWN NUMBER IS
? 4

THE DOWN NUMBER IS 1

YOUR  GUESS OF 4  IS NOT CORRECT-YOU LOSE
DO YOU WANT TO PLAY AGAIN? EYS
DO YOU WANT TO PLAY AGAIN? YES

YOUR HAND IS

 3  8  11  10  2

DO YOU WANT TO GO FIRST? YES


DO YOU WANT TO GUESS THE DOWN NUMBER? NO

WHAT NUMBER DO YOU WANT TO ASK ABOUT? 1

 1 IS IN MY HAND


DO YOU HAVE  3
? YES


DO YOU WANT TO GUESS THE DOWN NUMBER? NO

WHAT NUMBER DO YOU WANT TO ASK ABOUT? 9

 9 IS IN MY HAND


DO YOU HAVE 4
? NO


DO YOU WANT TO GUESS THE DOWN NUMBER? YES

WHAT DO YOU THINK THE DOWN NUMBER IS
? 4

THE DOWN NUMBER IS 5

YOUR  GUESS OF 4  IS NOT CORRECT-YOU LOSE
DO YOU WANT TO PLAY AGAIN? NO

YOU PLAYED 3 GAMES.  YOU LOST 2 YOU WON 1

BREAK IN 1580
OK
```

```
LIST

1 PRINT TAB(26)"GUESS-IT"
2 PRINTTAB(20)"CREATIVE COMPUTING"
3 PRINT TAB(18)"MORRISTOWN, NEW JERSEY"
4 PRINT
5 PRINT
10 PRINT
20 G1=0:C1=0
50 A1=RND(1)
70 H=5
80 DIM P(10,10)
90 FOR K=1 TO H
100 P(K,0)=1
110 P(0,K)=1/(K+1)
120 NEXT K
130 FOR I=1 TO H
140 FOR J=I TO H
150 P(I,J)=(1+J*P(J,I-1)*(1-P(J-1,I)))/(1+(J+2)*P(J,I-1))
160 P(J,I)=(1+I*P(I,J-1)*(1-P(I-1,J)))/(1+(I+1)*P(I,J-1))
170 NEXT J
180 NEXT I
190 Z=11
200 DIM U(Z),N(Z)
210 PRINT"DO YOU WANT INSTRUCTIONS-TYPE YES OR NO"
220 INPUT A$
230 IF A$="YES" THEN 1730
240 IF A$<>"NO" THEN 210
250 PRINT
260 G1=G1+1
270 FOR J=2 TO Z
280 U(J)=0
290 NEXT J
300 E=0:T=0:C=0:P=0:L=0
310 GOSUB 1630
320 REM N(1) TO N(H)= COMP HAND N(H+1)=TO N(Z)= OTHER HAND
330 D=(Z)
340 PRINT"YOUR HAND IS"
350 PRINT
360 FOR I=H+1 TO Z-1
370 PRINT N(I);
380 NEXT I
390 PRINT
400 PRINT
410 PRINT"DO YOU WANT TO GO FIRST";
420 INPUT A$
430 IF A$="YES" THEN 470
440 IF A$<>"NO" THEN 390
450 K=1
460 GOTO 480
470 K=0
480 K=K+1
490 M=H-C
500 N=H-P
510 PRINT
520 IF K=(INT(K/2))*2 THEN 860
530 PRINT
540 PRINT"DO YOU WANT TO GUESS THE DOWN NUMBER";
550 INPUT A$
560 IF A$="YES" THEN 1250
570 IF A$<>"NO" THEN 530
580 PRINT
590 PRINT"WHAT NUMBER DO YOU WANT TO ASK ABOUT";
600 INPUT E
610 FOR I=1 TO Z
620 IF E=U(I) THEN 650
630 NEXT I
640 GOTO 670
650 PRINT E;" WAS  ASKED BEFORE TRY AGAIN"
660 GOTO 580
670 FOR J=1 TO H
680 IF N(J)=E THEN 800
690 NEXT J
700 PRINT
710 PRINT;"IS NOT IN MY HAND"
720 IF M=0 THEN 1460
730 IF N=0 THEN 1440
740 Y=((M+1)*P(M,N-1)-M*P(M-1,N))/(1+(M+1)*P(M,N-1))
750 IF RND(1)<Y THEN 1380
760 GOSUB 1220
770 IF (H-P)=1 THEN 1460
780 P=P+1
790 GOTO 480
800 PRINT
810 PRINT E;"IS IN MY HAND"
820 C=C+1
830 GOSUB 1220
840 GOTO 480
850 REM COMP SEQ STARTS
860 IF T<>0 THEN 1410
870 IF H-C<>0 THEN 890
880 GOTO 1460
```

```
890 IF H-P<>0 THEN910
900 GOTO 1460
910 IF (2*H-2)-(P+C)<>0 THEN 930
920 GOTO 1460
930 REM RND DECISION TO BLUFF OR NOT ON ASKING FOR CARD
940 IF RND(1)>1/(1+(N+1)*P(N,M-1)) THEN 1060
950 PRINT
960 A=INT(H*RND(1))+1
970 FOR J=1 TO Z
980 IF N(A)=U(J) THEN 960
990 NEXT J
1000 PRINT"DO YOU HAVE";N(A)
1010 C=C+1
1020 INPUT A$
1030 E=N(A)
1040 GOSUB 1220
1050 GOTO 480
1060 GOSUB 1170
1070 PRINT
1080 PRINT"DO YOU HAVE ";N(A)
1090 INPUT A$
1100 IF A$="YES" THEN 1130
1110 T=1
1120 GOTO 480
1130 E=N(A)
1140 P=P+1
1150 GOSUB 1220
1160 GOTO 480
1170 A=INT((H+1)*RND(1))+(H+1)
1180 FOR J=1 TO Z
1190 IF N(A)=U(J) THEN GOTO 1170
1200 NEXT J
1210 RETURN
1220 L=L+1
1230 U(L)=E
1240 RETURN
1250 PRINT
1260 PRINT"WHAT DO YOU THINK THE DOWN NUMBER IS"
1270 INPUT B
1280 PRINT
1290 PRINT"THE DOWN NUMBER IS";N(Z)
1300 IF B=N(Z) THEN 1360
1310 PRINT
1320 PRINT"YOUR  GUESS OF";B;" IS NOT CORRECT-YOU LOSE"
1330 C1=C1+1
1340 GOTO 1520
1350 PRINT
1360 PRINT"YOUR GUESS OF ";B;"IS CORRECT - YOU WIN"
1370 GOTO 1520
1380 PRINT"I THINK YOU WERE  NOT BLUFFING WHEN YOU ASKED ABOUT";E
1390 G=E
1400 GOTO 1480
1410 PRINTN(A);"WAS NOT A BLUFF"
1420 G=N(A)
1430 GOTO 1480
1440 G=N(Z)
1450 GOTO 1480
1460 GOSUB 1170
1470 G=N(A)
1480 PRINT"I GUESS THE DOWN NUMBER IS";G
1490 IF G=N(Z) THEN 1590
1500 PRINT
1510 PRINT"THE DOWN NUMBER IS";N(Z);"I WAS WRONG... YOU WIN"
1520 PRINT"DO YOU WANT TO PLAY AGAIN";
1530 INPUT A$
1540 IF A$="YES" THEN 250
1550 IF A$<>"NO" THEN 1520
1560 PRINT
1570 PRINT"YOU PLAYED";G1;"GAMES.  YOU LOST";C1;"YOU WON";G1-C1
1580 STOP
1590 PRINT
1600 PRINT"THE DOWN NUMBER IS";N(Z);"I WAS CORRECT...YOU LOSE"
1610 C1=C1+1
1620 GOTO 1520
1630 FOR I=1 TO Z
1640 N(I)=I
1650 NEXT I
1660 FOR I=1 TO Z
1670 R=INT(RND(1)*((Z+1)-I))+I
1680 W=N(R)
1690 N(R)=N(I)
1700 N(I)=W
1710 NEXT I
1720 RETURN
1730 PRINT
1740 PRINT"THE OBJECT OF THIS GAME IS TO GUESS AN UNKNOWN NUMBER"
1750 PRINT"CALLED THE 'DOWN NUMBER'.  THE GAME IS PLAYED WITH THE"
1760 PRINT"NUMBERS 1 TO";Z;".  YOU WILL BE GIVEN A HAND OF ";H
1770 PRINT"RANDOMLY SELECTED NUMBERS BETWEEN 1 AND";Z;". THE "
1780 PRINT"COMPUTER WILL HAVE A SIMILAR HAND.  THE DOWN NUMBER WILL "
1785 PRINT"ALWAYS BE THE NUMBER NOT IN EITHER PLAYER HANDS."
1790 PRINT
1800 PRINT"YOU ALTERNATE MOVES WITH THE COMPUTER.  ON ANY MOVE THERE"
1810 PRINT"ARE TWO OPTIONS- GUESS THE DOWN NUMBER OR ASK ABOUT SOME "
1820 PRINT"NUMBER."
1830 PRINT
1840 PRINT"WHEN A PLAYER GUESSES THE DOWN NUMBER THE GAME STOPS."
1850 PRINT"IF THE GUESS IS CORRECT THAT PLAYER WINS."
1860 PRINT"IF THE GUESS IS NOT CORRECT THAT PLAYER LOSES."
1870 PRINT
1880 PRINT"ALL QUESTIONS ABOUT NUMBERS IN THE OTHER PLAYERS HAND"
1890 PRINT"MUST BE ANSWERED TRUTHFULLY.  A PLAYER MAY'BLUFF' BY"
1900 PRINT"ASKING ABOUT A NUMBER IN HIS OWN HAND.  THE COMPUTER"
1910 PRINT"WILL SOMETIMES DO THIS."
1920 PRINT
1930 PRINT"A NUMBER MAY BE ASKED ABOUT ONLY ONCE."
1940 PRINT
1950 PRINT"GOOD LUCK"
1960 GOTO 250
1970 END
OK
```

Your radar station picks up an enemy ICBM heading your way, telling you its coordinates (in miles north and miles east of your location). You launch a surface-to-air missile (SAM) to intercept it.

Your only control over the SAM is that you can aim it in any direction, both at launch, and in mid-air. Using the coordinates of the ICBM as a guide, you INPUT the direction (measured CCW from North) in which you want the SAM to travel.

At the next radar scan one minute later, you are given the new coordinates of the ICBM, the coordinates of your SAM, and the distance between the two. You can now make corrections in the course of your SAM by entering a new direction.

You have no control over the altitude of your SAM, as it is assumed that it will seek the same altitude as the ICBM.

As the two missiles draw closer, you make adjustments in the direction of the SAM so as to intercept the ICBM. It's not easy to hit, because the ICBM is programmed to make evasive maneuvers, by taking random deviations from the straight line course to your location. Also, its speed is not known, although it does not vary after being randomly selected at the start of the run.

You can destroy the ICBM by coming within 5 miles of it, at which time your SAM's heat-seeking sensors will come into action and direct it to its target. If you overshoot the ICBM it's possible to turn the SAM around and chase the ICBM back towards your location. But be careful; you may get both missiles in your lap.

There is also some element of chance involved, as several accidents have been programmed to occur randomly. These can work for you or against you.

Some ways to improve and expand the program are:

1. Operator control over SAM speed: In the present version the speed of the SAM is randomly selected by the computer at the start of the run, and remains constant thereafter. This often results in overshooting the ICBM. Modify the program so that you can input a new speed (within limits) at the same time you input the new direction.

2. Three dimensional version: Have the computer print the *altitude* of the ICBM, as well as its coordinates. The operator will then have to INPUT the angle his SAM is to make with the horizontal, when entering the other quantities.

3. Extend to all Quadrants. In the present version, the ICBM approaches only from the Northeast. You can expand this to include approach from any compass direction.

This game is derived from a program submitted by Chris Falco. The writeup is by Paul Calter and originally appeared in *Creative Computing*, May/Jun 1975.

```
                          ICBM
                    CREATIVE COMPUTING
                  MORRISTOWN, NEW JERSEY



-------MISSLE------          --------SAM--------          -----
MILES           MILES        MILES          MILES         HEADING
NORTH           EAST         NORTH          EAST          ?
-------------------------------------------------------------------
 201             975          0              0            ? 15
ICBM & SAM NOW 920 MILES APART
 198             920          48             12           ? 85
ICBM & SAM NOW 822 MILES APART
 200             870          52             61           ? 75
ICBM & SAM NOW 715 MILES APART
 196             812          64             109          ? 80
ICBM & SAM NOW 613 MILES APART
 180             762          72             158          ? 85
ICBM & SAM NOW 511 MILES APART
 169             710          76             207          ? 80
ICBM & SAM NOW 395 MILES APART
 157             645          84             256          ? 70
ICBM & SAM NOW 298 MILES APART
 157             595          101            302          ? 75
ICBM & SAM NOW 186 MILES APART
 140             535          113            350          ? 80
ICBM & SAM NOW 84 MILES APART
 126             483          121            399          ? 90
ICBM & SAM NOW 27 MILES APART
 113             423          121            449          ? 95
ICBM & SAM NOW 137 MILES APART
 113             361          116            498          ? -90
ICBM & SAM NOW 153 MILES APART
 110             295          116            448          ? -95
TOO BAD.  YOUR SAM FELL TO THE GROUND!
DO YOU WANT TO PLAY MORE? (Y OR N)? N
```

```
10 PRINT TAB(26);"ICBM"
20 PRINT TAB(20);"CREATIVE COMPUTING"
30 PRINT TAB(18);"MORRISTOWN, NEW JERSEY"
40 PRINT:PRINT:PRINT
110 X1=0:Y1=0
120 X=INT(RND(1)*800)+200:Y=INT(RND(1)*800)+200
130 S=INT(RND(1)*20+50):S1=INT(RND(1)*20+50)
170 PRINT "-------MISSLE------          ";
175 PRINT "--------SAM--------          -----"
180 PRINT "MILES","MILES","MILES","MILES","HEADING"
190 PRINT "NORTH","EAST","NORTH","EAST","?"
200 PRINT "-----------------------------------";
205 PRINT "----------------------------"
210 FOR N=1 TO 50
220 PRINT Y,X,Y1,X1,
230 IF X=0 THEN 550
240 INPUT T1
250 T1=T1/57.296
260 H=INT(RND(1)*200+1)
270 IF H>4 THEN 290
280 ON H GOTO 470,490,510,530
290 X1=INT(X1+S1*SIN(T1)):Y1=INT(Y1+S1*COS(T1))
310 IF SQR(X^2+Y^2)>S THEN 350
320 X=0:Y=0
340 GOTO 430
350 B=SQR(X^2+Y^2)/1000
360 T=ATN(Y/X)
370 X=INT(X-S*COS(T)+RND(1)*20+R)
380 Y=INT(Y-S*SIN(T)+RND(1)*20+R)
390 D=SQR((X-X1)^2+(Y-Y1)^2)
400 IF D=<5 THEN 440
410 D=INT(D)
420 PRINT "ICBM & SAM NOW"; D; "MILES APART"
430 NEXT N
440 PRINT "CONGRATULATIONS!  YOUR SAM CAME WITHIN";D;"MILES OF"
450 PRINT "THE ICBM AND DESTROYED IT!"
460 GOTO 560
470 PRINT "TOO BAD.  YOUR SAM FELL TO THE GROUND!"
480 GOTO 560
490 PRINT "YOUR SAM EXPLODED IN MIDAIR!"
500 GOTO 560
510 PRINT "GOOD LUCK-THE ICBM EXPLODED HARMLESSLY IN MIDAIR!"
520 GOTO 560
530 PRINT "GOOD LUCK-THE ICBM TURNED OUT TO BE A FRIENDLY AIRCRAFT!"
540 GOTO 560
550 PRINT "TOO BAD!"
555 PRINT "THE ICBM JUST HIT YOUR LOCATION!!"
560 PRINT "DO YOU WANT TO PLAY MORE? (Y OR N)";
570 INPUT A$
580 IF A$="Y" THEN 130
590 END
```

Inkblot

INKBLOT is a program that creates "inkblots" similar to those used in the famous Rorschach Inkblot Test. The program generates these inkblots randomly so that literally millions of different patterns can be produced. Many of these patterns are quite interesting and serve not only as conversation pieces, but also as good examples of computer "art."

In addition, INKBLOT is interesting from a mathematical point of view. This is because INKBLOT actually creates inkblots by plotting ellipses on the left side of the page and their mirror-images on the right side. The program first chooses the ellipses to be plotted by randomly selecting the values a, b, j, k and θ in the equation for a rotated ellipse:

$$\frac{[(x-j)\cos\theta + (y-k)\sin\theta]^2}{a^2} + \frac{[(y-k)\cos\theta - (x-j)\sin\theta]^2}{b^2} = 1$$

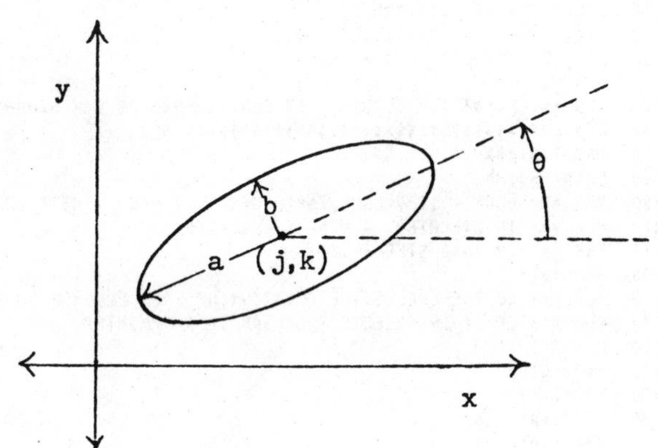

where a = the horizontal radius of the ellipse
b = the vertical radius of the ellipse
j = the distance from the ellipse center to the y-axis
k = the distance from the ellipse center to the x-axis
θ = the angle of rotation in radians

Since the actual method by which the program plots the ellipses is quite complicated, it won't be discussed here.

INKBLOT could be enhanced in several ways, for example allowing the user to specify which character is to be used in printing the inkblot. It could have an option to print the "negative" of an inkblot by filling in the area around the ellipses rather than the ellipses themselves. Finally, it is possible to build in a "repeatable randomness" feature so that exceptional outputs could be reproduced at any time. These enhancements are left for the ambitious programmer to make.

Program and description are by Scott Costello.

```
RUN
                                    INKBLOT
                               CREATIVE COMPUTING
                             MORRISTOWN, NEW JERSEY



$$$$$$$$$$$$$$$$$$$$$$$$$$$$$$$$$$$$$$$$$$$$$$$$$$$$$$$$$$$$$$$$$$$$$$$$$$$$$$$$
$$$$$$$$$$$$$$$$$$$$$$$$$$$$$$$$$$$$$$$$$$$$$$$$$$$$$$$$$$$$$$$$$$$$$$$$$$$$$$$$
$$                                                                            $$
$$                                                                            $$
$$$$$$$$$$$$$                                                      $$$$$$$$$$$$$
$$$$$$$$$$$$$$$$$                                              $$$$$$$$$$$$$$$$$
$$$$$$$$$$$$$$$$$$$                                          $$$$$$$$$$$$$$$$$$$
$$$$$$$$$$$$$$$$$$                                            $$$$$$$$$$$$$$$$$$
$$$$$$$$$$$$$$                                                    $$$$$$$$$$$$$$
$$$$$             $$$$$$$$$                          $$$$$$$$$             $$$$$
$$               $$$$$$$$$$$$                      $$$$$$$$$$$$               $$
$$              $$$$$$$$$$$$$$                    $$$$$$$$$$$$$$              $$
$$             $$$$$$$$$$$$$$$$                  $$$$$$$$$$$$$$$$             $$
$$             $$$$$$$$$$$$$$$$                  $$$$$$$$$$$$$$$$             $$
$$      $$$$$$$$$$$$$$$$$$$$$$$                  $$$$$$$$$$$$$$$$$$$$$$$      $$
$$    $$$$$$$$$$$$$$$$$$$$$$$$                    $$$$$$$$$$$$$$$$$$$$$$$$    $$
$$   $$$$$$$$$$$$$$$$$$$$$$$$$                    $$$$$$$$$$$$$$$$$$$$$$$$$   $$
$$   $$$$$$$$$$$$$$$$$$$$$$$                        $$$$$$$$$$$$$$$$$$$$$$$   $$
$$    $$$$$$$$$$$$$$$$$$$$                            $$$$$$$$$$$$$$$$$$$$    $$
$$     $$$$$$$$$$$$$$$$$$                              $$$$$$$$$$$$$$$$$$     $$
$$      $$$$$$$$$$$$$$$$$                              $$$$$$$$$$$$$$$$$      $$
$$        $$$$$$$$$$$$$$                                $$$$$$$$$$$$$$        $$
$$$$$$$$$$$   $$$$$$$$                                    $$$$$$$$   $$$$$$$$$$$
$$$$$$$$$$$$$                                                      $$$$$$$$$$$$$
$$$$$$$$$$$$$$$                                                  $$$$$$$$$$$$$$$
$$$$$$$$$$$$$$$$                                                $$$$$$$$$$$$$$$$
$$$$$$$$$$$$$$$$$                                              $$$$$$$$$$$$$$$$$
$$$$$$$$$$$$$$$$$                                              $$$$$$$$$$$$$$$$$
$$$$$$$$$$$$$$$$$$                                            $$$$$$$$$$$$$$$$$$
$$$$$$$$$$$$$$$$$$                                            $$$$$$$$$$$$$$$$$$
$$$$$$$$$$$$$$$$$$                                            $$$$$$$$$$$$$$$$$$
$$$$$$$$$$$$$$$$$                                              $$$$$$$$$$$$$$$$$
$$$$$$$$$$$$$$$$$                                              $$$$$$$$$$$$$$$$$
$$$$$$$$$$$$$$$$                                                $$$$$$$$$$$$$$$$
$$$$$$$$$$$$$$$                                                  $$$$$$$$$$$$$$$
$$$$$$$$$$$$$$                                                    $$$$$$$$$$$$$$
$$$$$$$$$$$$                                                        $$$$$$$$$$$$
$$$$$$$$$                                                              $$$$$$$$$
$$                                                                            $$
$$        $$$$$$$                                              $$$$$$$        $$
$$$$$  $$$$$$$$$$$                                            $$$$$$$$$$$  $$$$$
$$$$$$$$$$$$$$$$$$                                            $$$$$$$$$$$$$$$$$$
$$$$$$$$$$$$$$$$$                                              $$$$$$$$$$$$$$$$$
$$$$$$$$$$$$$$$                                                  $$$$$$$$$$$$$$$
$$    $$$$$$$                                                      $$$$$$$    $$
$$                                                                            $$
$$  $$$$$$$$$$$$$                                              $$$$$$$$$$$$$  $$
$$$$$$$$$$$$$$$$$$$$                                        $$$$$$$$$$$$$$$$$$$$
$$$$$$$$$$$$$$$$$$$$$$                                    $$$$$$$$$$$$$$$$$$$$$$
$$$$$$$$$$$$$$$$$$$$$$$                                  $$$$$$$$$$$$$$$$$$$$$$$
$$$$$$$$$$$$$$$$$$$$$$$$                                $$$$$$$$$$$$$$$$$$$$$$$$
$$$$$$$$$$$$$$$$$$$$$$$$                                $$$$$$$$$$$$$$$$$$$$$$$$
$$$$$$$$$$$$$$$$$$$$$$$$$$$$$$$$$$$$$$$$$$$$$$$$$$$$$$$$$$$$$$$$$$$$$$$$$$$$$$$$
$$$$$$$$$$$$$$$$$$$$$$$$$$$$$$$$$$$$$$$$$$$$$$$$$$$$$$$$$$$$$$$$$$$$$$$$$$$$$$$$
Ok
```

```
RUN
                          INKBLOT
                    CREATIVE COMPUTING
                  MORRISTOWN, NEW JERSEY



$$$$$$$$$$$$$$$$$$$$$$$$$$$$$$$$$$$$$$$$$$$$$$$$$$$$$$$$$$$$$$$$$$$$$$$$
$$$$$$$$$$$$$$$$$$$$$$$$$$$$$$$$$$$$$$$$$$$$$$$$$$$$$$$$$$$$$$$$$$$$$$$$
$$                        $$$$$$$$$$$$$$$$$$$$                        $$
$$                       $$$$$$$$$$$$$$$$$$$$$$                       $$
$$                      $$$$$$$$$$$$$$$$$$$$$$$$                      $$
$$                       $$$$$$$$$$  $$$$$$$$$$                       $$
$$                        $$$$$$$$    $$$$$$$$                        $$
$$                 $$$$$$$$$$$$$        $$$$$$$$$$$$$                 $$
$$              $$$$$$$$$$$$$$$$$$$  $$$$$$$$$$$$$$$$$$$              $$
$$            $$$$$$$$$$$$$$$$$$$$$$$$$$$$$$$$$$$$$$$$$$$$            $$
$$           $$$$$$$$$$$$$$$$$$$$$$$$$$$$$$$$$$$$$$$$$$$$$$           $$
$$          $$$$$$$$$$$$$$$$$$$$$$$$$$$$$$$$$$$$$$$$$$$$$$$$          $$
$$         $$$$$$$$$$$$$$$$$$$$$$$$$$$$$$$$$$$$$$$$$$$$$$$$$$         $$
$$        $$$$$$$$$$$$$$$$$$$$$$$$$$$$$$$$$$$$$$$$$$$$$$$$$$$$        $$
$$       $$$$$$$$$$$$$$$$$$$$$$$$$$$$$$$$$$$$$$$$$$$$$$$$$$$$$$       $$
$$       $$$$$$$$$$$$$$$$$$$$$$$$$$$$$$$$$$$$$$$$$$$$$$$$$$$$$$       $$
$$$$$$   $$$$$$$$$$$$$$$$$$$$$$$$$$$$$$$$$$$$$$$$$$$$$$$$$$$$$$   $$$$$$
$$$$$$$$$$$$$$$$$$$$$$$$$$$$$$$$$$$$$$$$$$$$$$$$$$$$$$$$$$$$$$$$$$$$$$$$
$$$$$$$$$$$$$$$$$$$$$$$$$$$$$$$$$$$$$$$$$$$$$$$$$$$$$$$$$$$$$$$$$$$$$$$$
$$$$$$$$$$$$$$$$$$$$$$$$$$$$$$$$$$$$$$$$$$$$$$$$$$$$$$$$$$$$$$$$$$$$$$$$
$$$$$$$$$$$$$$$$$$$$$$$$$$$$$$$$$$$$$$$$$$$$$$$$$$$$$$$$$$$$$$$$$$$$$$$$
$$$$$$$$$$$$$$$$$$$$$$$$$$$$$$$$$$$$$$$$$$$$$$$$$$$$$$$$$$$$$$$$$$$$$$$$
$$$$$$$$$$$$$$$$$$$$$$$$$$$$$$$$$$$$$$$$$$$$$$$$$$$$$$$$$$$$$$$$$$$$$$$$
$$$$$$$$$$$$$$$$$$$$$$$$$$$$$$$$$$$$$$$$$$$$$$$$$$$$$$$$$$$$$$$$$$$$$$$$
$$$$$$$$$$$$$$$$$$$$$$$$$$$$$$$$$$$$$$$$$$$$$$$$$$$$$$$$$$$$$$$$$$$$$$$$
$$$$$$$$$$$$$$$$$$$$$$$$$$$$$$$$$$    $$$$$$$$$$$$$$$$$$$$$$$$$$$$$$$$$$
$$$$$$$$$$$$$$$$$$$$$$$$$$$$$$          $$$$$$$$$$$$$$$$$$$$$$$$$$$$$$$
$$$$$$$$$$$$$$$$$$$$$$$$$$$$$              $$$$$$$$$$$$$$$$$$$$$$$$$$$$$
$$$$$$$$$$$$$$$$$$$$$$$$$$$$                $$$$$$$$$$$$$$$$$$$$$$$$$$$$
$$$$$$$$$$$$$$ $$$$$$$$$$                      $$$$$$$$$$ $$$$$$$$$$$$$$
$$$$$$$$$$$$                                                $$$$$$$$$$$$
$$$$$$$$$          $$$$$$$$$$$            $$$$$$$$$$$          $$$$$$$$$
$$               $$$$$$$$$$$$$$$        $$$$$$$$$$$$$$$               $$
$$             $$$$$$$$$$$$$$$$$$      $$$$$$$$$$$$$$$$$$             $$
$$             $$$$$$$$$$$$$$$$$$$    $$$$$$$$$$$$$$$$$$$             $$
$$            $$$$$$$$$$$$$$$$$$$$$  $$$$$$$$$$$$$$$$$$$$$            $$
$$            $$$$$$$$$$$$$$$$$$$$$  $$$$$$$$$$$$$$$$$$$$$            $$
$$           $$$$$$$$$$$$$$$$$$$$$$  $$$$$$$$$$$$$$$$$$$$$$           $$
$$            $$$$$$$$$$$$$$$$$$$$$  $$$$$$$$$$$$$$$$$$$$$            $$
$$            $$$$$$$$$$$$$$$$$$$$$  $$$$$$$$$$$$$$$$$$$$$            $$
$$             $$$$$$$$$$$$$$$$$$$    $$$$$$$$$$$$$$$$$$$             $$
$$             $$$$$$$$$$$$$$$$$$      $$$$$$$$$$$$$$$$$$             $$
$$               $$$$$$$$$$$$$$$        $$$$$$$$$$$$$$$               $$
$$                 $$$$$$$$$$$            $$$$$$$$$$$                 $$
$$                                                                    $$
$$                                                                    $$
$$                                                                    $$
$$                                                                    $$
$$                                                                    $$
$$                                                                    $$
$$                                                                    $$
$$                                                                    $$
$$$$$$$$$$$$$$$$$$$$$$$$$$$$$$$$$$$$$$$$$$$$$$$$$$$$$$$$$$$$$$$$$$$$$$$$
$$$$$$$$$$$$$$$$$$$$$$$$$$$$$$$$$$$$$$$$$$$$$$$$$$$$$$$$$$$$$$$$$$$$$$$$
Ok
```

```
LIST
100 PRINT TAB(26);"INKBLOT"
105 PRINT TAB(20);"CREATIVE COMPUTING"
110 PRINT TAB(18);"MORRISTOWN, NEW JERSEY"
115 PRINT:PRINT:PRINT
120  REM *** WORKS BY PLOTTING ELLIPSES AND THEIR MIRROR IMAGES
130 DIM A (12,13),B$(36),A$(36)
140  REM *** CHOOSE FROM 5 TO 12 ELLIPSES
150  M=INT(8*RND(1))+5
160  REM *** CREATE SIZE, LOCATION AND ANGLE OF M ELLIPSES
170  FOR L=1 TO M
180  A(L,1)=34*RND(1)
190  A(L,2)=80*RND(1)
200  A(L,3)=(15*RND(1)+2)^2
210  A(L,4)=(15*RND(1)+2)^2
220  T=3.14159*RND(1)
230  A(L,5)=COS(T)
240  A(L,6)=SIN(T)
250  A(L,7)=A(L,5)*A(L,6)
260  A(L,5)=A(L,5)*A(L,5)
270  A(L,6)=A(L,6)*A(L,6)
280  A(L,8)=A(L,1)*A(L,1)*A(L,6)
290  A(L,9)=A(L,1)*A(L,1)*A(L,5)
300  A(L,10)=A(L,1)*A(L,7)
310  A(L,11)=-2*A(L,1)*A(L,6)
320  A(L,12)=-2*A(L,1)*A(L,5)
330  A(L,13)=A(L,6)/A(L,4)+A(L,5)/A(L,3)
340  NEXT L
350  REM *** PRINT TOP BORDER;  B$ CONTAINS 36 DOLLAR SIGNS
360  B$="$$$$$$$$$$$$$$$$$$$$$$$$$$$$$$$$$$$$"
370  PRINT B$;B$
380  PRINT B$;B$
390  REM *** LOOP Y IS Y-COORDINATE OF PLOT; EACH TIME Y LOOP
400  REM *** IS EXECUTED, A LINE IS PRINTED
410  FOR Y=79.9 TO 0 STEP -1.6
420  A$="$$
430  REM *** LOOP E CHECKS THE EQUATION OF EACH ELLIPSE TO SEE
440  REM *** IF IT INTERSECTS THE LINE TO BE PRINTED
450  FOR E=1 TO M
460  Y1=Y-A(E,2)
470  Y2=Y1*Y1
480  Y3=Y1*A(E,10)
490  Y4=Y1*A(E,7)
500  B=(A(E,12)+Y4)/A(E,3)+(-Y4+A(E,11))/A(E,4)
510  C=(Y2*A(E,6)+A(E,9)-Y3)/A(E,3)+(Y2*A(E,5)+A(E,8)+Y3)/A(E,4)-1
520  REM *** R IS THE RADICAL IN THE STANDARD QUADRATIC FORMULA
530  R=B*B-4*A(E,13)*C
540  IF R<0 THEN 690
550  R=SQR(R)
560  REM *** FIND WHERE THE LINE INTERSECTS THE ELLIPSE
570  R1=INT(-(B+R)/2/A(E,13)+1)
580  IF R1>34 THEN 690
590  R2=INT((R-B)/2/A(E,13))
600  IF R2<1 THEN 690
610  IF R2<35 THEN 630
620  R2=34
630  IF R1>0 THEN 660
640  R1=1
650  REM *** FILL IN THE LINE WHERE IT CROSSES THE ELLIPSE
660  FOR J=R1+2 TO R2+2
670 A$=LEFT$(A$,J-1)+"$"+RIGHT$(A$,LEN(A$)-J)
680  NEXT J
690  NEXT E
700  REM *** PRINT LINE
710  PRINT A$;
720 FOR K=36 TO 1 STEP -1
730 PRINT MID$(A$,K,1);
740  NEXT K
750  NEXT Y
760  REM *** PRINT BOTTOM BORDER
770  PRINT B$;B$
780  PRINT B$;B$
790  END
Ok
```

Joust

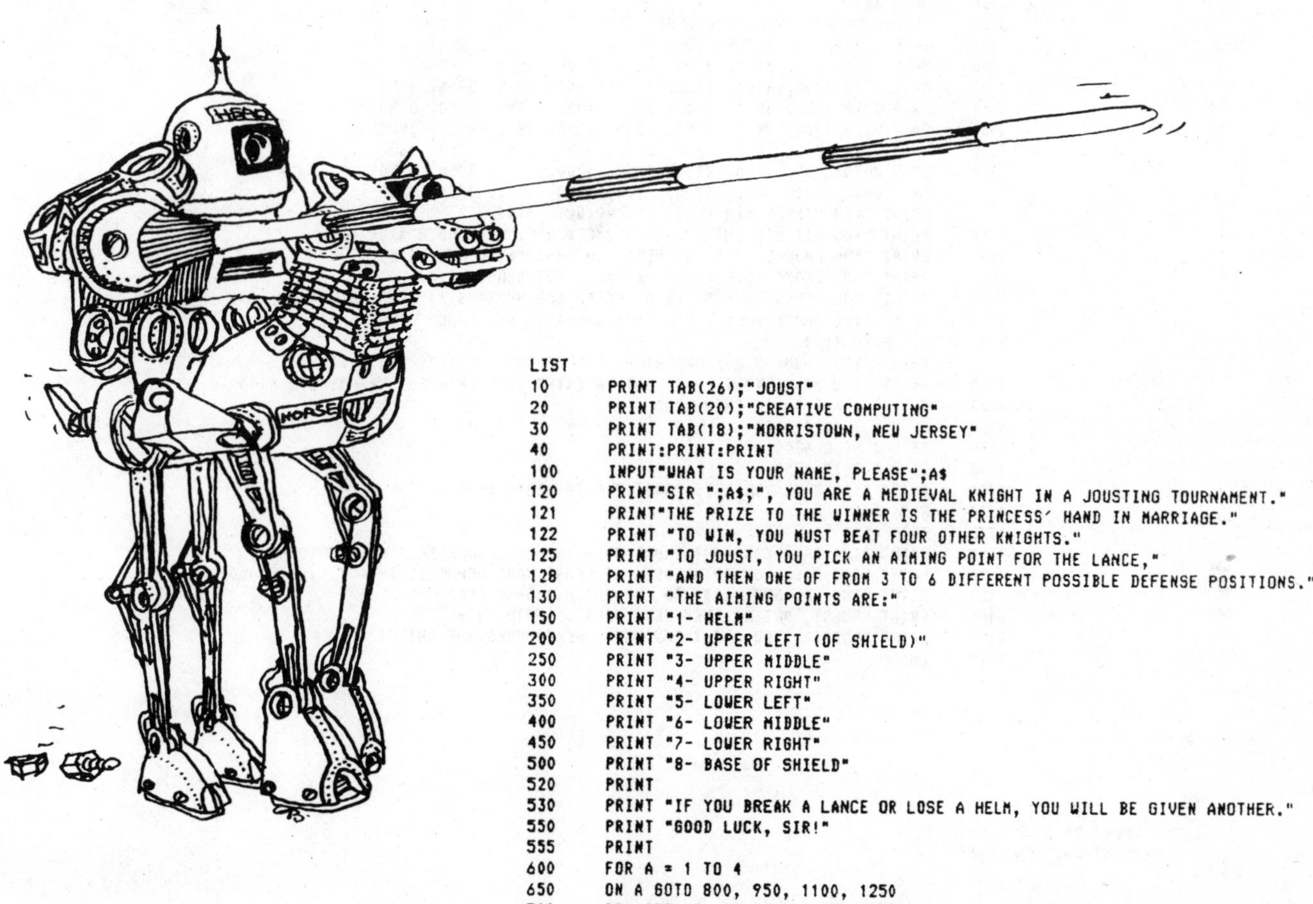

In this program you are a medieval knight in a jousting tournament. The prize to the winner of the tournament is the princess' hand in marriage. To win you must beat four other knights, the gold knight, the silver knight, the red knight, and the fierce black knight. On each pass of your opponent you must select one of eight different aiming points, such as the helm, lower left, face of shield, et cetera, and, based on your aiming point, you may select from three to six different defense positions such as a right lean or shield low.

As you proceed in the jousting tournament there are different intermediate outcomes such as getting knocked on the shield, breaking a spear, and so on. There are also some outcomes which end the contest such as your getting killed, or getting knocked from your horse.

This program was conceived and written by Alan Yarbrough.

```
LIST
10      PRINT TAB(26);"JOUST"
20      PRINT TAB(20);"CREATIVE COMPUTING"
30      PRINT TAB(18);"MORRISTOWN, NEW JERSEY"
40      PRINT:PRINT:PRINT
100     INPUT"WHAT IS YOUR NAME, PLEASE";A$
120     PRINT"SIR ";A$;", YOU ARE A MEDIEVAL KNIGHT IN A JOUSTING TOURNAMENT."
121     PRINT"THE PRIZE TO THE WINNER IS THE PRINCESS' HAND IN MARRIAGE."
122     PRINT "TO WIN, YOU MUST BEAT FOUR OTHER KNIGHTS."
125     PRINT "TO JOUST, YOU PICK AN AIMING POINT FOR THE LANCE,"
128     PRINT "AND THEN ONE OF FROM 3 TO 6 DIFFERENT POSSIBLE DEFENSE POSITIONS."
130     PRINT "THE AIMING POINTS ARE:"
150     PRINT "1- HELM"
200     PRINT "2- UPPER LEFT (OF SHIELD)"
250     PRINT "3- UPPER MIDDLE"
300     PRINT "4- UPPER RIGHT"
350     PRINT "5- LOWER LEFT"
400     PRINT "6- LOWER MIDDLE"
450     PRINT "7- LOWER RIGHT"
500     PRINT "8- BASE OF SHIELD"
520     PRINT
530     PRINT "IF YOU BREAK A LANCE OR LOSE A HELM, YOU WILL BE GIVEN ANOTHER."
550     PRINT "GOOD LUCK, SIR!"
555     PRINT
600     FOR A = 1 TO 4
650     ON A GOTO 800, 950, 1100, 1250
700     REM OFF YOU GO TO THE FOUR JOUSTS.
750     REM ------------------------------
800     PRINT "THIS IS YOUR FIRST JOUST. YOU ARE UP AGINST THE GOLD KNIGHT."
850     GOTO 1400
950     PRINT "THIS IS YOUR SECOND JOUST. YOUR OPPONENT IS THE SILVER KNIGHT."
1000    GOTO 1400
1100    PRINT "YOU ARE DOING WELL! YOUR THIRD JOUST IS AGAINST THE RED KNIGHT."
1150    GOTO 1400
1250    PRINT "THIS IS YOUR FINAL TEST!! IF YOU WIN THIS ONE THE PRINCESS"
1270    PRINT "IS YOURS!!! THIS FIGHT IS AGAINST THE FIERCE BLACK KNIGHT!!!!"
1400    INPUT "YOUR AIMING POINT(1-8)";B
1450    IF B <1 OR B>8 THEN 1400
1470    PRINT "YOU MAY USE ONE OF THESE DEFENSES:"
1500    ON B GOTO 1550, 1650, 1750, 1850, 1550, 1750, 1550, 1950
1550    PRINT " 4-STEADY SEAT, 5-SHIELD HIGH, 6-SHIELD LOW."
1600    GOTO 2000
1650    PRINT " 3-LEFT LEAN, 4-STEADY SEAT, 5-SHIELD HIGH, 6-SHIELD LOW."
1700    GOTO 2000
1750    PRINT " 1-LOWER HELM, 2-RIGHT LEAN, 3-LEFT LEAN, 4-STEADY SEAT, "
1755    PRINT " 5-SHIELD HIGH, 6-SHIELD LOW."
1800    GOTO 2000
1850    PRINT " 2-RIGHT LEAN, 4-STEADY SEAT, 5-SHIELD HIGH, 6-SHIELD LOW."
1900    GOTO 2000
1950    PRINT " 1-LOWER HELM, 4-STEADY SEAT, 5-SHIELD HIGH, 6-SHIELD LOW."
2000    INPUT "WHAT IS YOUR CHOICE"; C
2050    D = INT(RND(1)*8) + 1
2100    ON D GOTO 2150, 2200, 2250, 2300, 2350, 2400, 2450, 2500
2150    ON C GOTO 2600, 2600, 2600, 2700, 2800, 2600
2200    ON C GOTO 2800, 2750, 2600, 2750, 2750, 2600
2250    ON C GOTO 2850, 2800, 2650, 2750, 2950, 2900
2300    ON C GOTO 2650, 2600, 2750, 2650, 2650, 2800
2350    ON C GOTO 2750, 2950, 2600, 2750, 2600, 2750
2400    ON C GOTO 2950, 2650, 2750, 2950, 2850, 2750
2450    ON C GOTO 2650, 2600, 2950, 2650, 2650, 2650
2500    ON C GOTO 2750, 2650, 2850, 2750, 2850, 2750
```

```
2600    PRINT "HE MISSED YOU!":S=0:GOTO 3000
2650    PRINT "HE HIT YOUR SHIELD BUT IT GLANCED OFF.":S=0:GOTO 3000
2700    PRINT "HE KNOCKED OFF YOUR HELM!":S=0:GOTO 3000
2750    PRINT "HE BROKE HIS LANCE.":S=0:GOTO 3000
2800    PRINT "HE HAS UNSEATED YOU(THUD!)":S=5:GOTO 3000
2850    PRINT "HE HAS BROKEN HIS LANCE, INJURED AND UNSEATED YOU (OUCH!)"
2855    S=5:GOTO 3000
2900    PRINT "HE HAS INJURED AND UNSEATED YOU (CRASH!)":S=5:GOTO 3000
2950    PRINT "HE HAS BROKEN HIS LANCE AND UNSEATED YOU (CLANG!)":S=5
3000    E = INT(RND(1)*6) + 1
3050    ON D GOTO 3100,3150,3200,3250,3100,3200,3100,3300
3100    IF E<4 THEN 3000 ELSE 3350
3150    IF E<3 THEN 3000 ELSE 3350
3200    GOTO 3350
3250    IF E=1 OR E=3 THEN 3000 ELSE 3350
3300    IF E = 2 OR E = 3 THEN 3000
3350    ON E GOTO 3400, 3450, 3500, 3550, 3600, 3650
3400    ON B GOTO 3700, 3900, 3950, 3750, 3850, 4050, 3750, 3850
3450    ON B GOTO 3700, 3850, 3900, 3700, 4050, 3750, 3700, 3750
3500    ON B GOTO 3700, 3700, 3750, 3850, 3700, 3850, 4050, 3900
3550    ON B GOTO 3800, 3850, 3850, 3750, 3850, 4050, 3750, 3850
3600    ON B GOTO 3900, 3850, 4050, 3750, 3700, 3950, 3750, 3950
3650    ON B GOTO 3700, 3700, 4000, 3900, 3850, 3850, 3750, 3850
3700    PRINT "YOU MISSED HIM (HISS!)":T=0:GOTO 4100
3750    PRINT "YOU HIT HIS SHIELD BUT GLANCED OFF.":T=0:GOTO 4100
3800    PRINT "YOU KNOCKED OFF HIS HELM!(CHEERS!)":T=0:GOTO 4100
3850    PRINT "YOU BROKE YOUR LANCE(CRACK...)":T=0:GOTO 4100
3900    PRINT "YOU UNSEATED HIM (LOUD CHEERS AND HUZZAHS!!)":T=5:GOTO 4100
3950    PRINT "YOU BROKE YOUR LANCE, BUT UNSEATED AND INJURED YOUR FOE."
3955    T=5:GOTO 4100
4000    PRINT "YOU INJURED AND UNSEATED YOUR OPPONENT.":T=5:GOTO 4100
4050    PRINT "YOU BROKE YOUR LANCE BUT UNSEATED YOUR OPPONENT.":T=5:GOTO 4100
4100    IF S = T AND S = 0 THEN 4450
4150    IF S = T GOTO 4400
4200    IF S<T GOTO 4300
4250    IF S>T GOTO 4350
4300    PRINT "YOU HAVE WON THIS JOUST.":PRINT:GOTO 4320
4320    NEXT A
4330    GOTO 4550
4350    PRINT "TOO BAD, YOU LOST. HOPE YOUR INSURANCE WAS PAID UP.":GOTO 4500
4400    PRINT "TOO BAD, YOU BOTH LOST. AT LEAST YOUR HONOR IS INTACT.":GOTO 4500
4450    PRINT "YOU ARE NOW READY TO TRY AGAIN.":GOTO 1400
4500    PRINT "SORRY, BETTER LUCK NEXT JOUST.":GOTO 9999
4550    PRINT "HOORAY! YOU ARE THE WINNER. HERE COMES THE BRIDE!"
9999    END
Ok
```

```
RUN

                    JOUST
              CREATIVE COMPUTING
             MORRISTOWN, NEW JERSEY


WHAT IS YOUR NAME, PLEASE? STEVE
SIR STEVE, YOU ARE A MEDIEVAL KNIGHT IN A JOUSTING TOURNAMENT.
THE PRIZE TO THE WINNER IS THE PRINCESS' HAND IN MARRIAGE.
TO WIN, YOU MUST BEAT FOUR OTHER KNIGHTS.
TO JOUST, YOU PICK AN AIMING POINT FOR THE LANCE,
AND THEN ONE OF FROM 3 TO 6 DIFFERENT POSSIBLE DEFENSE POSITIONS.
THE AIMING POINTS ARE:
1- HELM
2- UPPER LEFT (OF SHIELD)
3- UPPER MIDDLE
4- UPPER RIGHT
5- LOWER LEFT
6- LOWER MIDDLE
7- LOWER RIGHT
8- BASE OF SHIELD

IF YOU BREAK A LANCE OR LOSE A HELM, YOU WILL BE GIVEN ANOTHER.
GOOD LUCK, SIR!

THIS IS YOUR FIRST JOUST. YOU ARE UP AGINST THE GOLD KNIGHT.
YOUR AIMING POINT(1-8)? 4
YOU MAY USE ONE OF THESE DEFENSES:
        2-RIGHT LEAN, 4-STEADY SEAT, 5-SHIELD HIGH, 6-SHIELD LOW.
WHAT IS YOUR CHOICE? 2
HE MISSED YOU!
YOU UNSEATED HIM (LOUD CHEERS AND HUZZAHS!!)
YOU HAVE WON THIS JOUST.

THIS IS YOUR SECOND JOUST. YOUR OPPONENT IS THE SILVER KNIGHT.
YOUR AIMING POINT(1-8)? 5
YOU MAY USE ONE OF THESE DEFENSES:
        4-STEADY SEAT, 5-SHIELD HIGH, 6-SHIELD LOW.
WHAT IS YOUR CHOICE? 4
HE BROKE HIS LANCE.
YOU BROKE YOUR LANCE(CRACK...)
YOU ARE NOW READY TO TRY AGAIN.
YOUR AIMING POINT(1-8)? 2
YOU MAY USE ONE OF THESE DEFENSES:
        3-LEFT LEAN, 4-STEADY SEAT, 5-SHIELD HIGH, 6-SHIELD LOW.
WHAT IS YOUR CHOICE? 3
HE BROKE HIS LANCE.
YOU MISSED HIM (HISS!)
YOU ARE NOW READY TO TRY AGAIN.
YOUR AIMING POINT(1-8)? 3
YOU MAY USE ONE OF THESE DEFENSES:
        1-LOWER HELM, 2-RIGHT LEAN, 3-LEFT LEAN, 4-STEADY SEAT,
        5-SHIELD HIGH, 6-SHIELD LOW.
WHAT IS YOUR CHOICE? 4
HE KNOCKED OFF YOUR HELM!
YOU BROKE YOUR LANCE(CRACK...)
YOU ARE NOW READY TO TRY AGAIN.
YOUR AIMING POINT(1-8)? 3
YOU MAY USE ONE OF THESE DEFENSES:
        1-LOWER HELM, 2-RIGHT LEAN, 3-LEFT LEAN, 4-STEADY SEAT,
        5-SHIELD HIGH, 6-SHIELD LOW.
WHAT IS YOUR CHOICE? 4
HE HIT YOUR SHIELD BUT IT GLANCED OFF.
YOU BROKE YOUR LANCE BUT UNSEATED YOUR OPPONENT.
YOU HAVE WON THIS JOUST.

YOU ARE DOING WELL! YOUR THIRD JOUST IS AGAINST THE RED KNIGHT.
YOUR AIMING POINT(1-8)? 8
YOU MAY USE ONE OF THESE DEFENSES:
        1-LOWER HELM, 4-STEADY SEAT, 5-SHIELD HIGH, 6-SHIELD LOW.
WHAT IS YOUR CHOICE? 1
HE HAS UNSEATED YOU(THUD!)
YOU BROKE YOUR LANCE(CRACK...)
TOO BAD, YOU LOST. HOPE YOUR INSURANCE WAS PAID UP.
SORRY, BETTER LUCK NEXT JOUST.
Ok
```

Jumping Balls

Jumping balls is a solitaire board game played with a board having nine holes in a line that can be filled with four white balls to the right end and four black balls to the left end. Without a board, it can be played with coins or chips. The object of the game is to reverse the position of the balls (or other objects) from one end of the board to the other.

You may make a move by moving a ball to the immediately adjacent empty hole or by jumping one other ball. You may not jump two or more balls. Holes are numbered from left to right. At the beginning of the game, hole number five is free. Consequently, a legitimate first move would be six to five, four to five, three to five, which would be a jump, or seven to five, another jump.

The computer does not rank your playing ability but, as a hint, you ought to be able to complete the game in fewer moves than are shown in our sample run.

The original author of this game was Anthony Rizzolo.

```
LIST
10 PRINT TAB(22);"JUMPING BALLS"
20 PRINT TAB(20);"CREATIVE COMPUTING"
30 PRINT TAB(18);"MORRISTOWN, NEW JERSEY"
40 PRINT:PRINT:PRINT
1040 DIM Q(9,1)
1050 PRINT "INSTRUCTIONS";
1060 INPUT A$
1070 IF LEFT$(A$,1)="N" THEN 1150
1080 PRINT "     IN THIS GAME YOU ARE GIVEN 8 BALLS ON A 9 HOLE"
1090 PRINT "BOARD.  THE OBJECT IS TO REVERSE THE ORDER OF THE BALLS"
1100 PRINT "THE 'S' ARE SILVER BALLS AND THE 'G' ARE GOLD."
1110 PRINT "YOU MUST GET THE SILVER TO WHERE THE GOLD ARE AND"
1120 PRINT "THE GOLD TO WHERE THE SILVER ARE.  THE SPACE IS"
1125 PRINT "A PERIOD ON THE BOARD."
1130 PRINT "GOOD LUCK!!  HERE IS THE BOARD:"
1140 S=0
1150 FOR X=1 TO 4
1160 LET Q(X,1)=1
1170 NEXT X
1180 LET Q(5,1)=0
1190  FOR X=6 TO 9
1200  LET Q(X,1)=2
1210  NEXT X
1220  LET A$=".SG"
1230  FOR X=1 TO 9
1240 PRINT MID$(A$,Q(X,1)+1,1);
1250  PRINT " ";
1260  NEXT X
1265 S=S+1
1270  PRINT "MOVE";
1280  INPUT M,M1
1290 IF M<=9 AND M>=1 AND M1<=9 AND M1>=1 THEN 1320
1300  PRINT "ILLEGAL MOVE"
1310  GOTO 1270
1320  REM:      CHECK FOR LEGAL MOVE
1330  IF M+1=M1 OR M-1=M1 THEN 1430
1340  REM:      SUBROUTINE FOR CHECKING JUMPS
1350  IF M=9 THEN 1390
1360  IF M=1 THEN 1410
1370  IF Q(M+1,1)=0 OR Q(M-1,1)=0 THEN 1300
1380  GOTO 1420
1390  IF Q(M-1,1)=0 THEN 1300
1400  GOTO 1420
1410  IF Q(M+1,1)=0 THEN 1300
1420  IF M+2<>M1 AND M-2<>M1 THEN 1300
1430  IF Q(M,1)<>0 THEN 1460
1440  PRINT "NOTHING AT SPACE";M
1450  GOTO 1270
1460  IF Q(M1,1)=0 THEN 1490
1470  PRINT "SPACE";M1;"IS OCCUPIED"
1480  GOTO 1270
1490  LET Q(M1,1)=Q(M,1)
1500  LET Q(M,1)=0
1510 X9=Q(1,1)+Q(2,1)+Q(3,1)+Q(4,1)
1512 Y9=Q(6,1)+Q(7,1)+Q(8,1)+Q(9,1)
1514 IF X9=8 AND Y9=4 THEN 1530
1520 GOTO 1230
1530  PRINT "YOU WIN!!!"
1535 PRINT "YOU COMPLETED THE GAME IN ";S;" MOVES!!!!"
1540  PRINT "AGAIN";
1550 INPUT A$
1560 IF LEFT$(A$,1)="Y" THEN 1130
1570  END
Ok
```

```
RUN
                      JUMPING BALLS
                    CREATIVE COMPUTING
                  MORRISTOWN, NEW JERSEY



INSTRUCTIONS? YES
     IN THIS GAME YOU ARE GIVEN 8 BALLS ON A 9 HOLE
BOARD.  THE OBJECT IS TO REVERSE THE ORDER OF THE BALLS
THE 'S' ARE SILVER BALLS AND THE 'G' ARE GOLD.
YOU MUST GET THE SILVER TO WHERE THE GOLD ARE AND
THE GOLD TO WHERE THE SILVER ARE.  THE SPACE IS
A PERIOD ON THE BOARD.
GOOD LUCK!!  HERE IS THE BOARD:
S S S S . G G G G MOVE? 6,5
S S S S G . G G G MOVE? 4,6
S S S . G S G G G MOVE? 5,4
S S S G . S G G G MOVE? 7,5
S S S G G S . G G MOVE? 6,7
S S S G G . S G G MOVE? 5,6
S S S G . G S G G MOVE? 6,5
S S S G G . S G G MOVE? 5,6
S S S G . G S G G MOVE? 3,5
S S . G S G S G G MOVE? 4,3
S S G . S G S G G MOVE? 6,4
S S G G S . S G G MOVE? 8,6
S S G G S G S . G MOVE? 7,8
S S G G S G . S G MOVE? 5,6
SPACE 6 IS OCCUPIED
MOVE? 5,7
S S G G . G S S G MOVE? 4,5
S S G . G G S S G MOVE? 2,4
S . G S G G S S G MOVE? 3,2
S G . S G G S S G MOVE? 1,3
. G S S G G S S G MOVE? 2,1
G . S S G G S S G MOVE? 3,2
G S . S G G S S G MOVE? 5,3
G S G S . G S S G MOVE? 6,5
G S G S G . S S G MOVE? 7,6
G S G S G S . S G MOVE? 9,7
G S G S G S G S . MOVE? 8,9
G S G S G S G . S MOVE? 6,8
G S G S G . G S S MOVE? 4,6
G S G . G S G S S MOVE? 2,4
G . G S G S G S S MOVE? 3,2
G G . S G S G S S MOVE? 5,3
G G G S . S G S S MOVE? 7,5
G G G S G S . S S MOVE? 6,7
G G G S G . S S S MOVE? 4,6
G G G . G S S S S MOVE? 5,4
YOU WIN!!!
YOU COMPLETED THE GAME IN  34  MOVES!!!!
AGAIN? NO
Ok
```

Keno

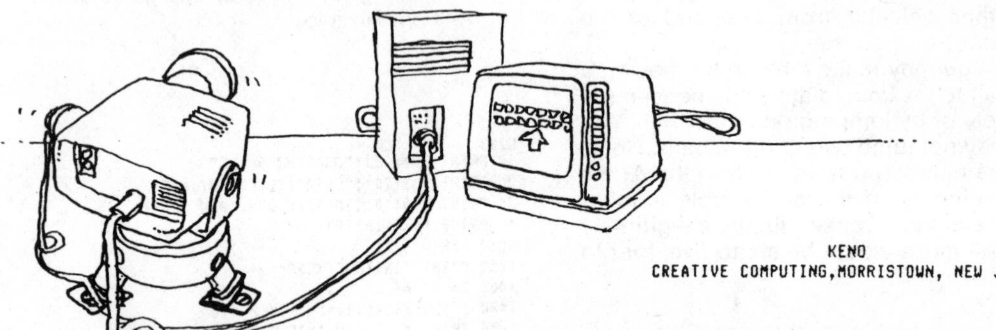

Keno is strictly an American invention that originated in the casinos in Nevada, perhaps in Reno. During the game, twenty numbers from one to eighty are selected at random. Prior to each game at the casino, the player may choose from one to fifteen numbers, or "spots" he thinks will be selected during the game. The player enters, or "marks," the desired spots and places a bet. At the end of each game, the spots marked by the player are compared with the twenty numbers and the payoff is computed accordingly. Keno seems to have a high attraction in Las Vegas because the betting is very simple and the maximum payoff is very high ($25,000). Nevertheless, the probability of winning is extremely low; indeed, Keno returns more to the house than virtually any other game.

In this particular computersized version of Keno, there is only one player and he has the option only of betting eight different spots. In Nevada the normal bet is in multiples of 60¢; however, in this game the bet will be $1.20 with no multiples possible. The payoff with eight spots marked is as follows:

Spots	Payoff
5	$10.00
6	$100.00
7	$2,200.00
8	$25,000.00

There is no payoff for zero, one, two, three, or four correct.

This version of Keno was originally written by Vincent Fazio.

```
                              KENO
               CREATIVE COMPUTING,MORRISTOWN, NEW JERSEY



KENO IS PLAYED IN MANY CASINOS IN LAS VEGAS.
PLAY KENO BY COMPUTER.  ONE VARIATION OF THE GAME, UTILIZES
THE RANDOM NUMBER GENERATOR.

THE PLAYER CHOOSES 8 DIFFERENT NUMBERS FROM 1 TO 80
INCLUSIVE, AND BETS $1.20.  THE COMPUTER WILL SELECT
20 NUMBERS AT RANDOM AND WILL ELIMINATE DUPLICATES WHICH
MAY OCCUR .  ANOTHER NUMBER  WILL BE INSERTED IN ITS PLACE
SO THAT THE COMPUTER WILL OUTPUT 20 DIFFERENT NUMBERS.




HERE WE GO!!!
THE COMPUTER WILL OUTPUT A ? MARK.  TYPE A NUMBER FROM
1 TO 80, INCLUSIVE, AND PRESS THE RETURN KEY. REPEAT THIS
PROCESS UNTIL THE ? MARK IS NO LONGER SHOWN.
? 1
? 23
? 24
? 35
? 46
? 77
? 65
? 2


 THE COMPUTER WILL SELECT 20 NUMBERS AT RANDOM.  THE BELL
TONE INDICATES IT IS IN THE PROCESS OF SELECTING THE NUMBERS.


YOUR NUMBERS ARE:
 1  23  24  35  46  77  65  2


THE COMPUTER HAS SELECTED THE FOLLOWING  NUMBERS:
33  5  74  69  44  7  45  48  80  36  45  50  26  25  38  77  6  49
15  51

THE PROGRAM WILL COMPARE YOUR NUMBERS WITH THE
NUMBERS THE COMPUTER HAS SELECTED.

LISTEN FOR THE BELL TONE--- EACH RING INDICATES ANOTHER
CORRECT GUESS BY YOU.
YOU HAVE GUESSED THE FOLLOWED NUMBERS:





 77


YOU CAUGHT 1 NUMBERS OUT OF 8--
NOT ENOUGH CORRECT GUESSES-- 'SO SOLLY', NO PAYOFF.
```

```
DO YOU WANT TO PLAY KENO AGAIN?
TYPE 'YES' OR 'NO'
? YES


HERE WE GO!!!
THE COMPUTER WILL OUTPUT A ? MARK.  TYPE A NUMBER FROM
1 TO 80, INCLUSIVE, AND PRESS THE RETURN KEY. REPEAT THIS
PROCESS UNTIL THE ? MARK IS NO LONGER SHOWN.
? 23
? 65
? 7
? 25
? 46
? 75
? 1
? 55


 THE COMPUTER WILL SELECT 20 NUMBERS AT RANDOM.  THE BELL
TONE INDICATES IT IS IN THE PROCESS OF SELECTING THE NUMBERS.


YOUR NUMBERS ARE:
 23  65  7  25  46  75  1  55


 THE COMPUTER HAS SELECTED THE FOLLOWING  NUMBERS:
 45  26  12  38  9  18  23  69  12  8  6  51  46  73  71  14  35  79
 61  58

THE PROGRAM WILL COMPARE YOUR NUMBERS WITH THE
NUMBERS THE COMPUTER HAS SELECTED.


LISTEN FOR THE BELL TONE--- EACH RING INDICATES ANOTHER
CORRECT GUESS BY YOU.
YOU HAVE GUESSED THE FOLLOWED NUMBERS:
 23



 46


YOU CAUGHT 2 NUMBERS OUT OF 8--
NOT ENOUGH CORRECT GUESSES-- 'SO SOLLY', NO PAYOFF.


DO YOU WANT TO PLAY KENO AGAIN?
TYPE 'YES' OR 'NO'
? NO
THAT'S ALL FOR NOW.  PLAY KENO AGAIN, BE SEEING YOU.
OK
```

```
 LIST

1 PRINT TAB(34)"KENO"
2 PRINT TAB(15)" CREATIVE COMPUTING,MORRISTOWN, NEW JERSEY"
3 DIM N(21),M(23),A(8)
9 PRINT:PRINT:PRINT
10 PRINT"KENO IS PLAYED IN MANY CASINOS IN LAS VEGAS."
13 PRINT "PLAY KENO BY COMPUTER.  ONE VARIATION OF THE GAME, UTILIZES"
16 PRINT"THE RANDOM NUMBER GENERATOR."
19 PRINT
20 PRINT"THE PLAYER CHOOSES 8 DIFFERENT NUMBERS FROM 1 TO 80"
23 PRINT"INCLUSIVE, AND BETS $1.20.  THE COMPUTER WILL SELECT"
26 PRINT"20 NUMBERS AT RANDOM AND WILL ELIMINATE DUPLICATES WHICH"
29 PRINT"MAY OCCUR .  ANOTHER NUMBER  WILL BE INSERTED IN ITS PLACE"
32 PRINT"SO THAT THE COMPUTER WILL OUTPUT 20 DIFFERENT NUMBERS."
35 PRINT:PRINT
38 PRINT:PRINT:PRINT "HERE WE GO!!!"
40 PRINT"THE COMPUTER WILL OUTPUT A ? MARK.  TYPE A NUMBER FROM "
43 PRINT"1 TO 80, INCLUSIVE, AND PRESS THE RETURN KEY. REPEAT THIS"
46 PRINT"PROCESS UNTIL THE ? MARK IS NO LONGER SHOWN."
48 FOR I=1 TO 8
50 INPUT A(I)
51 IF A(I)>80  THEN 56
53 IF A(I)=0 THEN 56
54 IF A(I)<0 THEN 56
55 GOTO 57
56 PRINT"TYPE A NUMBER FROM 1 TO 80 , INCLUSIVE, PLEASE.": GOTO 50
57 NEXT I
58 C=0:FOR K=1 TO7
59 FOR J=K TO 7
60 X=A(K):Y=A(J+1)
61 IF X<>Y THEN 72
62 C=C+1
63 PRINT"A DUPLICATE NUMBER HAS BEEN DETECTED IN YOUR INPUT."
64 PRINT"TYPE ANOTHER NUMBER, PLEASE.":INPUT Y
65 IF Y=0 THEN 70
66 IF Y>80 THEN 70
67 IF Y<0 THEN 70
68 A(J+1)=Y
69 GOTO 61
70 PRINT "TYPE A NUMBER FROM 1 TO 80, INCLUSIVE, PLEASE."
71 GOTO 64
72 NEXT J
73 NEXT K :PRINT:PRINT
75 IF C=0 THEN 88
76 GOTO 58
88 PRINT" THE COMPUTER WILL SELECT 20 NUMBERS AT RANDOM.  THE BELL "
91 PRINT"TONE INDICATES IT IS IN THE PROCESS OF SELECTING THE NUMBERS."
100 FOR L=1 TO 20
103 N(L)=INT(80*RND(80)+1)
106 M(L)=N(L)
109 NEXT L
110 L=21
112 FOR K=1 TO 20
115 FOR J=K TO L-1
118 X=M(K)
121 Y=M(J+1)
124 IF X<>Y  THEN 139
130 M(J+1)=INT(80*RND(1)+1)
133 Y=M(J+1)
136 GOTO 124
139 PRINT CHR$(7);
142 NEXT J
145 NEXT K
147 PRINT:PRINT
148 PRINT "YOUR NUMBERS ARE:"
151 FOR I=1 TO 8
154 PRINT A(I);
157 NEXT I: PRINT:PRINT:PRINT
160 PRINT" THE COMPUTER HAS SELECTED THE FOLLOWING  NUMBERS:"
163 FOR L=1 TO 20
167 PRINT M(L);
170 NEXT L:PRINT:PRINT
173 PRINT"THE PROGRAM WILL COMPARE YOUR NUMBERS WITH THE "
176 PRINT"NUMBERS THE COMPUTER HAS SELECTED."
179 PRINT:PRINT
182 PRINT"LISTEN FOR THE BELL TONE--- EACH RING INDICATES ANOTHER"
185 PRINT "CORRECT GUESS BY YOU.":
188 PRINT "YOU HAVE GUESSED THE FOLLOWED NUMBERS:"
191 G=0
194 I=1
197 FOR J=1 TO 20
200 X=A(I)
203 Y=M(J)
206 IF X=Y THEN 213
209 NEXT J
210 GOTO 225
213 PRINT CHR$(7);
216 FOR V1=1 TO 3976:NEXT V1
219 PRINT A(I);
222 G=G+1
225 I=I+1:PRINT:IF I<>8 THEN 197
228 IF G<5 THEN 242
231 IF G=5 THEN 261
234 IF G=6 THEN 267
237 IF G=7 THEN 273
240 IF G=8 THEN 279
242 PRINT "YOU CAUGHT";G;"NUMBERS OUT OF 8--"
243 PRINT "NOT ENOUGH CORRECT GUESSES-- 'SO SOLLY', NO PAYOFF."
245 PRINT:PRINT
246 PRINT "DO YOU WANT TO PLAY KENO AGAIN?"
249 PRINT "TYPE 'YES' OR 'NO'"
250 C=0
251 INPUT X$
252 IF X$= "YES" THEN 38
253 IF X$="NO" THEN 299
254 C=C+1
255 IF C=3 THEN 299
256 PRINT "TYPE 'YES' OR 'NO'"
257 GOTO 251
258 IF X$="NO" THEN 299
259 PRINT "TYPE YES OR NO PLEASE!!"
261 PRINT "YOU  CAUGHT";G;"NUMBERS OUT OF 8--YOU WIN $10.00"
264 PRINT:PRINT:GOTO 246
267 PRINT "YOU CAUGHT";G;"NUMBERS OUT OF 8--YOU WIN $100.00"
270 PRINT:PRINT:GOTO 246
273 PRINT "YOU CAUGHT ";G;"NUMBERS OUT OF 8--YOU WIN $2200.00"
276 PRINT:PRINT:GOTO246
279 PRINT "YOU CAUGHT ";G;"NUMBERS OUT OF 8--YOU WIN $25000.00"
282 PRINT "8 OUT OF 8 DOES NOT OCCUR TOO OFTEN, LUCKY."
285 PRINT:PRINT:GOTO 246
299 PRINT "THAT'S ALL FOR NOW.  PLAY KENO AGAIN, BE SEEING YOU."
300 END
OK
```

L Game

The L-game is a 2-player strategic game played on a 4x4 grid. It was originally devised by Edward de Bono and appeared in the book, "The Five-Day Course in Thinking." In the game, each player has one 'L' which covers four squares (3 high x 2 across). The two L's are labelled differently to avoid confusion. There are also two neutral 'boxes' each the size of a single square on the grid. To play the game with the computer the grid positions must be numbered as follows:

1	2	3	4
5	6	7	8
9	10	11	12
13	14	15	16

Play always begins with all the pieces on the board in this position:

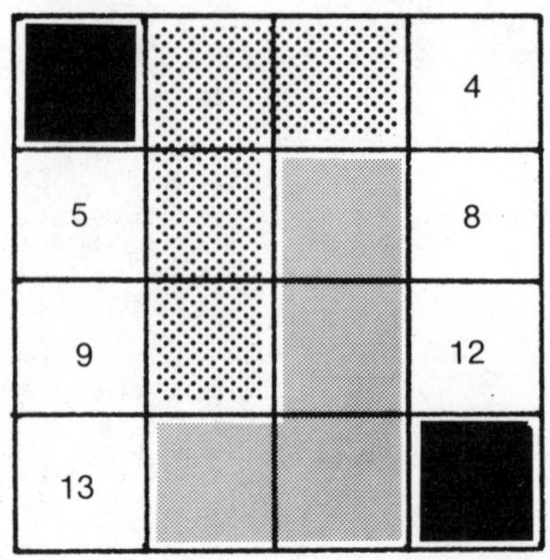

The object of the game is simply to position one's L and the neutral boxes to pin the other player's L. Each move is a mixture of offense and defense, for one is not only trying to pin the other player's L, but also trying to prevent his own L from being pinned.

Either player may move first. To move, one must pick up his L and move it to a different position on the board. The player may flip his L over, rotate it 90 degrees, etc. The L must not cover any other pieces or hang off the edge of the board. If a player is unable to move his L, or simply cannot find a move, he loses the game. Once the player has successfully moved his L to a new position on the board, he then has the option of moving the neutral boxes. He may move the boxes only to unoccupied positions and he has the option of moving one box, both boxes, or leaving the boxes where they are. By using the boxes effectively, one can block off moves for the other player's L and possibly pin him. After the player moves the boxes (or decides not to move one or both) it is the other player's turn and play continues in the same manner.

The computer version of the L Game was written by Bill Gardner.

```
RUN
                         L-GAME
                   CREATIVE COMPUTING
                 MORRISTOWN, NEW JERSEY


INSTRUCTIONS? YES

     L-game is a simple strategic game played on a 4x4
grid by two opposing players, in this case between you
and the computer.  The grid is numbered as follows:

================
: 1:: 2:: 3:: 4:
================
================
: 5:: 6:: 7:: 8:
================
================
: 9::10::11::12:
================
================
:13::14::15::16:
================

     The game is played with four pieces; both
you and the computer have one 'L', and there are
two 'BOXES' which are used by both players.
play always begins with the pieces on the board
in the following position:

****////////====
*  *////////: 4:
****////////====
====////0000====
: 5:////0000: 8:
====////0000====
====////0000====
: 9:////0000:12:
====////0000====
====00000000****
:13:00000000*  *
====00000000****

(computer is /, you are 0)
```

```
     The object of the game is to position your own
L and the boxes to prevent the computer from moving
its L.  Of course, it is trying to do the same to you!
To move, you must simply enter the four coordinates
where you want to place your L.  It must remain on the
board and must not cover any other pieces.  You must
move your L!  If you cannot find a new position
for your L, then the computer has effectively pinned your
L and it wins the game.
     Assuming you have successfully moved your L, you now
have the option of moving the boxes.  You may move one,
two, or none of the boxes by simply entering the coordinates
where you want to put them.  To leave a box where it is,
enter its present position.
     After you move the boxes, it is up to the computer
to find a move for its L and play continues in the same
manner.  Remember that you must not only try to pin the
computer's L but also keep your own L from being pinned.
Also, it is easier to play the game with your own board
than the computer printout.  To resign, enter 0,0,0,0
in place of your move.  GOOD LUCK!

BOARD PRINTOUT? YES
DO YOU WISH TO START? NO

COMPUTER MOVES TO  2   6   10   9
       MOVES BOXES TO  12  AND  16

====////========
: 1:////: 3:: 4:
====////========
====////0000====
: 5:////0000: 8:
====////0000====
////////0000****
////////0000*  *
////////0000****
====00000000****
:13:00000000*  *
====00000000****
```

```
YOUR MOVE FOR L? 4,3,7,11
YOUR MOVE FOR THE BOXES? 1,14
O.K.

****////00000000
*  *////00000000
****////00000000
====////0000====
: 5:////0000: 8:
====////0000====
////////0000====
////////0000:12:
////////0000====
====****========
:13:*  *:15::16:
====****========
```

```
YOUR MOVE FOR L? 3,7,11,12
YOUR MOVE FOR THE BOXES? 2,10
O.K.

====****0000====
: 1:*  *0000: 4:
====****0000====
////====0000====
////: 6:0000: 8:
////====0000====
////****00000000
////*  *00000000
////****00000000
////////========
////////:15::16:
////////========
```

LATER IN THE GAME

```
COMPUTER MOVES TO  5   9   13   6
        MOVES BOXES TO  10  AND  8

========0000====
: 1:: 2:0000: 4:
========0000====
////////0000****
////////0000*  *
////////0000****
////****00000000
////*  *00000000
////****00000000
////============
////:14::15::16:
////============


YOUR MOVE FOR L? 7,11,15,16
YOUR MOVE FOR THE BOXES? 10,3
O.K.

========****====
: 1:: 2:*  *: 4:
========****====
////////0000====
////////0000: 8:
////////0000====
////****0000====
////*  *0000:12:
////****0000====
////====00000000
////:14:00000000
////====00000000


COMPUTER MOVES TO  1   5   9   2
        MOVES BOXES TO  6  AND  10

////////========
////////: 3:: 4:
////////========
////****0000====
////*  *0000: 8:
////****0000====
////****0000====
////*  *0000:12:
////****0000====
========00000000
:13::14:00000000
========00000000


YOUR MOVE FOR L? 11,15,14,13
YOUR MOVE FOR THE BOXES? 6,10
O.K.

////////========
////////: 3:: 4:
////////========
////****========
////*  *: 7:: 8:
////****========
////****0000====
////*  *0000:12:
////****0000====
000000000000====
000000000000:16:
000000000000====


COMPUTER MOVES TO  1   2   3   7
        MOVES BOXES TO  6  AND  10

////////////====
////////////: 4:
////////////====
====****////====
: 5:*  *////: 8:
====****////====
====****0000====
: 9:*  *0000:12:
====****0000====
000000000000====
000000000000:16:
000000000000====


YOUR MOVE FOR L? 4,8,11,12
YOUR MOVE FOR THE BOXES? 6,14
O.K.

////////////0000
////////////0000
////////////0000
====****////0000
: 5:*  *////0000
====****////0000
========00000000
: 9::10:00000000
========00000000
====****========
:13:*  *:15::16:
====****========


COMPUTER MOVES TO  1   5   9   10
        MOVES BOXES TO  6  AND  7

////========0000
////: 2:: 3:0000
////========0000
////********0000
////*  **  *0000
////********0000
////////00000000
////////00000000
////////00000000
================
:13::14::15::16:
================


YOUR MOVE FOR L? 11,13,12,14
ILLEGAL MOVE FOR L.


YOUR MOVE FOR L? 11,13,14,15
YOUR MOVE FOR THE BOXES? 2,7
O.K.

////****========
////*  *: 3:: 4:
////****========
////====****====
////: 6:*  *: 8:
////====****====
////////0000====
////////0000:12:
////////0000====
000000000000====
000000000000:16:
000000000000====


COMPUTER MOVES TO  4   8   12   3
        MOVES BOXES TO  6  AND  7

========////////
: 1:: 2:////////
========////////
====********////
: 5:*  **  *////
====********////
========0000////
: 9::10:0000////
========0000////
000000000000====
000000000000:16:
000000000000====


YOUR MOVE FOR L? 5,9,10,11
YOUR MOVE FOR THE BOXES? 2,7
O.K.

====****////////
: 1:*  *////////
====****////////
0000====****////
0000: 6:*  *////
0000====****////
000000000000////
000000000000////
000000000000////
================
:13::14::15::16:
================


COMPUTER MOVES TO  8   12   16   15
        MOVES BOXES TO  6  AND  7

================
: 1:: 2:: 3:: 4:
================
0000********////
0000*  **  *////
0000********////
000000000000////
000000000000////
000000000000////
========////////
:13::14:////////
========////////


YOUR MOVE FOR L? 11,10,9,13
YOUR MOVE FOR THE BOXES? 3,7
O.K.

========****====
: 1:: 2:*  *: 4:
========****====
========****////
: 5:: 6:*  *////
========****////
000000000000////
000000000000////
000000000000////
0000====////////
0000:14:////////
0000====////////


COMPUTER MOVES TO  14   15   16   12
        MOVES BOXES TO  6  AND  7

================
: 1:: 2:: 3:: 4:
================
====********====
: 5:*  **  *: 8:
====********====
000000000000////
000000000000////
000000000000////
0000////////////
0000////////////
0000////////////


YOUR MOVE FOR L? 5,9,10,11
YOUR MOVE FOR THE BOXES? 3,8
O.K.

========****====
: 1:: 2:*  *: 4:
========****====
0000========****
0000: 6:: 7:*  *
0000========****
000000000000////
000000000000////
000000000000////
====////////////
:13:////////////
====////////////

CONGRATULATIONS! YOU HAVE WON.

PLAY AGAIN? NO
```

```
LIST
10 PRINT TAB(26);"L-GAME"
11 PRINT TAB(20);"CREATIVE COMPUTING"
12 PRINT TAB(18);"MORRISTOWN, NEW JERSEY"
13 PRINT:PRINT:PRINT
20 DIM C(4),O(4),T(4),B(16),N(16),M(100)
25 PRINT "INSTRUCTIONS";
30 INPUT A$
35 IF LEFT$(A$,1)="Y" THEN 3000
40 PRINT "BOARD PRINTOUT";
45 INPUT A$
50 IF LEFT$(A$,1)="N" THEN 65
55 LET F2=0
60 GOTO 70
65 LET F2=1
70 GOSUB 100
80 GOTO 210
100 REM INITIALIZE DATA
101 REM B1,B2 = POSITIONS OF BOXES
102 REM C(1,2,3,4) = COMPUTER'S POSITION (L)
103 REM O(1,2,3,4) = OPPONENT'S POSITION (L)
104 REM T(1,2,3,4) = 6,7,10,11 = CENTER POSITIONS
105 REM B(1,...16) = BOARD:
106 REM     B(X)=0   EMPTY
107 REM     B(X)=1   OPPONENT'S L
108 REM     B(X)=2   COMPUTER'S L
109 REM     B(X)=3   BOX
115 RESTORE
120 DATA 1,16,2,7,6,6,11,7,10,15,10,3,14,11
130 DATA 3,2,2,0,0,2,1,0,0,2,1,0,0,1,1,3
140 READ B1,B2
150 FOR X=1 TO 4
160 READ C(X),O(X),T(X)
170 NEXT X
180 FOR X=1 TO 16
190 READ B(X)
200 NEXT X
205 RETURN
210 PRINT "DO YOU WISH TO START";
215 INPUT A$
220 IF LEFT$(A$,1)="N" THEN 500
230 REM OPPONENT'S MOVE
235 GOSUB 2270
240 PRINT
245 PRINT "YOUR MOVE FOR L";
250 INPUT D(1),D(2),D(3),D(4)
255 IF ABS(D(1))+ABS(D(2))+ABS(D(3))+ABS(D(4))=0 THEN 1280
260 REM BUBBLE SORT
265 FOR X=1 TO 4
270 FOR Y=2 TO 4
275 IF D(Y)>D(Y-1) THEN 295
280 LET Z=D(Y)
285 LET D(Y)=D(Y-1)
290 LET D(Y-1)=Z
295 NEXT Y
300 NEXT X
305 REM CHECK LEGALITY
310 FOR X=1 TO 4
315 LET M(X)=D(X)
320 NEXT X
325 LET N1=4
330 LET F1=0
335 GOSUB 1800
340 IF M1<>4 THEN 1220
345 FOR X=1 TO 4
350 IF B(M(X))>1 THEN 1220
355 NEXT X
360 FOR X=1 TO 4
365 LET B(O(X))=0
370 NEXT X
375 FOR X=1 TO 4
380 LET B(M(X))=1
385 LET O(X)=M(X)
390 NEXT X
395 LET B(B1)=0
400 LET B(B2)=0
405 PRINT "YOUR MOVE FOR THE BOXES";
410 INPUT X,Y
415 IF ABS(X)+ABS(Y)<>X+Y THEN 1250
416 IF X=Y THEN 1250
420 IF B(X)+B(Y)>0 THEN 1250
430 LET B1=X
440 LET B2=Y
450 LET B(B1)=3
460 LET B(B2)=3
470 PRINT "O.K."
475 GOSUB 2270
480 REM COMPUTER'S MOVE
490 REM REMOVE C(1-4) FROM BOARD
500 FOR X=1 TO 4
510 LET B(C(X))=0
520 NEXT X
530 GOSUB 1420
540 LET F1=1
550 LET N1=Z
560 GOSUB 1800
570 IF M1=0 THEN 1300
580 REM FIND MOVE WITH BEST CENTER COVERAGE
585 GOSUB 1370
590 FOR E=0 TO M1-4 STEP 4
600 FOR F=1 TO 4
610 FOR G=1 TO 4
620 IF M(E+F)<>T(G) THEN 640
630 LET N(E/4+1)=N(E/4+1)+1
640 NEXT G
650 NEXT F
660 NEXT E
670 GOSUB 1500
680 REM PUT MOVE IN C(1-4)
690 LET Y=(Z-1)*4
700 FOR X=1 TO 4
710 LET C(X)=M(X+Y)
720 LET B(C(X))=2
730 NEXT X
740 PRINT
750 PRINT "COMPUTER MOVES TO ";C(1);" ";C(2);" ";C(3);" ";C(4)
760 REM FIND MOVES FOR BOXES
765 REM REMOVE BOXES FROM BOARD
770 LET B(B1)=0
780 LET B(B2)=0
790 REM IS OPPONENT IN CORNER?
800 FOR I=1 TO 4
810 FOR J=1 TO 4
820 IF O(I)=T(J) THEN 870
830 NEXT J
840 NEXT I
845 REM OPPONENT IN CORNER, IGNORE CENTER
850 GOTO 1020
860 REM OPPONENT NOT IN CORNER, FILL CENTER WITH BOXES
870 FOR X=1 TO 4
880 IF B(T(X))>0 THEN 920
890 LET B1=T(X)
900 LET B(B1)=3
910 GOTO 950
920 NEXT X
930 REM NO SPACES IN CENTER
940 GOTO 1020
950 FOR X=1 TO 4
960 IF B(T(X))>0 THEN 1000
970 LET B2=T(X)
980 LET B(B2)=3
990 GOTO 1080
1000 NEXT X
1005 REM CENTER FILLED
1010 GOTO 1050
1015 REM BOTH BOXES TO BE POSITIONED
1020 GOSUB 1610
1030 LET B1=B3
1040 LET B(B1)=3
1045 REM ONE BOX TO BE POSITIONED
1050 GOSUB 1610
1060 LET B2=B3
1070 LET B(B2)=3
1080 PRINT TAB(9);"MOVES BOXES TO ";B1;" AND ";B2
1081 FOR X=1 TO 4
1082 LET B(O(X))=1
1083 NEXT X
1085 GOSUB 2270
1090 REM CHECK FOR WIN
1100 FOR X=1 TO 4
1110 LET B(O(X))=0
1120 NEXT X
1130 GOSUB 1420
1140 LET F1=2
1150 LET N1=Z
1160 GOSUB 1800
1170 IF M1=0 THEN 1280
1180 FOR X=1 TO 4
1190 LET B(O(X))=1
1200 NEXT X
1210 GOTO 240
1220 PRINT "ILLEGAL MOVE FOR L."
1230 PRINT
1240 GOTO 240
```

```
1250 PRINT "ILLEGAL MOVE FOR BOX."
1260 PRINT
1270 GOTO 405
1280 PRINT "COMPUTER WINS!"
1290 GOTO 1310
1300 PRINT "CONGRATULATIONS! YOU HAVE WON."
1310 PRINT
1320 PRINT "PLAY AGAIN";
1325 INPUT A$
1330 IF LEFT$(A$,1)="Y" THEN 70
1340 GOTO 4000
1350 REM *** SUBROUTINES ***
1360 REM ERASE N(X)
1370 FOR X=1 TO 16
1380 LET N(X)=0
1390 NEXT X
1400 RETURN
1410 REM STORE LOCATIONS OF UNOCCUPIED POSITIONS IN N(X)
1420 LET Z=0
1430 FOR X=1 TO 16
1440 IF B(X)>0 THEN 1470
1450 LET Z=Z+1
1460 LET N(Z)=X
1470 NEXT X
1480 RETURN
1490 REM THIS SUBROUTINE RETURNS THE LOCATION OF THE LARGEST
1495 REM VALUE IN N(X).  IF A TIE EXISTS A RANDOM CHOICE IS MADE.
1500 LET Y=0
1510 LET Z=1
1520 FOR X=1 TO M1/4
1530 IF N(X)<Y THEN 1580
1540 IF N(X)>Y THEN 1560
1550 IF RND(1)>.5 THEN 1580
1560 LET Y=N(X)
1570 LET Z=X
1580 NEXT X
1590 RETURN
1600 REM BOX-FIND
1601 REM THIS SUBROUTINE FINDS THE MOVE FOR A BOX THAT WILL
1602 REM MOST RESTRICT THE OPPONENT'S L IN TERMS OF MOVES POSSIBLE.
1610 FOR X=1 TO 4
1620 LET B(O(X))=0
1630 NEXT X
1640 GOSUB 1420
1650 LET F1=2
1660 LET N1=Z
1670 GOSUB 1800
1680 GOSUB 1370
1690 FOR X=1 TO M1
1700 LET N(M(X))=N(M(X))+1
1710 NEXT X
1720 FOR X=1 TO 4
1730 LET N(O(X))=0
1740 NEXT X
1750 LET M1=64
1760 GOSUB 1500
1770 LET B3=Z
1780 RETURN
1790 REM L-FIND
1791 REM THIS SUBROUTINE CALCULATES ALL POSSIBLE MOVES FOR AN L GIVEN ALL
1792 REM EMPTY POSITIONS IN N(X).  IF F1=1, THE CURRENT POSITION OF THE
1793 REM COMPUTER'S L IS OMITTED.  OTHERWISE, THE CURRENT POSITION OF THE
1794 REM OPPONENT'S L IS OMITTED.  MOVES ARE RETURNED IN M(X), AND
1795 REM M1 IS THE LENGTH OF M(X).  (M1 = NUMBER OF MOVES * 4)
1800 LET M1=0
1810 LET J=4
1820 LET K=1
1830 GOSUB 1880
1840 LET J=1
1850 LET K=4
1860 GOSUB 1880
1870 RETURN
1880 LET P=0
1890 LET P=P+1
1900 LET A(1)=N(P)
1910 LET X=P
1920 LET X=X+1
1930 IF X>N1 THEN 2050
1940 IF N(X)-A(1)<>J THEN 1920
1950 LET A(2)=N(X)
1960 LET X=X+1
1970 IF X>N1 THEN 2050
1980 IF N(X)-A(2)<>J THEN 1960
1990 LET A(3)=N(X)
2000 FOR E=1 TO N1
2010 IF ABS(N(E)-A(1))=K THEN 2060
2020 IF ABS(N(E)-A(3))=K THEN 2060
2030 NEXT E
2040 GOTO 1890
2050 IF P<N1-2 THEN 1890
2055 RETURN
2060 LET A(4)=N(E)
2070 FOR F=1 TO 4
2080 IF A(F)/4<>INT(A(F)/4) THEN 2130
2090 FOR G=1 TO 4
2110 IF A(G)=A(F)+1 THEN 2030
2120 NEXT G
2130 NEXT F
2140 FOR Y=1 TO 4
2150 IF F1=1 THEN 2190
2160 IF A(Y)<>O(Y) THEN 2210
2170 NEXT Y
2180 GOTO 2030
2190 IF A(Y)<>C(Y) THEN 2210
2200 GOTO 2170
2210 FOR Y=1 TO 4
2220 LET M(M1+Y)=A(Y)
2230 NEXT Y
2240 LET M1=M1+4
2250 GOTO 2030
2260 REM BOARD PRINTOUT SUBROUTINE
2270 PRINT
2275 IF F2=1 THEN 2530
2280 FOR E=1 TO 13 STEP 4
2290 FOR F=1 TO 3
2300 FOR G=E TO E+3
2310 ON B(G)+1 GOTO 2320,2410,2430,2450
2320 IF F=2 THEN 2350
2330 PRINT "====";
2340 GOTO 2490
2350 PRINT ":";
2360 IF G>9 THEN 2390
2370 PRINT " ";CHR$(48+G);":";
2380 GOTO 2490
2390 PRINT "1";CHR$(38+G);":";
2400 GOTO 2490
2410 PRINT "OOOO";
2420 GOTO 2490
2430 PRINT "////";
2440 GOTO 2490
2450 IF F=2 THEN 2480
2460 PRINT "****";
2470 GOTO 2490
2480 PRINT "*  *";
2490 NEXT G
2500 PRINT
2510 NEXT F
2520 NEXT E
2530 PRINT
2540 RETURN
3000 REM INSTRUCTIONS
3010 PRINT
3020 PRINT "     L-game is a simple strategic game played on a 4x4"
3030 PRINT "grid by two opposing players, in this case between you"
3040 PRINT "and the computer.  The grid is numbered as follows:"
3050 LET F2=0
3060 FOR X=1 TO 16
3070 LET B(X)=0
3080 NEXT X
3090 GOSUB 2270
3100 PRINT "     The game is played with four pieces; both"
3110 PRINT "you and the computer have one 'L', and there are"
3120 PRINT "two 'BOXES' which are used by both players."
3130 PRINT "play always begins with the pieces on the board"
3140 PRINT "in the following position:"
3150 GOSUB 100
3160 GOSUB 2270
3165 PRINT "(computer is /, you are O)"
3166 PRINT
3170 PRINT "     The object of the game is to position your own"
3180 PRINT "L and the boxes to prevent the computer from moving"
3190 PRINT "its L.  Of course, it is trying to do the same to you!"
3200 PRINT "To move, you must simply enter the four coordinates"
3210 PRINT "where you want to place your L.  It must remain on the"
3220 PRINT "board and must not cover any other pieces.  You must"
3230 PRINT "move your L!  If you cannot find a new position"
3240 PRINT "for your L, then the computer has effectively pinned your"
3250 PRINT "L and it wins the game."
3260 PRINT "     Assuming you have successfully moved your L, you now"
3270 PRINT "have the option of moving the boxes.  You may move one,"
3280 PRINT "two, or none of the boxes by simply entering the coordinates"
3290 PRINT "where you want to put them.  To leave a box where it is,"
3300 PRINT "enter its present position."
3310 PRINT "     After you move the boxes, it is up to the computer"
3320 PRINT "to find a move for its L and play continues in the same"
3330 PRINT "manner.  Remember that you must not only try to pin the"
3340 PRINT "computer's L but also keep your own L from being pinned."
3350 PRINT "Also, it is easier to play the game with your own board"
3360 PRINT "than the computer printout.  To resign, enter 0,0,0,0"
3370 PRINT "in place of your move.  GOOD LUCK!"
3380 PRINT
3450 GOTO 40
4000 END
Ok
```

Life Expectancy

This program is a life-expectancy test derived from Peter Passell's book "How To." The test asks you a series of questions dealing with your life-style and environment. At the end of the questioning, the program gives your estimated life-expectancy and the percentage of the population you should outlive.

You may wish to experiment with certain variables to see what effect they will have on your lifespan. It's unlikely that you want to change your sex, but you may wish to check out the effect of smoking, drinking, mental attitude or weight.

This program was written by John E. Rogers.

```
RUN

                    LIFE EXPECTANCY
                   CREATIVE COMPUTING
                 MORRISTOWN, NEW JERSEY



THIS IS A LIFE EXPECTANCY TEST.
   DO YOU WISH INSTRUCTIONS? YES


   THIS IS A TEST TO PREDICT YOUR LIFE EXPECTANCY.  I
WILL ASK YOU A SERIES OF SHORT QUESTIONS, WHICH YOU WILL
REPLY BY TYPING IN THE CORRESPONDING ANSWER TO THE
QUESTION.

       EXAMPLE:  WHAT IS YOUR SEX?
              M=MALE
              F=FEMALE
'M' AND 'F' ARE THE POSSIBLE REPLIES TO THE QUESTION, ANSWER
LIKE THIS:
              CHOOSE ONE OF THE LETTERS ABOVE? M
TYPING AN 'M' SIGNIFIES YOU ARE A MALE.


  +++SEX+++
  ARE YOU MALE OR FEMALE?
  M= MALE.
  F= FEMALE.
CHOOSE ONE OF THE LETTERS ABOVE? M

  +++LIFE STYLE+++
  WHERE DO YOU LIVE?
  G= IF YOU LIVE IN AN URBAN AREA WITH A POPULATION OVER 2 MIL.
  K= IF YOU LIVE IN A TOWN UNDER 10,000, OR ON A FARM.
  I= NEITHER.
CHOOSE ONE OF THE LETTERS ABOVE? I

  HOW DO YOU WORK?
  M= IF YOU WORK BEHIND A DESK.
  L= IF YOUR WORK REQUIRES HEAVY PHYSICAL LABOR.
  I= NONE OF THE ABOVE.
CHOOSE ONE OF THE LETTERS ABOVE? I

  HOW LONG DO YOU EXERCISE STRENUOUSLY,
  (TENNIS, RUNNING, SWIMMING, ETC.)?
  F= FIVE TIMES A WEEK FOR AR LEAST A HALF HOUR.
  K= JUST TWO OR THREE TIMES A WEEK.
  I= DO NOT EXERCISE IN THIS FASHION.
CHOOSE ONE OF THE LETTERS ABOVE? K

  WHO DO YOU LIVE WITH?
  N= IF YOU LIVE WITH A SPOUSE, FRIEND, OR IN A FAMILY.
  H= IF YOU'VE LIVED ALONE FOR 1-10 YEARS SINCE AGE 25.
  G= FOR 11-20 YEARS.
  M= FOR 21-30 YEARS.
  E= FOR 31-40 YEARS.
  M= MORE THAN 40 YEARS.
CHOOSE ONE OF THE LETTERS ABOVE? N

  +++PSYCHE+++
  DO YOU SLEEP MORE THAN 10 HOURS A NIGHT?
  I= NO.
  E=YES.
CHOOSE ONE OF THE LETTERS ABOVE? I

  +++MENTAL STATE+++
  M= IF YOU ARE INTENSE, AGGRESSIVE, OR EASILY ANGERED.
  L= IF YOU ARE EASY GOING, RELAXED, OR A FOLLOWER.
  I= NEITHER.
CHOOSE ONE OF THE LETTERS ABOVE? L

  +++HOW YOU FEEL+++
  ARE YOU HAPPY OR UNHAPPY?
  J= HAPPY.
  G= UNHAPPY.
  I= NEITHER.
CHOOSE ONE OF THE LETTERS ABOVE? J

  +++FACTORS+++
  HAVE YOU HAD A SPEEDING TICKET IN THE LAST YEAR?
  H= YES.
  I=NO.
CHOOSE ONE OF THE LETTERS ABOVE? I

  +++INCOME+++
  DO YOU EARN MORE THAN $50,000 A YEAR?
  G= YES.
  I=NO.
CHOOSE ONE OF THE LETTERS ABOVE? IO

  +++SCHOOLING+++
  J= IF YOU HAVE FINISHED COLLEGE.
  L= IF YOU HAVE FINISHED COLLEGE WITH A GRADUATE
  OR PROFESSIONAL DEGREE.
  I= NOTHING LISTED.
CHOOSE ONE OF THE LETTERS ABOVE? I
```

```
+++AGE+++
 ARE YOU 65 OR OLDER AND STILL WORKING?
 L= YES.
 I= NO.
CHOOSE ONE OF THE LETTERS ABOVE? I

 +++HEREDITY+++
 K= IF ANY GRANDPARENTS LIVED TO 85 YEARS OLD.
 O= IF ALL FOUR GRANDPARENTS LIVED TO 80 YEARS OLD.
 I= NO GRANDPARENTS QUALIFY IN THE ABOVE.
CHOOSE ONE OF THE LETTERS ABOVE? I

 HAS ANY PARENT DIED OF A STROKE OR HEART ATTACK
 BEFORE THE AGE OF 50?
 E= YES.
 I= NO.
CHOOSE ONE OF THE LETTERS ABOVE? E

 +++FAMILY DISEASES+++
 ANY PARENT, BROTHER, OR SISTER UNDER 50 HAS (OR HAD)
 CANCER, A HEART CONDITION, OR DIABETES SINCE CHILDHOOD?
 M= YES.
 I= NO.
CHOOSE ONE OF THE LETTERS ABOVE? I

 +++HEALTH+++
 HOW MUCH DO YOU SMOKE?
 A= IF YOU SMOKE MORE THAN TWO PACKS A DAY.
 C= ONE TO TWO PACKS A DAY.
 M= ONE HALF TO ONE PACK A DAY.
 I= DON'T SMOKE.
CHOOSE ONE OF THE LETTERS ABOVE? I

 +++DRINK+++
 DO YOU DRINK THE EQUIVALENT OF A
 QUARTER BOTTLE OF ALCOHOLIC BEVERAGE A DAY?
 H= YES.
 I= NO.
CHOOSE ONE OF THE LETTERS ABOVE? I

 +++WEIGHT+++
 A= IF YOU ARE OVERWEIGHT BY 50 POUNDS OR MORE.
 E= OVER BY 30-50 POUNDS.
 G= OVER BY 10-30 POUNDS.
 I= NOT OVER WEIGHT.
CHOOSE ONE OF THE LETTERS ABOVE? I

 +++CHECKUPS+++
 DO YOU?  IF YOU ARE A MALE OVER 40 HAVE AN ANNUAL CHECKUP?
 K= YES.
 I= IF NO OR NOT A MALE OR UNDER 40 YEARS OLD.
CHOOSE ONE OF THE LETTERS ABOVE? I

 DO YOU? IF YOU ARE A WOMAN SEE A GYNECOLOGIST ONCE A YEAR?
 K= YES.
 I= IF NO OR NOT A WOMAN.
CHOOSE ONE OF THE LETTERS ABOVE? I

 +++CURRENT AGE+++
 K= IF YOU ARE BETWEEN 30 AND 40 YEARS OLD.
 L= BETWEEN 40 AND 50.
 F= BETWEEN 50 AND 70.
 N= OVER 70.
 I= UNDER 30.
CHOOSE ONE OF THE LETTERS ABOVE? I

YOU ARE EXPECTED TO LIVE TO THE AGE OF 76 YEARS
OUT LIVING 61% OF THE MEN AND 39% OF THE WOMEN.
Ok
```

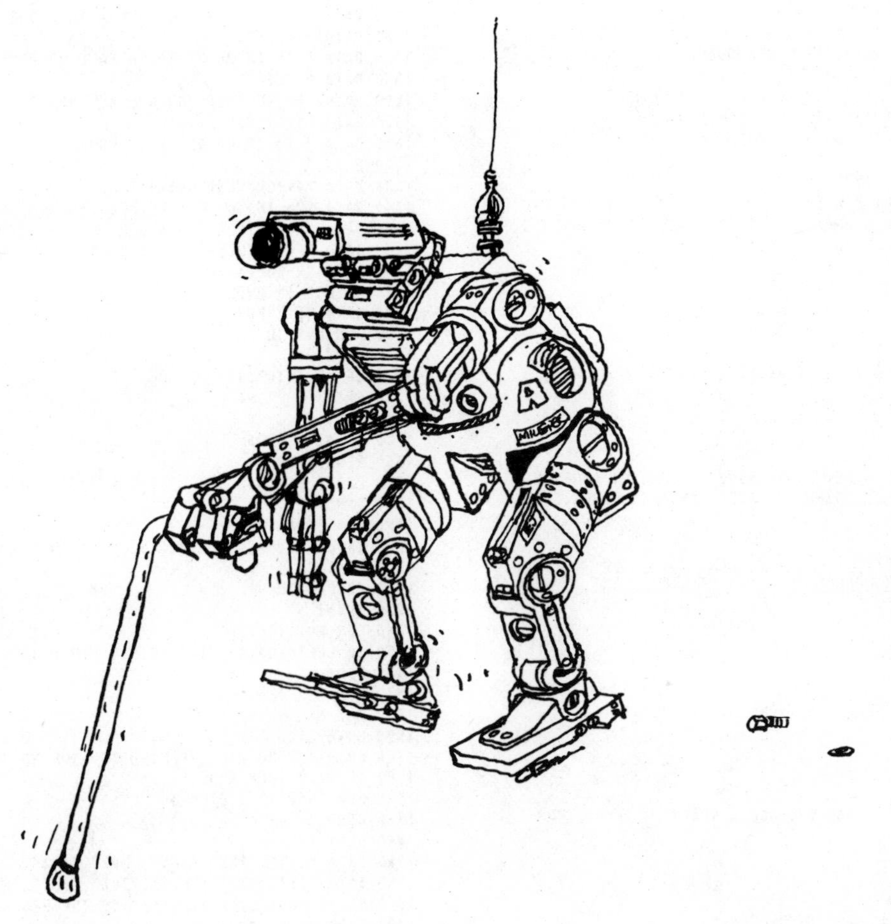

```
LIST
10 PRINT TAB(21);"LIFE EXPECTANCY"
20 PRINT TAB(20);"CREATIVE COMPUTING"
30 PRINT TAB(18);"MORRISTOWN, NEW JERSEY"
40 PRINT:PRINT:PRINT
270 PRINT :PRINT:PRINT
280 PRINT "THIS IS A LIFE EXPECTANCY TEST."
290 PRINT "   DO YOU WISH INSTRUCTIONS";
300 INPUT I$
310 IF LEFT$(I$,1)="N" THEN 470
320 PRINT:PRINT
340 PRINT "   THIS IS A TEST TO PREDICT YOUR LIFE EXPECTANCY.  I"
350 PRINT "WILL ASK YOU A SERIES OF SHORT QUESTIONS, WHICH YOU WILL"
360 PRINT "REPLY BY TYPING IN THE CORRESPONDING ANSWER TO THE"
370 PRINT "QUESTION."
380 PRINT
390 PRINT "        EXAMPLE:  WHAT IS YOUR SEX?"
400 PRINT "                  M=MALE"
410 PRINT "                  F=FEMALE"
420 PRINT "'M' AND 'F' ARE THE POSSIBLE REPLIES TO THE QUESTION, ANSWER"
430 PRINT "LIKE THIS:"
440 PRINT "              CHOOSE ONE OF THE LETTERS ABOVE? M"
450 PRINT "TYPING AN 'M' SIGNIFIES YOU ARE A MALE."
460 PRINT:PRINT:PRINT
470 R5=1
480 Z=72
490 A$="ABCDEMGHIJKLFNO"
500 GOTO 1700
510 R5=R5+1
520 IF R5>21 THEN 1900
530 DATA "+++SEX+++"
540 DATA "ARE YOU MALE OR FEMALE?"
550 DATA "M= MALE."
560 DATA " F= FEMALE."
570 DATA 2,"MF"
580 DATA "+++LIFE STYLE+++"
590   DATA "WHERE DO YOU LIVE?"
600 DATA "G= IF YOU LIVE IN AN URBAN AREA WITH A POPULATION OVER 2 MIL."
610 DATA "K= IF YOU LIVE IN A TOWN UNDER 10,000, OR ON A FARM."
620 DATA " I= NEITHER."
630 DATA 3,"GKI"
640 DATA "HOW DO YOU WORK?"
650 DATA "M= IF YOU WORK BEHIND A DESK."
660 DATA "L= IF YOUR WORK REQUIRES HEAVY PHYSICAL LABOR."
670 DATA " I= NONE OF THE ABOVE."
680 DATA 3,"MLI"
690 DATA "HOW LONG DO YOU EXERCISE STRENUOUSLY,"
700 DATA "(TENNIS, RUNNING, SWIMMING, ETC.)?"
710 DATA "F= FIVE TIMES A WEEK FOR AR LEAST A HALF HOUR."
720 DATA "K= JUST TWO OR THREE TIMES A WEEK."
730 DATA " I= DO NOT EXERCISE IN THIS FASHION."
740 DATA 3,"FKI"
750 DATA "WHO DO YOU LIVE WITH?"
760 DATA "N= IF YOU LIVE WITH A SPOUSE, FRIEND, OR IN A FAMILY."
770 DATA "H= IF YOU'VE LIVED ALONE FOR 1-10 YEARS SINCE AGE 25."
780 DATA "G= FOR 11-20 YEARS."
790 DATA "M= FOR 21-30 YEARS."
800 DATA "E= FOR 31-40 YEARS."
810 DATA " M= MORE THAN 40 YEARS."
820 DATA 6,"NHGMED"
830 DATA "+++PSYCHE+++"
840 DATA "DO YOU SLEEP MORE THAN 10 HOURS A NIGHT?"
850 DATA "I= NO."
860 DATA " E=YES."
870 DATA 2,"IE"
880 DATA "+++MENTAL STATE+++"
890 DATA "M= IF YOU ARE INTENSE, AGGRESSIVE, OR EASILY ANGERED."
900 DATA "L= IF YOU ARE EASY GOING, RELAXED, OR A FOLLOWER."
910 DATA " I= NEITHER."
920 DATA 3,"MLI"
930 DATA "+++HOW YOU FEEL+++"
940 DATA "ARE YOU HAPPY OR UNHAPPY?"
950 DATA "J= HAPPY."
960 DATA "G= UNHAPPY."
970 DATA " I= NEITHER."
980 DATA 3,"JGI"
990 DATA "+++FACTORS+++"
1000 DATA "HAVE YOU HAD A SPEEDING TICKET IN THE LAST YEAR?"
1010 DATA "H= YES."
1020 DATA " I=NO."
1030 DATA 2,"HI"
1040 DATA "+++INCOME+++"
1050 DATA "DO YOU EARN MORE THAN $50,000 A YEAR?"
1060 DATA "G= YES."
1070 DATA " I=NO."
1080 DATA 2,"GI"
1090 DATA "+++SCHOOLING+++"
1100 DATA "J= IF YOU HAVE FINISHED COLLEGE."
1110 DATA "L= IF YOU HAVE FINISHED COLLEGE WITH A GRADUATE"
1120 DATA "OR PROFESSIONAL DEGREE."
1130 DATA " I= NOTHING LISTED."
1140 DATA 3,"JLI"
1150 DATA  "+++AGE+++"
1160 DATA "ARE YOU 65 OR OLDER AND STILL WORKING?"
1170 DATA "L= YES."
1180 DATA " I= NO."
1190 DATA 2,"LI"
1200 DATA "+++HEREDITY+++"
1210 DATA "K= IF ANY GRANDPARENTS LIVED TO 85 YEARS OLD."
1220 DATA "O= IF ALL FOUR GRANDPARENTS LIVED TO 80 YEARS OLD."
1230 DATA " I= NO GRANDPARENTS QUALIFY IN THE ABOVE."
1240 DATA 3,"KOI"
1250 DATA "HAS ANY PARENT DIED OF A STROKE OR HEART ATTACK"
1260 DATA "BEFORE THE AGE OF 50?"
1270 DATA "E= YES."
1280 DATA " I= NO."
1290 DATA 2,"EI"
1300 DATA "+++FAMILY DISEASES+++"
1310 DATA "ANY PARENT, BROTHER, OR SISTER UNDER 50 HAS (OR HAD) "
1320 DATA "CANCER, A HEART CONDITION, OR DIABETES SINCE CHILDHOOD?"
1330 DATA "M= YES."
1340 DATA " I= NO."
1350 DATA 2,"MI"
1360 DATA "+++HEALTH+++"
1365 DATA "HOW MUCH DO YOU SMOKE?"
1370 DATA "A= IF YOU SMOKE MORE THAN TWO PACKS A DAY."
1380 DATA "C= ONE TO TWO PACKS A DAY."
1390 DATA "M= ONE HALF TO ONE PACK A DAY."
1400 DATA " I= DON'T SMOKE."
1410 DATA 4,"ACMI"
1420 DATA "+++DRINK+++"
1430 DATA "DO YOU DRINK THE EQUIVALENT OF A "
1440 DATA "QUARTER BOTTLE OF ALCOHOLIC BEVERAGE A DAY?"
1450 DATA "H= YES."
1460 DATA " I= NO."
1470 DATA 2,"HI"
1480 DATA "+++WEIGHT+++"
1490 DATA "A= IF YOU ARE OVERWEIGHT BY 50 POUNDS OR MORE."
1500 DATA "E= OVER BY 30-50 POUNDS."
1510 DATA "G= OVER BY 10-30 POUNDS."
1520 DATA " I= NOT OVER WEIGHT."
1530 DATA 4,"AEGI"
1540 DATA "+++CHECKUPS+++"
1550 DATA "DO YOU?  IF YOU ARE A MALE OVER 40 HAVE AN ANNUAL CHECKUP?"
1560 DATA "K= YES."
1570 DATA " I= IF NO OR NOT A MALE OR UNDER 40 YEARS OLD."
1580 DATA 2,"KI"
1590 DATA "DO YOU? IF YOU ARE A WOMAN SEE A GYNECOLOGIST ONCE A YEAR?"
1600 DATA "K= YES."
1610 DATA " I= IF NO OR NOT A WOMAN."
1620 DATA 2,"KI"
1630 DATA "+++CURRENT AGE+++"
1640 DATA "K= IF YOU ARE BETWEEN 30 AND 40 YEARS OLD."
1650 DATA "L= BETWEEN 40 AND 50."
1660 DATA "F= BETWEEN 50 AND 70."
1670 DATA "N= OVER 70."
1680 DATA " I= UNDER 30."
1690 DATA 5,"KLFNI"
1700 FOR Q=1 TO 7
1710 READ Q$
1720 IF LEFT$(Q$,1)=" " THEN 1750
1730 PRINT "  ";Q$
1740 NEXT Q
1750 PRINT " ";Q$
1760 READ C,C$
1770 PRINT "CHOOSE ONE OF THE LETTERS ABOVE";
1780 INPUT G$
1790 FOR C2=1 TO C
1800 IF LEFT$(G$,1)= MID$(C$,C2,1) THEN 1830
1810 NEXT C2
1820 GOTO 1770
1830 PRINT
1840 FOR N=1 TO 15
1850 IF LEFT$(G$,1)=MID$(A$,N,1) THEN 1870
1860 NEXT N
1870 M=N-9
1880 Z=Z+M
1890 GOTO 510
1900 PRINT  "YOU ARE EXPECTED TO LIVE TO THE AGE OF";Z;"YEARS"
1910 IF Z<60 THEN 1980
1920 FOR Y=60 TO Z STEP 5
1930 READ M$,F$
1940 NEXT Y
1950 DATA "26%","15%","36%","20%","48%","30%","61%","39%"
1960 DATA "75%","53%","87%","70%","96%","88%","99.9%","99.6%"
1970 PRINT "OUT LIVING ";M$;" OF THE MEN AND ";F$;" OF THE WOMEN."
1980 END
Ok
```

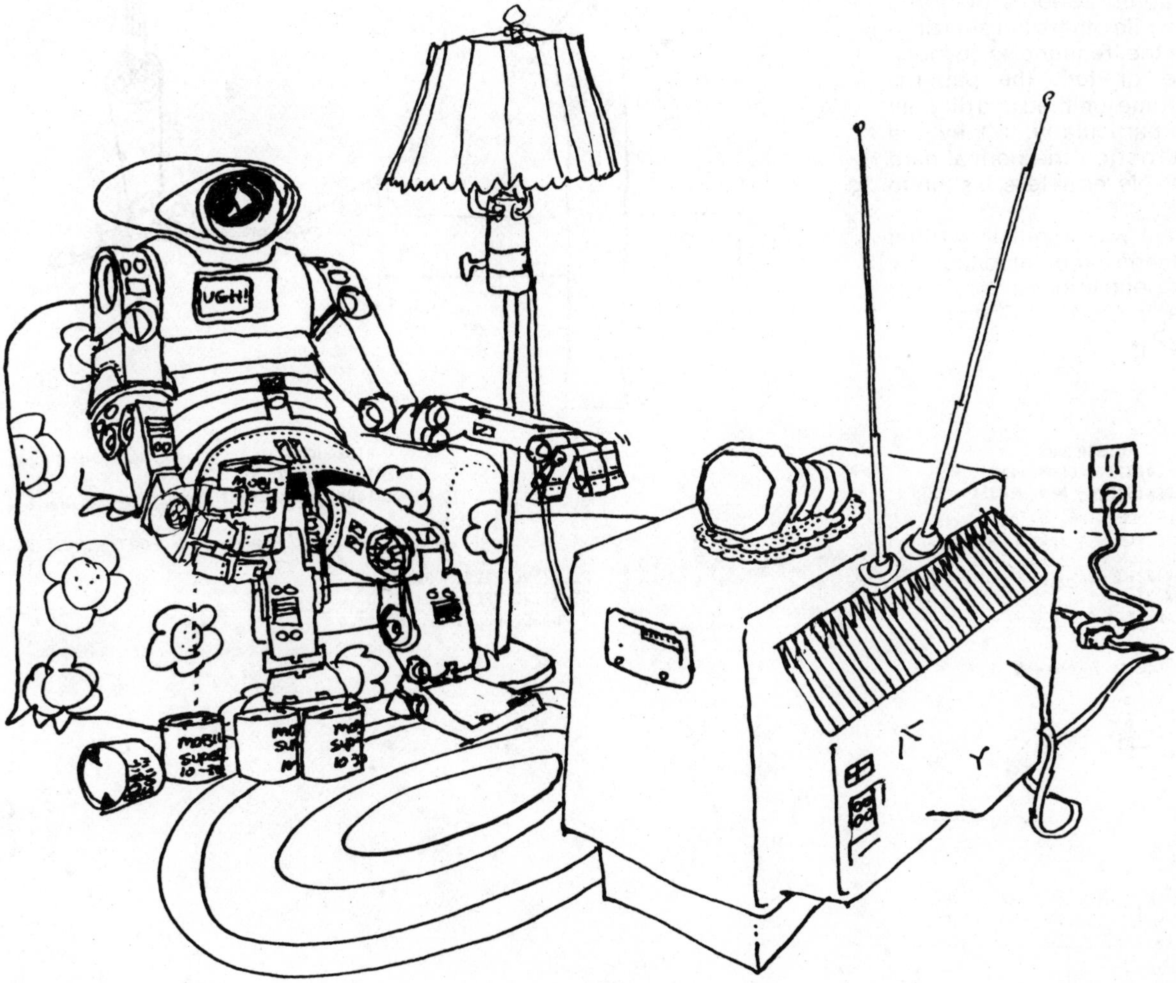

Lissajous

This program prints Lissajous patterns. You enter relative X and Y frequencies and the Y phase of pi. The relative frequencies for X and Y must be a positive number one or greater. The phase may be between zero and any number you want.

We have experimented with a wide range of relative frequencies and phases and come up with some startlingly beautiful patterns. Some are starkly plain while others are amazingly complex. If the frequencies go much beyond nine or ten, the patterns generally become jumbled and difficult to decipher particularly if they are being printed out on the normal hard copy terminal. Nevertheless, it's fun to experiment.

This program was originally written by Larry Ruane and modified by several other people along the line. It appeared first in *Creative Computing*, Sep/Oct 1977.

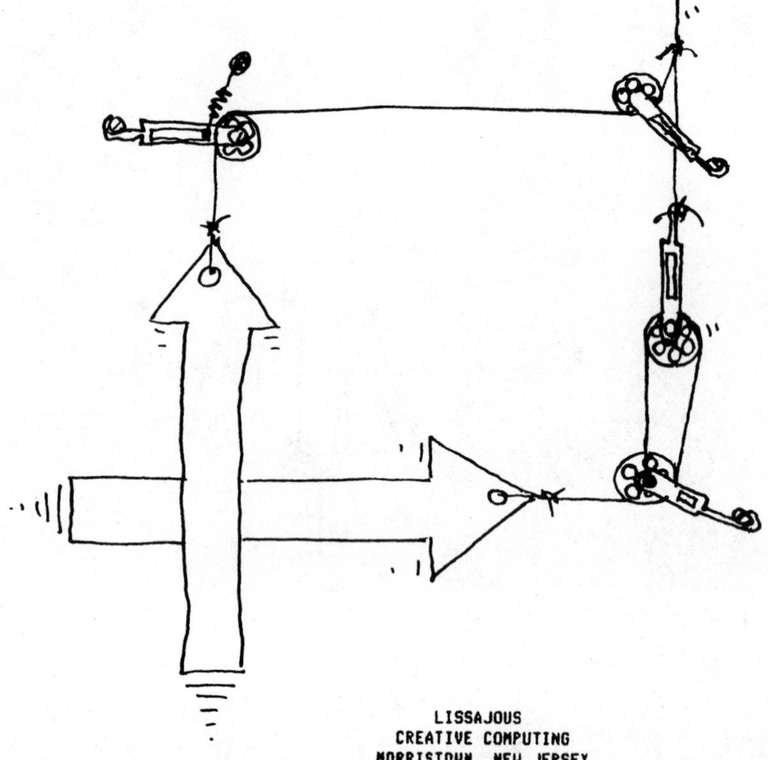

```
RUN
                    LISSAJOUS
               CREATIVE COMPUTING
              MORRISTOWN  NEW JERSEY


RELATIVE FREQ. FOR X? 3
RELATIVE FREQ. FOR Y? 6
Y PHASE, MULTIPLE OF PI? 0
```

```
                    LISSAJOUS
               CREATIVE COMPUTING
              MORRISTOWN  NEW JERSEY


RELATIVE FREQ. FOR X? 2
RELATIVE FREQ. FOR Y? 3
Y PHASE, MULTIPLE OF PI? 0
```

```
RUN
                      LISSAJOUS
                  CREATIVE COMPUTING
                MORRISTOWN  NEW JERSEY



RELATIVE FREQ. FOR X? 5
RELATIVE FREQ. FOR Y? 7
Y PHASE, MULTIPLE OF PI? 0
```

```
RELATIVE FREQ. FOR X? 1
RELATIVE FREQ. FOR Y? 1
Y PHASE, MULTIPLE OF PI? .5
```

```
LIST

10 PRINT TAB(22);"LISSAJOUS"
20 PRINT TAB(18);"CREATIVE COMPUTING"
30 PRINT TAB(16);"MORRISTOWN  NEW JERSEY"
40 PRINT:PRINT:PRINT
50 DIM Y(10)
100 REM. STEP-WISE LISSAJOUS
110 P=3.1415926
120 PRINT "RELATIVE FREQ. FOR X";:INPUT F1:IF INT(F1) < F1 THEN 120
122 IF F1 < 1 THEN 120
125 F=F1:F1=2*P*F1
130 PRINT "RELATIVE FREQ. FOR Y";:INPUT F2:IF INT(F2) < F2 THEN 130
132 IF F2 < 1 THEN 130
135 PRINT "Y PHASE, MULTIPLE OF PI";:INPUT P2:P2=P*P2
140 F2=2*P*F2
150 FOR X1=-18 TO 18
160 X=X1/18:GOSUB 1970:T1=X:T2=P-X
162 FOR I=0 TO F-1
165 T3=(T1+2*I*P)/F1:T4=(T2+2*I*P)/F1
170 Y1=30*SIN(F2*T3+P2):Y2=30*SIN(F2*T4+P2)
180 Y1=SGN(Y1)*INT(ABS(Y1)+.5):Y2=SGN(Y2)*INT(ABS(Y2)+.5)
190 Y(2*I)=Y1:Y(2*I+1)=Y2
200 NEXT I
210 FOR J=1 TO 2*F-1:I=J-1:T=Y(J)
220 IF T >= Y(I) THEN 240
230 Y(I+1)=Y(I):I=I-1:IF I >=0 THEN 220
240 Y(I+1)=T:NEXT J
250 FOR I=0 TO 2*F-1
260 IF I=0 THEN 280
270 IF Y(I)=Y(I-1) THEN 290
280 PRINT TAB(36+Y(I));"*";
290 NEXT I
300 PRINT
310 NEXT X1
1890 STOP
1960 REM:-------------------------------------
1970 IF ABS(X) < .1 THEN 2020
1980 X=X/(SQR(1+X)+SQR(1-X))
1990 GOSUB 1970
2000 X=2*X
2010 RETURN
2020 X=X+X^3/6+.075*X^5+X^7/22.4
2030 RETURN
2040 END
OK
```

Magic Square

We've all seen examples of magic squares. The most common one is a 3x3 square using the integers 1 through 9 in which the sum of each row, column and diagonal totals 15.

In the computer game of "Magic Square" the goal is to form a sum 15 magic square with you and the computer alternately filling in the integers between 1 and 9. If one player stumbles and puts a number in which causes the sum of a row, column, or diagonal to be something other than 15, he loses.

In forming a sum 15 magic square, there is only one fundamental solution. However, it can be rotated and reversed to form 8 solutions. Because the computer does not play a particularly creative game, all eight solutions cannot be obtained. How many can be?

Can you modify the computer program to play a more interesting game which permits all eight solutions? (Hint: Try randomizing the move position and number generators in Statements 400 and 410.)

This program was created by David Ahl and originally appeared in *Creative Computing*, Jan/Feb 1975.

```
RUN
                                MAGIC SQUARE
                 CREATIVE COMPUTING  MORRISTOWN NEW JERSEY



GAME OF MAGIC SQUARE

PLAYERS ALTERNATLEY CHOOSE AN INTEGER (1 TO 9)
THAT HAS NOT BEEN PREVIOUSLY USED AND PLACE IT
IN ANY UNFILLED CELL OF A TIC-TAC-TOE BOARD.
THE GOAL IS TO MAKE THE SUM OF EACH ROW, COLUMN,
AND DIAGONAL EQUAL TO 15.

THAT PLAYER LOSES WHO FIRST MAKES THE SUM OF THE
THREE FIGURES IN ANY ROW, COLUMN, OR DIAGONAL
SOMETHING OTHER THAN 15.

A TIE GAME DRAWS A MAGIC SQUARE!!

THE COMPUTER WILL ASK YOU ON EACH MOVE WHICH
CELL YOU WISH TO OCCUPY, AND THE NUMBER YOU WISH
LIKE '3,7' IF YOU WISHED TO PUT A 7 IN CELL 3.

HERE ARE THE CELL NUMBERS:

1 2 3
4 5 6
7 8 9

INPUT YOUR MOVE --- CELL AND NUMBER? 1,1

1              0              0
0              0              0
0              0              0

I MOVE TO CELL  2  WITH A  2

1              2              0
0              0              0
0              0              0


INPUT YOUR MOVE --- CELL AND NUMBER? 5,9

1              2              0
0              9              0
0              0              0

I MOVE TO CELL  4  WITH A  3

1              2              0
3              9              0
0              0              0


INPUT YOUR MOVE --- CELL AND NUMBER? 3,5

1              2              5
3              9              0
0              0              0

SORRY, YOU LOSE -- NICE TRY.
```

```
LET'S PLAY AGAIN. . .

INPUT YOUR MOVE --- CELL AND NUMBER? 1,1

 1              0              0
 0              0              0
 0              0              0

I MOVE TO CELL  2  WITH A  2

 1              2              0
 0              0              0
 0              0              0


INPUT YOUR MOVE --- CELL AND NUMBER? 9,9

 1              2              0
 0              0              0
 0              0              9

I MOVE TO CELL  4  WITH A  3

 1              2              0
 3              0              0
 0              0              9

INPUT YOUR MOVE --- CELL AND NUMBER? 6,5

 1              2              0
 3              0              5
 0              0              9

I MOVE TO CELL  8  WITH A  4

 1              2              0
 3              0              5
 0              4              9


INPUT YOUR MOVE --- CELL AND NUMBER? 5,7

 1              2              0
 3              7              5
 0              4              9

SORRY, YOU LOSE -- NICE TRY.
```

```
LIST
5 PRINT TAB(28);"MAGIC SQUARE"
10 PRINT TAB(15);"CREATIVE COMPUTING  MORRISTOWN NEW JERSEY"
12 DIM A(9),B(9)
15 PRINT
16 PRINT
17 PRINT
20 PRINT "GAME OF MAGIC SQUARE"
21 PRINT
25 PRINT "PLAYERS ALTERNATLEY CHOOSE AN INTEGER (1 TO 9)"
30 PRINT "THAT HAS NOT BEEN PREVIOUSLY USED AND PLACE IT"
35 PRINT "IN ANY UNFILLED CELL OF A TIC-TAC-TOE BOARD."
40 PRINT "THE GOAL IS TO MAKE THE SUM OF EACH ROW, COLUMN,"
45 PRINT "AND DIAGONAL EQUAL TO 15."
47 PRINT
50 PRINT "THAT PLAYER LOSES WHO FIRST MAKES THE SUM OF THE"
55 PRINT "THREE FIGURES IN ANY ROW, COLUMN, OR DIAGONAL"
60 PRINT "SOMETHING OTHER THAN 15."
62 PRINT
65 PRINT "A TIE GAME DRAWS A MAGIC SQUARE!!"
67 PRINT
70 PRINT "THE COMPUTER WILL ASK YOU ON EACH MOVE WHICH"
75 PRINT "CELL YOU WISH TO OCCUPY, AND THE NUMBER YOU WISH"
80 PRINT "LIKE '3,7' IF YOU WISHED TO PUT A 7 IN CELL 3."
85 PRINT
90 PRINT "HERE ARE THE CELL NUMBERS:"
92 PRINT
93 PRINT "1 2 3"
94 PRINT "4 5 6"
95 PRINT "7 8 9"
96 FOR I = 1 TO 9
97 A(I)=0
98 B(I)=0
99 NEXT I
100 M=0:W=0
103 PRINT
104 PRINT "INPUT YOUR MOVE --- CELL AND NUMBER";
105 INPUT I,N
110 IF I<1  OR I > 9 OR N < 1 OR N > 9 THEN 130
120 IF A(I)=0 AND B(N)=0 THEN 150
130 PRINT "ILLEGAL MOVE ... AGAIN"
135 GOTO 103
150 A(I)=N:B(N)=1:M=M+1
170 GOSUB 960
180 GOSUB 800
200 IF W=0 THEN 230
210 PRINT "SORRY, YOU LOSE -- NICE TRY."
211 GOTO 560
230 IF M < 5 THEN 400
240 PRINT "A TIE GAME -- BUT WE'VE DRAWN A MAGIC SQUARE!"
250 GOTO 560
400 FOR Q=1 TO 9
410 IF A(Q)> 0 THEN 480
420 FOR R=1 TO 9
430 IF B(R)>0 THEN 470
435 A(Q)=R
440 GOSUB 800
450 IF W=0 THEN 500
460 Q1=Q:R1=R:W=0:A(Q)=0
470 NEXT R
480 NEXT Q
490 W=1:R=R1:Q=Q1:A(Q)=R
500 B(R)=1
520 PRINT "I MOVE TO CELL ";Q;" WITH A ";R
530 GOSUB 960
540 IF W=0 THEN 103
550 PRINT "I LOSE --- YOU WIN!!"
560 PRINT
561 FOR I=1 TO 15
562 PRINT CHR$(7);
564 NEXT I
570 PRINT "LET'S PLAY AGAIN. . ."
575 GOTO 96
800 FOR X=1 TO 8
810 ON X GOTO 820,830,840,850,860,870,880,890
820 J=1:K=2:L=3:GOTO 900
830 K=4:L=7:GOTO 900
840 K=5:L=9:GOTO 900
850 J=4:L=6:GOTO 900
860 J=2:L=8:GOTO 900
870 J=3:L=7:GOTO 900
880 J=7:L=9:GOTO 900
890 J=7:K=8
900 IF A(J)=0 OR A(K)=0 OR A(L)=0 THEN 930
920 IF A(J)+A(K)+A(L) <> 15 THEN 940
930 NEXT X
935 GOTO 950
940 W=1
950 RETURN
960 PRINT
965 PRINT A(1),A(2),A(3)
970 PRINT A(4),A(5),A(6)
975 PRINT A(7),A(8),A(9)
980 PRINT
990 RETURN
999 END
Ok
```

Man-Eating Rabbit

In this game you are in a pit with a man-eating rabbit. The center of the pit, appropriately enough, is at 0,0, and it has a radius of ten. On each move, you can move in any one of eight different angles, 0, 45, 90, 135 ... etc. Unlike you, the rabbit can take more than one hop on a move. The object of the game is to avoid the rabbit for ten moves. If you do this successfully you'll be released and set free.

We're not sure what race of people on what planet dreamed up this diabolical sport, but we've found that it's extremely difficult to get away from the rabbit in more than about one out of ten games. You may, therefore, want to improve the odds somewhat by limiting the number of moves the rabbit can make on each turn to one or two. You'll find it interesting to graph the results of the program as you go along. To do this, you'll need a piece of quadrille paper at least 21 squares in each direction. Draw a circle with your compass ten units in diameter and then number the grid from minus ten to plus ten along the X and Y axes. Plot your moves as you go along and you'll see some interesting patterns develop.

This program was conceived and written by Philip Stanway.

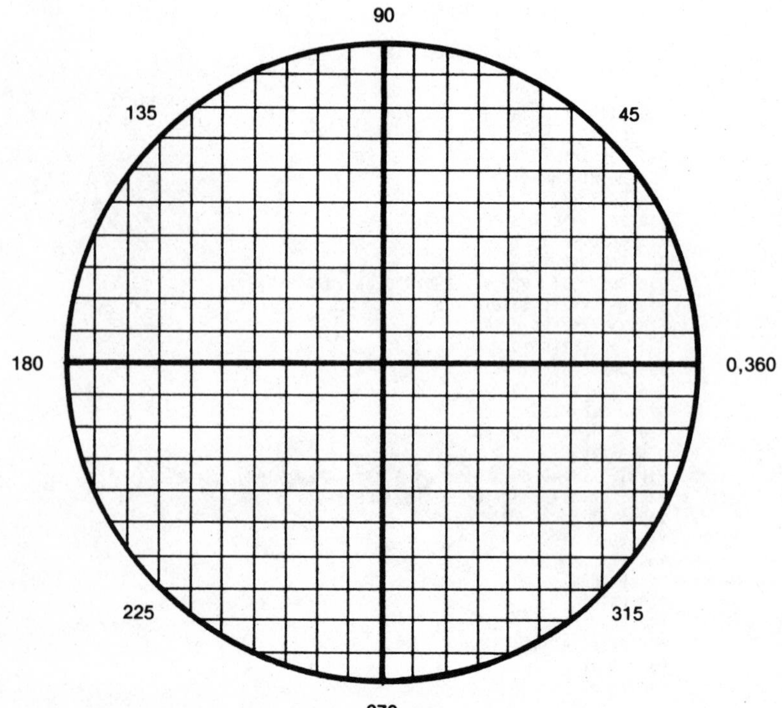


```
                    MAN-EATING RABBIT
                    CREATIVE COMPUTING
                  MORRISTOWN, NEW JERSEY


YOU ARE IN A PIT WITH A MAN-EATING RABBIT.
THE CENTER IS (0,0) AND IT HAS A RADIUS OF 10
IF YOU CAN AVOID THE RABBIT FOR 10 MOVES YOU WILL BE
RELEASED.  YOU AND THE RABBIT CAN MOVE ONLY 1 SPACE EACH
HOWEVER THE RABBIT CAN DO MULTIPLE JUMPS.
YOU CAN TRAVEL AT THESE ANGLES
0,45,90,135,180,225,270,315,360


WHERE WOULD YOU LIKE TO BE DROPPED? 2,3
RABBIT AT ( 2 , 7 ) AND DISTANCE  4

TURN # 1   HUMAN AT ( 2 , 3 )
AT WHAT ANGLE WILL YOU RUN ? 270
RUNNING ......HUMAN YOU ARE NOW AT ( 2 , 2 )
THE RABBIT IS POUNCING AT ANGLE..... 270
THE RABBIT IS POUNCING AT ANGLE..... 270
RABBIT AT ( 2 , 5 ) AND DISTANCE  3

TURN # 2   HUMAN AT ( 2 , 2 )
AT WHAT ANGLE WILL YOU RUN ? 225
RUNNING ......HUMAN YOU ARE NOW AT ( 1 , 1 )
THE RABBIT IS POUNCING AT ANGLE..... 270
THE RABBIT IS POUNCING AT ANGLE..... 270
RABBIT AT ( 2 , 3 ) AND DISTANCE  2.23607

TURN # 3   HUMAN AT ( 1 , 1 )
AT WHAT ANGLE WILL YOU RUN ? 225
RUNNING ......HUMAN YOU ARE NOW AT ( 0 , 0 )
THE RABBIT IS POUNCING AT ANGLE..... 225
RABBIT AT ( 1 , 2 ) AND DISTANCE  2.23607

TURN # 4   HUMAN AT ( 0 , 0 )
AT WHAT ANGLE WILL YOU RUN ? 225
RUNNING ......HUMAN YOU ARE NOW AT (-1 ,-1 )
THE RABBIT IS POUNCING AT ANGLE..... 225
RABBIT AT ( 0 , 1 ) AND DISTANCE  2.23607

TURN # 5   HUMAN AT (-1 ,-1 )
AT WHAT ANGLE WILL YOU RUN ? 270
RUNNING ......HUMAN YOU ARE NOW AT (-1 ,-2 )
THE RABBIT IS POUNCING AT ANGLE..... 270
RABBIT AT ( 0 , 0 ) AND DISTANCE  2.23607

TURN # 6   HUMAN AT (-1 ,-2 )
AT WHAT ANGLE WILL YOU RUN ? 225
RUNNING ......HUMAN YOU ARE NOW AT (-2 ,-3 )
THE RABBIT IS POUNCING AT ANGLE..... 225
THE RABBIT IS POUNCING AT ANGLE..... 225
THE RABBIT IS POUNCING AT ANGLE..... 270
RABBIT AT (-2 ,-3 ) AND DISTANCE  0
**CRUNCH** WELL R.I.P.
Ok
```

```
LIST
1 PRINT TAB(20);"MAN-EATING RABBIT"
2 PRINT TAB(20);"CREATIVE COMPUTING"
3 PRINT TAB(18);"MORRISTOWN, NEW JERSEY"
4 PRINT:PRINT:PRINT
10 PRINT "YOU ARE IN A PIT WITH A MAN-EATING RABBIT."
15 PRINT "THE CENTER IS (0,0) AND IT HAS A RADIUS OF 10"
20 PRINT "IF YOU CAN AVOID THE RABBIT FOR 10 MOVES YOU WILL BE"
25 PRINT "RELEASED.  YOU AND THE RABBIT CAN MOVE ONLY 1 SPACE EACH"
26 PRINT "HOWEVER THE RABBIT CAN DO MULTIPLE JUMPS."
27 PRINT "YOU CAN TRAVEL AT THESE ANGLES"
28 PRINT "0,45,90,135,180,225,270,315,360"
40 X=INT(21*RND(1)-10)
41 Y=INT(21*RND(1)-10)
45 D=SQR(ABS((X-X1)^2+(Y-Y1)^2))
46 IF D>10 THEN 40
47 PRINT
48 PRINT
50 PRINT "WHERE WOULD YOU LIKE TO BE DROPPED";
51 INPUT X1,Y1
60 IF SQR(ABS(X1^2+Y1^2))>10 THEN 50
65 IF X<>X1 THEN 70
66 IF Y<>Y1 THEN 70
67 PRINT "*****SQUISH*****"
69 PRINT "THE RABBIT IS DEAD!  YOU ARE SET FREE!":GOTO 340
70 FOR G=1 TO 10
71 D=SQR(ABS((X-X1)^2+(Y-Y1)^2))
80 PRINT "RABBIT AT (";X;",";Y;") AND DISTANCE ";D
90 IF D=0 THEN 330
91 PRINT:PRINT "TURN #";G;"  HUMAN AT (";X1;",";Y1;")"
100 PRINT "AT WHAT ANGLE WILL YOU RUN ";
101 INPUT A
110 IF A/45<>INT(A/45) THEN 100
111 PRINT "RUNNING ......";:P1=1
112 M=1:IF ABS((INT(A/10)*10)-A)<>5 THEN 120
113 M=SQR(2)
120 X2=(M*COS(A*(3.14159/180)))
121 Y2=(M*SIN(A*(3.14159/180)))
125 IF SQR(((X1+X2)^2+(Y1+Y2)^2))<=10 THEN 130
126 PRINT "YOU CAN'T GO INTO A WALL!!"
127 GOTO 100
130 X1=INT(X1*1000)/1000+X2
131 Y1=INT(Y1*1000)/1000+Y2
132 X1=INT(X1+.5)
133 Y1=INT(Y1+.5)
135 PRINT "HUMAN YOU ARE NOW AT (";X1;",";Y1;")"
136 IF X<>X1 THEN 140
137 IF Y<>Y1 THEN 140
138 PRINT "YOU RAN RIGHT INTO THE RABBIT!!"
139 GOTO 330
140 PRINT "THE RABBIT IS POUNCING AT ANGLE.....";:P1=P1+1
150 X2=X1-X:Y2=Y1-Y
151 IF X2=0 THEN 280
152 IF Y2=0 THEN 300
160 B=INT(ATN(ABS((Y2/X2)))/(3.14159/180))
170 ON SGN(X2)+2 GOTO 190,10,180
180 ON SGN(Y2)+2 GOTO 240,10,250
190 ON SGN(Y2)+2 GOTO 230,10,220
220 B=180-B:GOTO 250
230 B=B+180:GOTO 250
240 B=360-B
250 B=INT(B/45+.5)*45:PRINT B
255 M=1
256 IF ABS((INT(B/10)*10)-B)<>5 THEN 260
257 M=1.5
260 X2=(M*COS(B*(3.14159/180)))
261 Y2=(M*SIN(B*(3.14159/180)))
270 X=INT(X+X2+.5)
271 Y=INT(Y+Y2+.5)
272 GOTO 315
280 IF Y2<0 THEN 290
281 B=90:GOTO 315
290 B=270:GOTO 250
300 IF X2<0 THEN 310
301 B=1:GOTO 250
310 B=180:GOTO 250
315 IF SQR((X-X1)^2+(Y-Y1)^2)=0 THEN 323
320 P=INT(P1*RND(1)+1)
321 IF P<>1 THEN 323
322 GOTO 140
323 NEXT G:PRINT "YOU ARE RELEASED!":GOTO 340
330 PRINT "**CRUNCH** WELL R.I.P."
340 END
Ok
```

Maneuvers

In this game you are maneuvering in a corner of space shaped, interestingly enough, like a cube. The dimensions of the cube are ten parsecs on a side. The bases are at the corners as shown on the diagram with the sample run. There are four star bases located at corners of the cube which you must visit in order, A, B, C, and D, to deliver a message to them. While it is a fairly simple matter to get to Base A, the other bases sometimes prove somewhat elusive. One possibility would be to use a second computer to compute your course, or even compute the course before you start the game and then feed it in. Would this be cheating? I don't think so because the learning value in writing a program to compute your course will teach you more about the game than probably fifty plays of it. On the other hand, which is more fun? That's for you to find out.

This program was written by John C. Russ.

```
RUN
                         MANUEVERS
                     CREATIVE COMPUTING
                   MORRISTOWN, NEW JERSEY



DO YOU NEED INSTRUCTIONS? YES

YOU ARE THE PILOT OF THE ENTERPRISE'S SPACE SHUTTLE.
YOU MUST DELIVER A MESSAGE TO EACH OF FOUR STARBASES,
IN THE LEAST TOTAL TIME.  YOUR INITIAL POSITION IS AT
ONE CORNER OF A CUBE, TEN PARSECS ON A SIDE.  THE BASES
ARE AT THE CORNERS SHOWN BELOW, MARKED A, B, C, AND D IN
THE ORDER IN WHICH YOU MUST VISIT THEM.
```

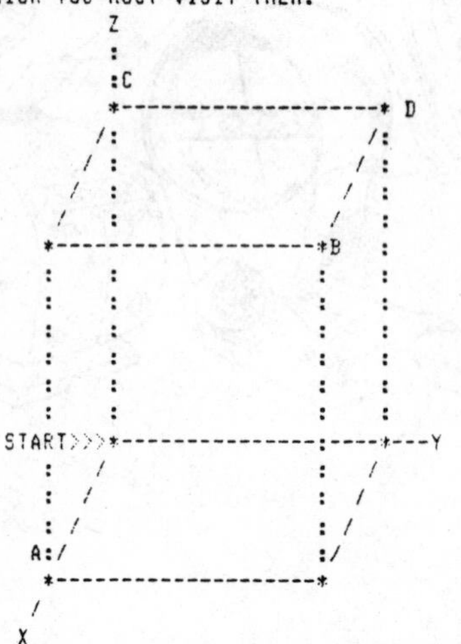


```
FOR YOUR SUBSPACE RADIO TO DELIVER THE MESSAGE, YOU
MUST PASS WITHIN ONE PARSEC OF EACH STARBASE.  YOUR
PROPULSION SYSTEM IS ALWAYS ON, GIVING YOU A CONSTANT
ACCELERATION OF 0.2 PARSECS PER STARDATE PER STARDATE.
YOU CAN ONLY CONTROL THE ORIENTATION OF YOUR SHIP, TO
DIRECT YOUR THRUST AND ACCELERATION.  YOU SPECIFY YOUR
SHIP'S ATTITUDE BY THE ANGLE THETA (THE CLOCKWISE ANGLE
IN THE X-Y PLANE STARTING AT THE X-AXIS) AND THE ANGLE
PSI (THE ANGLE OF INCLINATION ABOVE THE X-Y PLANE).
YOU INPUT NEW ANGLES EACH STARDATE.

ELAPSED  POSITION COORDINATES:              ORIENTATION
TIME      X          Y           Z          THETA  ,  PSI
 0        0          0           0          ? 0,0
 1        .1         0           0          ? 0,0
 2        .4         0           0          ? 0,0
 3        .9         0           0          ? 0,0
 4        1.6        0           0          ? 0,0
 5        2.5        0           0          ? 0,0
 6        3.6        0           0          ? 0,0
 7        4.9        0           0          ? 180,0
 8        6.2        0           0          ? 180,0
 9        7.3        0           0          ? 180,0
 10       8.2        0           0          ? 180,0
 11       8.9        0           0          ? 180,0
 12       9.4        0           0
MESSAGE DELIVERED TO BASE # 1
AT TIME 12.28                               ? 180,0
 13       9.7        0           0          ? 180,0
 14       9.8        0           0          ? 90,90
 15       9.8        0           .1         ? 90,90
 16       9.8        0           .4         ? 0,90
 17       9.8        0           .9         ? 90,45
 18       9.8        .071        1.571      ? 90,0
 19       9.8        .312        2.312      ? 90,0
 20       9.8        .754        3.054      ? 90,270
 21       9.8        1.295       3.695      ? 90,270
 22       9.8        1.836       4.136      ? 90,270
 23       9.8        2.378       4.378      ? 90,0
 24       9.8        3.019       4.519      ? 90,0
 25       9.8        3.861       4.661      ? 90,0
 26       9.8        4.902       4.802      ? 270,0
 27       9.8        5.944       4.944      ? 270,0
 28       9.8        6.785       5.085      ? 270,0
 29       9.8        7.426       5.226      ? 270,0
 30       9.8        7.868       5.368      ? 270,0
 31       9.8        8.109       5.509      ? 270,0
 32       9.8        8.151       5.651      ? 90,90
 33       9.8        8.092       5.892      ? 90,90
 34       9.8        8.034       6.333      ? 90,270
 35       9.8        7.975       6.775      ? 90,270
 36       9.8        7.916       7.016      ? 90,270
 37       9.8        7.858       7.058      ? 90,..\.\90
 38       9.8        7.799       7.099      ? 90,90
 39       9.8        7.741       7.341      ? 90,90
 40       9.8        7.682       7.782      ? 90,90
 41       9.8        7.623       8.423      ? 90,270
 42       9.8        7.565       9.065      ? 90,270
 43       9.8        7.506       9.506      ? 90,270
 44       9.8        7.448       9.748      ? 90,270
 45       9.8        7.389       9.789      ? 90,0
 46       9.8        7.431       9.731      ? 90,90
 47       9.8        7.572       9.772      ? 90,270
 48       9.8        7.713       9.813      ? 90,270
 49       9.8        7.855       9.655      ? 90,0
 50       9.8        8.096       9.396      ? 90,90
 51       9.8        8.438       9.238      ? 90,0
 52       9.8        8.879       9.179      ? 90,90
 53       9.8        9.421       9.22
MESSAGE DELIVERED TO BASE # 2
AT TIME 53.74                               ? 90,270
 54       9.8        9.962       9.262      ? 90,0
 55       9.8        10.603      9.203      ? 225,0
 56       9.729      11.274      9.145      ? 45,0
```

```
 57      9.659      11.945     9.086      ? 270,0
 58      9.659      12.586     9.028      ? 270,0
 59      9.659      13.028     8.969      ? 270,90
 60      9.659      13.369     9.01       ? 270,90
 61      9.659      13.71      9.252      ? 270,270
 62      9.659      14.052     9.493      ? 270,270
 63      9.659      14.393     9.535      ? 270,270
 64      9.658      14.735     9.376      ? 270,90
 65      9.658      15.076     9.218      ? 270,0
 66      9.658      15.318     9.159      ? 276,0
 67      9.669      15.36      9.1        ? 270,0
 68      9.69       15.202     9.042      ? 245,0
 69      9.668      14.854     8.983      ? 250,0
 70      9.571      14.321     8.925      ? 270,0
 71      9.439      13.595     8.866      ? 245,0
 72      9.264      12.677     8.807      ? 260,0
 73      9.03       11.571     8.749      ? 257,0
 74      8.757      10.268     8.69       ? 245,90
 75      8.46       8.869      8.732      ? 230,0
 76      8.1        7.392      8.873      ? 200,0
 77      7.581      5.805      9.015      ? 150,0
 78      6.882      4.234      9.156      ? 90,0
 79      6.096      2.812      9.297      ? 90,0
 80      5.31       1.591      9.439      ? 90,0
 81      4.524      .569       9.58       ? 90,0
 82      3.738      -.252      9.722      ? 90.0,0
 83      2.952      -.873      9.863      ? 45,0
 84      2.236      -1.324     10.005     ? 45,0
 85      1.663      -1.633     10.146     ? 45,0
 86      1.23       -1.801     10.287     ? 45,0
 87      .939       -1.827     10.429     ? 45,0
 88      .79        -1.712     10.57      ? 45,0
 89      .781       -1.456     10.712     ? 45,0
 90      .915       -1.058     10.853     ? 45,0
 91      1.189      -.519      10.994     ? 200,270
 92      1.535      .091       11.036     ? 180,270
 93      1.88       .701       10.877     ? 180,0
 94      2.126      1.311      10.619     ? 180,0
 95      2.171      1.921      10.36      ? 225,0
 96      2.046      2.46       10.102     ? 260,0
 97      1.832      2.83       9.843      ? 270,0
 98      1.602      3.002      9.584      ? 270,0
 99      1.371      2.974      9.326      ? 245
?? 0
 100     1.098      2.754      9.067      ? 260,90
 101     .782       2.445      8.909      ? 270,90
 102     .467       2.135      8.95       ? 285,0
 103     .178       1.729      9.092      ? 295,0
 104     -.043      1.135      9.233      ? 300,0
 105     -.172      .365       9.374
MESSAGE DELIVERED TO BASE # 3
AT TIME 105.48                            ? 90,0
 106     -.251      -.393      9.516      ? 75,0
 107     -.305      -.953      9.657      ? 80,0
 108     -.314      -1.319     9.799      ? 80,0
 109     -.29       -1.488     9.94       ? 80,0
 110     -.23       -1.459     10.081     ? 90,0
 111     -.153      -1.233     10.223     ? 90,0
 112     -.076      -.806      10.364     ? 90,0
 113     1E-03      -.179      10.506     ? 90,0
 114     .078       .648       10.647     ? 105,0
 115     .129       1.671      10.789     ? 103,270
 116     .154       2.791      10.83      ? 101,270
 117     .179       3.911      10.671     ? 99,0
 118     .189       5.13       10.413     ? 261,0
 119     .167       6.348      10.154     ? 270,90
 120     .13        7.468      9.996      ? 270,0
 121     .092       8.488      9.937      ? 260,90
 122     .055       9.408      9.979
MESSAGE DELIVERED TO BASE # 4
AT TIME 122.58                            GOOD JOB.  DO YOU WANT TO
TRY TO IMPROVE YOUR TIME? NO THANK YOU!
Ok
```

```
LIST
10 PRINT TAB(24);"MANUEVERS"
11 PRINT TAB(20);"CREATIVE COMPUTING"
12 PRINT TAB(18);"MORRISTOWN, NEW JERSEY"
13 PRINT:PRINT:PRINT
20 PRINT "DO YOU NEED INSTRUCTIONS";
30 INPUT X$
40 IF LEFT$(X$,1)="N" THEN 500
100 PRINT
110 PRINT "YOU ARE THE PILOT OF THE ENTERPRISE'S SPACE SHUTTLE."
120 PRINT "YOU MUST DELIVER A MESSAGE TO EACH OF FOUR STARBASES,"
130 PRINT "IN THE LEAST TOTAL TIME.  YOUR INITIAL POSITION IS AT"
140 PRINT "ONE CORNER OF A CUBE, TEN PARSECS ON A SIDE.  THE BASES"
150 PRINT "ARE AT THE CORNERS SHOWN BELOW, MARKED A, B, C, AND D IN"
160 PRINT "THE ORDER IN WHICH YOU MUST VISIT THEM."
170 PRINT "                     Z"
180 PRINT "                     :"
190 PRINT "                     :C"
200 PRINT "                     *------------------* D"
210 PRINT "                    /:                 /:"
220 PRINT "                   / :                / :"
230 PRINT "                  /  :               /  :"
240 PRINT "                 /   :              /   :"
250 PRINT "                *------------------*B   :"
260 PRINT "                :    :             :    :"
270 PRINT "                :    :             :    :"
275 PRINT "                :    :             :    :"
280 PRINT "                :    :             :    :"
285 PRINT "                :    :             :    :"
290 PRINT "                :    :             :    :"
300 PRINT "             START>>>*-------------:----*---Y"
310 PRINT "                :   /              :   /"
320 PRINT "                :  /               :  /"
330 PRINT "                : /                : /"
340 PRINT "               A:/                 :/"
350 PRINT "                *------------------*"
360 PRINT "               /"
370 PRINT "              X"
380 PRINT "FOR YOUR SUBSPACE RADIO TO DELIVER THE MESSAGE, YOU"
390 PRINT "MUST PASS WITHIN ONE PARSEC OF EACH STARBASE.  YOUR"
400 PRINT "PROPULSION SYSTEM IS ALWAYS ON, GIVING YOU A CONSTANT"
410 PRINT "ACCELERATION OF 0.2 PARSECS PER STARDATE PER STARDATE."
420 PRINT "YOU CAN ONLY CONTROL THE ORIENTATION OF YOUR SHIP, TO"
430 PRINT "DIRECT YOUR THRUST AND ACCELERATION.  YOU SPECIFY YOUR"
440 PRINT "SHIP'S ATTITUDE BY THE ANGLE THETA (THE CLOCKWISE ANGLE"
450 PRINT "IN THE X-Y PLANE STARTING AT THE X-AXIS) AND THE ANGLE"
460 PRINT "PSI (THE ANGLE OF INCLINATION ABOVE THE X-Y PLANE)."
470 PRINT "YOU INPUT NEW ANGLES EACH STARDATE."
500 PRINT
505 LET P=3.14159/180
510 LET J=1
520 DIM T(4,3),C(3)
530 FOR X=1 TO 4
540   FOR Y=1 TO 3
550     READ T(X,Y)
560   NEXT Y
570 NEXT X
580 DATA 10,0,0,10,10,10,0,0,10,0,10,10
590 LET A=.2
600 LET X1=0
610 LET Y1=0
620 LET Z1=0
630 LET V1=0
640 LET V2=0
650 LET V3=0
660 LET T0=0
670 LET B1=1E-03
680 LET B2=1E-03
700 PRINT "ELAPSED  POSITION COORDINATES:";
710 PRINT TAB(38);"ORIENTATION"
720 PRINT "TIME      X          Y          Z";
730 PRINT TAB(38);"THETA  ,  PSI"
800 PRINT T0;TAB(8);INT(1000*X1+.5)/1000;TAB(18);
805 PRINT INT(1000*Y1+.5)/1000;TAB(28);INT(1000*Z1+.5)/1000;
806 PRINT TAB(38);
810 FOR K=0 TO 1 STEP .02
820   LET C(1)=X+K*V1+A/2*K*K*COS(B2*P)*COS(B1*P)
830   LET C(2)=Y+K*V2+A/2*K*K*COS(B2*P)*SIN(B1*P)
840   LET C(3)=Z+K*V3+A/2*K*K*SIN(B2*P)
850   LET D=0
860   FOR L=1 TO 3
870     LET D=D+(T(J,L)-C(L))*(T(J,L)-C(L))
880   NEXT L
890   IF SQR(D)>1 GOTO 950
900   PRINT:PRINT  "MESSAGE DELIVERED TO BASE #";J
910   PRINT "AT TIME";T0+K;TAB(38);
920   IF J=4 GOTO 1100
930   LET J=J+1
940   GOTO 960
950 NEXT K
960 LET X=X1
970 LET Y=Y1
980 LET Z=Z1
985 LET T0=T0+1
990 INPUT  B1,B2
1030 LET X1=X+V1+A/2*COS(B2*P)*COS(B1*P)
1040 LET Y1=Y+V2+A/2*COS(B2*P)*SIN(B1*P)
1050 LET Z1=Z+V3+A/2*SIN(B2*P)
1060 LET V1=V1+A*COS(B2*P)*COS(B1*P)
1070 LET V2=V2+A*COS(B2*P)*SIN(B1*P)
1080 LET V3=V3+A*SIN(B2*P)
1090 GOTO 800
1100 PRINT "GOOD JOB.  DO YOU WANT TO"
1110 PRINT "TRY TO IMPROVE YOUR TIME";
1120 INPUT X$
1130 IF LEFT$(X$,1)="Y" THEN 500
1140 END
Ok
```

Mastermind®

The original invention of Mastermind is credited to an amateur mathematician, Mordechai Meirovich, who first displayed it at the 1971 Nurenburg Toy Fair.* Rights to the game were bought by Invicta who had moderate success with the game for 2½ years until the Christmas season of 1975 when it was the most popular packaged game. Sales surpassed even the old standby, Monopoly.

In its most basic form, Mastermind consists of a plastic game board, a dozen or so pegs which can be grouped into six basic colors, and two groups of black and white key pegs (sometimes called "inference pegs".) The game board resembles the figure below.

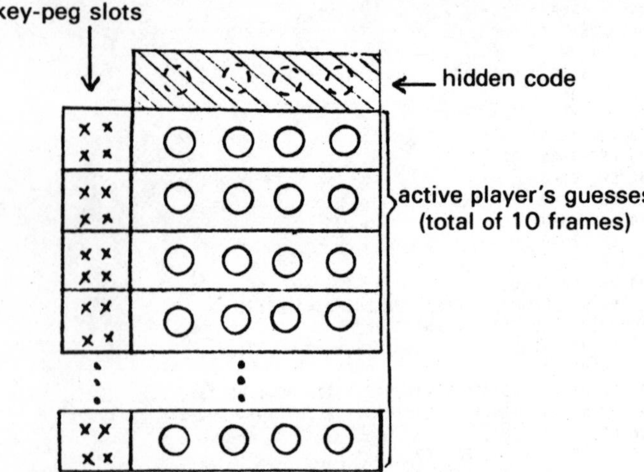

The game is played by two people, whom we shall designate as the "active" player and the "passive" player. The first step before play actually commences is to have the passive player (in our case, the computer) choose a total of four colored pegs at random from any of the six basic color groups (duplicate colors allowed, of course.) He then conceals these colors from the active player by placing the four pegs in the "hidden code"portion of the game board. It is now up to the active player to determine, in ten moves or less, the exact color and location of each of the four pegs comprising the hidden code.

To aid the active player in determining the hidden code, the passive player must award the active player a number of key pegs (inference pegs) after each guess, according to the following scheme: for *each* peg in the active player's current guess which corresponds exactly (in color *and* position) to a peg in the hidden code, the passive person places one *black* peg in the key-peg square adjacent to the passive player's current guess frame. Placing of the key pegs within the square is arbitrary since the relative position of the key peg carries no meaning. Clearly, when four black pegs are obtained, the hidden code is broken.

Secondly, the passive player must place one *white* key peg in the current key-peg square for *each* peg in the active player's current guess which matches (in color, but *not* position) a peg in the hidden code. Keep in mind that once a color peg in the player's current guess has been awarded a key peg, its function in determining the remaining number of key pegs to award for the current guess is finished. For example, suppose the hidden code were:

R B Y G

corresponding to red, blue, yellow, green, and the active player's current guess were:

G B B P

corresponding to green, blue, blue and purple.

The passive player should subsequently award one black and one white key peg for the following reasons: the blue color peg in position 2 of the current guess matches exactly in color and position with the hidden code. Secondly, the green color peg in position 1 of the current guess matches the color of the peg in position 4 of the hidden code. But since the *location* of the green peg is not exact, only a white peg is awarded. The blue and purple pegs in positions 3 and 4, respectively, of the current guess do not match either the color or position of the remaining pegs in the hidden code (positions 1 and 3) and hence, no other key pegs are awarded.

The game proceeds in this manner until the hidden code is broken or all ten frames have been filled. As noted earlier, the computer will play the passive player in our computer version, generating a hidden code and awarding the black and white key pegs after each guess.

The program offers the user two options, QUIT and BOARD, which may be entered at any time *after* the first move. QUIT instructs the program that you are fed up with playing Mastermind for the time being and wish to terminate the session. BOARD instructs the program to print out a summary of the moves prior to the time that the BOARD command was issued, including the guesses and key pegs awarded for each frame. Some players find that an arrangement of frames such as that provided by BOARD is easier to visualize and subsequently analyze. Beginners will find it most useful.

The program and this description were written by David G. Struble of the University of Dayton. It first appeared in *Creative Computing*, Mar/Apr 1976.

*Ed. Note—
To anyone familiar with children's games, it is obvious that Mastermind is simply a commercial adaptation (using colors rather than numbers) of the game Bulls and Cows. This game, much more popular in England than the U.S. is not, to my knowledge, commercially packaged. —DHA

```
RUN
                        MASTERMIND
                    CREATIVE COMPUTING
                  MORRISTOWN, NEW JERSEY



THE GAME OF MASTERMIND

COLOR CODES:
               R=RED     O=ORANGE     Y=YELLOW
               G=GREEN   B=BLUE       P=PURPLE


MOVE NUMBER 1 ? RRGG
 0  BLACK PEGS
 1  WHITE PEGS

MOVE NUMBER 2 ? OOBB
 0  BLACK PEGS
 0  WHITE PEGS

MOVE NUMBER 3 ? YYPP
 3  BLACK PEGS
 0  WHITE PEGS

MOVE NUMBER 4 ? YYPR
 2  BLACK PEGS
 0  WHITE PEGS

MOVE NUMBER 5 ? GYPP
 2  BLACK PEGS
 2  WHITE PEGS

MOVE NUMBER 6 ? YGPP
YOU WIN!!
WANT TO PLAY AGAIN? YES

MOVE NUMBER 1 ? RROO
 0  BLACK PEGS
 0  WHITE PEGS

MOVE NUMBER 2 ? GGYY
 1  BLACK PEGS
 1  WHITE PEGS

MOVE NUMBER 3 ? BBPP
 2  BLACK PEGS
 0  WHITE PEGS

MOVE NUMBER 4 ? BBGY
YOU WIN!!
WANT TO PLAY AGAIN? NO

Ok
```

```
LIST
10 PRINT TAB(24);"MASTERMIND"
20 PRINT TAB(20);"CREATIVE COMPUTING"
30 PRINT TAB(18);"MORRISTOWN, NEW JERSEY"
40 PRINT:PRINT:PRINT
100 PRINT "THE GAME OF MASTERMIND"
110 PRINT
130 PRINT "COLOR CODES:"
140 PRINT "                R=RED     O=ORANGE     Y=YELLOW"
150 PRINT "                G=GREEN   B=BLUE       P=PURPLE"
160 PRINT
170 DIM B$(10),Y(10),Z(10)
180 C(0)=4
190 FOR N=1 TO 4
200 C(N)=INT(6*RND(1)+1)
210 NEXT N
220 FOR N=1 TO 4
230 X=C(N)
240 GOSUB 730
250 C(N)=X
260 NEXT N
270 P$=""
273 FOR X1=1 TO 4
275 P$=P$+CHR$(C(X1))
277 NEXT X1
280 FOR P=1 TO 10
290 PRINT
300 PRINT "MOVE NUMBER";P;
310 INPUT G$
320 IF G$= "BOARD" THEN 910
330 IF G$="QUIT" THEN 440
340 B$(P)=G$
350 GOSUB 520
360 IF B=4 THEN 1010
370 GOSUB 600
380 PRINT B;" BLACK PEGS"
390 Y(P)=B
400 PRINT W;" WHITE PEGS"
410 Z(P)=W
420 NEXT P
430 PRINT "SORRY, YOU LOSE"
440 PRINT "THE CORRECT CODE WAS:";P$
450 PRINT "WANT TO PLAY AGAIN";
460 INPUT A$
480 IF A$="YES" THEN 190
490 PRINT
500 END
510 REM COMPUTE BLACK PEGS
520 FOR X1=1 TO 4
523 G(X1)=ASC(MID$(G$,X1,1))
525 NEXT X1
530 B=0
540 FOR K=1 TO 4
550 IF G(K) <> C(K) THEN 570
560 B=B+1
570 NEXT K
580 RETURN
590 REM COMPUTE WHITE PEGS
600 FOR X1=1 TO 4
603 R(X1)=ASC(MID$(P$,X1,1))
605 NEXT X1
610 W=0
620 FOR I=1 TO 4
630 FOR J=1 TO 4
640 IF G(I) <> R(J) THEN 680
650 W=W+1
660 R(J)=0
670 GOTO 690
680 NEXT J
690 NEXT I
700 W=W-B
710 RETURN
720 REM TRANSLATE COLOR CODES TO NUMERICS
730 IF X <> 1 THEN 760
740 X=89
750 RETURN
760 IF X <> 2 THEN 790
770 X=82
780 RETURN
790 IF X <> 3 THEN 820
800 X=80
810 RETURN
820 IF X <> 4 THEN 850
830 X=79
840 RETURN
850 IF X <> 5 THEN 880
860 X=71
870 RETURN
880 X=66
890 RETURN
900 REM PRINT BOARD SUMMARY
910 V=P-1
920 PRINT "GUESS","BLACKS","WHITES"
930 PRINT "-----","------","------"
960 FOR I=1 TO V
970 PRINT B$(I),Y(I),Z(I)
990 NEXT I
1000 GOTO 290
1010 PRINT "YOU WIN!!"
1020 GOTO 450
9999 END
Ok
```

Masterbagels

This is a fascinating, general-purpose, deductive logic game. It rolls Bagels, Mastermind, bulls and cows, et cetera, into one general deductive logic game. If you want to play Bagels, set the inputs to N,3,9 (N is the number of games you wish to play). If you want to play mastermind, set the inputs to N,4,6. Of course, many of the games that it plays are entirely new altogether such as N,7,4 or N,5,5.

To make it into a really general-purpose game, you might want to put in a modification in the digit selection routine (statements 300-320) with a parameter that either allows or disallows duplicate digits. As it is right now, the game does allow duplicate digits so that, for example, it could select a three digit number such as 223 or even 444. Another change you might want to add is in statement 750; it sets the maximum allowable trials for getting the answer. You may find that it is not giving you enough tries and you might want to increase the value of I.

Masterbagels was created by H.R. Hamilton and originally appeared in *Creative Computing*, Jan/Feb 1977.

```
RUN
                         MASTERBAGELS
                      CREATIVE COMPUTING
                    MORRISTOWN, NEW JERSEY
TEACH? YES
 HI, THIS IS A LOGIC GAME DESIGNED TO TEST YOUR DEDUCTIVE
ABILITY.  I WILL CHOOSE A RANDOM NUMBER AND YOU ISOLATE IT.
WHEN PROMPTED, ENTER A VALID NUMBER, AND I WILL THEN RESPOND
WITH THE # OF DIGITS THAT ARE RIGHT AND IN THE RIGHT POSITION
AND THE # RIGHT BUT IN THE WRONG POSITION.  IF I THINK YOU
ARE HOPELESSLY LOST, I WILL TELL YOU THE ANSWER AND WE
WILL GO ON TO THE NEXT NUMBER.  TO RECAP YOUR ENTRIES
ENTER A 0, TO QUIT ON A NUMBER ENTER 1, AND TO STOP ENTER 2

HOW MANY #'S(1-100), # DIGITS(2-6), AND MAX VALUE(2-9)? 2,2,4
GUESS? 12
 0 , 1
GUESS? 31
 0 , 0
GUESS? 24
 3 TRIES, 3 AVERAGE FOR 1 NUMBERS
GUESS? 24
 0 , 1
GUESS? 32
 1 , 0
GUESS? 22
 1 , 0
GUESS? 12
 4 TRIES, 3.5 AVERAGE FOR 2 NUMBERS
RUN AGAIN? YES

HOW MANY #'S(1-100), # DIGITS(2-6), AND MAX VALUE(2-9)? 1,4,6
GUESS? 1122
 1 , 1
GUESS? 1234
 2 , 0
GUESS? 3456
 0 , 2
GUESS? 1265
 1 , 1
GUESS? 2134
 1 , 1
GUESS? 0
 1 , 1 = 1122
 2 , 0 = 1234
 0 , 2 = 3456
 1 , 1 = 1265
 1 , 1 = 2134
GUESS? 2236
 1 , 2
GUESS? 2235
 1 , 1
GUESS? 1
ANSWER IS 6224
 10 TRIES, 10 AVERAGE FOR 1 NUMBERS
RUN AGAIN? NO
OK
```

```
LIST

5 PRINT TAB(23);"MASTERBAGELS"
6 PRINT TAB(20);"CREATIVE COMPUTING"
7 PRINT TAB(18);"MORRISTOWN, NEW JERSEY"
10 DIM F(9),M(9),T(9),H(18,3)
20 INPUT "TEACH";S$
30 IF LEFT$(S$,1)="N" THEN 130
50 PRINT "  HI, THIS IS A LOGIC GAME DESIGNED TO TEST YOUR DEDUCTIVE"
60 PRINT "ABILITY.  I WILL CHOOSE A RANDOM NUMBER AND YOU ISOLATE IT."
70 PRINT "WHEN PROMPTED, ENTER A VALID NUMBER, AND I WILL THEN RESPOND"
80 PRINT "WITH THE # OF DIGITS THAT ARE RIGHT AND IN THE RIGHT POSITION
90 PRINT "AND THE # RIGHT BUT IN THE WRONG POSITION.  IF I THINK YOU"
100 PRINT "ARE HOPELESSLY LOST, I WILL TELL YOU THE ANSWER AND WE"
110 PRINT "WILL GO ON TO THE NEXT NUMBER.  TO RECAP YOUR ENTRIES"
120 PRINT "ENTER A 0, TO QUIT ON A NUMBER ENTER 1, AND TO STOP ENTER 2"
130 S=0
140 PRINT
150 PRINT "HOW MANY #'S(1-100), # DIGITS(2-6), AND MAX VALUE(2-9)";
160 INPUT J,A,B
180 IF A<=0 THEN 220
190 IF A>6 THEN 220
200 IF B<2 THEN 220
210 IF B<10 THEN 240
220 PRINT "ILLEGAL RANGE, RE-ENTER RUN PARAMETERS"
230 GOTO 160
240 IF J<100 THEN 260
250 J=100
260 FOR X=0 TO J+A+B
270 I=RND(1)
280 NEXT X
290 FOR N=1 TO J
300 FOR X=0 TO A
310 T(X)=INT(RND(1)*B+1)
320 NEXT X
330 FOR I=1 TO A+B+1
340 FOR X=1 TO A
350 F(X)=0
360 NEXT X
370 F1=0
380 F2=0
390 INPUT "GUESS";V
400 IF V<> 0 THEN 450
410 FOR X=1 TO I-1
420 PRINT H(X,1)","H(X,2)"="H(X,3)
430 NEXT X
440 GOTO 390
450 IF V=1 THEN 750
460 IF V=2 THEN 920
470 T1=V
480 FOR X=1 TO A
490 M(X)=INT(T1/(10^(A-X)))
500 T1=T1-M(X)*(10^(A-X))+((SGN(A-(X+1))-1)*-.5)
510 IF M(X)<1 THEN 530
520 IF M(X)<B+1 THEN 550
530 PRINT "BAD NUMBER IN"V
540 GOTO 340
550 IF M(X)<>T(X) THEN 580
560 F(X)=1
570 F1=F1+1
580 NEXT X
590 IF F1=A THEN 810
600 FOR Y=1 TO A
610 IF T(Y)=M(Y) THEN 690
620 FOR X=1 TO A
630 IF M(Y)<>T(X) THEN 680
640 IF F(X)=1 THEN 680
650 F(X)=1
660 F2=F2+1
670 GOTO 690
680 NEXT X
690 NEXT Y
700 PRINT F1","F2
710 H(I,1)=F1
720 H(I,2)=F2
730 H(I,3)=V
740 NEXT I
750 I=A-1+B+1
760 V=0
770 FOR X=1 TO A
780 V=V+T(X)*(10^(A-X))
790 NEXT X
800 PRINT "ANSWER IS"V
810 S=S+I
820 PRINT I"TRIES,"S/N"AVERAGE FOR"N"NUMBERS"
830 Y=INT(RND(R)*I)
840 Y=INT(H(Y,2)/1024+4*RND(1))
850 FOR X=1 TO Y+1
860 I=RND(1)
870 NEXT X
880 NEXT N
890 INPUT "RUN AGAIN";S$
900 IF LEFT$(S$,1)="Y" THEN 130
920 END
OK
```

Matpuzzle

Ready to try something new? A game that isn't like STARTREK or Slot Machine? Then try MATPUZLE and enjoy the art of puzzle-making.

One benefit of puzzles is that they help develop a pattern of logic in one's thinking. In this puzzle you are given a matrix of letters, up to 6 x 6, and a board with dashes and a number above each of the dashes.

The matrix represents the letters of the words you typed in, each having the same length. The number of words and the length of the words are both limited to six, six words each six letters in length, but, both values don't have to be the same. The letters are then put in a matrix and randomly rearranged in lines 160-430.

The dashes on the board form the places for each letter of each word to be written in after it has been deciphered. The number above each dash, determined in lines 500-780, is the sum of the coordinates of where the letter of that dash is located in the matrix. The problem in solving the puzzle is that several coordinates have the same sum.

Since the answers appear above the puzzle itself, rip them off before you give it to a friend to try. They will have a great time trying to figure out your puzzle. Then let them make one for you or set up a relay. The possibilities are almost endless.

The program and description were written by Dave Schroeder.

```
RUN
                          MATPUZLE
                     CREATIVE COMPUTING
                   MORRISTOWN, NEW JERSEY

THIS IS A PUZZLE-MAKING GAME.
YOU INPUT UP TO SIX WORDS, UP TO SIX
LETTERS EACH, AND EQUAL IN LENGTH.
THE COMPUTER WILL SCRAMBLE THEM AND
PRINT THEM IN A MATRIX.  THE COMPUTER
WILL ALSO PRINT A CORRESPONDING NUMBER
BOARD.  WHEN IT STOPS TEAR IT AND GIVE IT
TO A FRIEND.
HOW MANY WORDS DO YOU WANT (UP TO 6)? 6
HOW MANY LETTERS IN EACH WORD (MUST BE SAME)? 6
TYPE ONE 6 LETTER WORD ON EACH LINE
? PARITY
? DUPLES\S\X
? MATRIX
? NUMBER
? LENGTH
? MOTHER

---------------------------- ( TEAR HERE ) ---------------------------
      1  2  3  4  5  6

  1   I  A  T  X  L  N

  2   E  E  R  M  H  I

  3   D  M  P  H  G  T

  4   U  L  O  A  R  B

  5   X  R  E  E  N  M

  6   T  T  U  P  Y  R



    6      3      5      2      7      11

  -----  -----  -----  -----  -----  -----
    4      5      10     6      4      5

  -----  -----  -----  -----  -----  -----
    6      8      4      9      8      6

  -----  -----  -----  -----  -----  -----
    7      9      11     10     8      7

  -----  -----  -----  -----  -----  -----
    6      3      10     8      8      7

  -----  -----  -----  -----  -----  -----
    5      7      9      7      9      12

  -----  -----  -----  -----  -----  -----

THE NUMBER ABOVE EACH DASH IS THE SUM OF TWO COORDINATES OF
THE POINT ON THE MATRIX WHERE THE CORRECT LETTER FOR THAT
SPOT WILL APPEAR.  THE PROBLEM IS THAT THE SUM OF SOME
COORDINATES ARE THE SAME SO SEVERAL LETTERS COULD FIT.  SO
TRY NOW TO FIND WHAT WORDS WERE USED AND SOLVE THE PUZZLE
-- GOOD LUCK
DO YOU WANT  ANOTHER RUN? YES
HOW MANY WORDS DO YOU WANT (UP TO 6)? 4
HOW MANY LETTERS IN EACH WORD (MUST BE SAME)? 5
TYPE ONE 5 LETTER WORD ON EACH LINE
? PRINT
? BASIC
? EQUAL
? POINT
```

```
---------------------------- ( TEAR HERE ) ---------------------------
      1   2   3   4   5

1     R   Q   C   U   E

2     I   T   A   N   L

3     I   I   S   B   P

4     O   N   T   P   A



   8       2       3       6       4

-----   -----   -----   -----   -----
   7       5       6       5       4

-----   -----   -----   -----   -----
   6       3       5       9       7

-----   -----   -----   -----   -----
   8       5       4       6       7

-----   -----   -----   -----   -----


THE NUMBER ABOVE EACH DASH IS THE SUM OF TWO COORDINATES OF
THE POINT ON THE MATRIX WHERE THE CORRECT LETTER FOR THAT
SPOT WILL APPEAR.  THE PROBLEM IS THAT THE SUM OF SOME
COORDINATES ARE THE SAME SO SEVERAL LETTERS COULD FIT.  SO
TRY NOW TO FIND WHAT WORDS WERE USED AND SOLVE THE PUZZLE
-- GOOD LUCK
DO YOU WANT  ANOTHER RUN? NO
OK
```

```
LIST

1 PRINT TAB(26)"MATPUZLE"
2 PRINTTAB(20)"CREATIVE COMPUTING"
3 PRINT TAB(18)"MORRISTOWN, NEW JERSEY"
4 PRINT:PRINT
10 DIM A$(6),B$(6,6),C(6,6),C$(6,6)
20 PRINT"THIS IS A PUZZLE-MAKING GAME."
30 PRINT"YOU INPUT UP TO SIX WORDS, UP TO SIX"
40 PRINT"LETTERS EACH, AND EQUAL IN LENGTH."
50 PRINT"THE COMPUTER WILL SCRAMBLE THEN AND"
60 PRINT"PRINT THEM IN A MATRIX.  THE COMPUTER "
70 PRINT"WILL ALSO PRINT A CORRESPONDING NUMBER"
80 PRINT"BOARD.  WHEN IT STOPS TEAR IT AND GIVE IT"
90 PRINT"TO A FRIEND."
100 PRINT"HOW MANY WORDS DO YOU WANT (UP TO 6)";
105 INPUT W
110 PRINT"HOW MANY LETTERS IN EACH WORD (MUST BE SAME)";
115 INPUT L
120 PRINT"TYPE ONE";L;"LETTER WORD ON EACH LINE"
130 FOR X=1 TO W
140 INPUT A$(X)
150 NEXT X
160 FOR X=1 TO W
170 FOR  Y=1 TO L
180 C$(X,Y)=MID$(A$(X),Y,1):B$(X,Y)=MID$(A$(X),Y,1)
190 NEXT Y
200 NEXT X
210 PRINT
215 FOR P=1 TO 28
220 PRINT"-";
221 NEXT P
225 PRINT TAB(29)"( TEAR HERE )";
226 FOR P1=1 TO 27
227 PRINT TAB(43)"-";
228 NEXT P1
230 PRINT
240 FOR Z=1 TO 60
250 F=INT(RND(1)*W+1)
260 D=INT(RND(1)*W+1)
270 G=INT(RND(1)*L+1)
280 E=INT(RND(1)*L+1)
290 J$=B$(F,G)
300 B$(F,G)=B$(D,E)
310 B$(D,E)=J$
320 NEXT Z
330 PRINT TAB(4);
340 FOR Z1=1 TO L
350 PRINT TAB(5);Z1;" ";
360 NEXT Z1
370 PRINT
380 PRINT
390 FOR Z2=1 TO W
400 PRINT Z2;"   ";
410 FOR Z3=1 TO L
420 PRINT B$(Z2,Z3);"   ";
430 NEXT Z3
440 PRINT
450 PRINT
460 NEXT Z2
470 PRINT
480 PRINT
490 PRINT
500 FOR P=1 TO L
510 FOR Q=1 TO W
520 T=0
530 FOR R=1 TO W
540 FOR S=1 TO L
550 IF T=1 THEN 600
560 IF B$(R,S)<>C$(Q,P)THEN 600
570 C(Q,P)=R+S
580 T=1
590 B$(R,S)=" "
600 NEXT S
610 NEXT R
620 NEXT Q
630 NEXT P
640 FOR X=1 TO W
650 PRINT TAB(3)
660 FOR M=1 TO L
670 IF C(X,M)>9 THEN 700
680 PRINT C(X,M);"     ";
690 GOTO 710
700 PRINT C(X,M);"    ";
710 NEXT M
720 PRINT:PRINT
730 PRINT TAB(2);
740 FOR M1=1 TO L
750 PRINT"-----";"   ";
760 NEXT M1
770 PRINT
780 NEXT X
790 PRINT
800 PRINT
810 PRINT"THE NUMBER ABOVE EACH DASH IS THE SUM OF TWO COORDINATES OF "
820 PRINT"THE POINT ON THE MATRIX WHERE THE CORRECT LETTER FOR THAT "
830 PRINT"SPOT WILL APPEAR.  THE PROBLEM IS THAT THE SUM OF SOME "
840 PRINT"COORDINATES ARE THE SAME SO SEVERAL LETTERS COULD FIT.  SO "
850 PRINT"TRY NOW TO FIND WHAT WORDS WERE USED AND SOLVE THE PUZZLE"
855 PRINT"-- GOOD LUCK"
860 PRINT"DO YOU WANT  ANOTHER RUN";
861 INPUT Y9$
870 IF Y9$="YES" THEN 100
880 END
OK
```

Maze

```
RUN

                         MAZE
                   CREATIVE COMPUTING
                 MORRISTOWN, NEW JERSEY



DO YOU NEED INSTRUCTIONS? YES


THIS PROGRAM WILL SIMULATE A NEAR-SIGHTED MOUSE IN
A MAZE.  YOU SELECT THE DIFFICULTY FACTOR - SIZE!
YOU MAY HAVE A MAZE OF ANY SIZE PERMITTED BY THE SIZE OF YOUR
SYSTEM. DIMENSIONS LESS THAN 5 ARE TOO TRIVIAL.
EACH MAZE IS DIFFERENT, AND HAS ONLY ONE WAY THROUGH IT.

WHAT ARE YOUR DIMENSIONS (HORIZONTAL, VERTICAL)? 10,10
```

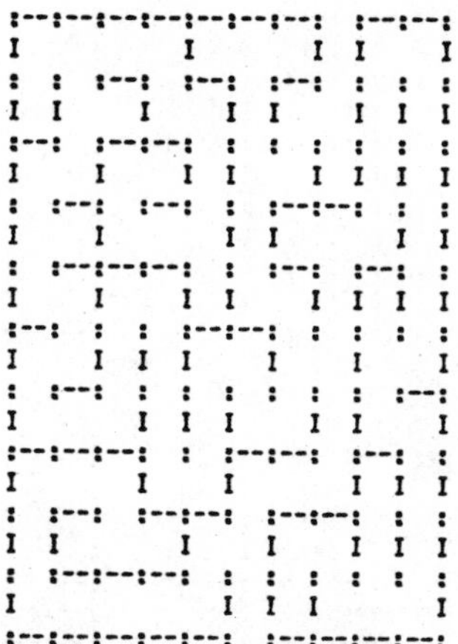

```
DO YOU WANT THE SOLUTION? YES
DO YOU WANT TO SEE EACH STEP? NO
```

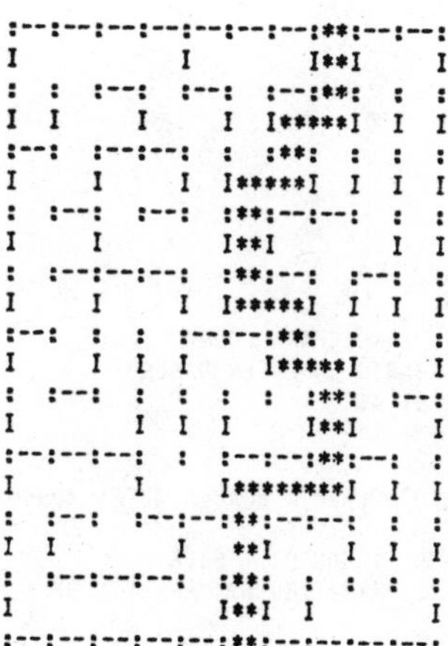

```
DO YOU WANT ANOTHER MAZE? YES

WHAT ARE YOUR DIMENSIONS (HORIZONTAL, VERTICAL)? 6,6
```

This is actually a two part game. In the first part, the program generates a maze which you can then try to find your way through with pencil and paper. Each path of the maze is three characters wide, hence the maximum width that will print on a standard seventy-two column width teletype or other hard copy printer is 24 for the horizontal dimension. A 132-column line printer could handle up to a horizontal dimension of 44. Naturally the vertical dimension can be anything since it's running the length of the paper. However, for really large mazes your computer system will probably be the limiting factor since several matrices are dimensioned with the horizontal and vertical dimensions of the maze.

In the second part of the program a near-sighted mouse is let loose in the maze and explores until he finds his way through. If you want to know what near-sighted means, run the program and ask to see the solution step by step as the mouse goes through the maze. If you elect not to see each step, you'll simply get a total solution for the maze itself.

With or without the mouse, it's a fun program and the larger mazes are frequently a real challenge to solve.

This program was conceived and written by Richard Schaal.

```
:--:--:--:  :--:--:
I              I  I
:  :  :--:--:  :  :
I  I        I     I
:--:--:--:--:  :  :
I              I  I
:  :--:--:--:--:  :
I        I     I  I
:  :--:  :  :  :  :
I  I     I  I  I  I
:  :  :--:  :  :  :
I  I     I  I     I
:--:--:  :--:--:--:
```

```
:--:--:--:**:--:--:
I         *****I  I
:  :  :--:--:**:  :
I  I        I**   I
:--:--:--:--:**:  :
I            **I  I
:  :--:--:--:--:  :
I        I     I  I
:  :--:  :  :  :  :
I  I     I  I  I  I
:  :  :--:  :  :  :
I  I     I  I     I
:--:--:  :--:--:--:
```

```
:--:--:--:**:--:--:
I         *****I  I
:  :  :--:--:**:  :
I  I        I**   I
:--:--:--:--:**:  :
I**************I  I
:  :--:--:--:--:  :
I        I     I  I
:  :--:  :  :  :  :
I  I     I  I  I  I
:  :  :--:  :  :  :
I  I     I  I     I
:--:--:  :--:--:--:
```

```
:--:--:--:**:--:--:
I         *****I  I
:  :  :--:--:**:  :
I  I        I**   I
:--:--:--:--:**:  :
I**************I  I
:**:--:--:--:--:  :
I**      I     I  I
:**:--:  :  :  :  :
I**I     I  I  I  I
:  :  :--:  :  :  :
I  I     I  I     I
:--:--:  :--:--:--:
```

```
:--:--:--:**:--:--:
I         *****I  I
:  :  :--:--:**:  :
I  I        I**   I
:--:--:--:--:**:  :
I**************I  I
:**:--:--:--:--:  :
I********I     I  I
:  :--:**:  :  :  :
I  I   **I  I  I  I
:  :  :--:  :  :  :
I  I     I  I     I
:--:--:  :--:--:--:
```

```
DO YOU WANT THE SOLUTION? YES
DO YOU WANT TO SEE EACH STEP? YES
```

```
:--:--:--:**:--:--:
I         **   I  I
:  :  :--:--:  :  :
I  I        I     I
:--:--:--:--:  :  :
I              I  I
:  :--:--:--:--:  :
I        I     I  I
:  :--:  :  :  :  :
I  I     I  I  I  I
:  :  :--:  :  :  :
I  I     I  I     I
:--:--:  :--:--:--:
```

```
:--:--:--:**:--:--:
I         *****I  I
:  :  :--:--:**:  :
I  I        I**   I
:--:--:--:--:**:  :
I         *****I  I
:  :--:--:--:--:  :
I        I     I  I
:  :--:  :  :  :  :
I  I     I  I  I  I
:  :  :--:  :  :  :
I  I     I  I     I
:--:--:  :--:--:--:
```

```
:--:--:--:**:--:--:
I         *****I  I
:  :  :--:--:**:  :
I  I        I**   I
:--:--:--:--:**:  :
I**************I  I
:**:--:--:--:--:  :
I**      I     I  I
:  :--:  :  :  :  :
I  I     I  I  I  I
:  :  :--:  :  :  :
I  I     I  I     I
:--:--:  :--:--:--:
```

```
:--:--:--:**:--:--:
I         *****I  I
:  :  :--:--:**:  :
I  I        I**   I
:--:--:--:--:**:  :
I**************I  I
:**:--:--:--:--:  :
I**      I     I  I
:  :--:  :  :  :  :
I  I     I  I  I  I
:  :  :--:  :  :  :
I  I     I  I     I
:--:--:  :--:--:--:
```

```
:--:--:--:**:--:--:
I         *****I  I
:  :  :--:--:**:  :
I  I        I**   I
:--:--:--:--:**:  :
I**************I  I
:**:--:--:--:--:  :
I********I     I  I
:  :--:**:  :  :  :
I  I*****I  I  I  I
:  :  :--:  :  :  :
I  I     I  I     I
:--:--:  :--:--:--:
```

```
:--:--:--:**:--:--:
I         *****I  I
:  :  :--:--:  :  :
I  I        I     I
:--:--:--:--:  :  :
I              I  I
:  :--:--:--:--:  :
I        I     I  I
:  :--:  :  :  :  :
I  I     I  I  I  I
:  :  :--:  :  :  :
I  I     I  I     I
:--:--:  :--:--:--:
```

```
:--:--:--:**:--:--:
I         *****I  I
:  :  :--:--:**:  :
I  I        I**   I
:--:--:--:--:**:  :
I      ********I  I
:  :--:--:--:--:  :
I        I     I  I
:  :--:  :  :  :  :
I  I     I  I  I  I
:  :  :--:  :  :  :
I  I     I  I     I
:--:--:  :--:--:--:
```

```
:--:--:--:**:--:--:
I         *****I  I
:  :  :--:--:**:  :
I  I        I**   I
:--:--:--:--:**:  :
I**************I  I
:**:--:--:--:--:  :
I**      I     I  I
:**:--:  :  :  :  :
I**I     I  I  I  I
:  :  :--:  :  :  :
I  I     I  I     I
:--:--:  :--:--:--:
```

```
:--:--:--:**:--:--:
I         *****I  I
:  :  :--:--:**:  :
I  I        I**   I
:--:--:--:--:**:  :
I**************I  I
:**:--:--:--:--:  :
I*****   I     I  I
:  :--:  :  :  :  :
I  I     I  I  I  I
:  :  :--:  :  :  :
I  I     I  I     I
:--:--:  :--:--:--:
```

```
:--:--:--:**:--:--:
I         *****I  I
:  :  :--:--:**:  :
I  I        I**   I
:--:--:--:--:**:  :
I**************I  I
:**:--:--:--:--:  :
I********I     I  I
:  :--:**:  :  :  :
I  I*****I  I  I  I
:  :**:--:  :  :  :
I  I**   I  I     I
:--:--:  :--:--:--:
```

```
:--:--:--:**:--:--:
I         *****I  I
:  :  :--:--:**:  :
I  I        I**   I
:--:--:--:--:  :  :
I              I  I
:  :--:--:--:--:  :
I        I     I  I
:  :--:  :  :  :  :
I  I     I  I  I  I
:  :  :--:  :  :  :
I  I     I  I     I
:--:--:  :--:--:--:
```

```
:--:--:--:**:--:--:
I         *****I  I
:  :  :--:--:**:  :
I  I        I**   I
:--:--:--:--:**:  :
I   ***********I  I
:  :--:--:--:--:  :
I        I     I  I
:  :--:  :  :  :  :
I  I     I  I  I  I
:  :  :--:  :  :  :
I  I     I  I     I
:--:--:  :--:--:--:
```

```
:--:--:--:**:--:--:
I         *****I  I
:  :  :--:--:**:  :
I  I        I**   I
:--:--:--:--:**:  :
I**************I  I
:**:--:--:--:--:  :
I**      I     I  I
:**:--:  :  :  :  :
I**I     I  I  I  I
:**:  :--:  :  :  :
I**I     I  I     I
:--:--:  :--:--:--:
```

```
:--:--:--:**:--:--:
I         *****I  I
:  :  :--:--:**:  :
I  I        I**   I
:--:--:--:--:**:  :
I**************I  I
:**:--:--:--:--:  :
I********I     I  I
:  :--:  :  :  :  :
I  I     I  I  I  I
:  :  :--:  :  :  :
I  I     I  I     I
:--:--:  :--:--:--:
```

```
:--:--:--:**:--:--:
I         *****I  I
:  :  :--:--:**:  :
I  I        I**   I
:--:--:--:--:**:  :
I**************I  I
:**:--:--:--:--:  :
I********I     I  I
:  :--:**:  :  :  :
I  I*****I  I  I  I
:  :**:--:  :  :  :
I  I*****I  I     I
:--:--:**:--:--:--:
```

```
LIST
10 PRINT TAB(27);"MAZE"
20 PRINT TAB(20);"CREATIVE COMPUTING"
30 PRINT TAB(18);"MORRISTOWN, NEW JERSEY"
40 PRINT:PRINT:PRINT
100 REM  MOUSE IN MAZE - SOLUTION SECTION BY RICHARD SCHAAL FMCC
110 REM  ORIGINAL MAZE PROGRAM FROM "101 BASIC COMPUTER GAMES"
120 PRINT "DO YOU NEED INSTRUCTIONS";:INPUT A$
130 IF LEFT$(A$,1)="Y" THEN 150
140 GOTO 200
150 PRINT:PRINT:PRINT "THIS PROGRAM WILL SIMULATE A NEAR-SIGHTED MOUSE I
N"
160 PRINT "A MAZE.  YOU SELECT THE DIFFICULTY FACTOR - SIZE!"
170 PRINT "YOU MAY HAVE A MAZE OF ANY SIZE PERMITTED BY THE SIZE OF YOUR
"
180 PRINT "SYSTEM. DIMENSIONS LESS THAN 5 ARE TOO TRIVIAL."
190 PRINT "EACH MAZE IS DIFFERENT, AND HAS ONLY ONE WAY THROUGH IT."
200 PRINT
210 PRINT "WHAT ARE YOUR DIMENSIONS (HORIZONTAL, VERTICAL)";
220 CLEAR 100: REM ERASE ALL ARRAYS AND VARIABLE VALUES
230 INPUT H,V
240 H=INT(ABS(H)):V=INT(ABS(V))
250 IF H>=5 AND V>=5 THEN 270
260 GOTO 150
270 DIM W(H,V),V(H,V)
280 PRINT:PRINT
290 Q=0:Z=0
300 X=INT(RND(1)*H+1)
310 FOR I=1 TO H
320 IF I=X THEN 350
330 PRINT ":--";
340 GOTO 360
350 PRINT ":  ";
360 NEXT I
370 PRINT ":"
380 C=1:W(X,1)=C:C=C+1:R=X:S=1
390 GOTO 470
400 IF R<>H THEN 450
410 IF S<>V THEN 440
420 R=1:S=1
430 GOTO 460
440 R=1:S=S+1:GOTO 460
450 R=R+1
460 IF W(R,S)=0 THEN 400
470 IF R=1 THEN 830
480 IF W(R-1,S)>0 THEN 830
490 IF S=1 THEN 640
500 IF W(R,S-1)<>0 THEN 640
510 IF R=H THEN 550
520 IF W(R+1,S)>0 THEN 550
530 X=INT(RND(1)*3+1)
540 ON X GOTO 1200,1240,1280
550 IF S<>V THEN 590
560 IF Z=1 THEN 620
570 Q=1
580 GOTO 600
590 IF W(R,S+1)>0 THEN 620
600 X=INT(RND(1)*3+1)
610 ON X GOTO 1200,1240,1370
620 X=INT(RND(1)*2+1)
630 ON X GOTO 1200,1240
640 IF R=H THEN 750
650 IF W(R+1,S)>0 THEN 750
660 IF S<>V THEN 700
670 IF Z=1 THEN 730
680 Q=1
690 GOTO 710
700 IF W(R,S+1)>0 THEN 730
710 X=INT(RND(1)*3+1)
720 ON X GOTO 1200,1280,1370
730 X=INT(RND(1)*2+1)
740 ON X GOTO 1200,1280
750 IF S<>V THEN 790
760 IF Z=1 THEN 820
770 Q=1
780 GOTO 800
790 IF W(R,S+1)>0 THEN 820
800 X=INT(RND(1)*2+1)
810 ON X GOTO 1200,1370
```

```
820 GOTO 1200
830 IF S=1 THEN 1040
840 IF W(R,S-1)>0 THEN 1040
850 IF R=H THEN 960
860 IF W(R+1,S)>0 THEN 960
870 IF S<>V THEN 910
880 IF Z=1 THEN 940
890 Q=1
900 GOTO 920
910 IF W(R,S+1)>0 THEN 940
920 X=INT(RND(1)*3+1)
930 ON X GOTO 1240,1280,1370
940 X=INT(RND(1)*2+1)
950 ON X GOTO 1240,1280
960 IF S<>V THEN 1000
970 IF Z=1 THEN 1030
980 Q=1
990 GOTO 1010
1000 IF W(R,S+1)>0 THEN 1030
1010 X=INT(RND(1)*2+1)
1020 ON X GOTO 1240,1370
1030 GOTO 1240
1040 IF R=H THEN 1140
1050 IF W(R+1,S)>0 THEN 1140
1060 IF S<>V THEN 1100
1070 IF Z=1 THEN 1130
1080 Q=1
1090 GOTO 1110
1100 IF W(R,S+1)>0 THEN 1130
1110 X=INT(RND(1)*2+1)
1120 ON X GOTO 1280,1370
1130 GOTO 1280
1140 IF S<>V THEN 1180
1150 IF Z=1 THEN 400
1160 Q=1
1170 GOTO 1190
1180 IF W(R,S+1)>0 THEN 400
1190 GOTO 1370
1200 W(R-1,S)=C:C=C+1:V(R-1,S)=2:R=R-1
1210 IF C=H*V+1 THEN 1510
1220 Q=0
1230 GOTO 470
1240 W(R,S-1)=C:C=C+1:V(R,S-1)=1:S=S-1
1250 IF C=H*V+1 THEN 1510
1260 Q=0
1270 GOTO 470
1280 W(R+1,S)=C:C=C+1
1290 IF V(R,S)=0 THEN 1320
1300 V(R,S)=3
1310 GOTO 1330
1320 V(R,S)=2
1330 R=R+1
1340 IF C=H*V+1 THEN 1510
1350 Q=0
1360 GOTO 830
1370 IF Q=1 THEN 1470
1380 W(R,S+1)=C
1390 C=C+1
1400 IF V(R,S)=0 THEN 1430
1410 V(R,S)=3
1420 GOTO 1440
1430 V(R,S)=1
1440 S=S+1
1450 IF C=H*V+1 THEN 1510
1460 GOTO 470
1470 Z=1
1480 IF V(R,S)=0 THEN 1500
1490 V(R,S)=3:Q=0:GOTO 400
1500 V(R,S)=1:Q=0:R=1:S=1:GOTO 460
1510 IF Z=1 THEN 1540
1520 R=INT(RND(1)*H)+1:S=V
1530 V(R,S)=V(R,S)+1
1540 GOSUB 2320
1550 PRINT "DO YOU WANT THE SOLUTION";:INPUT A$
1560 IF LEFT$(A$,1)<>"Y" THEN 2620
1570 PRINT "DO YOU WANT TO SEE EACH STEP";:INPUT A$:PRINT:PRINT
1580 FOR I=1 TO H:IF W(I,1)=1 THEN S=I:GOTO 1720
1590 NEXT I
1600 REM NOW WE CAN CLEAR W ARRAY AS ENTRY POINT IS FOUND.
1610 REM ELEMENTS IN V ARE EITHER 0,1,2 OR 3
1620 REM 0 IS CLOSED ON THE RIGHT AND AT THE BOTTOM
1630 REM 1 IS CLOSED ON THE RIGHT
1640 REM 2 IS CLOSED ON THE BOTTOM
1650 REM 3 IS OPEN ON THE RIGHT AND AT THE BOTTOM
1660 REM DIRECTIONS WILL BE CODED:
1670 REM  1 : UP
1680 REM  2 : DOWN
1690 SEM  4 : RIGHT
1700 REM  8 : LEFT
1710 REM SCAN V ARRAY FOR POSSIBLE MOVES IN ALL DIRECTIONS
1720 FOR I=1 TO H:FOR J=1 TO V
1730 W(I,J)=0
1740 REM TRY UP
1750 IF J=1 THEN 1780
1760 IF V(I,J-1)=1 OR V(I,J-1)=3 THEN W(I,J)=W(I,J)+1
1770 REM TRY DOWN
1780 IF J=V THEN 1810
1790 IF V(I,J)=1 OR V(I,J)=3 THEN W(I,J)=W(I,J)+2
1800 REM TRY RIGHT
1810 IF I=H THEN 1840
1820 IF V(I,J)=2 OR V(I,J)=3 THEN W(I,J)=W(I,J)+4
1830 REM TRY LEFT
1840 IF I=1 THEN 1860
1850 IF V(I-1,J)=2 OR V(I-1,J)=3 THEN W(I,J)=W(I,J)+8
1860 NEXT J
1870 NEXT I
1880 FOR I=1 TO H
1890 IF V(I,V)=1 OR V(I,V)=3 THEN W(I,V)=W(I,V)+2:E=I:GOTO 1920
1900 NEXT I
1910 REM HAVE TO GO DOWN FIRST
1920 Y=1:X=S
1930 V(X,Y)=V(X,Y)+4
1940 REM CHECK FOR POSSIBLE DIRECTIONS NOW...
1950 IF Y=V AND X=E THEN PRINT:GOSUB 2250:PRINT:PRINT:GOTO 2620
1960 GOSUB 2230
1970 REM CHECK POSSIBLE DIRECTIONS
1980 IF (W(X,Y) AND 2) <> 0 THEN 2030
1990 IF (W(X,Y) AND 4) <> 0 THEN 2080
2000 IF (W(X,Y) AND 8) <> 0 THEN 2130
2010 IF (W(X,Y) AND 1) <> 0 THEN 2180
2020 GOTO 1950
2030 IF (V(X,Y+1)>3) AND ((W(X,Y) AND 13)=0) THEN 2060
2040 IF V(X,Y+1)>3 THEN 1990
2050 Y=Y+1:V(X,Y)=V(X,Y)+4:GOTO 1950
2060 V(X,Y)=V(X,Y)-4:W(X,Y)=(W(X,Y) AND 13):Y=Y+1:W(X,Y)=(W(X,Y) AND 14)
2070 GOTO 1950
2080 IF (V(X+1,Y)>3) AND ((W(X,Y) AND 11)=0) THEN 2110
2090 IF V(X+1,Y)>3 THEN 2000
2100 X=X+1:V(X,Y)=V(X,Y)+4:GOTO 1950
2110 V(X,Y)=V(X,Y)-4:W(X,Y)=(W(X,Y) AND 11):X=X+1:W(X,Y)=(W(X,Y) AND 7)
2120 GOTO 1950
2130 IF (V(X-1,Y)>3) AND ((W(X,Y) AND 7)=0) THEN 2160
2140 IF V(X-1,Y)>3 THEN 2010
2150 X=X-1:V(X,Y)=V(X,Y)+4:GOTO 1950
2160 V(X,Y)=V(X,Y)-4:W(X,Y)=(W(X,Y) AND 7):X=X-1:W(X,Y)=(W(X,Y) AND 11)
2170 GOTO 1950
2180 IF (V(X,Y-1)>3) AND ((W(X,Y) AND 14)=0) THEN 2210
2190 IF V(X,Y-1)>3 THEN 1980
2200 Y=Y-1:V(X,Y)=V(X,Y)+4:GOTO 1950
2210 V(X,Y)=V(X,Y)-4:W(X,Y)=(W(X,Y) AND 14):Y=Y-1:W(X,Y)=(W(X,Y) AND 13)
2220 GOTO 1950
2230 IF LEFT$(A$,1)<>"Y" THEN RETURN
2240 PRINT
2250 FOR I=1 TO H
2260 IF I=S THEN 2290
2270 PRINT ":--";
2280 GOTO 2300
2290 PRINT ":**";
2300 NEXT I
2310 PRINT ":"
2320 FOR J=1 TO V
2330 PRINT "I";
2340 FOR I=1 TO H
2350 IF V(I,J)>3 THEN Z=V(I,J)-4:GOTO 2370
2360 Z=V(I,J)
2370 IF Z<2 THEN 2420
2380 IF Z<>V(I,J) AND V(I+1,J)>3 THEN PRINT "***";:GOTO 2440
2390 IF Z<>V(I,J) THEN PRINT "** ";:GOTO 2440
2400 PRINT "   ";
2410 GOTO 2440
2420 IF Z<>V(I,J) THEN PRINT "**I";:GOTO 2440
2430 PRINT "  I";
2440 NEXT I
2450 PRINT
2460 FOR I=1 TO H
2470 IF V(I,J)>3 THEN Z=V(I,J)-4:GOTO 2490
2480 Z=V(I,J)
2490 IF Z=0 THEN 2560
2500 IF Z=2 THEN 2560
2510 IF Z<>V(I,J) AND J=V THEN PRINT ":**";:GOTO 2570
2520 IF J=V THEN 2540
2530 IF Z<>V(I,J) AND V(I,J+1)>3 THEN PRINT ":**";:GOTO 2570
2540 PRINT ":  ";
2550 GOTO 2570
2560 PRINT ":--";
2570 NEXT I
2580 PRINT ":"
2590 NEXT J
2600 PRINT:PRINT
2610 RETURN
2620 PRINT:PRINT:PRINT "DO YOU WANT ANOTHER MAZE";:INPUT A$
2630 IF LEFT$(A$,1)="Y" THEN PRINT : GOTO 210
2640 PRINT:END
Ok
```

Millionaire

In this game, the computer takes you through your life from birth to death. Along the way, you're asked to make some petty and some other rather crucial decisions. Some of these decisions regard what kind of job you want, how much you bet in Las Vegas, whether you buy a valuable coin, whether you elect to take a vacation or a second job, stock purchases—buying and selling, automobile accidents, tornadoes, and the like.

At the end of your life (it goes by in a flash!) the computer tallies up your gains and your losses and tells you where you stand relative to becoming a millionaire. In ten plays of the game, the most we ever got was $379,000, somewhat short of being a millionaire, but probably, all things considered, more realistic.

Millionaire was conceived and written by Craig Gunnett, a dreamer to the very end.

```
RUN
                         MILLIONAIRE
                      CREATIVE COMPUTING
                    MORRISTOWN, NEW JERSEY


THIS IS THE GAME OF 'MILLIONAIRE'.  ALL YOU MUST DO IS
TYPE IN YOUR NAME AND ANSWER SOME QUESTIONS.  THE
DECISIONS YOU MAKE WILL DETERMINE HOW MUCH MONEY YOU
MAKE.  AT THE TIME OF YOUR DEATH, YOUR LIFE WILL BE
RATED BY THE AMOUNT OF MONEY YOU MADE THROUGHOUT
YOUR LIFE.  IF YOU HAVE MADE $1,000,000 , YOU WILL BE
A MILLIONAIRE AND WIN THE GAME.  NAME PLEASE? STEVE

O.K., STEVE, THIS IS YOUR NEW LIFE!
IN A SMALL TOWN, ON OCT 28 , 1980, STEVE IS BORN.
YOUR PARENTS ARE VERY POOR.  ON JUN 12 ,  1998 , YOU
LEAVE HOME WITH $ 410
YOU GOT A NEW JOB AS A FOOTBALL PLAYER.  YOU EARN $ 118031  A YEAR.
YOU ADJUST YOUR EXPENSES TO $ 110907  A YEAR.

SEP 27 , 2001
THE DOCTOR SAYS YOU NEED A VACATION.  DO YOU GO? YES

GOOD, THE VACATION COSTS $ 2671
YOU NOW HAVE $-2261

MAR 7 , 2011
THE INTEREST ON YOUR LOAN IS $ 1582 .  YOU HAVE $-3843
YOU GO TO LAS VEGAS TO GAMBLE.  HOW MUCH DO YOU BET? 100

YOU WON $ 138
YOU NOW HAVE $-3705
YOUR EARNINGS AND EXPENSES LEAVE YOU WITH $ 67535

AUG 6 , 2016
NEWS FLASH!!! A TORNADO HAS JUST HIT THE HOME OF STEVE
DAMAGES HAVE BEEN ESTIMATED AT $ 23999
YOU NOW HAVE $ 43536
YOUR EARNINGS AND EXPENSES LEAVE YOU WITH $ 79156

SEP 22 , 2025
YOUR GRANDFATHER GROVERS JUST DIED. (OH!)  HE LEFT
YOU $ 60773 , BUT FUNERAL EXPENSES ARE $ 12587
YOU NOW HAVE $ 127342
YOUR EARNINGS AND EXPENSES LEAVE YOU WITH $ 191458

SEP 20 , 2033
YOU JUST HAD A CAR ACCIDENT!  MEDICAL COSTS
ARE $ 1975 . REPAIRS COST $ 1584
YOU NOW HAVE $ 187899
YOUR EARNINGS AND EXPENSES LEAVE YOU WITH $ 244891

MAY 20 , 2038
YOUR HOME HAS BEEN ROBBED OF GOODS WORTH $ 13878
YOU NOW HAVE $ 231013
YOUR EARNINGS AND EXPENSES LEAVE YOU WITH $ 266633

MAY 1 , 2043
OH! YOU JUST GOT CANCER.  MEDICAL BILLS ARE $ 4638
YOU ARE DEAD (COULD'NT TELL, COULD YOU?) AT THE
AGE OF  63 .
YOU HAD $ 261995
NOT BAD, STEVE
THANKS FOR PLAYING 'MILLIONAIRE', STEVE!!!!
Ok
```

```
1 PRINT TAB(23);"MILLIONAIRE"
2 PRINT TAB(20);"CREATIVE COMPUTING"
3 PRINT TAB(18);"MORRISTOWN, NEW JERSEY"
4 PRINT:PRINT:PRINT
10 REM    MILLIONAIRE BY CRAIG GUNNETT
20 PRINT "THIS IS THE GAME OF 'MILLIONAIRE'.  ALL YOU MUST DO IS"
30 PRINT "TYPE IN YOUR NAME AND ANSWER SOME QUESTIONS.  THE"
40 PRINT "DECISIONS YOU MAKE WILL DETERMINE HOW MUCH MONEY YOU"
50 PRINT "MAKE.  AT THE TIME OF YOUR DEATH, YOUR LIFE WILL BE"
60 PRINT "RATED BY THE AMOUNT OF MONEY YOU MADE THROUGHOUT"
70 PRINT "YOUR LIFE.  IF YOU HAVE MADE $1,000,000 , YOU WILL BE"
80 PRINT "A MILLIONAIRE AND WIN THE GAME.  NAME PLEASE";
100 LET O=-1
110 DIM A$(20),Z$(1),M$(36),S(9),Q(16)
120 FOR I=1 TO 4
130   LET S(I)=150
140 NEXT I
150 INPUT A$
160 PRINT
170 PRINT "O.K., ";A$;", THIS IS YOUR NEW LIFE!"
180 LET M$="JANFEBMARAPRMAYJUNJULAUGSEPOCTNOVDEC"
190 IF RND(1)>.5 GOTO  220
200 PRINT "ON A BIG FARM";
210 GOTO 230
220 PRINT "IN A SMALL TOWN";
230 LET T=INT(RND(1)*12)+1
240 PRINT ", ON ";MID$(M$,3*T-2,3);INT(RND(1)*28)+1;", 1980,";
250 PRINT " ";A$;" IS BORN."
260 PRINT "YOUR PARENTS ARE VERY ";
270 IF RND(1)>.5 GOTO  310
280 PRINT "RICH.  ";
290 LET M=INT(RND(1)*5000)+10000
300 GOTO 330
310 PRINT "POOR.  ";
320 LET M=INT((RND(1)+RND(1))/2*1000)
330 LET T=INT(RND(1)*12)+1
```

```
340 LET Y=1996+INT(RND(1)*10)
350 PRINT "ON ";MID$(M$,T*3-2,3);T*2;", ";Y;", YOU"
360 PRINT "LEAVE HOME WITH $";M
370 LET Y=Y+INT(RND(1)*3)+1
380 GOSUB  680
390 FOR J=1 TO 13
400 IF (J/3)-INT(J/3)+E=0 THEN GOSUB 680
410   LET D=INT(28*RND(1))+1
420   LET M1=(INT(12*RND(1))+1)*3
430   PRINT
440 PRINT MID$(M$,M1-2,3);D;",";Y
450   IF Y-1980<70 GOTO  500
460   IF RND(1)>.5 GOTO  500
470   PRINT "YOU ARE DEAD (COULD'NT TELL, COULD YOU?) AT THE"
480   PRINT "AGE OF ";Y-1980;"."
490   GOTO 2370
500   IF M>=0 GOTO 540
510   LET I=INT(.07*Y9*(-M))
520   LET M=M-I
530   PRINT "THE INTEREST ON YOUR LOAN IS $";I;".  YOU HAVE $";M
540   LET Q=INT(13*RND(1))+1
550   IF Q(Q)=1 GOTO 540
560   LET Q(Q)=1
570   ON Q GOTO  890, 1010, 1100, 1220, 1280, 1430, 1530
580   ON (Q-7) GOTO  1850, 1930, 2060, 2120, 2240, 2280
590   PRINT "YOU NOW HAVE $";M
600   IF O=-2 GOTO 1530
610   IF J=1 GOTO  640
620   LET M=M+(E-C)*Y9
630   PRINT "YOUR EARNINGS AND EXPENSES LEAVE YOU WITH $";M
640   LET Y9=INT(RND(1)*6)+5
650   LET Y=Y+Y9
660 NEXT J
670 GOTO 470
680 REM      JOB SUB
690 PRINT "YOU GOT A NEW JOB AS A ";
```

```
700 ON INT(RND(1)*5)+1 GOTO  740, 770, 800, 830
710 PRINT "TEACHER";
720 LET E=INT(RND(1)*4000)+17000
730 GOTO 850
740 PRINT "LAWYER";
750 LET E=INT(RND(1)*40000)+80000
760 GOTO 850
770 PRINT "COMPUTER PROGRAMMER";
780 LET E=INT(RND(1)*5000)+20000
790 GOTO 850
800 PRINT "BUS DRIVER";
810 LET E=INT(RND(1)*2000)+16000
820 GOTO 850
830 PRINT "FOOTBALL PLAYER";
840 LET E=INT(RND(1)*100000)+100000
850 LET C=E-10000+INT((RND(1)+RND(1))*5000)
860 PRINT ".  YOU EARN $";E;" A YEAR."
870 PRINT "YOU ADJUST YOUR EXPENSES TO $";C;" A YEAR."
880 RETURN
890 PRINT "YOU GO TO LAS VEGAS TO GAMBLE.  HOW MUCH DO YOU BET";
900 INPUT S
910 PRINT
920 IF S<=0 GOTO 1000
930 IF RND(1)>.7 GOTO  970
940 LET S2=-INT(RND(1)*S)
950 PRINT "HA! HA! YOU LOST $";-S2
960 GOTO 990
970 LET S2=INT((RND(1)+RND(1))*S)
980 PRINT "YOU WON $";S2
990 LET M=M+S2
1000 GOTO 590
1010 PRINT "YOU ARE OFFERED A COIN SUPPOSEDLY WORTH $100,000."
1020 PRINT "DO YOU BUY IT";
1030 INPUT Z$
1040 PRINT
1050 LET V7=INT(RND(1)*200000)+1
1060 IF Z$<>"Y" GOTO  1080
1070 LET M=M-100000+V7
1080 PRINT "THE VALUE OF THE COIN IS $";V7
1090 GOTO 590
1100 PRINT "YOU ARE SERIOUSLY SICK.  (COULDN'T TELL, COULD YOU?)"
1110 PRINT "YOU HAVE ";
1120 ON (INT(RND(1)*3)+1) GOTO  1150, 1170
1130 PRINT "THE ASIO-DISPEPSIA REGIONALY HYPNOTIC FLU!(OH!)."
1140 GOTO 1180
1150 PRINT "COMPUTER ITIS."
1160 GOTO 1180
1170 PRINT "INFECTIOUS FATALY REOCCURING CHRONIC BAD BREATH."
1180 LET U=INT(RND(1)*1000)+500
1190 LET M=M-U
1200 PRINT "HEALTH EXPENSES COST YOU $";U
1210 GOTO 590
1220 LET F=INT(RND(1)*100000)
1230 LET C8=INT(F/2)-INT(RND(1)*(F/2))
1240 PRINT "YOUR GRANDFATHER GROVERS JUST DIED. (OH!)  HE LEFT"
1250 PRINT "YOU $";F;", BUT FUNERAL EXPENSES ARE $";C8
1260 LET M=M-C8+F
1270 GOTO 590
1280 IF E=0 GOTO  890
1290 PRINT "NEWS FROM YOUR BOSS:"
1300 ON (INT(RND(1)*3)+1) GOTO  1350, 1390
1310 LET L=INT(RND(1)*3000)+1
1320 LET E=E-L
1330 PRINT "YOU GOT A $";L;" DECREASE IN PAY.  YOU NOW EARN$";E
1340 GOTO 590
1350 PRINT "YOU'RE FIRED! (HA!)"
1360 LET E=0
1370 LET C=INT(C/4)
1380 GOTO 590
1390 LET R6=INT(RND(1)*5000)+1
1400 LET E=E+R6
1410 PRINT "YOU GOT A RAISE OF $";R6;".  YOU NOW EARN $";E
1420 GOTO 590
1430 PRINT "THE DOCTOR SAYS YOU NEED A VACATION.  DO YOU GO";
1440 INPUT Z$
1450 PRINT
1460 LET V=INT(RND(1)*2000)+1000
1470 IF Z$="N" GOTO 1500
1480 PRINT "GOOD, THE VACATION COSTS $";V
1490 GOTO 1510
1500 PRINT "YOU JUST HAD A NERVOUS BREAKDOWN.  MEDICAL COSTS - $";V
1510 LET M=M-V
1520 GOTO 590
1530 FOR I=1 TO 4
1540   LET S(I)=INT((INT(RND(1)*100)+100+2*S(I))/3)
1550 NEXT I
1560 PRINT "#            STOCK NAME          PRICE   SHARES OWNED"
1570 PRINT "1 IBM (INCREDIBLY BAD MACHINES) ";S(1);"    ";S(5)
1580 PRINT "2 USS (USELESS & STINKY STEEL)  ";S(2);"    ";S(6)
1590 PRINT "3 NCR (NO CASH RETURN)          ";S(3);"    ";S(7)
1600 PRINT "4 TWA (TOTAL WRECK AIRLINES)    ";S(4);"    ";S(8)
1610 IF S(9)=1 GOTO 2410
1620 PRINT "DO YOU BUY, SELL ($100 FEE), OR NOT (B,S, OR N)";
1630 INPUT Z$
1640 PRINT
1650 IF Z$="S" GOTO 1740
1660 IF Z$="N" GOTO 1810
1670 PRINT "STOCK # AND QUANTITY";
1680 INPUT S3,S(0)
1690 PRINT
1700 LET S(4+S3)=S(4+S3)+S(0)
1710 LET O=-2
1720 LET M=M-S(S3)*S(0)-100
1730 GOTO 1620
1740 PRINT "STOCK # AND QUANTITY";
1750 INPUT S2,S5
1760 IF RND(1)<.5 GOTO  1880
1770 IF S5>S(4+S2) GOTO 1740
1780 LET S(4+S2)=S(4+S2)-S5
1790 LET M=M+S(S2)*S5-100
1800 GOTO 1620
1810 LET S1=S(5)+S(6)+S(7)+S(8)
1820 IF S1>0 GOTO 610
1830 LET O=-1
1840 GOTO 610
1850 PRINT "NEWS FLASH!!! ";
1860 PRINT "A TORNADO HAS JUST HIT THE HOME OF ";A$
1870 GOTO 1890
1880 PRINT "AN AIRPLANE HAS JUST CRASHED INTO THE HOME OF ";A$
1890 LET D8=INT(RND(1)*50000)+1
1900 LET M=M-D8
1910 PRINT "DAMAGES HAVE BEEN ESTIMATED AT $";D8
1920 GOTO 590
1930 PRINT "OH! YOU JUST GOT ";
1940 IF Y-1980<55 GOTO  2000
1950 IF RND(1)>.4 GOTO  1980
1960 PRINT "CANCER";
1970 GOTO 2010
1980 PRINT "A HEART ATTACK";
1990 GOTO 2010
2000 PRINT "LEUKEMIA";
2010 LET M2=INT(RND(1)*5000)+1000
2020 LET M=M-M2
2030 PRINT ".  MEDICAL BILLS ARE $";M2
2040 IF RND(1)<.5 GOTO  470
2050 GOTO 590
2060 PRINT "YOU JUST HAD A CAR ACCIDENT!  MEDICAL COSTS"
2070 LET M3=INT(RND(1)*3000)+1000
2080 LET Q7=INT(RND(1)*5000)+100
2090 PRINT "ARE $";M3;". REPAIRS COST $";Q7
2100 LET M=M-M3-Q7
2110 GOTO 590
2120 IF E=0 GOTO  1010
2130 LET E2=10000+INT(RND(1)*5000)
2140 PRINT "YOU ARE OFFERED ANOTHER JOB FOR $";E2;" A YEAR."
2150 PRINT "WOULD YOU LIKE TO MOONLIGHT";
2160 INPUT Z$
2170 PRINT
2180 IF Z$="N" GOTO 590
2190 ON INT(RND(1)*3) GOTO  1350, 2220
2200 LET E=E+E2
2210 GOTO 590
2220 PRINT "FROM OVERWORK YOU GET ";
2230 GOTO 1980
2240 LET R2=INT(RND(1)*10000)+5000
2250 LET M=M-R2
2260 PRINT "YOUR HOME HAS BEEN ROBBED OF GOODS WORTH $";R2
2270 GOTO 590
2280 IF O=-1 GOTO 1430
2290 IF RND(1)>.7 GOTO  1430
2300 LET B4=INT(RND(1)*4)
2310 PRINT "STOCK MARKET CRASH!!!  EACH OF YOUR";S1;" SHARES OF"
2320 PRINT "STOCK IS WORTH $";B4;".  YOU MUST SELL ALL OF THEM"
2330 PRINT "FOR A TOTAL OF $";S1*B4
2340 LET M=M+S1*B4
2350 LET O=-1
2360 GOTO 590
2370 PRINT "YOU HAD $";M
2380 IF O=-1 GOTO 2430
2390 LET S(9)=1
2400 GOTO 1530
2410 LET M=M+S(1)*S(5)+S(2)*S(6)+S(3)*S(7)+S(4)*S(8)
2420 PRINT "WITH STOCK VALUE YOU HAVE $";M
2430 IF M<0 GOTO  2480
2440 IF M<500000 GOTO 2510
2450 IF M<1E+06 GOTO 2530
2460 PRINT A$;" WON!!  YOU ARE A MILLIONAIRE!!"
2470 GOTO 2540
2480 PRINT "YOU LOUSY #$%&'*!!! NOW YOUR POOR FAMILY HAS TO PAY"
2490 PRINT "OFF YOUR DEBTS.......................... "
2500 GOTO 2540
2510 PRINT "NOT BAD, ";A$
2520 GOTO 2540
2530 PRINT "CLOSE, ";A$;".  MAYBE NEXT LIFE."
2540 PRINT "THANKS FOR PLAYING 'MILLIONAIRE', ";A$;"!!!!"
2550 END
```

Minotaur

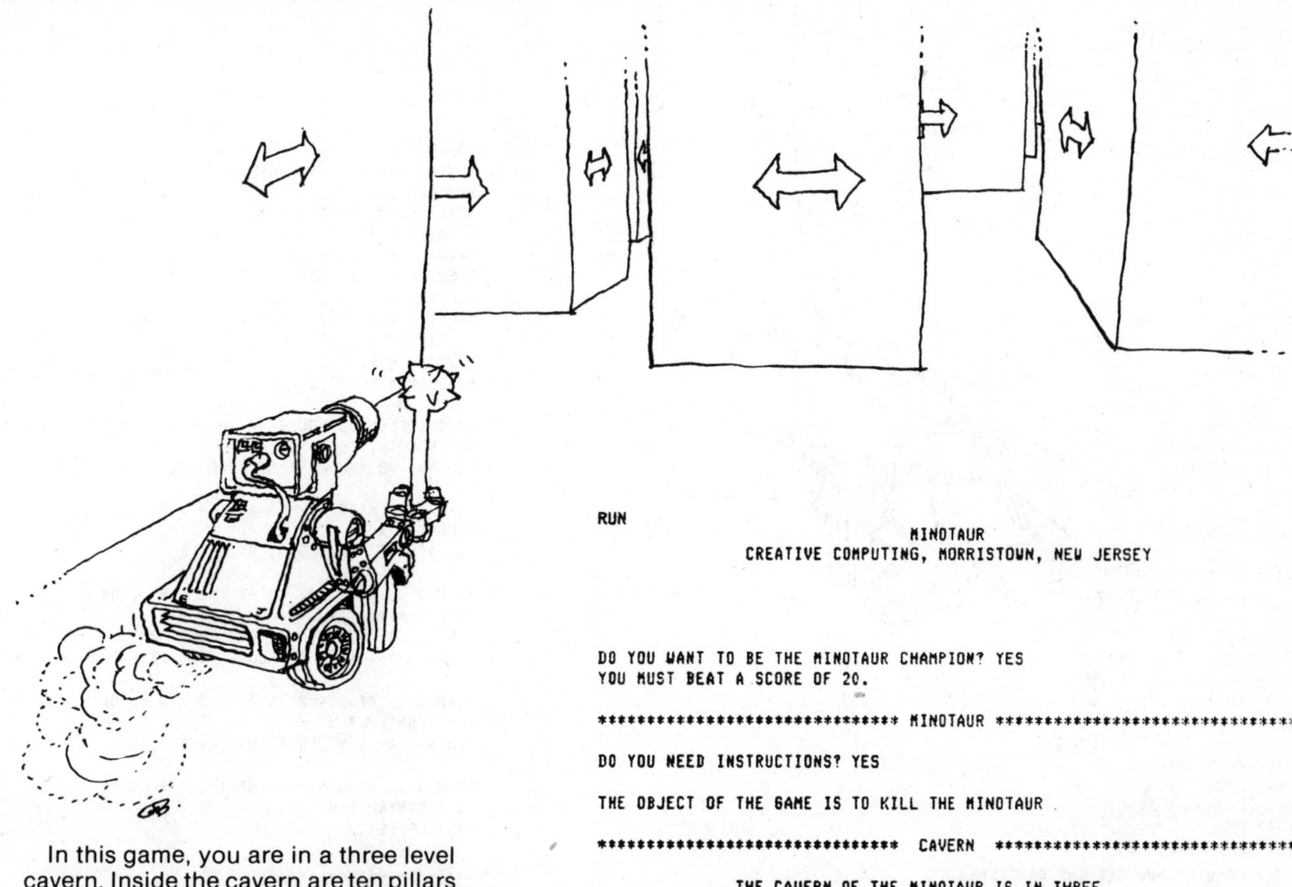

In this game, you are in a three level cavern. Inside the cavern are ten pillars which stretch through all three levels; they're electrified so that if you touch them you are immediately vaporized. Furthermore, there are trap doors which appear randomly and drop you down one level. The top level is three, the second level down is two, the first or lowest level is one. If a trap door appears in level one you are dropped into a bottomless pit and that ends the game. The minotaur itself also poses a hazard. If you wound him with your spear, he will charge you. Also, he randomly charges for no reason at all. However, he only charges in a straight line. Hint: keep at a slight diagonal from the minotaur until you are ready to throw your spear at him and you have a better chance of avoiding his charges. If you ask for a map, the axes are drawn in with X's. This does not indicate a barrier or fence; you are free to move across the X and Y coordinate planes. However, you are advised not to move out of any of the four edges as this represents yet a different form of bottomless pit and also ends the game. There are many, many additional hazards which are not shown in the sample run. Try it, and be surprised!

This program was conceived and written by Pete Klausler.

```
RUN
                              MINOTAUR
               CREATIVE COMPUTING, MORRISTOWN, NEW JERSEY



DO YOU WANT TO BE THE MINOTAUR CHAMPION? YES
YOU MUST BEAT A SCORE OF 20.

******************************** MINOTAUR ********************************

DO YOU NEED INSTRUCTIONS? YES

THE OBJECT OF THE GAME IS TO KILL THE MINOTAUR

******************************** CAVERN *******************************

     THE CAVERN OF THE MINOTAUR IS IN THREE
    LEVELS.  EACH LEVEL IS A COORDINATE PLANE
    OUTSIDE OF THE LEVELS THERE IS NOTHING BUT
    VACUUM.  THE PLANES STRETCH OUT 10 ON EACH AXIS
    FROM THE ORIGIN.

******************************** HAZARDS ******************************

                              BARRIERS

     INSIDE THE CAVERN ARE 10 ELECTRIFIED
    PILLARS STRETCHING THROUGH THE THREE
    LEVELS. THEY WILL DESTROY ANYTHING THAT
    TOUCHES THEM!!

                              TRAPDOORS

     TRAPDOORS WILL APPEAR OUT OF NOWHERE
    AND DROP YOU DOWN ONE LEVEL. IF YOU WERE
    ON LEVEL ONE, YOU LOSE!!


                         CHARGING MINOTAUR

     THE MINOTAUR WILL CHARGE IF YOU
    WOUND HIM WITH YOUR SPEAR.  ALSO, HE
    MAY CHARGE FOR NO REASON AT ALL!!!!


                   HERE ARE YOUR CONTROL FUNCTIONS
                        1) MOVING EAST
                        2) MOVING WEST
                        3) MOVING NORTH
                        4) MOVING SOUTH
                        5) MOVING UP A LEVEL
                        6) MOVING DOWN A LEVEL
                        7) THROWING YOUR SPEAR
                        8) GETTING A MAP


****************************** HAVE FUN ******************************
```

```
I WILL NOW SET THE BARRIERS.
BARRIER # 1 :(-7 , 5 ).
BARRIER # 2 :( 1 ,-3 ).
BARRIER # 3 :( 4 ,-1 ).
BARRIER # 4 :(-7 , 2 ).
BARRIER # 5 :( 0 , 3 ).
BARRIER # 6 :(-4 ,-6 ).
BARRIER # 7 :( 3 , 9 ).
BARRIER # 8 :(-7 ,-6 ).
BARRIER # 9 :( 1 ,-7 ).
BARRIER # 10 :(-1 , 4 ).

WHICH LEVEL DO YOU WANT TO START ON? 2
WHICH POINT? 0,0
HOW FAR DO YOU WANT TO MOVE PER A TURN? 4

TURN 1 .  MINOTAUR IS AT ( 10 , 10 ), ON L.  1 .
YOUR CONTROL? 6
YOU ARE AT ( 0 , 0 ), ON LEVEL  1 .

THE MINOTAUR IS CHARGING.
LEVEL 1
( 9 , 10 )
( 8 , 10 )
( 7 , 10 )
( 6 , 10 )
( 5 , 10 )
( 4 , 10 )
( 3 , 10 )
( 2 , 10 )
( 1 , 10 )
( 0 , 10 )
( 0 , 9 )
( 0 , 8 )
( 0 , 7 )
( 0 , 6 )
( 0 , 5 )
( 0 , 4 )
BZZZZZZZZZZZZZZZZZZZZZZOWNT MINOTAUR JUST FRIED HIMSELF
YOU WIN,  YOU LUCKY SCAB
YOU ARE NOW A QUALIFIED CHAMPION!
```

```
WOULD YOU LIKE TO PLAY AGAIN? YES
I WILL NOW SET THE BARRIERS.
BARRIER # 1 :(-3 , 10 ).
BARRIER # 2 :(-1 , 9 ).
BARRIER # 3 :( 1 , 4 ).
BARRIER # 4 :( 1 , 6 ).
BARRIER # 5 :( 10 ,-1 ).
BARRIER # 6 :(-2 ,-10 ).
BARRIER # 7 :( 3 , 3 ).
BARRIER # 8 :(-7 , 9 ).
BARRIER # 9 :( 6 , 7 ).
BARRIER # 10 :( 5 ,-8 ).

WHICH LEVEL DO YOU WANT TO START ON? 2
WHICH POINT? 0,0
HOW FAR DO YOU WANT TO MOVE PER A TURN? 5

TURN 1 .  MINOTAUR IS AT (-4 , 8 ), ON L.  3 .
YOUR CONTROL? 5
YOU ARE AT ( 0 , 0 ), ON LEVEL  3 .

TURN 2 .  MINOTAUR IS AT (-3 , 8 ), ON L.  3 .
YOUR CONTROL? 1
YOU ARE AT ( 5 , 0 ), ON LEVEL  3 .
YAAAAAAAAAAAAAAH TRAPDOOR, YOU FELL DOWN ONE LEVEL

TURN 3 .  MINOTAUR IS AT (-2 , 8 ), ON L.  3 .
YOUR CONTROL? 5
YOU ARE AT ( 5 , 0 ), ON LEVEL  3 .

TURN 4 .  MINOTAUR IS AT (-2 , 8 ), ON L.  2 .
YOUR CONTROL? 8
WHAT LEVEL? 2
.......B..X..........
...B.....BX..........
........M.X..........
..........X.....B....
..........XB.........
..........X..........
..........XB.........
..........X..B.......
..........X..........
..........X..........
XXXXXXXXXXOXXXXXXXXXX
..........X.........B
..........X..........
..........X..........
..........X..........
..........X..........
..........X..........
..........X..........
..........X....B.....
..........X..........
........B.X..........

LEVEL: 2
                                KEY
                                Y=YOU
                                M=MINOTAUR
                                S=SPEAR
                                B=BARRIER
                                O=ORIGIN
                                X=AXIS


TURN 5 .  MINOTAUR IS AT (-2 , 8 ), ON L.  2 .
YOUR CONTROL? 6
YOU ARE AT ( 5 , 0 ), ON LEVEL  2 .

THE MINOTAUR IS CHARGING.
BZZZZZZZZZZZZZZZZZZZZZZOWNT MINOTAUR JUST FRIED HIMSELF
YOU WIN,  YOU LUCKY SCAB
YOU ARE NOW A QUALIFIED CHAMPION!
WOULD YOU LIKE TO PLAY AGAIN? NO
Ok
```

```
LIST
100 PRINT TAB(32)"MINOTAUR"
120 PRINT TAB(15)"CREATIVE COMPUTING, MORRISTOWN, NEW JERSEY"
130 PRINT:PRINT:PRINT
160 L1=INT(RND(1)*3)+1
170 X1=INT(RND(1)*(-21))+11
180 Y1=INT(RND(1)*(-21))+11
190 PRINT
195 DIM B(15),C(15)
200 GOSUB 1350
210 REM INSTRUCTIONS
220 GOSUB 1660
230 REM BARRIERS
240 GOSUB 2330
250 REM PLACE PLAYER
260 GOSUB 2420
270 REM START GAME
280 REM SPEAR
290 IF X2=S1 AND Y2=S2 AND L2=S3 AND T>1 THEN 3690
300 REM  IS HE EATEN?
310 IF X1=X2 AND Y2=1 AND L1=L2 THEN 3670
320 REM CHARGING
330 IF RND(1)<.1 THEN 2850
340 REM TURN #
350 T=T+1
360 PRINT"TURN";T;".  MINOTAUR IS AT (";X1;",";Y1;"), ON L. ";L1;"."
370 PRINT "YOUR CONTROL";
380 INPUT Z
390 ON Z GOTO 400,430,450,480,500,530,550,3270
400 X2=X2+F
410 IF ABS(X2)>10 THEN 1160
420 GOTO 1180
430 X2=X2-F
440 GOTO 410
450 Y2=Y2+F
460 IF ABS(Y2)>10 THEN 1160
470 GOTO 420
480 Y2=Y2-F
490 GOTO 460
500 L2=L2+1
510 IF L2>3 OR L2<1 THEN 1330
520 GOTO 420
530 L2=L2-1
540 GOTO 510
550 REM  SPEAR-THROWING
560 IF L1<>L2 THEN 1080
570 IF X1<>X2 AND Y1<>Y2 THEN 1100
580 IF X1<>X2 AND ABS(Y1-Y2)>10 THEN 1120
590 IF ABS(X1-X2)>10 THEN 1120
600 IF S9=1 THEN 3720
610 PRINT"IN WHICH DIRECTION WOULD YOU LIKE TO THROW(USE 1,2,3,4)"
620 INPUT H1
630 PRINT"HOW FAR";
640 INPUT H2
650 S5=X2
660 S6=Y2
670 FOR H3=1 TO H2
680 ON H1 GOTO 690,720,740,770
690 S5=S5+1
700 IF ABS(S5)>10 THEN 860
710 GOTO 790
720 S5=S5-1
730 GOTO 700
740 S6=S6-1
750 IF ABS(S6)>10 THEN 860
760 GOTO 790
770 S6=S6-1
780 GOTO 750
790 PRINT"SPEAR IS AT (";S5;",";S6")."
800 REM TEST FOR BARRIERS
810 FOR A=1 TO 10
820 IF S5=B(A) AND S6=C(A) THEN 850
830 NEXT A
840 GOTO 870
850 PRINT "SMASH SPEAR SPLITERED AGAINST BARRIER #";A;""
860 GOTO 1140
870 NEXT H3
880 IF S5<>X1 OR S6<>Y1 THEN 1010
890 X=INT(RND(1)*3)+1
900 ON X GOTO 910,1010,1070
910 PRINT"YOU KILLED THE MINOTAUR IN";T;"TURNS."
920 GOTO 1450
930 PRINT"WOULD YOU LIKE TO PLAY AGAIN";
940 INPUT X$
950 IF X$<>"YES" THEN 3760
960 T=0
970 L1=INT(RND(1)*3)+1
980 X1=INT(RND(1)*(-21))+11
990 Y1=INT(RND(1)*(-21))+11
1000 GOTO 230
1010 PRINT"YOU MISSED.  SPEAR IS AT (";S5;",";S6;"). YOU MUST GET IT."
1020 S1=S5
1030 S2=S6
1040 S3=L2
1050 S9=1
1060 GOTO 280
1070 GOSUB 2840
1080 PRINT"YOU ARE NOT ON THE SAME LEVEL. YOU CANNOT THROW."
1090 GOTO 420
1100 PRINT"YOU ARE NOT ON THE SAME XOR Y LINE.  YOU CANNOT THROW."
1110 GOTO 420
1120 PRINT"YOU ARE NOT WITHIN 10. YOU CANNOT THROW."
1130 GOTO 420
1140 PRINT"YOU ARE NOW WEAPONLESS. YOU LOSE, SUCKER!"
1150 GOTO 930
1160 PRINT"YAAAAAAAAAAAAAAAAH YOU FELL OFF THE EDGE"
1170 GOTO 1150
1180 PRINT"YOU ARE AT (";X2;",";Y2;"), ON LEVEL ";L2;"."
1190 REM TEST FOR BARRIERS
1200 FOR A=1 TO 10
1210 IF X2=B(A) AND Y2=C(A) THEN 1240
1220 NEXT A
1230 GOTO 1260
1240 PRINT"YOU HAVE JUST FRIED YOURSELF ON AN ELECTRIFIED BARRIER."
1250 GOTO 1150
1260 REM TRAPDOORS
1270 X=INT(RND(1)*10)+1
1280 IF X=5 THEN 1300
1290 GOTO 2510
1300 PRINT"YAAAAAAAAAAAAAAH TRAPDOOR, YOU FELL DOWN ONE LEVEL"
1310 L2=L2-1
1320 IF L2>0 THEN 1290
1330 PRINT"YOU FELL OUT OF THE CAVERN. YOU LOSE."
1340 GOTO 1150
1350 PRINT"DO YOU WANT TO BE THE MINOTAUR CHAMPION";
1360 INPUT X9$
1370 IF X9$<>"YES" THEN 1440
1380 C2=20
1390 PRINT"YOU MUST BEAT A SCORE OF 20."
1391 DIM C3$(72)
1419 DIM C4$(72)
1440 RETURN
1450 IF X9$<>"YES" THEN 930
1460 C3=(1/T)*100
1470 IF C3<20 THEN 1630
1480 PRINT"YOU ARE NOW A QUALIFIED CHAMPION!"
1620 GOTO 930
1630 PRINT"SORRY ,YOU DID NOT BEAT THE CHAMPION."
1640 PRINT"DO YOU WANT TO PLAY AGAIN";
1650 GOTO 940
1660 REM INSTRUCTIONS
1670 PRINT
1672 FORV7=1 TO 31
1673 PRINT"*";
1675 NEXT V7
1680 PRINT TAB(32)"MINOTAUR";
1681 FOR V8=1 TO 31
1682 PRINT TAB(41)"*";
1683 NEXT V8
1720 PRINT
1730 PRINT
1740 PRINT"DO YOU NEED INSTRUCTIONS";
1760 INPUT X$
1770 IF X$<>"YES" THEN 2320
1780 PRINT
1800 PRINT "THE OBJECT OF THE GAME IS TO KILL THE MINOTAUR"
1820 PRINT
1825 FOR V9=1TO 31
1826 PRINT"*";
1827 NEXT V9
1830 PRINTTAB(33)"CAVERN";
1832 FOR V10=1 TO 31
1833 PRINT TAB(41)"*";
1835 NEXT V10
1836 PRINT
1837 PRINT
1840 PRINT TAB(12)"  THE CAVERN OF THE MINOTAUR IS IN THREE"
1850 PRINT TAB(12)"LEVELS.  EACH LEVEL IS A COORDINATE PLANE ."
1860 PRINT TAB(12)"OUTSIDE OF THE LEVELS THERE IS NOTHING BUT "
1870 PRINT TAB(12)"VACUUM.  THE PLANES STRETCH OUT 10 ON EACH AXIS"
1880 PRINT TAB(12)"FROM THE ORIGIN."
1890 PRINT
1910 FOR V11=1 TO 31
1920 PRINT"*";
1930 NEXT V11
1940 PRINT TAB(32)"HAZARDS";
1945 FOR V12=1 TO 31
1947 PRINT TAB(41)"*";
1948 NEXT V12
1950 PRINT
1955 PRINT
1960 PRINT TAB(32)"BARRIERS"
```

```
1965 PRINT
1970 PRINT TAB(12)"  INSIDE THE CAVERN ARE 10 ELECTRIFIED"
1980 PRINT TAB(12)"PILLARS STRETCHING THROUGH THE THREE"
1990 PRINT TAB(12)"LEVELS. THEY WILL DESTROY ANYTHING THAT"
2000 PRINT TAB(12)"TOUCHES THEM!!"
2010 PRINT
2020 PRINT TAB(32)"TRAPDOORS"
2025 PRINT
2030 PRINT TAB(12)"  TRAPDOORS WILL APPEAR OUT OF NOWHERE"
2040 PRINT TAB(12)"AND DROP YOU DOWN ONE LEVEL. IF YOU WERE"
2050 PRINT TAB(12)"ON LEVEL ONE, YOU LOSE!!"
2060 PRINT:PRINT
2070 PRINT TAB(27)"CHARGING  MINOTAUR"
2071 PRINT
2080 PRINT TAB(12)"  THE MINOTAUR WILL CHARGE IF YOU"
2090 PRINT TAB(12)"WOUND HIM WITH YOUR SPEAR.  ALSO, HE"
2100 PRINT TAB(12)"MAY CHARGE FOR NO REASON AT ALL!!!!"
2110 PRINT
2120 PRINT
2130 PRINTTAB(21)" HERE ARE YOUR CONTROL FUNCTIONS"
2140 PRINT TAB(27)"1) MOVING EAST"
2150 PRINT TAB(27)"2) MOVING WEST"
2160 PRINT TAB(27)"3) MOVING NORTH"
2170 PRINT TAB(27)"4) MOVING SOUTH"
2180 PRINT TAB(27)"5) MOVING UP A LEVEL"
2190 PRINT TAB(27)"6) MOVING DOWN A LEVEL"
2200 PRINT TAB(27)"7) THROWING YOUR SPEAR"
2210 PRINT TAB(27)"8) GETTING A MAP"
2220 PRINT
2230 PRINT
2240 FOR V13=1 TO 29
2250 PRINT"*";
2260 NEXT V13
2270 PRINTTAB(31)"HAVE FUN";
2280 FOR V14=1 TO 30
2290 PRINT TAB(41)"*";
2300 NEXT V14
2310 PRINT
2320 RETURN
2330 REM BARRIERS
2340 PRINT "I WILL NOW SET THE BARRIERS."
2350 FOR A=1 TO 10
2360 B(A)= INT(RND(1)*(-21))+11
2370 C(A)=INT(RND(1)*(-21))+11
2380 PRINT"BARRIER #";A;":(";B(A);",";C(A);")."
2390 NEXT A
2400 PRINT
2410 RETURN
2420 REM PLACE PLAYER
2430 PRINT"WHICH LEVEL DO YOU WANT TO START ON";
2440 INPUT L2
2450 PRINT"WHICH POINT";
2460 INPUT X2,Y2
2470 PRINT"HOW FAR DO YOU WANT TO MOVE PER A TURN";
2480 INPUT F
2490 PRINT
2500 RETURN
2510 REM MOVE MINOTAUR
2520 X4=X1
2530 Y4=Y1
2540 L4=L1
2550 X3=INT(RND(1)*6)+1
2560 ON X3 GOTO 2570,2620,2640,2690,2710,2760
2570 X1=X1+1
2580 IF ABS(X1)>10 THEN 2600
2590 GOTO 2780
2600 X1=X4
2610 GOTO 2550
2620 X1=X1-1
2630 GOTO 2580
2640 Y1=Y1+1
2650 IF ABS(Y1)>10 THEN 2670
2660 GOTO 2780
2670 Y1=Y4
2680 GOTO 2550
2690 IF X1=B(A) AND Y1=C(A) THEN 2550
2700 GOTO 2650
2710 L1=L1+1
2720 IF L1>3 OR L1<1 THEN 2740
2730 GOTO 2780
2740 L1=L4
2750 GOTO 2550
2760 L1=L1-1
2770 GOTO 2720
2780 FOR A=1 TO 10
2790 IF X1=B(A) AND Y1=C(A) THEN 255
2800 NEXT A
2810 PRINT
2820 GOTO280
2830 PRINT
2840 PRINT"YOU WOUNDED THE MINOTAUR"
2850 PRINT"THE MINOTAUR IS CHARGING."
2860 IF X1>X2 THEN 2890
2870 X3=1
2880 GOTO 2910
2890 X3=-1
2900 GOTO 2910
2910 IF Y1>Y2 THEN 2940
2920 Y3=1
2930 GOTO 2960
2940 Y3=-1
2950 GOTO2960
2960 IF L1>L2 THEN 2990
2970 L3=1
2980 GOTO 3000
2990 L3=-1
3000 IF L1=L2 THEN 3050
3010 L1=L1+L3
3020 PRINT"LEVEL";L1;""
3030 GOTO 3000
3040 REM HI THERE
3050 IF X1=X2 THEN 3100
3060 X1=X1+X3
3070 GOSUB 3140
3080 PRINT"(";X1;",";Y1;")"
3090 GOTO 3050
3100 IF Y1=Y2 THEN 3210
3110 Y1=Y1+Y3
3120 GOSUB 3140
3130 GOTO 3080
3140 FOR P=1 TO 10
3150 IF B(P)=X1 AND C(P)=Y1 THEN 3180
3160 NEXT P
3170 RETURN
3180 PRINT"BZZZZZZZZZZZZZZZZZZZZZOWNT MINOTAUR JUST FRIED HIMSELF"
3190 PRINT"YOU WIN,  YOU LUCKY SCAB"
3200 GOTO 1450
3210 PRINT"BITE "
3220 PRINT"CHEW"
3230 PRINT"CHOMP"
3240 PRINT"GULP"
3250 PRINT"YOU LOSE ,SUCKER"
3260 GOTO930
3270 PRINT"WHAT LEVEL";
3280 INPUT L4
3290 FOR Y4=10 TO -10 STEP -1
3300 FOR X4=-10 TO 10
3310 IF X4=X2 AND Y4=Y2 AND L4=L2 THEN 3410
3320 IF X4=X1 AND Y4=Y1 AND L4=L1 THEN 3430
3330 IF L4=S1 AND Y4=S2 AND L4=S3 THEN 3450
3340 FOR A=1 TO 10
3350 IF B(A)=X4 AND C(A)=Y4 THEN 3480
3360 NEXT A
3370 IF X4=0AND Y4=0 THEN 3500
3380 IF X4=0 OR Y4=0 THEN 3520
3390 PRINT".";
3400 GOTO 3530
3410 PRINT"Y";
3420 GOTO 3400
3430 PRINT"M";
3440 GOTO 3400
3450 IF S9=0 THEN 3340
3460 PRINT"S";
3470 GOTO 3400
3480 PRINT"B";
3490 GOTO 3400
3500 PRINT"O";
3510 GOTO 3400
3520 PRINT"X";
3530 NEXT X4
3540 PRINT
3550 NEXT Y4
3560 PRINT
3570 PRINT"LEVEL:";L4
3580 PRINT TAB(34)"KEY"
3590 PRINT TAB(31)"Y=YOU"
3600 PRINT TAB(31)"M=MINOTAUR"
3610 PRINT TAB(31)"S=SPEAR"
3620 PRINT TAB(31)"B=BARRIER"
3630 PRINT TAB(31)"O=ORIGIN"
3640 PRINT TAB(31)"X=AXIS"
3650 PRINT
3660 GOTO 2510
3670 PRINT"MINOTAUR MOVED TO YOUR SPOT; HE SAID YOU TASTED GREAT!!"
3680 GOTO 930
3690 PRINT"YOU HAVE YOUR SPEAR"
3700 S9=0
3710 GOTO 300
3720 PRINT"HOW CAN YOU THROW YOUR SPEAR IF YOU DON'T HAVE ONE?"
3730 PRINT"SPEAR IS AT(";S1;",";S2;") ON LEVEL ";S3
3740 GOTO 420
3750 STOP
3760 END
Ok
```

Motorcycle Jump

This program, originally titled EVILK permits you to act out your fantasies of being a motorcycle daredevil! The game is a simple motorcycle jump over several busses, which takes into account both gravity and drag forces. The ramp angle and motorcycle speed determine the distance jumped. Note that the injury penalty is greater for long jumps than for short ones, and that there is a chance for a crash even on a jump of the right length. This probability, initially set at .20, can be modified in line 560 to make survival more or less likely.

This program was written by Charles Aylworth and originally appeared in *Creative Computing*, Jul/Aug 1978.

```
RUN

                    MOTORCYCLE JUMP
                   CREATIVE COMPUTING
                 MORRISTOWN, NEW JERSEY


WE'RE AT THE SCENE OF THE BIG MOTORCYCLE JUMP!
HOW MANY BUSSES WILL YOU TRY TO JUMP? 5
 5  BUSSES!  THAT'S  75  FEET!
WHAT RAMP ANGLE WILL YOU USE? 90
 90  DEGREES?  THAT'S IMPOSSIBLE.  COME ON NOW,
WHAT RAMP ANGLE WILL YOU USE? 22
HOW FAST WILL YOU LEAVE THE RAMP? 0
      GOOD LUCK!
A PRACTICE JUMP!
OK, THIS TIME HOW FAST WILL YOU LEAVE THE RAMP? 54
      GOOD LUCK!
THERE HE GOES!!!!
*****************HE JUMPED TOO FAR!
HE MISSED THE RAMP.
I THINK HE'S HURT......
WELL, KILLER, THE DOCTOR SAYS YOU BROKE YOUR:
L.LEG
RIBS
BIKE
NECK
WANT TO JUMP AGAIN? YES


HOW MANY BUSSES WILL YOU TRY TO JUMP? 5
 5  BUSSES!  THAT'S  75  FEET!
WHAT RAMP ANGLE WILL YOU USE? 22
HOW FAST WILL YOU LEAVE THE RAMP? 46
      GOOD LUCK!
THERE HE GOES!!!!
*************HE'S SHORT OF THE RAMP .....
I THINK HE'S HURT......
WELL, KILLER, THE DOCTOR SAYS YOU BROKE YOUR:
R.ARM
PRIDE
L.ARM
BACK
BUTT
WANT TO JUMP AGAIN? YES


HOW MANY BUSSES WILL YOU TRY TO JUMP? 5
 5  BUSSES!  THAT'S  75  FEET!
WHAT RAMP ANGLE WILL YOU USE? 22
HOW FAST WILL YOU LEAVE THE RAMP? 47
      GOOD LUCK!
THERE HE GOES!!!!
**************HE MADE IT !  GREAT JUMP, KILLER!
WANT TO JUMP AGAIN? NO
YOU MADE IT  1  OUT OF  3  ATTEMPTS.
BE CAREFUL, NOW.
OK
```

```
10 PRINT TAB(21);"MOTORCYCLE JUMP"
20 PRINT TAB(20);"CREATIVE COMPUTING"
30 PRINT TAB(18);"MORRISTOWN, NEW JERSEY"
40 PRINT:PRINT:PRINT
50 DIM I2(14),I$(84)
90 I$="R.ARM L.ARM R.LEG L.LEG BACK  NECK  SKULL RIBS  KNEE  BUTT  "
100 I$=I$+"FACE  PELVISPRIDE BIKE  "
110 T=.1
130 T2=0
140 T3=0
150 PRINT "WE'RE AT THE SCENE OF THE BIG MOTORCYCLE JUMP!"
160 INPUT "HOW MANY BUSSES WILL YOU TRY TO JUMP";N
170 J=N*15
180 PRINT N;" BUSSES!  THAT'S ";J;" FEET!"
190 INPUT "WHAT RAMP ANGLE WILL YOU USE";A2
200 IF A2<90 AND A2>0 THEN 230
210 PRINT A2;" DEGREES?  THAT'S IMPOSSIBLE.  COME ON NOW, "
220 GOTO 190
230 A=A2*.01745
240 INPUT "HOW FAST WILL YOU LEAVE THE RAMP";S
250 PRINT "      GOOD LUCK!"
260 IF S>0 THEN 300
270 PRINT "A PRACTICE JUMP!"
280 PRINT "OK, THIS TIME ";
290 GOTO 240
300 H=6
310 D=0
320 G=6
330 R2=0
340 S2=0
350 S=S*1.5
360 PRINT "THERE HE GOES!!!!"
380 S=S-S2
390 F=S*T
400 D2=F*COS(A)
410 R=F*SIN(A)
420 R2=R2+(32*T)
430 R3=R2*T
440 H=H+R-R3
450 D=D+D2
460 PRINT "*";
480 S2=(S/120)*32*T
490 IF D>=J THEN G=6-R
510 IF G<=0 THEN G=0
520 IF H>G THEN 380
530 IF D<J THEN 600
540 IF D>J+20 THEN 640
550 L=((D-J)/30)+RND(1)
560 IF L>.8 THEN 650
570 PRINT "HE MADE IT !  GREAT JUMP, KILLER!"
580 T2=T2+1
590 GOTO 920
600 PRINT "HE'S SHORT OF THE RAMP ....."
620 L2=INT((((J-D)/5)*2)+(RND(1)*5)+.5)
630 GOTO 670
640 PRINT "HE JUMPED TOO FAR!"
650 PRINT "HE MISSED THE RAMP."
660 L2=INT(((D+20-J)/20)+(RND(1)*5))
670 PRINT "I THINK HE'S HURT......"
680 FOR K=1 TO 14
690 I2(K)=K
700 NEXT K
710 K2=14
720 IF L2>14 THEN L2=14
730 IF L2<=0 THEN L2=1
760 FOR K=1 TO L2
770 V=INT(RND(1)*1000)
780 V=(V-(INT(V/K2)*K2))+1
790 H2=I2(V)
800 I2(V)=I2(K2)
810 I2(K2)=H2
820 K2=K2-1
830 NEXT K
840 PRINT "WELL, KILLER, THE DOCTOR SAYS YOU BROKE YOUR:"
860 FOR K=(15-L2) TO 14
880 P=(6*I2(K))-5
890 A$=MID$(I$,P,6)
900 PRINT A$
910 NEXT K
920 T3=T3+1
930 INPUT "WANT TO JUMP AGAIN";A$
940 IF LEFT$(A$,1)="Y" THEN PRINT:PRINT:GOTO 160
950 PRINT "YOU MADE IT ";T2;" OUT OF ";T3;" ATTEMPTS."
960 PRINT "BE CAREFUL, NOW."
970 END
```

Nomad

"Gramma Nomad" is a person who doesn't really know where she wants to live, so she moves to a new house every game. Then she sends you a telegram asking you to visit her. The object of the game is to successfully navigate your way through the streets of Garbonzo City to Gramma's house. See the game for more details. A map of Garbonzo City is provided for your reference.

Nomad was written by Steve Trapp and first appeared in *Creative Computing*, Sep/Oct 1977.

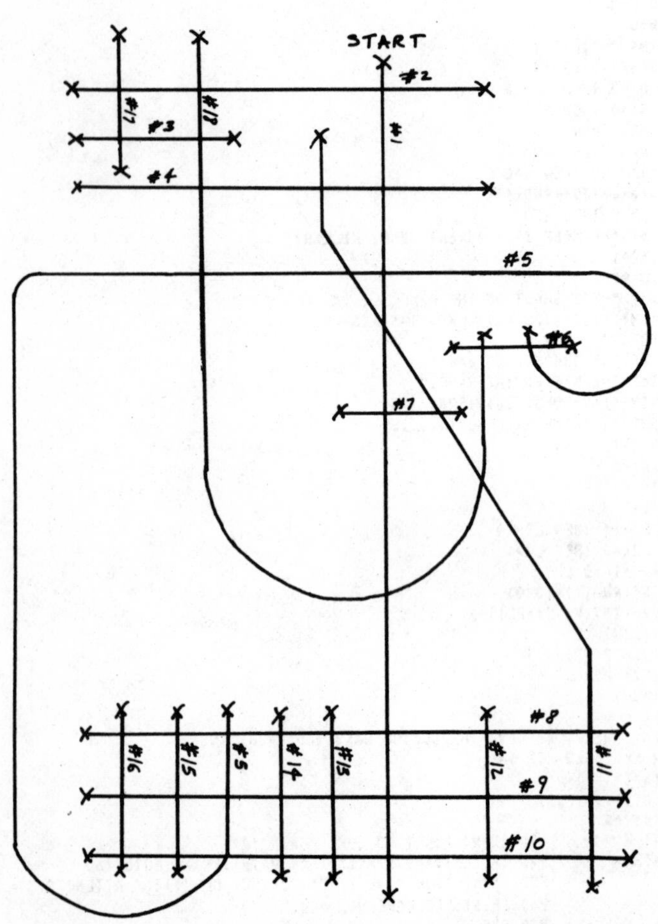


```
RUN
                         NOMAD
                   CREATIVE COMPUTING
                 MORRISTOWN, NEW JERSEY
RULES? YES

GRAMMA NOMAD IS A NICE OLD LADY WHO HAS NOT QUITE
MADE UP HER MIND WHERE SHE WANTS TO LIVE.
SHE HAS NARROWED IT DOWN TO SOMEWHERE IN GARBONZO CITY
AND ON A STREET CORNER.

AT THE BEGINNING, THE MAILMAN GIVES YOU A TELEGRAM WRITTEN
BY GRAMMA TELLING YOU WHERE SHE LIVES.
(I WILL READ IT TO YOU).

YOU GET INTO YOUR CAR IT LRAC NILKNARF NAMGREB LODGE.
FROM THEEEEERE YOU GO TO GRAMMAS HOUSE.

YOU TRY TO GET THERE WITHOUT:
CRASHUPS
TICKETS
FLAT TIRES
RUNNING OUT OF GAS
DEAD ENDS

THERE IS AN 8-MAN POLICE FORCE ENFORCING THE LAWS
OF GARBONZO CITY.

THERE ARE 2-DRUNKS ON THE STREETS OF GARBONZO
CITY.

IF A POLICEMAN CATCHES A DRUNK, HE HAS TO
TESTIFY IN COURT
(WHICH TAKES THE REST OF THE GAME)

IF A DRUNK DRIVER HITS YOU, YOU LOSE.

AT EACH JUNCTION, I WILL TELL YOU:
THE DIRECTION YOU ARE GOING
THE ROAD YOU ARE ON
THE ROAD CROSSING

I WILL ASK YOU:
THE WAY YOU WANT TO TURN (IE LEFT)
SPEED (IN MPH)

AN OVERPASS IS NOT A JUNCTION, SO IT IS
MERELY SKIPPED OVER.  IT IS UNANNOUNCED.

*THAT IS ALL*

WHAT IS YOUR NAME? STEVE

*GOOD LUCK*

DEAR STEVE,
HOW ARE YOU?  I LIVE AT THE CORNER
OF ROAD # 15  & # 9 !!!
COME ON OVER.
                    LOVE,
                    GRAMMA
((TELEGRAMMA CORP. TELEGRAM CO.))
```

```
GOING SOUTH ON ROAD # 1
JUNCTION: ROAD # 1  & # 2
FORWARD, LEFT, RIGHT OR U-TURN? F
SPEED? 40
SMOOSH...BUS FLATTENED YOUR CAR.

AGAIN? YES
WHAT IS YOUR NAME? STEVE

*GOOD LUCK*

DEAR STEVE,
HOW ARE YOU?  I LIVE AT THE CORNER
OF ROAD # 1  & # 8 !!!
COME ON OVER.
                    LOVE,
                    GRAMMA
((TELEGRAMMA CORP. TELEGRAM CO.))


GOING SOUTH ON ROAD # 1
JUNCTION: ROAD # 1  & # 2
FORWARD, LEFT, RIGHT OR U-TURN? F
SPEED? 30

GOING SOUTH ON ROAD # 1
JUNCTION: ROAD # 1  & # 4
FORWARD, LEFT, RIGHT OR U-TURN? F
SPEED? 30
POP...BULLDOG ATE YOUR TIRE!
```

```
AGAIN? YES
WHAT IS YOUR NAME? STEVE

*GOOD LUCK*

DEAR STEVE,
HOW ARE YOU?  I LIVE AT THE CORNER
OF ROAD # 11  & # 4 !!!
COME ON OVER.
                    LOVE,
                    GRAMMA
((TELEGRAMMA CORP. TELEGRAM CO.))


GOING SOUTH ON ROAD # 1
JUNCTION: ROAD # 1  & # 2
FORWARD, LEFT, RIGHT OR U-TURN? R
SPEED? 30

GOING WEST ON ROAD # 2
JUNCTION: ROAD # 2  & # 18
FORWARD, LEFT, RIGHT OR U-TURN? L
SPEED? 56
*SPEEDING*
NOT CAUGHT

GOING SOUTH ON ROAD # 18
JUNCTION: ROAD # 18  & # 3
FORWARD, LEFT, RIGHT OR U-TURN? F
SPEED? 45

GOING SOUTH ON ROAD # 18
JUNCTION: ROAD # 18  & # 4
FORWARD, LEFT, RIGHT OR U-TURN? L
*SPEED*   I DARE YOU   *SPEED*   I DARE YOU
SPEED? 100
*SPEEDING*
NOT CAUGHT

GOING EAST ON ROAD # 4
YOU MADE IT TO GRAMMAS HOUSE!!!!!!! !!

AGAIN? NO

*SEE YOU*
Ok
```

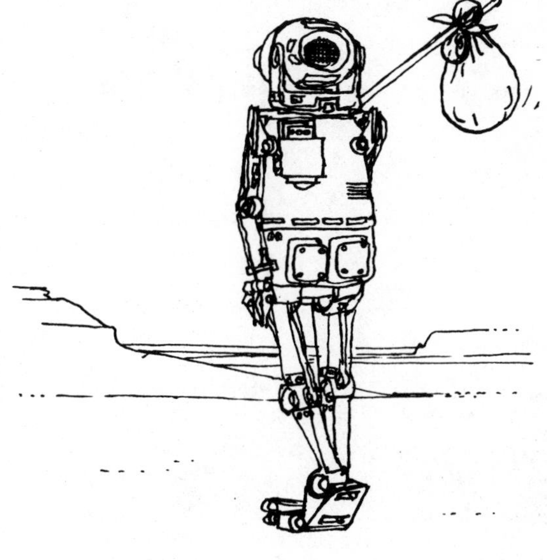

```
list
10 PRINT TAB(26);"NOMAD"
20 PRINT TAB(20);"CREATIVE COMPUTING"
30 PRINT TAB(18);"MORRISTOWN, NEW JERSEY"
1160 DIM K$(30),D(2,2),R(30,30),E(30,30),P(8,2),C(30)
1170 DIM W(30)
1180 DIM N$(30)
1190 REM GOSUB RULES
1200 GOSUB 3340
1210 REM RANDOM NUMBERS
1220 DEF FNA(X)=INT(RND(1)*X)+1
1230 REM # OF ROADS
1240 READ N
1250 FOR R=1 TO N
1260 REM # OF INTERSEC
1270 READ Q
1280 C(R)=ABS(Q)
1290 IF Q<0 THEN 1320
1300 W(R)=1
1310 GOTO 1330
1320 W(R)=-1
1330 REM DIREC, ROAD
1340 FOR J=1 TO C(R)
1350 READ E(R,J),R(R,J)
1360 NEXT J
1370 NEXT R
1380 REM NAME?
1390 PRINT "WHAT IS YOUR NAME";
1400 INPUT N$
1410 REM OPENING STATEMENT
1420 PRINT
1430 PRINT "*GOOD LUCK*"
1440 REM GRAMMAS HOUSE
1450 H1=FNA(N)
1460 H2=FNA(C(H1))
1470 REM DRUNK DRIVERS
1490 REM POLICE
1500 FOR A=1 TO 8
1510 P(A,1)=FNA(N)
1520 P(A,2)=FNA(C(P(A,1)))
1530 NEXT A
1540 REM LRAC NILKNARF NAMGREB LODGE
1550 R=1
1560 J=0
1570 I=1
1580 REM GOSUB CHECK
1590 GOSUB 2520
1600 REM GOSUB TELEGRAM
1610 GOSUB 2570
1620 REM ADD INCREMENT
1630 J=J+I
1640 REM NEED REPAIR?
1650 IF FNA(10)=1 THEN 2940
1660 REM DEAD END?
1670 IF J>C(R) OR J=0 THEN 3060
1680 REM DIRECTION
1690 IF I=-1 THEN 1720
1700 D=E(R,J)
1710 GOTO 1730
1720 D=9-E(R,J)
1730 REM ROAD CROSSING
1740 C=R(R,J)
1750 REM SKIP LINE
1760 PRINT
1770 REM GOSUB *DIREC, ROAD ON* PRINT
1780 GOSUB 2680
1790 REM AT GRAMMAS?
1800 IF H1=R AND R(R,J)=R(H1,H2) THEN 2880
1810 IF H1=R(R,J) AND R=R(H1,H2) THEN 2880
1820 REM JUNCTION
1830 PRINT "JUNCTION: ROAD #";R;" & #";C
1840 REM ASK WHAT WAY TO TURN
1850 PRINT "FORWARD, LEFT, RIGHT OR U-TURN";
1860 INPUT I$
1880 IF LEFT$(I$,1)="F" THEN 2080
1890 IF LEFT$(I$,1)="R" THEN 1970
1900 IF LEFT$(I$,1)="L" THEN 1990
1910 IF LEFT$(I$,1)="U" THEN 1950
1920 REM GOOFED
1930 PRINT "**YOU GOOFED**"
1940 GOTO 1850
1950 I=1*I
1960 GOTO 2080
1970 I=W(R)*I
1980 GOTO 2000
1990 I=-1*W(R)*I
2000 FOR A=1 TO C(C)
2010 IF R(C,A)=R THEN 2040
2020 NEXT A
2030 GOTO 4210
2040 R=C
2050 J=A
2060 REM DARE?
2070 IF FNA(4)=1 THEN 2360
2080 REM SPEED
2090 PRINT "SPEED";
2100 INPUT S
2110 REM DANGEROUSITY CRASH CHECKS
2120 IF S>100 THEN 3190
2130 IF S<30 THEN 3220
2140 REM ILLEGAL?
2150 IF S>55 THEN 3090
2160 REM DRUNK DRIVERS DRIVE.
2170 FOR A=1 TO 2
2180 IF D(A,1)=0 THEN 2210
2190 D(A,1)=FNA(N)
2200 D(A,2)=FNA(C(D(A,1)))
2210 NEXT A
2220 REM HIT BY DRUNK DRIVER?
```

```
2230 FOR A=1 TO 2
2240 IF D(A,1)=0 THEN 2270
2250 IF D(A,1)=R AND R(R,J)=R(D(A,1),D(A,2)) THEN 2910
2260 IF D(A,1)=R(R,J) AND R(D(A,1),D(A,2))=R THEN 2910
2270 NEXT A
2280 REM IS DRIVER CAUGHT?
2290 FOR A=1 TO 2
2300 IF D(A,1)=0 THEN 2340
2310 FOR B=1 TO 8
2320 IF D(A,1)=P(B,1) AND D(A,2)=P(B,2) THEN 2400
2330 NEXT B
2340 NEXT A
2350 GOTO 1620
2360 REM SPEED DARE PRINT
2370 ON FNA(3) GOTO 2380,2400,2420
2380 PRINT "I DARE YOU TO SPEED ** (DAREDEVIL)"
2390 GOTO 2430
2400 PRINT "*SPEEDING* IS FUN (SO DO IT)!!"
2410 GOTO 2430
2420 PRINT "*SPEED*   I DARE YOU   *SPEED*   I DARE YOU"
2430 GOTO 2080
2440 REM DRUNK CAUGHT
2450 PRINT "A DRUNK DRIVER HAS BEEN CAUGHT.  THE POLICEMAN WHO"
2460 PRINT "ARRESTED HIM WILL BE TESTIFYING AT COURT FOR"
2470 PRINT "THE REST OF THE GAME."
2480 PRINT
2490 D(A,1)=0:D(A,2)=0:P(B,1)=0:P(B,2)=0
2500 GOTO 1620
2510 REM CHECK
2520 FOR A=1 TO 8
2530 IF H1=P(A,1) AND R(H1,H2)=R(P(A,1),P(A,2)) THEN 1440
2540 IF H1=R(P(A,1),P(A,2)) AND R(H1,H2)=P(A,1) THEN 1440
2550 NEXT A
2560 RETURN
2570 REM TELEGRAM PRINT-UP
2580 PRINT
2590 PRINT "DEAR ";N$;","
2600 PRINT "HOW ARE YOU?  I LIVE AT THE CORNER"
2610 PRINT "OF ROAD #";H1;" & #";R(H1,H2);"!!!"
2620 PRINT "COME ON OVER."
2630 PRINT "                        LOVE,"
2640 PRINT "                        GRAMMA"
2650 PRINT "((TELEGRAMMA CORP. TELEGRAM CO.))"
2660 PRINT
2670 RETURN
2680 REM *DIREC. ROAD ON* PRINT-UP
2690 PRINT "GOING ";
2700 ON D GOTO 2710,2730,2750,2770,2790,2810,2830,2850
2710 PRINT "NORTH";
2720 GOTO 2860
2730 PRINT "WEST";
2740 GOTO 2860
2750 PRINT "NORTHEAST";
2760 GOTO 2860
2770 PRINT "SOUTHEAST";
2780 GOTO 2860
2790 PRINT "NORTHWEST";
2800 GOTO 2860
2810 PRINT "SOUTHWEST";
2820 GOTO 2860
2830 PRINT "EAST";
2840 GOTO 2860
2850 PRINT "SOUTH";
2860 PRINT " ON ROAD #";R
2872 RETURN
2880 REM AT GRAMMAS *PRINT*
2890 PRINT "YOU MADE IT TO GRAMMAS HOUSE!!!!!!! !!"
2900 GOTO 3240
2910 REM DRUNK HIT YOUR CAR *PRINT*
2920 PRINT "KERSPLATT--DRUNK DRIVER HIT YOUR CAR."
2930 GOTO 3240
2940 REM CAR NEEDS FIXING *PRINT-UP*
2950 ON FNA(5) GOTO 2960,2980,3000,3020,3040
2960 PRINT "POP...FLAT TIRE"
2970 GOTO 3050
2980 PRINT "FLIP...YOUR CAR DID A SUMERSALT"
2990 GOTO 3050
3000 PRINT "*OUT OF GAS*"
3010 GOTO 3050
3020 PRINT "SMOOSH...BUS FLATTENED YOUR CAR."
3030 GOTO 3050
3040 PRINT "POP...BULLDOG ATE YOUR TIRE!"
3050 GOTO 3240
3060 REM DEAD END PRINT
3070 PRINT "*DEAD END*"
3080 GOTO 3240
3090 REM SPEEDING
3100 PRINT "*SPEEDING*"
3110 REM CAUGHT BY POLICE?
3120 FOR X=1 TO 8
3130 IF P(X,1)=R AND P(X,1)=J THEN 3170
3140 NEXT X
3150 PRINT "NOT CAUGHT"
3160 GOTO 2160
3170 PRINT "CAUGHT SPEEDING BY THE POLICE!!"
3180 GOTO 3240
3190 REM TOO FAST *CRASH*
3200 PRINT "KERSMOUSHIIEEEE...WENT TOO FAST !!!!"
3210 GOTO 3240
3220 REM TOO SLOW *CRASH*
3230 PRINT "-*<(KRUNCH)>*-  TOO SLOW...CAR BEHIND RAN INTO YOU!"
3240 REM AGAIN?
3250 PRINT
3260 PRINT "AGAIN";
3270 INPUT I$
3290 IF LEFT$(I$,1)="Y" THEN 1380
3300 REM CLOSING STATEMENT
3310 PRINT
3320 PRINT "*SEE YOU*"
3330 GOTO 4210
3340 REM RULES?
3350 PRINT "RULES";
3360 INPUT I$
3380 IF LEFT$(I$,1)="N" THEN 3950
3390 PRINT
3400 PRINT "GRAMMA NOMAD IS A NICE OLD LADY WHO HAS NOT QUITE"
3410 PRINT "MADE UP HER MIND WHERE SHE WANTS TO LIVE."
3420 PRINT "SHE HAS NARROWED IT DOWN TO SOMEWHERE IN GARBONZO CITY"
3430 PRINT "AND ON A STREET CORNER."
3440 PRINT
3450 PRINT "AT THE BEGINNING, THE MAILMAN GIVES YOU A TELEGRAM WRITTEN"
3460 PRINT "BY GRAMMA TELLING YOU WHERE SHE LIVES."
3470 PRINT "(I WILL READ IT TO YOU)."
3480 PRINT
3490 PRINT "YOU GET INTO YOUR CAR IT LRAC NILKNARF NAMGREB LODGE."
3500 PRINT "FROM THEEEEERE YOU GO TO GRAMMAS HOUSE."
3510 PRINT
3520 PRINT "YOU TRY TO GET THERE WITHOUT:"
3530 PRINT "CRASHUPS"
3540 PRINT "TICKETS"
3550 PRINT "FLAT TIRES"
3560 PRINT "RUNNING OUT OF GAS"
3570 PRINT "DEAD ENDS"
3580 PRINT
3590 PRINT "THERE IS AN 8-MAN POLICE FORCE ENFORCING THE LAWS"
3600 PRINT "OF GARBONZO CITY."
3610 PRINT
3620 PRINT "THERE ARE 2-DRUNKS ON THE STREETS OF GARBONZO"
3630 PRINT "CITY."
3640 PRINT
3650 PRINT "IF A POLICEMAN CATCHES A DRUNK, HE HAS TO"
3660 PRINT "TESTIFY IN COURT"
3670 PRINT "(WHICH TAKES THE REST OF THE GAME)"
3680 PRINT
3690 PRINT "IF A DRUNK DRIVER HITS YOU, YOU LOSE."
3700 PRINT
3810 PRINT "AT EACH JUNCTION, I WILL TELL YOU:"
3820 PRINT "THE DIRECTION YOU ARE GOING"
3830 PRINT "THE ROAD YOU ARE ON"
3840 PRINT "THE ROAD CROSSING"
3850 PRINT
3860 PRINT "I WILL ASK YOU:"
3870 PRINT "THE WAY YOU WANT TO TURN (IE LEFT)"
3880 PRINT "SPEED (IN MPH)"
3890 PRINT
3900 PRINT "AN OVERPASS IS NOT A JUNCTION, SO IT IS"
3910 PRINT "MERELY SKIPPED OVER.  IT IS UNANNOUNCED."
3920 PRINT
3930 PRINT "*THAT IS ALL*"
3940 PRINT
3950 RETURN
3960 REM DATA LINES
3970 DATA 18
3980 DATA -8,8,2,8,4,8,5,8,11,8,7,8,8,8,9,8,10
3990 DATA 3,7,17,7,18,7,1
4000 DATA 2,7,17,7,18
4010 DATA 3,7,18,7,11,7,1
4020 DATA 7,8,8,8,9,8,10,7,18,7,11,7,1,1,6
4030 DATA -2,7,18,7,5
4040 DATA 2,7,1,7,11
4050 DATA 8,7,16,7,15,7,5,7,14,7,13,7,1,7,12,7,11
4060 DATA 8,7,16,7,15,7,5,7,14,7,13,7,1,7,12,7,11
4070 DATA 8,7,16,7,15,7,5,7,14,7,13,7,1,7,12,7,11
4080 DATA -7,4,4,4,5,4,1,4,7,8,8,8,9,8,10
4090 DATA -3,8,8,8,9,8,10
4100 DATA -3,8,8,8,9,8,10
4110 DATA -3,8,8,8,9,8,10
4120 DATA -3,8,8,8,9,8,10
4130 DATA -3,8,8,8,9,8,10
4140 DATA -2,8,2,8,3
4150 DATA -5,8,2,8,3,8,4,8,5,1,6
4160 DATA 0,0,0,0,0,0
4210 END
Ok
```

Not One

The game, Not One, sometimes known as Pig, is played with two players and a pair of dice. There are ten rounds in the game; one round consisting of one turn for each player. Players add the score that they attain on each round and the player with the highest score after ten rounds is the winner.

On each turn, the player may roll the two dice from one to as many times as he wishes. If the total of the dice on any roll after the first equals the total shown on the first roll, his score is then zero for that entire turn and the dice pass to the other player. On the other hand, if the total on his dice is anything different from the total on the first turn, he continues to roll and adds the totals of the dice to his score. After each successful roll, the player can decide whether to roll again or stop and score the number of points already obtained.

You'll find that the computer plays a surprisingly good game of Not One. To beat it, you'll need some knowledge of probabilities and a little bit of luck on your side.

Not One was written in response to a challenge that appeared in the charter issue of *Creative Computing*. The game was written by Robert Puopolo and first appeared in *Creative Computing*, Mar/Apr 1975.

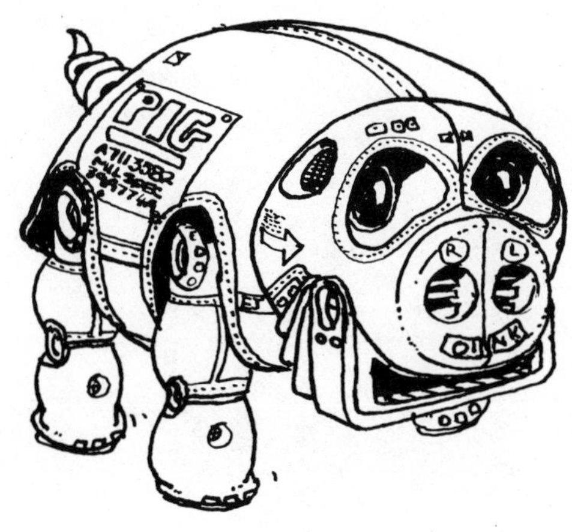


```
RUN
                    NOTONE

               CREATIVE COMPUTING
             MORRISTOWN NEW JERSEY


WOULD YOU LIKE THE INSTRUCTIONS? YES

THE GAME OF NOTONE IS PLAYED WITH
TWO PLAYERS AND A PAIR OF DICE. THERE ARE
TEN ROUNDS IN THE GAME ONE ROUND CONSISTING
OF ONE TURN FOR EACH PLAYER. PLAYERS
(YOURSELF AND THE COMPUTER) ADD THE SCORE
THEY ATTAIN ON EACH ROUND, AND THE PLAYER
WITH THE HIGHEST SCORE AFTER TEN ROUNDS IS THE WINNER

ON EACH TURN THE PLAYER MAY ROLL THE TWO
DICE FROM 1 TO N TIMES. IF TI IS THE TOTAL OF DICE ON
THE ITH ROLL, THEN THE PLAYERS SCORE FOR THE TURN IS
T(1)+T(2)+T(3)+........+T(N).  HOWEVER,
AND HERE'S THE CATCH, IF ANY T(I) IS EQUAL TO T(1) THEN
THE TURN IS OVER AND HIS SCORE FOR THAT ROUND IS ZERO
AFTER EACH ROLL THAT DOESN'T EQUAL T(1), THE PLAYER CAN
DECIDE WHETHER TO ROLL AGAIN OR STOP AND
SCORE THE NUMBER OF POINTS ALREADY OBTAINED.

ROUND  1
 7
ROLL AGAIN ? YES
 7
YOU GET A ZERO FOR THIS ROUND

                COMPUTERS MOVE

COMPUTER'S ROLL 1 : 7
COMPUTER'S ROLL 2 : 5
COMPUTER'S ROLL 3 : 11
COMPUTER'S ROLL 4 : 12
COMPUTER'S ROLL 5 : 8
COMPUTER'S ROLL 6 : 3

COMPUTER:  46                 YOU:  0

ROUND  2
 12
ROLL AGAIN ? YES
 4
ROLL AGAIN ? YES
 6
ROLL AGAIN ? YES
 7
ROLL AGAIN ? YES
 10
ROLL AGAIN ? YES
 7
ROLL AGAIN ? YES
 8
ROLL AGAIN ? YES
 9
ROLL AGAIN ? YES
 11
ROLL AGAIN ? YES
 11
ROLL AGAIN ? YES
 4
ROLL AGAIN ? NO

                COMPUTERS MOVE

COMPUTER'S ROLL 1 : 6
COMPUTER'S ROLL 2 : 9
COMPUTER'S ROLL 3 : 7
COMPUTER'S ROLL 4 : 7
COMPUTER'S ROLL 5 : 4
COMPUTER'S ROLL 6 : 7

YOU:  89        COMPUTER:  86

ROUND  3
 8
ROLL AGAIN ? YES
 4
ROLL AGAIN ? YS_ES
 5
ROLL AGAIN ? YES
 6
ROLL AGAIN ? NO

                COMPUTERS MOVE

COMPUTER'S ROLL 1 : 8
COMPUTER'S ROLL 2 : 7
COMPUTER'S ROLL 3 : 3
COMPUTER'S ROLL 4 : 6
COMPUTER'S ROLL 5 : 4
COMPUTER'S ROLL 6 : 7

COMPUTER:  121                YOU:  112

ROUND  4
 11
ROLL AGAIN ? YES
 3
ROLL AGAIN ? YES
 12
ROLL AGAIN ? YES
 3
ROLL AGAIN ? YES
 6
ROLL AGAIN ? YES
 7
ROLL AGAIN ? YES
 8
ROLL AGAIN ? YES
 10
ROLL AGAIN ? NO

                COMPUTERS MOVE

COMPUTER'S ROLL 1 : 5
COMPUTER'S ROLL 2 : 9
COMPUTER'S ROLL 3 : 12
COMPUTER'S ROLL 4 : 8
COMPUTER'S ROLL 5 : 7
COMPUTER'S ROLL 6 : 4
COMPUTER'S ROLL 7 : 6
COMPUTER'S ROLL 8 : 11
COMPUTER'S ROLL 9 : 6

COMPUTER:  189                YOU:  172

ROUND  5
 11
ROLL AGAIN ? YES
 7
ROLL AGAIN ? YES
 5
```

```
ROLL AGAIN ? YES
 3
ROLL AGAIN ? YES
 7
ROLL AGAIN ? YES
 11
YOU GET A ZERO FOR THIS ROUND

               COMPUTERS MOVE

COMPUTER'S ROLL 1 : 8
COMPUTER'S ROLL 2 : 6
COMPUTER'S ROLL 3 : 2
COMPUTER'S ROLL 4 : 9
COMPUTER'S ROLL 5 : 12
COMPUTER'S ROLL 6 : 6

COMPUTER:  232              YOU:  172

ROUND  6
 4
ROLL AGAIN ? YES
 5
ROLL AGAIN ? YES
 9
ROLL AGAIN ? YES
 8
ROLL AGAIN ? YES
 7
ROLL AGAIN ? YES
 10
ROLL AGAIN ? YES
 7
ROLL AGAIN ? YES
 7
ROLL AGAIN ? NO

               COMPUTERS MOVE

COMPUTER'S ROLL 1 : 10
COMPUTER'S ROLL 2 : 6
COMPUTER'S ROLL 3 : 5
COMPUTER'S ROLL 4 : 7
COMPUTER'S ROLL 5 : 8
COMPUTER'S ROLL 6 : 4
COMPUTER'S ROLL 7 : 7
COMPUTER'S ROLL 8 : 4
COMPUTER'S ROLL 9 : 6

COMPUTER:  289              YOU:  229

ROUND  7
 6
ROLL AGAIN ? YES
 11
ROLL AGAIN ? YES
 6
YOU GET A ZERO FOR THIS ROUND

               COMPUTERS MOVE

COMPUTER'S ROLL 1 : 6
COMPUTER'S ROLL 2 : 3
COMPUTER'S ROLL 3 : 8
COMPUTER'S ROLL 4 : 11
COMPUTER'S ROLL 5 : 7
COMPUTER'S ROLL 6 : 2

COMPUTER:  326              YOU:  229

ROUND  8
 8
ROLL AGAIN ? YES
 8
YOU GET A ZERO FOR THIS ROUND

               COMPUTERS MOVE

COMPUTER'S ROLL 1 : 7
COMPUTER'S ROLL 2 : 11
COMPUTER'S ROLL 3 : 10
COMPUTER'S ROLL 4 : 10
COMPUTER'S ROLL 5 : 6
COMPUTER'S ROLL 6 : 6

COMPUTER:  376              YOU:  229

ROUND  9
 3
ROLL AGAIN ? YES
 8
ROLL AGAIN ? YES
 7
ROLL AGAIN ? YES
 12
ROLL AGAIN ? YES
 2
ROLL AGAIN ? YES
 7
ROLL AGAIN ? YES
 5
ROLL AGAIN ? YES
 8
ROLL AGAIN ? YES
 7
ROLL AGAIN ? YES
 8
ROLL AGAIN ? YES
 5
ROLL AGAIN ? YES
 8
ROLL AGAIN ? YES
 6
ROLL AGAIN ? YES
 9
ROLL AGAIN ? NO

               COMPUTERS MOVE

COMPUTER'S ROLL 1 : 8
COMPUTER'S ROLL 2 : 8
THE COMPUTER GETS A ZERO FOR THE TURN!

COMPUTER:  376              YOU:  324

ROUND  10
 7
ROLL AGAIN ? YES
 10
ROLL AGAIN ? YES
 5
ROLL AGAIN ? YES
 7
YOU GET A ZERO FOR THIS ROUND

               COMPUTERS MOVE

COMPUTER'S ROLL 1 : 6
COMPUTER'S ROLL 2 : 11
COMPUTER'S ROLL 3 : 11
COMPUTER'S ROLL 4 : 8
COMPUTER'S ROLL 5 : 3
COMPUTER'S ROLL 6 : 6
THE COMPUTER GETS A ZERO FOR THE TURN!

FINAL SCORE

COMPUTER:  376              YOU:  324

SCORING SUMMARY

ROUND          YOU       COMPUTER

 1              0         46
 2              89        40
 3              23        35
 4              60        68
 5              0         43
 6              57        57
 7              0         37
 8              0         50
 9              95        0
 10             0         0

TOTALS:         324       376

OK
```

```
LIST

3 PRINT TAB(26);"NOTONE":PRINT
5 PRINT TAB(20);"CREATIVE COMPUTING"
6 PRINT TAB(19);"MORRISTOWN NEW JERSEY"
7 PRINT:PRINT:PRINT
10 DIM T(50),R(10),C(10),L(12)
15 INPUT "WOULD YOU LIKE THE INSTRUCTIONS";A$
20 IF A$="YES" THEN 35
25 IF A$="NO" THEN 100
30 PRINT:PRINT "ANSWER YES OR NO!!":PRINT:GOTO 15
35 PRINT:PRINT "THE GAME OF NOTONE IS PLAYED WITH"
40 PRINT "TWO PLAYERS AND A PAIR OF DICE. THERE ARE"
45 PRINT "TEN ROUNDS IN THE GAME ONE ROUND CONSISTING"
50 PRINT "OF ONE TURN FOR EACH PLAYER. PLAYERS"
55 PRINT "(YOURSELF AND THE COMPUTER) ADD THE SCORE"
60 PRINT "THEY ATTAIN ON EACH ROUND, AND THE PLAYER"
62 PRINT "WITH THE HIGHEST SCORE AFTER TEN ROUNDS IS THE WINNER":PRINT
67 PRINT "ON EACH TURN THE PLAYER MAY ROLL THE TWO"
69 PRINT "DICE FROM 1 TO N TIMES. IF T1 IS THE TOTAL OF DICE ON"
72 PRINT "THE ITH ROLL, THEN THE PLAYERS SCORE FOR THE TURN IS"
75 PRINT "T(1)+T(2)+T(3)+........+T(N).  HOWEVER,"
77 PRINT "AND HERE'S THE CATCH, IF ANY T(I) IS EQUAL TO T(1) THEN"
80 PRINT "THE TURN IS OVER AND HIS SCORE FOR THAT ROUND IS ZERO"
82 PRINT "AFTER EACH ROLL THAT DOESN'T EQUAL T(1), THE PLAYER CAN"
88 PRINT "DECIDE WHETHER TO ROLL AGAIN OR STOP AND "
90 PRINT "SCORE THE NUMBER OF POINTS ALREADY OBTAINED."
100 FOR T=1 TO 10:PRINT:PRINT "ROUND ";T
110 X=X+1:R1=INT(6*RND(1))+1
115 R2=INT(6*RND(1))+1:PRINT R1+R2
120 IF X>1 THEN 130
125 T(1)=R1+R2:GOTO 135
130 T(X)=R1+R2
131 IF T(1)<>T(X) THEN  135
132 PRINT "YOU GET A ZERO FOR THIS ROUND"
133 X=0:T1=0:GOTO 200
135 T1=T1+T(X)
140 INPUT "ROLL AGAIN ";B$
145 IF B$="YES" THEN 110
150 IF B$="NO" THEN R(T)=T1:X=0:T1=0:FOR A=1 TO 50:T(A)=0:NEXT:GOTO 200
160 PRINT:PRINT "ANSWER YES OR NO!!":PRINT: GOTO 140
200 PRINT:PRINT TAB(15);"COMPUTERS MOVE":PRINT
201 RESTORE
202 R1=INT(6*RND(1))+1:R2=INT(6*RND(1))+1
204 FOR D=2 TO R1+R2:READ L(D):NEXT:D=R1+R2
205 FOR C=1 TO L(D):IF C=1 THEN 215
210 R1=INT(6*RND(1))+1:R2=INT(6*RND(1))+1
215 PRINT "COMPUTER'S ROLL"C":";R1+R2
220 IF C>1 THEN 230
225 T(1)=R1+R2:GOTO 242
230 T(C)=R1+R2
235 IF T(C)<>T(1) GOTO 242
236 PRINT "THE COMPUTER GETS A ZERO FOR THE TURN!!"
237 T1=0:GOTO 245
242 T1=T1+T(C):NEXT C
245 C(T)=T1:T1=0:X=0
250 C2=C2+C(T):C1=C1+R(T)
253 PRINT:FOR B=1 TO 50:T(B)=0:NEXT
255 IF T=10 THEN PRINT "FINAL SCORE":PRINT
260 IF C2<C1 THEN 270
263 PRINT"COMPUTER: ";C2,"YOU: ";C1:GOTO 300
270 PRINT "YOU: ";C1,"COMPUTER: ";C2
300 NEXT T
305 DATA 18,18,9,9,6,6,6,9,9,18,18
310 PRINT:PRINT "SCORING SUMMARY":PRINT
315 PRINT "ROUND";TAB(15);"YOU";TAB(25);"COMPUTER":PRINT
320 FOR E=1 TO 10:PRINT E;TAB(16);R(E);TAB(26);C(E):NEXT
325 PRINT:PRINT "TOTALS: ";TAB(16);C1;TAB(26);C2:PRINT
OK
```

Obstacle

The game OBSTACLE is an obstacle course game played on a 9x40 grid.

A car is represented by the character '*', the obstacles are the walls (represented by exclamation points and hyphens) and spaces are where the car may travel. The car may not pass over or occupy a wall or obstacle. The character 'S' at the upper left corner, indicates where the car starts from, and the character in the lower right corner, the 'F', is the space the car must occupy at the finish to win. If the car tries to occupy or pass through a wall the game is lost. When the car lands on the space occupied by the character 'F', the car has finished the course, and the game is over, and a time is calculated.

Line-by-line, here's how the program works:

Line 610 dimensions the matrix M for 15 rows by 50 columns (allowing an adequate margin for modification).

Line 620-680 initializes all necessary variables.

Line 700-780, through the use of a random number generator, generates the obstacle course, where I is the row matrix index and J is the column matrix index and R1 is the random number. Line 720 generates a random number between 0 and 1, multiplies it by a density of 1.2 (to increase density factor by a few decimal points) and removes everything right of the decimal point. R1 is now either 0 or 1. If it is 0 the matrix memory location M (I,J) inside the For-Next Loop is assigned the value of a space, if it is 1, it is assigned the value of an exclamation point.

Lines 840 and 850 assign the walls to the course.

Line 890 stores the values of I and J into K and L, these act as value holders. After the print routine has been executed, I and J are reassigned their old values stored in K and L at line 970.

Lines 910-960, through use of a For-Next Loop (as in the initialization course set up routine), print out the characters represented by values in matrix M, Line 930, the CHR$ Function turns the values of the memory location into their ASCII character equivalent.

Line 990 checks if the car has moved yet, by checking D1. If D1>0 then it skips the query option and continues with the main body. If D1=0 then it executes the option query, asking whether a new course, or this course or end the game and then executes the respective option.

Line 1130 checks if D1 is not equal to 1 and if so continues with the movement routine. If not then it starts the car at matrix position 2,2 and continues with the movement routine.

Line 1080 starts the main program body, 1100 queries the direction and 1110 checks the input D if it is a valid direction. Line 1120 inputs the speed 'S' and Line 1130 initializes the counters S1 and D1. Lines 1160-1180 direct control to the proper movement routine (1 is up, 2 is right to left, 3 is down).

Line 1190-1220 is the movement routine for direction 1. Line 1190 erases the car from the previous position keeping track of I and J. Line 1200 and 1210 check each character position between matrix position I,J, and I-S,J for a wall (exclamation or hyphen); if one is encountered the game is over. If no walls are encountered, the move is legal and Line 1220 assigns the car to matrix position I-1,J and jumps to 1310 to check matrix position 10,41 if it contains a car. If so, the game is won and the End of Run routine is executed. If matrix position 10,41 is not occupied the game is not over and control jumps to 870, the matrix print routine. The Loop can only be exited by losing (crashing into an obstacle) or by getting the car to matrix position 10,41 where it executes the End of Run routine.

Line 1380 calculates the time by dividing total number of turns by total number of character spaces covered by the car and multiplies it by 100. Line 1390 prints the time and Line 1400 and 1410 query as to whether to play the game again.

The program and these notes were written by Eric Erickson.

```
RUN
                          OBSTACLE
                     CREATIVE COMPUTING
                   MORRISTOWN, NEW JERSEY



DO YOU WANT INSTRUCTIONS? YES
THE OBJECT OF THIS GAME IS TO MOVE YOUR CAR'*'
 BEGINNING AT'S' AND NAVIGATE THROUGH THE OBSTACLES
'!'&'-' WALLS TO THE SPACE MARKED 'F', YOU MUST LAND
ON THE SPACE MARKED 'F' ON THE EXACT AMOUNT OF SPACES
THERE ARE NO DIAGONAL MOVES.
THERE ARE NO RIGHT TO LEFT MOVES.
DIRECTIONS NO.1 IS UP.
DIRECTION NO.2 IS LEFT TO RIGHT
DIRECTION NO.3 IS DOWN.

SPEED IS THE NO. OF SPACES IN A GIVEN DIRECTION

            ----------------------------------------
            !S    !     ! !  !      ! !    !    !  !
            !   ! !    !          !    !           !
            ! !      ! !                  !    !   !
            !    !        !           !!!          !
            !!      !   !!    !   !           !    !
            !   !!          !    !           !  !! !
            !  !      !       !!  !    !      ! !! !
            !       !   !      !!    !         !!! !
            !        !     !    ! !   !!  !       F!
            ----------------------------------------
            OPTION :(A=CONTINUE,B=NEW COURSE,C=STOP)? A
            DIRECTION? 3

            SPEED? 4
            ILLEGAL MOVE...... YOU LOSE!!

            DO YOU WISH TO PLAY AGAIN? YES

            ----------------------------------------
            !S  !! !           !      ! ! !     !! !
            !   !            !                     !
            !    ! ! !!   !       !       !        !
            !     ! ! !            !    !     !    !
            !!           !       !    !   !   !    !
            !       !  ! !           !!  !  !      !
            !   ! !     !  !    !  !! ! !   !! !  !!
            !!           !        !!   !!       !! !
            !                ! ! !             !! F!
            ----------------------------------------
            OPTION :(A=CONTINUE,B=NEW COURSE,C=STOP)? A
            DIRECTION? 2

            SPEED? 1

            ----------------------------------------
            ! * !! !           !      ! ! !     !! !
            !   !            !                     !
            !    ! ! !!   !       !       !        !
            !     ! ! !            !    !     !    !
            !!           !       !    !   !   !    !
            !       !  ! !           !!  !  !      !
            !   ! !     !  !    !  !! ! !   !! !  !!
            !!           !        !!   !!       !! !
            !                ! ! !             !! F!
            ----------------------------------------
            DIRECTION? 3

            SPEED? 4

            ----------------------------------------
            !   !! !           !      ! ! !     !! !
            !   !            !                     !
            !    ! ! !!   !       !       !        !
            !     ! ! !            !    !     !    !
            !!*          !       !    !   !   !    !
            !       !  ! !           !!  !  !      !
            !   ! !     !  !    !  !! ! !   !! !  !!
            !!           !        !!   !!       !! !
            !                ! ! !             !! F!
            ----------------------------------------
```

Later in the Run

```
DIRECTION? 1

SPEED? 2

------------------------------------------
!   !!  !           !      !  ! !     !! !
!   !             !*                     !
!    ! ! !!    !       !        !        !
!     ! ! !             !     !     !    !
!!            !       !     !   !   !    !
!        !  ! !           !!   !  !      !
!   ! !      !  !    !  !!  ! !   !! !  !!
!!            !        !!    !!       !! !
!                 ! ! !              !! F!
------------------------------------------
```

```
DIRECTION? 2

SPEED? 6

------------------------------------------
!   !!  !           !      !  ! !     !! !
!   !             !      *               !
!    ! ! !!    !       !        !        !
!     ! ! !             !     !     !    !
!!            !       !     !   !   !    !
!        !  ! !           !!   !  !      !
!   ! !      !  !    !  !!  ! !   !! !  !!
!!            !        !!    !!       !! !
!                 ! ! !              !! F!
------------------------------------------
```

```
DIRECTION? 2

SPEED? `\`\8

------------------------------------------
!   !!  !           !      !  ! !     !! !
!   !             !              *       !
!    ! ! !!    !       !        !        !
!     ! ! !             !     !     !    !
!!            !       !     !   !   !    !
!        !  ! !           !!   !  !      !
!   ! !      !  !    !  !!  ! !   !! !  !!
!!            !        !!    !!       !! !
!                 ! ! !              !! F!
------------------------------------------
DIRECTION? 3

SPEED? 8
ILLEGAL MOVE...... YOU LOSE!!

DO YOU WISH TO PLAY AGAIN? NO
OK
```

```
LIST

10 PRINT TAB(26)"OBSTACLE"
20 PRINTTAB(20)"CREATIVE COMPUTING"
30 PRINTTAB(18)"MORRISTOWN, NEW JERSEY"
150 REM VARIABLES          USAGE
160 REM ----------------------------------------------------------------
170 REM   A1                 DECIMAL VALUE FOR THE CHARACTER´*´
180 REM   A2                 DECIMAL VALUE FOR THE CHARACTER ´ ´
190 REM   A3                 DECIMAL VALUE FOR THE CHARACTER ´!´
200 REM   A4                 DECIMAL VALUE FOR THE CHARACTER ´S´
210 REM   A5                 DECIMAL VALUE FOR THE CHARACTER ´F´
220 REM   A6                 DECIMAL VALUE FOR THE CHARACTER ´-´
230 REM   D                  DIRECTION
240 REM   D1                 TOTAL NO. OF TURNS TAKEN
250 REM   I                  ROW MATRIX
260 REM   J                  COLUMN MATRIX INDEX
270 REM   K                  PLACE HOLDER FOR THE VARIABLE I
280 REM   L                  PLACE HOLDER FOR THE VARIABLE J
290 REM   M                  MATRIX VARIBLE
300 REM   N$                 INPUT TO YES-NO QUESTIONS
310 REM   R1                 RANDOM NUMBER GENERATOR VARIABLE
320 REM   S                  SPEED
330 REM   S1                 TOTAL SPEED COUNTER
340 REM   T                  ´TIME´ RATIO (D1/S1)*100
350 REM
360 REM                           START PROGRAM
370 REM
380 REM
390 REM          INSTRUCTIONS
400 REM
410 PRINT
420 PRINT
430 PRINT
440 PRINT
450 PRINT "DO YOU WANT INSTRUCTIONS";:INPUT N$
460 IF N$<>"YES" THEN 610
470 PRINT"THE OBJECT OF THIS GAME IS TO MOVE YOUR CAR´*´"
480 PRINT" BEGINNING AT´S´ AND NAVIGATE THROUGH THE OBSTACLES"
490 PRINT"´!´&´-´ WALLS TO THE SPACE MARKED ´F´, YOU MUST LAND"
500 PRINT"ON THE SPACE MARKED ´F´ ON THE EXACT AMOUNT OF SPACES"
510 PRINT"THERE ARE NO DIAGONAL MOVES."
520 PRINT"THERE ARE NO RIGHT TO LEFT MOVES."
530 PRINT"DIRECTIONS NO.1 IS UP."
540 PRINT "DIRECTION NO.2 IS LEFT TO RIGHT"
550 PRINT"DIRECTION NO.3 IS DOWN."
560 PRINT
570 PRINT"SPEED IS THE NO. OF SPACES IN A GIVEN DIRECTION"
580 REM
590 REM                  INITIALATION
600 REM
610 DIM M(15,50)
620 A1=ASC("*")
630 A2=ASC("!")
640 A3=ASC(" ")
650 A4=ASC("S")
660 A5=ASC("F")
670 A6=ASC("-")
680 D1=0:S1=0
690 REM    *** NOTE - COURSE SET UP ROUTINE
700 FOR I=1 TO 10
710 FOR J=1 TO 42
720 R1=INT(RND(1)*1.2)
730 IF R1=0 THEN 760
740 M(I,J)=A2
750 GOTO 770
760 M(I,J)=A3
770 NEXT J
780 NEXT I
790 M(2,2)=A4
800 M(10,40)=A3
810 M(10,41)=A5
820 M(2,3)=A3
830 M(3,2)=A3
840 FOR I=1 TO 10:M(I,1)=A2:M(I,42)=A2:NEXT I
850 FOR J=1 TO 42:M(1,J)=A6:M(11,J)=A6:NEXT J
860 REM
870 REM          ** PRINTING ROUTINE **
880 REM
890 K=I:L=J
900 PRINT
910 FOR I=1 TO 11
920 FOR J=1 TO 42
930 PRINT CHR$(M(I,J));
940 NEXT J
950 PRINT
960 NEXT I
970 I=K:J=L
980 REM          88 NOTE- NEW COURSE OPTION**
990 IF D1>0 THEN 1080
1000 PRINT"OPTION :(A=CONTINUE,B=NEW COURSE,C=STOP)";
1010 INPUT N$
1020 IF N$="A" THEN 1080
1030 IF N$="B" THEN 670
1040 IF N$="C" THEN 1420
1050 PRINT"INVALID OPTION"
1060 GOTO 1000
1070 REM
1080 REM              ** MAIN PROGRAM BODY **
1090 REM
1100 PRINT"DIRECTION";:INPUT D:D=INT(ABS(D))
1110 IF D<1 THEN 1100
1111 IF D>3 THEN 1100
1120 PRINT:PRINT"SPEED";:INPUT S:S=INT(ABS(S))
1130 D1=D1+1:S1=S1+S:IF D1<>1 THEN 1160
1140 REM              ** NOTE - CAR STARTS AT POSITION 2,2
1150 J=2:I=2
1160 IF D=1 THEN 1190
1170 IF D=2 THEN 1230
1180 IF D=3 THEN 1270
1190 M(I,J)=A3:REM       ** WIPES OUT PREVIOUS CHARACTER **
1200 FOR C=1 TO S:I=ABS(I-1):IF M(I,J)=A2 THEN 1340
1210 IF M(I,J)=A6 THEN 1340
1215 NEXT C
1220 M(I,J)=A1: GOTO 1310
1230 M(I,J)=A3
1240 FOR C=1 TO S:J=J+1:IF M(I,J)=A2THEN 1340
1250 IF M(I,J)=A6 THEN 1340
1255 NEXT C
1260 M(I,J)=A1: GOTO 1310
1270 M(I,J)=A3
1280 FOR C=1 TO S: I=I+1:IF M(I,J)=A2 THEN 1340
1290 IF M(I,J)=A6 THEN 1340
1295 NEXT C
1300 M(I,J)=A1
1310 REM        ** NOTE - WINNING CHECK**
1320 IF M(10,41)<>A1 THEN 870
1330 GOTO 1360
1340 PRINT"ILLEGAL MOVE...... YOU LOSE!!":GOTO 1400
1350 REM
1360 REM          ** END OF REN ROUTINE **
1370 REM
1380 T=(D1/S1)*100
1390 PRINT "YOU WON!! AND YOUR TIME IS ";T
1400 PRINT:PRINT"DO YOU WISH TO PLAY AGAIN";:INPUT N$
1410 IF N$="YES" THEN 670
1420 END
```

Octrix

This is a card game for up to four players, or three players plus the computer. A deck of 32 cards is used with ace through eight in each of the four suits. All 32 of the cards are dealt out at the beginning of the game, eight to each player. On each hand, each player discards one card depending on the rules of the game (see the rules at the beginning of the sample game) either the high card discard or the low card discard wins that trick. After eight tricks a new hand is dealt and play proceeds as before. Perhaps the easiest way to learn Octrix is to play a few games with you and the computer or with several people and the computer. Observe what happens and before long you'll be able to work out a reasonable strategy for playing the game.

Octrix was written by Rogers Hamilton.

```
RUN
                                  OCTRIX
                            CREATIVE COMPUTING
                          MORRISTOWN, NEW JERSEY



TEACH GAME(Y OR N)? Y
  THIS  IS A GAME CALLED OCTRIX.  EACH PLAYER IS DEALT 8
CARDS RANGING FROM ACE THROUGH EIGHT.  THE CARDS ARE
RANKED ACCORDING TO BRIDGE SUITS WITH THE ACE OF CLUBS THE
LOWEST AND THE EIGHT OF SPADES HIGHEST.  THE OBJECT IS TO
WIN AS MANY OF THE EIGHT TRICKS AS POSSIBLE.  EACH TRICK
PLAYED DETERMINES THE PLAY OF THE NEXT TRICK.  IF THE HIGH
AND LOW CARDS PLAYED MATCH COLOR THE NEXT TRICK WILL BE
HIGH AND IF THEY DO NOT MATCH IT WILL BE LOW.  IT IS IM-
PORTANT TO SET STRATEGY TO WIN CONSECUTIVE TRICKS IN THAT
SCORING IS 1 POINT PER TRICK, 4 FOR TWO IN A ROW,9 FOR 3, UP
TO 64 FOR ALL EIGHT.

    RESPOND TO THE INPUT PROMPT WITH THE CARD YOU WANT TO
PLAY IN A TWO CHARACTER FORMAT WITH THE VALUE(A-8) AS THE
FIRST CHARACTER, AND SUIT(C,D,H,S) AS THE SECOND CHARACTER.
    (TO SEE THE REMAINING CARDS, ENTER A'P' IN
    RESPONSE TO THE 'WHAT CARD' QUERY)

THAT'S IT, GOOD LUCK!!
HOW MANY POINTS (0 ENTRY GIVES STANDARD 88)? 0
HOW MANY PLAYERS? 3
ENTER PLAYER'S NAME? JEFF
ENTER PLAYER'S NAME? BRUCE
ENTER PLAYER'S NAME? STEVE
SHOULD I PLAY TOO(Y OR N)? Y
                JEFF'S HAND                      BRUCE'S HAND                      STEVE'S HAND                   COMPUTER'S HAND
       CLB    DIA    HRT    SPD          CLB    DIA    HRT    SPD          CLB    DIA    HRT    SPD          CLB    DIA    HRT    SPD
!A    !      !      !      !*     !!A   !      !*     !      !      !!A   !      !      !*     !      !!A   !*     !      !      !      !A
!2    !      !*     !*     !      !!2   !      !      !      !*     !!2   !*     !      !      !      !!2   !      !      !      !      !2
!3    !      !      !      !      !!3   !*     !      !      !      !!3   !      !      !      !      !!3   !      !*     !*     !*     !3
!4    !*     !      !      !      !!4   !      !      !      !      !!4   !      !      !*     !*     !!4   !      !*     !      !      !4
!5    !      !      !      !*     !!5   !*     !      !      !      !!5   !      !*     !      !      !!5   !      !      !*     !      !5
!6    !      !*     !      !      !!6   !*     !      !      !      !!6   !      !      !      !*     !!6   !      !      !*     !      !6
!7    !*     !      !      !      !!7   !      !*     !*     !      !!7   !      !      !      !*     !!7   !      !      !      !      !7
!8    !      !      !      !*     !!8   !      !      !*     !      !!8   !*     !      !      !      !!8   !      !*     !      !      !8

TRICK # 1 (HIGH CARD WINS)
WHAT CARD, JEFF
████
WHAT CARD, BRUCE
████
WHAT CARD, STEVE
████
JEFF PLAYED THE EIGHT OF SPADES
BRUCE PLAYED THE FIVE OF CLUBS
STEVE PLAYED THE FIVE OF DIAMONDS
I PLAYED THE SIX OF HEARTS
JEFF WON TRICK # 1
TRICK # 2 (HIGH CARD WINS)
WHAT CARD, JEFF
████
WHAT CARD, BRUCE
████
WHAT CARD, STEVE
████
JEFF PLAYED THE FIVE OF SPADES
BRUCE PLAYED THE TWO OF SPADES
STEVE PLAYED THE FOUR OF SPADES
I PLAYED THE EIGHT OF DIAMONDS
I WON TRICK # 2
TRICK # 3 (LOW CARD WINS)
WHAT CARD, JEFF
████
WHAT CARD, BRUCE
████
WHAT CARD, STEVE
████
JEFF PLAYED THE FOUR OF CLUBS
BRUCE PLAYED THE SIX OF CLUBS
STEVE PLAYED THE SIX OF SPADES
I PLAYED THE ACE OF CLUBS
I WON TRICK # 3
TRICK # 4 (HIGH CARD WINS)
WHAT CARD, JEFF
████
```

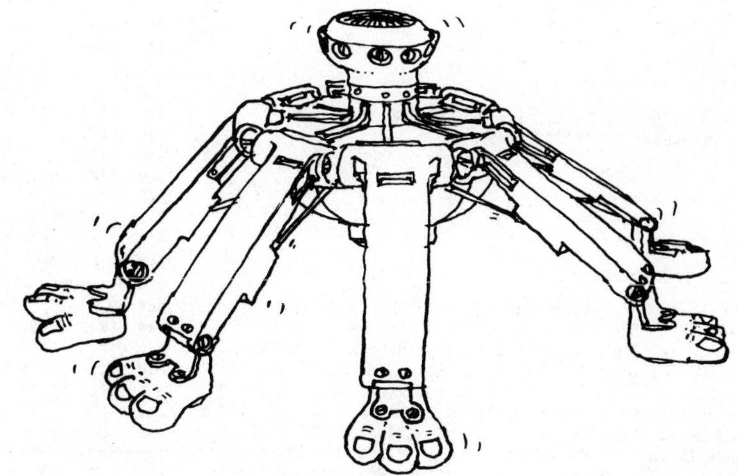

```
                JEFF'S HAND                             BRUCE'S HAND                            STEVE'S HAND                           COMPUTER'S HAND
          CLB     DIA     HRT    SPD            CLB     DIA     HRT    SPD            CLB     DIA     HRT    SPD            CLB     DIA     HRT    SPD
!A        !       !       !      !* !!A         !       !*      !      !  !!A         !       !       !*     !  !!A         !       !       !      !  !A
!2        !       !*      !*     !  !!2         !       !       !      !  !!2         !*      !       !      !  !!2         !       !       !      !  !2
!3        !       !       !      !  !!3         !*      !       !      !  !!3         !       !       !      !  !!3         !       !*      !*     !* !3
!4        !       !       !      !  !!4         !       !       !      !  !!4         !       !       !*     !  !!4         !       !*      !      !  !4
!5        !       !       !      !  !!5         !       !       !      !  !!5         !       !       !      !  !!5         !       !       !*     !  !5
!6        !       !*      !      !  !!6         !       !       !      !  !!6         !       !       !      !  !!6         !       !       !      !  !6
!7        !*      !       !      !  !!7         !       !*      !*     !  !!7         !       !       !      !* !!7         !       !       !      !  !7
!8        !       !       !      !  !!8         !       !       !*     !  !!8         !*      !       !      !  !!8         !       !       !      !  !8
```

```
WHAT CARD, JEFF
████
WHAT CARD, BRUCE
████
WHAT CARD, STEVE
████
JEFF PLAYED THE SIX OF DIAMONDS
BRUCE PLAYED THE EIGHT OF HEARTS
STEVE PLAYED THE FOUR OF HEARTS
I PLAYED THE FIVE OF HEARTS
BRUCE WON TRICK # 4
TRICK # 5 (HIGH CARD WINS)
WHAT CARD, JEFF
████
WHAT CARD, BRUCE
████
WHAT CARD, STEVE
████
JEFF PLAYED THE SEVEN OF CLUBS
BRUCE PLAYED THE SEVEN OF HEARTS
STEVE PLAYED THE EIGHT OF CLUBS
I PLAYED THE FOUR OF DIAMONDS
STEVE WON TRICK # 5
TRICK # 6 (LOW CARD WINS)
WHAT CARD, JEFF
████
WHAT CARD, BRUCE
████
WHAT CARD, STEVE
████
JEFF PLAYED THE TWO OF HEARTS
BRUCE PLAYED THE THREE OF CLUBS
STEVE PLAYED THE ACE OF HEARTS
I PLAYED THE THREE OF SPADES
STEVE WON TRICK # 6
TRICK # 7 (LOW CARD WINS)
WHAT CARD, JEFF
████
WHAT CARD, BRUCE
████
WHAT CARD, STEVE
████
JEFF PLAYED THE TWO OF DIAMONDS
BRUCE PLAYED THE ACE OF DIAMONDS
STEVE PLAYED THE SEVEN OF SPADES
I PLAYED THE THREE OF DIAMONDS
BRUCE WON TRICK # 7
JEFF PLAYED THE ACE OF SPADES
BRUCE PLAYED THE SEVEN OF DIAMONDS
STEVE PLAYED THE TWO OF CLUBS
I PLAYED THE THREE OF HEARTS
JEFF WON TRICK # 8
THAT HAND JEFF SCORED  2 POINTS FOR A 2 TOTAL
BRUCE SCORED  2 POINTS FOR A 2 TOTAL
STEVE SCORED  4 POINTS FOR A 4 TOTAL
I SCORED  4 POINTS FOR A 4 TOTAL
                JEFF'S HAND                             BRUCE'S HAND                            STEVE'S HAND
          CLB     DIA     HRT    SPD            CLB     DIA     HRT    SPD            CLB     DIA     HRT    SPD
!A        !       !       !*     !  !!A         !       !       !      !  !!A         !       !       !      !* !!A
!2        !       !       !      !  !!2         !       !*      !      !  !!2         !       !       !*     !* !!2
!3        !       !       !*     !  !!3         !       !       !      !* !!3         !*      !       !      !  !!3
!4        !       !*      !      !  !!4         !       !       !*     !* !!4         !       !       !      !  !!4
!5        !*      !       !      !  !!5         !       !       !      !  !!5         !       !       !*     !  !!5
!6        !*      !       !      !* !!6         !       !       !*     !  !!6         !       !       !      !  !!6
!7        !       !       !      !  !!7         !*      !       !*     !  !!7         !       !*      !      !* !!7
!8        !*      !       !*     !  !!8         !       !*      !      !  !!8         !       !       !      !* !!8

TRICK # 1 (HIGH CARD WINS)
WHAT CARD, JEFF
████
WHAT CARD, BRUCE
████
WHAT CARD, STEVE
████
JEFF PLAYED THE SIX OF CLUBS
BRUCE PLAYED THE FOUR OF SPADES
STEVE PLAYED THE EIGHT OF SPADES
I PLAYED THE SIX OF DIAMONDS
STEVE WON TRICK # 1
```

```
LIST
1 PRINT TAB(27)"OCTRIX"
2 PRINT TAB(20)"CREATIVE COMPUTING"
3 PRINT TAB(18)"MORRISTOWN, NEW JERSEY"
5 PRINT
6 PRINT
7 PRINT
10 DIM A(32),P(4,9),C$(255),Q(4,11),T$(72)
11 DIM N$(72),Y(72)
40 RESTORE
50 FOR X=0 TO7
60 READY$(X)
70 NEXT X
80 FOR X=0 TO 3
90 READ X$(X)
100 NEXT X
110 DATA"ACE","TWO","THREE","FOUR","FIVE","SIX","SEVEN","EIGHT"
120 DATA"CLUBS","DIAMONDS","HEARTS","SPADES"
130 FOR X=0 TO 9
140 READ T$(X)
150 DATA "A","2","3","4","5","6","7","8","LOW","HIGH"
160 NEXT X
170 PRINT"TEACH GAME(Y OR N)";
180 INPUT Z$
190 IF Z$<>"Y" THEN 380
200 PRINT"  THIS  IS A GAME CALLED OCTRIX.  EACH PLAYER IS DEALT 8"
210 PRINT"CARDS RANGING FROM ACE THROUGH EIGHT.  THE CARDS ARE"
220 PRINT"RANKED ACCORDING TO BRIDGE SUITS WITH THE ACE OF CLUBS THE"
230 PRINT"LOWEST AND THE EIGHT OF SPADES HIGHEST.  THE OBJECT IS TO"
240 PRINT"WIN AS MANY OF THE EIGHT TRICKS AS POSSIBLE.  EACH TRICK "
250 PRINT"PLAYED DETERMINES THE PLAY OF THE NEXT TRICK.  IF THE HIGH "
260 PRINT"AND LOW CARDS PLAYED MATCH COLOR THE NEXT TRICK WILL BE "
270 PRINT"HIGH AND IF THEY DO NOT MATCH IT WILL BE LOW.  IT IS IM-"
280 PRINT"PORTANT TO SET STRATEGY TO WIN CONSECUTIVE TRICKS IN THAT "
290 PRINT"SCORING IS 1 POINT PER TRICK, 4 FOR TWO IN A ROW,9 FOR 3, UP"
300 PRINT"TO 64 FOR ALL EIGHT."
305 PRINT
310 PRINT"     RESPOND TO THE INPUT PROMPT WITH THE CARD YOU WANT TO"
320 PRINT"PLAY IN A TWO CHARACTER FORMAT WITH THE VALUE(A-8) AS THE "
330 PRINT"FIRST CHARACTER, AND SUIT(C,D,H,S) AS THE SECOND CHARACTER."
340 PRINT"    (TO SEE THE REMAINING CARDS, ENTER A'P' IN"
350 PRINT"    RESPONSE TO THE 'WHAT CARD' QUERY)"
360 PRINT
370 PRINT"THAT'S IT, GOOD LUCK!!"
380 REM
390 FOR X=1 TO 15
400 READ Z
410 M$=M$+CHR$(Z)
420 NEXT X
430 DATA 35,35,35,35,13,72,72,72,72,13,73,73,73,73,13
440 Z9=88
450 PRINT"HOW MANY POINTS (0 ENTRY GIVES STANDARD 88)";
460  INPUT Z
470 IF Z=0 THEN 490
480 Z9=Z
490 FOR X=0 TO 31
500 A(X)=X
510 NEXT X
520 PRINT"HOW MANY PLAYERS";
530 INPUT N
540 N=INT(N)
550 IF N>4 THEN 570
560 IF N>0 THEN 590
570 PRINT"ONLY ONE TO FOUR PLAYERS ALLOWED, RE-ENTER"
580 GOTO 520
590 FOR X=0 TO N-1
600 Q(X,0)=0
610 PRINT"ENTER PLAYER'S NAME";
620 INPUT N$(X)
630 Y=LEN(N$(X))
640 FOR Z=1 TO Y
650 T$=MID$(N$(X),1,Z-1)
660 IF T$=" " THEN 680
670 NEXT Z
680 IF Z>1 THEN 710
690 PRINT"DON'T START NAME WITH SPACE,RE-";
700 GOTO 610
710 S$(X)=MID$(N$(X),1,Z-1)
```

```
720 NEXT X
730 FOR J=0 TO 127
740 C$(J)=" "
750 NEXT J
760 IF N=4 THEN 850
770 IF N=1 THEN 810
780 PRINT"SHOULD I PLAY TOO(Y OR N)";
790 INPUT Z$
800 IF Z$<>"Y" THEN 850
810 S$(N)="COMPUTER"
820 N$(N)="I"
830 Q(N,0)=0
840 N=N+1
850 FOR I=0 TO 31
860 X=A(I)
870 Y=INT(RND(1)*(32-I)+I)
880 A(I)=A(Y)
890 A(Y)=X
900 NEXT I
910 FOR Y=0 TO 7
920 FOR X=0 TO N-1
930 P(X,Y)=A(Y*4+X)
940 C$(X*32+P(X,Y))="*"
950 NEXT X
960 NEXT Y
970 H=1
980 GOSUB 1680
990 FOR R=1 TO 7
1000 PRINT"TRICK #";R;"("T$(8+H)" CARD WINS)"
1010 FOR X=0 TO N-1
1020 IF S$(X)="COMPUTER"THEN 2090
1030 Z=Z*Z
1040 PRINT"WHAT CARD, "S$(X)
1050 PRINT M$;
1060 INPUT E$
1070 IF E$<>"P" THEN 1100
1080 GOSUB 1680
1090 GOTO 1040
1100 Y=LEN(E$)
1110 IF Y=2 THEN 1140
1120 PRINT"BAD INPUT,RE-ENTER"
1130 GOTO 1050
1140 Y$=MID$(E$,1,1)
1150 Z$=MID$(E$,2,1)
1160 IF VAL(Y$)>0 THEN 1190
1170 IF Y$<>"A" THEN 1120
1180 Y$="1"
1190 Y=VAL(Y$)
1200 IF Y=0 THEN 1120
1210 IF Y>8 THEN 1120
1220 Z=0
1230 Q(X,10)=0
1240 IF Z$="C" THEN 1320
1250 Z=3
1260 IF Z$="S" THEN 1320
1270 Q(X,10)=1
1280 Z=1
1290 IF Z$="D" THEN 1320
1300 Z=2
1310 IF Z$<>"H" THEN 1120
1320 Y=(Y-1)*4+Z
1330 IF C$(X*32+Y)<>"*" THEN 1120
1340 Q(X,9)=Y
1350 NEXT X
1360 GOSUB 1880
1370 NEXT R
1380 FOR X=0 TO N-1
1390 FOR Z=0 TO 31
1400 IF C$(32*X+Z)="*" THEN 1430
1410 NEXT Z
1420 PRINT"BAD SCAN"
1430 C$(32*X+Z)=" "
1440 Q(X,9)=Z
1450 NEXT X
1460 R=8
1470 GOSUB 1880
1480 H1=0
1490 PRINT"THAT HAND ";
1500 FOR X=0 TO N-1
1510 Q(X,9)=0
1520 Y=0
1530 Z=0
1540 FOR R=1 TO 8
1550 Z=Z+Q(X,R)
1560 Q(X,R)=0
1570 IF Q(X,R+1)<>0 THEN 1600
1580 Y=Y+Z*Z
1590 Z=0
1600 NEXT R
1610 Q(X,0)=Q(X,0)+Y
1620 PRINT N$(X)" SCORED ";Y;"POINTS FOR A";Q(X,0);"TOTAL"
1630 IF Q(H1,0)>Q(X,0) THEN 1650
1640 H1=X
1650 NEXT X
1660 IF Q(H1,0)>=Z9 THEN 2450
1670 GOTO 850
1680 FOR S=0 TO N-1
1681 S8=0
1682 S9=23-(LEN(S$(S))+7)
1684 IF INT(S9/2)*2<>S9 THEN S8=1
1686 S9=INT(S9/2)
1690 PRINT SPC(9+S9);S$(S);"'S HAND";SPC(S9+S8);
1700 NEXT S
1710 PRINT
1720 FOR S=0 TO N-1
1730 PRINT"        CLB    DIA    HRT   SPD";
1740 NEXT S
1750 PRINT
1760 FOR S=0 TO 7
1770 FOR Y=0 TO N-1
1780 Z=Y*32+S*4
1790 PRINT"!";T$(S);"      !";C$(Z);"      !";C$(Z+1);"      !";C$(Z+2);
1791 PRINT"      !";C$(Z+3);" !";
1800 NEXT Y
1810 PRINT T$(S)
1820 NEXT S
1830 PRINT
1840 RETURN
1880 L1=0:H1=0
1890 FOR X=0 TO N-1
1900 Y=INT(Q(X,9)/4)
1910 Z=Q(X,9)-Y*4
1920 PRINT N$(X)" PLAYED THE "Y$(Y)" OF "X$(Z)
1930 C$(X*32+Q(X,9))=" "
1940 IF Q(X,9)>Q(L1,9) THEN 1960
1950 L1=X
1960 IF Q(X,9)<Q(H1,9) THEN 1980
1970 H1=X
1980 NEXT X
1990 IF H=1 THEN 2030
2000 Q(L1,R)=1
2010 PRINT N$(L1)" WON TRICK #";R
2020 GOTO 2050
2030 Q(H1,R)=1
2040 PRINT N$(H1)" WON TRICK #";R
2050 H=0
2060 IF Q(L1,10)<>Q(H1,10) THEN 2080
2070 H=1
2080 RETURN
2090 L1=0:L2=0:H1=0:H2=0
2100 FOR S=0 TO N-2
2110 FOR S1=0 TO 7
2120 IF P(S,S1)>P(L1,L2) THEN 2160
2130 IF C$(S*43+P(S,S1))=" " THEN 2160
2140 L1=S
2150 L2=S1
2160 IF P(S,S1)<P(H1,H2) THEN 2200
2170 IF C$(S*32+P(S,S1))=" " THEN 2200
2180 H1=S
2190 H2=S1
2200 NEXT S1
2210 NEXT S
2220 FOR S=R-1 TO 7
2230 IF H=1 THEN 2280
2240 IF P(N-1,S)<P(L1,L2) THEN 2260
2250 GOTO 2290
2260 IF RND(1)>.3 THEN 2380
2270 GOTO 2300
2280 IF P(N-1,S)>P(H1,H2) THEN 2260
2290 NEXT S
2300 H1=32
2310 Y=INT(RND(1)*16+H*16)
2320 FOR S1=R-1 TO 7
2330 L1=ABS(P(N-1,S1)-Y)
2340 IF H1<L1 THEN 2370
2350 H1=L1
2360 S=S1
2370 NEXT S1
2380 Q(X,9)=P(N-1,S)
2390 P(N-1,S)=P(N-1,R-1)
2400 Z=Q(X,9)-(INT(Q(X,9)/4)*4)
2410 IF Z<2 THEN 2430
2420 Z=ABS(Z-3)
2430 Q(X,10)=Z
2440 GOTO 1360
2450 IF H1>N-2 THEN 2510
2460 FOR X=H1+1 TO N-1
2470 IF Q(H1,0)>Q(X,0) THEN 2500
2480 PRINT"GAME TIED AFTER REGULATION, ENTERING SUDDEN DEATH"
2490 GOTO 850
2500 NEXT X
2510 PRINT N$(H1)"WON THE GAME, CONGRATULATIONS "S$(H1)
2520 END
Ok
```

Pasart

Description:

This program generates artistic patterns based on Pascal's triangle.

Comments:

Pascal's triangle is one of the most famous number patterns in mathematics. The triangle is very easy to construct. The first two rows consist of only 1's. Each of the subsequent have a 1 at either end of the row, but all other numbers in the pattern are the sum of the two numbers to the right and left in the row above. An example, illustrating the first 6 rows of the triangle, is shown below:

```
          1
        1   1
      1   2   1
    1   3   3   1
  1   4   6   4   1
1   5   10  10  5   1
```

The program provides the user with three options during the course of a RUN.

They are:

1. A single "Pascal's triangle"
2. Two "Pascal's triangles"
3. Four "Pascal's triangles"

A user may also specify the size of the array and the multiples of the number to be eliminated.

Option 1 simply allows a user to examine an artistic picture of the relative positions of the multiples of any number in the array. The apex of the array will appear in the upper left corner of the page.

An example of how the machine uses a "triangle" to create a design based on eliminating the multiples of two is shown below.

```
1 1 1  1              * * * *
1 2 3  4              *   *
1 3 6  10             * *
1 4 10 20             *
Before Printing       After Printing
```

Option 2 allows a user to create a picture based on two Pascal's triangles in opposite corners of a square array. An example of how the machine uses two Pascal's triangles in the corners of a square to create a design based on eliminating the multiples of 2 is shown below:

```
1 1 1 1 0             * * * *
1 2 3 0 1             *   *   *
1 3 0 3 1             * *   * *
1 0 3 2 1             *   *   *
0 1 1 1 1               * * * *
Before Printing       After Printing
```

Option 3 creates a design based on Pascal's triangles in the four corners of a square. An example of how the machine uses four Pascal's triangles in the corners of an 8x8 array to create an artistic design based on eliminating the multiples of 2 is shown below.

```
1 1 1 1 1 1 1 1       * * * * * * * *
1 2 3     3 2 1       *   *     *   *
1 3         3 1       * *         * *
1             1       *             *
1 3         3 1       * *         * *
1 2 3     3 2 1       *   *     *   *
1 1 1 1 1 1 1 1       * * * * * * * *
Before Printing       After Printing
```

Approximately 5 minutes of terminal time is required to print a design with dimensions of 36x36.

PASART and this description written by Charles A. Lund. They first appeared in *Creative Computing*, Mar/Apr 1977.

```
RUN
                              PASART
                         CREATIVE COMPUTING
                        MORRISTOWN  NEW JERSEY


THIS PROGRAM CREATES ARTIST DESIGNS BASED ON PASCAL'S TRIANGLE.
YOU HAVE 3 BASIC TYPES OF DESIGNS TO SELECT FROM:
1. A SINGLE PASCAL'S TRIANGLE (PLAYED WITH AN ARTISTIC FLARE)
2. TWO 'ARTSY' PASCAL'S TRIANGLES PRINTED BACK TO BACK
3. FOUR 'ARTSY' TRIANGLES IN THE CORNER OF
   A SQUARE ARRAY.
WHAT'S YOUR PLEASURE? 1, 2 OR 3? 2
WHICH MULTIPLES DO YOU WANT REPRESENTED WITH BLANKS? 2
HOW MANY ROWS AND COLUMS IN THE ARRAY (36 IS MAXIMUM)? 36
* * * * * * * * * * * * * * * * * * * * * * * * * * * * * * * * * * * *
*   *   *   *   *   *   *   *   *   *   *   *   *   *   *   *   *     *
* *     * *     * *     * *     * *     * *     * *     * *     *     *
*       *       *       *       *       *       *       *         * * *
* * * *         * * * *         * * * *         * * * *               *
*   *           *   *           *   *           *   *               * *
* *             * *             * *             * *               *   *
*               *               *               *               * * * *
* * * * * * * *                 * * * * * * * *               *       *
*   *   *   *                   *   *   *                   * *     * *
* *     * *                     * *                       *   *   *   *
*       *                       *                       * * * * * * * *
* * * *                                               *               *
*   *                                                 *             * *
* *                                                   *           *   *
*                                                   * *         * * * *
* * * * * * * * * * * *                               *       *       *
*   *   *   *   *   *                               * *     * *     * *
* *     * *     * *                               *   *   *   *   *   *
*       *       *                               * * * * * * * * * * * *
* * * *         * *                                                   *
*   *           *                                                   * *
* *             *                                                 *   *
*               *                                               * * * *
* * * * * * * *                       *                       *       *
*   *   *   *                       * *                     * *     * *
* *     * *                   *   *   *                   *   *   *   *
*       *               * * * * * * * *                 * * * * * * * *
* * * *               *               *               *               *
*   *               * *             * *             * *             * *
* *               *   *           *   *           *   *           *   *
*               * * * *         * * * *         * * * *         * * * *
* * *         *       *       *       *       *       *       *       *
*     *     * *     * *     * *     * *     * *     * *     * *     * *
*     *   *   *   *   *   *   *   *   *   *   *   *   *   *   *   *   *
* * * * * * * * * * * * * * * * * * * * * * * * * * * * * * * * * * * *
OK
```

PASART
CREATIVE COMPUTING
MORRISTOWN   NEW JERSEY

```
THIS PROGRAM CREATES ARTIST DESIGNS BASED ON PASCAL'S TRIANGLE.
YOU HAVE 3 BASIC TYPES OF DESIGNS TO SELECT FROM:
1. A SINGLE PASCAL'S TRIANGLE (PLAYED WITH AN ARTISTIC FLARE)
2. TWO 'ARTSY' PASCAL'S TRIANGLES PRINTED BACK TO BACK
3. FOUR 'ARTSY' TRIANGLES IN THE CORNER OF
   A SQUARE ARRAY.
WHAT'S YOUR PLEASURE? 1, 2 OR 3? 1
WHICH MULTIPLES DO YOU WANT REPRESENTED WITH BLANKS? 2
HOW MANY ROWS AND COLUMS IN THE ARRAY (36 IS MAXIMUM)? 36
* * * * * * * * * * * * * * * * * * * * * * * * * * * * * * * * * * * *
*   *   *   *   *   *   *   *   *   *   *   *   *   *   *   *   *   *
* *     * *     * *     * *     * *     * *     * *     * *     * *
*       *       *       *       *       *       *       *       *
* * * *         * * * *         * * * *         * * * *         * * * *
*   *           *   *           *   *           *   *           *   *
* *             * *             * *             * *             * *
*               *               *               *               *
* * * * * * * *                 * * * * * * * *
*   *   *   *                   *   *   *
* *     * *                     * *
*       *                       *
* * * *
*   *
* *
*
* * * * * * * * * * * *
*   *   *   *   *   *
* *     * *     * *
*       *       *
* * * *         * *
*   *           *
* *             *
*               *
* * * * * * * *
*   *   *   *
* *     * *
*       *
* * * *
*   *
* *
*
* * * * * * * *
*   *   *   *
* *     * *
*       *
```

```
WHAT'S YOUR PLEASURE? 1, 2 OR 3? 3
WHICH MULTIPLES DO YOU WANT REPRESENTED WITH BLANKS? 3
HOW MANY ROWS AND COLUMS IN THE ARRAY (36 IS MAXIMUM)? 36
* * * * * * * * * * * * * * * * * * * * * * * * * * * * * * * * * * * *
* *   * *   * *   * *   * *   * *     * *   * *   * *   * *   * *   * *
*     *     *     *     *     *         *     *     *     *     *     *
* * * * * *       * * * * * *             * * * * * *       * * * * * *
* *   * *         * *   * *                 * *   * *         * *   * *
*     *           *     *                     *     *           *     *
* * *             * * *                         * * *             * * *
* *               * *                             * *               * *
*                 *                                 *                 *
* * * * * * * * *                                     * * * * * * * * *
* *   * *   * *                                         * *   * *   * *
*     *     *                                             *     *     *
* * * * * *                                                 * * * * * *
* *   * *                                                     * *   * *
*     *                                                         *     *
* * *                                                             * * *
* *                                                                 * *
*                                                                     *
*                                                                     *
* *                                                                 * *
* * *                                                             * * *
*     *                                                         *     *
* *   * *                                                     * *   * *
* * * * * *                                                 * * * * * *
*     *     *                                             *     *     *
* *   * *   * *                                         * *   * *   * *
* * * * * * * * *                                     * * * * * * * * *
*                 *                                 *                 *
* *               * *                             * *               * *
* * *             * * *                         * * *             * * *
*     *           *     *                     *     *           *     *
* *   * *         * *   * *                 * *   * *         * *   * *
* * * * * *       * * * * * *             * * * * * *       * * * * * *
*     *     *     *     *     *         *     *     *     *     *     *
* *   * *   * *   * *   * *   * *     * *   * *   * *   * *   * *   * *
* * * * * * * * * * * * * * * * * * * * * * * * * * * * * * * * * * * *
```

PASART
CREATIVE COMPUTING
MORRISTOWN   NEW JERSEY

```
THIS PROGRAM CREATES ARTIST DESIGNS BASED ON PASCAL'S TRIANGLE.
YOU HAVE 3 BASIC TYPES OF DESIGNS TO SELECT FROM:
1. A SINGLE PASCAL'S TRIANGLE (PLAYED WITH AN ARTISTIC FLARE)
2. TWO 'ARTSY' PASCAL'S TRIANGLES PRINTED BACK TO BACK
3. FOUR 'ARTSY' TRIANGLES IN THE CORNER OF
   A SQUARE ARRAY.
WHAT'S YOUR PLEASURE? 1, 2 OR 3? 3
WHICH MULTIPLES DO YOU WANT REPRESENTED WITH BLANKS? 10
HOW MANY ROWS AND COLUMS IN THE ARRAY (36 IS MAXIMUM)? 36
* * * * * * * * * * * * * * * * * * * * * * * * * * * * * * * * * * * *
* * * * * * * * *   * * * * * * *     * * * * * * *   * * * * * * * * *
* * *   * * * * * * * * * *   *         *   * * * * * * * * * *   * * *
* *     * * *   *   * * *                     * * *   *   * * *     * *
* * * *   *     * * * *                         * * * *     *   * * * *
* * * * * * * * * * * * *                     * * * * * * * * * * * * *
* * * *   * * * * * * *                         * * * * * * *   * * * *
* * *     * * * *   *                             *   * * * *     * * *
* * * * * * * *                                         * * * * * * * *
*   *   * * *                                             * * *   *   *
* * * * * * * *                                         * * * * * * * *
* * * * * * *                                             * * * * * * *
* * * *   *                                                 *   * * * *
* * *                                                             * * *
* *                                                                 * *
* * *                                                             * * *
* *                                                                 * *
*                                                                     *
*                                                                     *
* *                                                                 * *
* * *                                                             * * *
* *                                                                 * *
* * *                                                             * * *
* * * *   *                                                 *   * * * *
* * * * * * *                                             * * * * * * *
* * * * * * * *                                         * * * * * * * *
*   *   * * *                                             * * *   *   *
* * * * * * * *                                         * * * * * * * *
* * *     * * * *   *                             *   * * * *     * * *
* * * *   * * * * * * *                         * * * * * * *   * * * *
* * * * * * * * * * * * *                     * * * * * * * * * * * * *
* * * *   *     * * * *                         * * * *     *   * * * *
* *     * * *   *   * * *                     * * *   *   * * *     * *
* * *   * * * * * * * * * *   *         *   * * * * * * * * * *   * * *
* * * * * * * * *   * * * * * * *     * * * * * * *   * * * * * * * * *
* * * * * * * * * * * * * * * * * * * * * * * * * * * * * * * * * * * *
```

```
WHAT'S YOUR PLEASURE? 1, 2 OR 3? 1
WHICH MULTIPLES DO YOU WANT REPRESENTED WITH BLANKS? 10
HOW MANY ROWS AND COLUMS IN THE ARRAY (36 IS MAXIMUM)? 36
* * * * * * * * * * * * * * * * * * * * * * * * * * * * * * * * * * * *
* * * * * * * * *   * * * * * * * * *   * * * * * * * * *   * * * * * *
* * *   * * * * * * * * * *   * * *     * * *   * * * * * * * * * *   *
* *     * * *   *   * * *     * *       * *     * * *   *   * * *     *
* * * *   *     * * * *       * * * * * *       * * * *     *   * * * *
* * * * * * * * * * * * * * * * * * * *         * * * * * * * * * * * *
* * * *   * * * * * * * * *   * * * *           * * * * *   * * * *   *
* * *     * * * *   * * *     * * *             * * * *     * * *     *
* * * * * * * *     * *       * * * * * * * * *   * *
*   *   * * *       *         * *   *   *   * * *   *
* * * * * * * * * * * * * * *   * *     *   *
* * * * * * * * *   * * * *     *   * *
* * * *   * * *     * * *       * *
* * *     * *       * *
* *       *         *
* * * * * * * * * *
* * * * * * * * * * * * *
* * *   * * * * *   *   *
* *     * * *   * *   *
*       * *     *     *
* * * * *       * * *
* * * *         *
* * *           * * *
* *             * *
* * * * * * * *   *
* * * * * * * * *
* * * * * * * * * *
* * *   * * * *
* * * *   * *
*   *     *
* * * * * * * *
* * * *   * * *
* * * * * * * *
* * *   * * *
* *     * *
* * * * * * * *
```

```
THIS PROGRAM CREATES ARTIST DESIGNS BASED ON PASCAL'S TRIANGLE.
YOU HAVE 3 BASIC TYPES OF DESIGNS TO SELECT FROM:
1. A SINGLE PASCAL'S TRIANGLE (PLAYED WITH AN ARTISTIC FLARE)
2. TWO 'ARTSY' PASCAL'S TRIANGLES PRINTED BACK TO BACK
3. FOUR 'ARTSY' TRIANGLES IN THE CORNER OF
   A SQUARE ARRAY.
WHAT'S YOUR PLEASURE? 1, 2 OR 3? 3
WHICH MULTIPLES DO YOU WANT REPRESENTED WITH BLANKS? 17
HOW MANY ROWS AND COLUMS IN THE ARRAY (36 IS MAXIMUM)? 36
* * * * * * * * * * * * * * * * * * * * * * * * * * * * * * * * * * * *
* * * * * * * * * * * * * * * *         * * * * * * * * * * * * * * * *
* * * * * * * * * * * * * * *             * * * * * * * * * * * * * * *
* * * * * * * * * * * * * *                 * * * * * * * * * * * * * *
* * * * * * * * * * * * *                     * * * * * * * * * * * * *
* * * * * * * * * * * *                         * * * * * * * * * * * *
* * * * * * * * * * *                             * * * * * * * * * * *
* * * * * * * * * *                                 * * * * * * * * * *
* * * * * * * * *                                     * * * * * * * * *
* * * * * * * *                                         * * * * * * * *
* * * * * * *                                             * * * * * * *
* * * * * *                                                 * * * * * *
* * * * *                                                     * * * * *
* * * *                                                         * * * *
* * *                                                             * * *
* *                                                                 * *
*                                                                     *
*                                                                     *
*                                                                     *
*                                                                     *
* *                                                                 * *
* * *                                                             * * *
* * * *                                                         * * * *
* * * * *                                                     * * * * *
* * * * * *                                                 * * * * * *
* * * * * * *                                             * * * * * * *
* * * * * * * *                                         * * * * * * * *
* * * * * * * * *                                     * * * * * * * * *
* * * * * * * * * *                                 * * * * * * * * * *
* * * * * * * * * * *                             * * * * * * * * * * *
* * * * * * * * * * * *                         * * * * * * * * * * * *
* * * * * * * * * * * * *                     * * * * * * * * * * * * *
* * * * * * * * * * * * * *                 * * * * * * * * * * * * * *
* * * * * * * * * * * * * * *             * * * * * * * * * * * * * * *
* * * * * * * * * * * * * * * *         * * * * * * * * * * * * * * * *
* * * * * * * * * * * * * * * * * * * * * * * * * * * * * * * * * * * *
```

```
LIST

2 PRINT TAB(24);"PASART"
4 PRINT TAB(18);"CREATIVE COMPUTING"
6 PRINT TAB(16);"MORRISTOWN   NEW JERSEY"
8 PRINT:PRINT:PRINT
20 DIM P(36,36)
22 FOR B1=1 TO 36
24 FOR B2=1 TO 36
26 P(B1,B2)=0
28 NEXT B2
30 NEXT B1
40 PRINT "THIS PROGRAM CREATES ARTIST DESIGNS BASED ON PASCAL'S TRIAN";
42 PRINT "GLE."
50 PRINT "YOU HAVE 3 BASIC TYPES OF DESIGNS TO SELECT FROM:"
60 PRINT "1. A SINGLE PASCAL'S TRIANGLE (PLAYED WITH AN ARTISTIC FLAR";
65 PRINT "E)"
70 PRINT "2. TWO 'ARTSY' PASCAL'S TRIANGLES PRINTED BACK TO BACK"
80 PRINT "3. FOUR 'ARTSY' TRIANGLES IN THE CORNER OF"
90 PRINT "   A SQUARE ARRAY."
100 PRINT "WHAT'S YOUR PLEASURE? 1, 2 OR 3";
110 INPUT O
120 IF (O-1)*(O-2)*(O-3) <> 0 THEN 100
130 PRINT "WHICH MULTIPLES DO YOU WANT REPRESENTED WITH BLANKS";
140 INPUT Q
150 PRINT "HOW MANY ROWS AND COLUMS IN THE ARRAY (36 IS MAXIMUM)";
160 INPUT T
170 IF T*(36-T) < 0 THEN 150
180 ON O GOTO 230,440,690
190 REM
200 REM
210 REM TIME TO CREATE AND PRINT A SINGLE PIECE OF PASART
220 REM FIRST BUILD THE PASCALS TRIANGLE
230 FOR R=1 TO T
240 FOR C=1 TO T
250 IF (R-1)*(C-1)=0 THEN 280
260 P(R,C)=P(R,C-1)+P(R-1,C)
270 GOTO 290
280 P(R,C)=1
290 NEXT C
300 NEXT R
310 REM TIME TO PLAY BACK THE TRIANGLE WITH AN ARTISTIC FLARE.
320 FOR R=1 TO T
330 FOR C=1 TO T
340 IF P(R,C)=0 THEN 380
350 IF (P(R,C)/Q)=INT(P(R,C)/Q) THEN 380
360 PRINT "* ";
370 GOTO 390
380 PRINT "  ";
390 NEXT C
400 PRINT
410 NEXT R
420 END
430 REM TIME TO CREATE AND PRINT DOUBLE PIECE OF PASART
440 Z=T
450 REM BUILD THE UPPER LEFT HAND HALF OF THE ARRAY.
460 LET N=Z
470 FOR R=1 TO N
480 FOR C=1 TO Z-1
490 IF (R-1)*(C-1)=0 THEN 520
500 P(R,C)=P(R,C-1)+P(R-1,C)
510 GOTO 530
520 P(R,C)=1
530 NEXT C
540 Z=Z-1
550 NEXT R
560 REM BUILD THE LOWER RIGHT HALF OF THE ARRAY.
570 Z=N
580 N=2
590 FOR R=Z TO 1 STEP -1
600 FOR C=Z TO N STEP -1
610 IF (R-Z)*(C-Z)=0 THEN 640
620 P(R,C)=P(R,C+1)+P(R+1,C)
630 GOTO 650
640 P(R,C)=1
650 NEXT C
660 N=N+1
670 NEXT R
680 GOTO 320
690 M=Q
700 REM BUILD THE UPPER LEFT HALF CORNER OF THE ARRAY.
710 Y=T
720 Z=INT(Y/2)
730 B5=Z*2
740 Z1=Z
750 Z2=Z1
760 Z3=Z2
770 X4=Z3
780 X5=X4
790 FOR I=1 TO Z1
800 FOR J=1 TO Z
810 IF (J-1)*(I-1)=0 THEN 840
820 P(I,J)=P(I,J-1)+P(I-1,J)
830 GOTO 850
840 P(I,J)=1
850 NEXT J
860 Z=Z-1
870 NEXT I
880 N=Z1
890 REM BUILD THE UPPER RIGHT HAND CORNER OF THE ARRAY.
900 FOR I=1 TO Z1
910 FOR J=Y TO X5+1 STEP -1
920 IF I=1 THEN 960
930 IF J=Y THEN 960
940 P(I,J)=P(I,J+1)+P(I-1,J)
950 GOTO 970
960 P(I,J)=1
970 NEXT J
980 X5=X5+1
990 NEXT I
1000 N=Z2
1010 REM BUILD THE LOWER LEFT CORNER OF THE ARRAY
1020 FOR I=Y TO X4+1 STEP -1
1030 FOR J=1 TO Z2
1040 IF J=1 THEN 1080
1050 IF I=Y THEN 1080
1060 P(I,J)=P(I,J-1)+P(I+1,J)
1070 GOTO 1090
1080 P(I,J)=1
1090 NEXT J
1100 Z2=Z2-1
1110 NEXT I
1120 N=Z3
1130 REM BUILD THE LOWER RIGHT CORNER OF THE ARRAY.
1140 FOR I=Y TO N+1 STEP -1
1150 FOR J=Y TO Z3+1 STEP -1
1160 IF J=Y THEN 1200
1170 IF I=Y THEN 1200
1180 P(I,J)=P(I+1,J)+P(I,J+1)
1190 GOTO 1210
1200 P(I,J)=1
1210 NEXT J
1220 Z3=Z3+1
1230 NEXT I
1240 GOTO 320
1250 END
OK
```

Pasart 2

This program is a major extension of the original Pasart program. It incorporates many new options including printing a calendar for any year from 1600 to 2300. It allows a user to enter any desired pair of printing characters. The size of the output is expanded to 72 by 72 with an option to expand it further by dividing the final triangle into 72 by 72 chunks that may be taped together. Another option provides the user with the opportunity to create a picture based on four Pascal's tables (option 6).

There wasn't room to show the output from all of these options on these pages. Try them out yourself and we're sure you'll be pleased with the rather spectacular results.

Pasart 2 was also written by Charles H. Lund.

```
RUN
                          PASART2
                     CREATIVE COMPUTING
                   MORRISTOWN, NEW JERSEY



  THIS PROGRAM CREATES ARTIST DESIGNS BASED ON
PASCAL'S TRIANGLE.
DO YOU WANT A LIST OF OPTIONS? YES
PLEASE TEAR OFF THIS LIST AND SAVE OR POST FOR FUTURE REFERENCE
----------------------------------------------------------------
1. A SINGLE PASCALS TRIANGLE PLAYED BACK LIKE THIS:
        BEFORE PRINTING     AFTER PRINTING
            1 1 1               ***
            1 2 3               * *
            1 3 6               **
2. A SINGLE PASCALS TRIANGLE PLAYED BACK LIKE THIS:
        BEFORE PRINTING     AFTER PRINTING
              1                  *
              1 1                **
              1 2 1              * *
3. A SINGLE PASCALS TRIANGLE PLAYED BACK LIKE THIS:
        BEFORE PRINTING     AFTER PRINTING
              1                  *
            1 2 1              *   *
           1 3 3 1            * * * *
4. TWO PASCALS TRIANGLES PRINTED BACK TO BACK LIKE THIS:
        BEFORE PRINTING     AFTER PRINTING
            1 1 1 0             ***
            1 2 0 1             *  *
            1 0 2 1             *  *
            0 1 1 1              ***
5. FOUR PASCAL TRIANGLES PRINTED IN A SQUARE LIKE THIS:
        BEFORE PRINTING     AFTER PRINTING
           1 1 1 1 1 1        ******
           1 2       2 1      *    *
           1           1      *    *
           1           1      *    *
           1 2       2 1      *    *
           1 1 1 1 1 1        ******
6. FOUR PASCALS TRIANGLES PRINTED IN A SQUARE LIKE THIS:
        BEFORE PRINTING     AFTER PRINTING
           1 1 1 1 1 1        ******
           1 2 3 3 2 1        * ** *
           1 3 6 6 3 1        **  **
           1 3 6 6 3 1        **  **
           1 2 3 3 2 1        * ** *
           1 1 1 1 1 1        ******
7. STARTING PASCALS TRIANGLE IN ANY DESIRED ROW & COLUMN
   SO THAT A USER CAN TAPE TOGETHER SEVERAL PICTURES
   TO MAKE A LARGER DESIGN.  THIS OPTION EXTENDS
   PICTURES LIKE THOSE SHOWN IN OPTION 1 IN 36 X 36 CHARACTER
   CHUNKS.  ENTRIES UP TO 1000 ROWS AND COLUMNS ARE ACCEPTED.
----------------------------------------------------------------
```

```
WHAT'S YOUR PLEASURE (1,2,3,4,5,6 OR 7)? 4
YOUR PICTURE SHOULD HIGHLIGHT THE MULTIPLES OF WHAT NUMBER? 4
WHAT CHARACTER WOULD YOU LIKE THE COMPUTER TO TYPE REPRESENTING
THE MULTIPLES OF  4 (ENTER '' '' FOR A BLANK)? " "
WHAT CHARACTER WOULD  YOU LIKE THE COMPUTER TO TYPE REPRESENTING
EACH OF THE OTHER NUMBERS IN THE PATTERN (ENTER '' '' FOR A BLANK)? *
HOW MANY ROWS AND COLUMNS IN THE ARRAY (36 IS MAX.)? 36
WOULD YOU LIKE A CALENDAR PRINTED WITH YOUR PICTURE? YES
WHAT YEAR BETWEEN 1600 AND 2300 WOULD YOU LIKE? 1979
************************************
*** *** *** *** *** *** *** *** ** *
******  ******  ******  ******  * **
* * *   * * *   * * *   * * *    ***
************    ************       *
*** * * ***     *** * * ***       **
**  **  **      **  **  **       ***
*   *   *       *   *   *       ****
************************       * * *
*** *** * * * * *** ***       ******
******  **  **  ******       *** ***
* * *   *   *   * * *       ********
****    ****    ****       *   *   *
***     * *     ***       **  **  **
**      **      **       *** * * ***
*       *       *       ************
********************   * * *   * * *
*** *** *** *** *  *  ******  ******
******  ******  *  * *** *** *** ***
* * *   * * *    *******************
************       *       *       *
*** * * ***       **      **      **
**  **  **       ***     * *     ***
*   *   *       ****    ****    ****
********       * * *   *   *   * * *
*** ***       ******  **  **  ******
******       *** *** * * * * *** ***
* * *       ************************
****       *   *   *       *   *   *
***       **  **  **      **  **  **
**       *** * * ***     *** * * ***
*       ************    ************
***    * * *   * * *   * * *   * * *
** *  ******  ******  ******  ******
* ** *** *** *** *** *** *** *** ***
************************************

                JANUARY  1979
==========================================
!SUN   MON   TUE   WED   THU   FRI   SAT!
==========================================
        1     2     3     4     5     6
 7      8     9     10    11    12    13
 14     15    16    17    18    19    20
 21     22    23    24    25    26    27
 28     29    30    31
==========================================


                FEBRUARY  1979
==========================================
!SUN   MON   TUE   WED   THU   FRI   SAT!
==========================================
                          1     2     3
 4      5     6     7     8     9     10
 11     12    13    14    15    16    17
 18     19    20    21    22    23    24
 25     26    27    28
==========================================


                 MARCH  1979
==========================================
!SUN   MON   TUE   WED   THU   FRI   SAT!
==========================================
                          1     2     3
 4      5     6     7     8     9     10
 11     12    13    14    15    16    17
 18     19    20    21    22    23    24
 25     26    27    28    29    30    31

==========================================
```

```
LIST
10 PRINT TAB(25);"PASART2"
20 PRINT TAB(20);"CREATIVE COMPUTING"
30 PRINT TAB(18);"MORRISTOWN, NEW JERSEY"
40 PRINT:PRINT:PRINT
50 REM *** THIS PROGRAM REQUIRES AROUND 16K FREE WORK SPACE
60 REM *** TO OBTAIN LARGER PICTURES, EXPAND THE ARRAY IN LINE
70 REM *** 110 TO P(72,72)
110 DIM P(36,36)
130 PRINT "  THIS PROGRAM CREATES ARTIST DESIGNS BASED ON"
135 PRINT "PASCAL'S TRIANGLE."
140 PRINT "DO YOU WANT A LIST OF OPTIONS";
150 INPUT S1$
170 IF LEFT$(S1$,1)<>"Y" THEN 630
180 PRINT "PLEASE TEAR OFF THIS LIST AND SAVE OR POST FOR FUTURE REFERENCE"
190 PRINT "---------------------------------------------------------------"
200 PRINT "1. A SINGLE PASCALS TRIANGLE PLAYED BACK LIKE THIS:"
210 PRINT "         BEFORE PRINTING     AFTER PRINTING"
220 PRINT "              1 1 1              ***"
230 PRINT "              1 2 3              * *"
240 PRINT "              1 3 6             **"
250 PRINT "2. A SINGLE PASCALS TRIANGLE PLAYED BACK LIKE THIS:"
260 PRINT "         BEFORE PRINTING     AFTER PRINTING"
270 PRINT "                1                 *"
280 PRINT "                1 1               **"
290 PRINT "                1 2 1             * *"
300 PRINT "3. A SINGLE PASCALS TRIANGLE PLAYED BACK LIKE THIS:"
310 PRINT "         BEFORE PRINTING     AFTER PRINTING"
320 PRINT "                1                  *"
330 PRINT "              1 2 1              *    *"
340 PRINT "             1 3 3 1            * * * *"
350 PRINT "4. TWO PASCALS TRIANGLES PRINTED BACK TO BACK LIKE THIS:"
360 PRINT "         BEFORE PRINTING     AFTER PRINTING"
370 PRINT "             1 1 1 0             ***"
380 PRINT "             1 2 0 1             *  *"
390 PRINT "             1 0 2 1             *  *"
400 PRINT "             0 1 1 1              ***"
410 PRINT "5. FOUR PASCAL TRIANGLES PRINTED IN A SQUARE LIKE THIS:"
420 PRINT "         BEFORE PRINTING     AFTER PRINTING"
430 PRINT "            1 1 1 1 1 1        ******"
440 PRINT "            1 2     2 1        *    *"
450 PRINT "            1         1        *    *"
460 PRINT "            1         1        *    *"
470 PRINT "            1 2     2 1        *    *"
480 PRINT "            1 1 1 1 1 1        ******"
490 PRINT "6. FOUR PASCALS TRIANGLES PRINTED IN A SQUARE LIKE THIS:"
500 PRINT "         BEFORE PRINTING     AFTER PRINTING"
510 PRINT "            1 1 1 1 1 1        ******"
520 PRINT "            1 2 3 3 2 1        * ** *"
530 PRINT "            1 3 6 6 3 1        **  **"
540 PRINT "            1 3 6 6 3 1        **  **"
550 PRINT "            1 2 3 3 2 1        * ** *"
560 PRINT "            1 1 1 1 1 1        ******"
570 PRINT "7. STARTING PASCALS TRIANGLE IN ANY DESIRED ROW & COLUMN"
580 PRINT "   SO THAT A USER CAN TAPE TOGETHER SEVERAL PICTURES"
590 PRINT "   TO MAKE A LARGER DESIGN.  THIS OPTION EXTENDS"
600 PRINT "   PICTURES LIKE THOSE SHOWN IN OPTION 1 IN 36 X 36 CHARACTER"
610 PRINT "   CHUNKS.  ENTRIES UP TO 1000 ROWS AND COLUMNS ARE ACCEPTED."
620 PRINT "---------------------------------------------------------------"
630 PRINT "WHAT'S YOUR PLEASURE (1,2,3,4,5,6 OR 7)";
640 INPUT O
650 IF O<=7 AND O>=1 THEN 660
655 PRINT "I'M SUPPOSED TO BE YOUR FRIEND, SO HOW ABOUT IT:":GOTO 630
660 PRINT "YOUR PICTURE SHOULD HIGHLIGHT THE MULTIPLES OF WHAT NUMBER";
670 INPUT Q
680 PRINT "WHAT CHARACTER WOULD YOU LIKE THE COMPUTER TO TYPE REPRESENTING"
690 PRINT "THE MULTIPLES OF ";Q; "(ENTER '' '' FOR A BLANK)";
700 INPUT S$
710 PRINT "WHAT CHARACTER WOULD  YOU LIKE THE COMPUTER TO TYPE REPRESENTING"
720 PRINT "EACH OF THE OTHER NUMBERS IN THE PATTERN (ENTER '' '' FOR A BLANK)";
730 INPUT T$
740 IF O=7 THEN 780
750 PRINT "HOW MANY ROWS AND COLUMNS IN THE ARRAY (36 IS MAX.)";
760 INPUT T
770 IF T>36 THEN PRINT "BE REASONABLE!":GOTO 750
780 PRINT "WOULD YOU LIKE A CALENDAR PRINTED WITH YOUR PICTURE";
800 INPUT R5$
810 IF LEFT$(R5$,1)<>"Y" THEN 850
820 PRINT "WHAT YEAR BETWEEN 1600 AND 2300 WOULD YOU LIKE";
830 INPUT Y9
840 IF Y9*(3099-Y9)<=0 THEN PRINT "EVEN I MAKE MISTAKES!":GOTO 820
850 ON O GOTO 940,2190,2330,1210,1510,1510,2550
920 REM TIME TO CREATE AND PRINT A SINGLE PIECE OF PASART
930 REM FIRST BUILD THE PASCALS TRIANGLE
940 FOR R=1 TO T
950 FOR C=1 TO T
960 IF (R-1)*(C-1)=0 THEN 1010
970 P(R,C)=P(R-1,C)+P(R,C-1)
980 IF P(R,C)<Q*Q*Q THEN 1020
990 P(R,C)=P(R,C)-Q*Q
1000 GOTO 980
1010 P(R,C)=1
1020 NEXT C
1030 NEXT R
1040 REM TIME TO PLAY BACK THE TRIANGLE WITH AN ARTISTIC FLARE
1050 IF O<>3 THEN 1070
1060 LET T=T*2-1
1070 FOR R=1 TO T
1080 FOR C=1 TO T
1090 IF P(R,C)=0 THEN 1130
1100 IF(P(R,C)/Q-INT(P(R,C)/Q))*Q<.95 THEN 1130
1110 PRINT T$;
1120 GOTO 1140
1130 PRINT S$;
1140 NEXT C
1150 PRINT
1160 NEXT R
1170 IF LEFT$(R5$,1)="Y" THEN 3260
1180 GOTO 3710
1190 REM OPTION 4 LINES 1210-1490
1200 REM TIME TO CREATE AND PRINT A DOUBLE PIECE OF PASART
1210 Z=T
1220 REM BUILD THE UPPER LEFT HAND CORNER OF THE ARRAY
1230 LET N=Z
1240 FOR R=1 TO N
1250 FOR C=1 TO Z-1
1260 IF (R-1)*(C-1)=0 THEN 1310
1270 P(R,C)=P(R-1,C)+P(R,C-1)
1280 IF P(R,C)<Q*Q*Q THEN 1320
1290 P(R,C)=P(R,C)-Q*Q
1300 GOTO 1280
1310 P(R,C)=1
1320 NEXT C
1330 Z=Z-1
1340 NEXT R
1350 REM BUILD THE LOWER RIGHT HALF OF THE ARRAY
1360 Z=N
1370 N=2
1380 FOR R=Z TO 1 STEP -1
1390 FOR C=Z TO N STEP -1
1400 IF (R-Z)*(C-Z)=0 THEN 1450
1410 P(R,C)=P(R,C+1)+P(R+1,C)
1420 IF P(R,C)<Q*Q*Q THEN 1460
1430 P(R,C)=P(R,C)-Q*Q
1440 GOTO 1420
1450 P(R,C)=1
1460 NEXT C
1470 N=N+1
1480 NEXT R
1490 GOTO 1070
1500 REM OPTIONS 5 AND 6 LINES 1500-2120
1510 M=Q
1520 REM BUILD THE UPPER LEFT CORNER OF THE ARRAY
1530 Y=T
1540 Z=INT(Y/2)
1550 B5=Z*2
1560 Z1=Z
1570 Z2=Z1
1580 Z3=Z2
1590 X4=Z3
1600 X5=X4
1610 FOR I=1 TO Z1
1620 FOR J=1 TO Z
1630 IF (J-1)*(I-1)=0 THEN 1680
1640 P(I,J)=P(I,J-1)+P(I-1,J)
1650 IF P(I,J)<Q*Q*Q THEN 1690
1660 P(I,J)=P(I,J)-Q*Q
1670 GOTO 1650
1680 P(I,J)=1
1690 NEXT J
1700 IF O=6 THEN 1720
1710 Z=Z-1
1720 NEXT I
1730 N=Z1
1740 REM BUILD THE UPPER RIGHT CORNER OF THE ARRAY
1750 FOR I=1 TO Z1
1760 FOR J=Y TO X5+1 STEP -1
1770 IF I=1 THEN 1830
1780 IF J=Y THEN 1830
1790 P(I,J)=P(I,J+1)+P(I-1,J)
1800 IF P(I,J)<Q*Q*Q THEN 1840
1810 P(I,J)=P(I,J)=Q*Q
1820 GOTO 1800
1830 P(I,J)=1
1840 NEXT J
1850 IF O=6 THEN 1870
1860 X5=X5+1
```

```
1870 NEXT I
1880 N=Z2
1890 REM BUILD THE LOWER LEFT CORNER OF THE ARRAY
1900 FOR I=Y TO X4+1 STEP -1
1910 FOR J=1 TO Z2
1920 IF J=1 THEN 1980
1930 IF I=Y THEN 1980
1940 P(I,J)=P(I,J-1)+P(I+1,J)
1950 IF P(I,J)<Q*Q*Q THEN 1990
1960 P(I,J)=P(I,J)-Q*Q
1970 GOTO 1950
1980 P(I,J)=1
1990 NEXT J
2000 IF O=6 THEN 2020
2010 Z2=Z2-1
2020 NEXT I
2030 N=Z3
2040 REM BUILD THE LOWER RIGHT CORNER OF THE ARRAY
2050 FOR I=Y TO N+1 STEP -1
2060 FOR J=Y TO Z3+1 STEP -1
2070 IF J=Y THEN 2130
2080 IF I=Y THEN 2130
2090 P(I,J)=P(I+1,J)+P(I,J+1)
2100 IF P(I,J)<Q*Q*Q THEN 2140
2110 P(I,J)=P(I,J)-Q*Q
2120 GOTO 2100
2130 P(I,J)=1
2140 NEXT J
2150 IF O=6 THEN 2170
2160 Z3=Z3+1
2170 NEXT I
2180 GOTO 1070
2190 REM PASFORM C OPTION 2 LINES 2150-2260
2200 FOR R=1 TO T
2210 FOR C=1 TO T
2220 IF C>R THEN 2300
2230 IF(C-1)=0 THEN 2290
2240 IF R=C THEN 2290
2250 LET P(R,C)=P(R-1,C-1)+P(R-1,C)
2260 IF P(R,C)<Q*Q*Q THEN 2300
2270 LET P(R,C)=P(R,C)-Q*Q
2280 GOTO 2260
2290 LET P(R,C)=1
2300 NEXT C
2310 NEXT R
2320 GOTO 1040
2330 REM PASFORM A OPTION 3 LINES 2290-2480
2340 IF T<=36 THEN 2370
2350 PRINT "MAX. OF 36 ROWS ALLOWED WITH THIS OPTION...HERE THEY COME"
2360 LET T=36
2370 LET P(1,T)=1
2380 FOR R=2 TO T
2390 LET C=1
2400 IF C>T*2-1 THEN 2530
2410 IF R+C=T+1 THEN 2470
2420 IF C=1 THEN 2480
2430 LET P(R,C)=P(R-1,C-1)+P(R-1,C+1)
2440 IF P(R,C)<Q*Q*Q THEN 2480
2450 LET P(R,C)=P(R,C)-Q*Q
2460 GOTO 2440
2470 LET P(R,C)=1
2480 IF R+C<T+1 THEN 2510
2490 LET C=C+2
2500 GOTO 2400
2510 LET C=C+1
2520 GOTO 2400
2530 NEXT R
2540 GOTO 1040
2550 REM OPTION 7 LINES 2540-3190
2570 REM PUSHES THE BOUNDARIES WAY OUT
2580 REM NOTE THE PROTECTION AGAINST THE TIME OUT PROBLEM ON UNIV 1110
2590 PRINT "WHAT WILL BE THE COORDINATES (R,C) OF THE UPPER LEFT CORNER"
2600 PRINT "OF THIS SECTION";
2610 INPUT R1,C1
2620 DIM R(1000),C(1000)
2630 REM *** T=TIM(1)
2640 FOR L1=1 TO 72:FOR L2=1 TO 72:P(L1,L2)=0:NEXT L2:NEXT L1
2650 FOR L2=1 TO 1000:R(L2)=1:C(L2)=1:NEXT L2
2670 IF R1=1 THEN 2780
2680 FOR R=2 TO R1
2690 FOR C=2 TO C1+72
2700 R(C)=R(C)+R(C-1)
2710 IF R(C)<Q*Q*Q THEN 2740
2720 R(C)=R(C)-Q*Q
2730 GOTO 2710
2740 NEXT C
2750 REM *** IF TIM(1)-T<6 THEN 2770
2760 GOSUB 3210
2770 NEXT R
2780 IF C1=1 THEN 2900
2790 FOR C=2 TO C1
2800 C(R1)=R(C)
2810 FoR R=R1+1 TO R1+72
2820 C(R)=C(R)+C(R-1)
2830 IF C(R)<Q*Q*Q THEN 2860
2840 C(R)=C(R)-Q*Q
2850 GOTO 2830
2860 NEXT R
2870 REM *** IF TIM(1)-T<6 THEN 2890
2880 GOSUB 3210
2890 NEXT C
2900 FOR C=1 TO 72
2910 P(1,C)=R(C+C1-1)
2920 P(C,1)=C(C+R1-1)
2930 NEXT C
2940 FOR R=2 TO 72
2950 FOR C=2 TO 72
2960 P(R,C)=P(R-1,C)+P(R,C-1)
2970 IF P(R,C)<Q*Q*Q THEN 3000
2980 P(R,C)=P(R,C)-Q*Q
2990 GOTO 2970
3000 NEXT C
3010 REM *** IF TIM(1)-T<6 THEN 3030
3020 GOSUB 3210
3030 NNEXT R
3040 GOSUB 3210
3050 PRINT
3060 PRINT
3070 FOR R=1 TO 70
3080 FOR C=1 TO 70
3090 IF (P(R,C)/Q-INT(P(R,C)/Q))*Q<.98 THEN 3120
3100 PRINT T$;
3110 GOTO 3130
3120 PRINT S$;
3130 NEXT C
3140 REM *** IF TIM(1)-T<6 THEN 3160
3150 GOSUB 3210
3160 PRINT
3170 NEXT R
3180 PRINT
3190 PRINT
3200 GOTO 1170
3210 PRINT " ";
3220 REM *** LINPUT A$
3230 REM *** T=TIM(1)
3240 RETURN
3250 GOTO 1170
3260 REM CALENDAR
3270 LET X=Y9
3280 REM LINES 3240-3640 PRODUCE A CALENDAR
3290 REM PROGRAM IS A SUBROUTINE THAT USES VARIABLE X=YEAR OF CALENDAR
3300 REM
3310 C=6
3320 FOR J=1600 TO X STEP 1
3330 IF J=X THEN 3390
3340 IF J/4 <> INT(J/4) THEN 3380
3350 IF (J-1700)*(J-1800)*(J-1900)*(J-2100)*(J-2200)*(J-2300)=0 THEN 3380
3360 C=C+2
3370 GOTO 3390
3380 C=C+1
3390 IF C<7 THEN 3410
3400 C=C-7
3410 NEXT J
3420 PRINT
3430 FOR R=1 TO 12
3440 READ A$
3450 PRINT TAB(17);A$;" ";X
3460 READ B
3470 IF X/4 <> INT(X/4) THEN 3500
3480 IF A$ <> "FEBRUARY" THEN 3500
3490 LET B=B+1
3500 REM TIME TO PRINT THE CALENDAR FOR THE YEAR X
3510 PRINT "=========================================="
3520 PRINT "!SUN   MON   TUE   WED   THU   FRI   SAT!"
3530 PRINT "=========================================="
3540 FOR D=1 TO B
3550 PRINT TAB(6*C);D;
3560 LET C=C+1
3570 IF C<7 THEN 3600
3580 PRINT
3590 C=0
3600 NEXT D
3610 PRINT
3620 PRINT "=========================================="
3630 FOR P=1 TO 3
3640 PRINT
3650 NEXT P
3660 NEXT R
3670 DATA "JANUARY",31,"FEBRUARY",28,"MARCH",31,"APRIL",30,"MAY",31
3680 DATA "JUNE",30,"JULY",31,"AUGUST",31,"SEPTEMBER",30,"OCTOBER",31
3690 DATA "NOVEMBER",30,"DECEMBER",31
3700 REM THE END
3710 END
Ok
```

Pinball

PINBALL is, naturally enough, a simulated pinball game—complete with bells if your terminal has them—in which the computer serves as the pinball machine. However, you don't need any quarters! The program is divided up into ten small routines contained within the whole. Each subprogram performs one task in simulating a pinball game.

Details on each task/subprogram are as follows.

1) Starting and monitoring the game.
This task is performed by the master function PINBAL, which is contained in lines 1-600 of the program. Pinbal asks if the user wants instructions or a picture at the start of the game, puts each new ball into play, moves the ball until it comes into contact with an object on the table, and tells the user when he is finished and if he has broken the table record.

2) Printing instructions.
This subprogram is on the lines numbered 1010-1999, and its major task is to print the instructions of the pinball game and then to branch to the picture program to print a picture of the table (see below). After the picture of the table is completed, this subroutine explains the function of each figure on the table.

3) Registering "hits" and computing new scores.
Lines 2010-3999 are in charge of taking action each time the space occupied by the ball on the table is not blank. These lines also prepare the table to take action on the next task, namely flipping the table's flippers when the ball approaches them.

4) Flipping the flippers.
This task is accomplished by the lines in the four thousand range. These lines also set up indicators for the monitor routine (1 above) to put the next ball into play if necessary and branch to the routine that adds bonus points for tags (letters A-J) knocked down during that ball's play.

5) Bonus points at the end of a ball's play.
Lines in the five thousand range handle this task and then branch back to the monitor routine to put the next ball into play. If all ten tabs are knocked down in one ball, the program immediately awards a bonus of 250 points and an extra ball to the player and resets the tabs for further play. Normally, bonus points are awarded at the rate of ten per tab at the end of a ball.

6) Printing pictures of the table.
Lines in the six thousand range print a picture of the pinball table, either at the beginning of play or randomly, at the rate of one picture for every twenty-five "hits."

7) Bouncing the ball off bumpers and the jackpot.
The ball is "bounced" by the routine beginning at line 7850.

8) Initializing the table.
The table is initialized at the beginning of the game by lines in the nine thousand range.

Suggestions for improvement and change.

1) Change the table as you wish by inserting or deleting bumpers, jackpot(s), gates (numbers, now 1-9 and 0), etc. You may also move the positions of any item on the table except the three flippers.
2) Program in new sorts of table objects.
3) If your system is so equipped, rig in the program with some synthesizer music to heighten realism!

Pinball was conceived and written by Donald-Bruce Abrams.

```
RUN
                        PINBALL
                  CREATIVE COMPUTING
                MORRISTOWN, NEW JERSEY



WELCOME TO COMPUTER PINBALL!!
WOULD YOU LIKE INSTRUCTIONS TO THIS
FANTASTIC GAME? YES


THE RULES OF COMPUTER PINBALL ARE FAIRLY SIMPLE.  YOU GET A TOTAL OF
FIVE BALLS.  IF YOU SCORE MORE THAN 1600, YOU GET A SIXTH BALL.  IF
YOUR SIX BALL SCORE IS MORE THAN 2200, YOU GET A SEVENTH BALL.

THIS TABLE HAS THREE FLIPPERS, EACH OF OF WHICH PROTECT AN OUT CHUTE.
HOWEVER, THIS SET DIFFERS FROM OTHER SETS, SINCE YOU MAY ONLY FLIP
TWO OF THE FLIPPERS ANY TIME THE BALL APPROACHES THE CHUTE.
NOTA BENE:  YOU DO NOT!!! KNOW FOR SURE WHERE THE BALL IS!!
SO, IF YOU FLIP THE WRONG TWO FLIPPERS, YOU LOSE THE BALL, AND THE
NEXT BALL IS PUT INTO PLAY.
     YOU CAN GET A PICTURE OF THE TABLE EVERY TIME THE BALL HITS
AN OBJECT, SO THAT MAY HELP YOU SOMEWHAT.  ALSO, YOU ARE TOLD WHERE
THE BALL IS EACH TIME IT HITS(EVEN IF YOU DON'T GET A PICTURE).
THERE IS SOME LOGIC TO THE CHOICE OF FLIPPERS, BUT SOME LUCK IS INVOLVED, TOO.
THE FLIPPERS ARE NUMBERED 1,2, AND 3 FROM LEFT TO RIGHT, AND ARE SHOWN
ON THE PICTURE BELOW AS '!' MARKS.
SINCE LUCK PLAYS ONLY A SMALL PART IN CHOOSING THE CORRECT FLIPPER,
YOU WILL DO POORLY IF YOU JUST GUESS WHICH FLIPPER THE BALL IS
HEADED TOWARD...


THE TABLE LOOKS LIKE THIS:
****************


  DDDDDDDDDDDD
 0            0
0   *  *  *    0
0  A  B  C  D  0
0    *   *     0
0 * *  $  *  * 0
0    *   *     0
0* E  F  G  H *0
0   *  *  *    0
0===        ===0
0  1 2 3 4 5   0
0 * 6 7 8 9  * 0
0===   0    ===0
0  0   0    0  0
!!!          !!!
0  \        /  0
0   \  I J /   0
0    \    /    0
0     \  /     0
\------!!----^-/
```

```
****************
THE CENTER BUMPER($) IS THE JACKPOT!
THE BALL IS PUT INTO PLAY THROUGH THE UP ARROW(^), AND GOES UP AND
AROUND, WHERE IT IS DEPOSITED ON THE UPPER HALF OF THE TABLE.  THE BALL
MAY BOUNCE FROM THE SIDE OF THE TABLE, AND MAY BOUNCE UP FROM THE
LINES ON THE SIDE(=) AND FROM THE DIAGONALS(\ AND /) AT THE BOTTOM
OF THE TABLE.  THE BUMPERS ARE INDICATED BY STARS(*).
     FLIPPERS ARE SHOWN AS EXCLAMATION POINTS(! OR !!).
THE BALL MAY GO OUT OF PLAY THROUGH ONE OF THE FOUR HOLES IN THE BOARD(O),
IN WHICH CASE YOU WILL GET A BONUS BUT LOSE THE BALL.
     GATES ARE SHOWN BY THE NUMBERS 1-9, AND KNOCK-DOWN TABS ARE SHOWN
AS THE LETTERS A-J.  YOU GET A BONUS FOR THESE AT THE END OF
A BALL, AND IF YOU KNOCK ALL OF THEM DOWN YOU GET A SPECIAL BONUS...

***EVERY ONCE IN A WHILE, I WILL SHOW YOU A PICTURE OF THE
TABLE AS IT HITS SOMETHING.  THE BALL IS SHOWN AS THE #.




THE BALL IS NOW AT ( 2 , 11 ).
YOU RECEIVE  15  POINTS FROM THE BUMPER AT  5 , 10 .
SCORE:  15


TAB H DOWN...
YOU RECEIVE  8  POINTS FROM THE BUMPER AT  6 , 14 .
SCORE:  23
YOU RECEIVE  12  POINTS FROM THE BUMPER AT  9 , 8 .
SCORE:  35
BALL APPROACHING FLIPPERS.  ENTER THE TWO FLIPPERS YOU WISH TO FLIP
IN THE FORM: X,Y ? 2,3
THE BALL IS NOW AT ( 7 , 10 ).
YOU RECEIVE  54  POINTS FROM THE BUMPER AT  7 , 10 .
SCORE:  89




TAB H DOWN...
YOU RECEIVE  51  POINTS FROM THE BUMPER AT  9 , 11 .
SCORE:  1283

YOU GET  60  POINTS FROM GATE 4
SCORE:  1343
BALL APPROACHING FLIPPERS.  ENTER THE TWO FLIPPERS YOU WISH TO FLIP
IN THE FORM: X,Y ? 2,3
THE BALL IS NOW AT ( 8 , 2 ).
YOU RECEIVE  26  POINTS FROM THE BUMPER AT  8 , 2 .
SCORE:  1369
YOU RECEIVE  37  POINTS FROM THE BUMPER AT  8 , 2 .
SCORE:  1406


TAB A DOWN...
YOU GET  45  POINTS FROM GATE 2
SCORE:  1451


TAB F DOWN...
YOU RECEIVE  10  POINTS FROM THE BUMPER AT  9 , 8 .
SCORE:  1461
BALL APPROACHING FLIPPERS.  ENTER THE TWO FLIPPERS YOU WISH TO FLIP
IN THE FORM: X,Y ? 1,2
THE BALL IS NOW AT ( 3 , 6 ).
YOU RECEIVE  15  POINTS FROM THE BUMPER AT  6 , 5 .
SCORE:  1476
YOU RECEIVE  49  POINTS FROM THE BUMPER AT  3 , 5 .
SCORE:  1525


TAB E DOWN...

TOO BAD... YOU HAVE GONE STRAIGHT OUT A CHUTE HOLE('O' ON THE TABLE).
TO CONSOLE YOU, I WILL GIVE YOU AN EXTRA
 13  POINTS, TO BRING YOUR TOTAL TO  1538 .
YOU NOW HAVE HAVE  1  BALLS LEFT.
YOUR BALL KNOCKED DOWN  4  TAGS!!
FOR THIS STELLAR PERFORMANCE, YOU ARE AWARDED
***** 40 *****  POINTS!!
SCORE:  1578

THE BALL IS NOW AT ( 2 , 10 ).
YOU GET  75  POINTS FROM GATE 3
SCORE:  1653
YOU RECEIVE  1  POINTS FROM THE BUMPER AT  7 , 10 .
SCORE:  1654
BALL APPROACHING FLIPPERS.  ENTER THE TWO FLIPPERS YOU WISH TO FLIP
IN THE FORM: X,Y ? 1,2
THE BALL IS NOW AT ( 5 , 10 ).
YOU RECEIVE  5  POINTS FROM THE BUMPER AT  5 , 10 .
SCORE:  1659
```

— more —

```
LIST
1 PRINT TAB(25);"PINBALL"
2 PRINT TAB(20);"CREATIVE COMPUTING"
3 PRINT TAB(18);"MORRISTOWN, NEW JERSEY"
4 PRINT:PRINT:PRINT
8 DIM R$(10),P$(20),L(2)
9 GOSUB 9500
10 A1=0:A0=0:X9=0
20 PRINT "WELCOME TO COMPUTER PINBALL!!"
30 PRINT "WOULD YOU LIKE INSTRUCTIONS TO THIS "
35 PRINT "FANTASTIC GAME";
40 INPUT Q$:IF LEFT$(Q$,1)="Y" THEN GOSUB 1010:GOTO 50
45 PRINT:PRINT "HOW ABOUT A PICTURE OF THE TABLE";
46 INPUT Q$:IF LEFT$(Q$,1)="Y" THEN GOSUB 6010
50 PRINT:PRINT:B=5
55 S=0:P=0
60 T$="ABCDEFGHIJ":PRINT
61 FOR Z=1 TO 10:R$(Z)=" ":NEXT Z:Z3=0
70 A1=0
71 A7=0
80 IF B<=0 THEN 290
100 L(1)=2+INT(RND(1)*6):L(2)=INT(RND(1)*14)+1
110 C=1+INT(RND(1)*7):A1=0
120 PRINT "THE BALL IS NOW AT (";L(1);",";L(2);")."
130 IF MID$(P$(L(1)),L(2),1)=" "THEN 150
140 GOSUB 2010
150 IF A7=7 THEN 280
160 IF A1<>4 THEN 180
170 GOTO 260
180 L(1)=L(1)+1
190 A1=0
200 L(2)=L(2)+INT(1+RND(1)*3)-2
210 IF L(2)<2 OR L(2)>15 THEN L(1)=L(1)+INT(1+RND(1)*3)-2
215 IF L(2)<2 OR L(2)>15 THEN L(2)=INT(2+RND(1)*13)
230 IF L(1)>=2 AND L(1)<=20 THEN GOTO 130
240 L(1)=INT(1+RND(1)*7)
250 GOTO 130
260 GOSUB 4010
270 IF A0=1 THEN 400
280 ON X9+1 GOTO 60,340
285 PRINT"YOU HAVE PLAYED YOUR SEVENTH BALL AND SCORED ";P;" POINTS!"
286 PRINT"YOU'RE VERY GOOD!":GOTO 9999
290 PRINT "YOU HAVE PLAYED YOUR FIVE BALLS, AND HAVE SCORED"
293 PRINT "A TOTAL OF ";P;" POINTS."
300 IF P<1600 THEN 9999
305 PRINT:PRINT "*** BONUS BALL ***"
310 B=B+1
320 X9=1
330 GOTO 60
340 PRINT "YOU HAVE PLAYED YOUR SIXTH BALL AND SCORED ";P;" POINTS!"
341 X9=2
350 IF P<2200 THEN 9999
355 PRINT:PRINT "*** BONUS BALL ***"
360 B=B+1:S=3
370 GOTO 60
380 GOTO 2010
390 GOTO 150
400 L(1)=2+INT(RND(1)*7)
405 L(2)=2+INT(RND(1)*13):X=0:Y=0
410 GOTO 110
1010 PRINT:PRINT
```

```
1030 PRINT "THE RULES OF COMPUTER PINBALL ARE FAIRLY SIMPLE.  YOU GET A TOTAL OF"
1040 PRINT "FIVE BALLS.  IF YOU SCORE MORE THAN 1600, YOU GET A SIXTH BALL.  IF"
1045 PRINT "YOUR SIX BALL SCORE IS MORE THAN 2200, YOU GET A SEVENTH BALL."
1060 PRINT:PRINT "THIS TABLE HAS THREE FLIPPERS, EACH OF OF WHICH PROTECT AN OUT CHUTE."
1070 PRINT "HOWEVER, THIS SET DIFFERS FROM OTHER SETS, SINCE YOU MAY ONLY FLIP"
1080 PRINT "TWO OF THE FLIPPERS ANY TIME THE BALL APPROACHES THE CHUTE."
1090 PRINT "NOTA BENE:  YOU DO NOT!!! KNOW FOR SURE WHERE THE BALL IS!!"
1093 PRINT "SO, IF YOU FLIP THE WRONG TWO FLIPPERS, YOU LOSE THE BALL, AND THE"
1095 PRINT "NEXT BALL IS PUT INTO PLAY."
1097 PRINT "     YOU CAN GET A PICTURE OF THE TABLE EVERY TIME THE BALL HITS"
1098 PRINT "AN OBJECT, SO THAT MAY HELP YOU SOMEWHAT.  ALSO, YOU ARE TOLD WHERE"
1099 PRINT "THE BALL IS EACH TIME IT HITS(EVEN IF YOU DON'T GET A PICTURE)."
1100 PRINT "THERE IS SOME LOGIC TO THE CHOICE OF FLIPPERS, BUT SOME LUCK IS INVOLVED, TOO."
1110 PRINT "THE FLIPPERS ARE NUMBERED 1,2, AND 3 FROM LEFT TO RIGHT, AND ARE SHOWN"
1120 PRINT "ON THE PICTURE BELOW AS '!' MARKS."
1123 PRINT "SINCE LUCK PLAYS ONLY A SMALL PART IN CHOOSING THE CORRECT FLIPPER,"
1125 PRINT "YOU WILL DO POORLY IF YOU JUST GUESS WHICH FLIPPER THE BALL IS"
1127 PRINT "HEADED TOWARD...":PRINT:PRINT:PRINT"THE TABLE LOOKS LIKE THIS:"
1130 PRINT "****************":PRINT:PRINT:FOR Z=1TO20:PRINTP$(Z):NEXT Z
1140 PRINT:PRINT:PRINT"****************"
1230 PRINT "THE CENTER BUMPER($) IS THE JACKPOT!"
1240 PRINT "THE BALL IS PUT INTO PLAY THROUGH THE UP ARROW(^), AND GOES UP AND "
1250 PRINT "AROUND, WHERE IT IS DEPOSITED ON THE UPPER HALF OF THE TABLE.  THE BALL"
1260 PRINT "MAY BOUNCE FROM THE SIDE OF THE TABLE, AND MAY BOUNCE UP FROM THE"
1263 PRINT "LINES ON THE SIDE(=) AND FROM THE DIAGONALS(\ AND /) AT THE BOTTOM"
1270 PRINT "OF THE TABLE.  THE BUMPERS ARE INDICATED BY STARS(*)."
1280 PRINT "     FLIPPERS ARE SHOWN AS EXCLAMATION POINTS(! OR !!).
1285 PRINT "THE BALL MAY GO OUT OF PLAY THROUGH ONE OF THE FOUR HOLES IN THE BOARD(O),"
1290 PRINT "IN WHICH CASE YOU WILL GET A BONUS BUT LOSE THE BALL."
1300 PRINT "     GATES ARE SHOWN BY THE NUMBERS 1-9, AND KNOCK-DOWN TABS ARE SHOWN"
1310 PRINT "AS THE LETTERS A-J.  YOU GET A BONUS FOR THESE AT THE END OF"
1320 PRINT "A BALL, AND IF YOU KNOCK ALL OF THEM DOWN YOU GET A SPECIAL BONUS..."
1330 PRINT:PRINT"***EVERY ONCE IN A WHILE, I WILL SHOW YOU A PICTURE OF THE"
1340 PRINT "TABLE AS IT HITS SOMETHING.  THE BALL IS SHOWN AS THE #."
1350 PRINT:PRINT:RETURN
```

Run continued

```
TAB C DOWN...
YOU RECEIVE  5  POINTS FROM THE BUMPER AT  6 , 14 .
SCORE: 1664


TAB H DOWN...
BALL APPROACHING FLIPPERS.  ENTER THE TWO FLIPPERS YOU WISH TO FLIP
IN THE FORM: X,Y ? 2,3
THE BALL IS NOW AT ( 8 , 9 ).
YOU RECEIVE  32  POINTS FROM THE BUMPER AT  9 , 8 .
SCORE:  1696
YOU GET  60  POINTS FROM GATE 8
SCORE:  1756
BALL APPROACHING FLIPPERS.  ENTER THE TWO FLIPPERS YOU WISH TO FLIP
IN THE FORM: X,Y ? 2,3
THE BALL IS NOW AT ( 5 , 3 ).
YOU RECEIVE  57  POINTS FROM THE BUMPER AT  6 , 3 .
SCORE:  1813
BALL APPROACHING FLIPPERS.  ENTER THE TWO FLIPPERS YOU WISH TO FLIP
IN THE FORM: X,Y ? 1,3
THE BALL IS NOW AT ( 6 , 6 ).
BALL APPROACHING FLIPPERS.  ENTER THE TWO FLIPPERS YOU WISH TO FLIP
IN THE FORM: X,Y ? 1,3
THE BALL IS NOW AT ( 6 , 12 ).
YOU GET  15  POINTS FROM GATE 4
SCORE:  1828
YOU GET  60  POINTS FROM GATE 4
SCORE:  1888
YOU GET  90  POINTS FROM GATE 3
SCORE:  1978
YOU GET  45  POINTS FROM GATE 3
SCORE:  2023
YOU GET  45  POINTS FROM GATE 4
SCORE:  2068
BALL APPROACHING FLIPPERS.  ENTER THE TWO FLIPPERS YOU WISH TO FLIP
IN THE FORM: X,Y ? 1,2
THE BALL IS NOW AT ( 5 , 14 ).
YOU RECEIVE  53  POINTS FROM THE BUMPER AT  6 , 14 .
SCORE:  2121
YOU RECEIVE  32  POINTS FROM THE BUMPER AT  9 , 8 .
SCORE:  2153


TAB I DOWN...
BALL APPROACHING FLIPPERS.  ENTER THE TWO FLIPPERS YOU WISH TO FLIP
IN THE FORM: X,Y ? 1,2
THE BALL IS NOW AT ( 4 , 9 ).


TAB F DOWN...
YOU GET  90  POINTS FROM GATE 3
SCORE:  2243
```

— more —

```
2010 IF MID$(P$(L(1)),L(2),1)="O" THEN 2070
2020 IF INT(RND(1)+.5)=<>1 THEN 2022
2021 IF MID$(P$(L(1)),L(2),1)="/"ORMID$(P$(L(1)),L(2),1)="\" THEN 2160
2022 S8=INT(RND(1)*6+1)
2023 FOR S7=1 TO S8:PRINT CHR$(7);:NEXT S7
2025 IF MID$(P$(L(1)),L(2),1)<="J"AND MID$(P$(L(1)),L(2),1)>="A" THEN 2190
2040 GOSUB 3010
2050 RETURN
2070 PRINT "TOO BAD... YOU HAVE GONE STRAIGHT OUT A CHUTE HOLE('O' ON THE TABLE)."
2075 PRINT "TO CONSOLE YOU, I WILL GIVE YOU AN EXTRA"
2090 Q=INT(RND(1)*141)
2100 P=P+Q
2110 PRINT Q;" POINTS, TO BRING YOUR TOTAL TO ";P;"."
2115 PRINT "YOU NOW HAVE HAVE ";B-1;" BALLS LEFT."
2120 B=B-1
2130 A7=7
2140 GOSUB 5010
2150 RETURN
2160 L(1)=L(1)+(1+INT(RND(1)*4))-(1+INT(RND(1)*4))
2170 L(2)=2+INT(RND(1)*14)
2180 RETURN
2190 PRINT
2200 FOR Q=1 TO 10
2203 IF R$(Q)=MID$(P$(L(1)),L(2),1) THEN 2275
2204 NEXT Q
2205 Z3=Z3+1:R$(Z3)=MID$(P$(L(1)),L(2),1)
2210 PRINT:PRINT "TAB ";R$(Z3);" DOWN..."
2255 IF Z3=10 THEN GOSUB 5010
2260 RETURN
2275 RETURN
3010 IF MID$(P$(L(1)),L(2),1)=CHR$(8) THEN RETURN
3015 IF MID$(P$(L(1)),L(2),1)="]" THEN RETURN
3017 IF MID$(P$(L(1)),L(2),1)="[" THEN RETURN
3018 IF MID$(P$(L(1)),L(2),1)="^" THEN 3110
3019 A1=0
3020 IF MID$(P$(L(1)),L(2),1)="=" THEN 3410
3030 C=C-1
3040 IF C=0 THEN 3110
3050 IF MID$(P$(L(1)),L(2),1)="!"ORMID$(P$(L(1)),L(2),1)="\"THEN 3110
3060 IF MID$(P$(L(1)),L(2),1)="/"ORMID$(P$(L(1)),L(2),1)="-"THEN 3110
3070 IF INT(1+RND(1)*25)=4 THEN GOSUB 6010
3080 IF MID$(P$(L(1)),L(2),1)="$" THEN 3230
3090 IF MID$(P$(L(1)),L(2),1)="*" THEN 3280
3100 GOTO 3320
```

— more —

Run Continued

```
 P I C T U R E
****************
  ▯▯▯▯▯▯▯▯▯▯▯▯
 0             0
0   *  *  *    0
0  A  B  C  D  0
0    *    *    0
0 * *  $  *  * 0
0    *    *    0
0* E  F  G  H *0
0   *  *  *    0
0===        ===0
0  1 # 3 4 5   0
0 * 6 7 8 9  * 0
0===   0    ===0
0  0   0    0  0
!!!           !!!
0  \        /  0
0    \ I J /   0
0     \   /    0
0      \ /     0
\------!!----^-/

THE BALL WAS AT THE '#'

****************
YOU GET  75  POINTS FROM GATE 2
SCORE:  2318
YOU GET  45  POINTS FROM GATE 1
SCORE:  2363


TAB E DOWN...
BALL APPROACHING FLIPPERS.  ENTER THE TWO FLIPPERS YOU WISH TO FLIP
IN THE FORM: X,Y ? 2,3
THE BALL IS NOW AT ( 2 , 3 ).
BALL APPROACHING FLIPPERS.  ENTER THE TWO FLIPPERS YOU WISH TO FLIP
IN THE FORM: X,Y ? 2,3
NO, YOU HAVE CHOSEN TO PROTECT THE WRONG FLIPPERS.  YOU NOW HAVE
 0  BALLS LEFT.
YOUR BALL KNOCKED DOWN  5  TAGS!!
FOR THIS STELLAR PERFORMANCE, YOU ARE AWARDED
***** 50 *****  POINTS!!
SCORE:  2413

YOU HAVE PLAYED YOUR FIVE BALLS, AND HAVE SCORED
A TOTAL OF  2413  POINTS.

*** BONUS BALL ***

THE BALL IS NOW AT ( 7 , 13 ).
YOU GET  75  POINTS FROM GATE 4
SCORE:  2488
BALL APPROACHING FLIPPERS.  ENTER THE TWO FLIPPERS YOU WISH TO FLIP
IN THE FORM: X,Y ? 1,2
THE BALL IS NOW AT ( 5 , 7 ).
YOU HAVE HIT THE JACKPOT!!!! YOU HAVE JUST WON  126  POINTS!!
YOU NOW HAVE  2614  POINTS!


TAB G DOWN...
YOU GET  60  POINTS FROM GATE 4
SCORE:  2674
YOU RECEIVE  50  POINTS FROM THE BUMPER AT  9 , 8 .
SCORE:  2724
YOU GET  75  POINTS FROM GATE 2
SCORE:  2799
TOO BAD... YOU HAVE GONE STRAIGHT OUT A CHUTE HOLE('0' ON THE TABLE).
TO CONSOLE YOU, I WILL GIVE YOU AN EXTRA
 41  POINTS, TO BRING YOUR TOTAL TO  2840 .
YOU NOW HAVE HAVE  0  BALLS LEFT.
YOUR BALL KNOCKED DOWN  1  TAGS!!
FOR THIS STELLAR PERFORMANCE, YOU ARE AWARDED
***** 10 *****  POINTS!!
SCORE:  2850
YOU HAVE PLAYED YOUR SIXTH BALL AND SCORED  2850  POINTS!

*** BONUS BALL ***

THE BALL IS NOW AT ( 5 , 13 ).
YOU GET  60  POINTS FROM GATE 5
SCORE:  2910
BALL APPROACHING FLIPPERS.  ENTER THE TWO FLIPPERS YOU WISH TO FLIP
IN THE FORM: X,Y ? 1,2
NO, YOU HAVE CHOSEN TO PROTECT THE WRONG FLIPPERS.  YOU NOW HAVE
 0  BALLS LEFT.
YOU HAVE PLAYED YOUR SEVENTH BALL AND SCORED  2910  POINTS!
YOU'RE VERY GOOD!
COME PLAY AGAIN SOMETIME!!
Ok
```

Listing continued

```
3110 A1=4
3120 GOTO 3390
3130 IF L(2)<6 THEN GOTO 3180
3140 IF L(2)<11 THEN 3200
3150 D=2:IF INT(1+RND(1)*2)=1 THEN D=D+(1+INT(RND(1)*3))-2:IF D>3 THEN D=D-3
3170 RETURN
3180 D=1:IF INT(1+RND(1)*2)=1 THEN D=INT(RND(1)*3)+D
3190 RETURN
3200 D=2:IF INT(1+RND(1)*2)=1 THEN D=D+INT(RND(1)*3):IFD>3THEN D=D-3
3210 RETURN
3230 Q=45+INT(RND(1)*146)
3240 PRINT "YOU HAVE HIT THE JACKPOT!!!! YOU HAVE JUST WON ";Q;" POINTS!!"
3250 P=P+Q
3260 PRINT "YOU NOW HAVE ";P;" POINTS!"
3270 GOTO 3360
3280 Q=INT(RND(1)*64)+1:P=P+Q
3290 PRINT "YOU RECEIVE ";Q;" POINTS FROM THE BUMPER AT ";L(1);",";L(2);"."
3300 PRINT "SCORE: ";P
3310 GOTO 3360
3320 Q=15*(1+INT(RND(1)*6)):P=P+Q
3330 PRINT "YOU GET ";Q;" POINTS FROM GATE ";MID$(P$(L(1)),L(2),1)
3340 PRINT "SCORE: ";P
3360 L(1)=(L(1)-INT(1+RND(1)*3))-INT(1+RND(1)*2)
3370 L(2)=L(2)-3+INT(RND(1)*5)+1
3380 RETURN
3390 GOSUB 7850
3400 GOTO 3130
3410 L(1)=L(1)-(1+INT(RND(1)*5))
3420 L(2)=L(2)-2+(1+INT(RND(1)*4))
3430 RETURN
4010 PRINT "BALL APPROACHING FLIPPERS.  ENTER THE TWO FLIPPERS YOU WISH TO FLIP"
4020 INPUT "IN THE FORM: X,Y ";V,W
4030 IF V=D OR W=D THEN 4110
4040 PRINT "NO, YOU HAVE CHOSEN TO PROTECT THE WRONG FLIPPERS.  YOU NOW HAVE"
4060 PRINT B-1;" BALLS LEFT."
4070 B=B-1
4080 A0=0
4090 GOSUB 5010
4100 RETURN
4110 A0=1
4120 C=INT(1+RND(1)*5)
4140 RETURN
5010 IF Z3=10 THEN 5090
5020 IF Z3=0 THEN RETURN
5030 PRINT "YOUR BALL KNOCKED DOWN ";Z3;" TAGS!!"
5040 PRINT "FOR THIS STELLAR PERFORMANCE, YOU ARE AWARDED "
5050 PRINT "*****";10*Z3;"*****";:PRINT"  POINTS!!"
5060 P=P+10*Z3
5080 GOTO 5120
5090 P=P+250
5100 PRINT "*****YOU KNOCKED DOWN ALL 10 TAGS!!!*****"
5110 PRINT "YOU ARE AWARDED 250 POINTS AND AN EXTRA BALL!!!"
5114 B=B+1
5120 PRINT "SCORE: ";P:RETURN
6010 PRINT
6020 PRINT:PRINT" P I C T U R E ":PRINT"****************"
6040 FOR Q=1 TO L(1)-1:PRINT P$(Q):NEXT Q
6044 PRINT MID$(P$(L(1)),1,L(2)-1);"#";MID$(P$(L(1)),L(2)+1,16-L(2))
6050 FOR Q=L(1)+1 TO 20:PRINT P$(Q):NEXT Q
6060 PRINT:PRINT"THE BALL WAS AT THE '#'":PRINT:PRINT"****************"
6100 RETURN
7850 L(2)=ABS(L(2)-2+INT(1+RND(1)*4))
7860 IF L(2)<=15 THEN RETURN
7870 L(2)=1+INT(RND(1)*15):RETURN
9500 P$(1)="  "
9501 FOR Q=1 TO 12:P$(1)=P$(1)+"["+CHR$(8)+"]":NEXT Q
9502 P$(1)=P$(1)+"  "
9510 P$(2)=" 0             0 "
9520 P$(3)="0   *  *  *    0"
9530 P$(4)="0  A  B  C  D  0"
9540 P$(5)="0    *    *    0"
9550 P$(6)="0 * *  $  *  * 0"
9560 P$(7)="0    *    *    0"
9570 P$(8)="0* E  F  G  H *0"
9580 P$(9)="0   *  *  *    0"
9590 P$(10)="0===        ===0"
9600 P$(11)="0  1 2 3 4 5   0"
9610 P$(12)="0 * 6 7 8 9  * 0"
9620 P$(13)="0===   0    ===0"
9630 P$(14)="0  0   0    0  0"
9640 P$(15)="!!!           !!!"
9650 P$(16)="0  \        /  0"
9660 P$(17)="0    \ I J /   0"
9670 P$(18)="0     \   /    0"
9680 P$(19)="0      \ /     0"
9690 P$(20)="\------!!----^-/"
9700 RETURN
9999 PRINT "COME PLAY AGAIN SOMETIME!!":END
Ok
```

Rabbit Chase

Seemingly, the purpose of this game is to chase-down and catch a rabbit. Now this rabbit is an elusive little devil—it can hop randomly in any direction. You can run at least as fast as the rabbit, maybe even faster (the computer will decide). You must get within 20 units of the rabbit to be able to catch him. Before each hop, the computer will print out your position, the rabbit's position, the direction the rabbit is going to jump, and your closest approach on the last hop. You are to tell the computer which direction you wish to run. All coordinates and directions are as a geometer would mark them on a standard Cartesian Coordinate System.

In addition to being good fun, this game gives you practice in using and visualizing an *x*-y coordinate plane. After each hop, consider the output and try to run the right direction. Try to do all the figuring in your head. Using scratch paper is considered to be cheating (except for maybe the first time you play).

Suggested Modifications

1. Change the program so that you can choose your own speed.
2. The game is much more challenging when the "capture distance" can be varied. A distance of 50 units is a cinch, 15 units may make you wish for scratch paper, 5 units will require you to use a protractor and graph paper.
3. See if you can invent a way to extend this game to 3 dimensions! 4 dimensions! etc.!
4. You might try limiting the total number of hops and/or having the computer give hints when requested.

Rabbit Chase was written by Ted C. Park of Pacific Union College. It first appeared in *Creative Computing*, Mar/Apr 1975.

```
LIST

10 PRINT TAB(29);"RABBIT CHASE"
20 PRINT TAB(15);"CREATIVE COMPUTING  MORRISTOWN NEW JERSEY"
30 PRINT
40 PRINT
50 PRINT
100 REM ('T' IS THE SQUARE OF THE CAPTURE DISTANCE)
105 LET T=400
115 REM --    INITALIZE VELOCITIES AND POSITIONS
125 LET V1=INT(RND(1)*10+.5)*10+50
130 LET V2=(INT(RND(1)*2+.5)+1)*V1
135 LET X1=(INT(RND(1)*400)+100)*SGN(RND(1)-.5)
140 LET Y1=(INT(RND(1)*400)+100)*SGN(RND(1)-.5)
145 IF Y1=0 OR X1=0 THEN 135
150 LET X2=0
155 LET Y2=0
160 PRINT "SPEEDS (UNITS/HOP):"
165 PRINT "RABBIT -";V1,"YOU -";V2
170 PRINT
175 PRINT
180 PRINT
185 LET C=(X2-X1)^2+(Y2-Y1)^2
190 LET P1=3.141592653589/180
195 LET H=1
200 REM --    PRINT OUT
215 LET D1=INT(RND(1)*359)
220 PRINT "HOP#: ";
225 LET Z=H
230 GOSUB 510
235 PRINT "  DISTANCE TO RABBIT: ";
240 LET Z=SQR((X2-X1)^2+(Y2-Y1)^2)
245 GOSUB 510
250 PRINT "   CLOSEST APPROACH: ";
255 LET Z=SQR(C)
260 GOSUB 510
265 PRINT
270 PRINT "RABBIT ---      POSITION: (";
275 LET Z=X1
280 GOSUB 520
285 PRINT ",";
290 LET Z=Y1
295 GOSUB 520
300 PRINT ")   AND DIRECTION:";
305 LET Z=D1
310 GOSUB 510
315 PRINT
320 PRINT "YOU ------      POSITION: (";
325 LET Z=X2
330 GOSUB 520
335 PRINT ",";
340 LET Z=Y2
345 GOSUB 520
350 PRINT ")   AND DIRECTION:";
355 INPUT D2
360 IF D2 < 0 OR D2 >=360 THEN 355
365 PRINT
370 PRINT
380 REM --    COMPUTE PATHS AND SEE IF THEY INTERSECT
390 LET X3=V1*COS(D1*P1)/100
395 LET Y3=V1*SIN(D1*P1)/100
400 LET X4=V2*COS(D2*P1)/100
405 LET Y4=V2*SIN(D2*P1)/100
410 LET C=(X2-X1)^2+(Y2-Y1)^2
415 FOR I=1 TO 100
420 LET X1=X1+X3
425 LET Y1=Y1+Y3
430 LET X2=X2+X4
435 LET Y2=Y2+Y4
440 IF C < (X2-X1)^2+(Y2-Y1)^2 THEN 445
443 C=(X2-X1)^2+(Y2-Y1)^2
445 NEXT I
450 LET H=H+1
455 IF C > T THEN 215
460 PRINT
465 PRINT
470 PRINT "**********"
475 PRINT "* GOT YA *"
480 PRINT "**********"
485 PRINT
490 PRINT
500 END
510 REM --    CONVERTS NUMBERS TO STRINGS FOR CLEANER OUTPUT
520 Z=INT(Z+.5)
525 PRINT RIGHT$("     "+STR$(Z),5);
585 RETURN
590 END
OK
```

```
RUN
                              RABBIT CHASE
               CREATIVE COMPUTING  MORRISTOWN NEW JERSEY



SPEEDS (UNITS/HOP):
RABBIT - 130  YOU - 130



HOP#:      1  DISTANCE TO RABBIT:   488   CLOSEST APPROACH:   488
RABBIT ---      POSITION: ( -190,  450)   AND DIRECTION:  203
YOU ------      POSITION: (    0,    0)   AND DIRECTION:? 135


HOP#:      2  DISTANCE TO RABBIT:   377   CLOSEST APPROACH:   377
RABBIT ---      POSITION: ( -310,  399)   AND DIRECTION:  130
YOU ------      POSITION: (  -92,   92)   AND DIRECTION:? 135


HOP#:      3  DISTANCE TO RABBIT:   378   CLOSEST APPROACH:   377
RABBIT ---      POSITION: ( -393,  499)   AND DIRECTION:   11
YOU ------      POSITION: ( -184,  184)   AND DIRECTION:? 90


HOP#:      4  DISTANCE TO RABBIT:   225   CLOSEST APPROACH:   225
RABBIT ---      POSITION: ( -266,  524)   AND DIRECTION:  314
YOU ------      POSITION: ( -184,  314)   AND DIRECTION:? 135


HOP#:      5  DISTANCE TO RABBIT:   103   CLOSEST APPROACH:    89
RABBIT ---      POSITION: ( -175,  430)   AND DIRECTION:  274
YOU ------      POSITION: ( -276,  406)   AND DIRECTION:? 0


HOP#:      6  DISTANCE TO RABBIT:   107   CLOSEST APPROACH:    57
RABBIT ---      POSITION: ( -166,  300)   AND DIRECTION:   72
YOU ------      POSITION: ( -146,  406)   AND DIRECTION:? 225


HOP#:      7  DISTANCE TO RABBIT:   157   CLOSEST APPROACH:    38
RABBIT ---      POSITION: ( -126,  424)   AND DIRECTION:  218
YOU ------      POSITION: ( -238,  314)   AND DIRECTION:? 0


HOP#:      8  DISTANCE TO RABBIT:   125   CLOSEST APPROACH:    68
RABBIT ---      POSITION: ( -229,  344)   AND DIRECTION:  134
YOU ------      POSITION: ( -108,  314)   AND DIRECTION:? 170
```

Roadrace

You are the driver of a race car on the notorious NY Route 20. You'll have to drive 5 miles with ½ gallon of gas, while keeping alert for changes in the road conditions, other cars, etc.

At the start you pick your car and course. During the race you control braking and acceleration.

Watch out for passing another car! If you try to go the same speed he's going, you're going to meet a Greyhound bus head-on!

The game is tough to win. I usually wipe out in a curve or run out of gas. You might want to increase your MPG rating...look at line 870.

Good luck!

This program originally appeared in *Creative Computing*, Jan/Feb 1975.

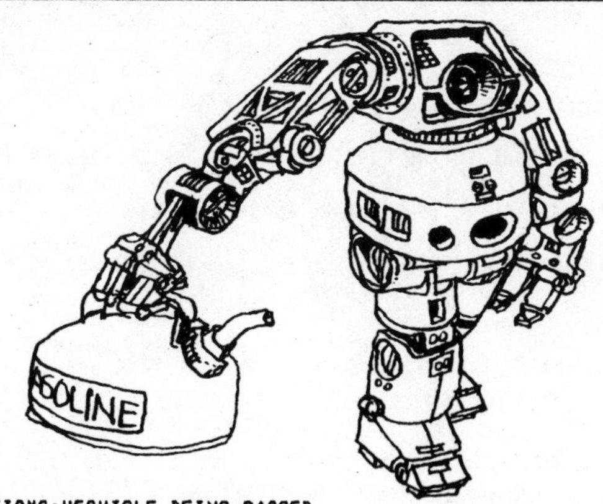


```
RUN
                         ROADRACE
         CREATIVE COMPUTING  MORRISTOWN NEW JERSEY


      THIS IS THE PITTSFIELD-ALBANY ROAD RALLY

WELCOME TO THE FIRST ANNUAL PITTSFIELD-ALBANY ROAD RALLY.
YOU'LL BE DRIVING RT. 20. TRYING TO WIN THE RACE AND
STAY ALIVE IN THE BARGIN. GOOD LUCK!!

YOY HAVE YOUR CHOICE OF: (1) A VW; (2) 283 NOVA;
(3) Z-28; OR (4) FERRARI

CHOOSE THE CAR YOU WANT BY THE NUMBER IN FRONT OF IT.
REMEMBER, THE BETTER THE CAR, THE MORE GAS IT USES.
WHICH CAR? 3

NOW YOU CHOOSE WHICH COURSE YOU WANT TO RACE ON.
THE EASIEST COURSE IS NUMBER 1, AND IS THE STRAIGHTEST
ROUTE. NUMBER 5 CONSISTS MOSTLY OF TURNS AND TWISTS.
WHICH ROUTE DO YOU WANT? 1

YOU WILL NEED TO TRAVEL 5 MILES WITH .5 GALLONS OF GAS.
YOUR STATUS WILL BE SHOWN EACH 10 SECONDS. AFTER EACH
STATUS CHECK YOU WILL BE ASKED FOR A NEW RATE OF GAS.
A RATE OF +10 IS HARD ACCELERATION, AND -10 IS HARD BRAKING
ANY NUMBER IN BETWEEN IS ALLOWABLE.

PRESENT VELOCITY = 0  NO. OF GALLONS = .5
NO. OF MILES = 0  TIME PASSED = 0 SECONDS
WHAT IS YOUR NEW RATE OF GAS ? 10

ROAD CONDITIONS:CLEAR AND STRAIGHT

PRESENT VELOCITY = 70  NO. OF GALLONS = .47
NO. OF MILES = .152174  TIME PASSED = 10 SECONDS
WHAT IS YOUR NEW RATE OF GAS ? 2

ROAD CONDITIONS:VECHICLE AHEAD 1000 FEET

PRESENT VELOCITY = 55  NO. OF GALLONS = .464
NO. OF MILES = .271739  TIME PASSED = 20 SECONDS
WHAT IS YOUR NEW RATE OF GAS ? 10

ROAD CONDITIONS:VECHICLE PASSED BY  75 MPH

PRESENT VELOCITY = 102  NO. OF GALLONS = .434
NO. OF MILES = .493478  TIME PASSED = 30 SECONDS
WHAT IS YOUR NEW RATE OF GAS ? 10

ROAD CONDITIONS:VECHICLE AHEAD 1000 FEET

PRESENT VELOCITY = 130  NO. OF GALLONS = .404
NO. OF MILES = .776087  TIME PASSED = 40 SECONDS
WHAT IS YOUR NEW RATE OF GAS ? -5

ROAD CONDITIONS:VECHICLE BEING PASSED
GREYHOUND BUS IN OTHER LANE DOING  64  MPH CRASH VELOCITY =  105
WHERE IS YOUR FUNERAL BEING HELD ?

YOU WANT TO TRY AGAIN, RIGHT !!!!
1-YES, 2-NO? 1
WHICH CAR? 3

WHICH ROUTE DO YOU WANT? 5

PRESENT VELOCITY = 0  NO. OF GALLONS = .5
NO. OF MILES = 0  TIME PASSED = 0 SECONDS
WHAT IS YOUR NEW RATE OF GAS ? 10

ROAD CONDITIONS: WARNING: CURVE AHEAD

PRESENT VELOCITY = 70  NO. OF GALLONS = .47
NO. OF MILES = .152174  TIME PASSED = 10 SECONDS
WHAT IS YOUR NEW RATE OF GAS ? 0

ROAD CONDITIONS:THROUGH CURVE

PRESENT VELOCITY = 41  NO. OF GALLONS = .47
NO. OF MILES = .241304  TIME PASSED = 20 SECONDS
WHAT IS YOUR NEW RATE OF GAS ? 7

ROAD CONDITIONS: WARNING: CURVE AHEAD

PRESENT VELOCITY = 73  NO. OF GALLONS = .449
NO. OF MILES = .4  TIME PASSED = 30 SECONDS
WHAT IS YOUR NEW RATE OF GAS ? -1

ROAD CONDITIONS:THROUGH CURVE

PRESENT VELOCITY = 36  NO. OF GALLONS = .449
NO. OF MILES = .478261  TIME PASSED = 40 SECONDS
WHAT IS YOUR NEW RATE OF GAS ? 10

ROAD CONDITIONS:CLEAR AND STRAIGHT

PRESENT VELOCITY = 91  NO. OF GALLONS = .419
NO. OF MILES = .676087  TIME PASSED = 50 SECONDS
WHAT IS YOUR NEW RATE OF GAS ? 5

ROAD CONDITIONS: WARNING: CURVE AHEAD

PRESENT VELOCITY = 88  NO. OF GALLONS = .404
NO. OF MILES = .867391  TIME PASSED = 60 SECONDS
WHAT IS YOUR NEW RATE OF GAS ? -4

ROAD CONDITIONS:THROUGH CURVE

PRESENT VELOCITY = 23  NO. OF GALLONS = .404
NO. OF MILES = .917391  TIME PASSED = 70 SECONDS
WHAT IS YOUR NEW RATE OF GAS ? 7

ROAD CONDITIONS: WARNING: CURVE AHEAD

PRESENT VELOCITY = 62  NO. OF GALLONS = .383
NO. OF MILES = 1.05217  TIME PASSED = 80 SECONDS
WHAT IS YOUR NEW RATE OF GAS ? -1

ROAD CONDITIONS:ARE TERRIBLE
 16  WAS THE SPEED THROUGH THE CURVE
 29  WAS YOUR SPEED, BY THE WAY WHERE IS YOUR FUNERAL BEING HELD ?
```

```
LIST
10 PRINT TAB(27);"ROADRACE"
20 PRINT TAB(15);"CREATIVE COMPUTING  MORRISTOWN NEW JERSEY"
30 PRINT
40 PRINT
50 PRINT
100 PRINT "       THIS IS THE PITTSFIELD-ALBANY ROAD RALLY"
120 PRINT
130 PRINT "WELCOME TO THE FIRST ANNUAL PITTSFIELD-ALBANY ROAD RALLY."
140 PRINT "YOU'LL BE DRIVING RT. 20. TRYING TO WIN THE RACE AND"
150 PRINT "STAY ALIVE IN THE BARGIN. GOOD LUCK!!"
160 PRINT
170 PRINT "YOY HAVE YOUR CHOICE OF: (1) A VW; (2) 283 NOVA;"
180 PRINT "(3) Z-28; OR (4) FERRARI"
190 PRINT
200 PRINT "CHOOSE THE CAR YOU WANT BY THE NUMBER IN FRONT OF IT."
210 PRINT "REMEMBER, THE BETTER THE CAR, THE MORE GAS IT USES."
220 PRINT "WHICH CAR";
230 INPUT C1
240 LET C1=INT(C1)
250 IF C1 > 4 THEN 280
260 IF C1 < 1 THEN 280
270 GOTO 300
280 PRINT "INVALID CAR NUMBER. NEW CAR ";
290 GOTO 230
300 PRINT
310 IF N2=1 THEN 345
320 PRINT "NOW YOU CHOOSE WHICH COURSE YOU WANT TO RACE ON."
330 PRINT "THE EASIEST COURSE IS NUMBER 1, AND IS THE STRAIGHTEST"
340 PRINT "ROUTE. NUMBER 5 CONSISTS MOSTLY OF TURNS AND TWISTS."
345 PRINT "WHICH ROUTE DO YOU WANT";
350 INPUT C2
360 LET C2=INT(C2)
380 IF C2 < 1 THEN 410
390 IF C2 > 5 THEN 410
400 GOTO 430
410 PRINT "INVALID COURSE NUMBER. NEW CHOICE ";
420 GOTO 350
430 IF N2=1 THEN 490
435 PRINT
440 PRINT "YOU WILL NEED TO TRAVEL 5 MILES WITH .5 GALLONS OF GAS."
450 PRINT "YOUR STATUS WILL BE SHOWN EACH 10 SECONDS. AFTER EACH "
460 PRINT "STATUS CHECK YOU WILL BE ASKED FOR A NEW RATE OF GAS. "
470 PRINT "A RATE OF +10 IS HARD ACCELERATION, AND -10 IS HARD BRAKING"
480 PRINT "ANY NUMBER IN BETWEEN IS ALLOWABLE."
490 FOR I=1 TO C1
500 READ B,M,S
510 LET B=B/10
520 NEXT I
530 LET A1=.5
540 LET M1=0
550 LET C1=C1/2
560 LET V=0
570 PRINT
580 LET R1=0
590 LET T=0
600 LET D=0
610 LET Q1=0
620 PRINT "PRESENT VELOCITY =";V;" NO. OF GALLONS =";A1
630 PRINT "NO. OF MILES =";M1;" TIME PASSED =";T;"SECONDS"
640 IF M1>= 5 THEN 1460
650 PRINT "WHAT IS YOUR NEW RATE OF GAS ";
660 INPUT G
670 IF G < -10 THEN 700
680 IF G > 10 THEN 700
690 GOTO 720
700 PRINT "NOT VALID. NEW RATE ";
710 GOTO 660
720 IF G < 9 THEN  780
730 LET Z=Z+1
740 IF Z> 4 THEN 760
750 GOTO 790
760 PRINT "YOUR ENGINE BLEW. YOU GOT HIT BY A PISTON."
770 GOTO 1270
780 LET Z=0
790 LET V=INT(B*G-M*V+V)
800 LET T=T+10
810 PRINT
820 PRINT "ROAD CONDITIONS:";
830 IF V > 0 THEN 850
840 LET V=0
850 LET M1=M1+V/460
860 IF G<0 THEN 890
870 LET A1=A1-(G*S)/5000
880 IF A1< 0 THEN 1380
890 IF R1=1 THEN 1050
900 IF Q1=1 THEN 980
910 LET Q=INT((C2+1)*RND(1))
920 LET R=INT((3.75-C2)*RND(1))
930 IF R > 0 THEN 1290
940 IF Q > 0 THEN 1340
950 PRINT "CLEAR AN STRAIGHT"
960 PRINT
970 GOTO 620
980 LET H=INT(15+35!*RND(1))
990 LET H=H+5*C1
1000 IF V>H THEN 1500
1010 PRINT "THROUGH CURVE"
1020 PRINT
1030 LET Q1=0
1040 GOTO 620
1050 LET E=E-(V-D)*3!
1060 IF E < 0 THEN 1100
1070 PRINT "VECHICLE ";E;" FEET AHEAD"
1080 PRINT
1090 GOTO 620
1100 IF V-D < 5 THEN 1180
1110 PRINT "VECHICLE PASSED BY ";
1120 LET D=V-D
1130 PRINT D;
1140 PRINT "MPH"
1150 PRINT
1160 LET R1=0
1170 GOTO 620
1180 PRINT "VECHICLE BEING PASSED "
1190 LET D=INT(25+40*RND(1))
1200 PRINT "GREYHOUND BUS IN OTHER LANE ";
1210 PRINT "DOING ";
1220 PRINT D;
1230 PRINT " MPH ";
1240 LET D=V+D
1250 PRINT "CRASH VELOCITY = ";D
1270 PRINT "WHERE IS YOUR FUNERAL BEING HELD ?"
1280 GOTO 1560
1290 PRINT "VECHICLE AHEAD 1000 FEET"
1300 PRINT
1310 LET D=INT(25+35*RND(1))
1320 LET R1=1
1330 GOTO 620
1340 PRINT " WARNING: CURVE AHEAD "
1350 LET Q1=1
1360 PRINT
1370 GOTO 620
1380 PRINT "EXCELLENT BUT WAIT!"
1390 PRINT
1400 PRINT "YOU RAN OUT OF GAS"
1410 GOTO 1550
1420 PRINT "BUT SOME HOW YOU MADE IT"
1430 PRINT
1440 LET R1=0
1450 GOTO 620
1460 PRINT
1470 PRINT
1480 PRINT "YOU MADE IT (LUCKY) !!!!!!!"
1490 GOTO 1560
1500 PRINT "ARE TERRIBLE"
1510 LET H=H-5*C1
1520 PRINT H;" WAS THE SPEED THROUGH THE CURVE"
1530 PRINT V;" WAS YOUR SPEED, BY THE WAY ";
1540 GOTO 1270
1550 PRINT "YOU LEAD FOOTED $%&''%$&$&&((&$&$'$($(($&'%#%#%%%"
1560 PRINT "YOU WANT TO TRY AGAIN, RIGHT !!!!"
1570 PRINT "1-YES, 2-NO";
1580 INPUT V
1590 IF V=2 THEN 1620
1600 N2=1
1610 GOTO 1640
1620 PRINT "CHICKEN"
1630 GOTO 1700
1640 RESTORE
1650 GOTO 220
1660 DATA 45,.53,10
1665 DATA 60,.5,13
1670 DATA 70,.41,15
1680 DATA 80,.39,18
1700 END
Ok
```

Rotate

The game of Rotate is played on a four-by-four board filled randomly with the letters A through P. In a sense it is like the little plastic games with sliding pieces bearing the numbers 1-15 or letters A-0.

The object of the game is to put the letters in alphabetical order. This is done by rotating groups of four letters clockwise one position. The group to be rotated is specified by the positional number of the letter in the upper left-hand corner of the group. You are also given one special move which permits you to exchange any two adjacent letters. You probably don't want to use this move too early in the game; indeed, sometimes it's not necessary at all, and since you get it only one time, once you use it you can't recover. Your only move then is to type a zero to give up.

Typically, a game will take from 20 to 30 moves to win. I haven't figured out the worst possible case (assuming an intelligent method of play); I'd be happy to hear from a reader on this. Have fun!

Rotate was written by me, David Ahl, and first appeared in *Creative Computing*, Sep/Oct 1977.

```
LIST

5 PRINT TAB(26);"ROTATE"
8 PRINT TAB(20);"CREATIVE COMPUTING"
10 PRINT TAB(18);"MORRISTOWN, NEW JERSEY":PRINT:PRINT:PRINT
11 DIM B(16),B$(16)
12 INPUT "INSTRUCTIONS";A$:PRINT:IF LEFT$(A$,1)="N" THEN 140
15 PRINT "IN THIS GAME THE BOARD IS LAID OUT AS FOLLOWS:"
25 FOR I=1 TO 16:B(I)=I:NEXT
30 PRINT:FOR I=1 TO 13 STEP 4
35 PRINT TAB(2);B(I);TAB(6);B(I+1);TAB(10);B(I+2);TAB(14);B(I+3)
40 NEXT I:PRINT
45 PRINT "BOARD POSITIONS ARE OCCUPIED RANDOMLY BY THE LETTERS A TO P."
50 PRINT "THE OBJECT OF THE GAME IS TO ORDER THE LETTERS BY ROTATING"
55 PRINT "ANY FOUR LETTERS CLOCKWISE ONE POSITION.  YOU SPECIFY THE"
60 PRINT "UPPER LEFT POSITION OF THE FOUR YOU WISH TO ROTATE, I.E.,"
65 PRINT "VALID MOVES ARE 1, 2, 3, 5, 6, 7, 9, 10 AND 11."
70 PRINT "CONSEQUENTLY, IF THE BOARD LOOKED LIKE:"
75 FOR I=1 TO 16:B$(I)=CHR$(I+64):NEXT:B$(2)="C":B$(3)="G"
80 B$(6)="B":B$(7)="F":GOSUB 400
85 PRINT "AND YOU ROTATED POSITION 2, THE BOARD WOULD BE:"
90 FOR I=2 TO 7:B$=CHR$(I+64):NEXT I:GOSUB 400
95 PRINT "AND YOU WOULD WIN !":PRINT
100 PRINT "YOU ALSO GET ONE 'SPECIAL' MOVE PER GAME WHICH YOU MAY OR"
105 PRINT "MAY NOT NEED.  THE SPECIAL MOVE ALLOWS YOU TO EXCHANGE"
110 PRINT "ANY TWO ADJACENT LETTERS IN A ROW.  TO MAKE THIS MOVE,"
115 PRINT "INPUT A '-1' AS YOUR MOVE AND YOU WILL BE ASKED FOR THE"
120 PRINT "POSITIONS OF THE TWO LETTERS TO EXCHANGE.  REMEMBER --"
125 PRINT "ONLY ONE SPECIAL MOVE PER GAME!":PRINT
130 PRINT "TO GIVE UP AT ANY TIME, TYPE A '0'.":PRINT:PRINT "GOOD LUCK !
":PRINT
140 FOR I=1 TO 16:B$(I)="0":NEXT I
150 FOR I=1 TO 16
160 T$=CHR$(INT(16*RND(1)+65))
165 FOR J=1 TO I
170 IF B$(J)=T$ THEN 160
175 NEXT J
180 B$(I)=T$:NEXT I
190 M=0:S=0:PRINT "HERE'S THE STARTING BOARD...":GOSUB 400
200 INPUT "POSITION TO ROTATE";I:IF I=0 THEN PRINT:PRINT:GOTO 140
205 IF I=-1 THEN 510
210 IF I=4 OR I=8 OR I>12 THEN PRINT "ILLEGAL.  AGAIN...":GOTO 200
220 M=M+1:T$=B$(I)
230 B$(I)=B$(I+4):B$(I+4)=B$(I+5):B$(I+5)=B$(I+1):B$(I+1)=T$
240 GOSUB 400
305 FOR I=1 TO 16
310 IF CHR$(I+64)<>B$(I) THEN 200
315 NEXT I
320 PRINT:PRINT "YOU ORDERED THE BOARD IN";M;" MOVES.":M1=M1+M:G=G+1
325 PRINT CHR$(7):FOR I=1 TO 15
330 PRINT:INPUT "PLAY AGAIN";A$:IF LEFT$(A$,1)="Y" THEN 140
340 PRINT:PRINT "YOU PLAYED";G;" GAMES AND ORDERED THE BOARD IN AN AVERA
GE"
350 PRINT "OF";M1/G;" MOVES PER GAME.":PRINT:GOTO 999
400 PRINT:FOR I=1 TO 13 STEP 4
410 PRINT B$(I)" "B$(I+1)" "B$(I+2)" "B$(I+3)
420 NEXT I:PRINT:RETURN
510 INPUT "EXCHANGE WHICH TWO POSITIONS";X,Y
520 IF X<>Y+1 AND X<>Y-1 THEN PRINT "ILLEGAL.  AGAIN...":GOTO 510
530 S=S+1:IF S>1 THEN PRINT "ONLY ONE SPECIAL MOVE PER GAME.":GOTO 200
540 T$=B$(X):B$(X)=B$(Y):B$(Y)=T$:GOTO 240
999 END
OK
```

```
RUN
                           ROTATE
                     CREATIVE COMPUTING
                   MORRISTOWN, NEW JERSEY



INSTRUCTIONS? YES

IN THIS GAME THE BOARD IS LAID OUT AS FOLLOWS:

   1   2   3   4
   5   6   7   8
   9   10  11  12
   13  14  15  16

BOARD POSITIONS ARE OCCUPIED RANDOMLY BY THE LETTERS A TO P.
THE OBJECT OF THE GAME IS TO ORDER THE LETTERS BY ROTATING
ANY FOUR LETTERS CLOCKWISE ONE POSITION.  YOU SPECIFY THE
UPPER LEFT POSITION OF THE FOUR YOU WISH TO ROTATE, I.E.,
VALID MOVES ARE 1, 2, 3, 5, 6, 7, 9, 10 AND 11.
CONSEQUENTLY, IF THE BOARD LOOKED LIKE:

A C G D
E B F H
I J K L
M N O P

AND YOU ROTATED POSITION 2, THE BOARD WOULD BE:

A C G D
E B F H
I J K L
M N O P

AND YOU WOULD WIN !

YOU ALSO GET ONE 'SPECIAL' MOVE PER GAME WHICH YOU MAY OR
MAY NOT NEED.  THE SPECIAL MOVE ALLOWS YOU TO EXCHANGE
ANY TWO ADJACENT LETTERS IN A ROW.  TO MAKE THIS MOVE,
INPUT A '-1' AS YOUR MOVE AND YOU WILL BE ASKED FOR THE
POSITIONS OF THE TWO LETTERS TO EXCHANGE.  REMEMBER --
ONLY ONE SPECIAL MOVE PER GAME!

TO GIVE UP AT ANY TIME, TYPE A '0'.

GOOD LUCK !

HERE'S THE STARTING BOARD...

E O C L
K G M A
F I P J
H N D B

POSITION TO ROTATE? 3

E O M C
K G A L
F I P J
H N D B
```

```
POSITION TO ROTATE? 2

E G O C
K A M L
F I P J
H N D B

POSITION TO ROTATE? 1

K E O C
A G M L
F I P J
H N D B

POSITION TO ROTATE? 1

A K O C
G E M L
F I P J
H N D B

POSITION TO ROTATE? 11

A K O C
G E M L
F I D P
H N B J

POSITION TO ROTATE? 10

A K O C
G E M L
F N I P
H B D J

POSITION TO ROTATE? 10

A K O C
G E M L
F B N P
H D I J

POSITION TO ROTATE? 6

A K O C
G B E L
F N M P
H D I J

POSITION TO ROTATE? 2

A B K C
G E O L
F N M P
H D I J

POSITION TO ROTATE? 10

A B K C
G E O L
F D N P
H I M J

POSITION TO ROTATE? 6

A B K C
G D E L
F N O P
H I M J

POSITION TO ROTATE? 6

A B K C
G N D L
F O E P
H I M J

POSITION TO ROTATE? 7

A B K C
G N E D
F O P L
H I M J

POSITION TO ROTATE? 3

A B E K
G N D C
F O P L
H I M J
```

```
POSITION TO ROTATE? 3

A B D E
G N C K
F O P L
H I M J

POSITION TO ROTATE? 3

A B C D
G N K E
F O P L
H I M J

POSITION TO ROTATE? 7

A B C D
G N P K
F O L E
H I M J

POSITION TO ROTATE? 7

A B C D
G N L P
F O E K
H I M J

POSITION TO ROTATE? 6

A B C D
G O N P
F E L K
H I M J

POSITION TO ROTATE? 5

A B C D
F G N P
E O L K
H I M J

POSITION TO ROTATE? 5

A B C D
E F N P
O G L K
H I M J

POSITION TO ROTATE? 10

A B C D
E F N P
O I G K
H M L J

POSITION TO ROTATE? 9

A B C D
E F N P
H O G K
M I L J

POSITION TO ROTATE? 9

A B C D
E F N P
M H G K
I O L J

POSITION TO ROTATE? 11

A B C D
E F N P
M H L G
I O J K

POSITION TO ROTATE? 10

A B C D
E F N P
M O H G
I J L K

POSITION TO ROTATE? 7

A B C D
E F H N
M O G P
I J L K
```

```
POSITION TO ROTATE? 7

A B C D
E F G H
M O P N
I J L K

POSITION TO ROTATE? 10

A B C D
E F G H
M J O N
I L P K

POSITION TO ROTATE? 11

A B C D
E F G H
M J P O
I L K N

POSITION TO ROTATE? 10

A B C D
E F G H
M L J O
I K P N

POSITION TO ROTATE? 9

A B C D
E F G H
I M J O
K L P N

POSITION TO ROTATE? 9

A B C D
E F G H
K I J O
L M P N

POSITION TO ROTATE? 11

A B C D
E F G H
K I P J
L M N O

POSITION TO ROTATE? 11

A B C D
E F G H
K I N P
L M O J

POSITION TO ROTATE? 10

A B C D
E F G H
K M I P
L O N J

POSITION TO ROTATE? 11

A B C D
E F G H
K M N I
L O J P

POSITION TO ROTATE? 11

A B C D
E F G H
K M J N
L O P I

POSITION TO ROTATE? 10

A B C D
E F G H
K O M N
L P J I

POSITION TO ROTATE? 11

A B C D
E F G H
K O J M
L P I N
```

Later in the Game

```
POSITION TO ROTATE? 9

A B C D
E F G H
J I K P
M L N O

POSITION TO ROTATE? 10

A B C D
E F G H
J L I P
M N K O

POSITION TO ROTATE? 9

A B C D
E F G H
M J I P
N L K O

POSITION TO ROTATE? 10

A B C D
E F G H
M L J P
N K I O

POSITION TO ROTATE? 10

A B C D
E F G H
M K L P
N I J O

POSITION TO ROTATE? 10

A B C D
E F G H
M I K P
N J L O

POSITION TO ROTATE? 9

A B C D
E F G H
N M K P
J I L O

POSITION TO ROTATE? 9

A B C D
E F G H
J N K P
I M L O

POSITION TO ROTATE? 9

A B C D
E F G H
I J K P
M N L O

POSITION TO ROTATE? 11

A B C D
E F G H
I J L K
M N O P

POSITION TO ROTATE? -1
EXCHANGE WHICH TWO POSITIONS? 11,12

A B C D
E F G H
I J K L
M N O P

YOU ORDERED THE BOARD IN 66  MOVES.

PLAY AGAIN? NO

YOU PLAYED 1  GAMES AND ORDERED THE BOARD IN
AN AVERAGE OF 66  MOVES PER GAME.

OK
```

Safe

In a sense, this is another game in the "guess a mystery number" family. However, it has quite a different "twist." In this game, you are trying to open a safe by turning or twisting a dial back and forth between one and ninety-nine or ninety-nine and one.

The instructions shown in the sample run are very complete. However, one hint that will help you when you start playing is that it is usually best to start at ninety-nine when going to the right because if you get a click, the number must be close. If not, you can step it down by eights or tens until you get the first click and then judge from there.

Safe was created and written by Kevin Ashley.

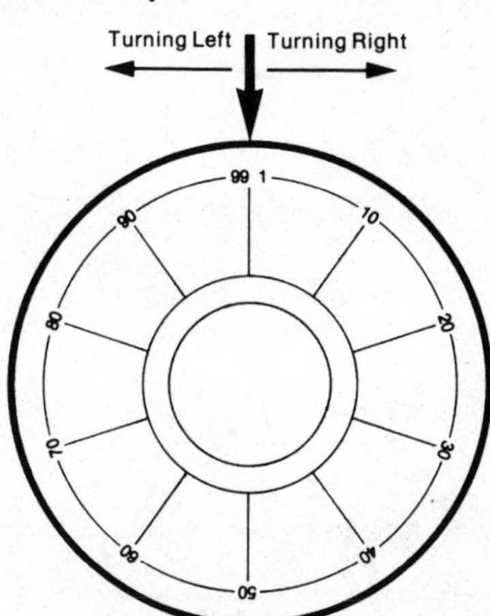

NOTE: There is no spot 0 (zero) and it spins back past the last number automatically as in most locks.

```
RUN
                              SAFE
                        CREATIVE COMPUTING
                      MORRISTOWN, NEW JERSEY


DO YOU WANT DIRECTIONS? YES


YOU ARE A BURGULAR AND HAVE ENCOUNTERED A SAFE.  YOU  MUST
OPEN THE SAFE TO GET THE SECRET PLANS THAT YOU  CAME FOR.
TO DO THIS , YOU MUST ENTER THE NUMBER OF WHAT YOU WANT THE
 DIAL TURNED TO, THE COMPUTER WILL ACT AS THE SAFE AND WILL
HELP YOU BY GIVING A SORT OF CLUE, THAT IS YOU WILL'HEAR'
A CLICK AT EVENLY SPACED NOTCHES AS YOU  MOVE TO THE PROPER
NUMBER.  THERE ARE FOUR OF THEM BEFORE THE FINAL CLICK IS
'HEARD'. AFTER THE FINAL ONE IS HEARD, YOU WILL GO ON TO
THE NEXT NUMBER.  THE COMPUTER WILL'SAY' 'CLICK' FOR EACH
NOTCH THAT YOU PASS AND '**CLICK**' WHEN  YOU REACH THE
PROPER NUMBER.  IF YOU PASS IT OR TAKE LONGER THAN TEN TRIES
ON ANY ONE NUMBER, YOU WILL ACTIVATE THE ALARM.
REMEMBER THAT WHEN YOU TURN THE DIAL TO THE LEFT, THE
NUMBERS GO FROM 1 -99 ,AND WHEN YOU GO TO THE RIGHT, THE
NUMBERS GO FROM 99-1
OKAY, START TO THE RIGHT,  SHHHHHH!!!!!!!!!!!!!!
ARE YOU READY? YES
OKAY, THEN LET'S START
? 89
? 79
CLICK
? 69
CLICK
? 59
CLICK
CLICK
? 49
CLICK
CLICK
CLICK
? 35
CLICK
CLICK
CLICK
CLICK
? 32
CLICK
CLICK
CLICK
CLICK
```

```
? 30
CLICK
CLICK
CLICK
CLICK
? 29
CLICK
CLICK
CLICK
CLICK
? 27
CLICK
CLICK
CLICK
CLICK
THE SENSOR HAS BEEN TRIGGERED
LEAVE WHILE YOU CAN BEFORE THE
POLICE GET HERE.
WANT TO TRY THE SAME SAFE? YES
ARE YOU READY? YES
OKAY, THEN LET'S START
? 25
CLICK
CLICK
CLICK
CLICK
? 23
CLICK
CLICK
CLICK
CLICK
? 19
THE SENSOR HAS BEEN TRIGGERED
LEAVE WHILE YOU CAN BEFORE THE
POLICE GET HERE.
WANT TO TRY THE SAME SAFE? YES
ARE YOU READY? YES
OKAY, THEN LET'S START
? 21
** CLICK **
AND NOW TO THE LEFT
? 5
CLICK
CLICK
CLICK
CLICK
? 10
? 30
? 50
? 60
? 70
? 80
? 90
? 95
? 97
THE SENSOR HAS BEEN TRIGGERED
LEAVE WHILE YOU CAN BEFORE THE
POLICE GET HERE.
WANT TO TRY THE SAME SAFE? YES
ARE YOU READY? YES
OKAY, THEN LET'S START
? 21
** CLICK **
AND NOW TO THE LEFT
? 1
CLICK
CLICK
CLICK
CLICK
? 5
? 6
? 7
? 8
? 12
? 14
? 16
? 18
** CLICK **
AND NOW TO THE RIGHT AGAIN
? 95
CLICK
CLICK
CLICK
? 89
CLICK
? 83
** CLICK **...YOU OPENED IT
BUT OH,OH, HE MUST HAVE MOVED IT
TRY THE ONE OVER THERE
OKAY, START TO THE RIGHT,  SHHHHHH!!!!!!!!!!!!!!
ARE YOU READY? NO
Ok
```

```
LIST
1 PRINT TAB(28)"SAFE"
2 PRINT TAB(20)"CREATIVE COMPUTING"
3 PRINT TAB(18)"MORRISTOWN, NEW JERSEY"
4 PRINT
5 PRINT
6 PRINT
10 DIM A1(4)
20 PRINT"DO YOU WANT DIRECTIONS";
30 INPUT A$
40 IF A$="YES" THEN 80
50 IF A$="NO" THEN 250
60 PRINT"ANSWER YES OR NO"
70 GOTO 20
80 PRINT
90 PRINT
100 PRINT"YOU ARE A BURGULAR AND HAVE ENCOUNTERED A SAFE.  YOU  MUST"
110 PRINT"OPEN THE SAFE TO GET THE SECRET PLANS THAT YOU  CAME FOR."
120 PRINT"TO DO THIS , YOU MUST ENTER THE NUMBER OF WHAT YOU WANT THE"
130 PRINT" DIAL TURNED TO, THE COMPUTER WILL ACT AS THE SAFE AND WILL"
140 PRINT"HELP YOU BY GIVING A SORT OF CLUE, THAT IS YOU WILL'HEAR'"
150 PRINT"A CLICK AT EVENLY SPACED NOTCHES AS YOU  MOVE TO THE PROPER"
160 PRINT"NUMBER.  THERE ARE FOUR OF THEM BEFORE THE FINAL CLICK IS"
170 PRINT"'HEARD'. AFTER THE FINAL ONE IS HEARD, YOU WILL GO ON TO"
180 PRINT"THE NEXT NUMBER.  THE COMPUTER WILL'SAY' 'CLICK' FOR EACH"
190 PRINT"NOTCH THAT YOU PASS AND '**CLICK**' WHEN  YOU REACH THE"
200 PRINT"PROPER NUMBER.  IF YOU PASS IT OR TAKE LONGER THAN TEN TRIES"
210 PRINT "ON ANY ONE NUMBER, YOU WILL ACTIVATE THE ALARM."
220 PRINT"REMEMBER THAT WHEN YOU TURN THE DIAL TO THE LEFT, THE"
230 PRINT"NUMBERS GO FROM 1 -99 ,AND WHEN YOU GO TO THE RIGHT, THE"
240 PRINT"NUMBERS GO FROM 99-1"
250 PRINT"OKAY, START TO THE RIGHT,  SHHHHHH!!!!!!!!!!!!!!"
260 A=INT(RND(1)*81)+10
270 B=INT(RND(1)*81)+10
280 C=INT(RND(1)*81)+10
290 PRINT"ARE YOU READY";
300 INPUT A$
310 IF A$="YES" THEN 340
320 IF A$<>"WHAT"THEN 990
330 PRINTA;B;C
340 L=100-A
350 FOR M=1 TO 4
360 A1(M)=(5-M)*L/5+A
370 NEXT M
380 J=1
390 PRINT"OKAY, THEN LET'S START"
400 INPUT M
410 ON SGN(M-A)+2 GOTO 500,570,420
420 FOR K=1 TO 4
430 IF M>A1(K) THEN 460
440 PRINT"CLICK"
460 NEXT K
470 IF J>=10 THEN 500
480 J=J+1
490 GOTO 400
500 PRINT"THE SENSOR HAS BEEN TRIGGERED"
510 PRINT"LEAVE WHILE YOU CAN BEFORE THE"
520 PRINT"POLICE GET HERE."
530 PRINT"WANT TO TRY THE SAME SAFE";
540 INPUT A$
550 IF A$="YES" THEN 280
560 GOTO 250
570 PRINT"** CLICK **"
580 L=L+B
590 FOR K=1 TO 4
600 A1(K)=K*L/5+B
610 NEXT K
620 PRINT"AND NOW TO THE LEFT"
630 J=1
640 INPUT M
650 ON SGN(M-A)+2 GOTO 660,500,680
660 ON SGN(M-B)+2 GOTO 670,760,500
670 M=M+100
680 FOR K=1 TO 4
690 IF M<A1(K) THEN 720
700 PRINT"CLICK"
710 A1(K)=200
720 NEXT K
730 IF J>=10 THEN 500
740 J=J+1
750 GOTO 640
760 PRINT"** CLICK **"
770 L=(100-C)+B
780 FOR K=1 TO 4
790 A1(K)=B+100-K*L/5
800 NEXT K
810 PRINT"AND NOW TO THE RIGHT AGAIN"
820 J=1
830 INPUT M
840 ON SGN(M-B)+2 GOTO 860,500,850
850 ONSGN(M-C)+2 GOTO 500,950,870
860 M=M+100
870 FOR K=1 TO 4
880 IF M>A1(K) THEN 910
890 PRINT"CLICK"
900 A1(K)=-200
910 NEXT K
920 IF J>=10 THEN 500
930 J=J+1
940 GOTO 830
950 PRINT"** CLICK **...YOU OPENED IT"
960 PRINT"BUT OH,OH, HE MUST HAVE MOVED IT"
970 PRINT"TRY THE ONE OVER THERE"
980 GOTO 250
990 END
Ok
```

Scales

This program tests your knowledge of different types of musical scales. It generates 11 types of scales: major, natural minor, harmonic minor, Hungarian minor, dorian, phygian, lydian, mixolydian, locrian, and whole tone.

Prior to running the program, test yourself off line on a sheet of paper by writing down several types of scales and 8 notes starting at a note chosen by you. Then run the program to check your answers.

When you run this program, you will be asked, "Which type of scale is wanted?" Respond by typing the first two letters of the name of the desired scale followed immediately by the desired key. Use a lower case 'b' for the flat and use '#' for the sharp. Sample in puts would be *phe* for phrygian starting on E, *maf#* for major on F-sharp, and *whg* for whole tone on G.

The author, Marvin S. Thostenson, is at the School of Music, University of Iowa. Scales first appeared in *Creative Computing*, Mar/Apr 1977.

```
RUN
                              SCALES
                         CREATIVE COMPUTING
                       MORRISTOWN, NEW JERSEY


ELEVEN SCALE TYPES -- MAJOR, MINOR, MODAL, AND WHOLE TONE

This program prints in letter names one octave upward, the major,
the natural, harmonic, melodic, and Hungarian minors, the
dorian, phrygian, lydian, mixolydian, and locrian modes, and
the whole tone scales.

Use a 3- or 4-character input: the first 2 char's are the scale
type, and the 3rd char'r is the single letter tonic, or the
last two char's are the tonic degree or the key signature.
SCALE TYPES-- ma na ha me do ph ly mi lo hu and wh
Input either a tonic or a signature.
EXAMPLES: macb lydb mieb whgb naf# hag# mea# loc# doc phd hue

      WHICH TYPE OF SCALE IS WANTED? whf#

           SCALE ASKED --------Whole tone scale on F#

  ANSWER (in letter names) ----------


      F#  G#  A#  B#  D   E   F#


      WHICH TYPE OF SCALE IS WANTED? nae

           SCALE ASKED --------Nat'l minor scale on E

  ANSWER (in letter names) ----------


      E   F#  G   A   B   C   D   E


      WHICH TYPE OF SCALE IS WANTED? whc

           SCALE ASKED --------Whole tone scale on C

  ANSWER (in letter names) ----------


      C   D   E   F#  Ab  Bb  C


      WHICH TYPE OF SCALE IS WANTED? hu2#

           SCALE ASKED --------Hung'n minor scale on B

  ANSWER (in letter names) ----------


      B   C#  D   E#  F#  G   A#  B


      WHICH TYPE OF SCALE IS WANTED? stop
OK
```

```
list

10 PRINT TAB(26);"SCALES"
20 PRINT TAB(20);"CREATIVE COMPUTING"
30 PRINT TAB(18);"MORRISTOWN, NEW JERSEY"
40 PRINT:PRINT:PRINT
100 A=0:B=0:C=0:D=0:E=0:H=0:K=0:L=0:M=0:N=0:O=0
200 W=4
210 PRINT "ELEVEN SCALE TYPES -- MAJOR, MINOR, MODAL, AND WHOLE TONE"
215 PRINT
220 PRINT "This program prints in letter names one octave upward, ";
225 PRINT "the major,"
227 PRINT "the natural, harmonic, melodic, and Hungarian minors, the"
228 PRINT "dorian, phrygian, lydian, mixolydian, and locrian modes, and"
229 PRINT "the whole tone scales.":PRINT
230 PRINT "Use a 3- or 4-character input: the first 2 char's are the sca
le"
232 PRINT "type, and the 3rd char'r is the single letter tonic, or the"
234 PRINT "last two char's are the tonic degree or the key signature."
240 PRINT "SCALE TYPES-- ma na ha me do ph ly mi lo hu and wh"
250 PRINT "Input either a tonic or a signature."
260 PRINT "EXAMPLES: macb lydb mieb whgb naf# hag# mea# loc# doc phd hue
"
270 B$="SCALE ASKED --------"
280 C$="ANSWER (in letter names) ----------"
290 O$="STRUCTURE---- "
300 K$=" tetrachords"
310 U=1
320 PRINT:PRINT:PRINT TAB(8);"WHICH TYPE OF SCALE IS WANTED";
330 INPUT A$
340 N=LEN(A$)
350 IF A$="stop" THEN 1290
360 E$="manahamedophlymilohuwh"
370 FOR X=1 TO 22 STEP 2
380 IF LEFT$(A$,2)=MID$(E$,X,2) THEN 400
390 NEXT X
400 Q=(X+1)/2
410 A0$=A$
420 X=ASC(LEFT$(A0$,1))-32
425 A0$=CHR$(X)+MID$(A0$,2,N)
430 READ D$
440 A0$=A$
450 X=ASC(LEFT$(A0$,1))-32
455 A0$=CHR$(X)+MID$(A0$,2,N)
460 IF LEFT$(D$,2)=LEFT$(A0$,2) THEN 480
470 GOTO 430
480 J$=D$
490 RESTORE
500 IF N<>3 THEN 530
520 A$=LEFT$(A$,3)+" "
530 IF Q=1 OR Q=7 OR Q=11 THEN 550
540 IF Q>=2 AND Q<=6 OR Q=9 OR Q=10 THEN 570
550 Y=1
560 GOTO 580
570 Y=2
580 F$="bxexaxdxgxcxfxb#e#a#d#g#c#f#b e a d g c f "
585 F$=F$+"bbebabdbgbcbfbbdedadddgdcd"
590 G$="BxExAxDxGxCxFxB#E#A#D#G#C#F#B E A D G C F "
595 G$=G$+"BbEbAbDbGbCbFbBdEdAdDdGdCd"
600 ON Y GOTO 610,630
610 H$="5t4t3t2t1t7x6x5x4x3x2x1x7#6#5#4#3#2#1#0#1b2b3b4b5b6b7b1d2d3d4d"
615 H$=H$+"5d6d7d"
620 GOTO 640
630 H$="2t1t7x6x5x4x3x2x1x7#6#5#4#3#2#1#0#1b2b3b4b5b6b7b1d2d3d4d"
635 H$=H$+"5d6d7d8d9d  "
640 FOR V=1 TO 68 STEP 2
650 IF MID$(A$,3,2)=MID$(F$,V,2) THEN 680
660 IF MID$(A$,3,2)=MID$(H$,V,2) THEN 680
670 NEXT V
680 C1$=MID$(G$,V,2)
690 T=T+1
700 IF T=9 THEN 1160
710 ON T GOTO 720,740,790,840,890,940,990,1040
720 R=0
730 GOTO 1060
740 IF Q=6 OR Q=9 THEN 770
750 R=-4
760 GOTO 1060
770 R=10
780 GOTO 1060
790 IF Q=1 OR Q=7 OR Q=8 OR Q=11 THEN 820
800 R=6
810 GOTO 1060
820 R=-8
830 GOTO 1060
840 IF Q=7 OR Q=10 OR Q=11 THEN 870
850 R=2
860 GOTO 1060
870 R=-12
880 GOTO 1060
890 IF Q=9 OR Q=11 THEN 920
900 R=-2
910 GOTO 1060
920 R=12
930 GOTO 1060
940 IF Q=1 OR Q=4 OR Q=5 OR Q=7 OR Q=8 THEN 970
950 R=8
960 GOTO 1060
970 R=-6
980 GOTO 1060
990 IF Q=1 OR Q=3 OR Q=4 OR Q=7 OR Q=10 THEN 1020
1000 R=4
1010 GOTO 1060
1020 R=-10
1030 GOTO 1060
1040 R=0
1060 IF Q=11 AND T=5 THEN 1090
1070 IF U=1 THEN I$=MID$(G$,V+R,2):GOTO 1100
1075 I$=LEFT$(I$,U-1)+MID$(G$,V+R,2)
1080 GOTO 1100
1090 GOTO 690
1100 I$=LEFT$(I$,U+1)+"  "
1110 IF MID$(I$,U+1,1)="d" THEN 1130
1120 GOTO 1140
1130 I$=LEFT$(I$,U)+"bb"
1140 U=U+4
1150 GOTO 690
1160 PRINT:PRINT TAB(3),B$;J$;C1$:PRINT
1170 PRINT TAB(3);C$:PRINT
1180 PRINT:PRINT TAB(8);I$
1190 C1$="":I$="":G$=""
1220 Q=0:T=0:R=0
1230 PRINT
1240 GOTO 310
1250 DATA "Major scale on ","Nat'l minor scale on "
1255 DATA "Harm'c minor scale on ","Mel'c minor scale on "
1260 DATA "Dorian mode on ","Phrygian mode on "
1270 DATA "Lydian mode on ","Mixolydian mode on ","Locrian mode on "
1280 DATA "Hung'n minor scale on ","Whole tone scale on "
1290 END
OK
```

Schmoo

Schmoos are imaginary creatures who love being splattered with juicy mudballs. You, being a schmoo lover, try to make schmoos happy by tossing mudballs at them. It will help you in playing this game to know a little bit about grids and angles like in the X,Y coordinate system 2,–3 means right 2 and down 3. If 0 degrees is the angle coinciding with the positive X axis, then 2,–3 would be in the fourth quadrant and would correspond to angles between 270 and 360 degrees.

If you're pretty good, you can "splat the schmoo" in about eight tries; but don't cheat and use the formula. And don't expect me to tell you where it's hidden in the program!

If you want to extend the Schmoo game, you might want to add a third dimension with flying schmoos. The program shouldn't be too hard and it would be a really neat game. If you want to try something easier, fix Schmoo so that it requires initial velocities as well as angles. You could even make a low-gravity (lunar version) of Schmoo.

Schmoo was conceived and written by Frederick H. Bell at the University of Pittsburgh. It first appeared in *Creative Computing*, Sep/Oct 1975.

```
RUN
                    SCHMOO
  CREATIVE COMPUTING  MORRISTOWN NEW JERSEY



THIS IS A NEW SCHMOO GAME.  SCHMOOS
ARE IMAGINARY CREATURES WHO LOVE
BEING SPLATTED WITH JUICY MUD BALLS.
YOU, BEING A SCHMOO LOVER, TRY TO
MAKE SCHMOOS HAPPY BY TOSSING MUD
BALLS AT THEM.  YOU HAVE A
MECHANICAL MUD SLINGER THAT WILL
SLING MUD TO A MAXIMUM DISTANCE
OF 46,500 INCHES. YOUR JOB IS TO
SET THE MUD SLINGER AT THE CORRECT
ELEVATION (0 TO 90) AND THE CORRECT
DIRECTIONAL ANGLE (0 TO 360) TO SPLAT THE
SCHMOO.  A HIT WITHIN 100 INCHES OF THE SCHMOO
WILL SPLATTER HIM.



COORDINATES OF THE SCHMOO ARE ( 29007 , 9760 ).

MUD SLINGER ELEVATION? 39
DIRECTIONAL ANGLE OF MUD SLINGER? 34
YOU MISSED THE SCHMOO AT ( 29007 , 9760 ).
YOUR MUD HIT ( 37707 , 25433 ).

MUD SLINGER ELEVATION? 23
DIRECTIONAL ANGLE OF MUD SLINGER? 31
YOU MISSED THE SCHMOO AT ( 29007 , 9760 ).
YOUR MUD HIT ( 28671 , 17227 ).

MUD SLINGER ELEVATION? 12
DIRECTIONAL ANGLE OF MUD SLINGER? 30
YOU MISSED THE SCHMOO AT ( 29007 , 9760 ).
YOUR MUD HIT ( 16379 , 9456 ).

MUD SLINGER ELEVATION? 18
DIRECTIONAL ANGLE OF MUD SLINGER? 27
YOU MISSED THE SCHMOO AT ( 29007 , 9760 ).
YOUR MUD HIT ( 24352 , 12408 ).

MUD SLINGER ELEVATION? 20
DIRECTIONAL ANGLE OF MUD SLINGER? 25
YOU MISSED THE SCHMOO AT ( 29007 , 9760 ).
YOUR MUD HIT ( 27088 , 12631 ).

MUD SLINGER ELEVATION? 20
DIRECTIONAL ANGLE OF MUD SLINGER? 21
YOU MISSED THE SCHMOO AT ( 29007 , 9760 ).
YOUR MUD HIT ( 27903 , 10711 ).

MUD SLINGER ELEVATION? 22
DIRECTIONAL ANGLE OF MUD SLINGER? 20
YOU MISSED THE SCHMOO AT ( 29007 , 9760 ).
YOUR MUD HIT ( 30353 , 11047 ).

MUD SLINGER ELEVATION? 21
DIRECTIONAL ANGLE OF MUD SLINGER? 17
YOU MISSED THE SCHMOO AT ( 29007 , 9760 ).
YOUR MUD HIT ( 29754 , 9096 ).

MUD SLINGER ELEVATION? 20
DIRECTIONAL ANGLE OF MUD SLINGER? 18
YOU MISSED THE SCHMOO AT ( 29007 , 9760 ).
YOUR MUD HIT ( 28426 , 9236 ).

MUD SLINGER ELEVATION? 21
DIRECTIONAL ANGLE OF MUD SLINGER? 18
YOU MISSED THE SCHMOO AT ( 29007 , 9760 ).
YOUR MUD HIT ( 29591 , 9614 ).

MUD SLINGER ELEVATION? 20
DIRECTIONAL ANGLE OF MUD SLINGER? 19
YOU MISSED THE SCHMOO AT ( 29007 , 9760 ).
YOUR MUD HIT ( 28260 , 9730 ).

MUD SLINGER ELEVATION? 22
DIRECTIONAL ANGLE OF MUD SLINGER? 18
YOU MISSED THE SCHMOO AT ( 29007 , 9760 ).
YOUR MUD HIT ( 30720 , 9981 ).

MUD SLINGER ELEVATION? 21
DIRECTIONAL ANGLE OF MUD SLINGER? 17.5
YOU MISSED THE SCHMOO AT ( 29007 , 9760 ).
YOUR MUD HIT ( 29673 , 9356 ).

MUD SLINGER ELEVATION? 21
DIRECTIONAL ANGLE OF MUD SLINGER? 18.4
YOU MISSED THE SCHMOO AT ( 29007 , 9760 ).
YOUR MUD HIT ( 29523 , 9821 ).

MUD SLINGER ELEVATION? 21
DIRECTIONAL ANGLE OF MUD SLINGER? 18.8
YOU MISSED THE SCHMOO AT ( 29007 , 9760 ).
YOUR MUD HIT ( 29454 , 10026 ).

MUD SLINGER ELEVATION? 20
DIRECTIONAL ANGLE OF MUD SLINGER? 18.6
YOU MISSED THE SCHMOO AT ( 29007 , 9760 ).
YOUR MUD HIT ( 28327 , 9533 ).

MUD SLINGER ELEVATION? 20.3
DIRECTIONAL ANGLE OF MUD SLINGER? 18.87
YOU MISSED THE SCHMOO AT ( 29007 , 9760 ).
YOUR MUD HIT ( 28633 , 9786 ).

MUD SLINGER ELEVATION? 20.5
DIRECTIONAL ANGLE OF MUD SLINGER? 18.87
YOU MISSED THE SCHMOO AT ( 29007 , 9760 ).
YOUR MUD HIT ( 28866 , 9866 ).
```

```
MUD SLINGER ELEVATION? 20.68
DIRECTIONAL ANGLE OF MUD SLINGER? 18.73
YOU MISSED THE SCHMOO AT ( 29007 , 9760 ).
YOUR MUD HIT ( 29098 , 9866 ).

MUD SLINGER ELEVATION? 20.68
DIRECTIONAL ANGLE OF MUD SLINGER? 18.69
YOU MISSED THE SCHMOO AT ( 29007 , 9760 ).
YOUR MUD HIT ( 29105 , 9846 ).

MUD SLINGER ELEVATION? 20.68
DIRECTIONAL ANGLE OF MUD SLINGER? 18.71
YOU MISSED THE SCHMOO AT ( 29007 , 9760 ).
YOUR MUD HIT ( 29102 , 9856 ).

MUD SLINGER ELEVATION? 20.62
DIRECTIONAL ANGLE OF MUD SLINGER? 18.71
*SCHMOO SPLATTED* 22  MUD BALLS TOSSED.

I SEE ANOTHER SCHMOO.  TO SPLAT
HIM, TYPE MUD.  TO QUIT, TYPE QUIT.

? MUD

COORDINATES OF THE SCHMOO ARE ( 6529 , 9167 ).
THE SCHMOO IS HAPPY TO BE SPLATTED.
TO MAKE YOU HAPPY TOO,
HE WILL THROW MUD AT YOU.

MUD SLINGER ELEVATION? 47
DIRECTIONAL ANGLE OF MUD SLINGER? 47
YOU MISSED THE SCHMOO AT ( 6529 , 9167 ).
YOUR MUD HIT ( 31635 , 33924 ).

SCHMOO MUD HIT  1010 INCHES FROM YOU.
MUD SLINGER ELEVATION? 10
DIRECTIONAL ANGLE OF MUD SLINGER? 47
YOU MISSED THE SCHMOO AT ( 6529 , 9167 ).
YOUR MUD HIT ( 10845 , 11630 ).

SCHMOO MUD HIT  910 INCHES FROM YOU.
MUD SLINGER ELEVATION? 7
DIRECTIONAL ANGLE OF MUD SLINGER? 51
YOU MISSED THE SCHMOO AT ( 6529 , 9167 ).
YOUR MUD HIT ( 7079 , 8742 ).

SCHMOO MUD HIT  1155 INCHES FROM YOU.
MUD SLINGER ELEVATION? 7.2
DIRECTIONAL ANGLE OF MUD SLINGER? 54
YOU MISSED THE SCHMOO AT ( 6529 , 9167 ).
YOUR MUD HIT ( 6797 , 9355 ).

SCHMOO MUD HIT  786 INCHES FROM YOU.
MUD SLINGER ELEVATION? 7.1
DIRECTIONAL ANGLE OF MUD SLINGER? 53.2
YOU MISSED THE SCHMOO AT ( 6529 , 9167 ).
YOUR MUD HIT ( 6832 , 9133 ).

SCHMOO MUD HIT  171 INCHES FROM YOU.
MUD SLINGER ELEVATION? 6.9
DIRECTIONAL ANGLE OF MUD SLINGER? 53.2
YOU MISSED THE SCHMOO AT ( 6529 , 9167 ).
YOUR MUD HIT ( 6643 , 8880 ).

SCHMOO MUD HIT  380 INCHES FROM YOU.
MUD SLINGER ELEVATION? 6.89
DIRECTIONAL ANGLE OF MUD SLINGER? 53.4
YOU MISSED THE SCHMOO AT ( 6529 , 9167 ).
YOUR MUD HIT ( 6603 , 8892 ).

SCHMOO MUD HIT  750 INCHES FROM YOU.
MUD SLINGER ELEVATION? 6.86
DIRECTIONAL ANGLE OF MUD SLINGER? 53.57
YOU MISSED THE SCHMOO AT ( 6529 , 9167 ).
YOUR MUD HIT ( 6548 , 8872 ).

SCHMOO MUD HIT  1219 INCHES FROM YOU.
MUD SLINGER ELEVATION? 6.91
DIRECTIONAL ANGLE OF MUD SLINGER? 53.54
YOU MISSED THE SCHMOO AT ( 6529 , 9167 ).
YOUR MUD HIT ( 6600 , 8933 ).

SCHMOO MUD HIT  1579 INCHES FROM YOU.
MUD SLINGER ELEVATION? 6.89
DIRECTIONAL ANGLE OF MUD SLINGER? 53.52
YOU MISSED THE SCHMOO AT ( 6529 , 9167 ).
YOUR MUD HIT ( 6585 , 8905 ).

THE SCHMOO HAS SPLATTED YOU!
CLEAN UP AND GOODBYE!
Ok
```

```
LIST
10 PRINT TAB(30);"SCHMOO"
20 PRINT TAB(15);"CREATIVE COMPUTING  MORRISTOWN NEW JERSEY"
21 PRINT
22 PRINT
23 PRINT
30 PRINT "THIS IS A NEW SCHMOO GAME.  SCHMOOS"
32 PRINT "ARE IMAGINARY CREATURES WHO LOVE"
34 PRINT "BEING SPLATTED WITH JUICY MUD BALLS."
36 PRINT "YOU, BEING A SCHMOO LOVER, TRY TO"
38 PRINT "MAKE SCHMOOS HAPPY BY TOSSING MUD"
40 PRINT "BALLS AT THEM.  YOU HAVE A"
42 PRINT "MECHANICAL MUD SLINGER THAT WILL"
44 PRINT "SLING MUD TO A MAXIMUM DISTANCE"
46 PRINT "OF 46,500 INCHES. YOUR JOB IS TO"
50 PRINT "SET THE MUD SLINGER AT THE CORRECT"
55 PRINT "ELEVATION (0 TO 90) AND THE CORRECT"
60 PRINT "DIRECTIONAL ANGLE (0 TO 360) TO SPLAT THE"
65 PRINT "SCHMOO.  A HIT WITHIN 100 INCHES OF THE SCHMOO"
70 PRINT "WILL SPLATTER HIM."
75 PRINT
90 PRINT
100 K1=0
110 Z=INT(1+RND(1)*4-1E-08)
120 ON Z GOTO 130,140,150,160
130 P=-1
135 Q=-1
138 GOTO 200
140 P=-1
145 Q=1
148 GOTO 200
150 P=1
155 Q=-1
158 GOTO 200
160 P=1
165 Q=1
200 X=(INT(26000*RND(1)+5000))*P
210 Y=(INT(26000*RND(1)+5000))*Q
220 S=0
230 K1=K1+1
240 IF K1 < 2 THEN 400
250 R=INT(7*RND(1)+5)
260 GOTO 400
300 PRINT "THE ELEVATION MUST BE BETWEEN 1 AND 90."
310 GOTO 500
320 PRINT "DIRECTIONAL ANGLE MUST BE FROM 0 TO 360."
340 GOTO 500
350 PRINT "*SCHMOO SPLATTED*";S;" MUD BALLS TOSSED."
351 PRINT
352 PRINT "I SEE ANOTHER SCHMOO.  TO SPLAT"
354 PRINT "HIM, TYPE MUD.  TO QUIT, TYPE QUIT."
356 PRINT
358 INPUT C$
360 IF C$="MUD" THEN 110
361 STOP
362 PRINT "YOU MISSED THE SCHMOO AT (";X;",";Y;")."
364 PRINT "YOUR MUD HIT (";INT(X1);",";INT(Y1);")."
366 PRINT
370 IF K1 < 2 THEN 500
380 IF S >= R THEN 800
390 PRINT "SCHMOO MUD HIT ";R2;"INCHES FROM YOU."
395 GOTO 500
400 PRINT
410 PRINT "COORDINATES OF THE SCHMOO ARE (";X;",";Y;")."
415 IF K1 < 2 THEN 420
417 PRINT "THE SCHMOO IS HAPPY TO BE SPLATTED."
418 PRINT "TO MAKE YOU HAPPY TOO,"
419 PRINT "HE WILL THROW MUD AT YOU."
420 PRINT
500 PRINT "MUD SLINGER ELEVATION";
502 INPUT B
504 PRINT "DIRECTIONAL ANGLE OF MUD SLINGER";
506 INPUT C
520 IF B = 90 THEN 700
530 IF B > 90 THEN 300
540 IF B < 1 THEN 300
550 IF C < 0 THEN 320
560 IF C > (360-(1E-08)) THEN 320
570 S=S+1
580 IF K1 < 2 THEN 595
590 R2=INT(ABS(300*RND(1)*(11-2*S))+90)
595 J=3.1415926535#/180
596 D=ABS(INT(93000!*SIN(B*J)*COS(B*J)))
610 X1=D*COS(C*3.1415926535#/180)
620 Y1=D*SIN(C*3.1415926535#/180)
630 D1=SQR((X-X1)^2+(Y-Y1)^2)
640 IF 100 >= D1 THEN 350
650 GOTO 362
700 PRINT "YOU DOPE!  YOU SPLATTED YOURSELF."
710 GOTO 900
800 PRINT "THE SCHMOO HAS SPLATTED YOU!"
802 PRINT "CLEAN UP AND GOODBYE!"
900 END
```

Seabattle

The object of the game of SEA BATTLE is quite simple. You are a submarine with a mission to seek out and destroy all of the enemy ships in your area, using whatever means are available. This includes torpedoes, Polaris missiles, sabotage, and suicide. The enemy, in turn, throws out depth charges in an attempt to destroy you. There are also some underwater mines which have a nasty habit of blowing you up when you run into them. Other hazards are some very hungry sea monsters lurking about who have a taste for submarine sandwiches.

I started writing this program two years ago, and finished my last modifications just recently. Of course, this doesn't mean I worked on it continuously for two years. There were some long 4-6 month stretches when I didn't do anything to it. It started out as a very simple program, and I just kept thinking of things to add to it.

I am currently a senior in Simley Senior High School in Inver Grove Heights, Minnesota, and am 18 years old. I have been working with computers since the ninth grade, and have written many programs, including this one.

This program always draws a crowd in our school computer room, even from kids who don't even know which end of a teletype to type on. I built every possible inconvenience into it, to keep people from winning too easily. I am happy to say that when a person wins now, it's headline news. There are always muttered oaths to beat the computer next time, and this alone brings me more enjoyment than playing the program.

As you can see, the program is quite long, and initially I had some storage problems, as I'm sure many of you will have, too. All I can say is to slice away at some of the more trivial commands and options until (hopefully) you cut it down to a reasonable size. If compiling space is a problem, you may have to divide the program into subprograms chained together. If you don't have this capability, you'll have to brainstorm your own ideas.

Here are some of the anomalies our HP 2000 system. Strings are dimensioned from one to 72 characters in length. Positions on the string are identified with two numbers. Ex. A$(2,4) A$ is the name of the string. The 2 tells the computer to begin the substring at the second character. The 4 tells the computer to end the substring at the fourth character of A$. So, A$(1,1) allocates the first character of A$. I used this for identifying 'Y' and 'N' in yes/no responses.

Line 590 is an example of logical operation. It tells the computer that if the expression is nonzero, to proceed to the line specified. If it is zero, it will fall through to the next line.

A slightly different type of logical operation is found in lines 3020-3050. In these lines the logical quantity is evaluated first, and if true, the quantity is set to 1. If it is false, it is set to 0. These can all be taken care of with IF-THEN statements if necessary.

I hope that the size of the program does not scare too many people away. It should be able to be made compatible with very little rewriting. If you have a few hours of free time to rewrite a little, it should be worth the effort.

I tried to throw a lot of random statements in there to make playing the game more uncertain. Cutting some of these out may save some space, if that's a problem for you.

Note: The writeup above, by Vincent Erickson, refers to the original HP version. The one presented here is in standard Microsoft Basic. Some conversion notes by Steve North are found in the listing, lines 90-230.

THIS IS THE GAME OF SEA BATTLE!!! THE OBJECT OF THE GAME IS TO DESTROY ALL OF THE ENEMY SHIPS IN YOUR 20 BY 20 AREA WITH THE VARIOUS WEAPONS IN YOUR SUBMARINE'S ARSENAL. YOU MUST DO THIS, HOWEVER, WITHOUT LETTING THE ENEMY DESTROY YOU FIRST!!

THERE ARE SEVERAL INTERESTING HAZARDS IN THE GAME. THEY INCLUDE:
.. DEPTH CHARGES FROM NEARBY ENEMY SHIPS.
.. VERY HUNGRY SEA MONSTERS!!
.. AND HIDDEN UNDERWATER MINES.

THE DEPTH CHARGES ARE EFFECTIVE TO ANY DEPTH, BUT THEY LOSE THEIR EFFECTIVNESS OVER DISTANCE, SO THE FARTHER YOU ARE FROM ANY SHIPS, THE BETTER!
THE SEA MONSTERS TAKE A MEANDERING COURSE THROUGH YOUR AREA THAT MAY BRING IT CLOSE ENOUGH TO ATTACK YOU. YOU RARELY SURVIVE. THEY ALSO LIKE TO EAT YOUR TORPEDOS, BUT MISSILES WILL KILL THEM.

THE ENEMY SHIPS MOVE ON EVERY TURN, IN A FIXED COURSE, UNLESS THEY ENCOUNTER OBSTACLES. THEY WILL GET BLOWN UP BY MINES, AND GET EATEN BY SEA MONSTERS TOO.

YOU HAVE TEN ORDERS THAT YOU MAY GIVE. THEY ARE:

```
    #0: NAVIGATION - THIS COMMAND ALLOWS YOU TO MOVE IN A
PARTICULAR DIRECTION AND DISTANCE ACROSS YOUR AREA. THE
 8 1 2  DIRECTION IS DETERMINED BY THE GRAPH AT LEFT. THERE
  \'/   ARE 8 DIRECTIONS TO MOVE IN, AND THEY ARE THE SAME
 7-*-3  ANYTIME YOU ARE ASKED FOR A COURSE. FOR EXAMPLE,
  /'\   TO MOVE NORTH, YOU WOULD USE COURSE #1. THE COMPUTER
 6 5 4  WILL ALSO ASK FOR AN AMOUNT OF POWER. IT TAKES 100 UNITS
OF POWER TO MOVE YOUR SUB 1 SPACE. BEWARE OF OBSTACLES!!
IF YOU USE MORE THAN 1000 UNITS IN A TURN, THERE IS AN OVERLOAD
DANGER, SO BE VERY CAREFUL!!
```

#1: SONAR - THIS COMMAND HAS TWO OPTIONS. OPTION #1 GIVES DIRECTIONAL INFORMATION, SHOWING THE DIRECTIONS AND DISTANCES IN WHICH THERE ARE ENEMY SHIPS. THIS IS USEFUL FOR SHOOTING AT LONG RANGES, WHERE IT IS DIFFICULT TO TELL IF A SHIP IS IN DIRECT LINE.

OPTION #0 PRINTS OUT A MAP OF YOUR AREA IN A SQUARE. (IT USES SYMBOLS FOR THE MAP) '*' INDICATES DRY LAND, '$' IS AN UNDERWATER MINE, '\S/' IS AN ENEMY SHIP. '-#-' IS A SEA MONSTER. '!H!' IS YOUR HEADQUARTERS, AND FINALLY, '(X)' IS YOU!!!

EVERY SO OFTEN, A '.' WILL APPEAR INSIDE THE SCREEN. THIS IS A SONAR MALFUNCTION, AND SO THE OBJECT THERE ISN'T IDENTIFIED. IF YOU ARE ABOVE 50 FEET, WAVES WILL SHOW UP AS '.'.

#2: TORPEDO CONTROL - THIS COMMAND ALLOWS YOU TO SHOOT 1 OF YOUR 10 TORPEDOS AT ENEMY SHIPS. THE COMPUTER WILL ONLY REQUIRE THE DIRECTION TO SHOOT, USING THE INDICATOR ABOVE. THEY HAVE A RANGE OF 7-13 SPACES. ONE TORPEDO GETS ONE SHIP.

#3: POLARIS MISSILE CONTROL - THIS COMMAND ALLOWS YOU TO LAUNCH ONE OF YOUR POLARIS MISSILES AGAINST THE ENEMY. THE COMPUTER WILL ASK FOR A COURSE AND FUEL. IT TAKES 75 LBS. OF FUEL TO BOOST A MISSILE 1 SPACE. SINCE THEY ARE SO MUCH MORE POWERFUL, THEY WILL COMPLETELY DESTROY THE SPACE THEY LAND ON, PLUS ALL OF THE IMMEDIATELY ADJACENT ONES. MISSILES DESTROY EVERYTHING!!!

#4: MANUEVERING - THIS COMMAND ALLOWS YOU TO CHANGE THE DEPTH YOU'RE AT. YOU MAY WANT TO DO THIS IF YOU ARE BADLY DAMAGED, BECAUSE REPAIRS GO ON TWICE AS QUICKLY BELOW 2500 FT. AND ABOVE 50 FT. THAN IN BETWEEN. YOU START THE GAME AT 100 FT. YOU USE UP ABOUT 1 POWER UNIT FOR EVERY 2 FT. YOU CHANGE.

#5: STATUS/DAMAGE REPORT - THIS COMMAND GIVES YOU THE STATUS OF YOUR SUB. IT TELLS YOU HOW MUCH IS LEFT IN YOUR ARSENAL, WHICH ITEMS ARE DAMAGED, AND HOW MUCH.

#6: HEADQUARTERS - THIS COMMAND ALLOWS SCUBA DIVERS FROM YOUR HEADQUARTERS TO REPLENISH YOUR SUPPLY OF WEAPONS AND MEN. YOU MUST BE AT 50 FT. OR LESS, AND 2 OR LESS SPACES AWAY TO DO THIS HOWEVER, AND YOU CAN ONLY DO IT TWICE.

#7: SABOTAGE (SCUBA) - THIS COMMAND ALLOWS YOU TO SEND MEN OUT ON A SABOTAGE MISSION AGAINST ENEMY SHIPS. YOU MAY ONLY GO AGAINST SHIPS WITHIN 3 SPACES OF YOU, AND YOU MUST LEAVE AT LEAST 10 MEN ON BOARD THE SUB TO RUN IT.

#8: POWER CONVERSION - THIS COMMAND ALLOWS YOU TO CHANGE FUEL TO POWER, OR VICE-VERSA.

#9: SURRENDER - THIS COMMAND IS ONLY FOR COWARDS AND TRAITORS!!

YOU START THE GAME WITH THE FOLLOWING SUPPLIES:
6000 UNITS OF POWER, 2500 LBS. OF ROCKET FUEL, 10 TORPEDOS
3 MISSILES, 1 HEADQUARTERS, AND A RANDOM NUMBER OF SHIPS.

I LEFT SOME INTERESTING DETAILS OUT OF THE INSTRUCTIONS, TO MAKE PLAYING THE GAME THE FIRST FEW TIMES MORE INTERESTING.

YOU START THE GAME IN THE ISLAND'S LAGOON, AND IT IS YOUR DUTY TO SEEK OUT AND DESTROY THE ENEMY AT ALL COSTS!!!

```
RUN
                                SEABAT
              CREATIVE COMPUTING  MORRISTOWN, NEW JERSEY



WHAT IS YOUR NAME? CAPTAIN AHAB

YOU MUST DESTROY 18 ENEMY SHIPS TO WIN CAPTAIN AHAB.


WHAT ARE YOUR ORDERS CAPTAIN AHAB? 1
OPTION #? 0

 . . . . . . . \S/ . . . . . . . . . . . . . . .
 .                                             .
 .    $      \S/                               .
 .                  \S/\S/         \S/    \S/  .
 .                        -#- . \S/            .
 .                                      $      .
 .      \S/     \S/*********                   .
 .          $    . ************-#-         \S/
 .    $         *********   ******             .
 .              ******  (X)   ***      $       .
 .              ******      ******             .
 .                ******  ***                  .
 .        \S/       ***               $        .
 .                                .            .
 .  $               \S/                        .
 .                                             .
 .                                             .
 .                           . $       \S/     .
 .                             $       \S/-#- .
 . . . . . . . . . . . . . . . . . . . . . \S/ .


WHAT ARE YOUR ORDERS CAPTAIN AHAB? 3
COURSE (1-8)? 1
FUEL (LBS.)? 450
YOU DESTROYED 2 ENEMY SHIPS CAPTAIN AHAB!!!
DEPTH CHARGES OFF STARBOARD SIDE CAPTAIN AHAB!!!
LIGHT, SUPERFICIAL DAMAGE CAPTAIN AHAB.


---*** RESULT OF LAST ENEMY MANUEVER ***---


WHAT ARE YOUR ORDERS CAPTAIN AHAB? 1
OPTION #? 0

 . . . \S/\S/\S/ . . \S/ . . . . . . . \S/ . \S/\S/\S/\S/
 .                                             .
 .   .                                         .
 .                            -#-              .
 .           .                                 .
 .          \S/                        $       .
 .                *********   -#-              .
 .          $ \S/   ************               .
 .    $         *********   ******             .
 .              ******  (X)   ***      $       .
 .              ******      ******             .
 .                ******  ***      \S/         .
 .                  ' ***               $      .
 .                                 !H!         .
 .  $                                          .
 .                              .              .
 .                                      \S/    .
 .                           $ .       \S/-#--#- .
 .                             $               .
 . . . . . . . . . . . . . . . . . . . . . . . .


WHAT ARE YOUR ORDERS CAPTAIN AHAB? 0
COURSE (1-8)? 5
POWER AVAILABLE= 5550 . POWER TO USE? 200
NAVIGATION COMPLETE. POWER LEFT= 5350 .
DEPTH CHARGES OFF PORT SIDE CAPTAIN AHAB!!!
LIGHT, SUPERFICIAL DAMAGE CAPTAIN AHAB.


---*** RESULT OF LAST ENEMY MANUEVER ***---
*** SHIP DESTROYED BY A MINE CAPTAIN AHAB!!!
*** SHIP EATEN BY A SEA MONSTER CAPTAIN AHAB!!


WHAT ARE YOUR ORDERS CAPTAIN AHAB? 5
# OF ENEMY SHIPS LEFT....... 14
# OF POWER UNITS LEFT....... 5300
# OF TORPEDOS LEFT.......... 10
# OF MISSILES LEFT.......... 2
# OF CREWMEN LEFT........... 30
LBS. OF FUEL LEFT........... 2050
```

```
WANT DAMAGE REPORT? YES
   ITEM          DAMAGE  (+ GOOD, 0 NUETRAL, - BAD)
   ----          ------
ENGINES         -.888657
SONAR            1.58997
TORPEDOS         4.77987
MISSILES         1.87385
MANUEVERING      3.22063
STATUS           4.54389
HEADQUARTERS     2.90217
SABOTAGE         3.82123
CONVERTER        0
YOU ARE AT LOCATION ( 12 , 10 ).



WHAT ARE YOUR ORDERS CAPTAIN AHAB? 1
OPTION #? 0
```

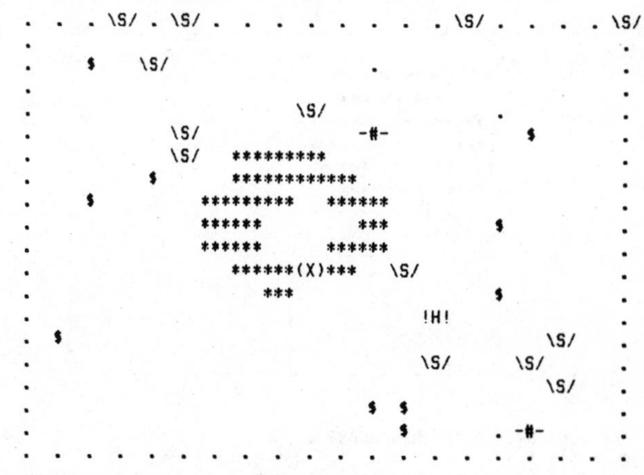

```
WHAT ARE YOUR ORDERS CAPTAIN AHAB? 0
ENGINES ARE UNDER REPAIR CAPTAIN AHAB.


WHAT ARE YOUR ORDERS CAPTAIN AHAB? 7
NO SHIPS IN RANGE CAPTAIN AHAB.


WHAT ARE YOUR ORDERS CAPTAIN AHAB? 4
NEW DEPTH? 50
MANUEVER COMPLETE. POWER LOSS= 25
DEPTH CHARGES OFF PORT SIDE CAPTAIN AHAB!!!
LIGHT, SUPERFICIAL DAMAGE CAPTAIN AHAB.


---*** RESULT OF LAST ENEMY MANUEVER ***---
*** SHIP DESTROYED BY A MINE CAPTAIN AHAB!!!


WHAT ARE YOUR ORDERS CAPTAIN AHAB? 1
OPTION #? 0
```

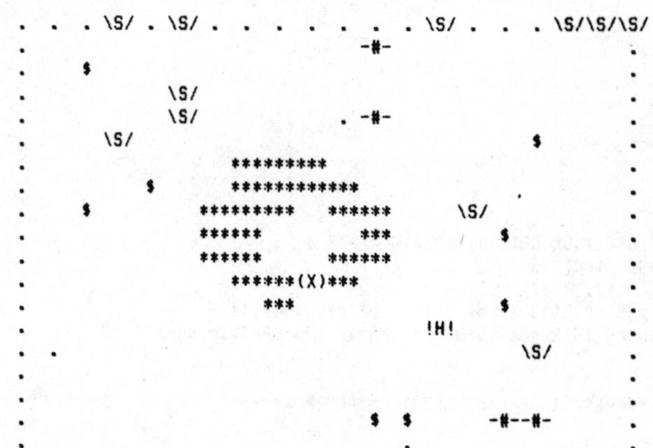

```
WHAT ARE YOUR ORDERS CAPTAIN AHAB? 5
# OF ENEMY SHIPS LEFT....... 13
# OF POWER UNITS LEFT....... 5125
# OF TORPEDOS LEFT.......... 10
# OF MISSILES LEFT.......... 2
# OF CREWMEN LEFT........... 30
LBS. OF FUEL LEFT........... 2050
```

```
---*** RESULT OF LAST ENEMY MANUEVER ***---

WHAT ARE YOUR ORDERS CAPTAIN AHAB? 0
COURSE (1-8)? 2
POWER AVAILABLE= 2021 . POWER TO USE? 500
NAVIGATION COMPLETE. POWER LEFT= 1521 .
NO SHIPS IN RANGE TO DEPTH CHARGE YOU CAPTAIN AHAB!!


---*** RESULT OF LAST ENEMY MANUEVER ***---


WHAT ARE YOUR ORDERS CAPTAIN AHAB? 1
OPTION #? 0

 .  .  .  .  .  .  .  .  .  .  .  .  .  .  .  .  . \S/\S/\S/
 .                         (X)                            .
 .     $                                                  .
 .                                                        .
 .                                                        .
 .                                              $         .
 .                   *********                            .
 .                   *************                        .
 .     $          *********   ******                      .
 .                ******         ***          $           .
 .                ******      ******                      .
 .                   ******   ***          .              .
 .             -#-      ***   -#- .  .        $           .
 .                                                        .
 .  $                                                     .
 .                                                        .
 .                                                        .
 .                                .  $                    .
 .                                   $                    .
 .  .  .  .  .  .  .  .  .  .  .  .  .  .  .  .  .  .  .  .


WHAT ARE YOUR ORDERS CAPTAIN AHAB? 0
COURSE (1-8)? 1
POWER AVAILABLE= 1471 . POWER TO USE? 100
NAVIGATION COMPLETE. POWER LEFT= 1371 .
NO SHIPS IN RANGE TO DEPTH CHARGE YOU CAPTAIN AHAB!!


---*** RESULT OF LAST ENEMY MANUEVER ***---


WHAT ARE YOUR ORDERS CAPTAIN AHAB? 1
OPTION #? 0

 .  .  .  .  .  .  .  .  . (X) .  .  .  . \S/ .  . \S/\S/ .
 .                                                        .
 .     .                                                  .
 .                                                        .
 .                                                        .
 .                                              $         .
 .                   *********                            .
 .                   *************                        .
 .     .          *********   ******                      .
 .                ******         ***          $           .
 .                ******      ******                      .
 .                   ******   ***                         .
 .          -#-         ***-#--#--#-          $           .
 .                                                        .
 .  $                                                     .
 .                                                        .
 .                                                        .
 .                                $  $                    .
 .                                   $                    .
 .  .  .  .  .  .  .  .  .  .  .  .  .  .  .  .  .  .  .  .


WHAT ARE YOUR ORDERS CAPTAIN AHAB? 3
COURSE (1-8)? 3
FUEL (LBS.)? 675
YOU DESTROYED 3 ENEMY SHIPS CAPTAIN AHAB!!!
NO SHIPS IN RANGE TO DEPTH CHARGE YOU CAPTAIN AHAB!!


---*** RESULT OF LAST ENEMY MANUEVER ***---


WHAT ARE YOUR ORDERS CAPTAIN AHAB? 2
COURSE (1-8)? 3
..!....!....!....!..OUCH!!!  YOU GOT ONE CAPTAIN AHAB!!
GOOD WORK CAPTAIN AHAB!!!  YOU GOT THEM ALL!!!
PROMOTION AND COMMENDATIONS WILL BE GIVEN IMMEDIATELY!!!
WANT ANOTHER GAME? NO
Break in 6250
Ok
```

LATER IN THE RUN

```
LIST
10  PRINT TAB(33);"SEABAT"
20  PRINT TAB(15);"CREATIVE COMPUTING  MORRISTOWN, NEW JERSEY"
30  PRINT:PRINT:PRINT
40  REM
50  REM  PROGRAM BY VINCENT ERIKSON
60  REM   ORIGINALLY IN H.P. BASIC
70  REM   CONVERTED TO MICROSOFT BASIC BY S.N.
80  REM
90  REM  NOTE THE FOLLOWING ABOUT CONVERSIONS:
100  REM  1)  RESTORE <LINE NUMBER> MEANS TO SET THE DATA
110  REM       POINTER TO THE SPECIFIED LINE.  THIS IS ONLY
120  REM       PRESENT IN TRS-80 LEVEL II AND CP/M BASIC.
130  REM       FOR OTHERS, IMPROVISE BY USING A RESTORE, AND
140  REM       FOR...NEXT WITH READ STATEMENTS TO SKIP OVER
150  REM       THE DATA THAT SHOULD BE IGNORED.
160  REM
170  REM  2)  LOGICAL EXPRESSIONS ARE USED OFTEN.  A TRUE
180  REM       EXPRESSION EVALUATES AS A (-1) AND A FALSE EXPRESSION
190  REM       EVALUATES AS A (0).  THUS IF THE PROGRAM SAYS:
200  REM            X = (D<50)
210  REM       IT MEANS, LET X=0 IF D>=50, AND LET X=-1 IF D<50.
220  REM       AGAIN, IMPROVISE IF YOUR BASIC DOESN'T HAVE THIS
230  REM       (BUT ALL MICROSOFT BASICS DO.)
240  REM
245  REM   The real name of this program is, "Underwater Pie Lob"
250  REM *** PROGRAM FOLLOWS ***
260  REM ***
270  DIM A(20,20),D(9)
280  PRINT "WHAT IS YOUR NAME";
290  INPUT N$
300  PRINT
310  REM *** SET UP AREA ***
320  FOR I=1 TO 20
322  FOR J=1 TO 20
324  A(I,J)=0
326  NEXT J
328  NEXT I
330  REM *** ISLAND ***
340  RESTORE 6300
350  FOR X=7 TO 13
360  FOR Y=7 TO 12
370  READ A(X,Y)
380  NEXT Y
390  NEXT X
400  REM *** SUB ***
410 S1=10: S2=10
420  A(S1,S2)=2
430  REM *** ENEMY SHIPS ***
440  S=INT(RND(1)*16)+15
450  RESTORE 6090
460  FOR X=1 TO (INT(RND(1)*4)+1)*2-1
470  READ D8,D9
480  NEXT X
490  FOR X=1 TO S
500  X1=INT(RND(1)*20)+1
510  X2=INT(RND(1)*20)+1
520  IF A(X1,X2)<>0 THEN 500
530  A(X1,X2)=3
540  NEXT X
550  PRINT "YOU MUST DESTROY";S;"ENEMY SHIPS TO WIN ";N$;"."
560  REM *** HEADQUARTERS ***
570  S3=INT(RND(1)*20)+1
580  S4=INT(RND(1)*20)+1
590  IF A(S3,S4)<>0 THEN 570
600  A(S3,S4)=4
610  REM *** UNDERWATER MINES ***
620  FOR X=1 TO INT(RND(1)*8)+8
630  X1=INT(RND(1)*20)+1
640  X2=INT(RND(1)*20)+1
650  IF A(X1,X2)<>0 THEN 630
660  A(X1,X2)=5
670  NEXT X
680  REM *** SEA MONSTERS ***
690  FOR X=1 TO 4
700  X1=INT(RND(1)*18)+2
710  X2=INT(RND(1)*18)+2
720  IF A(X1,X2)<>0 THEN 700
730  A(X1,X2)=6
740  RESTORE 6090
750  FOR Y=1 TO INT(RND(1)*8)+1
760  READ M1,M2
770  NEXT Y
780  NEXT X
790  REM *** SET STARTING VALUES ***
800  FOR I=1 TO 9
802  D(I)=0
804  NEXT I
810  C=30
820  P=6000
830  F=2500
840  T=10
850  M=3
```

```
860 D=100
870 D2=2
880 REM *** COMMAND SECTION ***
890 PRINT: PRINT: PRINT "WHAT ARE YOUR ORDERS ";N$;
900 INPUT O
910 ON INT(O+1) GOTO 1040,1680,2220,2680,3250,3410,3700,3880,4400,4660
920 PRINT "THE COMMANDS ARE:"
930 PRINT "      #0: NAVIGATION"
940 PRINT "      #1: SONAR"
950 PRINT "      #2: TORPEDO CONTROL"
960 PRINT "      #3: POLARIS MISSILE CONTROL"
970 PRINT "      #4: MANUEVERING"
980 PRINT "      #5: STATUS/DAMAGE REPORT"
990 PRINT "      #6: HEADQUARTERS"
1000 PRINT "      #7: SABOTAGE"
1010 PRINT "      #8: POWER CONVERSION"
1020 PRINT "      #9: SURRENDER"
1030 GOTO 880
1040 REM *** #0: NAVIGATION ***
1050 IF D(1) >= 0 THEN 1080
1060 PRINT "ENGINES ARE UNDER REPAIR ";N$;"."
1070 GOTO 880
1080 IF C>8 THEN 1110
1090 PRINT "NOT ENOUGH CREW TO MAN THE ENGINES ";N$;"."
1100 GOTO 880
1110 D1=1-((.23+RND(1)/10)*(-(D <= 50)))
1120 GOSUB 6080
1130 PRINT "POWER AVAILABLE=";P;". POWER TO USE";
1140 INPUT P1
1150 IF P1<0 OR P1>P THEN 1130
1160 IF P1 <= 1000 THEN 1210
1170 IF RND(1)<.43 THEN 1210
1180 PRINT "ATOMIC PILE GOES SUPERCRITICAL ";N$;"!!! HEADQUARTERS"
1190 PRINT "WILL WARN ALL SUBS TO STAY FROM RADIOACTIVE AREA!!!"
1200 GOTO 6180
1210 X=S1
1220 Y=S2
1230 Q1=1
1240 FOR X2=1 TO INT(INT(P1/100+.5)*D1+.5)
1250 IF X+X1>0 AND X+X1<21 AND Y+Y1>0 AND Y+Y1<21 THEN 1280
1260 PRINT "YOU CAN'T LEAVE THE AREA ";N$;"!!"
1270 GOTO 1340
1280 ON A(X+X1,Y+Y1)+1 GOTO 1290,1330,1630,1390,1440,1470,1490
1290 X=X+X1
1300 Y=Y+Y1
1310 P=P-100
1320 GOTO 1520
1330 PRINT "YOU ALMOST RAN AGROUND ";N$;"!!"
1340 A(X,Y)=2
1350 A(S1,S2)=0
1360 S1=X
1370 S2=Y
1380 GOTO 4690
1390 IF D>50 THEN 1290
1400 PRINT "YOU RAMMED A SHIP!!! YOU'RE BOTH SUNK ";N$;"!!"
1410 S=S-1
1420 IF S=0 THEN 6260
1430 GOTO 6180
1440 IF D>50 THEN 1290
1450 PRINT "YOU RAMMED YOUR HEADQUARTERS!! YOU'RE SUNK!!"
1460 GOTO 6180
1470 PRINT "YOU'VE BEEN BLOWN UP BY A MINE ";N$;"!!"
1480 GOTO 6180
1490 IF RND(1)<.21 THEN 1630
1500 PRINT "YOU WERE EATEN BY A SEA MONSTER, ";N$;"!!"
1510 GOTO 6180
1520 REM *** CHECK FOR NEARBY SEA MONSTERS ***
1530 FOR X3=X-2 TO X+2
1540 FOR Y3=Y-2 TO Y+2
1550 IF X3<1 OR X3>20 OR Y3<1 OR Y3>20 THEN 1610
1560 IF A(X,Y)<>6 THEN 1610
1570 IF RND(1)<.25 THEN 1500
1580 IF Q1=0 THEN 1610
1590 PRINT "YOU JUST HAD A NARROW ESCAPE WITH A SEA MONSTER ";N$;"!!"
1600  Q1=0
1610 NEXT Y3
1620 NEXT X3
1630 NEXT X2
1640 PRINT "NAVIGATION COMPLETE. POWER LEFT=";P;"."
1650 IF P>0 THEN 1340
1660 PRINT "ATOMIC PILE HAS GONE DEAD!!! SUB SINKS, CREW SUFFOCATES"
1670 GOTO 6180
1680 REM *** #1: SONAR ***
1690 IF D(2) >= 0 THEN 1720
1700 PRINT "SONAR IS UNDER REPAIR ";N$;"."
1710 GOTO 880
1720 IF C>5 THEN 1750
1730 PRINT "NOT ENOUGH CREW TO WORK SONAR ";N$;"."
1740 GOTO 880
1750 PRINT "OPTION #";
1760 INPUT O
1770 ON INT(O+1) GOTO 1790,2010
1780 GOTO 1750
1790 REM *** PRINT OUT MAP ***
1800 PRINT
1810 FOR X=1 TO 20
1820 FOR Y=1 TO 20
1830 DATA "   ","***","(X)","\S/","!H!"," $ ","-#-"
1840 IF A(X,Y)<>0 THEN 1880
1850 IF X<>1 AND X<>20 AND Y<>1 AND Y<>20 THEN 1880
1860 PRINT " . ";
1870 GOTO 1950
1880 RESTORE 1830
1890 FOR X1=1 TO A(X,Y)+1
1900 READ A$
1910 NEXT X1
1920 IF D<50 AND RND(1)<.23 AND A(X,Y)<>1 AND A(X,Y)<>2 THEN 1860
1930 IF RND(1)<.15 AND A(X,Y)>2 THEN 1860
1940 PRINT A$;
1950 NEXT Y
1960 PRINT
1970 NEXT X
1980 P=P-50
1990 IF P>0 THEN 880
2000 GOTO 1660
2010 REM *** DIRECTIONAL INFORMATION ***
2020 FOR I=1 TO 5
2022 B(I)=0
2024 NEXT I
2030 PRINT "DIRECTION   # OF SHIPS     DISTANCES"
2040 RESTORE 6090
2050 FOR X=1 TO 8
2060 READ X1,Y1
2070 X3=0
2080 FOR X4=1 TO 20
2090 IF S1+X1*X4<1 OR S1+X1*X4>20 OR S2+Y1*X4<1 OR S2+Y1*X4>20 THEN 2140
2100 IF A(S1+X1*X4,S2+Y1*X4)<>3 THEN 2130
2110 X3=X3+1
2120 B(X3)=X4
2130 NEXT X4
2140 IF X3=0 THEN 2200
2150 PRINT "   ";X,X3,
2160 FOR X4=1 TO X3
2170 PRINT B(X4);
2180 NEXT X4
2190 PRINT
2200 NEXT X
2210 GOTO 1980
2220 REM *** #2: TORPEDO CONTROL ***
2230 IF D(3) >= 0 THEN 2260
2240 PRINT "TORPEDO TUBES ARE UNDER REPAIR ";N$;"."
2250 GOTO 880
2260 IF C >= 10 THEN 2290
2270 PRINT "NOT ENOUGH CREW TO FIRE TORPEDO ";N$;"."
2280 GOTO 880
2290 IF T THEN 2320
2300 PRINT "NO TORPEDOS LEFT ";N$;"."
2310 GOTO 880
2320 IF D<2000 THEN 2360
2330 IF RND(1)>.5 THEN 2360
2340 PRINT "PRESSURE IMPLODES SUB UPON FIRING...YOU'RE CRUSHED!!"
2350 GOTO 6180
2360 GOSUB 6080
2370 X=S1
2380 Y=S2
2390 FOR X2=1 TO INT(7+5*(-(D>50))-RND(1)*4+.5)
2400 IF X+X1>0 AND X+X1<21 AND Y+Y1>0 AND Y+Y1<21 THEN 2460
2410 PRINT "TORPEDO OUT OF SONAR RANGE....INEFFECTUAL ";N$;"."
2420 T=T-1
2430 P=P-150
2440 IF P>0 THEN 4690
2450 GOTO 1660
2460 ON A(X+X1,Y+Y1)+1 GOTO 2470,2510,2650,2540,2580,2610,2630
2470 X=X+X1
2480 Y=Y+Y1
2490 PRINT "..!..";
2500 GOTO 2650
2510 PRINT "YOU TOOK OUT SOME ISLAND ";N$;"!"
2520 A(X+X1,Y+Y1)=0
2530 GOTO 2420
2540 PRINT "OUCH!!!  YOU GOT ONE ";N$;"!!"
2550 S=S-1
2560 IF S<>0 THEN 2520
2570 GOTO 6260
2580 PRINT "YOU BLEW UP YOUR HEADQUARTERS ";N$;"!!!"
2590 S3=0: S4=0: D2=0
2600 GOTO 2520
2610 PRINT "BLAM!! SHOT WASTED ON A MINE ";N$;"!!"
2620 GOTO 2520
2630 PRINT "A SEA MONSTER HAD A TORPEDO FOR LUNCH ";N$;"!!"
2640 GOTO 2420
2650 NEXT X2
2660 PRINT "DUD."
2670 GOTO 2420
2680 REM *** #3: POLARIS MISSILE CONTROL ***
```

```
2690  IF D(4) >= 0 THEN 2720
2700  PRINT "MISSILE SILOS ARE UNDER REPAIR ";N$;"."
2710  GOTO 880
2720  IF C>23 THEN 2750
2730  PRINT "NOT ENOUGH CREW TO LAUNCH A MISSILE ";N$;"."
2740  GOTO 880
2750  IF M<>0 THEN 2780
2760  PRINT "NO MISSILES LEFT ";N$;"."
2770  GOTO 880
2780  IF D>50 AND D<2000 THEN 2850
2790  PRINT "RECOMMEND THAT YOU DO NOT FIRE AT THIS DEPTH...PROCEED";
2800  INPUT A$
2810  IF LEFT$(A$,1)="N" THEN 880
2820  IF RND(1)<.5 THEN 2850
2830  PRINT "MISSILE EXPLODES UPON FIRING ";N$;"!! YOU'RE DEAD!!"
2840  GOTO 6180
2850  GOSUB 6080
2860  PRINT "FUEL (LBS.)";
2870  INPUT F1
2880  IF F1>0 AND F1 <= F THEN 2910
2890  PRINT "YOU HAVE";F;"LBS. LEFT ";N$;"."
2900  GOTO 2860
2910  F2=INT(F1/75+.5)
2920  IF S1+X1*F2>0 AND S1+X1*F2<21 AND S2+Y1*F2>0 AND S2+Y1*F2<21 THEN 2980
2930  PRINT "MISSILE OUT OF SONAR TRACKING ";N$;". MISSILE LOST."
2940  M=M-1
2950  F=F-F1
2960  P=P-300
2970  GOTO 2440
2980  D3=0: D4=0: D5=0: D6=0
2990  FOR X=S1+X1*F2-1 TO S1+X1*F2+1
3000  FOR Y=S2+Y1*F2-1 TO S2+Y1*F2+1
3010  IF X<1 OR X>20 OR Y<1 OR Y>20 THEN 3140
3020  D3=D3-(A(X,Y)=3)
3030  D4=D4-(A(X,Y)=6)
3040  D5=D5-(A(X,Y)=5)
3050  D6=D6-(A(X,Y)=1)
3060  IF A(X,Y)<>4 THEN 3100
3070  PRINT "YOU'VE DESTROYED YOUR HEADQUARTERS ";N$;"!!!"
3080  D3=0: S4=0: D2=0
3090  GOTO 3130
3100  IF A(X,Y)<>2 THEN 3130
3110  PRINT "YOU JUST DESTROYED YOURSELF ";N$;"!!!   DUMMY!!"
3120  GOTO 6180
3130  A(X,Y)=0
3140  NEXT Y
3150  NEXT X
3160  IF D6=0 THEN 3180
3170  PRINT "YOU BLEW OUT SOME ISLAND ";N$;"."
3180  IF D5=0 THEN 3200
3190  PRINT "YOU DESTROYED";D5;"MINES ";N$;"."
3200  IF D4=0 THEN 3220
3210  PRINT "YOU GOT";D4;"SEA MONSTERS ";N$;"!!!   GOOD WORK!!"
3220  PRINT "YOU DESTROYED";D3;"ENEMY SHIPS ";N$;"!!!"
3230  S=S-D3
3240  GOTO 2940
3250  REM *** MANUEVERING ***
3260  IF D(5) >= 0 THEN 3290
3270  PRINT "BALLAST CONTROLS ARE BEING REPAIRED ";N$;"."
3280  GOTO 880
3290  IF C>12 THEN 3320
3300  PRINT "THERE ARE NOT ENOUGH CREW TO WORK THE CONTROLS ";N$;"."
3310  GOTO 880
3320  PRINT "NEW DEPTH";
3330  INPUT D1
3340  IF D1 >= 0 AND D1<3000 THEN 3370
3350  PRINT "HULL CRUSHED BY PRESSURE ";N$;"!!"
3360  GOTO 6180
3370  P=P-INT(ABS((D-D1)/2+.5))
3380  PRINT "MANUEVER COMPLETE. POWER LOSS=";INT(ABS((D-D1)/2+.5))
3390  D=D1
3400  GOTO 4690
3410  REM *** #5: STATUS / DAMAGE REPORT ***
3420  IF D(6) >= 0 THEN 3450
3430  PRINT "NO REPORTS ARE ABLE TO GET THROUGH ";N$;"."
3440  GOTO 880
3450  IF C>3 THEN 3480
3460  PRINT "NO ONE LEFT TO GIVE THE REPORT ";N$;"."
3470  GOTO 880
3480  PRINT "# OF ENEMY SHIPS LEFT.......";S
3490  PRINT "# OF POWER UNITS LEFT.......";P
3500  PRINT "# OF TORPEDOS LEFT..........";T
3510  PRINT "# OF MISSILES LEFT..........";M
3520  PRINT "# OF CREWMEN LEFT...........";C
3530  PRINT "LBS. OF FUEL LEFT...........";F
3540  PRINT
3550  PRINT "WANT DAMAGE REPORT";
3560  INPUT A$
3570  IF LEFT$(A$,1)="N" THEN 3670
3580  PRINT "  ITEM          DAMAGE  (+ GOOD, 0 NUETRAL, - BAD)"
3590  PRINT "  ----          ------"
3600  DATA "ENGINES","SONAR","TORPEDOS","MISSILES","MANUEVERING"
3610  DATA "STATUS","HEADQUARTERS","SABOTAGE","CONVERTER"
3620  RESTORE 3600
3630  FOR X=1 TO 9
3640  READ A$
3650  PRINT A$,D(X)
3660  NEXT X
3670  PRINT "YOU ARE AT LOCATION (";S1;",";S2;")."
3680  PRINT
3690  GOTO 880
3700  REM *** #6: HEADQUARTERS ***
3710  IF D(7) >=0 THEN 3740
3720  PRINT "HEADQUARTERS IS DAMAGED.  UNABLE TO HELP ";N$;"."
3730  GOTO 880
3740  IF D2<>0 THEN 3770
3750  PRINT "HEADQUARTERS IS DESERTED ";N$;"."
3760  GOTO 880
3770  IF SQR((S1-S3)^2+(S2-S4)^2) <= 2 AND D<51 THEN 3800
3780  PRINT "UNABLE TO COMPLY WITH DOCKING ORDERS ";N$;"."
3790  GOTO 880
3800  PRINT "DIVERS FROM HEADQUARTERS BRING OUT SUPPLIES AND MEN."
3810  P=4000
3820  T=8
3830  M=2
3840  F=1500
3850  C=25
3860  D2=D2-1
3870  GOTO 4690
3880  REM *** #7: SABOTAGE ***
3890  IF D(8)>=0 THEN 3920
3900  PRINT "HATCHES INACCESSIBLE ";N$;".  NO SABOTAGES POSSIBLE."
3910  GOTO 880
3920  IF C>10 THEN 3950
3930  PRINT "NOT ENOUGH CREW TO GO ON A MISSION ";N$;"."
3940  GOTO 880
3950  D3=0: D4=0
3960  FOR X=S1-2 TO S1+2
3970  FOR Y=S2-2 TO S2+2
3980  IF X<1 OR X>20 OR Y<1 OR Y>20 THEN 4010
3990  D3=D3-(A(X,Y)=3)
4000  D4=D4-(A(X,Y)=6)
4010  NEXT Y
4020  NEXT X
4030  IF D3<>0 THEN 4060
4040  PRINT "NO SHIPS IN RANGE ";N$;"."
4050  GOTO 880
4060  PRINT "THERE ARE";D3;"SHIPS IN RANGE ";N$;"."
4070  PRINT "HOW MANY MEN ARE GOING ";N$;
4080  INPUT Q1
4090  IF C-Q1 >= 10 THEN 4120
4100  PRINT "YOU MUST LEAVE AT LEAST 10 MEN ON BOARD ";N$;"."
4110  GOTO 4070
4120  D5=INT(D3/Q1+.5)
4130  D6=0
4140  FOR X=S1-2 TO S1+2
4150  FOR Y=S2-2 TO S2+2
4160  IF D3/Q1>1-RND(1) AND RND(1)+D3/Q1<.9 THEN 4220
4170  IF A(X,Y)<>3 THEN 4220
4180  D6=D6+1
4190  A(X,Y)=0
4200  S=S-1
4210  IF S=0 THEN 6260
4220  NEXT Y
4230  NEXT X
4240  PRINT D6;"SHIPS WERE DESTROYED ";N$;"."
4250  D6=0: D7=0
4260  FOR X=1 TO Q1
4270  D7=D7-(RND(1)>.6)
4280  NEXT X
4290  FOR X=1 TO Q1-D7
4300  D6=D6-(RND(1)<.15)
4310  NEXT X
4320  IF D4=0 THEN 4360
4330  PRINT "A SEA MONSTER SMELLS THE MEN ON THE WAY BACK!!!"
4340  PRINT D7;"MEN WERE EATEN ";N$;"!!"
4350  C=C-D7
4360  PRINT D6;"MEN WERE LOST THROUGH ACCIDENTS ";N$;"."
4370  C=C-D6
4380  P=P-INT(10*Q1+RND(1)*10)
4390  GOTO 4690
4400  REM *** #8: POWER CONVERTER ***
4410  IF D(9) >= 0 THEN 4440
4420  PRINT "POWER CONVERTER IS DAMAGED ";N$;"."
4430  GOTO 880
4440  IF C>5 THEN 4470
4450  PRINT "NOT ENOUGH MEN TO WORK THE CONVERTER ";N$;"."
4460  GOTO 880
4470  PRINT "OPTION? (1=FUEL TO POWER, 2=POWER TO FUEL)";
4480  INPUT O
4490  ON O GOTO 4510,4580
4500  GOTO 4470
4510  REM *** FUEL TO POWER CONVERSION ***
4520  PRINT "FUEL AVAILABLE=";F;". CONVERT";
```

```
4530  INPUT C1
4540  IF C1>F OR C1<0 THEN 4520
4550  F=F-C1
4560  P=P+INT(C1/3)
4570  GOTO 4640
4580  REM *** POWER TO FUEL CONVERSION ***
4590  PRINT "POWER AVAILABLE=";P-1;". CONVERT";
4600  INPUT C1
4610  IF C1>P-1 OR C1<0 THEN 4590
4620  P=P-C1
4630  F=F+INT(C1*3)
4640  PRINT "CONVERSION COMPLETE. POWER=";P;". FUEL=";F;"."
4650  GOTO 4690
4660  REM *** #9: SURRENDER ***
4670  PRINT "COWARD!! YOU'RE NOT VERY PATRIOTIC ";N$;"!!!"
4680  GOTO 6180
4690  REM *** RETALIATION SECTION ***
4700  Q=0
4710  FOR X=S1-4 TO S1+4
4720  FOR Y=S2-4 TO S2+4
4730  IF X<1 OR X>20 OR Y<1 OR Y>20 THEN 4760
4740  IF A(X,Y)<>3 THEN 4760
4750  Q=Q+(RND(1)/SQR((S1-X)^2+(S2-Y)^2))
4760  NEXT Y
4770  NEXT X
4780  IF Q THEN 4810
4790  PRINT "NO SHIPS IN RANGE TO DEPTH CHARGE YOU ";N$;"!!"
4800  GOTO 5210
4810  PRINT "DEPTH CHARGES OFF ";
4820  IF RND(1)>.5 THEN 4850
4830  PRINT "PORT SIDE ";N$;"!!!"
4840  GOTO 4860
4850  PRINT "STARBOARD SIDE ";N$;"!!!"
4860  IF Q>.13 OR RND(1)>.92 THEN 4890
4870  PRINT "NO REAL DAMAGE SUSTAINED ";N$;"."
4880  GOTO 5210
4890  IF Q>.36 OR RND(1)>.96 THEN 4940
4900  PRINT "LIGHT, SUPERFICIAL DAMAGE ";N$;"."
4910  P=P-50
4920  D(INT(RND(1)*9)+1)=-RND(1)*2
4930  GOTO 5210
4940  IF Q>.6 OR RND(1)>.975 THEN 5020
4950  PRINT "MODERATE DAMAGE. REPAIRS NEEDED."
4960  P=P-75+INT(RND(1)*30)
4970  FOR Y=1 TO 2
4980  X=INT(RND(1)*9)+1
4990  D(X)=D(X)-RND(1)*8
5000  NEXT Y
5010  GOTO 5210
5020  IF Q>.9 OR RND(1)>.983 THEN 5100
5030  PRINT "HEAVY DAMAGE!! REPAIRS IMMEDIATE ";N$;"!!!"
5040  P=P-(200+INT(RND(1)*76))
5050  FOR X=1 TO 4+INT(RND(1)*2)
5060  Y=INT(RND(1)*9)+1
5070  D(Y)=D(Y)-RND(1)*11
5080  NEXT X
5090  GOTO 5210
5100  PRINT "DAMAGE CRITICAL!!!!   WE NEED HELP!!!"
5110  A$="VRAVUKXCNVPCRHFDRSAXQURLQTRHXYACVFZYITLCBSSYYKDQIPCAEGQGPCNOTSIO"
5120  X=INT(RND(1)*16)+1
5130  PRINT "SEND 'HELP' IN CODE. HERE IS THE CODE:";MID$(A$,X,4);
5132  REM  TIME DELAY AND THEN ERASE THE CODE
5134  FOR I=1 TO 300: NEXT I
5136  PRINT CHR$(13);TAB(38);"XXXX";CHR$(13);TAB(38);"****"
5140  INPUT "ENTER CODE";B$
5150  PRINT
5160  IF B$<>MID$(A$,X,4) THEN 5190
5170  PRINT "FAST WORK ";N$;"!! HELP ARRIVES IN TIME TO SAVE YOU!!!"
5180  GOTO 5040
5190  PRINT "MESSAGE GARBLED ";N$;"...NO HELP ARRIVES!!!"
5200  GOTO 6180
5210  REM *** MOVE SHIPS / SEA MONSTERS ***
5220  IF D(1) >= 0 OR D(3) >= 0 OR D(4) >= 0 OR D(5) >= 0 OR D(7) >= 0 THEN 5260
5230  IF D(8) >= 0 OR D(9) >= 0 THEN 5260
5240  PRINT "DAMAGE TOO MUCH ";N$;"!!!   YOU'RE SUNK!!"
5250  GOTO 6180
5260  REM *** MOVE SHIPS / SEA MONSTERS ***
5270  PRINT: PRINT: PRINT "---*** RESULT OF LAST ENEMY MANUEVER ***---"
5280  FOR X=1 TO 20
5290  FOR Y=1 TO 20
5300  IF A(X,Y)<>3 THEN 5690
5310  REM *** MOVE A SHIP ***
5320  W=D8
5330  V=D9
5340  IF X+W>0 AND X+W<21 AND Y+V>0 AND Y+V<21 THEN 5420
5350  FOR X0=19 TO 1 STEP -1
5360  IF A(X-W*X0,Y-V*X0)<>0 THEN 5400
5370  A(X-W*X0,Y-V*X0)=3
5380  A(X,Y)=0
5390  GOTO 6000
5400  NEXT X0
5410  STOP
5420  ON A(X+W,Y+V)+1 GOTO 5430,5460,5530,5460,5560,5600,5650
5430  A(X+W,Y+V)=3
5440  A(X,Y)=0
5450  GOTO 6000
5460  REM *** CHANGE DIRECTION ***
5470  RESTORE 6090
5480  FOR X0=1 TO INT(RND(1)*8)+1
5490  READ W,V
5500  NEXT X0
5510  IF X+W<1 OR X+W>20 OR Y+V<1 OR Y+V>20 THEN 5470
5520  GOTO 5420
5530  IF D>50 THEN 5460
5540  PRINT "*** YOU'VE BEEN RAMMED BY A SHIP ";N$;"!!!"
5550  GOTO 6180
5560  IF RND(1)<.15 THEN 5460
5570  PRINT "*** YOUR HEADQUARTERS WAS RAMMED ";N$;"!!!"
5580  S3=0: S4=0: D2=0: A(X+W,Y+V)=0
5590  GOTO 5620
5600  IF RND(1)<.7 THEN 5460
5610  PRINT "*** SHIP DESTROYED BY A MINE ";N$;"!!!"
5620  S=S-1
5630  IF S<>0 THEN 5440
5640  GOTO 6260
5650  IF RND(1)<.8 THEN 5460
5660  PRINT "*** SHIP EATEN BY A SEA MONSTER ";N$;"!!"
5670  S=S-1
5680  GOTO 5630
5690  REM *** MOVE A SEA MONSTER ***
5700  IF A(X,Y)<>6 THEN 6000
5710  IF X+M1<1 OR X+M1>20 OR Y+M2<1 OR Y+M2>20 THEN 5760
5720  ON A(X+M1,Y+M2)+1 GOTO 5730,5760,5830,5850,5900,5730,5930
5730  A(X+M1,Y+M2)=6
5740  A(X,Y)=0
5750  GOTO 6000
5760  REM *** CHANGE DIRECTION ***
5770  RESTORE 6090
5780  FOR X0=1 TO INT(RND(1)*8)+1
5790  READ M1,M2
5800  NEXT X0
5810  IF X+M1<1 OR X+M1>20 OR Y+M2<1 OR Y+M2>20 THEN 5760
5820  GOTO 5720
5830  PRINT "*** YOU'VE BEEN EATEN BY A SEA MONSTER ";N$;"!!"
5840  GOTO 6180
5850  IF RND(1)>.2 THEN 5760
5860  PRINT "*** SHIP EATEN BY A SEA MONSTER ";N$;"!!"
5870  S=S-1
5880  IF S<>0 THEN 5730
5890  GOTO 6260
5900  PRINT "*** A SEA MONSTER ATE YOUR HEADQUARTERS ";N$;"!!"
5910  S3=0: S4=0: D2=0
5920  GOTO 5730
5930  IF RND(1)<.75 THEN 5760
5940  PRINT "*** A SEA MONSTER FIGHT ";N$;"!!! ";
5950  IF RND(1)<.8 THEN 5980
5960  PRINT "AND ONE DIES!!"
5970  GOTO 5730
5980  PRINT "IT'S A TIE!!"
5990  GOTO 5760
6000  NEXT Y
6010  NEXT X
6020  REM *** MAKE REPAIRS ***
6030  FOR Y=1 TO 9
6040  X=INT(RND(1)*9)+1
6050  D(X)=D(X)+(RND(1)*(2+RND(1)*2))*(1+(-(D<51) OR -(D>2000)))*(-(D(X)<3))
6060  NEXT Y
6070  GOTO 880
6080  REM *** GOSUB FOR COURSE / DIRECTION ***
6090  DATA -1,0,-1,1,0,1,1,1,1,0,1,-1,0,-1,-1,-1
6100  PRINT "COURSE (1-8)";
6110  INPUT C1
6120  IF C1<1 OR C1>8 THEN 6100
6130  RESTORE 6090
6140  FOR X9=1 TO INT(C1+.5)
6150  READ X1,Y1
6160  NEXT X9
6170  RETURN
6180  REM *** DESTROYED ? ***
6190  PRINT "THERE ARE STILL";S;"ENEMY SHIPS LEFT ";N$;"."
6200  PRINT "YOU WILL BE DEMOTED TO RANK OF DECK SCRUBBER!!!"
6210  PRINT "WANT ANOTHER GAME";
6220  INPUT A$
6230  IF LEFT$(A$,1)<>"Y" THEN 6250
6240  GOTO 310
6250  STOP
6260  PRINT "GOOD WORK ";N$;"!!!  YOU GOT THEM ALL!!!"
6270  PRINT "PROMOTION AND COMMENDATIONS WILL BE GIVEN IMMEDIATELY!!!"
6280  GOTO 6210
6290  REM *** ISLAND DATA ***
6300  DATA 0,1,1,1,0,0,0,1,1,1,0,1,1,1,0,1,1,1,1,0,0,0,1
6310  DATA 1,1,0,0,1,1,0,1,1,0,1,0,0,0,1,0,0,0
6320  END
Ok
```

Seawar

You are the commander of a fleet of ships operating in enemy territory. Your task force consists of 9 ships, and the enemy has 9 ships. Whoever sinks all of the opponent's ships first wins the campaign.

You, as the commander, must provide the angle of elevation at which the guns will be fired, neglecting air resistance. Your instruments will read the range to the target, and the initial velocity is held constant at about 675 meters per second.

SEAWAR will help you learn about the paths of projectiles and what happens as the angle of elevation varies.

1. First, what do you think the path of the projectile looks like. Make a sketch. (If you're still not sure, do some research in the library—it will help you win the battle, commander!)
   a. What angle of elevation do you think will give the maximum range?
   b. What will happen if you fire the guns at 0°?
   c. What will happen to the projectile if you fire it straight up?
2. After becoming proficient at winning the battle, change the initial velocity of the projectile. How does this affect the range?

The original SEAWAR had a timing function that allowed only about 7 seconds to make your next move. If your computer has a timer, this would be a neat addition.

The origin of SEAWAR is unknown. It was revised and submitted to us by David S. Paxton. It was further revised and the writeup prepared by Mary T. Dobbs, Mathematics and Science Center, Glen Allen, Virginia. It first appeared in *Creative Computing*, May/Jun 1975.

```
RUN

                          SEAWAR
                     CREATIVE COMPUTING
                   MORRISTOWN, NEW JERSEY


YOU COMMAND A FLEET OF SHIPS OPERATING IN
ENEMY TERRITORY!!!
DO YOU NEED ANY ASSISTANCE? YES
YOU TELL YOUR GUN CREWS THE ELEVATION TO SET THEIR GUNS.
ELEVATION IS IN DEGREES FROM 0 TO 360.
YOUR TASK FORCE CONSISTS OF 3 DESTROYERS, 2 CRUISERS,
2 BATTLESHIPS, AND 2 HEAVY AIRCRAFT CARRIERS.
THE ENEMY HAS 9 SHIPS FOR HIS DEFENSE.
IF YOU SUCCEED IN SINKING ALL HIS SHIPS BEFORE HE SINKS
YOURS, YOU HAVE WON. HOWEVER, IF HE SINKS ALL YOUR SHIPS
BEFORE YOU HAVE DEFEATED HIM, YOU HAVE LOST!!
LET US BEGIN!!!

YOUR FLAGSHIP HAS DETECTED A U-BOAT APPROACHING AT 5 PHANTOMS.
YOUR SUBMARINE DETECTION EQUIPMENT READS THE RANGE TO THE TARGET
AS  39481  METERS.
THE U-BOAT HAS COMMENCED FIRING TORPEDOES AT YOUR SHIPS.
HIS FIRST TORPEDO EXPLODED  281  METERS BEHIND YOUR SHIP.
WHAT ELEVATION ** ? 38

-----FIRE!!!
DEPTH CHARGE EXPLODED  5637  METERS AFT OF TARGET.
THE ENEMY U-BOAT SANK ONE OF YOUR DESTROYERS!!
WHAT ELEVATION ** ? 32.4

-----FIRE!!!
DEPTH CHARGE EXPLODED  2592  METERS AFT OF TARGET.
THE ENEMY U-BOAT SANK YOUR HEAVY CRUISER!!
WHAT ELEVATION ** ? 29.9

-----FIRE!!!
DEPTH CHARGE EXPLODED  707  METERS AFT OF TARGET.
THE ENEMY TORPEDO EXPLODED  103 METERS IN
FRONT OF YOUR SHIP.
WHAT ELEVATION ** ? 29.2

-----FIRE!!!
DEPTH CHARGE EXPLODED  123  METERS AFT OF TARGET.
THE ENEMY U-BOAT SANK ANOTHER OF YOUR DESTROYERS!!
WHAT ELEVATION ** ? 29.07

-----FIRE!!!
DEPTH CHARGE EXPLODED RIGHT ON TOP OF THAT BABY!!!

TARGET DESTROYED!!!      ** 5  **  ROUNDS EXPENDED.
YOU HAVE LOST  3  SHIPS, AND THE ENEMY HAS LOST  1 .
```

```
YOUR FLAGSHIP REPORTS THE SIGHTING OF AN ENEMY 210 MM SHORE GUN
YOUR INSTRUMENTS READ THE RANGE TO THE TARGET AS  41020  METERS.
THE ENEMY 210 MM SHORE GUN IS FIRING ON YOUR SHIPS!
HIS FIRST ROUND FELL  113  METERS SHORT.
WHAT ELEVATION ** ? 32


-----FIRE!!!
SHELL OVERSHOT TARGET BY  773  METERS.
THE ENEMY 210 MM SHORE GUN SANK ONE OF YOUR BATTLESHIPS!!
WHAT ELEVATION ** ? 31.27


-----FIRE!!!
SHELL OVERSHOT TARGET BY  240  METERS.
THE ENEMY 210 MM SHORE GUN SANK YOUR LAST DESTROYER!!
WHAT ELEVATION ** ? 31./\/\07


-----FIRE!!!
  ** BOOM  **

TARGET DESTROYED!!!     ** 3  **  ROUNDS EXPENDED.
YOU HAVE LOST  5  SHIPS, AND THE ENEMY HAS LOST  2 .

YOUR FLAGSHIP REPORTS THE SIGHTING OF AN ENEMY 70,000 TON CRUISER
YOUR INSTRUMENTS READ THE RANGE TO THE TARGET AS  41009  METERS.
THE ENEMY 70,000 TON CRUISER IS FIRING ON YOUR SHIPS!
IN FACT, HE JUST SANK YOUR AIRCRAFT CARRIER!!
WHAT ELEVATION ** ? 32


-----FIRE!!!
SHELL OVERSHOT TARGET BY  784  METERS.
THE ENEMY 70,000 TON CRUISER SANK YOUR LIGHT CRUISER!!
WHAT ELEVATION ** ? 31.1


-----FIRE!!!
SHELL OVERSHOT TARGET BY  123  METERS.
THE ENEMY 70,000 TON CRUISER SANK YOUR LAST AIRCRAFT CARRIER!!
WHAT ELEVATION ** ? 30.9


-----FIRE!!!
  ** BOOM  **

TARGET DESTROYED!!!     ** 3  **  ROUNDS EXPENDED.
YOU HAVE LOST  8  SHIPS, AND THE ENEMY HAS LOST  3 .

YOUR FLAGSHIP REPORTS THE SIGHTING OF AN ENEMY BATTLESHIP
YOUR INSTRUMENTS READ THE RANGE TO THE TARGET AS  42864  METERS.
THE ENEMY BATTLESHIP IS FIRING ON YOUR SHIPS!
IN FACT, HE JUST SANK YOUR LAST BATTLESHIP!!
            ********  PEACE  ********



YOU FIRED       11             ROUNDS. THE ENEMY FIRED      10
 ROUNDS.
ALL OF YOUR SHIPS HAVE BEEN SUNK.  SO SORRY
THE BATTLE IS OVER..........THE ENEMY WINS!
OK




LIST

5 PRINT TAB(26);"SEAWAR"
6 PRINT TAB(20);"CREATIVE COMPUTING"
7 PRINT TAB(18) "MORRISTOWN, NEW JERSEY"
9 PRINT:PRINT:PRINT
10 PRINT "YOU COMMAND A FLEET OF SHIPS OPERATING IN"
15 PRINT "ENEMY TERRITORY!!!"
20 PRINT "DO YOU NEED ANY ASSISTANCE";
40 INPUT Q$
50 IF Q$="YES" THEN 90
60 IF Q$="NO" THEN 170
70 PRINT "INPUT 'YES' OR 'NO'"
80 GOTO 40
90 PRINT "YOU TELL YOUR GUN CREWS THE ELEVATION TO SET THEIR GUNS."
100 PRINT "ELEVATION IS IN DEGREES FROM 0 TO 360."
119 PRINT "YOUR TASK FORCE CONSISTS OF 3 DESTROYERS, 2 CRUISERS,"
120 PRINT "2 BATTLESHIPS, AND 2 HEAVY AIRCRAFT CARRIERS."
130 PRINT "THE ENEMY HAS 9 SHIPS FOR HIS DEFENSE."
140 PRINT "IF YOU SUCCEED IN SINKING ALL HIS SHIPS BEFORE HE SINKS"
150 PRINT"YOURS, YOU HAVE WON. HOWEVER, IF HE SINKS ALL YOUR SHIPS"
160 PRINT "BEFORE YOU HAVE DEFEATED HIM, YOU HAVE LOST!!"
170 PRINT "LET US BEGIN!!!"
210 PRINT ""
220 READ Z$
230 A=A+1
240 GOTO 320
250 RESTORE
260 IF O=9 OR A=9 THEN 840
270 FOR X=1 TO A
280 READ Z$
290 NEXT X
300 READ Z$
310 A=A+1
320 IF Z$="AIRCRAFT CARRIER" THEN 390
330 IF Z$="U-BOAT" THEN 2000
340 IF Z$="TORPEDO BOAT" THEN 360
350 P=1
360 GOTO 405
390 RESTORE
405 PRINT:PRINT "YOUR FLAGSHIP REPORTS THE SIGHTING OF AN ENEMY ";Z$
410 T=43000.-30000*RND(0)+(RND(0)*10)*.987654+102
420 IF T<10000 THEN 410
430 S=0:P2=0
440 T=INT(T)
450 IF Z$="U-BOAT" THEN 2030
460 PRINT "YOUR INSTRUMENTS READ THE RANGE TO THE TARGET AS ";T;" METERS
."
480 IF P=1 THEN 1480
490 IF S>4 THEN 510
500 GOTO 540
510 PRINT "ALL RIGHT, BAD SHOT, THE TARGET HAS MOVED OUT OF"
520 PRINT "RANGE !!! LET'S TRY IT AGAIN !!!"
525 S1=S1+S
530 GOTO 320
540 PRINT "WHAT ELEVATION ** ";
550 INPUT B
551 PRINT
570 PRINT ""
590 PRINT "-----FIRE!!!"
600 S=S+1
620 IF B>360 THEN 1410
630 IF B<0 THEN 750
640 IF B=0 THEN 770
650 IF B=90 THEN 980
660 IF B>330 THEN 770
670 IF B>180 THEN 1370
680 IF B>150 THEN 1300
690 IF B>90 THEN 1020
700 V1=675.285
705 E=INT(T-(V1^2/9.80665*SIN(2*B/57.3)))
710 IF ABS(E) <= 100 THEN 1050
720 IF E>100 THEN 1200
730 IF E<-100 THEN 1250
750 PRINT "GUN BACKFIRED, KILLING CREW!"
760 GOTO 820
770 PRINT "WHAT ARE YOU TRYING TO DO? KILLSOME FISH? THE SHELL"
780 PRINT "EXPLODED UNDER WATER FIFTY METERS FROM YOUR SHIP!!!"
790 GOTO 1590
820 PRINT "                 ADMIRAL PLEASE !!!!"
830 GOTO 1590
840 PRINT "              ********  PEACE  ********"
870 PRINT:PRINT:PRINT
890 PRINT "YOU FIRED ",S1," ROUNDS. THE ENEMY FIRED ",S2," ROUNDS."
900 IF O=9 THEN 920
910 IF A=9 THEN 950
920 PRINT "ALL OF YOUR SHIPS HAVE BEEN SUNK.  SO SORRY"
930 PRINT "THE BATTLE IS OVER..........THE ENEMY WINS!"
940 GOTO 2220
950 PRINT "YOU HAVE DECIMATED THE ENEMY..........THAT'S NICE"
960 PRINT "THE BATTLE IS OVER..........YOU WIN!!!!!"
970 GOTO 2220
980 PRINT "YOU IDIOT!! YOU SHOT STRAIGHT UP!!, AND THE SHELL"
990 PRINT "LANDED ON YOUR OWN GUN POSITION, DESTROYING IT!!!"
1000 GOTO 1590
1020 PRINT "HEY STUPID, YOU'RE FIRING ON YOUR OWN SHIPS!!!"
1030 GOTO 1590
1050 IF Z$="U-BOAT" THEN 1070
1060 GOTO 1090
1070 PRINT "DEPTH CHARGE EXPLODED RIGHT ON TOP OF THAT BABY!!!"
1080 GOTO 1100
1090 PRINT " ** BOOM  **"
1100 PRINT ""
1110 M$="TARGET DESTROYED!!!     **"
1120 N$=" **  ROUNDS EXPENDED."
1130 PRINT M$;S;N$
1142 PRINT "YOU HAVE LOST ";O;" SHIPS, AND THE ENEMY HAS LOST ";A;"."
1150 S1=S1+S
1160 PI=0
1190 GOTO 250
1200 IF Z$="U-BOAT" THEN 2130
1210 PRINT "SHOT FELL ";ABS(E);" METERS SHORT OF TARGET."
1230 GOTO 1590
1250 IF Z$="U-BOAT" THEN 2160
1260 PRINT "SHELL OVERSHOT TARGET BY ";ABS(E);" METERS."
1280 GOTO 1590
```

```
1310 PRINT "  YOU SHOT A PROJECTILE, INTO THE AIR,"
1320 PRINT "  IT FELL TO THE WATER, YOU KNOW NOT WHERE."
1330 PRINT "BUT I DO, YOU IDIOT, YOU JUST SANK YOUR OWN FLEET TANKER!!"
1340 S1=S1+1
1350 IF P=1 THEN 1590
1360 GOTO 490
1370 PRINT "WHAT ARE YOU TRYING TO DO?? DRILL A NEW HATCH?? THE SHELL"
1380 PRINT "EXPLODED IN YOUR SHIP, DESTROYING IT!!!"
1385 O=O+1
1386 IF O=9 THEN 840
1390 IF P=1 THEN 1590
1400 GOTO 820
1410 PRINT "WHERE DID U LEARN TO TYPE? ";B;"DEGREES EXCEEDS 360 BY"
1420 PRINT B-360;" DEGREES."
1430 S1=S1+1
1440 IF P=1 THEN 1590
1450 GOTO 490
1480 PRINT "THE ENEMY ";Z$;" IS FIRING ON YOUR SHIPS!"
1490 P4=1234*RND(RND(0))+(RND(0)*10)
1500 IF P4>500 THEN 1490
1510 IF P2=1 THEN 1600
1520 IF INT(P4)<100 THEN 1800
1530 IF Z$="U-BOAT" THEN 2100
1540 PRINT "HIS FIRST ROUND FELL ";INT(P4);" METERS SHORT."
1560 S2=S2+1
1570 GOTO 490
1590 IF P2=1 THEN 1490
1600 P1=1250*RND(RND(0))+(RND(0)*10)
1610 IF P1>P4 THEN 1600
1620 IF P1<(P4-400) THEN 1600
1630 IF P1<100 THEN 1710
1640 P4=P1
1650 S2=S2+1
1660 IF Z$="U-BOAT" THEN 2190
1670 PRINT "THE ENEMY ROUND FELL ";INT(P1);" METERS SHORT."
1700 GOTO 490
1710 S2=S2+1
1720 P2=1
1730 GOSUB 1850
1750 PRINT "THE ENEMY ";Z$;" SANK ";D$
1760 O=O+1
1770 IF O=9 THEN 840
1780 IF D$="YOUR LAST BATTLESHIP!!" THEN 840
1790 GOTO 490
1800 R2=1
1810 GOSUB 1850
1820 PRINT "IN FACT, HE JUST SANK ";D$
1830 O=O+1
1840 GOTO 1770
1850 RESTORE
1860 FOR C=1 TO (9+O)
1870 READ D$
1880 NEXT C
1890 READ D$
1920 DATA "U-BOAT","210 MM SHORE GUN","70,000 TON CRUISER"
1930 DATA "BATTLESHIP","TORPEDO BOAT","HEAVYFRIGATE"
1940 DATA "E-TYPE DESTROYER","GUIDED-MISSLE SHIP","AIRCRAFT CARRIER"
1950 DATA "ONE OF YOUR DESTROYERS!!","YOUR HEAVY CRUISER!!"
1960 DATA "ANOTHER OF YOUR DESTROYERS!!","ONE OF YOUR BATTLESHIPS!!"
1970 DATA "YOUR LAST DESTROYER!!","YOUR AIRCRAFT CARRIER!!"
1975 DATA "YOUR LIGHT CRUISER!!","YOUR LAST AIRCRAFT CARRIER!!"
1980 DATA "YOUR LAST BATTLESHIP!!"
1990 RETURN
2000 PRINT "YOUR FLAGSHIP HAS DETECTED A U-BOAT APPROACHING AT 5 ";
2005 PRINT "PHANTOMS."
2010 P=1
2020 GOTO 410
2030 PRINT "YOUR SUBMARINE DETECTION EQUIPMENT READS THE RANGE TO THE";
2031 PRINT " TARGET"
2040 T=INT(T-1500)
2050 IF T<0 THEN 410
2060 PRINT "AS ";T;" METERS."
2080 PRINT "THE U-BOAT HAS COMMENCED FIRING TORPEDOES AT YOUR SHIPS."
2090 GOTO 1490
2100 PRINT "HIS FIRST TORPEDO EXPLODED ";(INT(P4)-50);" METERS BEHIND";
2105 PRINT " YOUR SHIP."
2120 GOTO 1560
2130 PRINT "DEPTH CHARGE EXPLODED ";ABS(E);" METERS SHORT OF TARGET."
2150 GOTO 1590
2160 PRINT "DEPTH CHARGE EXPLODED ";ABS(E);" METERS AFT OF TARGET."
2180 GOTO 1590
2190 PRINT "THE ENEMY TORPEDO EXPLODED ";(INT(P1)-50);"METERS IN"
2201 PRINT "FRONT OF YOUR SHIP."
2210 GOTO 490
2220 END
OK
```

Shoot

The scene is some time in the near future. You and another individual on the other side of the planet are the only survivors of a total atomic war. (Yes, I know it's corny.) This war was fought totally with ground based atomic missiles. Both you and the surviving enemy have found the last missile bases left from each side. Fortunately (for me anyway), these missile grids are made and operated identically.

Each player moves on and is restricted to a 10 by 10 missile matrix. Every co-ordinate on the grid corresponds to a mini-missile base. At every base, there is a terminal tied into the main scanner computer, located safely many miles away. From each terminal, the player obtains information relevant to the current situation. Because of the way the missiles are constructed, the area left after lift-off is exposed to high doses of raw radiation and may not be occupied by life. The same is true of an area that has been struck by a missile, it is extremely lethal and would kill anything entering the vicinity.

Due to the fact that everyone else is dead, all machinery must be operated manually. This means that the players must set the target co-ordinates and latch the fuse for the missile to be shot off. After that, the players must flee the area. This is done in a small shuttle car, equipped with sensor devices to avoid dangerous areas. But due to its limited power reserves, it can go only two units in any direction, up, down, or diagonally, and no more or less. The danger involved is that while in flight, the player is away from a scanner computer terminal and will not know where the enemy missile is aimed to land.

In the time it takes to move to the new base, the missiles will be at the apex of their flight above the earth. There the computer will give out tracking information as to whether you hit the enemy, or he hit you, or both. If the missile is coming down to hit the player, there is no escape. The time required to recharge the shuttle car is longer than the time it takes for the missile to hit the ground. If either player is unfortunate enough to get trapped into a corner, the seeping radiation will eventually kill him.

So it is plainly a game of kill or be killed. However, don't be misled into thinking that it is simply a game of luck, several different strategies may be applied to destroy the enemy.

Line by line explanation.

Lines 440-490. I assemble three commonly used print strings. S$ becomes a string of fourteen spaces.

Lines 500-530. Here is the dimensioning of the four matrices, and the start-up and circle check data. The matrices "I" and "H" stand for player and enemy playing fields (I and HE). the "T" matrix is a temporary list for use by the enemy, and is part of the "smart" algorithm. It is loaded up during each pass with the possible places he could move to, or looking at the possible places where the player could move. The "P" matrix is filled with the eight possible co-ordinates that one may move to. I might say here that the program may be modified for a longer and more challenging game by changing the data in line 530. Change all the twos to ones and the two players may move only one unit away from their previous position, instead of the two used now.

Lines 540-730. I set up a random number to decide which pair of corner co-ordinates the enemy will be started in. I then proceed to set the pair from 550 to 570. I then digress to zero my matrices. Picking up where I left off, lines 640 to 680 peel away any unused, but unwanted data, keying on the unique first number of the last pair. From there the remaining data is dumped into "P."

Lines 740-820. Make the report that the enemy has been "fooling around." The starting co-ordinates for the player are then obtained and checked. From there the valid loop switch is set, a map is printed, and the program is thrust headlong into the main routine.

Lines 830-920. Here the co-ordinates for the missile and the new spot to sit on are obtained and verified of their validity.

Lines 930-1080. "Enemy" decides where player might be going from last position, and aims his missile in that direction.

Lines 1090-1280. The "enemy" looks for place to go. If he has cornered himself, say so, prepare him for his execution, and make it look like he hasn't fired a missile. Otherwise, he chooses a new co-ordinate to rest upon.

Lines 1290-1480. Now we move everyone around (where we can), and start to find out who got who, if anyone at all. Then from 1430-1480 there is a check to discover whether the player has a place to go or not. If not, another message is printed and player will die quietly after output.

Lines 1490-1780. Here the printing of the two matrices is done. A value of one or zero is tested for making the proper symbol. After the output is complete "Z" is checked to see if anyone died on the way. If no one had, return for another pass, else terminate the program.

I spent a lot of time debugging this program. After I finally got it to work, I found that it became somewhat addictive. The tension does seem to build when the game reaches the final possible moves. I found there are two different useful strategies that may be applied.

My favorite is building a fence around the enemy with missile shots. The idea is to cut off his movements while trying to keep out of his way. The other method is the one the enemy uses. Here the player shoots at where he thinks the opponent may be each time. Quite often the game is ended early, the odds of being hit become too great.

Any method you use, or another you may think of, will lend long hours of enjoyment. Have fun!

The program and description were written by David Spencer.

```
RUN
                    SHOOT
              CREATIVE COMPUTING
            MORRISTOWN, NEW JERSEY


DO YOU WANT INSTRUCTIONS? YES

 IT IS THE FINAL HOUR OF MAN. YOU AND A WARRING NATION
HAVE ENTERED INTO A LAST CONTEST. ALL THE LIFE NOW LEFT ON
EARTH ARE YOU AND YOUR ENEMY. BOTH HE AND YOU HAVE FOUND THE
LAST REMAINING ATOMIC MISSILE SILO MATRICES ESTABLISHED BY
THE NOW-DEAD SUPERPOWERS. HE, LIKE YOU, WISHES NOT TO DIE
BUT TO LIVE IN PEACE.
 HOWEVER IT HAS BECOME APPARENT THAT HE FEELS HIS PEACE
THREATENED AND IS PREPARING AN ATTACK. BOTH YOU AND HE HAVE
SCANNERS THAT WILL WARN YOU OF HIS MOVEMENTS AND TRACK THE
FLIGHT OF HIS ATOMIC MISSILES, THUS HE IS WORKING SLOWLY.
THE ENEMY, LIKE YOURSELF, HAS A MISSILE GRID NEARLY
IDENTICAL IN STRUCTURE AND OPERATION TO YOURS, BECAUSE YOU
ARE THE ONLY ONE LEFT, IT WILL BE NECESSARY TO FIRE ALL YOUR
MISSILES MANUALLY. ONCE THE FUSE IS SET, YOU MUST FLEE THE
AREA AND GET TWO GRID UNITS AWAY. YOU MAY NEVER RETURN TO
THIS SPOT, OR A SPOT WHERE A MISSILE HAS LANDED; THE
RADIATION IS INTENSE AND WOULD MEAN AN INSTANT, PAINFUL
DEATH.
 SO THE STAGE HAS BEEN SET. THERE IS PEACE UNTIL THE
SIGN THAT THE ENEMY HAS MOVED TO HIS MISSILE RANGE. HE WILL
FIRE EVERY TIME YOU WILL, AND DO SO UNTIL ONE OF YOU IS
DESTROYED.
 EACH TIME A ROUND OF MISSILES HAS BEEN FIRED, THE
SCANNERS WILL REPORT THE STATUS OF BOTH YOUR'S AND THE ENEMY'S
GRID TERRITORY. IT WILL SHOW ALL AREAS THAT HAVE HAD EITHER
A MISSILE HIT OR A MISSILE FIRED FROM IT. WITH THIS
CONTINUALLY UPDATED MAP, YOU MAY BE ABLE TO INDUCTIVELY
DISCOVER OR TRAP YOUR OPPONENT. BEWARE, HE WILL BE TRYING TO
DO THE SAME TO YOU.

SCANNER COMPUTER: ENEMY ACTIVITY ON GRID AT 10 , 1

YOUR STARTING CO-ORDINATES? 3,3

 YOUR TERRITORY            ENEMY TERRITORY

   12345678910               12345678910
 1 ::::::::::              1 ::::::::::
 2 ::::::::::              2 ::::::::::
 3 ::*:::::::              3 ::::::::::
 4 ::::::::::              4 ::::::::::
 5 ::::::::::              5 ::::::::::
 6 ::::::::::              6 ::::::::::
 7 ::::::::::              7 ::::::::::
 8 ::::::::::              8 ::::::::::
 9 ::::::::::              9 ::::::::::
10 ::::::::::             10 *:::::::::

MISSILE CO-ORDINATES? 10,4
WHERE TO MOVE TO? 3,5

SCANNER COMPUTER: HEY! YOU GOT HIM!!
 YOUR TERRITORY            ENEMY TERRITORY

   12345678910               12345678910
 1 ::::*:::::              1 ::::::::::
 2 ::::::::::              2 ::::::::::
 3 ::*:::::::              3 ::::::::::
 4 ::::::::::              4 ::::::::::
 5 ::::::::::              5 ::::::::::
 6 ::::::::::              6 ::::::::::
 7 ::::::::::              7 ::::::::::
 8 ::::::::::              8 ::::::::::
 9 ::::::::::              9 ::::::::::
10 ::::::::::             10 *::*::::::

OK
```

```
RUN
                    SHOOT
              CREATIVE COMPUTING
            MORRISTOWN, NEW JERSEY

DO YOU WANT INSTRUCTIONS? NO
SCANNER COMPUTER: ENEMY ACTIVITY ON GRID AT 1 , 1

YOUR STARTING CO-ORDINATES? 2,5

 YOUR TERRITORY            ENEMY TERRITORY

   12345678910               12345678910
 1 ::::::::::              1 *:::::::::
 2 ::::*:::::              2 ::::::::::
 3 ::::::::::              3 ::::::::::
 4 ::::::::::              4 ::::::::::
 5 ::::::::::              5 ::::::::::
 6 ::::::::::              6 ::::::::::
 7 ::::::::::              7 ::::::::::
 8 ::::::::::              8 ::::::::::
 9 ::::::::::              9 ::::::::::
10 ::::::::::             10 ::::::::::

MISSILE CO-ORDINATES? 4,1
WHERE TO MOVE TO? 2,7

 YOUR TERRITORY            ENEMY TERRITORY

   12345678910               12345678910
 1 ::::::::::              1 *:::::::::
 2 ::::*:::::              2 ::::::::::
 3 ::::::::::              3 ::::::::::
 4 ::*:::::::              4 *:::::::::
 5 ::::::::::              5 ::::::::::
 6 ::::::::::              6 ::::::::::
 7 ::::::::::              7 ::::::::::
 8 ::::::::::              8 ::::::::::
 9 ::::::::::              9 ::::::::::
10 ::::::::::             10 ::::::::::

MISSILE CO-ORDINATES? 1,5
WHERE TO MOVE TO? 2,9

 YOUR TERRITORY            ENEMY TERRITORY

   12345678910               12345678910
 1 ::::::::::              1 *:*:*:::::
 2 ::::*:*:*:              2 ::::::::::
 3 ::::::::::              3 ::::::::::
 4 ::*:::::::              4 *:::::::::
 5 ::::::::::              5 ::::::::::
 6 ::::::::::              6 ::::::::::
 7 ::::::::::              7 ::::::::::
 8 ::::::::::              8 ::::::::::
 9 ::::::::::              9 ::::::::::
10 ::::::::::             10 ::::::::::

MISSILE CO-ORDINATES? 3,4
WHERE TO MOVE TO? 3,9
WHERE TO MOVE TO? 4,9

 YOUR TERRITORY            ENEMY TERRITORY

   12345678910               12345678910
 1 ::::::::::              1 *:*:*:::::
 2 ::::*:*:*:              2 ::::::::::
 3 ::::::::::              3 ::**::::::
 4 ::*:::*:::              4 *:::::::::
 5 ::::::::::              5 ::::::::::
 6 ::::::::::              6 ::::::::::
 7 ::::::::::              7 ::::::::::
 8 ::::::::::              8 ::::::::::
 9 ::::::::::              9 ::::::::::
10 ::::::::::             10 ::::::::::

MISSILE CO-ORDINATES? 5,5
WHERE TO MOVE TO? 6,9

SCANNER COMPUTER: HEY! YOU GOT HIM!!
SCANNER COMPUTER: YOU MOVED RIGHT UNDER HIS MISSILE!!
 YOUR TERRITORY            ENEMY TERRITORY

   12345678910               12345678910
 1 ::::::::::              1 *:*:*:::::
 2 ::::*:*:*:              2 ::::::::::
 3 ::::::::::              3 ::***:::::
 4 ::*:::*:*:              4 *:::::::::
 5 ::::::::::              5 ::::*:::::
 6 ::::::::*:              6 ::::::::::
 7 ::::::::::              7 ::::::::::
 8 ::::::::::              8 ::::::::::
 9 ::::::::::              9 ::::::::::
10 ::::::::::             10 ::::::::::
```

```
LIST

10 PRINT TAB(26);"SHOOT"
20 PRINT TAB(20);"CREATIVE COMPUTING"
30 PRINT TAB(18);"MORRISTOWN, NEW JERSEY"
40 PRINT:PRINT:PRINT
110 INPUT "DO YOU WANT INSTRUCTIONS";A$
120 IF LEFT$(A$,1)<>"Y" GOTO 440
130 PRINT
140 PRINT " IT IS THE FINAL HOUR OF MAN. YOU AND A WARRING NATION"
150 PRINT "HAVE ENTERED INTO A LAST CONTEST. ALL THE LIFE NOW LEFT ON"
160 PRINT "EARTH ARE YOU AND YOUR ENEMY. BOTH HE AND YOU HAVE FOUND THE"
170 PRINT "LAST REMAINING ATOMIC MISSILE SILO MATRICES ESTABLISHED BY"
180 PRINT "THE NOW-DEAD SUPERPOWERS. HE, LIKE YOU, WISHES NOT TO DIE"
190 PRINT "BUT TO LIVE IN PEACE."
200 PRINT " HOWEVER IT HAS BECOME APPARENT THAT HE FEELS HIS PEACE"
210 PRINT "THREATENED AND IS PREPARING AN ATTACK. BOTH YOU AND HE HAVE"
220 PRINT "SCANNERS THAT WILL WARN YOU OF HIS MOVEMENTS AND TRACK THE"
230 PRINT "FLIGHT OF HIS ATOMIC MISSILES, THUS HE IS WORKING SLOWLY."
240 PRINT "THE ENEMY, LIKE YOURSELF, HAS A MISSILE GRID NEARLY"
250 PRINT "IDENTICAL IN STRUCTURE AND OPERATION TO YOURS, BECAUSE YOU"
260 PRINT "ARE THE ONLY ONE LEFT, IT WILL BE NECESSARY TO FIRE ALL YOUR"
270 PRINT "MISSILES MANUALLY. ONCE THE FUSE IS SET, YOU MUST FLEE THE"
280 PRINT "AREA AND GET TWO GRID UNITS AWAY. YOU MAY NEVER RETURN TO"
290 PRINT "THIS SPOT, OR A SPOT WHERE A MISSILE HAS LANDED; THE"
300 PRINT "RADIATION IS INTENSE AND WOULD MEAN AN INSTANT, PAINFUL"
310 PRINT "DEATH."
320 PRINT " SO THE STAGE HAS BEEN SET. THERE IS PEACE UNTIL THE"
330 PRINT "SIGN THAT THE ENEMY HAS MOVED TO HIS MISSILE RANGE. HE WILL"
340 PRINT "FIRE EVERY TIME YOU WILL, AND DO SO UNTIL ONE OF YOU IS"
350 PRINT "DESTROYED."
360 PRINT " EACH TIME A ROUND OF MISSILES HAS BEEN FIRED, THE"
370 PRINT "SCANNERS WILL REPORT THE STATUS OF BOTH YOUR'S AND THE ENEMY'
S"
380 PRINT "GRID TERRITORY. IT WILL SHOW ALL AREAS THAT HAVE HAD EITHER"
390 PRINT "A MISSILE HIT OR A MISSILE FIRED FROM IT. WITH THIS"
400 PRINT "CONTINUALLY UPDATED MAP, YOU MAY BE ABLE TO INDUCTIVELY"
410 PRINT "DISCOVER OR TRAP YOUR OPPONENT. BEWARE, HE WILL BE TRYING TO"
420 PRINT "DO THE SAME TO YOU."
430 PRINT
440 G$="  -12345678910"
450 C$="SCANNER COMPUTER: "
460 S$=""
470 FOR X=1 TO 14
480 S$=S$+" "
490 NEXT X
510 DIM I(10,10),H(10,10),T(8,2),P(8,2)
520 DATA 10,10 , 1,1 , 10,1 , 1,10 , 10,9 , 9,10 , 1,2 , 2,1
530 DATA -2,-2 , 0,-2, 2,-2, 2,0 , 2,2 , 0,2 ,-2,2 ,-2,0
540 R=INT(RND(1)*8+1)
550 FOR X=1 TO R
560 READ A,B
570 NEXT X
580 FOR X=1 TO 10
590 FOR Y=1 TO 10
600 I(X,Y)=0
610 H(X,Y)=0
620 NEXT Y
630 NEXT X
640 IF A=2 GOTO 690
650 FOR X=1 TO 8
660 READ C,D
670 IF C=2 GOTO 690
680 NEXT X
690 FOR X=1 TO 8
700 FOR Y=1 TO 2
710 READ P(X,Y)
720 NEXT Y
730 NEXT X
740 PRINT C$;"ENEMY ACTIVITY ON GRID AT";A;",";B
750 PRINT
760 INPUT "YOUR STARTING CO-ORDINATES";E,F
770 IF E<1 OR E>10 OR F<1 OR F>10 GOTO 760
780 Z=1
790 I(E,F)=1
800 H(A,B)=1
810 PRINT
820 GOTO 1490
830 INPUT "MISSILE CO-ORDINATES";M,N
840 IF M<1 OR M>10 OR N<1 OR N>10 GOTO 830
850 INPUT "WHERE TO MOVE TO";S,T
860 IF S<1 OR S>10 OR T<1 OR T>10 GOTO 850
870 IF I(S,T)=1 GOTO 850
880 FOR X=1 TO 8
890 IF P(X,1)+E=S AND P(X,2)+F=T GOTO 920
900 NEXT X
910 GOTO 850
920 PRINT
930 L=1
940 FOR X=1 TO 8
950 IF P(X,1)+E>10 OR P(X,1)+E<1 OR P(X,2)+F>10 OR P(X,2)+F<1 GOTO 1000
960 IF  I(P(X,1)+E,P(X,2)+F)=1 GOTO 1000
970 T(L,1)=P(X,1)+E
980 T(L,2)=P(X,2)+F
990 L=L+1
1000 NEXT X
1010 L=L-1
1020 IF L<>1 GOTO 1060
1030 C=T(L,1)
1040 D=T(L,2)
1050 GOTO 1090
1060 G=INT(RND(1)*L+1)
1070 C=T(G,1)
1080 D=T(G,2)
1090 L=1
1100 FOR X=1 TO 8
1110 IF P(X,1)+A>10ORP(X,1)+A<1 OR P(X,2)+B>10ORP(X,2)+B<1 GOTO 1160
1120 IF H(P(X,1)+A,P(X,2)+B)=1 GOTO 1160
1130 T(L,1)=P(X,1)+A
1140 T(L,2)=P(X,2)+B
1150 L=L+1
1160 NEXT X
1170 L=L-1
1180 IF L<>0 GOTO 1220
1190 PRINT C$;"THE ENEMY HAS CORNERED HIMSELF IN!!"
1200 Z=0
1204 C=E
1207 D=F
1210 GOTO 1290
1220 IF L<>1 GOTO 1260
1230 J=T(1,1)
1240 K=T(1,2)
1250 GOTO 1290
1260 G=INT(RND(1)*L+1)
1270 J=T(G,1)
1280 K=T(G,2)
1290 I(E,F)=1
1300 H(A,B)=1
1310 I(C,D)=1
1320 H(M,N)=1
1330 IF M<>J OR D<>T GOTO 1390
1340 PRINT C$;"HEY! YOU GOT HIM!!"
1350 Z=0
1360 IF C<>S OR D<>T GOTO 1390
1370 PRINT C$;"YOU MOVED RIGHT UNDER HIS MISSILE!!"
1380 Z=0
1390 E=S
1400 F=T
1410 A=J
1420 B=K
1430 FOR X=1 TO 8
1440 IF P(X,1)+E>10ORP(X,1)+E<1 OR P(X,2)+F>10ORP(X,2)+F<1 GOTO 1460
1450 IF I(P(X,1)+E,P(X,2)+F)=0 GOTO 1490
1460 NEXT X
1470 PRINT C$;"FOOL! YOU HAVE BOXED YOURSELF INTO A CORNER!!"
1480 Z=0
1490 PRINT " YOUR TERRITORY ","ENEMY TERRITORY"
1500 PRINT
1510 PRINT G$;S$;G$
1520 FOR X=1 TO 10
1530 IF X=10 GOTO 1560
1540 PRINT X;
1550 GOTO 1570
1560 PRINT "10 ";
1570 FOR Y=1 TO 10
1580 IF I(X,Y)=1 GOTO 1610
1590 PRINT ":";
1600 GOTO 1620
1610 PRINT "*";
1620 NEXT Y
1630 PRINT " ";S$;
1640 IF X=10 GOTO 1670
1650 PRINT X;
1660 GOTO 1680
1670 PRINT "10 ";
1680 FOR Y=1 TO 10
1690 IF H(X,Y)=1 GOTO 1720
1700 PRINT ":";
1710 GOTO 1730
1720 PRINT "*";
1730 NEXT Y
1740 PRINT
1750 NEXT X
1760 PRINT
1770 IF Z=1 GOTO 830
1780 END
OK
```

Smash

This game is a one-lap jalopy race. There is one big problem: you don't know the shape of the course or the safe speed with which you can go around the corners. Consequently you're likely to smash up fairly frequently or else go so slowly that you don't earn a good placing among the winners. However, after four or five plays of the game you'll begin to get the hang of it and you'll be able to whip around the course in grand fashion. The instructions in the program are quite detailed. Have fun!

SMASH was written by Scott Byron

```
RUN

                          SMASH
                    CREATIVE COMPUTING
                  MORRISTOWN, NEW JERSEY



DO YOU NEED INSTRUCTIONS? YES

THIS IS SMASH--THE GAME THAT SIMULATES A CAR RACE.
YOU WILL RESPOND WITH ONE OF THE FOLLOWING MANUEVERS
WHEN A '?' IS TYPED.  THE POSITION NUMBERS REFER TO THE
POINT AT WHICH YOU ARE ON THE TRACK-THEY GO AS FOLLOWS:

  1-THE START LINE
  2-MID STRAIGHT-AWAY
  3-COMING UP ON A LEFT TURN
  4-MID LEFT TURN
  5-COMING UP ON A RIGHT TURN
  6-MID-RIGHT TURN
  7-THE FINISH LINE

     MANEUVERS
  1-FLOOR IT
  2-ACCELERATE(MODERATE)
  3-BRAKE SLIGHT
  4-JAM ON THE BRAKES
  5-SHARP RIGHT
  6-MODERATE RIGHT
  7-SHARP LEFT
  8-MODERATE LEFT

TIME(SEC)      MILES TO GO    M.P.H.        POSITION      MOVE
 0              10             0             1            ? 1
 30             9.77167        27.4          4            ? 2
 60             9.32917        53.1          3            ? 2
 90             8.55292        93.15         4            ? 3
 120            7.9012         78.2062       2            ? 1
SMASH--YOU WENT RIGHT INTO THE WALL!
DO YOU WANT TO PLAY AGAIN? YES

TIME(SEC)      MILES TO GO    M.P.H.        POSITION      MOVE
 0              11             0             1            ? 1
 30             10.8217        21.4          2            ? 1
 60             10.1008        86.5          2            ? 1
SMASH--YOU WENT RIGHT INTO THE WALL!
DO YOU WANT TO PLAY AGAIN? YES

TIME(SEC)      MILES TO GO    M.P.H.        POSITION      MOVE
 0              13             0             1            ? 1
 30             12.7742        27.1          3            ? 2
 60             12.3688        48.65         4            ? 2
 90             11.6623        84.775        5            ? 6
 120            10.9521        85.2287       6            ? 6
 150            10.3235        75.4221       6            ? 2
 180            9.31159        121.433       3            ? 3
 210            8.44864        103.554       4            ? 8
 240            7.56004        106.632       2            ? 2
 270            6.14713        169.549       3            ? 3
 300            4.93168        145.855       4            ? 7
 330            4.10717        98.9407       2            ? 2
 360            2.77708        159.611       3            ? 3
 390            1.63575        136.96        4            ? 7
 420            .737833        107.75        2            ? 2
 435.387        0              172.625       7
THAT ENDS THE RACE, YOU PLACED # 2
YOUR AVERAGE SPEED WAS 107.491 M.P.H.
DO YOU WANT TO PLAY AGAIN? NO
Ok
```

```
LIST
10 PRINT TAB(26);"SMASH"
20 PRINT TAB(20);"CREATIVE COMPUTING"
30 PRINT TAB(18);"MORRISTOWN, NEW JERSEY"
40 PRINT:PRINT:PRINT
50 DIM A(7),J(6)
70 PRINT"DO YOU NEED INSTRUCTIONS";
80 INPUT Z$
90 PRINT
100 FOR X=1 TO 7:READ A(X):NEXT X
105 FOR X=1 TO 6:READ J(X):NEXT X
120 IF LEFT$(Z$,1)="N" THEN 350
130 PRINT"THIS IS SMASH--THE GAME THAT SIMULATES A CAR RACE."
140 PRINT"YOU WILL RESPOND WITH ONE OF THE FOLLOWING MANUEVERS"
150 PRINT "WHEN A '?' IS TYPED.  THE POSITION NUMBERS REFER TO THE"
160 PRINT"POINT AT WHICH YOU ARE ON THE TRACK-THEY GO AS FOLLOWS:"
170 PRINT
180 PRINT "  1-THE START LINE"
190 PRINT "  2-MID STRAIGHT-AWAY"
200 PRINT "  3-COMING UP ON A LEFT TURN"
210 PRINT "  4-MID LEFT TURN"
220 PRINT "  5-COMING UP ON A RIGHT TURN"
230 PRINT "  6-MID-RIGHT TURN"
240 PRINT "  7-THE FINISH LINE"
250 PRINT
260 PRINT"     MANEUVERS"
270 PRINT"  1-FLOOR IT"
280 PRINT"  2-ACCELERATE(MODERATE)"
290 PRINT"  3-BRAKE SLIGHT"
300 PRINT"  4-JAM ON THE BRAKES"
310 PRINT"  5-SHARP RIGHT"
320 PRINT"  6-MODERATE RIGHT"
330 PRINT"  7-SHARP LEFT"
340 PRINT"  8-MODERATE LEFT"
350 PRINT
360 PRINT"TIME(SEC)","MILES TO GO","M.P.H.","POSITION","MOVE"
370 LET A=INT(10+RND(1)*5):Y=A
380 LET B=0:T=0
390 LET C=1
400 GOTO 420
410 LET C=(INT(2+RND(1)*5))
```

```
420 PRINT T,A,B,C,
430 INPUT D
440 IF D<>INT(D) THEN 470
450 IF D>8 THEN 470
460 IF D>=1 THEN 490
470 PRINT"ONE THRU EIGHT ONLY"
480 GOTO 420
490 IF D<>1 THEN 510
500 LET B=3*B+20+INT(10+RND(1)*91)/10
510 IF D<>2 THEN 530
520 LET B=3*B/2+7+INT(10+RND(1)*61)/10
530 IF D<>3 THEN 550
540 LET B=7*B/8-6+INT(10+RND(1)*41)/10
550 IF D<>4 THEN 570
560 LET B=4*B/7-26+INT(10+RND(1)*81)/10
570 IF D=7 THEN 590
580 IF D<>5 THEN 600
590 LET B=9*B/10*(.7+RND(1)*.6)
600 IF D=8 THEN 620
610 IF D<>6 THEN 630
620 LET B=13*B/14*(.7+RND(1)*.6)
630 IF B>0 THEN 650
640 LET B=0
650 IF A-B/120>0 THEN 730
660 LET T=T+A*3600/B
670 PRINT T,0,B,7
680 PRINT"THAT ENDS THE RACE, YOU PLACED #"INT(T/(20*Y)+.5)
690 PRINT"YOUR AVERAGE SPEED WAS"Y*3600/T"M.P.H."
700 IF INT(T/(20*Y)+.5)<>1 THEN 980
710 PRINT"THAT WAS A PERFECT RACE, CHAMP!"
720 GOTO 980
730 IF C<>2 THEN 760
740 IF D=7 THEN 960
750 IF D=5 THEN 960
760 IF C=3 THEN 780
770 IF C<>4 THEN 800
780 IF D=5 THEN 960
790 IF D=6 THEN 960
800 IF C=6 THEN 820
810 IF C<>5 THEN 840
820 IF D=7 THEN 960
830 IF D=8 THEN 960
840 IF B>J(C) THEN 970
850 IF INT(1+RND(0)*77)<>40 THEN 880
860 PRINT"SMASH--YOU HAVE BEEN HIT BY ANOTHER CAR!!"
870 GOTO 980
880 LET T=T+30
890 LET A=A-B/120
900 IF C=1 THEN 410
910 IF C=4 THEN 410
920 IF C=2 THEN 410
930 IF C=6 THEN 410
940 LET C=C+1
950 GOTO 420
960 PRINT"BAD MOVE!"
970 PRINT "SMASH--YOU WENT RIGHT INTO THE WALL!"
980 PRINT"DO YOU WANT TO PLAY AGAIN";
990 INPUT Z$
1000 IF LEFT$(Z$,1)="Y" THEN 350
1020 DATA 2,3,5,2,3,5,2,200,240,180,170,180,170
1030 END
Ok
```

Strike 9

This is a simple game based on the numbers 1 through 9, and a pair of dice. First, the computer rolls a random number for your "dice." Then you must take that number from the total of your board numbers 1-9. To win you must remove all of your board numbers. With each roll you must remove the total number of that roll from the board or you lose.

One strategy is to remove the largest numbers possible with each roll, or you can try to get the most numbers removed. For example, if the roll is 10, you might want to remove the 1, 2, 3 and 4 instead of the 1 and 9.

You may want to have competition and players can alternate with rolls. Then the player who can't remove all numbers from his/her roll loses.

Strike 9 was conceived by Bruce Grembowski and first appeared in *Creative Computing*, Jan/Feb 1977.

```
RUN

                         STRIKE 9
                   CREATIVE COMPUTING
                  MORRISTOWN  NEW JERSEY



DO YOU NEED INSTRUCTIONS ? YES
STRIKE NINE IS PLAYED WITH A PAIR OF DICE AND A
BOARD WITH NINE NUMBERS: 1 2 3 4 5 6 7 8 9. YOU
ARE GIVEN A ROLL AND CAN KNOCK OFF UP TO 4 NUMBERS.
IF YOU INPUT THAT YOU WANT TO REMOVE 5 NUMBERS, YOU
WILL BE GIVEN A CHART OF THE NUMBERS YOU HAVE LEFT
TO REMOVE. NEXT YOU INPUT HOW MANY NUMBERS YOU WANT
TO REMOVE, AND THEN INPUT THE NUMBERS YOU WANT TO
TAKE OFF, ONE AT A TIME. THE NUMBERS YOU TAKE OFF
MUST ADD UP TO THE ROLL. YOU WIN BY REMOVING EVERY
NUMBER FROM THE BOARD. YOU LOSE IF YOU CANNOT
REMOVE ALL NUMBERS WITH THE ROLL YOU HAVE.

READY TO PLAY?

HERE IS THE BOARD:   1  2  3  4  5  6  7  8  9
YOUR ROLL IS    8
# OF NUMBERS TO REMOVE ? 1
WHAT IS THE NUMBER? 8
YOUR ROLL IS    3
# OF NUMBERS TO REMOVE ? 2
WHAT IS THE NUMBER? 2
? 1
YOUR ROLL IS    6
# OF NUMBERS TO REMOVE ? 1
WHAT IS THE NUMBER? 6
YOUR ROLL IS    9
# OF NUMBERS TO REMOVE ? 1
WHAT IS THE NUMBER? 9
YOUR ROLL IS    7
# OF NUMBERS TO REMOVE ? 1
WHAT IS THE NUMBER? 7
YOUR ROLL IS    9
# OF NUMBERS TO REMOVE ? 5
THE NUMBERS YOU HAVE LEFT TO REMOVE ARE:   3  4  5
# OF NUMBERS TO REMOVE ? 2
WHAT IS THE NUMBER? 5
? 4
YOUR ROLL IS    7
SORRY, YOU LOST THIS TIME.
THERE ARE  1  NUMBERS LEFT ON THE BOARD:     3
WANT TO TRY AGAIN (YES OR NO)? NO
OK
```

```
LIST

10 PRINT TAB(25);"STRIKE 9"
20 PRINT TAB(19);"CREATIVE COMPUTING"
30 PRINT TAB(18);"MORRISTOWN  NEW JERSEY"
90 DIM A(9),D(4)
110 PRINT:PRINT:PRINT
170 PRINT "DO YOU NEED INSTRUCTIONS ";
180 INPUT R$
190 IF R$ ="NO" THEN 340
200 IF R$ <> "YES" THEN 170
210 PRINT "STRIKE NINE IS PLAYED WITH A PAIR OF DICE AND A"
220 PRINT "BOARD WITH NINE NUMBERS: 1 2 3 4 5 6 7 8 9. YOU"
230 PRINT "ARE GIVEN A ROLL AND CAN KNOCK OFF UP TO 4 NUMBERS."
240 PRINT "IF YOU INPUT THAT YOU WANT TO REMOVE 5 NUMBERS, YOU"
250 PRINT "WILL BE GIVEN A CHART OF THE NUMBERS YOU HAVE LEFT"
260 PRINT "TO REMOVE. NEXT YOU INPUT HOW MANY NUMBERS YOU WANT"
270 PRINT "TO REMOVE, AND THEN INPUT THE NUMBERS YOU WANT TO "
280 PRINT "TAKE OFF, ONE AT A TIME. THE NUMBERS YOU TAKE OFF"
290 PRINT "MUST ADD UP TO THE ROLL. YOU WIN BY REMOVING EVERY"
300 PRINT "NUMBER FROM THE BOARD. YOU LOSE IF YOU CANNOT"
310 PRINT "REMOVE ALL NUMBERS WITH THE ROLL YOU HAVE."
320 PRINT
340 PRINT "READY TO PLAY?"
350 PRINT
355 PRINT "HERE IS THE BOARD:  ";
360 REM SET UP THE BOARD
370 FOR B=1 TO 9
380 PRINT B;
390 A(B)=B
400 NEXT B
405 PRINT
410 C=INT(RND(1)*6+1)+INT(RND(1)*6+1)
420 PRINT "YOUR ROLL IS ",C
430 T=0
440 FOR X=1 TO 9
450 T=T+A(X)
460 NEXT X
465 REM CHECK FOR LOSS
470 IF C > T THEN 950
480 IF C=T THEN 1120
490 FOR K=1 TO 9
500 FOR L=1 TO 9
510 FOR M=1 TO 9
520 FOR N=1 TO 9
530 IF N=K THEN 630
540 IF N=L THEN 630
550 IF N=M THEN 630
560 IF M=K THEN 640
570 IF M=L THEN 640
```

```
580 IF L=K THEN 650
590 IF C-A(K)=0 THEN 680
600 IF C-A(K)=A(N) THEN 680
610 IF C-A(K)-A(L)=A(N) THEN 680
620 IF C-A(K)-A(M)=A(N) THEN 680
630 NEXT N
640 NEXT M
650 NEXT L
660 NEXT K
670 GOTO 950
680 FOR X=1 TO 4
690 D(X)=0
700 NEXT X
710 PRINT "# OF NUMBERS TO REMOVE ";
720 INPUT E
730 IF INT(E) <> E THEN 760
740 IF E < 1 THEN 760
750 IF E>4 THEN 880
755 GOTO 770
760 PRINT "ANSWER 1, 2, 3, OR 4 (5 FOR THE BOARD)"
765 GOTO 710
770 PRINT "WHAT IS THE NUMBER";
780 FOR F=1 TO E
790 INPUT D(F)
800 IF A(D(F)) <> 0 THEN 825
810 PRINT "YOU REMOVED IT BEFORE, TRY AGAN."
820 GOTO 710
825 NEXT F
830 IF C <> D(1)+D(2)+D(3)+D(4) THEN 870
835 FOR F=1 TO E
840 A(D(F))=0
850 NEXT F
860 GOTO 410
870 PRINT "THOSE NUMBERS DON'T ADD UP TO YOUR ROLL, TRY AGAIN"
875 GOTO 710
880 PRINT "THE NUMBERS YOU HAVE LEFT TO REMOVE ARE:  ";
890 FOR B=1 TO 9
900 IF A(B)=0 THEN 920
910 PRINT A(B);
920 NEXT B
930 PRINT
940 GOTO 710
950 PRINT "SORRY, YOU LOST THIS TIME."
960 T=0
970 FOR B=1 TO 9
980 IF A(B)=0 THEN 1000
990 T=T+1
1000 NEXT B
1010 PRINT "THERE ARE ";T;" NUMBERS LEFT ON THE BOARD:    ";
1020 FOR X=1 TO 9
1030 IF A(X)=0 THEN 1050
1040 PRINT A(X);
1050 NEXT X
1060 PRINT
1070 PRINT "WANT TO TRY AGAIN (YES OR NO)";
1080 INPUT G$
1090 IF G$="YES" THEN 170
1100 IF G$ <> "NO" THEN 1070
1110 END
1120 PRINT "* * * CONGRATULATIONS * * *"
1130 PRINT "* YOU WON *"
1140 PRINT
1150 PRINT
1160 PRINT "PLAY ANOTHER GAME (YES OR NO)";
1170 INPUT H$
1180 IF H$="YES" THEN 170
1190 IF H$ <> "NO" THEN 1160
1200 END
OK
```

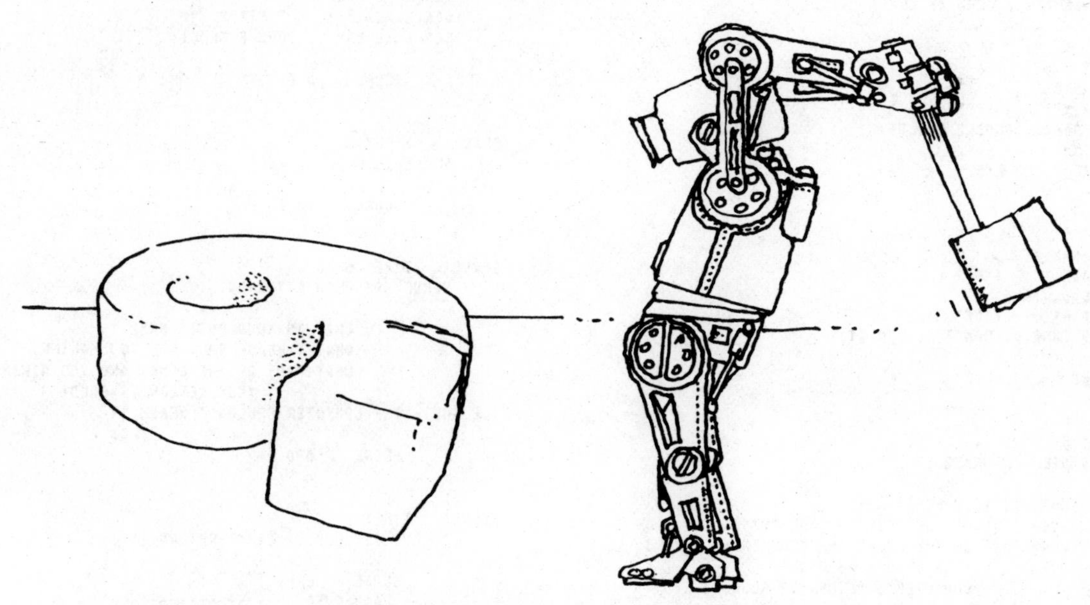

Tennis

Tennis is, as its name implies, a tennis match. In this game you have several options available to you as the position on the court that you wish to play from, the placement of your shot that you're trying for, and the speed or type of shot. As in normal tennis, you don't always make the shot that you try for. The program lets you play, more or less, at the intermediate level. If you think that it allows you to play too well or too poorly, you could always change some of the random factors that determine how often a shot is missed.

Tennis was written by Victor Nahigian and David Ahl.

```
RUN
                              TENNIS MATCH
            CREATIVE COMPUTING, MORRISTOWN, NEW JERSEY


THERE ARE SEVERAL OPTIONS AVAILABLE TO YOU AS TO POSITION,
PLACEMENT OF SHOT, AND SPEED (TYPE) OF SHOT.  THE KEY THAT
YOU WILL USE IS...
     POSITION(PLACEMENT, TOO): L.BACKCOURT(1);R.BACK-
COURT(2); L. FORECOURT(3); R. FORECOURT(4).
     SPEED (TYPE) OF SHOT: FAST-SLAM(S);SLOWLOB(L).
   BACKHANDS AND FOREHANDS WILL MERELY BE ASSUMED AS YOU
SHOOT FROM A CERTAIN SECTION OF THE COURT.
     ON SERVES, YOU CANNOT HAVE PLACEMENT OPTIONS, BUT YOU
WILL BE ABLE TO ALTER THE SPEED OF IT.  BY THE WAY, YOU
WILL BE ALLOWED TO SERVE FIRST IN ALL GAMES.
          ARE YOU READY?... HERE WE GO!!!


     SERVE!   TYPE? S
          SERVE IS BAD
          SERVE AGAIN!!    TYPE? S
          SERVE IS BAD... DOUBLE FAULT!

               SCORE    LOVE15


     SERVE!   TYPE? S
          SERVE IS BAD
          SERVE AGAIN!!    TYPE? S
          LET SERVE... TAKE 1
          SERVE AGAIN!!    TYPE? S
           SERVE IS GOOD... CAN'T RETURN IT!!

               SCORE    15 - 15


     SERVE!   TYPE? S
          SERVE HAS BEEN RETURNED...

                    WHAT IS YOUR POSITION?? 1
                    WHAT TYPE OF SHOT ARE YOU MAKING? S
                    WHAT PART OF THE COURT ARE YOU AIMING FOR? 3
                              YOUR RETURN IS GOOD!
                              COMPUTER'S RETURN IS GOOD!

                    WHAT IS YOUR POSITION?? 1
                    WHAT TYPE OF SHOT ARE YOU MAKING? S
                    WHAT PART OF THE COURT ARE YOU AIMING FOR? 2
                              YOUR RETURN IS GOOD!
                              COMPUTER'S RETURN IS GOOD!

                    WHAT IS YOUR POSITION?? 2
     NICE TRY-YOU WERE UNABLE TO REACH THAT SHOT-COURT # 3

               SCORE    15 - 30

SERVE!   TYPE? S
     SERVE IS BAD
     SERVE AGAIN!!    TYPE? S
      SERVE IS GOOD... CAN'T RETURN IT!!

          SCORE    DUCE


SERVE!   TYPE? S
      SERVE IS GOOD... CAN'T RETURN IT!!

          SCORE    ADD IN


SERVE!   TYPE? S
     SERVE IS BAD
     SERVE AGAIN!!    TYPE? S
     SERVE IS BAD... DOUBLE FAULT!

          SCORE    DUCE


SERVE!   TYPE? S
     SERVE IS BAD
     SERVE AGAIN!!    TYPE? S
     SERVE IS BAD... DOUBLE FAULT!

          SCORE    ADD OUT


SERVE!   TYPE? S
     SERVE HAS BEEN RETURNED...

               WHAT IS YOUR POSITION?? 1
               WHAT TYPE OF SHOT ARE YOU MAKING? L
               WHAT PART OF THE COURT ARE YOU AIMING FOR? 4
                         YOUR RETURN IS GOOD!
NICE SHOT- THE COMPUTER COULDN'T REACH IT

          SCORE    DUCE


SERVE!   TYPE? S
     SERVE IS BAD
     SERVE AGAIN!!    TYPE? S
     SERVE IS BAD... DOUBLE FAULT!

          SCORE    ADD OUT


SERVE!   TYPE? S
     SERVE IS GOOD... ACE!!

          SCORE    DUCE


SERVE!   TYPE? S
     SERVE HAS BEEN RETURNED...

               WHAT IS YOUR POSITION?? 1
               WHAT TYPE OF SHOT ARE YOU MAKING? S
               WHAT PART OF THE COURT ARE YOU AIMING FOR? 3
                         YOUR RETURN IS GOOD!
NICE SHOT- THE COMPUTER COULDN'T REACH IT

          SCORE    ADD IN


SERVE!   TYPE? S
      SERVE IS GOOD... CAN'T RETURN IT!!

          SCORE    GAME
--------------- GAME OVER ----------------
          SCORE-GAMES        YOU...ME
                              1     0


SERVE!   TYPE? S
     LET SERVE...TAKE 2
SERVE!   TYPE? S
      SERVE IS GOOD... CAN'T RETURN IT!!

          SCORE    15 - LOVE
```

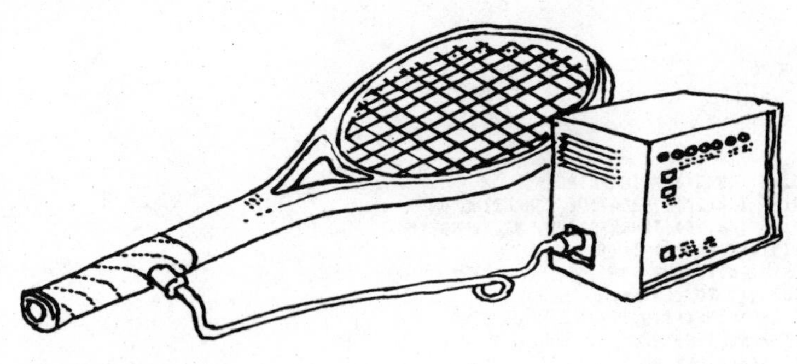

```
LIST
1 PRINT TAB(30)"TENNIS MATCH"
2 PRINT TAB(15)"CREATIVE COMPUTING, MORRISTOWN, NEW JERSEY"
10 PRINT:PRINT:PRINT
21 PRINT "THERE ARE SEVERAL OPTIONS AVAILABLE TO YOU AS TO POSITION,"
22 PRINT "PLACEMENT OF SHOT, AND SPEED (TYPE) OF SHOT.  THE KEY THAT "
23 PRINT "YOU WILL USE IS..."
24 PRINT TAB(5)"POSITION(PLACEMENT, TOO): L.BACKCOURT(1);R.BACK-"
25 PRINT "COURT(2); L. FORECOURT(3); R. FORECOURT(4)."
26 PRINT TAB(5)"SPEED (TYPE) OF SHOT: FAST-SLAM(S);SLOWLOB(L)."
27 PRINT TAB(3)"BACKHANDS AND FOREHANDS WILL MERELY BE ASSUMED AS YOU "
28 PRINT "SHOOT FROM A CERTAIN SECTION OF THE COURT."
29 PRINT TAB(5) "ON SERVES, YOU CANNOT HAVE PLACEMENT OPTIONS, BUT YOU"
30 PRINT "WILL BE ABLE TO ALTER THE SPEED OF IT.  BY THE WAY, YOU"
31 PRINT "WILL BE ALLOWED TO SERVE FIRST IN ALL GAMES."
32 PRINT TAB(10);"ARE YOU READY?... HERE WE GO!!!"
35 Y=0
36 Z=0
38 PRINT
39 PRINT
40 PRINT "      SERVE!   TYPE";
41 INPUT A$: IF A$<>"L" AND A$<>"S" THEN PRINT "'L' OR 'S'": GOTO 40
42 A=100*RND (1)
43 IF A$="L" THEN 52
44 C=6
45 D=51
46 IF A<C THEN 50
47 IF A<D THEN 70
48 PRINT TAB(10);"SERVE IS BAD"
49 GOTO 55
50 PRINT TAB(10);"LET SERVE...TAKE 2"
51 GOTO 40
52 C=4
53 D=66
54 GOTO 46
55 PRINT TAB(10);"SERVE AGAIN!!    TYPE";
56 INPUT B$: IF B$<>"L" AND B$<>"S" THEN PRINT "'L' OR 'S'": GOTO 55
57 E=100*RND(1)
58 IF B$="L" THEN 67
59 G=5
60 H=41
61 IF E<G THEN 65
62 IF E<H THEN 70
63 PRINT TAB(10);"SERVE IS BAD... DOUBLE FAULT!"
64 GOTO 130
65 PRINT TAB(10);"LET SERVE... TAKE 1"
66 GOTO 55
67 G=3
68 H=76
69 GOTO61
70 I=100 * RND(1)
71 IF I>6 THEN 74
72 PRINT TAB(10);"SERVE IS GOOD... ACE!!"
73 GOTO 128
74 K=100*RND (1)
75 IF A$="L" THEN 81
76 IF B$="L" THEN 81
77 N=61
78 IF K<N THEN 85
79 PRINT TAB(10); " SERVE IS GOOD... CAN'T RETURN IT!!"
80 GOTO 128
81 N=76
82 GOTO 78
85 PRINT TAB(10);"SERVE HAS BEEN RETURNED..."
86 PRINT
87 O=INT (4*RND(1))+1
88 PRINT TAB(20);"WHAT IS YOUR POSITION?";
89 INPUT Q
90 IF O+Q=5 THEN 124
91 PRINT TAB(20);"WHAT TYPE OF SHOT ARE YOU MAKING";
92 INPUT C$
93 PRINT TAB(20);"WHAT PART OF THE COURT ARE YOU AIMING FOR";
94 INPUT R
95 S=100*RND(1)
96 IF C$="L" THEN 99
97 IF S<81 THEN 107
98 GOTO 100
99 IF S<91 THEN 107
100 U=4*RND(1)
101 PRINT TAB(30);"YOUR RETURN IS BAD..."
102 IF U<2 THEN 105
103 PRINT TAB(33);"HIT OUT-OF-BOUNDS"
104 GOTO 130
105 PRINT TAB(33);"HIT INTO NET"
106 GOTO 130
107 PRINT TAB(30);"YOUR RETURN IS GOOD!"
108 A1=INT(4*RND(1))
109 IF R+A1=5 THEN 127
110 W=100*RND(1)
111 IF C$="L" THEN 112
112 IF W<84 THEN 122
113 GOTO 115
114 IF W<84 THEN 122
115 C1=4*RND(1)
116 PRINT TAB(30);"COMPUTER'S RETURN IS BAD"
117 IF B<2 THEN 120
118 PRINT TAB(33);"HIT OUT-OF-BOUNDS"
119 GOTO 128
120 PRINT TAB(33);"HIT INTO NET"
121 GOTO 128
122 PRINT TAB(30);"COMPUTER'S RETURN IS GOOD!"
123 GOTO 86
124 PRINT "     NICE TRY-YOU WERE UNABLE TO REACH THAT SHOT-COURT #"O
125 GOTO 130
127 PRINT "     NICE SHOT- THE COMPUTER COULDN'T REACH IT"
128 Y=Y+1
129 GOTO 131
130 Z=Z+1
131 PRINT:GOSUB 200
132 PRINT TAB(15);"SCORE     "S$
134 IF Y>=4 AND Y>Z+1 THEN 137
135 IF Z>=4 AND Z>Y+1 THEN 139
16 GOTO 38
137 Y1=Y1+1
138 GOTO 140
139 Z1=Z1+1
140 PRINT"--------------- GAME OVER ----------------"
141 PRINT TAB(15);"SCORE-GAMES       YOU...ME"
142  PRINT TAB(32);Y1;"  ";Z1
143 IF Y1>=6 AND Y1>Z1+1 THEN 146
144 IF Z1>=6 AND Z1>Y1+1 THEN 149
145 GOTO 35
146 PRINT
147 PRINT "*****CONGRATULATIONS...YOU WON*****"
148 GOTO 151
149 PRINT
150 PRINT "*****AS PREDICTED, THE COMPUTER IS AGAIN TRIUMPHANT!*****"
151 PRINT
152 PRINT"   I'D LIKE TO PLAY YOU AGAIN SOMETIME, BUT RIGHT NOW, I"
153 PRINT "HAVE TO REST.........BYE!!!"
154 PRINT
200 IF Y>=2 AND Z>=2 THEN 300
210 IF Y=4 OR Z=4 THEN S$="GAME": GOTO 400
220 IF Y=0 THEN Y$="LOVE"
230 IF Y=1 THEN Y$="15 - "
240 IF Y=2 THEN Y$="30 - "
245 IF Y=3 THEN Y$="40 - "
250 IF Z=0 THEN Z$="LOVE"
255 IF Z=1 THEN Z$="15"
260 IF Z=2 THEN Z$="30"
265 IF Z=3 THEN Z$="40"
270 S$=Y$+Z$:GOTO 400
300 IF Y=Z THEN S$="DUCE":GOTO 400
310 IF Y=Z+1 THEN S$="ADD IN ": GOTO 400
320 IF Y=Z-1 THEN S$="ADD OUT": GOTO 400
330 IF Y=Z+2 OR Z=Y+2 THEN S$="GAME"
400 RETURN
500 END
Ok
```

Tickertape

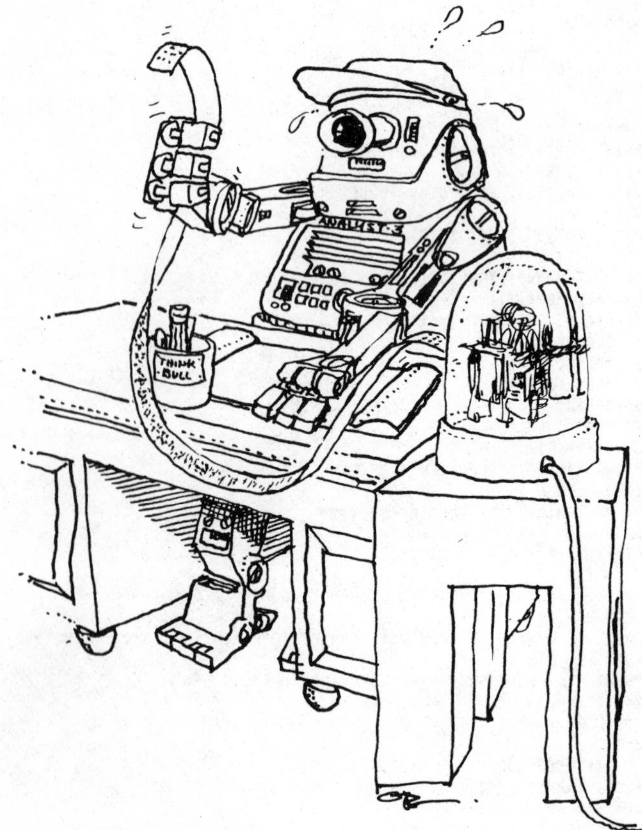

```
LIST

5 PRINT TAB(24);"TICKERTAPE"
6 PRINT TAB(20);"CREATIVE COMPUTING"
7 PRINT TAB(18);"MORRISTOWN, NEW JERSEY"
9 PRINT:PRINT:PRINT
10 INPUT A$:GOSUB 80
20 FOR N=1 TO LEN(A$)
25 B=ASC(MID$(A$,N,1))
30 IF B>90 THEN 47
33 IF B<65 THEN 40
35 B=B-64
37 GOTO 50
40 IF B>57 OR B<48 THEN 47
43 B=B-20
45 GOTO 50
47 B=27
50 FOR S=0 TO (B-1)*5:READ A:NEXT S
60 FOR S=1 TO 5:READ A:PRINT CHR$(A);:NEXT S
65 PRINT CHR$(0);:RESTORE
70 NEXT N
75 GOSUB 80:END
80 FOR N=1 TO 30:PRINT CHR$(0);:NEXT N
90 RETURN
110 DATA 0,254,9,9,9,254,255,137,137,137,118,126,129,129,129,129
120 DATA 255,129,129,129,126,255,137,137,137,137,255,9,9,9,1
130 DATA 126,129,129,145,243,255,8,8,8,255,129,129,255,129,129
140 DATA 96,128,129,127,1,255,8,20,34,193,255,128,128,128,128
150 DATA 255,2,12,2,255,255,2,60,64,255,126,129,129,129,126
160 DATA 255,9,9,9,6,126,129,161,65,190
170 DATA 255,25,41,73,134,134,137,137,137,113,1,1,255,1,1
180 DATA 127,128,128,128,127,63,96,192,96,63,127,128,112,128,127
215 DATA 195,36,24,36,195,3,4,248,4,3,193,161,145,137,135
220 DATA 0,0,0,0,0,126,161,137,133,126,132,130,255,128,128,194,161,145
230 DATA 137,134,66,137,137,137,118,12,10,137,255,136,199,137,137,137
240 DATA 248,126,137,137,137,114,1,1,249,5,2,118,137,137,137,118
250 DATA 70,137,137,137,126
OK
```

This program inputs a line of characters from a Teletype, and then punches the shape of each letter on paper tape. This program can handle all of the letters and numbers and the space, but there is no reason why it could not be modified to handle various symbols also.

The operation of this program is fairly straightforward. After each character is converted to a number equivalent to its place in the alphabet (A=1, B=2, Z=26, space=27), a simple table look-up is performed to find the correct numbers to punch onto the tape. These numbers are stored in the DATA statements.

The original program was designed for a PDP-8; the one here runs in Microsoft Basic, however it would not be difficult to modify the program for virtually any Basic-speaking computer.

Written by Bill Gardner and Jim Larus, Tickertape first appeared in *Creative Computing*, May/Jun 1977.

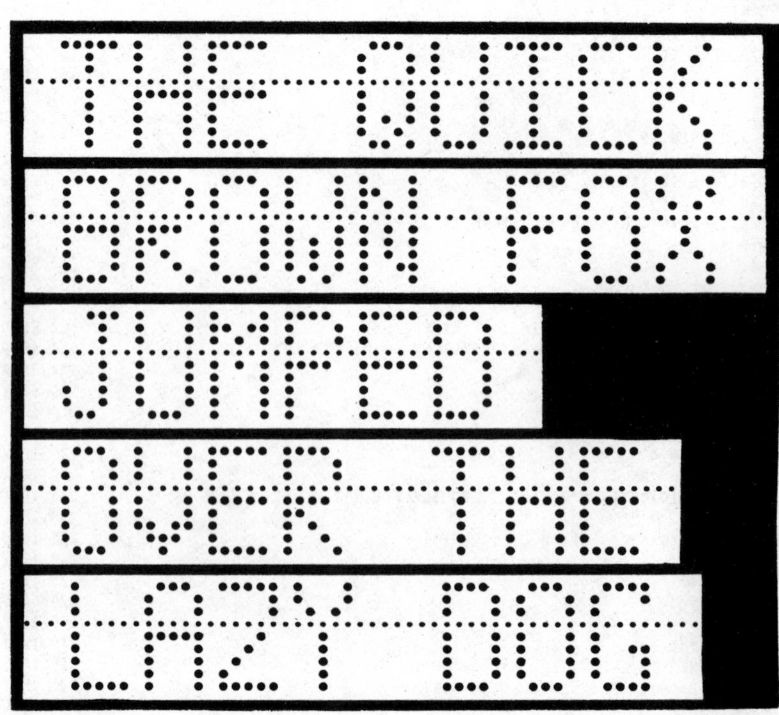

TV Plot

This program automatically devises plots for television shows or series guaranteed to appeal to the masses and win high Nielsen ratings. By substituting appropriate words in the various parts of the program it could be easily modified for many other useful purposes such as devising names for new breakfast cereals, preparing PhD theses, or naming government agencies and their corresponding projects.

This program was originally written in FOCAL by Mary Cole and converted to BASIC by David Ahl.

```
LIST
10 PRINT TAB(26);"TVPLOT"
20 PRINT TAB(20);"CREATIVE COMPUTING"
40 PRINT TAB(18);"MORRISTOWN, NEW JERSEY"
50 PRINT:PRINT:PRINT
55 PRINT "THIS PROGRAM AUTOMATICALLY COMES UP WITH TELEVISION"
60 PRINT "SHOWS GUARANTEED TO APPEAL TO THE MASSES AND WIN"
70 PRINT "HIGH NEILSEN RATINGS.":PRINT
80 PRINT "HERE IS THE FIRST PLOT:"
100 PRINT:GOSUB 800
110 ON X GOTO 120,130,140,150,160,120,130,140,150,160
120 A$="PROGRAM":GOTO 170
130 A$="REPORT":GOTO 170
140 A$="SPECIAL":GOTO 170
150 A$="SERIES":GOTO 170
160 A$="STORY"
170 GOSUB 800
180 ON X GOTO 190,200,210,220,230,240,250,260,270,280
190 B$="SWINGING":GOTO 290
200 B$="BRILLIANT":GOTO 290
210 B$="SALTY":GOTO 290
220 B$="HILARIOUS":GOTO 290
230 B$="SENSITIVE":GOTO 290
240 B$="DODDERING":GOTO 290
250 B$="HENPECKED":GOTO 290
260 B$="DEDICATED":GOTO 290
270 B$="THOUGHTFUL":GOTO 290
280 B$="HEAVY"
290 GOSUB 800
300 ON X GOTO 310,320,330,340,350,360,370,380,390,400
310 C$="GIRL COWHAND":GOTO 410
320 C$="LITTLE BOY":GOTO 410
330 C$="SCIENTEST":GOTO 410
340 C$="LAWYER":GOTO 410
350 C$="TOWN MARSHALL":GOTO 410
360 C$="DENTIST":GOTO 410
370 C$="BUS DRIVER":GOTO 410
380 C$="JUNGLE MAN":GOTO 410
390 C$="SECRET AGENT":GOTO 410
400 C$="COLLIE"
410 GOSUB 800
420 ON X GOTO 430,440,450,460,470,430,440,450,460,470
430 D$="A WHIZ":GOTO 480
440 D$="A FLOP":GOTO 480
450 D$="MEDIOCRE":GOTO 440
460 D$="A SUCCESS":GOTO 440
470 D$="A DISASTER"
480 GOSUB 800
490 ON X GOTO 500,510,520,530,540,550,560,570,580,590
500 E$="SOLVING CRIMES":GOTO 600
510 E$="ROPING COWS":GOTO 600
520 E$="COOKING HEALTH FOOD":GOTO 600
530 E$="PITCHING WOO":GOTO 600
540 E$="PROTECTING ECOLOGY":GOTO 600
550 E$="HELPING CHILDREN":GOTO 600
560 E$="TWO-FISTED DRINKING":GOTO 600
570 E$="FIGHTING FIRES":GOTO 600
580 E$="HERDING ELEPHANTS":GOTO 600
590 E$="WINNING RACES":GOTO 600
600 GOSUB 800
610 ON X GOTO 620,630,640,650,660,670,680,690,700,710
620 F$="RECOVERS THE JEWELS":GOTO 720
630 F$="FOILS THE SPIES":GOTO 720
640 F$="DESTROYS THE CITY":GOTO 720
650 F$="FINDS LOVE":GOTO 720
660 F$="SAVES THE ANIMALS":GOTO 720
670 F$="CONFESSES":GOTO 720
680 F$="DISCOVERS THE SECRET":GOTO 720
690 F$="STOPS THE FLOOD":GOTO 720
700 F$="HELPS THE DOG":GOTO 720
710 F$="MAKES THE SACRIFICE"
720 PRINT "THE ";A$;" IS ABOUT A ";B$;" ";C$;" WHO IS ";D$;" AT"
730 PRINT E$;" AND WHO ";F$;".":PRINT:PRINT
740 INPUT "ANOTHER (YES OR NO)";A$
750 IF A$="NO" THEN 999
760 GOTO 100
800 X=INT(10*RND(1)+1):RETURN
999 PRINT:PRINT "O.K.  HOPE YOU HAVE A SUCCESSFUL TV SHOW!!":END
Ok
```

```
RUN
                          TVPLOT
                    CREATIVE COMPUTING
                  MORRISTOWN, NEW JERSEY



THIS PROGRAM AUTOMATICALLY COMES UP WITH TELEVISION
SHOWS GUARANTEED TO APPEAL TO THE MASSES AND WIN
HIGH NEILSEN RATINGS.

HERE IS THE FIRST PLOT:

THE SPECIAL IS ABOUT A HILARIOUS LAWYER WHO IS A WHIZ AT
SOLVING CRIMES AND WHO STOPS THE FLOOD.


ANOTHER (YES OR NO)? YES

THE PROGRAM IS ABOUT A THOUGHTFUL COLLIE WHO IS A FLOP AT
HERDING ELEPHANTS AND WHO CONFESSES.


ANOTHER (YES OR NO)? YES

THE PROGRAM IS ABOUT A SENSITIVE SECRET AGENT WHO IS A WHIZ AT
TWO-FISTED DRINKING AND WHO STOPS THE FLOOD.


ANOTHER (YES OR NO)? YES

THE SPECIAL IS ABOUT A DEDICATED LITTLE BOY WHO IS A FLOP AT
COOKING HEALTH FOOD AND WHO HELPS THE DOG.


ANOTHER (YES OR NO)? YES

THE SERIES IS ABOUT A DODDERING LAWYER WHO IS A WHIZ AT
HERDING ELEPHANTS AND WHO STOPS THE FLOOD.


ANOTHER (YES OR NO)? YES

THE SPECIAL IS ABOUT A HENPECKED LAWYER WHO IS A FLOP AT
FIGHTING FIRES AND WHO DESTROYS THE CITY.


ANOTHER (YES OR NO)? YES

THE STORY IS ABOUT A SENSITIVE GIRL COWHAND WHO IS A FLOP AT
SOLVING CRIMES AND WHO RECOVERS THE JEWELS.


ANOTHER (YES OR NO)? NO

O.K.  HOPE YOU HAVE A SUCCESSFUL TV SHOW!!
Ok
```

Twonky

The computer will set up a 15x15 playing field in which you are randomly located. Also inside the field is an objective square, 30 blocked squares (walls), 22 relocation squares, and 1 super special new maze square, and, of course, the Twonky (which is no relation to a creme-filled cupcake).

To win the game, you must reach the objective square before the Twonky gets you, by moving one square at a time, forward, backward, right or left. Unfortunately, you are hindered by several things:

RELOCATION squares, when moved on, cause you to be randomly transported to another position in the maze.

WALLS; you can't move into these squares, and lose your turn when you hit one.

SUPER-MAZE-SQUARE; essentially an instant loss, since when you move here a completely new maze is set up.

TWONKY; after every move, the Twonky moves toward you. (He is impervious to all traps, even walls). When he gets too close to you (2 or fewer squares), you lose. However, you are equipped with a de-materializing ray gun. You have the option of using this on your turn. If you hit the Twonky he de-materializes and then re-materializes on a different square of the maze to resume his quest after you. (CAUTION: he could be dropped into your lap!).

After each move pair (you and Twonky), your distance from both the Twonky and the objective square are printed. There is no board printout — you play blind. However, using the distances, you can home in to the approximate position of both Twonky and objective.

When shooting at the Twonky, you do *not* have a shot if the distance he is from you is not an integer. For example: If the Twonky is 2.23606 units away, you don't have a direct shot. If he is 4 units away, you do have a shot. Exceptions to this rule are distances of 5, 10, 13, and 17. (A review of the Pythagorean Theorem will show why this is true.) Hence, if the distance is 5, 10, or 13 (but not 17), you may or may not have a direct shot. Likewise, this set of rules applies to the direction of the objective.

If you watch your distances before and after moving, you should be able to tell where the Twonky is in relation to you, e.g., forward and to the right, or backward and to the left. Take the distance you are from the Twonky, square it, say $2.23606^2 = 4.999998$ approx. = 5. Then find two integers that when squared and added together equal this (2 and 1). If the Twonky is forward and to the right, you now know that he is either up 2, over 1, or up 1, over 2.

The thing that makes Twonky unique, is that it can be played on two levels, one in which you play for fun, moving haphazardly; or you can play while figuring out exact positions, and calculating moves in advance for a challenging (as well as fun) game.

Twonky was written by Mark Capella and first appeared in *Creative Computing*, May/Jun 1977.

```
RUN
                         TWONKY
                   CREATIVE COMPUTING
                  MORRISTOWN  NEW JERSEY



DO YOU WANT INSTRUCTIONS (Y/N)? Y



THIS IS THE GAME OF TWONKY.
YOU HAVE LANDED ON THE PLANET OF TWINKY AND
ITS KING (KONG:THEIR KING IS KING KONG) HAS
CAPTURED YOU. HE HAS PUT YOU IN A MAZE THAT IS
15 * 15 UNITS LONG. YOU ARE IN THE DARK AND CANNOT
SEE... YOU MUST GET TO THE OBJECTIVE SQUARE AND
BE SET FREE.

     HAZARDS INCLUDE:
SQUARES THAT YOU CANNOT GO INTO (30).
SQUARES THAT RANDOMLY THROW YOU AROUND THE MAZE (22).
SQUARE THAT SETS UP A NEW MAZE AND ALL THAT'S IN IT (1)
MONSTER CALLED TWONKY THAT CHASES YOU AND WILL
    ABSORB YOU IF THE DISTANCE IT IS FROM YOU FALLS
    BELOW 2 UNITS.
    TWONKY IS ALSO IMMUNE TO ALL TRAPS INCLUDING
     WALLS.

    YOU CAN:
MOVE ONE SQUARE AT A TIME TO FIND THE OBJECTIVE
     OR ESCAPE FROM THE TWONKY.
SHOOT AT THE TWONKY ONE DIRECTION AT A TIME.
  IF THE TWONKY IS HIT, HE WILL BE REPLACED IN THE
       MAZE RANDOMLY.

IF THE TWONKY ABSORBS YOU...YOU LOSE.
 IF YOU LAND ON THE OBJECTIVE SQUARE YOU WIN.

GOOD LUCK!

------------------------------------


THE TWONKY IS  8.06226  UNITS AWAY.
THE OBJECTIVE IS  9.48683  UNITS AWAY.


MOVE OR SHOOT (M/S)? M
WHICH WAY (F/B/R/L)? F
MOVE ALLOWED.

THE TWONKY IS  7.2111  UNITS AWAY.
THE OBJECTIVE IS  8.54401  UNITS AWAY.

TWONKY MOVES....

THE TWONKY IS  6.70821  UNITS AWAY.
THE OBJECTIVE IS  8.54401  UNITS AWAY.


MOVE OR SHOOT (M/S)? M
WHICH WAY (F/B/R/L)? R
MOVE ALLOWED.

THE TWONKY IS  7.2111  UNITS AWAY.
THE OBJECTIVE IS  8.94428  UNITS AWAY.

TWONKY MOVES....

THE TWONKY IS  6.70821  UNITS AWAY.
THE OBJECTIVE IS  8.94428  UNITS AWAY.
```

```
MOVE OR SHOOT (M/S)? M
WHICH WAY (F/B/R/L)? L
MOVE ALLOWED.

THE TWONKY IS  6.32456  UNITS AWAY.
THE OBJECTIVE IS  8.54401  UNITS AWAY.

TWONKY MOVES....

THE TWONKY IS  6.08276  UNITS AWAY.
THE OBJECTIVE IS  8.54401  UNITS AWAY.


MOVE OR SHOOT (M/S)? M
WHICH WAY (F/B/R/L)? F
MOVE ALLOWED.

THE TWONKY IS  5.09902  UNITS AWAY.
THE OBJECTIVE IS  7.61577  UNITS AWAY.

TWONKY MOVES....

THE TWONKY IS  5  UNITS AWAY.
THE OBJECTIVE IS  7.61577  UNITS AWAY.


MOVE OR SHOOT (M/S)? S
WHICH WAY (F/B/R/L)? F
Z A P --Z A P --Z A P --Z A P --BLAST!!!!
YOU HIT WALL.
SHOT MISSED.

THE TWONKY IS  5  UNITS AWAY.
THE OBJECTIVE IS  7.61577  UNITS AWAY.

TWONKY MOVES....

THE TWONKY IS  4  UNITS AWAY.
THE OBJECTIVE IS  7.61577  UNITS AWAY.


MOVE OR SHOOT (M/S)? S
WHICH WAY (F/B/R/L)? B
Z A P --Z A P --Z A P --Z A P --Z A P --Z A P --Z A P --FIZZLE...
SHOT LEFT MAZE.
SHOT MISSED.

THE TWONKY IS  4  UNITS AWAY.
THE OBJECTIVE IS  7.61577  UNITS AWAY.

TWONKY MOVES....

THE TWONKY IS  3  UNITS AWAY.
THE OBJECTIVE IS  7.61577  UNITS AWAY.


MOVE OR SHOOT (M/S)? S
WHICH WAY (F/B/R/L)? R
Z A P --Z A P --FIZZLE...
SHOT LEFT MAZE.
SHOT MISSED.

THE TWONKY IS  3  UNITS AWAY.
THE OBJECTIVE IS  7.61577  UNITS AWAY.

TWONKY MOVES....

THE TWONKY IS  2  UNITS AWAY.
THE OBJECTIVE IS  7.61577  UNITS AWAY.


MOVE OR SHOOT (M/S)? S
WHICH WAY (F/B/R/L)? L
Z A P --Z A P --Z A P --Z A P --BLAST!!!!
YOU HIT WALL.
SHOT MISSED.

THE TWONKY IS  2  UNITS AWAY.
THE OBJECTIVE IS  7.61577  UNITS AWAY.

TWONKY MOVES....

THE TWONKY IS  1  UNITS AWAY.
THE OBJECTIVE IS  7.61577  UNITS AWAY.


> > > SCHLOORP !!! < < <
THE TWONKY JUST ABSORBED YOU !! YOU LOSE.


TRY AGAIN (Y/N)? N
OK
```

```
LIST

10 PRINT TAB(24);"TWONKY"
20 PRINT TAB(18);"CREATIVE COMPUTING"
30 PRINT TAB(16);"MORRISTOWN  NEW JERSEY"
40 PRINT:PRINT:PRINT
140 GOSUB 2250
150 DIM A(15,15)
160 LET R9=0
170 GOSUB 1830
180 PRINT "-------------------------------------"
190 PRINT
200 GOSUB 1450
210 PRINT
220 PRINT "MOVE OR SHOOT (M/S)";
230 INPUT Q8$
240 IF Q8$="M" THEN 270
250 IF Q8$="S" THEN 950
260 GOTO 210
270 PRINT "WHICH WAY (F/B/R/L)";
280 INPUT Q$
290 IF Q$="F" THEN 340
300 IF Q$="B" THEN 370
310 IF Q$="L" THEN 400
320 IF Q$="R" THEN 430
330 GOTO 210
340 LET X5=X
350 LET Y5=Y-1
360 GOTO 460
370 LET X5=X
380 LET Y5=Y+1
390 GOTO 460
400 LET X5=X-1
410 LET Y5=Y
420 GOTO 460
430 LET X5=X+1
440 LET Y5=Y
450 GOTO 460
460 IF X5<1 THEN 510
470 IF X5>15 THEN 510
480 IF Y5<1 THEN 510
490 IF Y5>15 THEN 510
500 GOTO 540
510 PRINT "THAT MOVE TAKES YOU OUT OF THE MAZE."
520 PRINT "MOVE NOT ALLOWED."
530 GOTO 1430
540 ON (A(X5,Y5)+1) GOTO 550,620,630,660,760,800,920
550 REM *** EMPTY SPACE
560 LET A(X,Y)=0
570 LET A(X5,Y5)=1
580 LET X=X5
590 LET Y=Y5
600 PRINT "MOVE ALLOWED."
610 GOTO 1430
620 REM *** IMPOSSIBLE TO GET HERE
630 REM *** BLOCKED SPACE ROUTINE.
640 PRINT "THAT SPACE IS BLOCKED."
650 GOTO 1430
660 REM *** RELOCATION ROUTINE.
670 PRINT "YOU'VE BEEN   R E L O C A T E D !!!"
680 GOSUB 2710
690 IF A(Z,W)>2 THEN 540
700 IF A(Z,W) <> 0 THEN 680
710 LET A(Z,W)=1
720 LET A(X,Y)=0
730 LET X=Z
740 LET Y=W
750 GOTO 1430
760 REM *** CHANGE ALL, SUPER TRAP.
770 PRINT "   YOU HIT THE SUPER TRAP!! YOU GET A NEW MAZE."
780 GOSUB 1830
790 GOTO 1430
800 REM *** HE WON!
810 PRINT
820 PRINT "I DON'T BELIEVE IT BUT YOU WON THE GAME!"
830 PRINT "YOU GOT TO THE OBJECTIVE BEFORE"
840 PRINT "   THE TWONKY GOT YOU!!"
850 PRINT
```

```
860 PRINT
870 PRINT "TRY AGAIN (Y/N)";
880 INPUT Q$
890 IF Q$="Y" THEN 160
900 IF Q$="N" THEN 2750
910 GOTO 870
920 REM *** HE LANDED ON TWONKY!]
930 PRINT "YOU STEPPED ON THE TWONKY!"
940 GOTO 1790
950 REM *** SHOOT ROUTINE
960 PRINT "WHICH WAY (F/B/R/L)";
970 INPUT Q$
980 IF Q$="F" THEN 1030
990 IF Q$="B" THEN 1060
1000 IF Q$="R" THEN 1120
1010 IF Q$="L" THEN 1090
1020 GOTO 210
1030 LET S1=0
1040 LET S2=-1
1050 GOTO 1140
1060 LET S1=0
1070 LET S2=1
1080 GOTO 1140
1090 LET S1=-1
1100 LET S2=0
1110 GOTO 1140
1120 LET S1=1
1130 LET S2=0
1140 LET R1=X
1150 LET R2=Y
1160 LET R1=R1+S1
1170 LET R2=R2+S2
1180 PRINT "Z A P --";
1190 IF R1 < 1 THEN 1240
1200 IF R1 > 15 THEN 1240
1210 IF R2 < 1 THEN 1240
1220 IF R2 > 15 THEN 1240
1230 GOTO 1280
1240 PRINT "FIZZLE..."
1250 PRINT "SHOT LEFT MAZE."
1260 PRINT "SHOT MISSED."
1270 GOTO 1430
1280 IF A(R1,R2) <>2 THEN 1330
1290 PRINT "BLAST!!!!"
1300 PRINT "YOU HIT WALL."
1310 PRINT "SHOT MISSED."
1320 GOTO 1430
1330 IF A(R1,R2) <> 6 THEN 1160
1340 PRINT " OUCH!!"
1350 PRINT "TWONKY RETREATES."
1360 LET A (R1,R2)=R9
1370 GOSUB 2710
1380 IF A(Z,W) <> 0 THEN 1370
1390 LET A(Z,W)=6
1410 LET X1=Z
1420 LET Y1=W
1430 GOSUB 1450
1440 GOTO 1570
1450 REM *** PRIBNT TWONKY AND OBJECTIVE DISTANCE
1455 PRINT
1460 PRINT "THE TWONKY IS ";
1470 D=(SQR(ABS((X1-X)^2+(Y1-Y)^2)))
1490 PRINT D;
1500 PRINT " UNITS AWAY."
1510 PRINT "THE OBJECTIVE IS ";
1520 D1=(SQR(ABS(X2-X)^2+(Y2-Y)^2))
1530 PRINT D1;
1540 PRINT " UNITS AWAY."
1550 PRINT
1560 RETURN
1570 REM *** TWONKYS LOGIC
1580 IF D<2 THEN 1790
1590 LET Z2=Y1
1600 LET Z1=X1
1610 IF X < X1 THEN 1680
1620 IF X > X1 THEN 1700
1630 IF Y < Y1 THEN 1660
1640 LET Z2=Y1+1
1650 GOTO 1710
1660 LET Z2=Y1-1
1670 GOTO 1710
1680 LET Z1=X1-1
1690 GOTO 1710
1700 LET Z1=X1+1
1710 LET A(X1,Y1)=R9
1720 LET R9=A(Z1,Z2)
1730 LET A(Z1,Z2)=6
1740 LET X1=Z1
1750 LET Y1=Z2
1760 PRINT "TWONKY MOVES...."
1770 GOSUB 1450
1780 IF D >= 2 THEN 210
1790 PRINT
1800 PRINT "> > > SCHLOORP !!! < < <"
1810 PRINT "THE TWONKY JUST ABSORBED YOU !! YOU LOSE."
1820 GOTO 850
1830 REM *** SET UP NEW MAZE ROUTINE
1840 REM *** 1=PLAYER, 2=BLOCKED SPACES
1850 REM *** 3=RELOCATIONS, 4=SUPER TRAP
1860 REM *** 5=OBJECTIVE, 6=TWONKY
1870 REM *** 0=EMPTY SPACES
1880 REM *** CLEAR MAZE
1883 FOR B0=1 TO 15
1885 FOR B1=1 TO 15
1890 LET A(B0,B1)=0
1893 NEXT B1
1895 NEXT B0
1910 FOR I=1 TO 30
1920 GOSUB 2710
1930 IF A(Z,W) <> 0 THEN 1920
1940 LET A(Z,W)=2
1950 NEXT I
1960 REM *** PLACE RELOCATIONS
1970 FOR I=1 TO 22
1980 GOSUB 2710
1990 IF A(Z,W) <> 0 THEN 1980
2000 LET A(Z,W)=3
2010 NEXT I
2020 REM *** PLACE THE SPECIAL TRAP
2030 GOSUB 2710
2040 IF A(Z,W) <> 0 THEN 2030
2050 LET A(Z,W)=4
2060 REM *** PLACE THE PLAYER
2070 GOSUB 2710
2080 IF A(Z,W) <> 0 THEN 2070
2090 LET A(Z,W)=1
2100 LET X=Z
2110 LET Y=W
2120 REM *** PLACE THE OBJECTIVE
2130 GOSUB 2710
2140 IF A(Z,W) <> 0 THEN 2130
2150 LET A(Z,W)=5
2160 LET X2=Z
2170 LET Y2=W
2180 REM *** PLACE THE TWONKY
2190 GOSUB 2710
2200 IF A(Z,W) <> 0 THEN 2190
2210 LET A(Z,W)=6
2220 LET X1=Z
2230 LET Y1=W
2240 RETURN
2250 REM
2310 PRINT "DO YOU WANT INSTRUCTIONS (Y/N)";
2320 INPUT Q$
2330 IF Q$="N" THEN 2700
2340 IF Q$ <> "Y" THEN 2310
2350 PRINT:PRINT:PRINT
2380 PRINT "THIS IS THE GAME OF TWONKY."
2410 PRINT "YOU HAVE LANDED ON THE PLANET OF TWINKY AND"
2420 PRINT "ITS KING (KONG:THEIR KING IS KING KONG) HAS "
2430 PRINT "CAPTURED YOU. HE HAS PUT YOU IN A MAZE THAT IS"
2440 PRINT "15 * 15 UNITS LONG. YOU ARE IN THE DARK AND CANNOT"
2450 PRINT "SEE... YOU MUST GET TO THE OBJECTIVE SQUARE AND"
2460 PRINT "BE SET FREE."
2470 PRINT
2480 PRINT "      HAZARDS INCLUDE:"
2490 PRINT "SQUARES THAT YOU CANNOT GO INTO (30)."
2500 PRINT "SQUARES THAT RANDOMLY THROW YOU AROUND THE MAZE (22)."
2510 PRINT "SQUARE THAT SETS UP A NEW MAZE AND ALL THAT'S IN IT (1)"
2520 PRINT "MONSTER CALLED TWONKY THAT CHASES YOU AND WILL"
2530 PRINT "    ABSORB YOU IF THE DISTANCE IT IS FROM YOU FALLS"
2540 PRINT "    BELOW 2 UNITS."
2550 PRINT "    TWONKY IS ALSO IMMUNE TO ALL TRAPS INCLUDING"
2560 PRINT "      WALLS."
2570 PRINT
2590 PRINT "    YOU CAN:"
2600 PRINT "MOVE ONE SQUARE AT A TIME TO FIND THE OBJECTIVE"
2610 PRINT "     OR ESCAPE FROM THE TWONKY."
2620 PRINT "SHOOT AT THE TWONKY ONE DIRECTION AT A TIME."
2630 PRINT "  IF THE TWONKY IS HIT, HE WILL BE REPLACED IN THE"
2640 PRINT "         MAZE RANDOMLY."
2645 PRINT
2650 PRINT "IF THE TWONKY ABSORBS YOU...YOU LOSE."
2660 PRINT " IF YOU LAND ON THE OBJECTIVE SQUARE YOU WIN."
2670 PRINT
2680 PRINT "GOOD LUCK!"
2690 PRINT
2700 RETURN
2710 REM *** SUBROUTINE TO GET 2 RANDOM NUMBERS
2720 LET Z=INT(RND(1)*15+1)
2730 LET W=INT(RND(1)*15+1)
2740 RETURN
2750 END
OK
```

Two-to-Ten

Two-to-Ten is a game of chance played with a special deck of cards with only the cards 2-10. The game is similar to blackjack in that you are drawing cards and trying to come as close as possible to a goal number (chosen at random before each round) without going over it. You must come within a certain number of points of the goal number determined by a "lucky-limit" card. The catch to the game is that you are not given the exact value of the goal number but rather a clue that is only within 15% of the goal.

Can you think of a way to make Two-to-Ten more interesting? Perhaps playing it against the computer as an opponent?

Two-to-Ten appeared in *Creative Computing*, Nov/Dec 1976.

```
                         TWO TO TEN
              CREATIVE COMPUTING  MORRISTOWN NEW JERSEY

WELCOME TO THE GAME OF TWO TO TEN.  THAT NAME COMES FROM THE
SPECIAL 'DECK OF CARDS' USED. THERE ARE NO FACE CARDS - ONLY
THE CARDS 2-10.  THIS GAME IS EASY AND FUN TO PLAY IF YOU
UNDERSTAND WHAT YOU ARE DOING SO READ THE INSTRUCTIONS
CAREFULLY.
AT THE START OF THE GAME, YOU BET ON WINNING.  TYPE IN ANY
NUMBER BETWEEN 0 AND 200.  I THEN PICK A RANDOM NUMBER
YOU ARE TO REACH BY THE SUM TOTAL OF MORE CARDS CHOSEN.
BECAUSE OF THE RARE CHANCE OF YOU GETTING TO THAT NUMBER
EXACTLY, YOU ARE GIVEN AN ALLOWANCE CARD.  THE OBJECT OF
THE GAME OF TO GET THE TOTAL OF CARDS WITHIN THE MYSTERY
NUMBER WITHOUT GOING OVER.
YOU ARE GIVEN A HINT AS TO WHAT THE NUMBER IS.  THIS IS NOT
THE EXACT NUMBER ONLY ONE CLOSE. ALL YOU DO IN THIS GAME IS
DECIDE WHEN TO STOP.  AT THIS POINT YOUR TOTAL IS COMPARED
WITH THE NUMBER AND YOUR WINNINGS ARE DETERMINED.

PLACE YOUR BET . . . YOU HAVE $ 200  TO SPEND.? 50

YOUR 'LUCKY LIMIT' CARD IS A  8
YOU MUST COME WITHIN  8  WITHOUT GOING OVER TO WIN.

HERE WE GO


CARD # 1  IS A  3 .YOU ARE TRYING TO COME NEAR  28
YOUR TOTAL IS  3   DO YOU WANT TO CONTINUE? YES


CARD # 2  IS A  3 .YOU ARE TRYING TO COME NEAR  28
YOUR TOTAL IS  6   DO YOU WANT TO CONTINUE? YES


CARD # 3  IS A  9 .YOU ARE TRYING TO COME NEAR  28
YOUR TOTAL IS  15   DO YOU WANT TO CONTINUE? YES


CARD # 4  IS A  6 .YOU ARE TRYING TO COME NEAR  28
YOUR TOTAL IS  21   DO YOU WANT TO CONTINUE? YES


CARD # 5  IS A  10 .YOU ARE TRYING TO COME NEAR  28
YOUR TOTAL IS  31   DO YOU WANT TO CONTINUE? NO

YOU WIN!  THE NUMBER WAS  32  YOUR GUESS TOTAL WAS 31
WITHIN YOUR LIMIT CARD.
YOU NOW HAVE $ 250  IN CASH TO BET IN THE NEXT GAME!
WOULD YOU LIKE TO PLAY THE NEXT GAME? NO
HOPE YOU HAD FUN.
```

```
10 PRINT TAB(28);"TWO TO TEN"
20 PRINT TAB(15);"CREATIVE COMPUTING  MORRISTOWN NEW JERSEY"
30 PRINT
40 PRINT
50 PRINT
60 PRINT "WELCOME TO THE GAME OF TWO TO TEN.  THAT NAME COMES FROM THE"
70 PRINT "SPECIAL 'DECK OF CARDS' USED. THERE ARE NO FACE CARDS - ONLY"
80 PRINT "THE CARDS 2-10.  THIS GAME IS EASY AND FUN TO PLAY IF YOU"
90 PRINT "UNDERSTAND WHAT YOU ARE DOING SO READ THE INSTRUCTIONS"
100 PRINT "CAREFULLY."
110 PRINT "AT THE START OF THE GAME, YOU BET ON WINNING.  TYPE IN ANY"
120 PRINT "NUMBER BETWEEN 0 AND 200.  I THEN PICK A RANDOM NUMBER"
130 PRINT "YOU ARE TO REACH BY THE SUM TOTAL OF MORE CARDS CHOSEN."
140 PRINT "BECAUSE OF THE RARE CHANCE OF YOU GETTING TO THAT NUMBER"
150 PRINT "EXACTLY, YOU ARE GIVEN AN ALLOWANCE CARD.  THE OBJECT OF"
160 PRINT "THE GAME OF TO GET THE TOTAL OF CARDS WITHIN THE MYSTERY"
170 PRINT "NUMBER WITHOUT GOING OVER."
180 PRINT "YOU ARE GIVEN A HINT AS TO WHAT THE NUMBER IS.  THIS IS NOT"
190 PRINT "THE EXACT NUMBER ONLY ONE CLOSE. ALL YOU DO IN THIS GAME IS"
200 PRINT "DECIDE WHEN TO STOP.  AT THIS POINT YOUR TOTAL IS COMPARED"
210 PRINT "WITH THE NUMBER AND YOUR WINNINGS ARE DETERMINED."
220 M=200
223 D=0
225 T=0
227 O=INT(10*RND(1))+25
229 N=INT(O*RND(1))+O
230 R=(INT(15*RND(1))+1)/100
250 S=INT(2*RND(1)+1)
260 IF S <> 1 THEN 270
262 E=INT(N-(N*R))
265 GOTO 280
270 E=INT(N+(N*R))
280 A=INT(9*RND(1)+2)
283 PRINT
285 PRINT "PLACE YOUR BET . . . YOU HAVE $";M;" TO SPEND.";
287 INPUT B
288 PRINT
289 IF B < 0 THEN 297
290 IF M >= B THEN 300
293 PRINT "YOU CAN'T BET MORE THAT YOU'VE GOT!"
295 GOTO 285
297 PRINT "YOU MAY NOT BET AGAINST YOURSELF."
298 GOTO 285
300 PRINT "YOUR 'LUCKY LIMIT' CARD IS A ";A
310 PRINT "YOU MUST COME WITHIN ";A;" WITHOUT GOING OVER TO WIN."
315 PRINT
320 PRINT "HERE WE GO"
322 PRINT
324 PRINT
340 D=D+1
350 C=INT(9*RND(1)+2)
360 PRINT "CARD #";D;" IS A ";C;".YOU ARE TRYING TO COME NEAR ";E
365 T=T+C
370 IF T <= N THEN 380
375 PRINT "YOUR TOTAL IS OVER THE NUMBER";N;" AN AUTOMATIC LOSS!"
377 GOTO 570
380 PRINT "YOUR TOTAL IS ";T;"  DO YOU WANT TO CONTINUE";
385 INPUT Q$
387 PRINT
390 IF LEFT$(Q$,1)="Y" THEN 322
410 IF T < N-A  OR T > N THEN 550
500 PRINT "YOU WIN!  THE NUMBER WAS ";N;" YOUR GUESS TOTAL WAS";T
510 PRINT "WITHIN YOUR LIMIT CARD."
520 M=M+B
540 GOTO 600
550 PRINT "YOU BLEW IT!  THE NUMBER WAS ";N;", OUTSIDE YOUR LIMIT BY ";
560 PRINT (N-A)-T
565 PRINT
570 M=M-B
600 PRINT "YOU NOW HAVE $";M;" IN CASH TO BET IN THE NEXT GAME!"
605 IF M <= 0 THEN 655
610 PRINT "WOULD YOU LIKE TO PLAY THE NEXT GAME";
615 INPUT Q$
620 IF LEFT$(Q$,1)="Y" THEN 223
630 PRINT "HOPE YOU HAD FUN."
640 GOTO 999
650 PRINT
655 PRINT CHR$(7);
660 PRINT "YOU ARE BROKE!!  YOU MAY NOT PLAY ANYMORE!!"
999 END
Ok
```

UFO

UFO is a strategy game in which you play against the computer in a life-and-death struggle for superiority of space. It takes place after a space war with another planet in which both earth and the attacker's planet are destroyed. Both planets—basically similar in strength, social structure, and scientific awareness—realizing they are doomed, launch a "lifeboat" into space. The lifeboats are equally armed and powered.

However, the aliens are much better marksmen, hitting once out of every two shots (in lines 880-890, the computer's odds are set). The reason is as follows. The enemy ship's decision is made by the program; the enemy will only retreat if he feels you are ramming and will approach only if you are running and/or his fuel is running out (smaller weaponry eats up less fuel). He will only use option 6 (no move but gains fuel) if his energy is below a certain point. In other words, you can think, while he cannot. You have the advantage of your mind, so the alien has been given the advantage of a good steady aim.

The game is set in the future: civilization is destroyed, 150 people are left, and you are in command. The enemy has never truly been seen, as many enemies are never truly seen, but nevertheless you must destroy him or be destroyed. Your weapons are explained and the game begins. In your command ship is a control which will not allow you to make an illegal move. This control waits after you fire for the shot to reach the other ship and for the explosion reports to reach the ship. It then gives a full report of power drain of both ships. If your power is not negative you are still in the game but once it drops below zero your crew dies (the energy level is the amount of energy left to counteract the attack. If more energy hits the ship than was repulsed, the ship is destroyed. If the amounts are equal then the ship had exactly the same amount of energy as the attack drained.) If in any game you can get close enough to your enemy to use your heavy guns without frightening off the enemy (5000-11000), the game will last for quite a long time. Theoretically this game will last forever if played logically.

Written by Raymond J. Kernay, UFO first appeared in *Creative Computing* in Jul/Aug 1977. A modified version called Star Wars appeared in Sep/Oct 1978.

```
RUN
                          UFO
                   CREATIVE COMPUTING
                  MORRISTOWN NEW JERSEY


 DO YOU WANT INSTRUCTIONS? YES
YOU ARE ABOUT TO RECEIVE HIGH SECURITY INFORMATION
PLEASE EAT THE COMPUTER READ OUT AFTER READING


THIS IS THE YEAR 2000...CIVILIZATION AS YOU KNOW IT HAS
BEEN DESTROYED...NATIONS HAVE BEEN REDUCED TO RUBBLE
IN A MASSIVE SPACE WAR
YOU ARE ONBOARD A SPACE SHIP WHOSE SOLE PURPOSE
IS TO SAFE GUARD THE 150 PEOPLE ON YOUR SHIP...THE
SOLE SURVIVORS...YOUR MISSION: FIND A PLANET SUITABLE
FOR YOUR COLONISTS.....PROBLEM: THE ENEMY OF EARTH STILL
EXISTS. STRANGE CREATURES NEVER SEEN BY MAN

BY THE TIME YOU READ THIS EARTH WILL NO LONGER EXIST.......
HERE IS YOUR VITAL DATUM:
            YOU ARE EQUIPT WITH 10000 UNITS OF ENERGY
            WHEN YOU RUN OUT THE ALIENS WILL DESTROY YOU


                        WEAPONRY
TYPE DESCRIPTION CAPACITY FUEL DRAIN
  1  HEAVY GUNS  0-11000    10 UNITS
  2  WARHEADS 10000-100000 100 UNITS
  3  LASER   10000-20000   1000 UNITS

                        OPTIONS
  4  APPROACH     ---------100 UNITS
  5  RETREAT      ---------100 UNITS
  6  BY TYPING 6 YOU CAN PASS AND GAIN 100 UNITS
     (LABORERS WORK TO PRODUCE POWER)


                         ENEMY

THE ENEMY HAS THE SAME CAPABILITIES THAT YOU HAVE
EACH TIME A SHIP IS HIT ITS ENERGY DRAIN IS EQUAL TO
THE AMOUNT OF ENERGY SPENT*10 (EXCEPT LASER WHICH EQUALS
                              THE AMOUNT SPENT*3 UNITS)
BOTH SHIPS ARE ON THE SAME MISSION, DESTINATION AND BOTH
ARE ON EQUAL TERMS
UNFORTUNATLY YOU MUST KILL EACH OTHER TO WIN
YOUR MAXIMUM SPEED IS A JUMP OF 50000 UNITS, HOWEVER
SPEEDS VARY BETWEEN 10000-50000
WARHEADS TRAVEL AT 35000 FEET PER SEC...SHELLS 1000 PER SECOND
THIS MESSAGE WAS RECORDED EARTH IS DEAD...GOOD LUCK


THIS IS COMPUTER CONTROL WHAT IS YOUR NAME? BRUCE B. S.
VERY GOOD BRUCE B. S.
LEAVING PLANETARY ORBIT BRUCE B. S. SHIP APPROACHING AT
 180025 MILES
WHAT ARE YOUR ORDERS BRUCE B. S.? 2
LETS NOT CRACK UNDER PRESSURE
WHAT ARE YOUR ORDERS BRUCE B. S.? 3
LASER FIRED
DIRECT HIT.....ENEMY SHIP'S POWER DOWN
ENEMY SHIP REPORT
RANGE= 180025   POWER= 7000
ENEMY FIRES LASER
DIRECT HIT..... POWER DOWN
```

```
        STATUS OF SHIP
RANGE= 180025 POWER SUPPLY= 6000
WHAT ARE YOUR ORDERS BRUCE B. S.? 3
LASER FIRED
DIRECT HIT.....ENEMY SHIP'S POWER DOWN
ENEMY SHIP REPORT
RANGE= 180025   POWER= 3000
ENEMY FIRES LASER
DIRECT HIT..... POWER DOWN

        STATUS OF SHIP
RANGE= 180025 POWER SUPPLY= 2000
WHAT ARE YOUR ORDERS BRUCE B. S.? 3
LASER FIRED
MISSED TOO BAD
ENEMY SHIP REPORT
RANGE= 180025   POWER= 2000
ENEMY FIRES LASER
DIRECT HIT..... POWER DOWN


        STATUS OF SHIP
RANGE= 180025 POWER SUPPLY=-2000
ENEMY IS VICTOR LIFE SUPPORT FADING CREW DYING



PLAY AGAIN? NO
OK
```

```
LIST

10 PRINT TAB(26);"UFO"
20 PRINT TAB(19);"CREATIVE COMPUTING"
30 PRINT TAB(18);"MORRISTOWN NEW JERSEY"
40 PRINT:PRINT:PRINT
60 DIM P(1)
80 REM UFO
90 PRINT " DO YOU WANT INSTRUCTIONS";
100 INPUT A$
102 IF LEFT$(A$,1)="N" THEN 480
104 IF LEFT$(A$,1)="Y" THEN 110
106 GOTO 90
110 PRINT "YOU ARE ABOUT TO RECEIVE HIGH SECURITY INFORMATION"
120 PRINT "PLEASE EAT THE COMPUTER READ OUT AFTER READING"
130 PRINT:PRINT:PRINT
140 PRINT "THIS IS THE YEAR 2000...CIVILIZATION AS YOU KNOW IT HAS"
150 PRINT "BEEN DESTROYED...NATIONS HAVE BEEN REDUCED TO RUBBLE"
160 PRINT "IN A MASSIVE SPACE WAR"
170 PRINT "YOU ARE ONBOARD A SPACE SHIP WHOSE SOLE PURPOSE"
180 PRINT "IS TO SAFE GUARD THE 150 PEOPLE ON YOUR SHIP...THE"
190 PRINT "SOLE SURVIVORS...YOUR MISSION: FIND A PLANET SUITABLE"
200 PRINT "FOR YOUR COLONISTS.....PROBLEM: THE ENEMY OF EARTH STILL"
210 PRINT "EXISTS. STRANGE CREATURES NEVER SEEN BY MAN":PRINT
220 PRINT "BY THE TIME YOU READ THIS EARTH WILL NO LONGER EXIST......."
230 PRINT "HERE IS YOUR VITAL DATUM:"
240 PRINT TAB(10);"YOU ARE EQUIPT WITH 10000 UNITS OF ENERGY"
250 PRINT TAB(10);"WHEN YOU RUN OUT THE ALIENS WILL DESTROY YOU"
260 PRINT:PRINT:PRINT:PRINT TAB(25);"WEAPONRY"
270 PRINT "TYPE";TAB(5);"DESCRIPTION";TAB(17);"CAPACITY";TAB(26);
275 PRINT "FUEL DRAIN"
280 PRINT "  1";TAB(5);"HEAVY GUNS";TAB(17);"0-11000";TAB(27);
285 PRINT "10 UNITS"
290 PRINT "  2";TAB(5);"WARHEADS";TAB(14);"10000-100000";TAB(27);
295 PRINT "100 UNITS"
300 PRINT "  3";TAB(5);"LASER";TAB(13);"10000-20000";TAB(27);
305 PRINT "1000 UNITS"
310 PRINT:PRINT:PRINT TAB(25);"OPTIONS"
320 PRINT "  4";TAB(5);"APPROACH";TAB(17);"---------";TAB(26);
325 PRINT "100 UNITS"
327 PRINT "  5";TAB(5);"RETREAT";TAB(17);"---------";TAB(26);
328 PRINT "100 UNITS"
330 PRINT "  6";TAB(5);"BY TYPING 6 YOU CAN PASS AND GAIN 100 UNITS"
350 PRINT TAB(5);"(LABORERS WORK TO PRODUCE POWER)"
360 PRINT:PRINT:PRINT TAB(25);"ENEMY"
370 PRINT:PRINT "THE ENEMY HAS THE SAME CAPABILITIES THAT YOU HAVE"
380 PRINT "EACH TIME A SHIP IS HIT ITS ENERGY DRAIN IS EQUAL TO"
390 PRINT "THE AMOUNT OF ENERGY SPENT*10 (EXCEPT LASER WHICH EQUALS"
400 PRINT TAB(30);"THE AMOUNT SPENT*3 UNITS)"
410 PRINT "BOTH SHIPS ARE ON THE SAME MISSION, DESTINATION AND BOTH"
420 PRINT "ARE ON EQUAL TERMS"
430 PRINT "UNFORTUNATLY YOU MUST KILL EACH OTHER TO WIN"
440 PRINT "YOUR MAXIMUM SPEED IS A JUMP OF 50000 UNITS, HOWEVER"
450 PRINT "SPEEDS VARY BETWEEN 10000-50000"
460 PRINT "WARHEADS TRAVEL AT 35000 FEET PER SEC...SHELLS 1000";
465 PRINT " PER SECOND"
470 PRINT "THIS MESSAGE WAS RECORDED EARTH IS DEAD...GOOD LUCK"
480 PRINT:PRINT:PRINT:PRINT "THIS IS COMPUTER CONTROL WHAT IS YOUR NAME";
490 INPUT A$:PRINT "VERY GOOD ";A$
500 P=10000:P(1)=10000:A=RND(1)*200000
510 PRINT "LEAVING PLANETARY ORBIT ";A$;B$;C$;" SHIP APPROACHING AT";
512 PRINT
515 PRINT A;"MILES"
520 PRINT "WHAT ARE YOUR ORDERS ";A$;B$;C$;:INPUT C
530 O=INT(RND(1)*2)+1
540 ON C GOTO 570,650,710,750,780,820
560 PRINT "LETS NOT CRACK UNDER PRESSURE":GOTO 520
570 IF A>11005 THEN 560
580 P=P-10
590 PRINT "GUNS FIRED":
595 FOR X=1 TO A*2 STEP 1000
600 NEXT X
610 IF O=1 THEN 630
620 PRINT "MISSED TO BAD":GOTO 830
630 PRINT "DIRECT HIT.......ENEMY SHIP'S POWER DOWN"
640 P(1)=P(1)-100:GOTO 830
650 IF A > 100000 THEN 560
655 IF A < 10000 THEN 560
660 P=P-100:PRINT "WARHEAD LAUNCHED":FOR X=1 TO A*2 STEP 35000
670 NEXT X
680 IF O=1 THEN 690:PRINT "MISSED TOO BAD":GOTO 830
690 PRINT "DIRECT HIT.....ENEMY SHIP'S POWER DOWN"
700 P(1)=P(1)-1000
705 GOTO 830
710 IF A < 100000 THEN 560
714 P=P-1000
716 PRINT "LASER FIRED"
720 IF O=1 THEN 730
725 PRINT "MISSED TOO BAD":GOTO 830
730 PRINT "DIRECT HIT.....ENEMY SHIP'S POWER DOWN"
740 P(1)=P(1)-3000:GOTO 830
750 B=RND(1)*40000+10000:A=A-B:P=P-100:IF A<1 THEN 770
760 GOTO 830
770 PRINT "***COLLISION***":PRINT "BOTH SHIPS DESTROYED":GOTO 1080
780 B=RND(1)*40000+10000:A=A+B:P=P-100:IF A > 200050 THEN 800
790 GOTO 830
800 PRINT A$;" YOUR RANGE IS ";A;"BUT WE CANNOT RUN, RANGE IS NOW ";
805 PRINT "200000"
810 A=200000:GOTO 830
820 P=P+100
830 PRINT "ENEMY SHIP REPORT":PRINT "RANGE=";A;"  POWER=";P(1)
840 IF P(1) < 1 THEN 1110
850 IF P(1) < 500 THEN 1040
860 IF A < 5000 THEN 1070
870 R=INT(RND(1)*3)+1:O=INT(RND(1)*2+1)
880 ON R GOTO 970,920
885 IF R=2 THEN
890 IF A < 100000 THEN 870
892 P(1)=P(1)-1000
894 PRINT "ENEMY FIRES LASER"
900 IF O=1 THEN 910: PRINT "MISSED...WHEW!!":GOTO 1010
910 PRINT "DIRECT HIT..... POWER DOWN": P=P-3000:GOTO 1010
920 IF A > 100000 THEN 870: IF A < 10000 THEN 870
930 P(1)=P(1)-100: PRINT "ENEMY WARHEAD FIRED"
940 FOR D=1 TO A STEP 35000: NEXT D
950 IF O=1 THEN 960: PRINT "MISSED... WHEW!":GOTO 1010
960 P=P-1000: PRINT "DIRECT HIT!...POWER DOWN":GOTO 1010
970 IF A > 11000 THEN 870: (1)=P(1)-10:PRINT "ENEMY FIRES SHELL"
980 FOR D=1 TO A STEP 1000: NEXT D
990 IF O=1 THEN 1000:PRINT "MISSED...WHEW!":GOTO 1010
1000 PRINT "DIRECT HIT .....POWER DOWN":P=P-100
1010 PRINT:PRINT:PRINT TAB(10);"STATUS OF SHIP"
1020 PRINT "RANGE=";A;"POWER SUPPLY=";P: IF P<1 THEN 1130
1030 GOTO 520
1040 P(1)=P(1)+100: PRINT "ENEMY SHIP RESTING":GOTO 1010
1050 B=INT(RND(1)*40000+10000:A=A-B:PRINT "ENEMY SHIP APPROACHING  ";A$; B$;
1055 PRINT C$
1060 GOTO 1010
1070 B=RND(1)*40000+10000:A=A+B:PRINT "ENEMY SHIP RETREATING":GOTO 1010
1080 PRINT "THAT WAS A PRETTY DUMB THING TO DO ";A$;B$;C$
1090 PRINT "YOUR MISSION IS TO PROTECT YOUR PASSENGERS NOT DESTROY"
1100 GOTO 1140
1110 PRINT "ENEMY SHIPS POWER GONE NO LIFE PRESENT"
1120 PRINT "MISSION SUCCESSFUL":GOTO 1210
1130 PRINT "ENEMY IS VICTOR LIFE SUPPORT FADING CREW DYING"
1140 REM
1150 PRINT
1160 PRINT
1170 PRINT
1180 PRINT "PLAY AGAIN";
1190 INPUT A$
1200 IF LEFT$(A$,1)="Y" THEN 80
1210 END
```

Under & Over

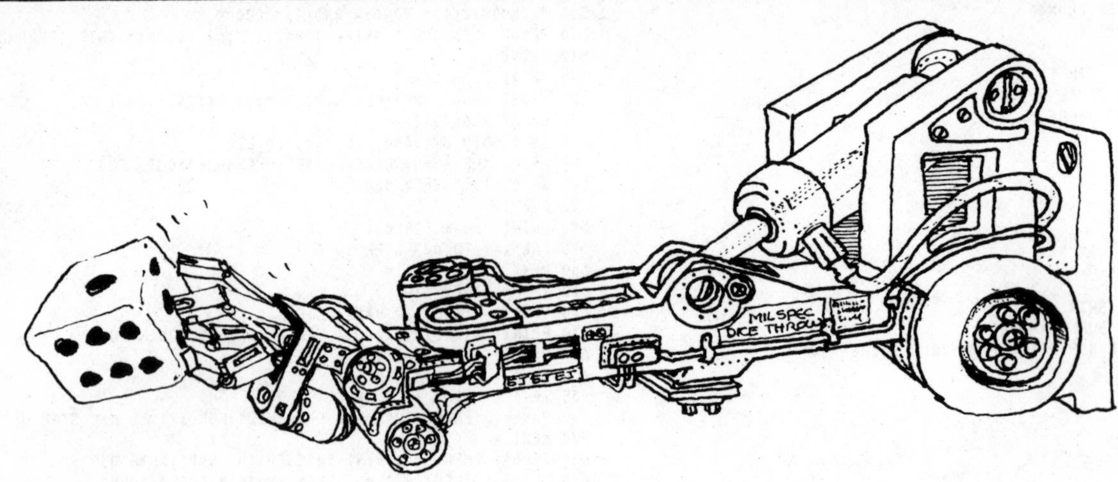

This is a funny little dice game in which you're betting on the outcome of rolling two dice. You may bet on any number from two to twelve. If your number is exactly the same as shown on the sum of the dice, you win at four to one odds. If your number is under seven and the roll of the dice is under seven, you win even money. If your number is over seven and the roll of the dice is over seven, you also win even money. Only a bet on seven itself can win at four to one. The program goes on until you run out of money or until you interrupt it.

```
RUN
                         UNDER OR OVER
                       CREATIVE COMPUTING
                     MORRISTOWN, NEW JERSEY


THIS IS A GAME OF UNDER AND OVER. IF YOU PICK
UNDER OR OVER SEVEN, YOU WILL WIN EVEN MONEY.
IF YOU PICK EVEN YOU WILL WIN MONEY AT FOUR TO ONE
ODDS. YOU HAVE $100 TO START WITH. GOOD LUCK!


WHAT NUMBER DO YOU WISH TO PLAY AND HOW MUCH
DO YOU WANT TO BET ON THE NUMBER? 4,10

THE DICE HAVE NOW BEEN THROWN. THE RESULTS
ARE AS FOLLOWS:
 DIE #1        DIE #2        SUM          YOUR#         TOSS
 2             5             7            4             EVEN

                    !!!!!YOU LOSE!!!!!
THE AMOUNT YOU NOW HAVE IS 100

WHAT NUMBER DO YOU WISH TO PLAY AND HOW MUCH
DO YOU WANT TO BET ON THE NUMBER? 4,10

THE DICE HAVE NOW BEEN THROWN. THE RESULTS
ARE AS FOLLOWS:
 DIE #1        DIE #2        SUM          YOUR#         TOSS
 1             4             5            4             UNDER

                    ********YOU WIN EVEN MONEY********
THE AMOUNT YOU NOW HAVE IS 110
```

```
WHAT NUMBER DO YOU WISH TO PLAY AND HOW MUCH
DO YOU WANT TO BET ON THE NUMBER? 7,20

THE DICE HAVE NOW BEEN THROWN. THE RESULTS
ARE AS FOLLOWS:
 DIE #1        DIE #2        SUM           YOUR#         TOSS
 5             6             11            7             OVER

                   !!!!!YOU LOSE!!!!!
THE AMOUNT YOU NOW HAVE IS 90

WHAT NUMBER DO YOU WISH TO PLAY AND HOW MUCH
DO YOU WANT TO BET ON THE NUMBER? 8,10

THE DICE HAVE NOW BEEN THROWN. THE RESULTS
ARE AS FOLLOWS:
 DIE #1        DIE #2        SUM           YOUR#         TOSS
 2             1             3             8             UNDER

                   !!!!!YOU LOSE!!!!!
THE AMOUNT YOU NOW HAVE IS 80
WHAT NUMBER DO YOU WISH TO PLAY AND HOW MUCH
DO YOU WANT TO BET ON THE NUMBER? 9,20

THE DICE HAVE NOW BEEN THROWN. THE RESULTS
ARE AS FOLLOWS:
 DIE #1        DIE #2        SUM           YOUR#         TOSS
 2             1             3             9             UNDER

                   !!!!!YOU LOSE!!!!!
THE AMOUNT YOU NOW HAVE IS 60

WHAT NUMBER DO YOU WISH TO PLAY AND HOW MUCH
DO YOU WANT TO BET ON THE NUMBER? 5,10

THE DICE HAVE NOW BEEN THROWN. THE RESULTS
ARE AS FOLLOWS:
 DIE #1        DIE #2        SUM           YOUR#         TOSS
 5             5             10            5             OVER

                   !!!!!YOU LOSE!!!!!
THE AMOUNT YOU NOW HAVE IS 50

WHAT NUMBER DO YOU WISH TO PLAY AND HOW MUCH
DO YOU WANT TO BET ON THE NUMBER? 6,10

THE DICE HAVE NOW BEEN THROWN. THE RESULTS
ARE AS FOLLOWS:
 DIE #1        DIE #2        SUM           YOUR#         TOSS
 4             2             6             6             UNDER

                   ********YOU WIN 4 TO 1********
THE AMOUNT YOU NOW HAVE IS 90

WHAT NUMBER DO YOU WISH TO PLAY AND HOW MUCH
DO YOU WANT TO BET ON THE NUMBER? 8,90

THE DICE HAVE NOW BEEN THROWN. THE RESULTS
ARE AS FOLLOWS:
 DIE #1        DIE #2        SUM           YOUR#         TOSS
 5             3             8             8             OVER

                   ********YOU WIN 4 TO 1********
THE AMOUNT YOU NOW HAVE IS 450

WHAT NUMBER DO YOU WISH TO PLAY AND HOW MUCH
DO YOU WANT TO BET ON THE NUMBER? 7,450

THE DICE HAVE NOW BEEN THROWN. THE RESULTS
ARE AS FOLLOWS:
 DIE #1        DIE #2        SUM           YOUR#         TOSS
 6             1             7             7             EVEN

                   ********YOU WIN 4 TO 1********
THE AMOUNT YOU NOW HAVE IS 2250

WHAT NUMBER DO YOU WISH TO PLAY AND HOW MUCH
DO YOU WANT TO BET ON THE NUMBER? 4,2250

THE DICE HAVE NOW BEEN THROWN. THE RESULTS
ARE AS FOLLOWS:
 DIE #1        DIE #2        SUM           YOUR#         TOSS
 6             1             7             4             EVEN

                   !!!!!YOU LOSE!!!!!
THE AMOUNT YOU NOW HAVE IS 2250

WHAT NUMBER DO YOU WISH TO PLAY AND HOW MUCH
DO YOU WANT TO BET ON THE NUMBER? 4,2250

THE DICE HAVE NOW BEEN THROWN. THE RESULTS
ARE AS FOLLOWS:
 DIE #1        DIE #2        SUM           YOUR#         TOSS
 1             5             6             4             UNDER

                   ********YOU WIN EVEN MONEY********
THE AMOUNT YOU NOW HAVE IS 4500

WHAT NUMBER DO YOU WISH TO PLAY AND HOW MUCH
DO YOU WANT TO BET ON THE NUMBER? 7,4500

THE DICE HAVE NOW BEEN THROWN. THE RESULTS
ARE AS FOLLOWS:
 DIE #1        DIE #2        SUM           YOUR#         TOSS
 3             5             8             7             OVER

                   !!!!!YOU LOSE!!!!!
THE AMOUNT YOU NOW HAVE IS 0

THE GAME IS OVER AND YOU ARE FLAT BROKE. SORRY CHARLIE
THIS PROVES THAT IT IS NOT GOOD TO GAMBLE
DO YOU WANT TO PLAY AGAIN? NO
Ok
```

```
100 PRINT TAB(22);"UNDER OR OVER"
110 PRINT TAB(20);"CREATIVE COMPUTING"
120 PRINT TAB(18);"MORRISTOWN, NEW JERSEY"
130 PRINT:PRINT:PRINT
140 PRINT"THIS IS A GAME OF UNDER AND OVER. IF YOU PICK"
150 PRINT"UNDER OR OVER SEVEN, YOU WILL WIN EVEN MONEY."
160 PRINT"IF YOU PICK EVEN YOU WILL WIN MONEY AT FOUR TO ONE"
170 PRINT"ODDS. YOU HAVE $100 TO START WITH. GOOD LUCK!":PRINT:PRINT
180 A=100
190 RESTORE
200 REM
210 READ A$,B$,C$
220 DATA "UNDER","OVER","EVEN"
230 PRINT"WHAT NUMBER DO YOU WISH TO PLAY AND HOW MUCH"
240 PRINT"DO YOU WANT TO BET ON THE NUMBER";:INPUT B,C
250 PRINT:PRINT"THE DICE HAVE NOW BEEN THROWN. THE RESULTS"
260 PRINT"ARE AS FOLLOWS:"
270 Q=INT(6*RND(1)+1):R=INT(6*RND(1)+1)
280 PRINT " DIE #1","DIE #2","SUM","YOUR#","TOSS"
290 IF Q+R>7 THEN 310
295 IF Q+R=7 THEN 320
300 PRINT Q,R,Q+R,B,A$:PRINT
303 IF B=Q+R THEN 350
305 IF B<7 THEN 380
307 GOTO 410
310 PRINT Q,R,Q+R,B,B$:PRINT
313 IF B=Q+R THEN 350
315 IF B>7 THEN 380
317 GOTO 410
320 PRINT Q,R,Q+R,B,C$:PRINT
330 IF B=Q+R THEN 350
340 GOTO 420
350 A=A+(4*C)
360 PRINT TAB(20)"********YOU WIN 4 TO 1********"
370 PRINT"THE AMOUNT YOU NOW HAVE IS" A :PRINT:GOTO 440
380 A=A+C
390 PRINT TAB(20)"********YOU WIN EVEN MONEY********"
400 PRINT"THE AMOUNT YOU NOW HAVE IS" A :PRINT:GOTO 440
410 A=A-C
420 PRINT TAB(20)"!!!!!YOU LOSE!!!!!"
430 PRINT"THE AMOUNT YOU NOW HAVE IS" A :PRINT
440 IF A>0 THEN 190
450 PRINT"THE GAME IS OVER AND YOU ARE FLAT BROKE. SORRY CHARLIE"
460 PRINT"THIS PROVES THAT IT IS NOT GOOD TO GAMBLE"
470 PRINT"DO YOU WANT TO PLAY AGAIN";:INPUT W$
480 IF LEFT$(W$,1)="Y" THEN 180
490 END
Ok
```

Van Gam

VAN GAM is a simple game with an interesting solution set. The winning sequence pairs are formed by certain mutually exclusive *sequences*, using the golden mean,

$$\frac{1+\sqrt{5}}{2}$$

as an irrational generator. See explanation, lines 40-130.

$$\text{IF } T = \frac{1+\sqrt{5}}{2}$$

$$\text{and } X = T + 1,\ Y = \frac{1}{T} + 1$$

then for integers N the winning sequence generators are

INT (N * X) 2 5 7 10 13 . . . .

INT (N * Y) 1 3 4 6 8 . . . .

It is interesting to note that the union of these sequences is the set of integers, and their intersection is empty. That is the case, in fact, for *any* irrational generator, but only T will produce winning VAN GAM pairs. The game is not much fun in that the average user will never be able to beat the computer in non-trivial cases, unless he has been taught the winning sequences.

This program by Alan Brown first appeared in *Creative Computing*, Jan/Feb 1978.

```
RUN
                         VANGAM
                   CREATIVE COMPUTING
                 MORRISTOWN, NEW JERSEY



VAN WYTHOFF'S GAME: DO YOU WANT INSTRUCTIONS? YES
YOU ARE TO CREATE TWO PILES OF MATCHES, EACH CONTAINING 100
OR LESS.  YOU PLAY ALTERNATELY WITH ME, AND OUR MOVES CONSIST
OF:
         (A) TAKING AWAY 1 OR MORE MATCHES FROM ONE PILE ONLY, OR
         (B) TAKING AWAY THE SAME NUMBER FROM EACH PILE.
THE ONE WHO TAKES AWAY THE LAST MATCH OF ALL WINS.
ENTER YOUR MOVES IN THIS MANNER:
          2L - (2 LEFT) TAKE TWO FROM LEFT PILE
          3R - (3 RIGHT) TAKE THREE FROM RIGHT PILE
          5B - (5 BOTH) TAKE FIVE FROM EACH PILE



DESIRED PILE SIZES (NUMBER,NUMBER)? 17,22
DO YOU WANT TO GO FIRST? YES
                          LEFT  RIGHT
                           17    22

YOUR MOVE:  ? 3L
                  LEAVING  14    22
HM.. I TAKE : 2B  LEAVING  12    20

YOUR MOVE:  ? 3B
                  LEAVING  9     17
HM.. I TAKE : 2R  LEAVING  9     15

YOUR MOVE:  ? 5R
                  LEAVING  9     10
HM.. I TAKE : 3L  LEAVING  6     10

YOUR MOVE:  ? 3B
                  LEAVING  3     7
HM.. I TAKE : 2R  LEAVING  3     5

YOUR MOVE:  ? 3R
                  LEAVING  3     2
HM.. I TAKE : 2L  LEAVING  1     2

YOUR MOVE:  ? 1R
                  LEAVING  1     1
HM.. I TAKE : 1B  LEAVING  0     0

SORRY - I WIN.  DON'T FEEL BADLY - I'M AN EXPERT.

DO YOU WANT TO PLAY AGAIN? YES


DESIRED PILE SIZES (NUMBER,NUMBER)? 26,16
DO YOU WANT TO GO FIRST? NO
                          LEFT  RIGHT
                           26    16
I TAKE :       1L  LEAVING  25    16

YOUR MOVE:  ? 2B
                  LEAVING  23    14
HM.. I TAKE : 1L  LEAVING  22    14

YOUR MOVE:  ? 2B
                  LEAVING  20    12
HM.. I TAKE : 1L  LEAVING  19    12

YOUR MOVE:  ? 1B
                  LEAVING  18    11
HM.. I TAKE : 1L  LEAVING  17    11

YOUR MOVE:  ? 2B
                  LEAVING  15    9
HM.. I TAKE : 1L  LEAVING  14    9

YOUR MOVE:  ? 1B
                  LEAVING  13    8
HM.. I TAKE : 1L  LEAVING  12    8

YOUR MOVE:  ? 2B
                  LEAVING  10    6
HM.. I TAKE : 1L  LEAVING  9     6

YOUR MOVE:  ? 2B
                  LEAVING  7     4
HM.. I TAKE : 1L  LEAVING  6     4

YOUR MOVE:  ? 1B
                  LEAVING  5     3
HM.. I TAKE : 1L  LEAVING  4     3

YOUR MOVE:  ? 2B
                  LEAVING  2     1
HM.. I TAKE : 1L  LEAVING  1     1

YOUR MOVE:  ? 1B
                  LEAVING  0     0
HM..

YOU WIN!!

CONGRADULATIONS.  YOU ARE A VERY CLEVER VAN WYTHOFF'S
GAMESMAN.

DO YOU WANT TO PLAY AGAIN? NO

O.K.  BYE NOW.
OK
```

```
LIST

5 PRINT TAB(26);"VANGAM"
6 PRINT TAB(20);"CREATIVE COMPUTING"
7 PRINT TAB(18);"MORRISTOWN, NEW JERSEY"
8 PRINT:PRINT:PRINT
10 DIM Q(200)
15 X=(1+SQR(5))/2:Y=1+1/X:X=1+X
16 FOR I=0 TO 99
17 Q(I*2)=INT(I*X):Q(I*2+1)=INT(I*Y)
18 NEXT I:T=0
20 PRINT "VAN WYTHOFF'S GAME: DO YOU WANT INSTRUCTIONS";
30 INPUT B$:IF LEFT$(B$,1)="N" THEN 130
40 PRINT "YOU ARE TO CREATE TWO PILES OF MATCHES, EACH CONTAINING 100"
50 PRINT "OR LESS.  YOU PLAY ALTERNATELY WITH ME, AND OUR MOVES CONSIST"
60 PRINT "OF:"
65 PRINT TAB(10);"(A) TAKING AWAY 1 OR MORE MATCHES";
67 PRINT " FROM ONE PILE ONLY, OR"
70 PRINT TAB(10);"(B) TAKING AWAY THE SAME NUMBER FROM EACH PILE."
80 PRINT "THE ONE WHO TAKES AWAY THE LAST MATCH OF ALL WINS."
90 PRINT "ENTER YOUR MOVES IN THIS MANNER:"
100 PRINT TAB(10);"2L - (2 LEFT) TAKE TWO FROM LEFT PILE"
110 PRINT TAB(10);"3R - (3 RIGHT) TAKE THREE FROM RIGHT PILE"
120 PRINT TAB(10);"5B - (5 BOTH) TAKE FIVE FROM EACH PILE"
130 PRINT:PRINT:PRINT
200 INPUT "DESIRED PILE SIZES (NUMBER,NUMBER)";S1,S2
210 L=S1:R=S2
220 IF L+R>5 THEN 240
230 PRINT "OH, YOU'RE A SPORT, YOU ARE."
240 INPUT "DO YOU WANT TO GO FIRST";B$
255 PRINT TAB(27);"LEFT  RIGHT"
257 PRINT TAB(27);L;TAB(33);R
260 P=L*2:IF L>R THEN 400
270 P=R*2
400 IF LEFT$(B$,1)="N" THEN 690
405 IF L=R THEN PRINT "YOU LIKE SITTING DUCKS, DON'T YOU?"
410 PRINT:INPUT "YOUR MOVE:  ";B$
415 FOR X=1 TO LEN(B$)
420 IF ASC(MID$(B$,X,1))<48 OR ASC(MID$(B$,X,1))>57 THEN 425
423 NEXT X
425 S3=VAL(MID$(B$,1,X-1))
427 IF S3=0 THEN 460
430 IF MID$(B$,X,1)="L" THEN 550
440 IF MID$(B$,X,1)="R" THEN 570
450 IF MID$(B$,X,1)="B" THEN 590
460 T=T+1:IF T>2 THEN 1940
470 PRINT:PRINT "IMPROPER ENTRY, STOP FOOLING AROUND.":GOTO 410
550 IF S3>L THEN 460
555 L=L-S3:GOTO 610
570 IF S3>R THEN 460
575 R=R-S3:GOTO 610
590 IF S3>L THEN 460
600 L=L-S3:GOTO 570
610 PRINT TAB(19);"LEAVING";TAB(27);L;TAB(33);R
614 PRINT "HM.. ";
615 FOR I=1 TO 500:A=A+I:NEXT I
620 IF L+R>0 THEN 690
630 PRINT:PRINT:PRINT "YOU WIN!!":PRINT
635 PRINT "CONGRADULATIONS.  YOU ARE A VERY CLEVER VAN WYTHOFF'S"
637 PRINT "GAMESMAN."
640 GOTO 1900
690 I=0:M=0
700 IF Q(I)=L THEN 760
710 IF Q(I+1)=L THEN 780
720 IF Q(I)=R THEN 800
730 IF Q(I+1)=R THEN 820
740 I=I+2:GOTO 700
760 L1=I:L2=1:IF M=1 THEN 840
770 M=1:GOTO 720
780 L1=I:L2=0:IF M=1 THEN 840
790 M=1:GOTO 720
800 R1=I:R2=1:IF M=1 THEN 840
810 M=1: GOTO 740
820 R1=I:R2=0:IF M=1 THEN 840
830 M=1: GOTO 740
840 IF L=R THEN 895
845 IF R1=L1 THEN 1080
850 IF L1>R1 THEN 900
860 P=L1+L2
880 IF Q(P)>R THEN 940
890 M=R-Q(P):R=Q(P):A$="R":GOTO 1110
895 M=L:L=0:R=0:A$="B":GOTO 1110
900 P=R1+R2
920 IF Q(P)>L THEN 940
930 M=L-Q(P):L=Q(P):A$="L":GOTO 1110
940 M=0:A$="B"
950 P=L1:IF R1<L1 THEN P=R1
960 P=P-2:G=0
965 M=M+1:L=L-1:R=R-1
970 FOR I=P TO 0 STEP -2
990 IF Q(I)=L THEN 1040
1000 IF Q(I+1)=L THEN 1050
1010 IF Q(I)=R THEN 1060
1020 IF Q(I+1)=R THEN 1070
1030 NEXT I:GOTO 965
1040 IF Q(I+1)=R THEN 1110
1045 GOTO 1075
1050 IF Q(I)=R THEN 1110
1055 GOTO 1075
1060 IF Q(I+1)=L THEN 1110
1065 GOTO 1075
1070 IF Q(I)=L THEN 1110
1075 IF G=1 THEN 960
1077 G=1:GOTO 965
1080 IF L>R THEN 1100
1090 R=R-1:M=1:A$="R":GOTO 1110
1100 L=L-1:M=1:A$="L"
1110 B$="":IF M>9 THEN 1930
1113 B$=CHR$(M+48)
1114 B$=B$+A$
1115 PRINT "I TAKE :";TAB(14);B$;TAB(19);"LEAVING";TAB(27);L;TAB(33);R
1120 IF L+R>0 THEN 410
1130 PRINT:PRINT "SORRY - I WIN.  DON'T FEEL BADLY - I'M AN EXPERT."
1900 PRINT:INPUT "DO YOU WANT TO PLAY AGAIN";B$
1910 IF LEFT$(B$,1)="Y" THEN 130
1920 GOTO 1970
1930 B$=CHR$(INT(M/10)+48):B$=B$+CHR$(M-INT(M/10)*10+48)
1935 GOTO 1114
1940 PRINT:PRINT "LOOK, YOU JUST WON'T STOP FOOLING ABOUT.  BUZZ OFF."
1945 GOTO 1970
1970 PRINT:PRINT "O.K.  BYE NOW."
1980 END
OK
```

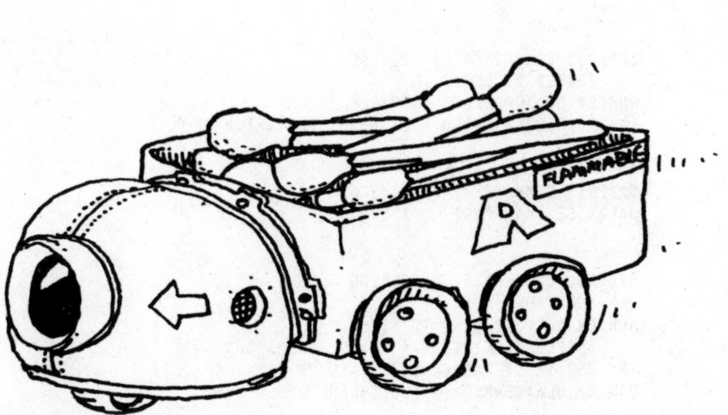

Warfish

In this game, you're the commander of an American submarine with a mission to seek out and destroy as many Japanese ships as possible during World War II.

You may up your periscope to search for Japanese ships, you may launch your torpedoes, or you may dive to avoid Japanese ships that are attacking you.

For the most part, this is a game of random probabilities. To make it more interesting, you might wish to introduce a skill factor in terms of aiming your submarine or distance away from an enemy ship, size of the enemy ship, and so on.

Warfish was written by Randy Wit.

```
RUN
                              WARFISH
                        CREATIVE COMPUTING
                      MORRISTOWN, NEW JERSEY


DO YOU DESIRE THE RULES OF WARFISH ? YES

YOU COMMAND AN AMERICAN SUBMARINE THAT BEEN SENT OUT
TO ATTACK JAPANESE SHIPS AT SEA DURING WORLD WAR TWO

 THE ORDERS THAT CAN BE GIVEN ARE THE FOLLOWING:
PERISCOPE  - TO SEARCH FOR JAPANESE SHIPS
TORPEDO - TO LAUNCH TORPEDOES AT JAPANESE SHIPS
DIVE - TO ESCAPE JAPANESE SHIPS THAT ARE ATTACKING

THESE ARE SOME HISTORIC U.S. NAVY SUBMARINES -
      TAUTOG, SILVERSIDES, CAVALLA, BLUEFISH, THRESHER
        SWORDFISH, FLASHER, TROUT,ARCHER
SELECT ONE OF THE ABOVE, OR USE A NAME OF YOUR CHOICE
PRINT THE NAME OF YOUR SUBMARINE ? TROUT


JAPANESE TORPEDO BOAT IS ATTACKING


ORDERS, COMMANDER  ? DIVE
DISTANCE OF JAPANESE TORPEDO BOAT            DEPTH OF USS TROUT
 1500 YARDS                                    0 FEET
 1250 YARDS                                    25 FEET
 1000 YARDS                                    50 FEET
 750 YARDS                                    75 FEET
 500 YARDS                                    100 FEET
 250 YARDS                                    125 FEET
 0 YARDS                                    150 FEET
THE USS TROUT IS UNHURT


ORDERS, COMMANDER  ? PERISCOPE
JAPANESE FREIGHTER -  7500  TONS


ORDERS, COMMANDER  ? TORPEDO
 26  TORPEDOES LEFT
NUMBER OF TORPEDOES TO FIRE? 2
 2  TORPEDOES FIRED - 0  HITS


ORDERS, COMMANDER  ? TORPEDO
 24  TORPEDOES LEFT
NUMBER OF TORPEDOES TO FIRE? 3
 3  TORPEDOES FIRED - 0  HITS

ORDERS, COMMANDER  ? TORPEDO
 21  TORPEDOES LEFT
NUMBER OF TORPEDOES TO FIRE? 3
 3  TORPEDOES FIRED - 1  HITS -FREIGHTER SUNK


ORDERS, COMMANDER  ? PERISCOPE
JAPANESE TRANSPORT -  11500  TONS


ORDERS, COMMANDER  ? TORPEDO
 18  TORPEDOES LEFT
NUMBER OF TORPEDOES TO FIRE? 3
 3  TORPEDOES FIRED - 2  HITS -TRANSPORT SUNK


ORDERS, COMMANDER  ? PERISCOPE
JAPANESE AMMUNITION SHIP -  9650  TONS


ORDERS, COMMANDER  ? TORPEDO
 15  TORPEDOES LEFT
NUMBER OF TORPEDOES TO FIRE? 2
 2  TORPEDOES FIRED - 0  HITS


ORDERS, COMMANDER  ? TORPEDO
 13  TORPEDOES LEFT
NUMBER OF TORPEDOES TO FIRE? 3
 3  TORPEDOES FIRED - 2  HITS -AMMUNITION SHIP SUNK


ORDERS, COMMANDER  ? PERISCOPE
JAPANESE AMMUNITION SHIP -  9650  TONS


ORDERS, COMMANDER  ? TORPEDO
 10  TORPEDOES LEFT
NUMBER OF TORPEDOES TO FIRE? 2
 2  TORPEDOES FIRED - 1  HITS -AMMUNITION SHIP SUNK


ORDERS, COMMANDER  ? PERISCOPE
JAPANESE FREIGHTER -  8100  TONS


ORDERS, COMMANDER  ? TORPEDO
 8  TORPEDOES LEFT
NUMBER OF TORPEDOES TO FIRE? 2
 2  TORPEDOES FIRED - 0  HITS


ORDERS, COMMANDER  ? TORPEDO
 6  TORPEDOES LEFT
NUMBER OF TORPEDOES TO FIRE? 3
 3  TORPEDOES FIRED - 0  HITS


ORDERS, COMMANDER  ? TORPEDO
 3  TORPEDOES LEFT
NUMBER OF TORPEDOES TO FIRE? 2
 2  TORPEDOES FIRED - 2  HITS -FREIGHTER SUNK


ORDERS, COMMANDER  ? PERISCOPE
JAPANESE TRANSPORT -  11500  TONS


ORDERS, COMMANDER  ? TORPEDO
 1  TORPEDOES LEFT
NUMBER OF TORPEDOES TO FIRE? 1
 1  TORPEDOES FIRED - 1  HITS -TRANSPORT SUNK
THE USS TROUT HAS EXPENDED ALL OF ITS TORPEDOES
CONGRATULATIONS ON A SUCCESSFUL DEPLOYMENT

 THE SUBMARINE USS TROUT HAS SUNK A TOTAL OF 6  SHIPS
 THE ENEMY TONNAGE SUNK IS  57900  TONS
OK
```

```
LIST

1 PRINT TAB(25)"WARFISH"
2 PRINT TAB(20)"CREATIVE COMPUTING"
3 PRINT TAB(18)"MORRISTOWN, NEW JERSEY"
5 PRINT
6 PRINT
7 PRINT
8 PRINT
9 DIM A$(72)
10 Q0=RND(1)
30 PRINT"DO YOU DESIRE THE RULES OF WARFISH ";
40 INPUT X$
50 IF X$="NO" THEN 200
51 IF X$="YES" THEN 60
52 PRINT"YES OR NO ONLY, PLEASE."
53 GOTO 30
60 PRINT
70 PRINT"YOU COMMAND AN AMERICAN SUBMARINE THAT BEEN SENT OUT"
80 PRINT"TO ATTACK JAPANESE SHIPS AT SEA DURING WORLD WAR TWO"
90 PRINT
100 PRINT" THE ORDERS THAT CAN BE GIVEN ARE THE FOLLOWING:"
110 PRINT"PERISCOPE  - TO SEARCH FOR JAPANESE SHIPS"
120 PRINT"TORPEDO - TO LAUNCH TORPEDOES AT JAPANESE SHIPS"
130 PRINT "DIVE - TO ESCAPE JAPANESE SHIPS THAT ARE ATTACKING"
140 PRINT
150 PRINT"THESE ARE SOME HISTORIC U.S. NAVY SUBMARINES -"
160 PRINT"       TAUTOG, SILVERSIDES, CAVALLA, BLUEFISH, THRESHER"
170 PRINT"       SWORDFISH, FLASHER, TROUT,ARCHER"
180 PRINT"SELECT ONE OF THE ABOVE, OR USE A NAME OF YOUR CHOICE"
200 PRINT"PRINT THE NAME OF YOUR SUBMARINE ";
210 INPUT A$
220 T=26
230 D=INT(RND(1)*10)
240 IF D<6 THEN 330
250 IF D<>6 AND D<> 7 THEN 270
255 R$="DESTROYER"
260 W=2100
270 IF D<>8 THEN290
271 R$="DESTROYER ESCORT"
280 W=1350
290 IF D<>9 THEN 310
291 R$="TORPEDO BOAT"
300 W=70
310 IF D=6  OR D=7 THEN 313
311 Q=1
312 GOTO 314
313 Q=2
314 PRINT
315 PRINT
320 PRINT"JAPANESE ";R$;" IS ATTACKING"
330 IF D>= 6 THEN 340
335 A=INT(RND(1)*10)
340 PRINT
350 PRINT
360 PRINT"ORDERS, COMMANDER  ";
370 INPUT C$
371 C$=MID$(C$,1,1)
380 IF C$="P" THEN 420
390 IF C$="T" THEN 780
400 IF C$="D" THEN 990
410 GOTO 360
420 IF D>5 OR Q>0 THEN 760
430 IF A>=4 THEN 470
435 R$="FREIGHTER"
440 IF A<>0 AND A<>1 THEN 450
445 W=6500
450 IF A<> 2 THEN 460
455 W=7500
460 IF A<>3 THEN 470
465 W=8100
470 IF A<>7 AND A<>8 THEN 490
475 R$="TANKER"
480 IF A<>8 THEN 485
481 W=10000
482 GOTO 490
485 W=9500
490 IF A<>4 AND A<>5 THEN 510
491 R$="TRANSPORT"
500 IF A<>5 THEN 505
501 W=11500
502 GOTO 510
505 W=8800
510 IF A<>6 THEN 530
515 R$="AMMUNITION SHIP"
520 W=9650
530 IF A>=9 OR A=6 THEN 540
535 Q=1
540 IF A<>6 THEN 550
545 Q=1
550 IF A<9 THEN 760
560 E=INT(RND(1)*10)
570 IF E<>0 THEN 590
575 R$="BATTLESHIP"
580 W=33500
590 IF E<>1 THEN 610
595 R$="AIRCRAFT CARRIER"
600 W=25700
610 IF E<>2 THEN 630
615 R$="HEAVY CRUISER"
620 W= 9900
630 IF E<>3 THEN 650
635 R$="LIGHT CRUISER"
640 W=9600
650 IF E<>4 AND E<>5 THEN 670
655 R$="DESTROYER"
660 W=2100
670 IF E<>6 AND E<>7 THEN 690
675 R$="SUBMARINE"
680 W=1500
690 IF E<>8 AND E<>9 THEN 710
700 W=1350
710 IF E<=5 THEN 720
715 Q=1
720 IF E<>4 ANDE<>5 THEN 730
725 Q=2
730 IF E<>2 AND E<>3 THEN 740
735 Q=3
740 IF E<>1 THEN 750
745 W=4
750 IFE<>0 THEN 760
755 Q=6
760 PRINT"JAPANESE ";R$;" - ";W;" TONS"
770 GOTO 340
780 IF Q>=1 THEN 800
785 PRINT" NO JAPANESE SHIPS IN SIGHT - JUST OCEAN"
790 IF Q<1 THEN 360
800 PRINT T;" TORPEDOES LEFT"
810 PRINT"NUMBER OF TORPEDOES TO FIRE";
820 INPUT R
830 IF R<0 OR T-R<0 THEN 810
840 IF R<>INT(R) THEN 810
850 T=T-R
860 S=INT(RND(1)*10)
870 IF S>R THEN 860
880 Q=Q-S
890 IF Q<=0 THEN 900
895 Q$="DAMAGED"
900 IF Q>=1 THEN 930
905 Q$="SUNK"
910 O=O+W
920 L=L+1
930 PRINT R;" TORPEDOES FIRED -";S;" HITS";
940 IF S<>0 THEN 950
945 PRINT
950 IF S<=0 THEN 960
955 PRINT" -"; R$;" ";Q$
960 IF D>5 AND Q>0 THEN 1140
970 IF T<1 THEN 1160
980 IF Q<1 THEN 230
985 GOTO 340
990 IF D>=6 THEN 1000
995 PRINT" THEN USS ";A$;" IS NOT UNDER ATTACK"
1000 IF D<6 THEN 360
1010 U=INT(RND(1)*10)*250+500
1020 PRINT "DISTANCE OF JAPANESE ";R$;"                    DEPTH OF USS ";A$
1030 PRINT U;"YARDS                                              ";Z;"FEET"
1040 U=U-250
1050 Z=Z+25
1060 IF U>-250 THEN 1030
1070 IF R$="TORPEDO BOAT " THEN 1100
1080 N=INT(RND(1)*10)*25+50
1090 IF N+26>Z AND N-26<Z THEN 1120
1099 U=Z=0
1100 PRINT"THE USS ";A$;" IS UNHURT"
1110 Q=0
1111 GOTO 230
1120 PRINT"THE USS ";A$;" HAS BEEN SUNK BY DEPTH CHARGES"
1130 GOTO 1180
1140 PRINT"THE USS "A$;" HAS BEEN SUNK BY GUNFIRE"
1150 GOTO 1180
1160 PRINT"THE USS ";A$;" HAS EXPENDED ALL OF ITS TORPEDOES"
1170 IF O<=0 THEN 1180
1175 PRINT"CONGRATULATIONS ON A SUCCESSFUL DEPLOYMENT"
1180 PRINT
1190 PRINT" THE SUBMARINE USS ";A$;" HAS SUNK A TOTAL OF";L;" SHIPS"
1200 PRINT" THE ENEMY TONNAGE SUNK IS ";O;" TONS"
1210 END
OK
```

Word Search Puzzle

This program generates the immensely popular word-search puzzles containing names of Presidents, states, types of animals, fish, and every manner of objects. It asks you the length and width of the puzzle you wish generated and then the number of words to be hidden in the puzzle. As the instructions note, occasionally the computer may find that it can't hide a particular word in the puzzle and will ask you if it should start over or if you want that particular word deleted. If you start over, try giving it fewer words or larger puzzle dimensions. The program hides the words fairly efficiently although you can usually improve on it slightly when you get the final puzzle out. Since you're probably just using this program for fun, it's generally more than adequate.

This word search puzzle generator was originated by Leor Zolman.

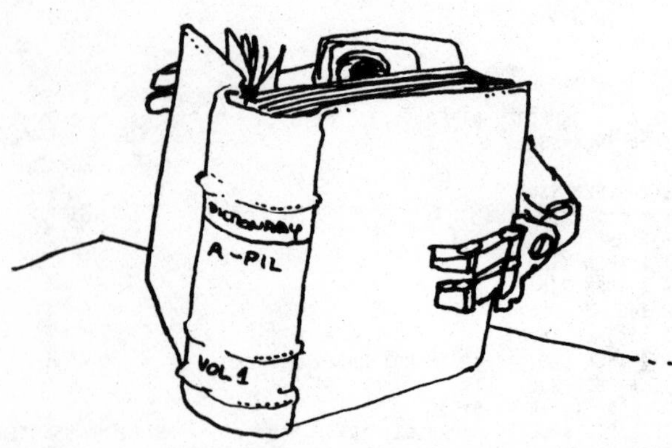


```
RUN
                         WORD SEARCH PUZZLE
                         CREATIVE COMPUTING
                       MORRISTOWN, NEW JERSEY


  THIS PROGRAM IS A WORD SEARCH PUZZLE GENERATOR!!
THE PROGRAM TAKES A SET OF INPUT STRINGS, PURGES ALL
NON-ALPHABETIC CHARACTERS OUT OF THEM, AND INCORPORATES
THEM INTO A WORD SEARCH PUZZLE.

  IN THE COURSE OF MAKING THE PUZZLE, THE MACHINE MAY
FIND THAT IT CAN'T PUT A PARTICULAR WORD ANYWHERE, AND
SO WILL ASK YOU IF IT SHOULD START THE WHOLE PUZZLE
OVER.  IF YOU DON'T WANT IT TO START OVER, TYPING 'NO'
WILL THROW AWAY THAT PARTICULAR WORD.  IF THIS PERSISTS,
TRY EITHER GIVING LESS WORDS OR BIGGER PUZZLE DIMENSIONS!

HOW MANY COLUMNS DOES YOUR PRINTER HAVE? 72
DO YOU WANT A SOLUTION PRINTOUT? YES
WHAT IS TO BE THE WIDTH OF THE PUZZLE? 15
THE LENGTH? 15
WHAT IS THE MAXIMUM NUMBER OF WORDS IN THE PUZZLE? 10

NOW ENTER A HEADING THAT WILL BE PRINTED OVER THE PUZZLE:
( 72 CHARACTERS MAXIMUM! )
? COMPUTER LANGUAGES
OK . . . ENTER A WORD AT EACH QUESTION MARK.
TO REDO THE PREVIOUS WORD, TYPE A HYPHEN (-).
WHEN YOU RUN OUT OF WORDS, TYPE A PERIOD (.).
? BAS*&^%$  IC
-basic-
? FOR)(*&TRAN
-fortran-
? P L I
-pli-
? C O B O L++=';
-cobol-
? ASSEMBNLER
-assembnler-
? -
REDO assembnler. . .
? ASSEMBLER
-assembler-
? RPG
-rpg-
? ALGOL
-algol-
? LISP
-lisp-
? SNOBOL
-snobol-
? PILOT
-pilot-
THAT'S IT... 10 WORDS.
NOW LET ME PONDER THIS......
HOW MANY COPIES OF THIS PUZZLE DO YOU WANT? 1
FOR EACH COPY, HIT RETURN TO BEGIN PRINTING...
?




                         COMPUTER LANGUAGES


                B I U R W I X N R S K A T T Z
                O G O M L G S L R E P A O Y S
                Y V Y P F F A Z O I Z K C F P
                P M T T R H P P L G O S S S Y
                Z S R I H B S O J Y L N B X X
                E A C E K R T H S I O A H F N
                D F Q I L U K K Q B B F B R J
                D L Q T S B V A O H W W F G C
                Q I L Y D A M L K U P O V P A
                K X P O G Z B E X M R R F U D
                M V C S B P S Y S T I L X S U
                I I I D I O R G R S V A Y T Y
                E H N D A L C A N U A Z W J K
                L A C R Y L N V K T F Z O W C
                F V Q Y U A J F U G P Q J B V


FIND THESE HIDDEN WORDS IN THE ABOVE PUZZLE:

algol          assembler      basic          cobol          fortran
lisp           pilot          pli            rpg            snobol
```

```
                    HERE IS THE ANSWER KEY:


       . . . . . I . . . . . . . . .
       . . . . L . . L . . P . . . .
       . . . P . . . . O I . . . . .
       . . . . . . . . L G . . S . .
       . . R . . . . O . . L N . . .
       . . C E . . T . . . O A . . .
       . . . I L . . . . B . . . . .
       . . . . S B . . O . . . F . .
       . . L . . A M L . . . O . . .
       . . P O G . B E . . R . . . .
       . . . S B P . . S T . . . . .
       . . . . I O R . R S . . . . .
       . . . . . L C A . . A . . . .
       . . . . . . N . . . . . . . .
       . . . . . . . . . . . . . . .


FIND THESE HIDDEN WORDS IN THE ABOVE PUZZLE:

algol          assembler      basic          cobol          fortran
lisp           pilot          pli            rpg            snobol
```

```
LIST
10 PRINT TAB(20);"WORD SEARCH PUZZLE"
20 PRINT TAB(20);"CREATIVE COMPUTING"
30 PRINT TAB(18);"MORRISTOWN, NEW JERSEY"
40 PRINT:PRINT:PRINT
50 PRINT "  THIS PROGRAM IS A WORD SEARCH PUZZLE GENERATOR!!"
60 PRINT "THE PROGRAM TAKES A SET OF INPUT STRINGS, PURGES ALL"
70 PRINT "NON-ALPHABETIC CHARACTERS OUT OF THEM, AND INCORPORATES"
80 PRINT "THEM INTO A WORD SEARCH PUZZLE."
90 PRINT
100 PRINT "  IN THE COURSE OF MAKING THE PUZZLE, THE MACHINE MAY"
110 PRINT "FIND THAT IT CAN'T PUT A PARTICULAR WORD ANYWHERE, AND"
120 PRINT "SO WILL ASK YOU IF IT SHOULD START THE WHOLE PUZZLE"
130 PRINT "OVER.  IF YOU DON'T WANT IT TO START OVER, TYPING 'NO'"
140 PRINT "WILL THROW AWAY THAT PARTICULAR WORD.  IF THIS PERSISTS,"
150 PRINT "TRY EITHER GIVING LESS WORDS OR BIGGER PUZZLE DIMENSIONS!"
160 PRINT:PRINT
280 CLEAR 3000
300 DEF FNA(Z)=INT(RND(1)*Z+1)
310 INPUT "HOW MANY COLUMNS DOES YOUR PRINTER HAVE";TW
320 INPUT "DO YOU WANT A SOLUTION PRINTOUT";X$
330 INPUT "WHAT IS TO BE THE WIDTH OF THE PUZZLE";W:MD=W
340 IF W*2<=TW THEN 345
343 PRINT "THAT WILL NOT FIT IN";TW;" COLUMNS.":GOTO 330
345 IF W<1 THEN 330
350 INPUT "THE LENGTH";L:IF L>W THEN MD=L
355 IF L<1 THEN 350
360 INPUT "WHAT IS THE MAXIMUM NUMBER OF WORDS IN THE PUZZLE";M
370 IF M>=2 THEN 380
375 PRINT "SORRY; THERE MUST BE AT LEAST 2 WORDS.":GOTO 360
380 PRINT
390 DIM A$(L,W),W$(M)
400 DIM W(M,3),DXY(8,2),DD(28)
410 PRINT "NOW ENTER A HEADING THAT WILL BE PRINTED OVER THE PUZZLE:"
420 PRINT "(";TW;"CHARACTERS MAXIMUM! )"
430 INPUT XY$
440 PRINT "OK . . . ENTER A WORD AT EACH QUESTION MARK."
450 PRINT "TO REDO THE PREVIOUS WORD, TYPE A HYPHEN (-)."
460 PRINT "WHEN YOU RUN OUT OF WORDS, TYPE A PERIOD (.)."
470 FOR I=1 TO M
480 INPUT T$:IF T$="-" THENI=I-1:PRINT "REDO ";W$(I);". . .":GOTO 480
490 IF T$="." THEN M=I-1:GOTO 660
500 IF LEN(T$)=0 THEN PRINT "INPUT ERROR; REDO:":GOTO 480
510 J=1
520 TE$=MID$(T$,J,1):IF TE$>="a" AND TE$<="z" THEN   570
525 IF TE$<"A" OR TE$>"Z" THEN 530
527 T$=LEFT$(T$,J-1)+CHR$(ASC(MID$(T$,J,1))+32)+RIGHT$(T$,LEN(T$)-J)
530 IF TE$=T$ THEN T$="": GOTO 500
540 IF J=LEN(T$) THEN T$=LEFT$(T$,J-1):GOTO 580            :GOTO570
550 IF J=1 THEN T$=RIGHT$(T$,LEN(T$)-1):J=J-1:GOTO 570
560 T$=LEFT$(T$,J-1)+RIGHT$(T$,LEN(T$)-J):J=J-1
570 J=J+1:IF J<=LEN(T$) THEN 520
580 PRINT "-";T$;"-"
600 IF LEN(T$)<=MD THEN 610
605 PRINT "THAT'S TOO LONG, I'M AFRAID.";
607 PRINT " TRY ANOTHER ONE:":GOTO 480
610 FOR IZ=1 TO I-1: IF W$(IZ)<>T$ THEN NEXT:GOTO 630
620 PRINT "YOU ENTERED THAT ONE ALREADY. TRY ANOTHER:":GOTO 480
630 W$(I)=T$
640 NEXT I
650 PRINT "THAT'S IT...";M;"WORDS."
660 PRINT "NOW LET ME PONDER THIS......"
680 FOR I=1 TO M-1
685 FOR J=I+1 TO M
690 IF LEN(W$(I)) < LEN(W$(J)) THEN HZ$=W$(I):W$(I)=W$(J):W$(J)=HZ$
700 NEXT:NEXT
710 FOR I=1 TO 8:READ DXY(I,1),DXY(I,2):NEXT
720 FOR I=1 TO 28:READ DD(I):NEXT
730 DATA 0,1,1,1,1,0,1,-1,0,-1,-1,-1,-1,0,-1,1
740 DATA 2,4,6,8,2,4,6,8,2,4,6,8,2,4,6,8,2,4,6,8,2,4,6,8,1,3,5,7
750 FOR I=1 TO M
760 LN=LEN(W$(I))
770 NT=0
790 SD=DD(FNA(28))
800 SX=FNA(W):X1=SX+(LN-1)*DXY(SD,1):IF X1<1 OR X1>W THEN 790
810 SY=FNA(L):X1=SY+(LN-1)*DXY(SD,2):IF X1<1 OR X1>L THEN 790
820 NT=NT+1:IF NT<>W*L*2 THEN 850
830 PRINT "COULDN'T FIT  '";W$(I);"'  IN THE PUZZLE."
832 INPUT "DO YOU WANT ME TO START OVER";A$
834 IF LEFT$(A$,1)="y" THEN 750
836 W$(I)="":GOTO 950
850 J=SY:K=SX
860 FOR P=1 TO LN
870 IF LEN(A$(J,K)) AND A$(J,K)<>MID$(W$(I),P,1) THEN 790
880 J=J+DXY(SD,2):K=K+DXY(SD,1):NEXT P
900 J=SY:K=SX
910 FOR P=1 TO LN:A$(J,K)=MID$(W$(I),P,1)
920 J=J+DXY(SD,2):K=K+DXY(SD,1):NEXT
940 W(I,1)=SX:W(I,2)=SY:W(I,3)=SD
950 NEXT I
970 FOR I=1 TO L
975 FOR J=1 TO W
980 IF A$(I,J)="" THEN A$(I,J)=CHR$(FNA(26)+96)
990 NEXT:NEXT
1010 FOR I=1 TO M-1:FOR J=I+1 TO M
1020 IF W$(I)<=W$(J) THEN 1030
1021 HZ$=W$(I):W$(I)=W$(J):W$(J)=HZ$
1025 FOR K=1 TO 3:HZ=W(I,K):W(I,K)=W(J,K):W(J,K)=HZ:NEXT K
1030 NEXTJ:NEXT I
1040 INPUT "HOW MANY COPIES OF THIS PUZZLE DO YOU WANT";N
1050 PRINT "FOR EACH COPY, HIT RETURN TO BEGIN PRINTING..."
1060 FOR C=1 TO N:GOSUB 1070:NEXT:GOTO 1230
1070 INPUT A$:PRINT
1080 T=(TW-2*W)/2:PRINT
1090 PRINT
1100 PRINT TAB((TW-LEN(XY$))/2);XY$
1110 PRINT:PRINT
1120 FOR J=1 TO L:PRINT TAB(T);
1130 FOR K=1 TO W:IF A$(J,K)="." THEN PRINT ". ";:GOTO 1140
1135 PRINT CHR$(ASC(A$(J,K))-32);" ";
1140 NEXT:PRINT:NEXT
1150 PRINT:PRINT
1160 PRINT "FIND THESE HIDDEN WORDS IN THE ABOVE PUZZLE:"
1170 PRINT
1180 FOR J=1 TO M:IF LEN(W$(J))=0 THEN 1210
1190 IF POS(0) + LEN(W$(J)) > TW-2 THEN PRINT
1200 PRINT W$(J),
1210 NEXT:PRINT:PRINT:PRINT:PRINT
1220 RETURN
1230 IF LEFT$(X$,1)="Y" OR LEFT$(X$,1)="y" THEN 1250
1240 END
1250 REM
1260 FOR I=1 TO L:FOR J=1 TO W:A$(I,J)=".":NEXTJ:NEXTI
1270 FOR I=1 TO M
1280 LN=LEN(W$(I)):J=W(I,2):K=W(I,1)
1290 FOR P=1 TO LN
1300 A$(J,K)=MID$(W$(I),P,1)
1310 J=J+DXY(W(I,3),2):K=K+DXY(W(I,3),1):NEXT P
1320 NEXT I
1330 XY$="HERE IS THE ANSWER KEY:"
1340 GOSUB 1070
1350 PRINT:PRINT
1360 END
Ok
```

Wumpus 1

The Genesis of Wumpus

Two years ago I happened by People's Computer Company (PCC) and saw some of their computer games — such as Hurkle, Snark, and Mugwump. My reaction was: "EECH!!" Each of these games was based on a 10 x 10 grid in Cartesian co-ordinates and three of them was too much for me. I started to think along the lines of: "There has to be a hide and seek computer game without that (exp. deleted) grid!!" In fact, why not a topological computer game — imagine a set of points connected in some way and the player moves about the set via the interconnections.

That afternoon in meditation the phrase "Hunt the Wumpus" arrived, and Wumpus was born. He's still a bit vague in physical detail as most dedicated Wumpus hunters know, but appearances are part of the game. (If you like, send me a picture of your version of a Wumpus. Perhaps friendly Dave, our editor, will publish the best one in *Creative Computing*.) The grid I chose was the vertices of a dodecahedron — simply because it's my favorite Platonic solid and once, ages ago, I made a kite shaped like one. The edges became the connecting tunnels between the caves which were the set of points for the game.

My basic idea at this time was for the player to approach the Wumpus, back off, and come up to him by going around the dodecahedron. To my knowledge, this has never happened . . . most players adopt other strategies rather than this cold-blooded approach.

Anyway . . . how to get the Wumpus! How about an arrow which could turn corners as it goes from room to room. Let the hunter tell the arrow where to go and let it fly. The shortest round trip without reversals is 5 caves — and thus the Crooked Arrow.

Hmmm . . . How does one sense the Wumpus? It's dark in yonder cave, and light would wake him up. If one got one cave away, the wumpus's distinct smell would serve as a warning. So far, so good . . . but Wumpus is still too easy, so let's find some appropriate hazards for the caves.

Bottomless pits were easy. Any imaginary cave would have a few of those around the place. Superbats were harder to come by. It took me a day or two to get that idea. The Superbats are a sort of rapid transit system gone a little batty (sorry about that one). They take you a random distance to a random cave and leave you there. If that's a pit or a Wumpus, well, you are in Fate's hands.

Around this time, I saw that Map-making would be a regular activity of Wumpus-hunters. I numbered the caves and made the scheme fixed in the hopes a practised player might notice this and make himself a permanent map of the caverns. (Another unrealised hope — as an exercise, make yourself such a map on a Squashed Dodecahedron).

To start the game fairly, Wumpus, Hazards, and Hunter are located on different points at the start of the game. Each game starts with random choices of location, but the hunter may restart with the same set-up if he chooses. This allows re-plays if the hunter, say, fell into a pit on the first move.

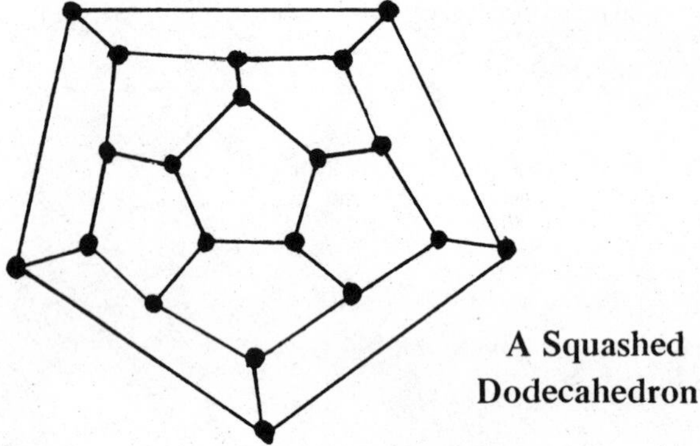

A Squashed Dodecahedron

Wumpus was nearly done in my mind . . . (hint to a games-writer: Have a clear notion of your game before you start coding it. This saves MUCH confusion.) yet I felt it was a bit dull. Once you found the Wumpus all you had to do was shoot it. To fix this, the Wumpus was given a little life. If you shot an arrow or moved into his cave, he woke up and chose to move to a neighboring room or to the same room (one of 4 choices). If you and the Wumpus were in the same room after he moved, he ATE YOU UP!!

Around here I noticed that the pits and the bats didn't affect the Wumpus. To explain this, I added some color by making him heavy and with the legendary sucker feet. After all, evolution works in strange ways!! If you are a Wumpus fiend, make a version of Wumpus in which he avoids pits and superbats can carry him only one room (with the possibility of being dumped into your cave). This can be done by making the wumpus moving procedure a subroutine.

I wrote Wumpus and dropped it off at PCC. Then I went home and dreamed up Wumpus 2.

The Birth of Wumpus

Around a month later, I went to the Synergy conference at Stanford, where many of the far-out folk were gathered to share their visions of improving the world. PCC had a few terminals running in a conference room and I dropped by. To my vast surprise, all of the terminals were running Wumpus and scraps of paper on the floor with scrawled numbers and lines testified that much dedicated Wumpus-hunting was in progress. I had spawned a hit computer game!!!

Later, PCC published Wumpus in its newsletter, and *Creative Computing* published it in their Sep/Oct 1975 issue.

Wumpus and this writeup are the products of the talented and creative Gregory Yob.

```
RUN
                                 WUMPUS
              CREATIVE COMPUTING  MORRISTOWN, NEW JERSEY



INSTRUCTIONS (Y-N)? Y
WELCOME TO 'HUNT THE WUMPUS'
  THE WUMPUS LIVES IN A CAVE OF 20 ROOMS. EACH ROOM
HAS 3 TUNNELS LEADING TO OTHER ROOMS. (LOOK AT A
DODECAHEDRON TO SEE HOW THIS WORKS-IF YOU DON'T KNOW
WHAT A DODECHADRON IS, ASK SOMEONE)

     HAZARDS:
BOTTOMLESS PITS - TWO ROOMS HAVE BOTTOMLESS PITS IN THEM
     IF YOU GO THERE, YOU FALL INTO THE PIT (& LOSE!)
SUPERBATS - TWO OTHER ROOMS HAVE SUPER BATS. IF YOU
     GO THERE, A BAT GRABS YOU AND TAKES YOU TO SOME OTHER
     ROOM AT RANDOM. (WHICH MIGHT BE TROUBLESOME)

     WUMPUS:
THE WUMPUS IS NOT BOTHERED BY THE HAZARDS (HE HAS SUCKER
FEET AND IS TOO BIG FOR A BAT TO LIFT). USUALLY
HE IS ASLEEP. TWO THINGS THAT WAKE HIM UP: YOUR ENTERING
HIS ROOM OR YOUR SHOOTING AN ARROW.
     IF THE WUMPUS WAKES, HE MOVES (P=.75) ONE ROOM
OR STAYS STILL (P=.25). AFTER THAT, IF HE IS WHERE YOU
ARE, HE EATS YOU UP (& YOU LOSE!)

     YOU:
EACH TURN YOU MAY MOVE OR SHOOT A CROOKED ARROW
     MOVING: YOU CAN GO ONE ROOM (THRU ONE TUNNEL)
     ARROWS: YOU HAVE 5 ARROWS. YOU LOSE WHEN YOU RUN OUT.
     EACH ARROW CAN GO FROM 1 TO 5 ROOMS. YOU AIM BY TELLING
     THE COMPUTER TTHE ROOM#S YOU WANT THE ARROW TO GO TO.
     IF THE ARROW CAN'T GO THAT WAY (IE NO TUNNEL) IT MOVES
     AT RANDOM TO THE NEXT ROOM.
       IF THE ARROW HITS THE WUMPUS, YOU WIN.
       IF THE ARROW HITS YOU, YOU LOSE.

     WARNINGS:
      WHEN YOU ARE ONE ROOM AWAY FROM WUMPUS OR HAZARD,
     THE COMPUTER SAYS:
WUMPUS-   'I SMELL A WUMPUS'
BAT   -   'BATS NEARBY'
PIT   -   'I FEEL A DRAFT'

HUNT THE WUMPUS

BATS NEARBY!
YOU ARE IN ROOM  7
TUNNELS LEAD TO  6  8  17

SHOOT OR MOVE (S-M)? M
WHERE TO? 8
ZAP--SUPER BAT SNATCH! ELSEWHEREVILLE FOR YOU!

I FEEL A DRAFT!
YOU ARE IN ROOM  20
TUNNELS LEAD TO  13  16  19

SHOOT OR MOVE (S-M)? M
WHERE TO? 13

YOU ARE IN ROOM  13
TUNNELS LEAD TO  12  14  20

SHOOT OR MOVE (S-M)? M
WHERE TO? 14

YOU ARE IN ROOM  14
TUNNELS LEAD TO  4  13  15

SHOOT OR MOVE (S-M)? M
WHERE TO? 15

I FEEL A DRAFT!
YOU ARE IN ROOM  15
TUNNELS LEAD TO  6  14  16

SHOOT OR MOVE (S-M)? 6
SHOOT OR MOVE (S-M)? M
WHERE TO? 6

YOU ARE IN ROOM  6
TUNNELS LEAD TO  5  7  15

SHOOT OR MOVE (S-M)? 5
SHOOT OR MOVE (S-M)? M
WHERE TO? 5

YOU ARE IN ROOM  5
TUNNELS LEAD TO  1  4  6
SHOOT OR MOVE (S-M)? M
WHERE TO? 4

YOU ARE IN ROOM  4
TUNNELS LEAD TO  3  5  14

SHOOT OR MOVE (S-M)? M
WHERE TO? 3

I FEEL A DRAFT!
YOU ARE IN ROOM  3
TUNNELS LEAD TO  2  4  12

SHOOT OR MOVE (S-M)? M
WHERE TO? 12

I SMELL A WUMPUS!
YOU ARE IN ROOM  12
TUNNELS LEAD TO  3  11  13

SHOOT OR MOVE (S-M)? S
NO. OF ROOMS(1-5)? 1
ROOM #? 11
AHA! YOU GOT THE WUMPUS!
HEE HEE HEE - THE WUMPUS'LL GETCHA NEXT TIME!!
```

```
LIST
10 PRINT TAB(33);"WUMPUS"
20 PRINT TAB(15);"CREATIVE COMPUTING  MORRISTOWN, NEW JERSEY"
22 PRINT
24 PRINT
26 PRINT
30 PRINT "INSTRUCTIONS (Y-N)";
40 INPUT I$
50 IF I$="N" THEN 60
55 GOSUB 1000
60 REM- SET UP CAVE (DODECAHEDRAL NODE LIST)
70 DIM S(20,3)
80 FOR J=1 TO 20
90 FOR K=1 TO 3
100 READ S(J,K)
110 NEXT K
120 NEXT J
130 DATA 2,5,8,1,3,10,2,4,12,3,5,14,1,4,6
140 DATA 5,7,15,6,8,17,1,7,9,8,10,18,2,9,11
150 DATA 10,12,19,3,11,13,12,14,20,4,13,15,6,14,16
160 DATA 15,17,20,7,16,18,9,17,19,11,18,20,13,16,19
170 DEF FNA(X)=INT(20*RND(1))+1
180 DEF FNB(X)=INT(3*RND(1))+1
190 DEF FNC(X)=INT(4*RND(1))+1
200 REM- LOCATE L ARRAY ITEMS
210 REM- 1-YOU,2-WUMPUS,3&4-PITS,5&6-BATS
220 DIM L(6),M(6)
230 FOR J=1 TO 6
240 L(J)=FNA(0)
260 M(J)=L(J)
270 NEXT J
280 REM- CHECK FOR CROSSOVERS (IE L(1)=L(2) ETC)
290 FOR J=1 TO 6
300 FOR K=J TO 6
310 IF J=K THEN 330
320 IF L(J)=L(K) THEN 240
330 NEXT K
340 NEXT J
350 REM- SET# ARROS
```

```
360 A=5
365 L=L(1)
370 REM- RUN THE GAME
375 PRINT "HUNT THE WUMPUS"
380 REM- HAZARD WARNINGS & LOCATIONS
390 GOSUB 2000
400 REM- MOVE OR SHOOT
410 GOSUB 2500
420 ON O GOTO 440,480
430 REM- SHOOT
440 GOSUB 3000
450 IF F=0 THEN 390
460 GOTO 500
470 REM- MOVE
480 GOSUB 4000
490 IF F=0 THEN 390
500 IF F>0 THEN 550
510 REM- LOSE
520 PRINT "HA HA HA - YOU LOSE!"
530 GOTO 560
540 REM- WIN
550 PRINT "HEE HEE HEE - THE WUMPUS'LL GETCHA NEXT TIME!!"
560 FOR J=1 TO 6
570 L(J)=M(J)
580 NEXT J
590 PRINT "SAME SET-UP (Y-N)";
600 INPUT I$
610 IF I$ <> "Y" THEN 230
620 GOTO 360
1000 REM- INSTRUCTIONS
1010 PRINT "WELCOME TO 'HUNT THE WUMPUS'"
1020 PRINT "  THE WUMPUS LIVES IN A CAVE OF 20 ROOMS. EACH ROOM"
1030 PRINT "HAS 3 TUNNELS LEADING TO OTHER ROOMS. (LOOK AT A"
1040 PRINT "DODECAHEDRON TO SEE HOW THIS WORKS-IF YOU DON'T KNOW"
1050 PRINT "WHAT A DODECHADRON IS, ASK SOMEONE)"
1060 PRINT
1070 PRINT "     HAZARDS:"
1080 PRINT "BOTTOMLESS PITS - TWO ROOMS HAVE BOTTOMLESS PITS IN THEM"
1090 PRINT "     IF YOU GO THERE, YOU FALL INTO THE PIT (& LOSE!)"
1100 PRINT "SUPERBATS - TWO OTHER ROOMS HAVE SUPER BATS. IF YOU"
1110 PRINT "     GO THERE, A BAT GRABS YOU AND TAKES YOU TO SOME";
1115 PRINT " OTHER"
1120 PRINT "     ROOM AT RANDOM. (WHICH MIGHT BE TROUBLESOME)"
1130 PRINT
1140 PRINT "     WUMPUS:"
1150 PRINT "THE WUMPUS IS NOT BOTHERED BY THE HAZARDS (HE HAS SUCKER"
1160 PRINT "FEET AND IS TOO BIG FOR A BAT TO LIFT). USUALLY"
1170 PRINT "HE IS ASLEEP. TWO THINGS THAT WAKE HIM UP: YOUR ENTERING"
1180 PRINT "HIS ROOM OR YOUR SHOOTING AN ARROW."
1190 PRINT "     IF THE WUMPUS WAKES, HE MOVES (P=.75) ONE ROOM"
1200 PRINT "OR STAYS STILL (P=.25). AFTER THAT, IF HE IS WHERE YOU"
1210 PRINT "ARE, HE EATS YOU UP (& YOU LOSE!)"
1220 PRINT
1230 PRINT "     YOU:"
1240 PRINT "EACH TURN YOU MAY MOVE OR SHOOT A CROOKED ARROW"
1250 PRINT "     MOVING: YOU CAN GO ONE ROOM (THRU ONE TUNNEL)"
1260 PRINT "     ARROWS: YOU HAVE 5 ARROWS. YOU LOSE WHEN YOU RUN OUT."
1270 PRINT "     EACH ARROW CAN GO FROM 1 TO 5 ROOMS. YOU AIM BY ";
1275 PRINT "TELLING"
1280 PRINT "     THE COMPUTER TTHE ROOM#S YOU WANT THE ARROW TO GO TO."
1290 PRINT "     IF THE ARROW CAN'T GO THAT WAY (IE NO TUNNEL) IT ";
1295 PRINT "MOVES"
1300 PRINT "     AT RANDOM TO THE NEXT ROOM."
1310 PRINT "       IF THE ARROW HITS THE WUMPUS, YOU WIN."
1320 PRINT "       IF THE ARROW HITS YOU, YOU LOSE."
1330 PRINT
1340 PRINT "     WARNINGS:"
1350 PRINT "      WHEN YOU ARE ONE ROOM AWAY FROM WUMPUS OR HAZARD,"
1360 PRINT "     THE COMPUTER SAYS:"
1370 PRINT "WUMPUS-   'I SMELL A WUMPUS'"
1380 PRINT "BAT   -   'BATS NEARBY'"
1390 PRINT "PIT   -   'I FEEL A DRAFT'"
1400 PRINT
1410 RETURN
2000 REM- PRINT  LOCATION & HAZARD WARNINGS
2010 PRINT
2020 FOR J= 2 TO 6
2030 FOR K=1 TO 3
2040 IF S(L(1),K)<>L(J) THEN 2110
2050 ON J-1 GOTO 2060,2080,2080,2100,2100
2060 PRINT "I SMELL A WUMPUS!"
2070 GOTO 2110
2080 PRINT "I FEEL A DRAFT!"
2090 GOTO 2110
2100 PRINT "BATS NEARBY!"
2110 NEXT K
2120 NEXT J
2130 PRINT "YOU ARE IN ROOM ";L(1)
2140 PRINT "TUNNELS LEAD TO ";S(L,1);S(L,2);S(L,3)
2150 PRINT
2160 RETURN
2500 REM- CHOOSE OPTION
2510 PRINT "SHOOT OR MOVE (S-M)";
2520 INPUT I$
2530 IF I$ <> "S" THEN 2560
2540 O=1
2550 RETURN
2560 IF I$ <> "M" THEN 2510
2570 O=2
2580 RETURN
3000 REM- ARROW ROUTINE
3010 F=0
3020 REM- PATH OF ARROW
3030 L=L(1)
3040 PRINT "NO. OF ROOMS(1-5)";
3050 INPUT J9
3060 IF J9<1 OR J9>5 THEN 3040
3070 FOR K=1 TO J9
3080 PRINT "ROOM #";
3090 INPUT P(K)
3095 IF K <= 2 THEN 3115
3100 IF P(K) <> P(K-2) THEN 3115
3105 PRINT "ARROWS AREN'T THA TCORRKED - TRY ANOTHER ROOM"
3110 GOTO 3080
3115 NEXT K
3120 REM- SHOOT ARROW
3140 FOR K=1 TO J9
3150 FOR K1=1 TO 3
3160 IF S(L,K1)=P(K) THEN 3295
3170 NEXT K1
3180 REM- NO TUNNEL FOR ARROW
3190 L=S(L,FNB(1))
3200 GOTO 3300
3210 NEXT K
3220 PRINT "MISSED"
3225 L=L(1)
3230 REM- MOVE WUMPUS
3240 GOSUB 3370
3250 REM- AMMO CHECK
3255 A=A-1
3260 IF A>0 THEN 3280
3270 F=-1
3280 RETURN
3290 REM- SEE IF ARROW IS AT L(1) OR L(2)
3295 L=P(K)
3300 IF L <> L(2) THEN 3340
3310 PRINT "AHA! YOU GOT THE WUMPUS!"
3320 F=1
3330 RETURN
3340 IF L <> L(1) THEN 3210
3350 PRINT "OUCH! ARROW GOT YOU!"
3360 GOTO 3270
3370 REM- MOVE WUMPUS ROUTINE
3380 K=FNC(0)
3390 IF K=4 THEN 3410
3400 L(2)=S(L(2),K)
3410 IF L(2) <> L THEN 3440
3420 PRINT "TSK TSK TSK - WUMPUS GOT YOU!"
3430 F=-1
3440 RETURN
4000 REM- MOVE ROUTINE
4010 F=0
4020 PRINT "WHERE TO";
4030 INPUT L
4040 IF L<1 OR L>20 THEN 4020
4050 FOR K=1 TO 3
4060 REM- CHECK IF LEGAL MOVE
4070 IF S(L(1),K)=L THEN 4130
4080 NEXT K
4090 IF L=L(1) THEN 4130
4100 PRINT "NOT POSSIBLE -";
4110 GOTO 4020
4120 REM- CHECK FOR HAZARDS
4130 L(1)=L
4140 REM- WUMPUS
4150 IF L <> L(2) THEN 4220
4160 PRINT "... OOPS! BUMPED A WUMPUS!"
4170 REM- MOVE WUMPUS
4180 GOSUB 3380
4190 IF F=0 THEN 4220
4200 RETURN
4210 REM- PIT
4220 IF L <> L(3) AND L <> L(4) THEN 4270
4230 PRINT "YYYIIIIEEEE . . . FELL IN PIT"
4240 F=-1
4250 RETURN
4260 REM- BATS
4270 IF L <> L(5) AND L <> L(6) THEN 4310
4280 PRINT "ZAP--SUPER BAT SNATCH! ELSEWHEREVILLE FOR YOU!"
4290 L=FNA(1)
4300 GOTO 4130
4310 RETURN
5000 END
Ok
```

Wumpus 2

Hark!! The weary Wumpus hunter, wan from 50 days in the Terminal Caverns, exhausted and with all of his arrows expended — — — (A groaning Teletype roars at a sleepy student. Maps litter the floor covered with circles and integers. With callused fingers, the immortal Wumpus player looks up with bloodshot eyes and implores: "How do I get out of here?")

I suspected that the dodecahedron may prove a bit boring after a few thousand games, so I wrote Wumpus 2 to extend your pleasure. Some of the more mathematical minded may have noticed there are lots of ways to link caves with three tunnels apiece. Some of these patterns are topologically interesting . . . .

Wumpus 2 is the same old Wumpus in different settings — including those of your own design. As you play in the different caves, you will notice that the game changes in difficulty and strategy. Now to a description of the various caves in Wumpus 2.

CAVE 0 (Dodecahedron)

This is the same old Wumpus with which you are familiar.

CAVE 1 (Mobius Strip)

Since my original vision was topological, here is the first wonder of topology, the Mobius strip. Take a strip of paper, give it a half-twist and join the ends into a loop. The result has just one side and one edge (if you disbelieve, take a pencil and go around the thing).

A perceptive player will note that the placement of the pits influence the game. Two pits placed just right (around 5% of the games have this) will force a detour back around the strip in certain cases. Getting around is slower than in Cave 0, but it is easier to search the place.

CAVE 2 (String of Beads)

See the diagram for this one. Here, placement of the pits will often make parts of the caves inaccessible except by bat-express. (Can you see why?) Play in this cave is frustrating until you have gone to the trouble of making a reference map; otherwise you keep coming back to your starting point. (Look at the diagram and see how this may be so.)

CAVE 3 (Hex Network)

This is my attempt at a torus (doughnut). If you can visualise a hexagon net like a honeycomb or a tile floor and stretch it onto a doughnut, you've got it!! The drawing tries to show this, but if you prefer, think of it as a complicated molecule of some sort. Play in this one is very similar to CAVE 0.

CAVE 4 (Dendrite)

Up to now, each tunnel leads to another cave and only one tunnel connects a pair of caves. This need not be a strict rule and the next two caves illustrate variations on this. The dendrite is a branching pattern like a tree or a plant. At the ends of the plant are "leaves" which are caves leading to themselves or multiple tunnels. This cave is especially susceptible to severance by pits and getting stuck in corners near the wumpus. A nice thing is that you often will know exactly where the Wumpus is when you come near him.

CAVE 5 (one way streets)

This is the extreme example of all tunnels are one-way. You will find that getting about this cave is like travel in Los Angeles — much going to get to the neighbor's house. If you overshoot, you must travel all the way around, just like missing a freeway offramp.

CAVE 6 (Do Your OWN)

Draw up a map of caves, each cave with tunnels GOING TO three (exactly three) caves (same or different). Then the computer will ask you for the numbers of the destination tunnels for each of the 20 caves in Wumpus. When you have it entered, play Wumpus on your own caves. Let me know of your favorite ones, and your most frustrating ones!!!

FINIS

In any case, Wumpus has spawned several versions and spread about the computer games-dom really nicely. For myself, the soul of the game is in the idea and fun of it rather than the program or the computer which hosts it. I feel that all really good games will turn programmers on enough for them to write it for their system from the idea alone and encourage games writers to think carefully on the art and esthetics of their games before writing a line of code.

Wumpus-2 and this description are products of Gregory Yob. They appeared previously in *Creative Computing*, Jan/Feb 1976 and the game in *People's Computer Co.*

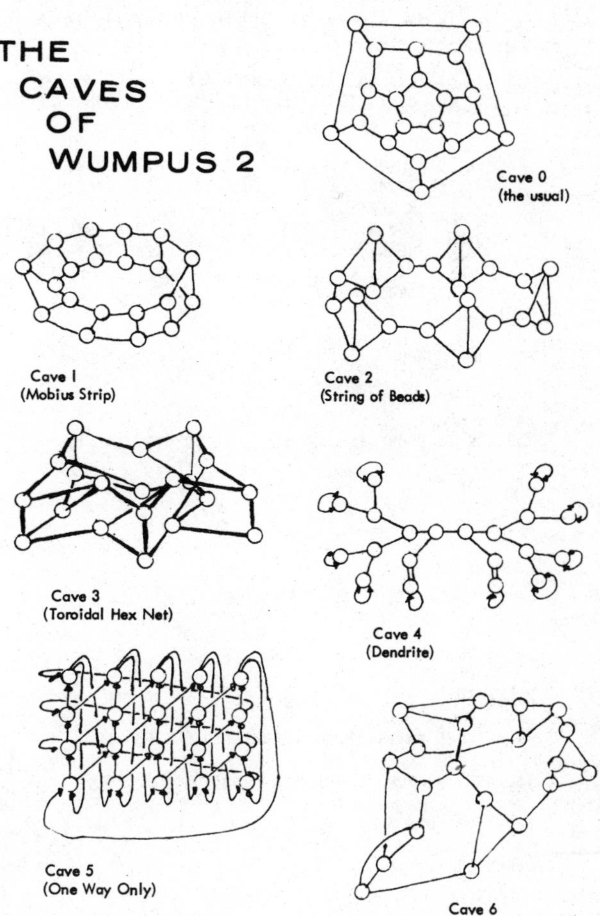

```
RUN
                          WUMPUS 2
                     CREATIVE COMPUTING
                   MORRISTOWN  NEW JERSEY



INSTRUCTIONS? YES

WELCOME TO WUMPUS II
THIS VERSION HAS THE SAME RULES AS 'HUNT THE WUMPUS'.
HOWEVER, YOU NOW HAVE A CHOICE OF CAVES TO PLAY IN.
SOME CAVES ARE EASIER THAN OTHERS. ALL CAVES HAVE 20
ROOMS AND 3 TUNNELS LEADING FROM ONE ROOM TO OTHER ROOMS.
THE CAVES ARE:
  0  -  DODECAHEDRON   THE ROOMS OF THIS CAVE ARE ON A
        12-SIDED OBJECT, EACH FORMING A PENTAGON.
        THE ROOMS ARE AT THE CORNERS OF THE PENTAGONS.
        EACH ROOM HAVING TUNNELS THAT LEAD TO 3 OTHER ROOMS

  1  -  MOBIUS STRIP   THIS CAVE IS TWO ROOMS
        WIDE AND 10 ROOMS AROUND (LIKE A BELT)
        YOU WILL NOTICE THERE IS A HALF TWIST
        SOMEWHERE.

  2  -  STRING OF BEADS     FIVE BEADS IN A CIRCLE.
        EACH BEAD IS A DIAMOND WITH A VERTICAL
        CROSS-BAR. THE RIGHT & LEFT CORNERS LEAD
        TO NEIGHBORING BEADS. (THIS ONE IS DIFFICULT
        TO PLAY)

  3  -  HEX NEWORK     IMAGINE A HEX TILE FLOOR. TAKE
        A RECTANGLE WITH 20 POINTS (INTERSECTIONS)
        INSIDE (4X4). JOIN RIGHT & LEFT SIDES TO MAKE A
        CYLINDER. THEN JOIN TOP & BOTTOM TO FORM A
        TORUS (DOUGHNUT).
        HAVE FUN IMAGINING THIS ONE!!

  CAVES 1-3 ARE REGULAR IN A SENSE THAT EACH ROOM
GOES TO THREE OTHER ROOMS & TUNNELS ALLOW TWO-
WAY TRAFFIC. HERE ARE SOME 'IRREGULAR' CAVES:

  4  -  DENDRITE WITH DEGENERACIES   PULL A PLANT FROM
        THE GROUND. THE ROOTS & BRANCHES FORM A
        DENDRITE - IE., THERE ARE NO LOOPING PATHS
        DEGENERACY MEANS A) SOME ROOMS CONNECT TO
        THEMSELVES AND B) SOME ROOMS HAVE MORE THAN ONE
        TUNNEL TO THE SAME OTHER ROOM IE, 12 HAS
        TWO TUNNELS TO 13.

  5  -  ONE WAY LATTICE      HERE ALL TUNNELS GO ONE
        WAY ONLY. TO RETURN, YOU MUST GO AROUND THE CAVE
        (ABOUT 5 MOVES).

  6  -  ENTER YOUR OWN CAVE    THE COMPUTER WILL ASK YOU
        THE ROOMS NEXT TO EACH ROOM IN THE CAVE.
          FOR EXAMPLE:
            ROOM #1     ? 2,3,4        - YOUR REPLY OF 2,3,4
              MEANS ROOM 1 HAS TUNNELS GOING TO ROOMS:
              2, 3, & 4.
  HAPPY HUNTING!
CAVE #(0-6) ? 4

HUNT THE WUMPUS

I SMELL A WUMPUS!
BATS NEARBY!
YOU ARE IN ROOM  11  TUNNELS LEAD TO  13  14  12

SHOOT OR MOVE ? S

NO. OF ROOMS ? 1

ROOM #? 13


MISSED
SHOOT OR MOVE ? M

WHERE TO ? 13

ZAP--SUPER BAT SNATCH! ELSEWHERESVILLE FOR YOU!

YOU ARE IN ROOM  6  TUNNELS LEAD TO  4  7  5

SHOOT OR MOVE ? M

WHERE TO ? 4
```

```
BATS NEARBY!
YOU ARE IN ROOM  4  TUNNELS LEAD TO  4  6  1

SHOOT OR MOVE ? M

WHERE TO ? 4


BATS NEARBY!
YOU ARE IN ROOM  4  TUNNELS LEAD TO  4  6  1

SHOOT OR MOVE ? M

WHERE TO ? 6


YOU ARE IN ROOM  6  TUNNELS LEAD TO  4  7  5

SHOOT OR MOVE ? M

WHERE TO ? 5


YOU ARE IN ROOM  5  TUNNELS LEAD TO  2  7  3

SHOOT OR MOVE ? M

WHERE TO ? 2


YOU ARE IN ROOM  2  TUNNELS LEAD TO  2  5  3

SHOOT OR MOVE ? M

WHERE TO ? 3


YOU ARE IN ROOM  3  TUNNELS LEAD TO  3  6  4

SHOOT OR MOVE ? M

WHERE TO ? 6


YOU ARE IN ROOM  6  TUNNELS LEAD TO  4  7  5

SHOOT OR MOVE ? M

WHERE TO ? 7


YOU ARE IN ROOM  7  TUNNELS LEAD TO  6  10  8

SHOOT OR MOVE ? M

WHERE TO ? 10


I FEEL A DRAFT!
YOU ARE IN ROOM  10  TUNNELS LEAD TO  9  11  10

SHOOT OR MOVE ? M

WHERE TO ? 11


I SMELL A WUMPUS!
BATS NEARBY!
YOU ARE IN ROOM  11  TUNNELS LEAD TO  13  14  12

SHOOT OR MOVE ? S

NO. OF ROOMS ? 1

ROOM #? 12


AHA! YOU GOT THE WUMPUS! HE WAS IN ROOM 12
HEE HEE HEE - THE WUMPUS'LL GET YOU NEXT TIME!!
PLAY AGAIN? NO

Ok
```

```
LIST
3 PRINT TAB(25);"WUMPUS 2"
4 PRINT TAB(20);"CREATIVE COMPUTING"
5 PRINT TAB(18);"MORRISTOWN  NEW JERSEY"
7 PRINT
10 PRINT
15 PRINT
20 REM- WUMPUS VERSION 2
30 DIM S(20,3)
40 DIM L(6),M(6),P(5)
50 PRINT "INSTRUCTIONS";
60 INPUT I$
70 PRINT
80 IF LEFT$(I$,1) <> "Y" THEN 130
100 GOSUB 700
110 REM- CHOOSE AND SET UP CAVE
130 GOSUB 2530
140 DEF FNA(X)=INT(20*RND(1))+1
150 DEF FNB(X)=INT(3*RND(1))+1
160 DEF FNC(X)=INT(4*RND(1))+1
170 REM LOCATE L ARRAY ITEMS
180 REM 1-YOU, 2-WUMPUS, 3&4-PITS, 5&6-BATS
210 FOR J=1 TO 6
220 L(J)=FNA(0)
230 M(J)=L(J)
240 NEXT J
250 REM CHECK FOR CROSSOVERS (IE L(1)=L(2) ETC)
260 FOR J=1 TO 6
270 FOR K=J TO 6
280 IF J=K THEN 300
290 IF L(J)=L(K) THEN 210
300 NEXT K
310 NEXT J
320 REM SET # ARROWS
330 A=5
340 L=L(1)
350 REM- RUN THE GAME
360 PRINT "HUNT THE WUMPUS"
370 REM-HAZARDS WARNINGS AND LOCATION
380 GOSUB 1230
390 REM MOVE OR SHOOT
400 GOSUB 1400
410 ON O GOTO 430,470
420 REM SHOOT
430 GOSUB 1550
440 IF F=0 THEN 400
450 GOTO 490
460 REM MOVE
470 GOSUB 2150
480 IF F=0 THEN 380
490 IF F > 0 THEN 540
500 REM LOSE
510 PRINT "HA HA HA - YOU LOOSE!"
520 GOTO 550
530 REM WIN
540 PRINT "HEE HEE HEE - THE WUMPUS'LL GET YOU NEXT TIME!!"
550 FOR J=1 TO 6
560 L(J)=M(J)
570 NEXT J
580 PRINT "PLAY AGAIN";
590 INPUT I$
595 PRINT
600 PRINT
620 IF LEFT$(I$,1) <> "Y" THEN 3310
640 PRINT "SAME SET-UP ";
650 INPUT I$
660 PRINT
670 IF LEFT$(I$,1) <> "Y" THEN 130
680 GOTO 330
700 REM- INSTRUCTIONS
710 PRINT "WELCOME TO WUMPUS II"
720 PRINT "THIS VERSION HAS THE SAME RULES AS 'HUNT THE WUMPUS'."
730 PRINT "HOWEVER, YOU NOW HAVE A CHOICE OF CAVES TO PLAY IN."
740 PRINT "SOME CAVES ARE EASIER THAN OTHERS. ALL CAVES HAVE 20"
750 PRINT "ROOMS AND 3 TUNNELS LEADING FROM ONE ROOM TO OTHER ROOMS."
760 PRINT "THE CAVES ARE:"
770 PRINT "  0  -  DODECAHEDRON   THE ROOMS OF THIS CAVE ARE ON A"
780 PRINT "        12-SIDED OBJECT, EACH FORMING A PENTAGON."
790 PRINT "        THE ROOMS ARE AT THE CORNERS OF THE PENTAGONS."
800 PRINT "        EACH ROOM HAVING TUNNELS THAT LEAD TO 3 OTHER ROOMS"
805 PRINT
810 PRINT "  1  -  MOBIUS STRIP   THIS CAVE IS TWO ROOMS"
820 PRINT "        WIDE AND 10 ROOMS AROUND (LIKE A BELT)"
830 PRINT "        YOU WILL NOTICE THERE IS A HALF TWIST"
840 PRINT "        SOMEWHERE."
850 PRINT
860 PRINT "  2  -  STRING OF BEADS    FIVE BEADS IN A CIRCLE."
870 PRINT "        EACH BEAD IS A DIAMOND WITH A VERTICAL"
880 PRINT "        CROSS-BAR. THE RIGHT & LEFT CORNERS LEAD"
890 PRINT "        TO NEIGHBORING BEADS. (THIS ONE IS DIFFICULT"
900 PRINT "        TO PLAY)"
910 PRINT
920 PRINT "  3  -  HEX NEWORK    IMAGINE A HEX TILE FLOOR. TAKE"
930 PRINT "        A RECTANGLE WITH 20 POINTS (INTERSECTIONS)"
940 PRINT "        INSIDE (4X4). JOIN RIGHT & LEFT SIDES TO MAKE A"
950 PRINT "        CYLINDER. THEN JOIN TOP & BOTTOM TO FORM A"
960 PRINT "        TORUS (DOUGHNUT)."
970 PRINT "        HAVE FUN IMAGINING THIS ONE!!"
980 PRINT
990 PRINT "  CAVES 1-3 ARE REGULAR IN A SENSE THAT EACH ROOM"
1000 PRINT "GOES TO THREE OTHER ROOMS & TUNNELS ALLOW TWO-"
1010 PRINT "WAY TRAFFIC. HERE ARE SOME 'IRREGULAR' CAVES:"
1020 PRINT
1030 PRINT "  4  -  DENDRITE WITH DEGENERACIES   PULL A PLANT FROM"
1040 PRINT "        THE GROUND. THE ROOTS & BRANCHES FORM A "
1050 PRINT "        DENDRITE - IE., THERE ARE NO LOOPING PATHS"
1060 PRINT "        DEGENERACY MEANS A) SOME ROOMS CONNECT TO"
1070 PRINT "        THEMSELVES AND B) SOME ROOMS HAVE MORE THAN ONE"
1080 PRINT "        TUNNEL TO THE SAME OTHER ROOM IE, 12 HAS "
1090 PRINT "        TWO TUNNELS TO 13."
1100 PRINT
1110 PRINT "  5  -  ONE WAY LATTICE     HERE ALL TUNNELS GO ONE"
1120 PRINT "        WAY ONLY. TO RETURN, YOU MUST GO AROUND THE CAVE"
1130 PRINT "        (ABOUT 5 MOVES)."
1140 PRINT
1160 PRINT "  6  -  ENTER YOUR OWN CAVE    THE COMPUTER WILL ASK YOU"
1170 PRINT "        THE ROOMS NEXT TO EACH ROOM IN THE CAVE."
1180 PRINT "          FOR EXAMPLE:"
1190 PRINT "            ROOM #1     ? 2,3,4       - YOUR REPLY OF 2,3,4
1200 PRINT "             MEANS ROOM 1 HAS TUNNELS GOING TO ROOMS:"
1210 PRINT "             2, 3, & 4."
1220 PRINT "  HAPPY HUNTING!"
1225 RETURN
1230 REM
1240 PRINT
1250 FOR J=2 TO 6
1260 FOR K=1 TO 3
1270 IF S(L(1),K) <> L(J) THEN 1340
1280 ON J-1 GOTO 1290,1310,1310,1330,1330
1290 PRINT "I SMELL A WUMPUS!"
1300 GOTO 1340
1310 PRINT "I FEEL A DRAFT!"
1320 GOTO 1340
1330 PRINT "BATS NEARBY!"
1340 NEXT K
1350 NEXT J
1360 PRINT "YOU ARE IN ROOM ";L(1);
1370 PRINT " TUNNELS LEAD TO ";S(L,1);S(L,2);S(L,3)
1380 PRINT
1390 RETURN
1400 REM- CHOOSE OPTION
1410 GOTO 1450
1420 PRINT "ERROR   ";
1430 INPUT Z9
1440 PRINT "";
1450 PRINT "SHOOT OR MOVE ";
1460 INPUT I$
1470 PRINT
1490 IF LEFT$(I$,1) <> "S" THEN 1520
1500 O=1
1510 RETURN
1520 IF LEFT$(I$,1) <> "M" THEN 1420
1530 O=2
1540 RETURN
1550 REM- ARROW ROUTINE
1560 F=0
1570 REM- PATH OF ARROW
1590 GOTO 1630
1600 PRINT "ERROR   ";
1610 INPUT Z9
1620 PRINT "";
1630 PRINT "NO. OF ROOMS ";
1640 INPUT J9
1650 PRINT
1670 IF J9 < 1 OR J9 > 5 OR INT(J9) <> ABS(J9) THEN 1600
```

```
1680 FOR K=1 TO J9
1690 PRINT "ROOM #";
1700 INPUT P(K)
1710 PRINT
1730 IF P(K) > 0 AND P(K) < 21 AND INT(P(K))=ABS(P(K)) THEN 1780
1740 PRINT "ERROR  ";
1750 INPUT Z9
1760 PRINT "";
1770 GOTO 1690
1780 NEXT K
1790 PRINT
1800 REM -  SHOOT ARROW
1810 A=A-J9
1820 A9=L(1)
1830 FOR K=1 TO J9
1840 FOR K1=1 TO 3
1850 IF S(A9,K1)=P(K) THEN 1990
1860 NEXT K1
1870 REM -  NO TUNNEL FOR THE ARROW
1880 A9=S(A9,FNB(1))
1890 GOTO 2000
1900 NEXT K
1910 PRINT "MISSED"
1920 REM -  MOVE WUMPUS
1930 GOSUB 2070
1940 REM -  AMMO CHECK
1950 IF A > 0 THEN 1970
1955 PRINT "YOU HAVE USED ALL OF YOUR ARROWS."
1960 F=-1
1970 RETURN
1980 REM -  SEE IF ARROW IS AT L[1] OT L[2]
1990 A9=P(K)
2000 IF A9 <> L(2) THEN 2040
2010 PRINT "AHA! YOU GOT THE WUMPUS! HE WAS IN ROOM";L(2)
2020 F=1
2030 RETURN
2040 IF A9 <> L(1) THEN 1900
2050 PRINT "OUCH! ARROW GOT YOU!"
2060 GOTO 1960
2070 REM -  MOVE WUMPUS ROUTINE
2080 K=FNC(0)
2090 IF K=4 THEN 2140
2100 L(2)=S(L(2),K)
2110 IF L(2) <> L THEN 2140
2120 PRINT "TSK TSK TSK- WUMPUS GOT YOU!"
2130 F=-1
2140 RETURN
2150 REM -  MOVE ROUTINE
2160 F=0
2170 GOTO 2210
2180 PRINT "ERROR   ";
2190 INPUT Z9
2200 PRINT "";
2210 PRINT "WHERE TO ";
2220 INPUT L
2230 PRINT
2240 IF L < 1 OR L > 20 OR ABS(L) <> INT(L) THEN 2180
2250 FOR K=1 TO 3
2260 REM -  CHECK IF LEGAL MOVE
2270 IF S(L(1),K)=L THEN 2350
2280 NEXT K
2290 IF L=L(1) THEN 2350
2300 PRINT "NOT POSSIBLE - ";
2310 INPUT Z9
2320 PRINT "";
2330 GOTO 2210
2340 REM -  CHECK FOR HAZARDS
2350 L(1)=L
2360 REM -  WUMPUS
2370 IF L <> L(2) THEN 2430
2380 PRINT "... OOPS! BUMPED A WUMPUS!"
2390 REM -   MOVE A WUMPUS
2400 GOSUB 2080
2410 IF F=0 THEN 2430
2420 REM -  PIT
2430 IF L <> L(3) AND L <> L(4) THEN 2480
2440 PRINT "YYYIIIEEEE . . . FELL IN A PIT"
2450 F=-1
2460 RETURN
2470 REM -  BATS
2480 IF L <> L(5) AND L <> L(6) THEN 2520
2490 PRINT "ZAP--SUPER BAT SNATCH! ELSEWHERESVILLE FOR YOU!"
2500 L=FNA(1)
2510 GOTO 2350
2520 RETURN
2530 REM -  SELECT CAVE
2540 GOTO 2580
2550 PRINT "ERROR   ";
2560 INPUT Z9
2570 PRINT "";
2580 PRINT "CAVE #(0-6) ";
2585 RESTORE
2590 INPUT N
2600 PRINT
2620 IF N<0 OR N>6 OR INT(N) <> ABS(N) THEN 2550
2630 ON N+1 GOSUB 2750,2730,2810,2890,2970,3050,3130
2640 RETURN
2650 REM -  DODECAHEDRON
2670 DATA 2,5,8,1,3,10,2,4,12,3,5,14,1,4,6
2680 DATA 5,7,15,6,8,17,1,7,9,8,10,18,2,9,11
2690 DATA 10,12,19,3,11,13,12,14,20,4,13,15,6,4,16
2700 DATA 15,17,20,7,16,18,9,17,19,11,18,20,1316,19
2710 GOSUB 3240
2720 RETURN
2730 REM -  MOBIUS STRIP
2735 FOR B1=1 TO 1
2737 FOR B2=1 TO 60
2740 READ B0
2742 NEXT B2
2744 NEXT B1
2750 DATA 20,2,3,19,1,4,1,4,5,2,3,6,3,6,7
2760 DATA 4,5,8,5,8,9,6,7,10,7,10,11,8,9,12
2770 DATA 9,12,13,10,11,14,11,14,15,12,13,16,12,16,17
2780 DATA 14,15,18,15,18,19,16,17,20,2,17,20,1,18,19
2790 GOSUB 3240
2800 RETURN
2810 REM -  STRING OF BEADS
2815 FOR B1=1 TO 2
2817 FOR B2=1 TO 60
2820 READ B0
2822 NEXT B2
2824 NEXT B1
2830 DATA 2,3,20,1,3,4,1,2,4,2,3,5,4,6,7
2840 DATA 5,7,8,5,6,8,6,7,9,8,10,11,9,11,12
2850 DATA 9,10,12,10,11,13,12,14,15,13,15,16,13,14,16
2860 DATA 14,15,17,16,18,19,17,19,20,17,18,20,1,18,19
2870 GOSUB 3240
2880 RETURN
2890 REM -  HEX NUT ON TORUS
2895 FOR B1=1 TO 3
2897 FOR B2=1 TO 60
2900 READ B0
2902 NEXT B2
2904 NEXT B1
2910 DATA 6,10,16,6,7,17,7,8,18,8,9,19,9,10,20
2920 DATA 1,2,15,2,3,11,3,4,12,4,5,13,5,6,14
2930 DATA 7,16,20,8,16,17,9,17,18,10,18,19,6,19,20
2940 DATA 1,11,12,2,12,13,3,13,14,4,14,15,5,11,15
2950 GOSUB 3240
2960 RETURN
2970 REM -  DENDRITE W/ DEGENERACIES
2975 FOR B1=1 TO 4
2977 FOR B2=1 TO 60
2980 READ B0
2982 NEXT B2
2984 NEXT B1
2990 DATA 1,1,5,2,2,5,3,3,6,4,4,6,1,2,7
3000 DATA 3,4,7,5,6,10,8,9,9,8,8,10,7,9,11
3010 DATA 10,13,14,12,13,13,11,12,12,11,15,16,14,17,18
3020 DATA 14,19,20,15,17,17,15,18,18,16,19,19,16,20,20
3030 GOSUB 3240
3040 RETURN
3050 REM -  ONE WAY LATTICE
3055 FOR B1=1 TO 5
3057 FOR B2=1 TO 60
3060 READ B0
3062 NEXT B2
3064 NEXT B1
3070 DATA 5,4,8,1,5,6,2,6,7,3,7,8,8,9,12
3080 DATA 5,9,10,6,10,11,7,11,12,12,13,16,9,13,14
3090 DATA 10,14,15,11,15,16,16,17,20,13,17,18,14,18,19
3100 DATA 15,19,20,1,4,20,1,2,17,2,3,18,3,4,19
3110 GOSUB 3240
3120 RETURN
3130 REM -   INPUT YOUR OWN CAVE
3140 FOR J=1  TO 20
3150 PRINT "ROOM #";J;
3160 INPUT S(J,1),S(J,2),S(J,3)
3170 FOR K=1 TO 3
3180 IF S(J,K) > 0 AND S(J,K) < 21 AND ABS(S(J,K))=ABS(S(J,K)) THEN3210
3190 PRINT "***** ERROR!!!!!"
3200 GOTO 3150
3210 NEXT K
3220 NEXT J
3230 RETURN
3240 REM -  INPUT CAVE
3250 FOR J=1 TO 20
3260 FOR K=1 TO 3
3270 READ S(J,K)
3280 NEXT K
3290 NEXT J
3300 RETURN
3310 END
Ok
```

TENNIS BUM 3
OIL